ADDICTION COUNSELING REVIEW

Preparing for Comprehensive Certification and
licensing examinations

ADDICTION COUNSELING REVIEW
Preparing for Comprehensive, Certification and Licensing Examinations

Edited by

Robert Holman Coombs
UCLA School of Medicine

LEA
LAWRENCE ERLBAUM ASSOCIATES, PUBLISHERS
2005 Mahwah, New Jersey   London

Senior Consulting Editor:	Susan Milmoe
Editorial Assistant:	Kristen Depken
Cover Design:	Kathryn Houghtaling Lacey
Textbook Production Manager:	Paul Smolenski
Full-Service Compositor:	TechBooks
Text and Cover Printer:	Hamilton Printing Company

This book was typeset in 10/12 pt. Times New Roman, Bold, and Italic.
The heads were typeset in Sabon, Sabon Bold, and Sabon Bold Italic.

Lahaska Press, a unique collaboration between the Houghton Mifflin College Division and Lawrence Erlbaum Associates, is dedicated to publishing books and offering services for the academic and professional counseling communities. Houghton Mifflin and Lawrence Erlbaum will focus on becoming a major conduit for educational and academic materials in the psychological and educational counseling fields. The partnership of Lahaska Press was formed in late 1999. The name "Lahaska" is a Native American Lenape word meaning "source of much writing." It is also a small town in eastern Pennsylvania, named by the Lenape.

Lawrence Erlbaum Associates, Inc., Publishers
10 Industrial Avenue
Mahwah, New Jersey 07430
www.erlbaum.com

Library of Congress Cataloging-in-Publication Data

Addiction counseling review : preparing for comprehensive, certification and licensing
    examinations / edited by Robert H. Coombs.
        p.   cm.
    Includes index.
    ISBN 0-8058-4311-6 (case : alk. paper)—ISBN 0-8058-5463-0 (pbk: alk. paper)
        1. Drug abuse counseling—Examinations, questions, etc.   2. Drug abuse counselors—
    Licenses—Study guides.   3. Drug abuse counselors—Certification.   I. Coombs, Robert H.
    RC564.A2816   2005
    362.29′186—dc22
                                                                      2004016810

Books published by Lawrence Erlbaum Associates are printed on acid-free paper, and their bindings are chosen for strength and durability.

Printed in the United States of America
10   9   8   7   6   5   4   3   2   1

for
Loni and Steve

Contents

Preface

Addiction, the most serious public health problem in the United States, affects millions of individuals. More than 19 million Americans—8.3% of the U.S. population age 12 or older—currently use illicit drugs. In addition, 54 million are regularly binge drinkers.

These results come from the federal government's *Household Survey*—recently renamed *The National Survey on Drug Use and Health*—a very large national study that in 2002 interviewed 68,126 respondents—representative of 98% of the U.S. population age 12 or older. All were interviewed in their homes (including dormitories or homeless shelters). The homeless, military personnel on active duty, and those in prisons or other institutionalized settings were not included (Office of Applied Studies, 2003).

Conducted by the federal government's Substance Abuse and Mental Health Services Administration (SAMHSA) in the Department of Health and Human Services, this study found that alcohol is the most commonly used *psychoactive* drug and marijuana, used by 14.6 million Americans, is the most commonly used *illicit* drug. About one-third of marijuana users (4.8 million people) used it twenty or more days in the past month.

Prescription medications, the third most frequently used drug, were used illegally by 6.2 million people (2.6% of the population ages 12 or older). Of these, about 4.4 million used narcotic pain relievers, 1.8 million used anti-anxiety medications (i.e., tranquilizers), 1.2 million used stimulants, and 0.4 million used sedatives.

Current illicit drug use is highest among young adults age 18 to 25, 20% of whom used psychoactive substances. Among 10.7 million people age 12 to 20 (28.8% of the latter age group) reported drinking alcohol in the month prior to the survey interview. Of these, 7.2 million were binge drinkers (19.3%) and 2.3 million heavy drinkers (6.2%).

More than 4 million adults have both a substance use disorder and serious mental illness. In 2002, 17.5 million adults over age 18 (8.3 % of all adults) had a serious mental illness. Adults who used illicit drugs were more than twice as likely to have serious mental illness as those who did not.

This survey also reports that 18.6 million (7.9% of the population age 12 or older) need treatment for a serious alcohol problem and 7.7 million people (3.3% of the total population) need treatment for a diagnosable drug problem other than alcohol. Yet, only 1.5 million received treatment for alcohol problems and only 1.4 million received specialized substance abuse treatment for an illicit drug problem.

Interestingly, more than 94% of those with chemical abuse disorders thought that they didn't need treatment. "A denial gap of over 94% is intolerable," noted John Walters, White House Director of National Drug Control Policy.

> *People need to understand the addictive nature of drugs and not presume that they are 'all right' when everyone around them knows better. Families and friends need to urge their loved ones to seek treatment when they experience the toll that addiction takes on loved ones and communities. (News Release, September 5, 2003, p. 1)*

Of the 362,000 Americans who recognized they needed treatment for substance abuse, 266,000 had unsuccessfully attempted to obtain treatment for *alcohol* abuse and another 88,000 had been unsuccessful in getting treatment for addiction to *other psychoactive drugs*. "There is no other medical condition for which we would tolerate such huge numbers unable to obtain the treatment they need," said HHS Secretary Tommmy G. Thompson (News Release. September 5, 2003, p. 1).

Another disturbing statistic, during the year prior to interview, 33.5 million Americans, about one in seven (14.2%), drove under the influence of *alcohol* at least once and 11 million (4.7%) were under the influence of an *illicit drug*! People 21 years of age had the highest rate of driving while drug impaired (18%).

These alarming statistics, only the tip of the iceberg, make clear that addiction and its related problems put all of us in harm's way. Substance abuse also devitalizes American industries where an estimated $60–100 billion is lost each year in work productivity through, absenteeism, drug-related accidents, medical claims, and theft. Other drug-related problems include family disintegration, health-care costs, and drug-related crime.

The Federal Office of Management and Budget estimates that drug abuse costs our country $300 billion a year, including government anti-drug programs as well as the costs of crime, healthcare, accidents, and lost productivity. Though billions have been spent trying to curtail illicit drug supplies, drugs are cheaper and more plentiful today than ever before.

Most federal and state funding to combat drug use is allocated to enforcement efforts that swell prison populations—today equaling the size of Houston, Texas, our fourth largest urban city. Keeping 1.35 million Americans behind bars costs the American public more than $25 billion each year. Astonishingly, one out of every 147 American citizens now resides in jail. And of these, more than 80%—nearly 1.2 million prisoners—are currently imprisoned for drug offenses.

These sad statistics reflect the draconian drug policies foisted on the American public by self-serving politicians and government bureaucrats, policies which misunderstand the nature of drug problems, are ineffective, and create additional hardships for users, their families, and communities. This continually failing federal drug policy, based on the criminal justice approach of catch-'em-and-lock-'em-up, spends billions per year of taxpayer money. Yet problems have increased, not subsided. "We're bigger, better, and more efficient," a criminal justice official observed, "but the problem just seems to grow at an astronomical rate" (personal communication).

Not surprisingly, a veritable army of workers now earn their living, directly or indirectly, dealing with substance abuse problems. Among these are at least 115,000 drug counselors (the combined membership of *only two of several* prominent drug counseling organizations). Drug counselors work in such places as private treatment facilities (both inpatient and outpatient), detoxification facilities, halfway houses, prisons and jails, the courts, schools, hospitals, churches, and governmental facilities.

As the client base for addiction counselors escalates, so does the need to adequately train them.

Prior to the 1970s, alcoholism and other drug dependencies were considered separate problems, and this division still lingers in some quarters. Two federal agencies, for example, still sponsor separate addiction programs: the National Institute on Alcoholism and Alcohol Abuse and the National Institute on Drug Abuse. Although progress has been slow in viewing alcohol as a psychoactive drug, the designation "alcohol and other drug dependencies" (AOD) now conveys a correct concept.

During the 1970s, standards were established to certify alcoholism counselors. But it wasn't until the 1980s that more insightful addictionologists defined alcoholism as an addiction similar to other addictions. At this time, both alcoholism counseling and counseling with clients addicted to other drugs began to be considered under a single set of standards, and private volunteer boards were created to establish and maintain standards for assessing clinical competencies.

Because standards and laws differ so widely from state to state, professional associations stepped up to establish national standards. In 1981, the International Certification and Reciprocity Consortium/Alcohol and Other Drug Abuse, Inc. (IC&RC/AODA) formed to standardize the certification of AOD counselors. A not-for-profit voluntary membership organization based in Falls Church, Virginia (6402 Arlington Blvd. #1200, Falls Church, VA 22042-2356; Telephone: 703-294-5827; Fax: 875-8867; e-mail: info@crcaada.org; Web site: www.icrcaoda.org), IC&RC/AODA is comprised of certifying agencies involved in credentialing alcohol and drug abuse counselors, clinical supervisors, and prevention specialists. Comprised of seventy agencies representing more than 35,000 certified professionals, IC&RC member boards are currently located in forty states, the District of Columbia, and ten countries outside the United States. Members also include the U.S. Army, U.S Air Force, U.S. Navy, Marines, the Indian Health Services, and the U.S. Administrative Office of the Courts (Coombs and Howatt, 2005).

Committed to public protection, IC&RC/AODA and its members provide quality, competency-based certification programs for professionals engaged in the prevention and treatment of addictions and related problems. The organization also promotes the establishment and recognition of minimum standards.

IC&RC/AODA offers five certifications: (a) Alcohol and Drug Counselor, (b) Advanced Alcohol and Drug Counselor, (c) Certified Clinical Supervisor, (d) Criminal Justice Addictions Professional, and (e) Certified Prevention Specialist.

Certification for Alcohol and Drug Counseloring requires the following:

1. *Experience*: Three years (6,000 hours) of documented supervised work experience with a Certified Alcohol and Drug Counselor in a paid or voluntary capacity providing direct counseling services to AOD clients (those with a diagnosis of alcohol and/or other drug dependency). One year of the three-year requirement may be exchanged with a bachelor's or other advanced degree in behavioral science.

2. *Education*: A total of 270 hours of documented formal classroom education, with six of these hours in professional ethics and responsibilities.

3. *Training*: Three hundred hours in a formal, systematic process that focuses on skill development and integration of knowledge in a setting where AOD counseling is provided.

4. *International Written Exam*: All certification boards must use the organization's international written exam in their processes of certifying new applicants.

5. *Case Presentation Method* (CPM): A standardized process by which an applicant's competence in the twelve core functions is measured by peers through an oral examination (these are spelled out in federal government publications, Such as *Addiction Counseling Competencies: The Knowledge, Skills, and Attitudes of Professional Practice*, SAMHSA Center for Substance Abuse Treatment, Technical Assistance Publication Series 21).

6. *Code of Ethics*: Each applicant must sign a code that gives the board a written enforcement and appeals mechanism to maintain ethical standards.

7. *Re-certification*: Standards must be published and forty hours of continuing education earned every two years.

The Association For Addiction Professionals (NAADAC)—formerly called the National Association of Alcoholism and Drug Abuse Counseling (the Association still uses the initials NAADAC)—is based in Alexandria, Virginia (901 N. Washington St. Suite 600, Alexandria, VA 22314; Telephone: 703-741-7686 or 800-548-0497; Fax: 741-7698 or 800-377-1136; Web site: www.naadac.org). With nearly 14,000 members and forty-seven state affiliates representing more than 80,000 addiction counselors, NAADAC is the nation's largest network of alcoholism and drug abuse treatment professionals. Founded in 1972, NAADAC began with a primary focus on alcohol and drug addiction counselors but now recognizes tobacco and gambling addiction.

Among the organization's national certification programs are the National Certified Addiction Counselor and the Master Addiction Counselor (MAC) designations (more than 15,000 counselors have been credentialed in the last eight years). Two other credentials are Tobacco Addiction Specialist Certification and Substance Abuse Professional.

NAADAC offers the following three AOD certifications:

1. The *National Certified Addiction Counselor (Level 1)* requires a current state certification/licensure as an AOD counselor, three years of full time or 6,000 hours of supervised AOD counseling, 270 contact hours of AOD class work or related counseling topics (including six hours of ethics and six of HIV/AIDS), and a passing score on the National Exam, Level 1.

2. The *National Certified Addiction Counselor (Level 2)* requires a bachelor's degree, current state certification/licensure as an AOD counselor, five years of full time or 10,000 hours of supervised AOD counseling, 450 contact hours in AOD classes including six hours of ethics and six of HIV/AIDS and a passing score on the National Exam, Level 2.

3. *Master Addiction Counselor (MAC)* requires a master's degree in the healing arts of an AOD related field, three years of supervised AOD clinical experience (two at the post–master's degree level) 500 contact hours of AOD class work, and a passing score on the National Exam (Coombs and Howatt, 2005).

The American Academy of Health Providers in the Addictive Disorders (AAHPAD), one of the big three certifying organizations, certifies those with doctoral or advanced level training in the health professions. Based in Duluth, Minnesota (314 West Superior Street, Suite 702, Duluth, MN 55802; Telephone: 218-727-3940; Fax: 722-0346; e-mail: info@americanacademy.org; Web site: www.americanacademy.org), it is an international nonprofit credentialing body, organized to maintain quality standards for treating addictive disorders. The Academy provides competency standards for addiction treatment professionals throughout the world.

The Academy's Certified Addiction Specialist (CAS) credential unites clinicians from various disciplines—doctors, psychiatrists, psychologists, nurses, social workers and other counselors—under a single standard of health care. Not focused exclusively on alcoholism and other drug addictions, the CAS credential covers all addictive disorders, such as compulsive gambling, sex addiction, and eating disorders. Those specializing in gambling disorders receive the designation Gambling Specialist Certification. The Academy also offers a Tobacco Cessation Specialist Certification.

Minimal eligibility requirements for the CAS include the following:

1. A master's or doctoral degree from an accredited health care training program.

2. Three years of postgraduate, supervised experience providing direct health care services to clients who have an addictive disorder. Predoctoral or premaster's internships at an approved site may be applied toward one year.

3. A portfolio of clinical training with a minimum of 120 hours in basic counseling skills including assessment, interviewing, and diagnosis, and a minimum of 60 hours of training in each area of specialization.

4. Three professional recommendations, at least one of which must be from a supervisor who is personally familiar with the applicant's work and can document his or her health care experience.

5. A completed application with the application fee. Continuing education annual renewal requirement is 20 hours in addiction related coursework (Coombs and Howatt, 2005).

Other countries also provide certifications. In Canada, for example, the Addiction Intervention Association (AIA), formed in 1985, certifies alcohol and drug counselors in all Canadian Provinces and Districts. Located in Cambridge, Ontario (78 Cowansview Road, Cambridge ON N1R 7N3, Canada; Telephone: 866-624-1911; Fax: 519-624-9972; e-mail: aia@aia.ca; Web site: www.aia.ca), AIA is a voluntary nonprofit organization affiliated with the IC&RC/AODA. (In addition to overseeing certifying bodies in the U.S., IC&RC monitors certifying boards in eight other countries, including Canada). AOD counselors certified by the AIA meet rigorous standards that include a combination of education, work experience, clinical supervision, knowledge and skills specific to the specialized area of substance abuse disorders, and must pass an examination that has been psychometrically tested for reliability and validity. Regardless of world locations, each IC&RC member board accepts, without qualification, the eligibility certificates of its sister boards. This creates a level of mobility for the professional AOD counselor (Coombs and Howatt, 2005).

Large business associations also offer AOD certification through their employee assistance programs. The Employee Assistance Certification Commission (EACC)/Certification Department (2101 Wilson Blvd., Suite 500, Arlington, VA 22201) offers the designation Certified Employee Assistance Professional (CEAP). Candidates must pass the CEAP exam demonstrating knowledge at the "journeyman" level of EAP work, meet the EAP work experience requirements, earn Professional Development Hours (PDHs), and complete the CEAP advisement process prior to application. Option 1 includes 3,000 hours of work experience in an EAP setting and 60 PDHs. Option 2 requires a graduate degree and 15 PDHs. Certification is granted for three years (Coombs and Howatt, 2005).

Several U.S. professional organizations also offer certifications in drug counseling. These include the American Society of Addiction Medicine (ASAM), the American College of Addictionology and Compulsive Disorders (ACACD), the National Board for Certified Counselors, Inc. (NBCC), and the Substance Abuse Program Administrators Association or SAPAA (Coombs and Howatt, 2005).

The American Society of Addiction Medicine (ASAM), based in Chevy Chase, Maryland (4601 N. Park Avenue, Upper Arcade #101, Chevy Chase, MD 20815, Telephone: 301-656-3920; Fax: 301-656-3815, email: email@asam.org. Web site: www.asam.org) is the nation's medical specialty society dedicated to educating physicians and medical students. It seeks to improve the treatment of individuals suffering from alcoholism and other addictions, promote research and prevention, and enlighten and inform both the medical community and the public about these issues. Since its inception in 1986, ASAM has certified more than 3,300 physicians in the specialty of *addiction medicine*. ASAM also offers a subspecialty for physicians interested in being certified as Medical Review Officers.

The American College of Addictionology and Compulsive Disorders (ACACD), based in Miami Beach, Florida (3303 Flamingo Drive, Miami Beach, FL 33140; Telephone: 305-535-8803, 800-490-7714; Fax: 538-2204 Web site: www.acacd.com), offers the Board Certified Addictionologist Credential (CAd). The CAd indicates that those with this credential are prepared with the skills to be a primary intervention resource in addiction intervention, treatment, and management and allows them to function in hospitals, residential and outpatient treatment centers, federal, state, and county criminal justice programs, and private practice.

National Board for Certified Counselors, Inc. (NBCC), located in Greensboro, NC at the School of Education, University of North Carolina, Greensboro, (Telephone: 336-547-0607; e-mail: eubanks@nbcc.org or dilda@nbcc.org; Web site: www.nbcc.org) is an independent not-for-profit credentialing body for counselors. It was incorporated in 1982 by the American Counseling Association (ACA) as an independent credentialing body to monitor a national certification system, identify those counselors who have voluntarily sought and obtained certification, and maintain a register of those counselors. Although NBCC and ACA have strong historical ties and work together to further the profession of counseling, the two organizations are completely separate entities.

Since 1982, NBCC's certification program requires recognized counselors meet predetermined standards in their training, experience, and performance on the National Counselor Examination for Licensure and Certification (NCE), the most portable credentialing examination in counseling. NBCC has more than 31,000 certified counselors working in more than fifty countries. These examinations are used by more than forty states, the District of Columbia, and Guam to credential counselors on a state level.

NBCC's flagship credential is the National Certified Counselor (NCC). But it also offers specialty certification in several other areas: (a) School counseling—The National Certified School Counselor (NCSC), (b) Clinical mental health counseling—The Certified Clinical Mental Health Counselor (CCMHC), and (c) Addictions counseling—The Master Addictions Counselor (MAC). The NCC is a prerequisite or corequisite for specialty credentials such as the MAC Credential. The requirements for the MAC credential include the following:

1. Documentation of a minimum of 12 semester hours of graduate coursework in the area of addictions which may include coursework in group and/or marriage and family counseling (up to six semester hours) OR 500 continuing education specifically in addictions.

2. Three years supervised experience as an addictions counselor at no fewer than 20 hours per week. Two of the three years must have been completed after the counseling master's degree was conferred.

3. A passing score on the Examination for Master Addictions Counselors (EMAC).

The Substance Abuse Program Administrators Association or SAPAA (7220 SW Sylvan Ct., Portland, OR 97225; Telephone: 866-538-4788; Fax: 503-297-4748; e-mail: president@ sapacc.org; web site: www.sapacc.org) has the mission to establish, promote, and communicate high standards of quality, integrity, and professionalism in the administration of workplace substance abuse prevention programs through education, training, and the exchange of ideas. SAPAA's national standards are recognized as the credential for the substance abuse testing and program management industry professional.

The Substance Abuse Program Administrators' Certification Commission (SAPACC), the national certifying body for substance program administrators who have chosen to be recognized as specialists with demonstrated proficiency in their field, is a nonprofit corporation dedicated to enhancing the quality and level of professional knowledge and skills. It administers proficiency training and examination and certification programs.

The Certified Substance Abuse Program Administrators (C-SAPA) certifying examination, formalized in 1997, aids employment opportunities and has increased the professional stature of the many professionals who have earned it. To be recognized as a C-SAPA, an administrator must (a) have worked in the substance abuse field for 6000 hours for 4000 hours if he or she holds a bachelor's degree or higher, and (b) demonstrate experience, with time spent in at least four of the following seven areas:

1. Development of policies and procedures
2. Administration of random programs
3. Medical Review Officer (MRO) interaction/oversight
4. Oversight and/or performance of specimen collection procedures
5. Supervisory training
6. Compliance with federal and state laws
7. Interaction/oversight with substance abuse professionals

Although voluntary boards, such as those already mentioned, currently oversee the credentialing process and serve as ethics review committees for certified counselors, many states are now moving to regulate AOD counselors. At least thirteen states have passed licensure bills to regulate AOD counselors, eleven have introduced licensure legislation and sixteen others are reportedly drafting bills which will soon be discussed by state legislatures. For more information, visit www.addictionrecov.org/paradigm/P_PR_W99/Kaplan.html.

Licensing laws vary from state to state. Some states have a tiered system that allows for two or three levels of licensure. Independent practice usually requires a master's degree while some who are licensed must work under supervision. When state laws are enacted to monitor AOD counselors, a grand-parenting period usually permits experienced AOD counselors to continue their clinical practice.

Each state has its own laws defining what professions are licensed and which licensing boards regulate each profession. In addition, each state licensing board has its own continuing education requirements. While many states accept at least one of the national certifying board's approvals, there is still some variance regarding the approval and acceptability of audiotapes and home study, even with the national approvals.

Two examples of state licensing agencies are: (a) The California Association of Alcoholism and Drug Abuse Counselors (CAADAC) and (b) the California Association for Alcohol/Drug Educators (CAADE).

The CAADAC (3400 Bradshaw Road, Suite A5, Sacramento, CA 95827; Telephone: 916-368-9412; Fax 916-368-9424; Web site: http://caadac.org) uses a "career ladder" approach in which career-minded addiction professionals are "covered" throughout their working lives—from beginning and volunteer staff, to seasoned, certified counselors. CAADAC offers professional recognition, opportunities for career growth, a registry for employment verification, ethical standards enforcement, and networking that allows for an AODA treatment team approach.

The CAADE (Credentialing Coordinator, Box 9152, Oxnard, CA 93031-7152; Telephone: 805-485-5247; Web site: www.caade.org) is one of the credentialing organizations included in the State of California Department of Alcohol and Drug Programs directory that meets the minimum criteria for AOD counseling. The CAADE seeks to promote and support quality education in alcohol and drug studies through (a) the development and application of accreditation and application of accreditation standards for alcohol and drug education, (b) certification of alcohol and drug treatment specialists, (c) provision for continuing education and professional development, and (d) participation in forums for examination, discussion, and debate on subjects related to alcohol and drug studies. With 733 members, CAADE acts as a credentialing organization for more than sixty college and university programs as part of the State of California Department of Alcohol and Drug Programs. Most states have similar, easily accessed, organizations.

CAADE and sister state organizations, seeking to ensure the development and promotion of alcohol and drug studies programs, develop guidelines to assist colleges and universities in admitting students, selecting appropriate faculty, and developing courses to meet the training needs of program managers, counselors, mental health workers, nurses, employee assistance personnel, and a growing number of other professionals within the field of Health and Human Services.

The Certified Addictions Treatment Specialist (CATS) is a credential that identifies the academically trained specialist who is able to facilitate behavioral change for persons affected by AOD. It signifies to a potential employer, colleague, or client that the specialist has practical experience in the area of evaluation and assessment, treatment planning, pharmacology of alcohol and other drugs, cultural issues and their relevance, models of intervention, family issues, legal and ethical issues, and referrals and record keeping.

As states move to regulate AOD counselors via licensure, educational standards rise. Because many AOD counselors formerly came from the recovering community, a competency-based standard was initially utilized and counselors were expected to master a set of core functions. Credentialing/licensing requirements now require specific academic training, supervised experience and passing relevant examinations (college based and state/organizational certification/licensure exams).

In 1993 the Center for Substance Abuse Treatment (CSAT) created the Addiction Technology Transfer Center (ATTC) Program, comprised of eleven geographically dispersed centers covering twenty-four states and Puerto Rico, to foster improvements in the preparation of addiction treatment professionals. As part of that program, the ATTC National Curriculum Committee was established to evaluate existing curricula and establish priorities for curriculum development.

The Committee's first activity was to define the competencies essential to the effective practice of counseling for psychoactive substance use disorders. Those competencies could then be used as criteria for evaluating curriculum materials. The Committee published *Addiction Counselor Competencies* (National Curriculum Committee, 2000), which describes the knowledge, skills, and attitudes that characterize competent practice in addictions counseling. The Curriculum Committee developed the following list of basic knowledge, skills, and attitudes—transdisciplinary foundations—that should be taught in reputable AOD training programs:

Understanding Addiction

1. Understand a variety of models and theories of addiction and other problems related to substance use.
2. Recognize the social, political, economic, and cultural context within which addiction and substance abuse exist, including risk and resiliency factors that characterize individuals and groups and their living environments.
3. Describe the behavioral, psychological, physical health, and social effects of psychoactive substances on the user and significant others.

4. Recognize the potential for substance use disorders to mimic a variety of medical and psychological disorders and the potential for medical and psychological disorders to coexist with addiction and substance abuse.

Treatment Knowledge

1. Describe the philosophies, practices, policies, and outcomes of the most generally accepted and scientifically supported models of treatment, recovery, relapse prevention, and continuing care for addiction and other substance-related problems.
2. Recognize the importance of family, social networks, and community systems in the *systems* treatment and recovery process.
3. Understand the importance of research and outcome data and their application in clinical practice.
4. Understand the value of an interdisciplinary approach to addiction treatment.

Application to Practice

1. Understand the established diagnostic criteria for substance use disorders and describe treatment modalities and placement criteria within the continuum of care.
2. Describe a variety of helping strategies for reducing the negative effects of substance use, abuse, and dependence.
3. Tailor helping strategies and treatment modalities to the client's stage of dependence, change, or recovery.
4. Provide treatment services appropriate to the personal and cultural identity and language of the client.
5. Adapt practice to the range of treatment settings and modalities.
6. Be familiar with medical and pharmacological resources in the treatment of substance use disorders.
7. Understand the variety of insurance and health maintenance options available and the importance of helping clients access those benefits.
8. Recognize that crisis may indicate an underlying substance use disorder and may be a window of opportunity for change.
9. Understand the need for and the use of methods for measuring treatment outcome.

Professional Readiness

1. Understand diverse cultures and incorporate the relevant needs of culturally diverse groups, as well as people with disabilities, into clinical practice.
2. Understand the importance of self-awareness in ones' personal, professional, and cultural life.
3. Understand the addiction professional's obligations to adhere to ethical and behavioral standards of conduct in the helping relationship.
4. Understand the importance of ongoing supervision and continuing education in the delivery of client services.
5. Understand the obligation of the addiction professional to participate in prevention as well as treatment.
6. Understand and apply setting-specific policies and procedures for handling crises or dangerous situations, including safety measures for clients and staff.

The primary purpose of this book is to help AOD counseling students, interns, and trainees to prepare for two (possibly three) exams: (a) the comprehensive exams usually required for graduation in AOD college programs, and (b) the certification or licensing exam required by professional organizations and states. This book offers students enrolled in AOD courses a handy review guide.

Others who will find this book useful include program administrators, grant writers, researchers, and policy makers in the field of addiction. AOD educators, faculty in the behavioral sciences, counselors, clinical supervisors, mental health professionals, and all who work with drug and alcohol related problems—education, health, drug prevention, drug control, research, and public policy—who wish to update their knowledge will find this book attractive. Containing well-organized and current content information, this practical review volume provides a useful handbook. In short, this book is both a *professional handbook* and a *course textbook*.

Topical chapters, written by leading experts, cover the standard information usually tested on comprehensive and licensing exams. Organized into six sections, they address the following:

- *Addiction Basics*—addiction's defining features, the neurobiology of addiction, types of addictive drugs, and the history of addiction treatment, policy and recovery in America.
- *Personality Development and Drugs*—lifespan development and drugs, diverse drug abusing populations, psychopathology, and families and drugs.
- *Common Client Problems*—smoking, problem drinking, illicit drug use and prescription drug abuse, HIV/AIDS, and coexisting disorders.
- *Counseling Theories and Skills*—classical counseling models, contemporary counseling models, assessing, diagnosing and treatment planning, case management, and handling crises.
- *Treatment Resources*—addiction recovery tools, drug treatment and aftercare programs and networks, drug abuse prevention tools and programs, and harm reduction tools and programs.
- *Career Issues*—drugs and the law, professional ethics, professional development, and professional examinations in alcohol and other drug abuse counseling.

All twenty-six chapters have a parallel format, designed to enhance a comprehensive and personally rewarding review of AOD information. Special features include the following:

- *Truth or Fiction*—a list of fifteen true/false questions at the beginning of the chapter.
- *Insert Boxes*—thirty four-item multiple choice questions approximating questions routinely given on AOD certification exams that can be answered by reading the chapter.
- *Discussion Questions*—a list of provocative discussion questions at the end of the chapter.
- *Key Terms*—a list of key terms and their definitions.
- *Suggested Further Reading*—an annotated list of leading content sources for additional study.

In preparing for comprehensive or certification exams, I recommend that you master the important information in each chapter of this book by following these steps:

1. As a *pretest*, before reading the chapter, write down your answers to the true/false questions and the multiple choice questions.
2. Carefully read the chapter, making *written notes* as you go.
3. *Study your notes*.

4. Repeat Step 1 above and *compare results* with your pretest and the correct answers provided in the key at the end of the book.
5. Note weak areas and *re-study* these sections.
6. Using your notes, *meet with another interested student*—someone who will challenge you with questions—and review what you've learned. Then discuss the ten questions listed at chapter end.

To maximize your success, I recommend you read Kelman and Straker's paperback book, *Study Without Stress: Mastering Medical Sciences* (2000). One of nine books in my *Book Series on Medical Student Survival*, this practical study guide teaches beleaguered medical students how to master an overwhelming mountain of basic science materials. The techniques explained there will also help you.

If you follow these steps, I predict that you will confidently pass your examinations with flying colors the first time around.

SUGGESTED FURTHER READING

Bianco, D. P., Moran, A., & Bianco, D. J. (Eds.). (1996). *Professional and Occupational Licensing Directory: A Descriptive Guide to State and Federal Licensing, Registration, and Certification Requirements* (2nd ed.). Detroit MI: Gale Group.

Describes state and federal licensing, registration, and certification programs in various occupations.

Coombs, R. H., & Howatt, W. A. (2005). *The Addiction Counselor's Desk Reference: Practical Resources to Enhance Counseling Effectiveness*. New York: Wiley.

A great wealth of practical resource material pertinent to certifications and counseling. Much of the information presented here about certifying agencies comes from this book.

REFERENCES

Coombs, R. H., & Howatt, W. A. (2005). *The Addiction Counselor's Desk Reference: A Comprehensive Guide*. New York: Wiley.
Kelman, E. G., & Straker, K. C. (2000). *Study without stress: Mastering medical sciences*. Thousand Oaks, CA: Sage.
National Curriculum Committee, Center for Substance Abuse Treatment. (2000). *Addiction Counselor Competencies* (DHHS Pub. No. SMA 00-3468). Washington, DC: U.S. Government Printing Office.
News Release. *22 Million in U.S. Suffer From Substance Dependence or Abuse*, Press Office, Substance Abuse and Mental Health Services Administration, U.S. Department of Health and Human Services, Retrieved September 5, 2003, from www.hhs.gov/news.
Office of Applied Studies, Substance Abuse and Mental Health Services Administration, U.S. Department of Health and Human Services. (2003). *Overview of findings from the 2002 National Survey on Drug Use and Health*. (NHSDA series H-21, DHHS publication No. SMA 03-3774). Rockville, MD.

Acknowledgments

I gratefully acknowledge *Carla Cronkhite Vera*, my esteemed assistant at UCLA, for her expert help with every aspect of this book. She assisted me in developing the book proposal, selecting authors, providing clear author guidelines, and effectively networking with all authors. She also suggested ways to improve chapter manuscripts and handled myriad details and problems with characteristic efficiency and good cheer. *Carol Jean Coombs,* my life's partner, provided valued counsel and advice and suggested ways to effectively shorten lengthy chapter manuscripts without sacrificing important content. Sandra and Steve Brimhall prepared the subject and author indexes.

ADDICTION BASICS

1

Addiction's Defining Characteristics

Howard J. Shaffer and Mark J. Albanese

Division on Addictions, Harvard Medical School;
Department of Psychiatry, The Cambridge Health Alliance

TRUTH OR FICTION?

___ *1. Addiction can exist without drug taking.*
___ *2. Most addictions emerge from an early positive experience with the object of addiction.*
___ *3. Addiction is a formal diagnosis in the American Psychiatric Association's DSM–IV.*
___ *4. People often think that drugs cause addiction.*
___ *5. There is a gold standard that is available to identify the presence of addiction.*
___ *6. Clinicians should make diagnoses tentatively.*
___ *7. Formulations have little to do with how clinicians understand addictive behaviors.*
___ *8. Addiction can exist without physical dependence.*
___ *9. Addictive disorders are limited to alcohol and drug related problems.*
___ *10. The original use of the term* addiction *referred to a unique and excessive pattern of drug taking.*
___ *11. Dopamine has been implicated in the development of addiction.*
___ *12. All scientists agree that behavioral addictions exist.*
___ *13. Tolerance and withdrawal provide evidence of neuroadaptation.*
___ *14. Objects of addiction shift subjective experiences.*
___ *15. Clinicians find it easy to distinguish people who are overwhelmed by impulses to act from those who are not willing to resist these impulses.*

Addiction is ... an attachment to, or dependence upon, any substance, thing, person or idea so single-minded and intense that virtually all other realities are ignored or given second place—and consequences, even lethal ones, are disregarded. (Mack, 2002)[1]

---

[1] This definition can apply to individuals, groups and diverse collectives (e.g., cultures).

It is best to think of any affliction—a disease, a disability . . . —as a text and of "society" as its author. (Blum, 1985, p. 221)

DECONSTRUCTING ADDICTION

Despite simple working definitions of **addiction**, the essence of the term remains elusive. Without a clear definition, researchers will continue finding it very difficult, for example, to determine addiction prevalence rates, etiology, or the necessary and sufficient causes that stimulate recovery (Shaffer, 1997a, 1999). Also, without a precise definition of addiction, clinicians will encounter diagnostic and treatment matching difficulties, and satisfactory treatment outcome measures will remain lacking. Finally, without an agreed upon definition, public policy makers will find it difficult to establish regulatory legislation, determine treatment need, establish health care systems, and promulgate new guidelines for health care reimbursement.

In this chapter, we examine the idea of addiction and its consequences. We consider the meaning of addiction and the contemporary schemas for understanding, defining, identifying, and treating addiction. It is important to note that addiction is a dynamic process that waxes and wanes. People with addiction often go through phases of exacerbation and abstention; many also have episodes of controlled activity when they use the object of their addiction intermittently or more often but only to a limited extent. There is considerable evidence that people with addiction can recover with and without treatment. Despite the connotation of an "addict" as someone who cannot change and is resistant to the influence of treatment, people with addiction do change and often respond positively to treatment experiences.

The term *addict*, a pejorative term, is no longer acceptable in many journals (e.g., the *Journal of Substance Abuse Treatment* was one of the first publications to establish an editorial policy that avoids the use of the term *addict*). Just as the expression *addict* is increasingly unwelcome in scholarly and scientific journals, the term *addiction* has been unwelcome in diagnostic manuals (e.g., *Diagnostic and Statistical Manual of Mental Disorders*, American Psychiatric Association [APA], 1980, 1987, 1994, 2000).

A Paradigm Shift

From substance abuse to shopping (Baker, 2000; Catalano & Sonenberg, 1993; Christenson et al., 1994), eating carrots (Cerny & Cerny, 1992), drinking water to intoxication (Pickering & Hogan, 1971; Rowntree, 1923), committing anti-social or criminal acts (Hodge, McMurran, & Hollin, 1997), and using computers (O'Reilly, 1996; Shaffer, Hall, & Vander Bilt, 2000), social observers have applied the notion of addiction to many and varied human activities (Orford, 1985). Until recently, the contemporary use of addiction has been limited almost exclusively to substance using behavior patterns that evidence adverse consequences, often including the emergence of neuroadaptation (e.g., tolerance and withdrawal). When scientists began to consider the matter of behavioral addictions (Marks, 1990), the construct of addiction became more plastic and complex.

1. Which of the following statements is true?
   a. A precise definition of addiction remains elusive.
   b. People with addiction often go through phases of exacerbation and abstention.
   c. The term *addict* is considered pejorative and unacceptable by many professional journals.
   d. All of the above.

The negative consequences of addiction typically include biological, psychological, and social harms. The negative biological consequences often—but not always—include the emergence of neuroadaptation. ***Neuroadaptation*** is the technical term for the observation that (a) an increased dose is needed to experience the same subjective effects as with a previous lower dose, and (b) there is a stereotypical pattern of discomfort upon stopping use. These elements of neuroadaptation are ***tolerance*** and ***withdrawal***, respectively. Tolerance among heroin users, for example, refers to the observation that regular users require more heroin to get the same level of intoxication experienced previously at a lower dose; withdrawal means that these users get sick when they stop using the drug and that using the drug again can make this stereotypical pattern of illness stop.

2. When an increased dose is needed to experience the same subjective effects as with lower doses before, a person has developed:
   a. tolerance.
   b. withdrawal.
   c. abuse.
   d. dependence.

3. The stereotypical pattern of discomfort upon stopping use is known as:
   a. tolerance.
   b. withdrawal.
   c. abuse.
   d. dependence.

Pathological gambling and other patterns of behavioral excess also can show neuroadaptation despite the absence of drug ingestion. For example, disordered gamblers often evidence a pattern of increasing bets to achieve the same level of excitement they experienced before at a lower level of wagering; gamblers also report symptoms of withdrawal when they cut back or stop gambling (Wray & Dickerson, 1981). However, not all scientists accept the idea of behavioral addictions (Holden, 2001), and the consequence of this debate is conceptual chaos about the concept of addiction (Shaffer, 1997a).

The History of an Idea

The idea of **addiction** emerged long ago. Interestingly, early uses of the term were considerably less negative than its current use—although even today there still is a tendency to use addiction to describe passion and fervor for cars, foods, computers, and other objects of interest. According to the Oxford English Dictionary (Oxford University Press, 1971), the first use of addiction emerged during the seventeenth century (Roman law, 1625) when a formal sentence of court represented a surrender, or dedication, of any one to a master. Shortly thereafter (i.e., 1641), devotion to a habit or pursuit was considered the essence of addiction. Such habits or pursuits included reading and involvement with agricultural activities.

4. The notion of addiction has been applied to:
   a. shopping.
   b. substance abuse.
   c. using computers.
   d. all of the above.

5. Addiction first referred to:
   a. sexual perversion.
   b. alcohol misuse.
   c. dedication to a master.
   d. none of the above.

6. The idea of addiction began to refer to the state of being addicted to a drug during what century?
   a. sixteenth
   b. seventeenth
   c. eighteenth
   d. nineteenth

It wasn't until the eighteenth century that the idea of addiction began to refer to the compulsion or need to continue *taking a drug* as a result of taking it in the past. Contrary to conventional wisdom, the idea of addiction derives originally from the excessive habits and pursuits of everyday life—not the ingestion of **psychoactive** substances. Almost a century after addiction became linked to drug use, the Chinese language (i.e., Cantonese *yn*) reflected the state of craving. The forms *yin* and *ying* may reflect the Mandarin pronunciation *yn* of the same character (e.g., having a yin [1876] or yearning; Oxford University Press, 1971).

The concept of addiction has important consequences for understanding human behavior. Addiction implies that people have urges or cravings that make it difficult to control or manage their behavior. The presence of addiction suggests that sufferers might not be able to conform their behavior to the requirements of community life because of impulses beyond their control. Ultimately, the idea of addiction stimulates the development and sustains its conceptual alter-ego—control—which has its roots in fifteenth- and sixteenth-century language referring both to relationships with one's passions and to power relationships between people (Oxford University Press, 1971). In the United States' criminal justice system, these ideas have influenced the notion of *mens rea* or "evil mind" and serve as the architectural superstructure of insanity—but do not share the full exculpatory power of insanity since most states assume some modicum of responsibility for taking the drink or drug that led to a criminal act.

> *The concept of addiction currently is going through a renaissance and return to its origins. People toss around the term "addiction" to describe someone's relationship to a job, a boyfriend, or a computer. But scientists have traditionally confined their use of the term to substances—namely alcohol and other drugs—that clearly foster physical dependence in the user. That's changing, however. New knowledge about the brain's reward system, much gained by super refined brain scan technology, suggests that as far as the brain is concerned, a reward's a reward, regardless of whether it comes from a chemical or an experience. And where there's a reward, there's the risk of the vulnerable brain getting trapped in a compulsion. "Over the past 6 months, more and more people have been thinking that, contrary to earlier views, there is commonality between substance addictions and other compulsions," says Alan Leshner, head of the National Institute on Drug Abuse (NIDA) and incoming executive officer of the American Association for the Advancement of Science, publisher of Science. (Holden, 2001, p. 980)*

The Transformation of Addiction From an Idea to an Illness: The Emergence of a Paradigm

On Addiction: Current Status

Addiction is a lay term, often used by scientists, but not included in diagnostic manuals like *DSM–IV–TR* or *ICD–10* (APA, 2000; World Health Organization, 1992). Dependence is a more scientific construct, occasionally used by lay people. Recognizing the problems associated with the meaning of addiction, Vaillant (1982) suggested that, instead of seeking a strict operational definition, we should think of alcoholism like mountains and seasons: we know these things when we see them. Clinicians working with the full range of addictive disorders (e.g., substance, gambling, and other excessive patterns of activity) often apply similar subjective strategies as they try to determine whether addiction is present and if it requires treatment.

7. Addiction is:
   a. a lay term.
   b. a scientific term.
   c. included in *DSM–IV–TR*.
   d. included in *ICD–10*.

8. Substance dependence includes which of the following symptoms?
   a. cognitive
   b. behavioral
   c. physiological
   d. all of the above

9. Substance abuse is:
   a. less severe than substance dependence.
   b. a maladaptive pattern of substance use.
   c. both a and b.
   d. neither a nor b.

Despite some conceptual confusion, there are useful guidelines to help identify people struggling with addiction. For example, *DSM–IV–TR* discusses the long-term substance use disorders in terms of ***abuse*** and ***dependence*** (e.g., alcohol or drug abuse and dependence) and specifies the main features of substance *dependence* as "a cluster of cognitive, behavioral, and physiological symptoms indicating that the individual continues use of the substance despite significant substance-related problems" (APA, 2000, p. 192). *DSM–IV–TR* defines substance *abuse*—less serious than substance dependence—as "a maladaptive pattern of substance use manifested by recurrent and significant adverse consequences related to the repeated use of substances" (APA, 2000, p. 198). Before we consider this framework and the practical or applied aspects of this architecture for addiction treatment, it is important to understand the conceptual issues that influence clinical judgments about the assessment and treatment of addiction.

Distinguishing Use, Abuse, Dependence, and Addiction

In the absence of a consensual definition of addiction, clinicians and public policy makers often debate whether people who use drugs also "abuse" drugs. Treatment providers and programs commonly mistake drug users for "abusers;" and both of these drug using groups are readily mistaken for people who are drug dependent. Too often the results are unnecessary hospitalizations, increased medical costs, and patients who learn to distrust health care providers. Alternatively, absent a precise definition of addiction, some people fail to receive the care they require. As a result, practice guidelines in the addictions are equivocal and health care systems experience management and reimbursement chaos.

Even under most established constructions of addiction, not all drug dependent patients evidence addictive behavior.[2] For example, from a biological perspective, postoperative patients often receive opioids for the treatment of pain; many of these patients experience neuroadaptation, but never seek these drugs after their pain subsides. Patients sufficiently treated with opioid analgesics for an extended time typically do not behave as if they are addicted despite being drug dependent in the technical sense. Alternatively, from a psychosocial view, in most civilized countries, under nearly every traditional circumstance, people who are nicotine dependent do not evidence addiction—primarily because the substance is legal and readily available. However, when tobacco is recast as a socially or legally illicit substance, addictive behavior patterns emerge. To illustrate, during a political struggle in Italy, cigarettes were in short supply. The Reuters News Service reported the following:

> Over the past week, police have reported episodes they say are reminiscent of the days of wartime shortages. Prostitutes in some parts of the country, for example, have resorted to holding up two fingers to passing cars, meaning their price is two 200 cigarette cartons. In Florence on Saturday night one man was mugged with the threat: 'Your cigarettes or your life.' Lines of cars built up on the French and Swiss borders at the weekend as desperate smokers sought supplies. Pharmacists reported a run on nicotine patches. Street peddlers were doing a roaring trade in smuggled cigarettes, with newspapers reporting single packets of foreign cigarettes fetching $14.40 on the black market in many areas—six times the normal price. (Reuters News Service, 1992, p. 50)

Casual observers of this situation might have thought that such circumstances could only emerge from an addictive relationship with heroin or other opioids. Complicating conceptual matters further, physical dependence is not always necessary for the notion of addiction to apply. For example, upon stopping, pathological gamblers who do not use alcohol or other psychoactive drugs can reveal physical symptoms that appear to be very similar to either opioid, stimulant, or polysubstance withdrawal (Wray & Dickerson, 1981). Perhaps the patterns and experience of excessive behaviors are more important than the objects of these acts.

10. A chronic pain patient receives opioid analgesics for an extended period of time and gradually needs to increase the dose to get adequate pain relief. After the pain subsides, the patient stops the medication and never seeks it again. Words that describe the process that the patient experienced include all the following EXCEPT:
    a. addiction.
    b. dependence.
    c. neuroadaptation.
    d. tolerance.

Addiction With Dependence and Without Dependence

If addiction can exist with or without physical dependence, then the concept of addiction must be sufficiently broad to include human predicaments related to either substances or activities. Scientists and clinicians refer to nondrug addiction activities such as gambling or shopping—activities that do not involve the ingestion of psychoactive substances—as "process or behavioral addictions" (Shaffer, 1996, 1997a, 1999). Although we could debate whether we should include substance or process addictions within the kingdom of addiction, technically

---

[2] Although a full discussion of this matter is beyond the scope of this chapter, it also is important to note that not all people with addiction are impaired in every aspect of their daily life.

there is little choice. Just as ingested substances precipitate impostor molecules vying for receptor sites within the brain, human activities stimulate naturally occurring neurotransmitters (Hyman, 1994; Hyman & Nestler, 1993). The activity of these naturally occurring psychoactive substances likely will be determined to be the mediating cause of many process addictions. As we will see later, the biological substrate is similar for both.

11. Addiction can exist:
    a. with physical dependence.
    b. without physical dependence.
    c. both a and b.
    d. neither a nor b.

12. Nondrug addiction activities such as gambling or shopping are referred to as:
    a. process addictions.
    b. behavioral addictions.
    c. both a and b.
    d. neither a nor b.

The Neurochemistry of Addiction

Shifting Subjective States

If addiction can exist both with and without physical dependence, we might consider the objects of addiction as those things that reliably and robustly shift subjective experience, that is, those activities that consistently change experience in a desired direction (e.g., activities that always make people feel good).

The most reliable and robust "shifters" hold the greatest potential to stimulate the development of addictive disorders. However, since the strength and consistency of these activities to shift subjective states vary across individuals and settings, scientists are unable to predict with accuracy who will become addicted. Nevertheless, psychoactive drugs and certain other activities correlate highly with shifting subjective states because these activities reliably influence and change emotional experiences. Consequently, psychoactive drug use (Hyman, 1994) and certain other behaviors (e.g., gambling) tend to be ranked high among the activities that often are associated with addictive behaviors.

13. Shifters of subjective experience:
    a. are always drugs.
    b. change experience in a desired direction.
    c. do not include gambling.
    d. usually involve sex.

The most common conceptual error committed by clinicians, researchers, and public policy makers is to suppose that addiction is a latent property of an object (e.g., a drug or game of chance). Conventional wisdom, for example, refers to "addictive drugs" or "addictive gambling." However, addiction is not the product of a substance, game, or technology, though each of these has the capacity to influence human experience. Experience is the currency of addiction. When a particular pattern of behavior reliably and robustly changes emotional experience, the potential for addiction emerges. In other words, addiction is the description of a relationship between organisms and objects within their environment, not simply the result of an object's attributes. As such, the causes of addiction are multifactorial (Zinberg, 1984).

Final Common Pathways: The Currency of Addiction

Addictive behaviors are neurobiologically similar. To stimulate and sustain involvement with the various objects of addiction, the brain's **reward** system must be energized. Originally, the reward system likely existed to ensure the propagation of the species by implicitly teaching people that sex was pleasurable and should be repeated. The same reward system eventually became activated, for some people, by other pleasurable experiences (e.g., using psychoactive drugs, gambling, eating, shopping).

The reward system of the brain includes the ventral tegmental area (VTA), located in the anterior ventral midbrain and the nucleus accumbens (NA), located in the ventral forebrain. The dopaminergic neurons that have their cell bodies in the VTA and terminals in the NA are part of the brain's mesolimbic dopamine system. Dopamine is one class of neurotransmitters that scientists have implicated in the development and maintenance of addictive behaviors. The brain reward system is enhanced by substances such as alcohol, cocaine, and opiates. As Wise states: "The drugs known to synergize with brain stimulation reward . . . are, for the most part, drugs of abuse" (Wise, 1996, p. 327). Furthermore, functional neuroimaging studies, which display images of a living, functioning brain responding to a task, reveal that anticipation of cocaine, money, and beauty energize the reward system (Aharon et al., 2001; Breiter, Aharon, Kahneman, Dale, & Shizgal, 2001). The observation of disparate objects stimulating similar neurobiological pathways indicates that, regardless of the object of addiction, the brain is the final common pathway for addictive behaviors. When people do not experience the subjective pleasure associated with the stimulation of the brain's reward system, they typically stop engaging in these behaviors. Interestingly, while opiates enhance the reward system, opiate antagonists, such as naloxone and naltrexone diminish the system's operation.

14. The brain reward system includes:
    a. the ventral tegmental area.
    b. the nucleus accumbens.
    c. both a and b.
    d. neither a nor b.

15. Reward deficiency syndrome results from hypofunction of which system?
    a. dopamine
    b. serotonin
    c. epinephrine
    d. glutamate

16. Which of the following is true?
    a. Opiates act through the endogenous opioid system.
    b. Alcohol acts through the GABA system.
    c. Both a and b.
    d. Neither a nor b.

A *reward deficiency syndrome* has been implicated in vulnerability to addiction (Blum et al., 2000). This syndrome is a result of hypofunction of the dopamine system described above. People with such dysfunction fail to experience sufficient pleasure; they adapt to this circumstance by engaging in behaviors that stimulate the faulty reward circuitry. Further:

Epidemiological, genetic, and neurobiological evidence support the notion that vulnerability to addiction (as well as impulsive and compulsive behaviors) is genetically transmitted. It is not necessary to establish that all addiction is caused by genetic vulnerability. Heavy exposure to alcohol and other drugs may set in motion perturbators of neurochemistry and receptors which may have similar end results. (Blum et al., p. 2)

Also:

It does not seem to be the case that all habit-forming drugs activate the same reward mechanism in the brain. The evidence is good, however, that several . . . substances—the psychomotor stimulants, the opiates, nicotine, phencyclidine, and cannabis—synergize with rewarding medial forebrain bundle brain stimulation, and elevate—as does the stimulation itself— . . . dopamine concentrations in the nucleus accumbens and other dopamine terminal fields. (Wise, 1996)

It is vital to note that, given the variety of brain receptor systems affected by the assortment of abusable substances, other transmitter systems (e.g., norepinephrine, GABA, glutamate, serotonin) interact with the dopamine reward system. Ingested psychoactive substances—and human activities in general—exert their influence on subjective experience through the brain's endogenous neurotransmitter systems. For example, opiates function through the endogenous opioid system and alcohol through the GABA system. These neurotransmitter systems, as well as others, impinge upon and modulate the dopamine reward system.

Another important consideration in understanding the biological underpinnings of addiction is to consider the different routes of administration for substances of abuse. Cocaine offers a good example. It can be inhaled, ingested orally, snorted, or injected intravenously. When ingested orally, cocaine has slow onset and achieves relatively low peak concentration in the blood. Conversely, intravenous and inhaled cocaine exerts its effect within seconds and achieves high blood levels. Furthermore, all forms of cocaine use can have toxic effects, such as cardiac arrhythmia and myocardial infarction. While the quicker routes of cocaine administration might lead to higher rates of addiction compared to oral ingestion, cocaine is the substance in both instances; this observation reveals the importance of identifying and understanding the route of any drug administration. Regardless of route of administration, each class of psychoactive drugs ultimately interfaces with the brain's reward system in similar ways.

17. Orally ingested cocaine:
    a. has quicker onset than inhaled cocaine.
    b. has slower onset than inhaled cocaine.
    c. has higher peak blood concentration than inhaled cocaine.
    d. does not act through the brain's reward system.

Identifying the Primary Dimensions and Distinguishing Characteristics of Addiction

Contemporary addiction workers think of addictive behavior as having three primary components: (1) some element of craving or compulsion, (2) losing self-control, and (3) continuing the behavior in question in spite of associated adverse consequences. Though these dimensions provide a useful map for understanding the elements of addiction, we must remember that the map is not the territory (Shaffer, 1992, 1999; Shaffer & Robbins, 1991, 1995) and a diagnosis is not the disease (Shaffer & Robbins, 1991; Szasz, 1991).

Addiction can be distinguished from compulsive patterns of behavior by the quality of associated subjective states. Addictive behaviors tend to be *ego-syntonic*, particularly early in the development of an addiction. People experience ego-syntonic behaviors as consistent with their sense of self and do not anticipate that these activities will cause personal problems. In fact, most addictions emerge from positive experiences (e.g., winning a bet, relieving psychological or physical discomfort by ingesting drugs). People tend to experience other psychiatric illnesses as *ego-dystonic* (i.e., ego-alien). A person in an ego-dystonic state feels as if something—an "otherness"—is taking control against his or her will and directing behaviors toward undesirable ends. Despite not wanting to act on these renegade urges, people with compulsive disorders act to discharge the mounting pressure—then they feel some measure of tension relief. Clinicians often can distinguish obsessive-compulsive disorders from addiction by the extent of ego-dystonic thoughts and distress that accompany these disorders compared to addiction, which usually reveals subjective anguish only after the fact (Shaffer, 1994a).

18. A component of addictive behavior is:
    a. craving.
    b. loss of control.
    c. continued behavior despite adverse consequences.
    d. all of the above.

19. Early in their development, addictions tend to be:
    a. ego-syntonic.
    b. ego-dystonic.
    c. both a and b.
    d. neither a nor b.

Behavioral Excess as Evidence: Avoiding Tautologies

For scientists, the concept of addiction represents a troublesome tautology that has contributed to keeping addiction a very popular lay concept and not part of the diagnostic nomenclature. The tautology operates like this: when observers notice adverse consequences, stimulated by repetitive behavior patterns, apparently occurring against the actor's better judgment, they often infer the presence of addiction.

> *The problem is that there is no independent way to confirm that the "addict" cannot help himself and therefore the label is often used as a tautological explanation of the addiction. The habit is called an addiction because it is not under control but there is no way to distinguish a habit that is uncontrollable from one that is simply not controlled. (Akers, 1991, in Davies, 1996, p. S41)*

Even if we consider the substance use disorders and pathological gambling as the leading categorical candidates for addiction status in a new diagnostic classification system, these diagnostic manuals will remain inadequate on the matter of addiction if social consequences and self-report direct the nosological schema. As organized currently, diagnostic manuals like *DSM–IV* increase the likelihood that clinicians repeatedly can classify disorders like pathological gambling correctly. However, these systems fail to address the construct validity of what is being classified because the "addictive" disorders (e.g., pathological gambling and substance use disorders) are assumed to exist by inference from the consequences associated with the behaviors in question (Barron, 1998).

Diagnostic systems that rest upon a mix of self-report and corroborating perspectives do not resolve the problem. Individuals struggling with intemperate behavior suffer the burden of *fundamental attribution error* (Ross, 1977). This cognitive error leads people with addiction to the perception that an external object stimulated their excessive behavior (e.g., addictive drugs, or addictive gambling); conversely, observers tend to think the cause of intemperance is a relatively stable underlying trait (e.g., weak character or addictive personality). Both perspectives are biased.

ADDICTION AND GOLD STANDARDS

No Gold Standard Currently

A *gold standard* is a definitive index against which diagnosticians and researchers can judge the status of a clinical state. Many underlying conditions that cause illness—latent states—are invisible to the observer. Honesty, greediness, and integrity, for example, are invisible latent states that influence day-to-day behavior and are judged to be present only by their consequences. In medicine, the gold standard for the diagnosis of AIDS is a blood test that determines the extent of T-cells; for diabetes, it is a blood test that determines the blood glucose level. At present, there is no gold standard for judging the presence or absence of addiction. Even the existence of neuroadaptation—tolerance and withdrawal—does not represent a gold standard against which clinicians can judge the presence or absence of addiction. Neuroadaptive signs simply represent the development of physical dependence symptoms. Dependence is often positively correlated with the presence of addiction, but this relationship is not sufficiently reliable to be a gold standard.

> 20. Which of the following is the gold standard definition of addiction?
>   a. tolerance
>   b. withdrawal
>   c. neuroadaptation
>   d. none of the above

The Gold Standard Future

Like many psychiatric disorders, addiction does not have an independent gold standard. Absent a gold standard, addiction often suffers from the "myth of mental illness" stigma (Szasz, 1987, 1991). For addiction to emerge as a viable scientific construct, whether psychoactive drug use or pathological gambling, investigators need to establish a gold standard against which clinicians can judge the presence or absence of the disorder. Social consensus among scientists is insufficient to establish a gold standard, though it can yield a criterion to establish concurrent validity in the absence of a bona fide gold standard. To achieve gold status, the benchmark must be independent of the disorder being judged. If addiction represents an *uncontrollable impulse* and not an *uncontrolled habit*, then there must be independent validation of the irrepressible impulse or the impaired regulatory mechanisms[3] (Kipnis, 1997). The definition of addiction cannot be limited to intemperate behaviors that only result in adverse consequences. If addiction is a primary disorder, independent of its consequences, clinicians and scientists should be able to identify the disorder without knowing its consequences. Nevertheless, clinical significance and human suffering require that we attend to addictive behavior patterns whether or not we can distinguish it with precision.

---

[3] Pathological gambling is now classified in *DSM–IV* as an impulse disorder. From this perspective, it represents an irrepressible impulse—the hallmark of an impulse disorder. Unlike most characterizations of addiction as primarily ego-syntonic, clinicians consider impulse disorders, like obsessive-compulsive disorders, as primarily ego-dystonic.

An independent gold standard likely will come from neurogenetic or biobehavioral attributes. Early neuroscience research is encouraging. For example, altered dopaminergic and serotonergic functions have been found among pathological gamblers (Bergh, Sodersten, & Nordin, 1997; DeCaria, Begaz, & Hollander, 1998). Biogenetic vulnerabilities also have been identified among pathological gamblers (Comings, 1998), and there is evidence to suggest that there may be genetic markers for novelty seeking behavior among normals that can predispose people to take "chances" (Benjamin et al., 1996; Ebstein et al., 1996). Finally, as noted earlier, new evidence suggests that there are common reward circuits in the central nervous system responsible for the experiences associated with the anticipation of substance use effects, the acquisition of money, and the appreciation of beauty (Aharon et al., 2001; Breiter, 1999; Breiter et al., 2001).

Reconsidering Clinical Diagnoses as the "Gold Standard"

In the absence of a gold standard, some investigators assume that clinicians provide the proxy gold standard against which the accuracy of screening instruments can be measured (Lesieur & Blume, 1987; Volberg, 1996; WEFA Group, ICR Survey Research Group, Lesieur, & Thompson, 1997). For example, investigators often use the term *probable pathological gambling* rather than *pathological gambling*. "The term **probable** distinguishes the results of prevalence surveys, where classification is based on responses to questions in a telephone interview, from a clinical diagnosis" (Volberg, p. 3). Similarly, others conclude that:

> *Because only a clinical evaluation using DSM–IV can diagnose pathological gambling, we have used the term "probable" pathological gambling.... Since the survey is not a clinical diagnosis, we cannot say that respondents can be "diagnosed" as pathological gamblers, rather we use the term "probable" pathological gamblers. (WEFA Group et al., pp. 5-2–5-5)*

However, clinicians who perform diagnostic evaluations are not as reliable as many people assume (Meehl, 1954, 1973; Rosenhan, 1973; Ziskin, 1970). Clinicians are extremely vulnerable to biases in clinical judgment. Faraone and Tsuang emphasize the fact that psychiatric diagnoses should not be considered a gold standard and that it is important to assess the adequacy of these diagnoses (1994). We suggest that all diagnostic classification—whether clinician- or instrument-based—be held as tentative, and not the final word (Kleinman, 1987; Shaffer, 1986).

DSM–IV–TR

Diagnoses are tentative classifications: these groups of disorders are subject to change with new research and revisions of the diagnostic manuals. Also, diagnostic schemes often reflect implicit cultural conventions and community values. Consequently, clinicians often perceive diagnostic categories as diseases rather than a simplifying organizational scheme (Kleinman, 1987). For example:

> *If [classification] ... is applied as a tentative model, not an entifying map, with serious concern for its likely inadequacy to grasp the subtlety, ambiguity and obdurate humanity of the sick, if it is distrusted, received as a mere shorthand, regarded as one vision among others, then it is more likely to be adequate to what should be the humane core of clinical work. (Kleinman, p. 51–52)*

Keeping these conceptual and practical issues in mind, *DSM–IV–TR* provides an operational guide to making diagnoses. An especially appealing aspect of the *DSM* is its multidimensional formulation of disorders in terms of (a) biological, psychological, and social aspects, and (b) its appreciation for the spectrum of and heterogeneity in substance use problems (APA, 1987, 1904, 2000).

Biopsychosocial Formulations

Just as there is no gold standard for diagnosing addictive disorders, we must recognize that the values of a culture ebb and flow such that diagnostic criteria change over time. Despite these changes, diagnostic criteria have consistently rested upon biological, psychological, and social changes as well as concerns that the individual with such problems has been considered "sick" by onlookers. This has led to clinicians formulating their cases using the *biopsychosocial* model.

Earlier, we reviewed the *DSM–IV* substance abuse and dependence definitions. As we noted, the criteria used to diagnose individuals with these disorders acknowledge biological, psychological, and social factors. We already described two of the criteria, tolerance and withdrawal signs and symptoms, which refer to the biological neuroadaptive features of addiction. The other *DSM–IV–TR* criteria include psychosocial standards; that is: (a) important social, occupational, or recreational activities are given up or reduced because of the substance use; and (b) the substance use is continued despite knowledge of physical or psychological problems that are likely caused or exacerbated by the substance. Consider driving while intoxicated, a social consequence of addictive behavior and a pressing community concern.

21. Biological neuroadaptive features of addiction include:
    a. tolerance.
    b. withdrawal.
    c. both a and b.
    d. neither a nor b.

Focus on Social Consequences: Driving While Intoxicated

Thus far we have focused primarily on the individual consequences of addiction (e.g., neuroadaptation). Frequently, however, the reason addiction gets attention is its impact on society. The adverse consequences of excessive drug use stimulate the attention of the public; consequently, pressure is put on the makers of public policy and others to do something about drug use.

Driving while intoxicated (DWI) dramatically and powerfully illustrates the societal impact of drug abuse. A recent study (Lapham et al., 2001) found that 85% of women and 91% of men treated in a DWI program had alcohol dependence or abuse as defined by *DSM–IV*. The societal implications of this pattern of drug use are striking. The National Highway Traffic Safety Administration (NHTSA; 2000) reported that 15,786 of the 41,611 (38%) U.S. traffic fatalities during 1999 were alcohol related. In addition, the NHTSA calculated that between 1982 and 1999, 365,343 people died in alcohol-related crashes; in 1999, 308,000 people were injured in alcohol-related crashes. Of note, traffic crashes are the single greatest cause of death for every age from 6 to 33; almost half of these fatalities are in alcohol-related crashes. Miller et al. (1998) estimated that the annual cost of alcohol-related accidents in the United States is $120 billion. Furthermore, there is evidence that the majority of DWI offenders go undetected. For example, more than 80% of impaired drivers admitted to hospital emergency departments were not held responsible for their offense (Orsay, Doan-Wiggins, Lewis, Lucke, & RamaKrishnan, 1994). Also, though the number of licensed drivers increased 15% from 1990 to 1997, the number of DWI arrests decreased 18% (Bureau of Justice Statistics, 1999). Furthermore, the evidence reveals a significant reoffense rate (Albanese, Baker, Meagher, & Walters, 2001).

Social events influence the extent and perception of addiction. For example, the tragic social impact of DWI offenses lowers a community's capacity to tolerate drinking and driving. This growing intolerance increases the likelihood that drinking drivers will be considered deviant. Ultimately, the community will explain their aberrant behavior by considering them as suffering with addiction; they also might be viewed as criminal. These views emerge independent of the actual pattern (e.g., quantity) of alcohol consumption and are influenced primarily by the social consequences of their actions. The social consequences of DWI often determine how much blood alcohol content will be tolerated by a community. When the consequences of drinking (e.g., DWI) are perceived as socially severe and risky, observers consider the loss of control associated with such drinking as more pervasive. Less tolerant, the community will urge treatment providers and public policy makers to use clinical and regulatory measures to intervene (e.g., expand treatment, increase enforcement, and lower the legal limit of blood alcohol thresholds). Just as these cultural and community events shape the perception of drinking and driving, models of addiction influence the social perception of addiction in general and diagnostic activities in particular.

Spectrum of Disorders

As noted in *DSM–IV–TR*, the distribution and determinants of substance use vary among diverse populations. Some never use alcohol or drugs, some use occasionally, and others exhibit substance use disorders, abuse, or dependence. In addition to these disorders, the American Psychiatric Association has classified a variety of other substance-related disorders in their diagnostic manual (2000). For example, alcohol and drugs can cause intoxication and withdrawal, each of which suggests that there is an abuse or dependence problem, but neither of which is adequate to make such a diagnosis. Substance intoxication consists of: (a) development of a reversible substance-specific syndrome due to recent ingestion of a substance, and (b) clinically significant maladaptive behavioral or psychological changes due to the effect of the substance on the central nervous system which develop during or shortly after use of the substance. Similarly, withdrawal consists of: (a) development of a substance-specific syndrome due to the cessation of (or reduction in) substance use that has been of sufficient quantity and duration, and (b) clinically significant distress or impairment in social, occupational, or other important areas of functioning caused by the substance-specific syndrome (2000). In addition, there are numerous other substance-induced disorders, such as substance-induced delirium, psychosis, and mood disorders. Also, *DSM–IV–TR* classifies pathological gambling, which shares some features with substance dependence, as an impulse disorder.

22. The spectrum of *DSM–IV–TR* substance use disorders includes:
    a. intoxication.
    b. withdrawal.
    c. substance-induced mood disorder.
    d. all of the above.

MODELS OF ADDICTION

Importance of Ideologies

Whether articulated or not, researchers, clinicians, public policy makers, and lay people alike approach the idea of addiction with a fundamental ideology. Since ideologies provide a framework for understanding and approaching problems, you should be aware of these ideologies. Though these perspectives focus attention toward various addiction attributes, they also serve as blinders that might prevent you from acknowledging other characteristics of addiction essential to understanding or improving prevention or treatment efforts. For example, a biologically minded clinician can view recidivistic alcoholic behavior as a mainly neurochemical problem and treat it with naltrexone. While this is certainly a valid approach to treating alcohol dependence for some, it is important that you do not disregard other factors (e.g., family stress predisposing to relapse) that might also warrant additional treatment approaches (e.g., psychosocial interventions).

Clinicians apply their models of addiction to make sense of those who seek their care. The risk for clinicians is that they will view addiction only from their perspective, failing to recognize that their view serves as a lens through which clinical evidence is screened. Shaffer and Robbins (1991) illustrated this point by presenting three descriptions of "Ms. S," each formulation of which tells a different story about her problems based on the belief system(s) employed by the clinician. The first case summary describes a biological view of Ms. S., the second a psychological perspective, and the third a behavioral orientation.

Biological Formulation

Ms. S, a twenty-one-year-old woman with a four-year history of depression and cocaine addiction, experienced a major depression with severely impaired functioning prior to her use of cocaine. The patient has a positive family history for affective illness. Ms. S's mother has been hospitalized twice following depressive episodes, her maternal aunt has been diagnosed with bipolar illness, and her father's alcohol dependence might mask a depression.

23. A clinician concludes that depression in a forty-year-old man is a result of brain dopamine depletion from years of cocaine dependence. This formulation is:
   a. biological.
   b. psychological.
   c. behavioral.
   d. none of the above.

24. A clinician concludes that opiate dependence in a thirty-five-year-old man represents an attempt to self-medicate angry feelings. This formulation is:
   a. biological.
   b. psychological.
   c. behavioral.
   d. none of the above.

25. A clinician concludes that cocaine dependence has developed in a thirty-year-old woman because the drug positively reinforces her good emotional experiences. This formulation is:
   a. biological.
   b. psychological.
   c. behavioral.
   d. none of the above.

Psychological Formulation

Ms. S, a twenty-one-year-old woman with a four-year history of drug abuse and self-destructive behavior, has a background of physical and sexual abuse and emotional deprivation. This has left her with low self-esteem, poor object relations, and an inability to tolerate intense affect. The patient's cocaine use began at age 17 and continues to be her method of managing the demands of adult life for which she feels ill equipped.

Behavioral Formulation

Ms. S, a twenty-one-year-old woman who has been using cocaine excessively for the past four years, uses between .50 and .75 grams of cocaine two to three times daily. Her exclusive route of cocaine administration is intranasal. Ms. S reports that cocaine acts as a negative reinforcer by relieving her feelings of malaise and discomfort. Because she has few alternative activities that produce positive reinforcement, her repertoire of behaviors has become narrow. Consequently, she has withdrawn from her primary social support systems.

Ideology and Clinical Understanding

As in all narratives, each clinical account of Ms. S tells you as much about the clinician as it does about her. In addition, how you understand any narrative is influenced by your own frame of reference. In the language of psychotherapy, formulations (Perry, Cooper, & Michels, 1987; Shaffer, 1986; Weiner, 1975) such as those above reflect how various clinicians use different conceptual models to understand a case and identify a treatment plan (Lazare, 1976). Clinicians create, construct, or "tell" different stories with and about their patients depending on a complex transaction between personal, cultural, and professional ideologies. Sometimes, the disparity among these views can lead to a "babble of voices" (Havens, 1973, p. 2).

With the exception of transtheoretical approaches (Prochaska, DiClemente, & Norcross, 1992; Shaffer, 1992, 1997b; Shaffer & Robbins, 1995), the various models developed to help us understand addiction tend to focus on the biological, psychological, or social underpinnings of these disorders. These perspectives, however, are not mutually exclusive. For example, Khantzian's (1997) **self-medication** hypothesis (SMH) of addictions is a psychodynamic model that understands substance abuse as an attempt by those with self-regulation deficits in affect, self-care, self-esteem, and interpersonal relationships to provide some internal regulation (Albanese, 2003). At the same time, the SMH neither denies nor is at odds with biological, social, or other psychological understandings. In fact, the SMH makes clear that the combination of genetic predisposition and self-regulation deficits, mixed with substances of abuse, can lead to a substance use disorder (Khantzian, 1999).

The SMH does not purport to be the *only* understanding for *all* addictive behavior patterns. To our knowledge, nobody has articulated a unifying principle—biological, psychological, or social—that explains all of addiction. In his collected works, Khantzian (1999) stated that the SMH approach "should be considered in parallel with other approaches and not in competition with them. . . . I do not assume to have all the answers . . . only some special ones, answers that are often not enough considered in an era of biological psychiatry and empiricism" (p. 5). He continues:

> *As in any approach there are potentials and limitations. . . . I believe it is the obligation of all of us, however, to try and appreciate the potentials and limitations of the various approaches we adopt, to find complementarity when we can, and, when we cannot, to explore the advantages of other perspectives. (1999, pp. 5–6)*

Similarly, Zinberg (1975)—whose approach emphasized the interplay of (a) drug effect, (b) an individual's psychological set (i.e., expectations), and (c) the social setting within which drug use occurs in stimulating and sustaining the evolution of substance dependence—acknowledged that some people use illicit drugs to deal with painful affects. Of note, most people who experiment with substances do not develop a substance use disorder, probably because they have neither the biological predisposition nor the combination of biology and self-regulation deficits or vulnerabilities.

An Introduction to Models of Addiction

Engaging in pleasurable activities is not without risk. Although most people experience pleasure without developing adverse consequences, some develop a range of biological, psychological, and social problems related directly or indirectly to their experience of pleasure and how they manage or regulate these feelings. As illustrated earlier, how healthcare providers understand excessive behaviors determines how they will treat these behavior patterns. Though readily grouped into biological, psychological, and sociological perspectives, there are a variety of different clinical, scientific, and lay viewpoints toward addiction and addictive behavior patterns. These perspectives range from informal but still influential formulations about the nature of intemperance, to well-developed and reasoned theories. The majority of models clinicians use to guide their treatment efforts fall somewhere between these extremes. A brief review of these models reveals considerable breadth and diversity of ideas and implications. Table 1.1 illustrates a representative set of common perspectives used to explain a variety of addictive behaviors (Shaffer & Burglass, 1981). In addition to a moral view, these perspectives are loosely organized into biological, psychological, and social perspectives.

As Table 1.1 shows, clinicians can apply various and perhaps substantially different treatment strategies with patients seeking care depending upon their particular theoretical perspective(s). For example, treatment providers who view pathological gambling in wholly biological terms might suggest that pharmacotherapy is the best route to mental health; others who understand disordered gambling in terms of erroneous cognitions might suggest that a combination of education and cognitive behavioral therapy represent the best path to recovery.

Transforming Excessive Behavior From a Moral Weakness to Sickness: Moving From Preaching to Treating

To illustrate the evolution of models of addiction and how these models can change our understanding of the behaviors they explain, we briefly review the application of models to gambling. Excessive gambling has gone through a number of intellectual formulations and transformations in the short time it has been the object of scientific study. Early understandings of intemperate gambling tended to perceive this problem as a moral issue, rather than a clinical one. Gradually, and not without some controversy (Rosecrance, 1985), people began to regard immoderate gambling as a sickness instead of immoral self-guidance and depravity. Early works that considered the developmentally established and deep-seated psychodynamics of intemperate gambling transformed it from a moral to a mental health problem (Bergler, 1957; Freud, 1928/1961; Galdston, 1951). Instead of simply reflecting a greedy desire to get something for nothing, dynamically functional explanations emerged to suggest that gambling excesses had roots in sexual desire, sensation seeking, and biogenetic influences. As these ideas gained popularity, many people began to argue that the responsibility for treating problem gamblers lies not simply with moral leaders, but also with mental health care providers.

TABLE 1.1

Common Perspectives on Addictive Disorders

Perspective	Illustrative Publications	Conceptualization
Moral Turpitude	(Johnson, 1986; Quinn, 1891; Weems, 1812)	Addictive behavior is a moral problem that requires piety and values conversion.
Biological Models		
Disease or illness	Alcoholics Anonymous (AA), Narcotics Anonymous (NA), Gamblers Anonymous (GA) (Alcoholics Anonymous, 1976; Gamblers Anonymous, 2002)	Excessive behavior is viewed as a chronic disease for which there is no cure except abstinence.
Impulse control disorder	*DSM–IV* (APA, 1980, 1994; Bergh, Sodersten, & Nordin, 1997; Cardoso, 2002; Christenson et al., 1994; Comings et al., 1999; France, 1902; Hollander, Buchalter, & DeCaria, 2000; Marks, 1990)	Deficiencies or changes in neurobiological or genetic structures or activities influence regulatory problems that result in impulsive behavior patterns. Impulses are discharged too readily and bursts of behavior, of either short or prolonged duration, result.
Biogenetic vulnerability	(Comings, 1998; Comings et al., 1999; Crabbe, 2002)	Addictive disorders reflect a genetic susceptibility to impulsive and excessive behaviors.
Reward deficiency and neurophysiological adaptation	(Aharon et al., 2001; Bergh et al., 1997; Breiter et al., 2001; Ebstein et al., 1996; Wise, 1996)	Addiction results from shifts in the "reward" system and reflects changes in the pattern of activity among neurotransmitters or a deficit in the capacity of this system to yield pleasurable experiences.
Psychological Models		
Behavioral excess	(Seager, 1970; Skinner, 1969)	Social learning and reinforcement contingencies influence some gamblers (for example), otherwise healthy, into a pattern of excessive gambling.
Bad judgment	(Rosecrance, 1985, 1988)	Addictive disorders (e.g., gambling) represent poor strategies, usually displayed by naïve gamblers who do not fully understand the games they play.
Psychological deficiency and self-medication	(Jacobs, 1989; Khantzian, 1975, 1997; Rado, 1933)	Personality and emotional vulnerabilities invite addiction as an adaptive response that serves as an anodyne for these problems; under some conditions, these excessive behavior patterns can serve to keep people from regressing to a more primitive state. Addictive behavior patterns are viewed as an attempt to manage uncomfortable psychological states.

(Continued)

TABLE 1.1

(Continued)

Perspective	Illustrative Publications	Conceptualization
Psychological Models		
Psychodynamic neuroticism	(Dodes, 2002; Lindner, 1950)	Addictive behavior patterns result from intrapsychic conflicts that can have roots in earlier developmental stages, and the adaptations that follow.
Erroneous thought patterns	(Ladouceur, Paquet, & Dube, 1996; Ladouceur & Walker, 1998)	Gambling viewed as a product of illogical cognition concerning laws of probability.
Social Models		
Psychosocial	(Orford, 1985, 2001; Zinberg, 1984)	Cognition and behavior pertaining to excessive behaviors are influenced by numerous moral and social factors that are responsible for its development and maintenance.
Public health issue	(Korn & Shaffer, 1999; Marlatt, 1996; Marlatt, Baer, Donovan, & Kivlahan, 1988)	Addiction is a multidimensional health risk for which potential biological, psychological, economic, and social costs must be considered. Addiction develops within a social context and it likely has benefits as well as costs for the sufferer and the social setting.

Clinicians and public policy makers alike have argued this position for other addictive behaviors. For example, some have suggested that addiction to alcohol and drugs is best treated by psychologists because the prevalence of substance abuse among clinical populations is quite high and because most treatment approaches for addiction are psychologically rooted (Miller & Brown, 1997). The same might be said for pathological gambling. In any event, the first inclusion of pathological gambling in the APA's *Diagnostic and Statistical Manual of Mental Disorders* (i.e., *DSM–III*, 1980) completed the transformation of excessive gambling from a moral problem to a clinical disorder that required treatment instead of—or in addition to—piety (National Research Council, 1999).

26. Which of the following are biological models?
    a. biogenetic vulnerability
    b. reward deficiency
    c. both a and b
    d. neither a nor b

27. With regard to models of addiction, which of the following is *false*?
    a. The various models tend to focus on the biological, psychological, or social underpinnings of the addictions.
    b. The self-medication hypothesis is primarily a biological model.
    c. The models are not mutually exclusive.
    d. All of the above.

Treating Addiction as a Syndrome

Although it has unique elements, addiction shares many signs and symptoms with other disorders (e.g., anxiety, depression, impulsivity); consequently, addiction is best thought of as a syndrome. As a syndrome, addiction's common component (e.g., depression) is shared with other disorders (e.g., substance use or gambling disorders), while its unique component (e.g., betting increasing amounts of money) is specific to one type of disorder (e.g., pathological gambling). The shared component reflects broad individual differences that can vary along multiple dimensions (e.g., intensity and duration); the unique component distinguishes pathological gambling from other disorders and is specific only to it (Widiger & Clark, 2000). If we consider addiction as a syndrome, the most effective treatments for the variety of addictive behaviors will reflect a multimodal "cocktail" approach combined with patient-treatment matching.

THE COURSE AND STAGES OF ADDICTION

Although later chapters in this book will examine treatment specific issues in more detail, it is important and useful to examine the natural history of addiction and how it relates to prevention and treatment efforts; this sequence of events permits a better understanding of addiction by providing important insights into its course and treatment matching. Instead of examining these events from the perspective of a particular theoretical model, we use a meta or transtheoretical model known as *stage change* that integrates a variety of theoretical views (Prochaska, 1996; Prochaska et al., 1992; Shaffer, 1997b).

Stage change concepts have emerged as an important force in the treatment of addictive behaviors (Crowley, 1999; Prochaska et al., 1992; Prochaska, Norcross, & DiClemente, 1994; Quinn, 1891; Rollnick & Morgan, 1995; Shaffer, 1992, 1994b, 1997b; Shaffer & Robbins, 1995). Stage change theory suggests that an evaluation of a person's readiness to change and determination of their stage of change are important steps to formulating treatment strategies (Shaffer & Robbins, 1995).

Initiation and Positive Consequences

To become excessively involved with any object or activity, one must first begin a relationship with that object or activity. Initiation marks the first stage of this relationship. Primary prevention programs aim to stop initiation so that the opportunity for progression is interrupted. However, when the early experience with an object or activity is positive, the relationship is sustained and it tends to continue.

Negative Experiences: When Consequences Present Without Awareness (Precontemplation)

Before people with addiction seek treatment, they often experience many problems and have little awareness that their excessive behavior pattern is the primary cause of their difficulties. At this stage the person with addiction is not considering a behavioral change. Their drinking, drug use, or gambling still is viewed as a positive experience. Since this stage is characterized by lack of awareness of addiction as an entity or primary cause of distress, the major clinical challenges or themes are to *enhance awareness* of consequences and overcome *resistance* to change.

Contemplation: Adverse Consequences Enter Awareness

During this stage, treatment seekers recognize the pattern of addictive behavior as the primary cause of their problems and evidence some receptivity to the possibility of addressing these issues. The major clinical challenge is to address the person's *ambivalence* about whether there is a wish to alter their addictive behavior pattern and deal with the associated problems. The primary approach to stimulating the wish to want to change is to acknowledge that addiction provides positive benefits but also costs. The clinician must acknowledge that modifying the pattern of behavior that caused problems will require relinquishing some current activities. A decision balance exercise that explores the pluses and minuses of maintaining the behavior and the gains and losses of changing is the major vehicle for resolving the ambivalence about the value of curbing addictive behaviors. A seminal event such as the loss of a large sum of money, job loss, or health crisis, referred to as a *turning point*, often marks the treatment seeker's decision to commit to major changes.

Preparation: Turning Points and an Orientation to Change

At this stage, treatment seekers have accepted the notion that changes are necessary and worthwhile. The major clinical challenge is to help people struggling with addiction to see the array of alternatives available to them; *making choices* is central and the key treatment activity is planning. Therapist efforts focus on goal setting and planning for treatment and life changes. Together, the person with addiction and their treatment provider explore therapeutic options and appropriate action steps. Parameters to be considered include type of setting, program philosophy, level of care, kind and variety of therapeutic modalities, group or individual format, professional profile, and cost. Treatment matching is the important principle. Success at this stage is often linked to honoring the person's preferences and validating the acceptability of the person's choices.

Active Quitting: Taking Action for Change

At this stage of an addictive disorder and its treatment, the major theme is active *learning*. The clinical strategy focuses on encouraging people with addiction to initiate a range of *new behaviors* based on the acquisition of new knowledge, insight, attitudes, and skills. This is the beginning of psychological detoxification and restoration. Identifying and substituting a different leisure activity to replace the time spent gambling is an important component of a healthy recovery. For example, solution focused brief therapy has been implemented successfully in the substance abuse field; however, research with gambling and other addictive patterns is limited. The introduction of a support program such as the fellowship of Alcoholics Anonymous or Gamblers Anonymous and more involvement in spiritually enriching experiences also can be highly beneficial. Though clinicians can suggest these support systems, almost any that a recovering person chooses holds potential to be helpful.

Relapse Prevention and Change Maintenance

To achieve enduring treatment goals, the clinical focus at this stage of treatment is to *practice* the new competencies to sustain a balanced, healthy lifestyle. Adult learning theory recognizes that developing and mastering new behaviors requires training and repetition. Relapses can and often do occur; because this is a common part of recovery from gambling and other addictive behavior patterns, clinicians should pay particular attention to situational risk as a critical component of relapse (Marlatt & Gordon, 1985; McAulliffe & Ch'ien, 1986; Svanum & McAdoo, 1989; Vaillant, 1988).

TABLE 1.2

Matching Stages of Change to Treatment Modalities

Stages of Addictive Behaviors	Range of Possible Treatment Modality Matches
1. Initiation	Primary prevention (e.g., public education and information programs)
2. Positive Consequences	Secondary prevention (e.g., public education, counseling)
3. Adverse Consequences Enter Awareness	Tertiary prevention (e.g., counseling), outpatient psychotherapy services, self-help fellowships (to stimulate ambivalence, dissonance, and a readiness for change), acute inpatient services (when there is a need for medical and psychiatric crisis management)
4. Turning Point(s)	Acute inpatient and outpatient services (e.g., detoxification, partial care, 12-step, and self-help programs)
5. Active Quitting	Residential (only for chronic substance abusers who have little or no social support systems available), partial care, or outpatient services (e.g., chemical substitutions, counseling, 12-step, and self-help programs)
6. Relapse Prevention or Change Maintenance	Outpatient, 12-step, self-help, and residential (only for chronic substance abusers who have little or no social support systems available)

There is one major caveat regarding the stage change model and motivational enhancement counseling. Observers often incorrectly think that changes occur in a linear and progressive fashion. In reality, the change process is recursive with many opportunities to revisit earlier stages and successfully navigate the tasks of recovery necessary to grow as a person and rebuild one's life (Shaffer, 1992, 1997b; Shaffer & Robbins, 1995).

In addition to the specific treatment tasks associated with each stage of change or stage of the disorder's natural history, stages of change also provide public health workers with the framework to develop programs strategically. This population-based view of stage change represents a shift from individually based treatment tactics to a broader set of programs designed for the community (Tucker, Donovan, & Marlatt, 1999). Although a full discussion of the public health implications for stage change and program matching is beyond the scope of this chapter, Table 1.2 provides a summary of only some of the potential stage-modality matches that can be used to guide program development and implementation.

The idea of addiction is relatively new in the history of language. Almost four hundred years ago, the concept of addiction emerged. Its earliest applications applied principally to activities that engaged fervor and passion. Later, addiction was chiefly used to describe behaviors that involved the ingestion of psychoactive drugs. Currently, addiction is being transformed by new theory and neuroimaging technology to describe a wide range of behaviors that include both patterns of excessive activity without psychoactive drug use (e.g., pathological gambling) and the substance use disorders (Holden, 2001; Shaffer, 1997a, 1999).

28. During which stage is there little awareness that adverse consequences have resulted from excessive alcohol use?
    a. precontemplation
    b. contemplation
    c. preparation
    d. action

29. In which stage do clinicians help the alcohol-dependent person choose which treatment is best?
    a. precontemplation
    b. contemplation
    c. preparation
    d. action

30. During which stage do clinicians help pathological gamblers initiate new, alternative behaviors?
    a. precontemplation
    b. contemplation
    c. preparation
    d. action

Depicting the concept of addiction is like trying to shoot a fish with a bow and arrow in a clear, calm pool of water. The fish is easy to see, but refraction makes the task nearly impossible. Similarly, addiction has many defining characteristics. These are very difficult to operationalize since the attributes of addiction, in part, are a function of the sociocultural setting within which they occur. Attributes of the setting influence how the behavior is experienced and the extent to which adverse consequences accrue. Most contemporary addiction workers acknowledge that there are biological, psychological, and social characteristics that define addiction; however, these observers tend to disagree about the extent to which each of these factors is causal in producing addiction or influential in sustaining addiction. Not everyone with a biogenetic vulnerability will develop addiction; similarly, not everyone without such predisposing risk factors will avoid addiction.

Addiction is a dynamic process that waxes and wanes. People with addiction typically go through phases of exacerbation and abstention. Many people struggling with addiction also have episodes of controlled activity whereby they use the object of their addiction intermittently or more often, but only to a limited extent. Addiction has not yet been accepted in diagnostic manuals as a formal class of disease—though substance use, gambling, and other excessive patterns are included under other classifications. Clinicians attempting to diagnose addiction are faced with a complex set of assessment tasks: they must distinguish a person's overwhelming impulses to act from their unwillingness to resist these impulses. Despite these conceptual and practical difficulties, there also is considerable evidence that people with addiction can recover both with and without treatment (e.g., McLellan, 1994; McLellan et al., 1992; Shaffer & Jones, 1989; Sobell, Cunningham, & Sobell, 1996; Sobell, Ellingstad, & Sobell, 2000).

KEY TERMS

abuse: A maladaptive pattern of behavior or substance use that can lead to clinically significant impairment or distress; a less severe disorder than dependence in the spectrum of substance use disorders.

addiction: Difficult-to-define lay term that indicates continued use of a substance or participation in a behavior despite adverse consequences; typically addiction also involves some level of craving and loss of control.

dependence: A cluster of cognitive, behavioral, and physiological symptoms representing a circumstance where an individual continues use of a substance or participates in a behavior despite significant adverse consequences; this state is more severe than abuse in the spectrum of substance use disorders.

gold standard: A definitive independent index against which diagnosticians and researchers can judge the status of a clinical state.

neuroadaptation: A technical term referring to underlying brain changes that can lead to, or be associated with, the development of tolerance and withdrawal.

psychoactive: A substance or experience that activates the brain's reward system.

reward: The subjective experience of pleasure associated with activation of the brain system stimulated by certain psychoactive substances or behavior patterns.

self-medication: A psychodynamic model that views addiction as an attempt by those with self-regulation deficits in affect, self-care, self-esteem, and interpersonal relationships to provide some internal regulation.

tolerance: A diminished biological or behavioral response to repeated administration of the same amount of a substance or participation in the same level of behavior; or, the need for an increased amount of a substance or level of behavior to achieve the same subjective effects.

withdrawal: A stereotypical syndrome of physical and/or psychological disturbances that follows the abrupt discontinuation of substance use or behavior activities, or pharmacological blockade of the actions of a substance.

DISCUSSION QUESTIONS

1. How is addiction similar and different from dependence?
2. What is meant by a "gold standard" for the identification of addiction?
3. What is the value of making diagnoses tentatively?
4. Compare and contrast three models of addiction.
5. Describe the spectrum of *DSM–IV–TR* substance use disorders.
6. Describe the history of the term *addiction*.
7. Describe the stages of recovery from addiction.
8. What is "reward deficiency syndrome"?
9. How is the concept of "addict" pejorative?
10. Describe a biopsychosocial treatment plan for a client with alcohol dependence and depression.

ACKNOWLEDGMENT

This work was supported in part by funding from the National Center for Responsible Gaming, the Institute for Research on Pathological Gambling and Related Disorders at Harvard Medical School's Division on Addictions and the Arcadia Charitable Trust. The authors extend special thanks to Chris Freed, Edward Khantzian, Rachel Kidman, David Korn, Richard LaBrie, Debi LaPlante, Erin Parker, Christine Reilly, and Christine Thurmond for their important contributions to this chapter.

SUGGESTED FURTHER READING

Hyman, S. E. (1994). Why does the brain prefer opium to broccoli? *Harvard Review of Psychiatry, 2*(1): 43–46.

> This elegantly written and readily accessible article describes the fundamental neurobiological aspects of psychoactive drug effects. Understanding what makes a drug psychoactive is an essential building block for all addiction treatment providers.

Khantzian, E. J. (1999). *Treating addiction as a human process*. Northvale, NJ: Jason Aronson.

There always has been a tendency to blame people with addiction for bringing the problem on; this circumstance can lead to oppressive and less-than-productive treatment strategies. In this sensitive and insightful book, Khantzian provides the foundation for an empathic treatment approach that will help clinicians better understand the experience and meaning of addiction so they can more effectively deal with the difficulties and conflicts so often observed among people struggling with addiction.

Marlatt, G. A., & Gordon, J. (Eds.). (1985). *Relapse prevention*. New York, Guilford Press.

This book represents the pioneering work that provided the foundation for relapse prevention treatment throughout the field. The authors provide the first comprehensive theoretical and clinical strategies for understanding and dealing with relapse. Every clinician needs to have this knowledge in their clinical tool kit.

Shaffer, H. J., & Burglass, M. E. (Eds.). (1981). *Classic contributions in the addictions*. New York: Brunner/ Mazel.

This edited volume includes some of the classic papers upon which the field of addiction studies and treatment rests. These seminal papers include: Sandor Rado's "Psychoanalysis of Pharmacothymia (Drug Addiction)," which was the first major paper to transform addiction from a moral problem to a clinical concern; George Vaillant's "Sociopathy as a Human Process," which we recommend for repeated reading by addiction treatment providers; Norman Zinberg's "High States" and his "Addiction and Ego Function"; and Edward Khantzian's "Self-Selection and Progression in Drug Dependence," which is the foundation of the contemporary self-medication hypothesis.

Vaillant, G. E. (1983). *The natural history of alcoholism: Causes, patterns, and paths to recovery*. Cambridge: Harvard University Press.

A rare prospective study, this volume is one of the most important publications on alcoholism ever written. This is essential reading for anyone working in the field of addiction treatment.

REFERENCES

Aharon, I., Etcoff, N., Ariely, D., Chabris, C. F., O'Connor, E., & Breiter, H. C. (2001). Beautiful faces have variable reward value: fMRI and behavioral evidence. *Neuron, 32*, 537–551.

Albanese, M. J. (2003). The self-medication hypothesis: Epidemiology, clinical findings and implications. *Psychiatric Times, 20*(4), 57–64.

Albanese, M. J., Baker, G., Meagher, E., & Walters, E. (2001, December). *Reoffense in a DWI population*. Paper presented at the American Academy of Addiction Psychiatry, Amelia Island, FL.

Alcoholics Anonymous. (1976). *Alcoholics anonymous: the story of how many thousands of men and women have recovered from alcoholism* (3rd ed.). New York: Alcoholics Anonymous World Services.

American Psychiatric Association. (1980). *Diagnostic and statistical manual of mental disorders* (3rd ed.). Washington, DC: Author.

American Psychiatric Association. (1987). *Diagnostic and statistical manual of mental disorders* (3rd ed. rev.). Washington, DC: Author.

American Psychiatric Association. (1994). *Diagnostic and statistical manual of mental disorders* (4th ed.). Washington, DC: Author.

American Psychiatric Association. (2000). *Diagnostic and statistical manual of mental disorders* (text rev.). Washington, DC: Author.

Baker, A. (Ed.). (2000). *Serious shopping*. London: Free Association Books.

Barron, J. (Ed.). (1998). *Making diagnosis meaningful: Enhancing evaluation and treatment of psychological disorders*. Washington, DC: American Psychological Association.

Benjamin, J., Lin, L., Patterson, C., Greenberg, B. D., Murphy, D. L., & Hamer, D. H. (1996). Population and familial association between the D4 dopamine receptor gene and measures of novelty seeking. *Nature Genetics, 12*(January), 81–83.

Bergh, C., Sodersten, E. P., & Nordin, C. (1997). Altered dopamine function in pathological gambling. *Psychological Medicine, 27*, 473–475.

Bergler, E. (1957). *The psychology of gambling*. New York: Hill and Wang.

Blum, A. (1985). The collective representation of affliction: Some reflections on disability and disease as social facts. *Theoretical Medicine, 6*, 221–232.

Blum, K., Braverman, E. R., Holder, M. M., Lubar, J. F., Monastra, V. J., Miller, D., et al. (2000). Reward deficiency syndrome: A biogenetic model for the diagnosis and treatment of impulsive, addictive, and compulsive behaviors. *Journal of Psychoactive Drugs, 32*(Suppl.), 1–112.

Breiter, H. C. (1999, February 5). *Neurobiology of gambling.* Paper presented at the New Directions in Gambling Addiction Research, George Washington University, Washington, DC.

Breiter, H. C., Aharon, I., Kahneman, D., Dale, A., & Shizgal, P. (2001). Functional imaging of neural responses to expectancy and experience of monetary gains and losses. *Neuron, 30,* 619–639.

Bureau of Justice Statistics. (1999). *Drunk driving.* Washington, DC: U.S. Department of Justice.

Cardoso, S. H. (n.d.). *Kleptomania (pathological stealing).* Retrieved March 3, 2002, from http://www.epub.org.br/cm/n11/doencas/per-impulso-clepto-i.htm

Catalano, E. M., & Sonenberg, N. (1993). *Consuming passions: Help for compulsive shoppers.* Oakland, CA: New Harbinger Publications.

Cerny, L., & Cerny, K. (1992). Can carrots be addictive? An extraordinary form of drug dependence. *British Journal of Addiction, 87,* 1195–1197.

Christenson, G. A., Faber, R. J., de Zwaan, M., Raymond, N. C., Specker, S. M., Edern, M. D., et al. (1994). Compulsive buying: Descriptive characteristics and psychiatric comorbidity. *The Journal of Clinical Psychiatry, 55*(1), 5–11.

Comings, D. E. (1998). The molecular genetics of pathological gambling. *CNS Spectrums, 3*(6), 20–37.

Comings, D. E., Gonzalez, N., Wu, S., Gade, R., Muhleman, D., Saucier, G., et al. (1999). Studies of the 48 bp repeat polymorphism of the DRD4 gene in impulsive, compulsive, addictive behaviors: Tourette syndrome, ADHD, pathological gambling, and substance abuse. *American Journal of Medical Genetics. Neuropsychiatric Genetics, 88*(4), 358–368.

Crabbe, J. C. (2002). Genetic contributions to addiction. *Annual Review of Psychology, 53*(1), 435–462.

Crowley, J. W. (Ed.). (1999). *The drunkard's progress: Narratives of addiction, despair, and recovery.* Baltimore: John Hopkins University Press.

Davies, J. B. (1996). Reasons and causes: Understanding substance users' explanations for their behavior. *Human Psychopharmacology, 11,* S39–S48.

DeCaria, C. M., Begaz, T., & Hollander, E. (1998). Serotonergic and noradrenergic function in pathological gambling. *CNS Spectrums, 3*(6), 38–47.

Dodes, L. (2002). *The heart of addiction.* New York: Harper Collins.

Ebstein, R. P., Novick, O., Umansky, R., Priel, B., Osher, Y., Blaine, D., et al. (1996). Dopamine D4 receptor (D4DR) exon III polymorphism associated with the human personality trait of novelty seeking. *Nature Genetics, 12*(January), 78–80.

Faraone, S. V., & Tsuang, M. T. (1994). Measuring diagnostic accuracy in the absence of a "gold standard." *American Journal of Psychiatry, 151*(5), 650–657.

France, C. J. (1902). The gambling impulse. *American Journal of Psychology, 13,* 364–407.

Freud, S. (1961). Dostoevsky and parricide. In J. Strachey (Ed. & Trans.), *The standard edition of the complete psychological works of Sigmund Freud* (Vol. 21, pp. 175–196). London: Hogarth Press. (Original work published 1928)

Galdston, I. (1951). The psychodynamics of the triad, alcoholism, gambling, and superstition. *Mental Hygiene, 35,* 589–598.

Gamblers Anonymous. (2002). *12 step program.* Retrieved January 26, 2002, from http://www.gamblersanonymous.org/recovery.html

Havens, L. L. (1973). *Approaches to the mind: Movement of the psychiatric schools from sects toward science.* Boston: Little-Brown.

Hodge, J. E., McMurran, M., & Hollin, C. R. (Eds.). (1997). *Addicted to crime?* West Sussex, England: Wiley.

Holden, C. (2001). Behavioral addictions: Do they exist? *Science, 294,* 980–982.

Hollander, E., Buchalter, A. J., & DeCaria, C. M. (2000). Pathological gambling. *Psychiatric Clinics of North America, 23*(3), 629–642.

Hyman, S. E. (1994). Why does the brain prefer opium to broccoli? *Harvard Review of Psychiatry, 2*(1), 43–46.

Hyman, S. E., & Nestler, E. J. (1993). *The molecular foundations of psychiatry.* Washington, DC: American Psychiatric Association.

Jacobs, D. F. (1989). A general theory of addictions: rationale for and evidence supporting a new approach for understanding and treating addictive behaviors. In H. J. Shaffer, S. Stein, B. Gambino, & T. N. Cummings (Eds.), *Compulsive gambling: Theory, research & practice* (pp. 35–64). Lexington, MA: Lexington Books.

Johnson, V. E. (1986). *Intervention: How to help someone who doesn't want help.* Minneapolis: Johnson Institute Books.

Khantzian, E. J. (1975). Self selection and progression in drug dependence. *Psychiatry Digest, 36,* 19–22.

Khantzian, E. J. (1997). The self-medication hypothesis of substance use disorders: A reconsideration and recent applications. *Harvard Review of Psychiatry, 4*(5), 231–244.

Khantzian, E. J. (1999). *Treating addiction as a human process*. Northvale, NJ: Jason Aronson.

Kipnis, D. (1997). Ghosts, taxonomies, and social psychology. *American Psychologist, 52*(3), 205–211.

Kleinman, A. (1987). Culture and clinical reality: Commentary on culture-bound syndromes and international disease classifications. *Culture, Medicine and Psychiatry, 11*(1), 49–52.

Korn, D. A., & Shaffer, H. J. (1999). Gambling and the health of the public: Adopting a public health perspective. *Journal of Gambling Studies, 15*(4), 289–365.

Ladouceur, R., Paquet, C., & Dube, D. (1996). Erroneous perceptions in generating sequences of random events. *Journal of Applied Social Psychology, 26*(24), 2157–2166.

Ladouceur, R., & Walker, M. (1998). The cognitive approach to understanding and treating pathological gambling. In A. S. Bellack & M. Hersen (Eds.), *Comprehensive Clinical Psychology* (pp. 588–601). New York: Pergamon.

Lapham, S. C., Smith, E., Baca, J. C., Chang, I., Skipper, B. J., Baum, G., et al. (2001). Prevalence of psychiatric disorders among persons convicted of driving while impaired. *Archives of General Psychiatry, 58*, 943–949.

Lazare, A. (1976). The psychiatric examination in the walk-in clinic. *Archives of General Psychiatry, 33*, 96–102.

Lesieur, H. R., & Blume, S. B. (1987). The South Oaks Gambling Screen (SOGS): A new instrument for the identification of pathological gamblers. *American Journal of Psychiatry, 144*(9), 1184–1188.

Lindner, R. M. (1950). The psychodynamics of gambling. *Annals of the American Academy of Political and Social Science, 269*, 93–107.

Mack, J. E. (2002, February 2). *Addictions: Individual and societal.* Paper presented at the 25 Years of Addiction Treatment, Boston, MA.

Marks, I. (1990). Behavioural (non-chemical) addictions. *British Journal of Addiction, 85*, 1389–1394.

Marlatt, G. A. (1996). Harm reduction: Come as you are. *Addictive Behaviors, 21*(6), 779–788.

Marlatt, G. A., Baer, J. S., Donovan, D. M., & Kivlahan, D. R. (1988). Addictive behaviors: Etiology and treatment. *Annual Review of Psychology, 39*, 223–252.

Marlatt, G. A., & Gordon, J. (Eds.). (1985). *Relapse prevention*. New York: Guilford Press.

McAulliffe, W. E., & Ch'ien, J. M. N. (1986). Recovery training and self help: A relapse-prevention program for treated opiate addicts. *Journal of Substance Abuse Treatment, 3*, 9–20.

McLellan, A. T. (1994, October 2–5). *Is treating substance abuse worth it?* Paper presented at the Training About Alcohol and Substance Abuse for All Primary Care Physicians Conference, Phoenix, AZ.

McLellan, A. T., O'Brien, C. P., Metzger, D., Alterman, A. I., Cornish, J., & Urschel, H. (1992). How effective is substance abuse treatment—compared to what? In C. P. O'Brien & J. H. Jaffe (Eds.), *Addictive states* (pp. 231–252). New York: Raven Press.

Meehl, P. E. (1954). *Clinical versus statistical prediction: A theoretical analysis and a review of the evidence*. Minneapolis: University of Minnesota Press.

Meehl, P. E. (1973). *Psychodiagnosis: Selected papers*. New York: Norton.

Miller, T. R., Lestina, D. C., & Spicer, R. S. (1998). Highway crash costs in the United States by driver age, blood alcohol level, victim age, and restraint use. *Accident Analysis And Prevention, 30*(2), 137–150.

Miller, W. R., & Brown, S. A. (1997). Why psychologists should treat alcohol and drug problems. *American Psychologist, 52*(12), 1269–1279.

National Highway Traffic Safety Administration. (2000). *Traffic safety facts 1999: A compilation of motor vehicle crash data from the fatality analysis reporting system and the general estimates system* (Publication No. DOT HS 809 100). Washington, DC: U.S. Department of Transportation, NHTSA.

National Research Council. (1999). *Pathological gambling: A critical review*. Washington DC: National Academy Press.

O'Reilly, M. (1996). Internet addiction: A new disorder enters the medical lexicon. *Canadian Medical Association Journal, 154*(12), 1882–1883.

Orford, J. (1985). *Excessive appetites: A psychological view of addictions*. New York: Wiley.

Orford, J. (2001). *Excessive appetites: A psychological view of addictions* (2nd ed.). New York: Wiley.

Orsay, E. M., Doan-Wiggins, L., Lewis, R., Lucke, R., & RamaKrishnan, V. (1994). The impaired driver: hospital and police detection of alcohol and other drugs of abuse in motor vehicle crashes. *Annals of Emergency Medicine, 24*, 51–55.

Oxford University Press. (1971). *The compact edition of the Oxford English dictionary* (Vol. I). London: Author.

Perry, S., Cooper, A. M., & Michels, R. (1987). The psychodynamic formulation: Its purpose, structure, and clinical application. *American Journal of Psychiatry, 144*, 543–550.

Pickering, L. K., & Hogan, G. R. (1971). Voluntary water intoxication in a normal child. *Journal of Pediatrics, 78*, 316–318.

Prochaska, J. O. (1996). A stage paradigm for integrating clinical and public health approaches to smoking cessation. *Addictive Behaviors, 21*(6), 721–732.

Prochaska, J. O., DiClemente, C. C., & Norcross, J. C. (1992). In search of how people change: Applications to addictive behaviors. *American Psychologist, 47*, 1102–1114.

Prochaska, J. O., Norcross, J. C., & DiClemente, C. C. (1994). *Changing for good: A revolutionary six-stage program for overcoming bad habits and moving your life positively forward.* New York: Avon.

Quinn, J. P. (1891). *Fools of fortune.* Chicago: The Anti-Gambling Association.

Rado, S. (1933). The psychoanalysis of pharmacothymia (drug addiction). *Psychoanalytic Quarterly, 2,* 1–23.

Reuters News Service. (1992, November 25). Cigarette shortage in Italy draws tobacconist protest. *Boston Globe,* p. 50.

Rollnick, S., & Morgan, M. (1995). Motivational interviewing: Increasing readiness for change. In A. M. Washton (Ed.), *Psychotherapy and substance abuse: A practitioner's handbook* (pp. 179–191). New York: Guilford Press.

Rosecrance, J. (1985). Compulsive gambling and the medicalization of deviance. *Social Problems, 32,* 275–284.

Rosecrance, J. (1988). *Gambling without guilt: The legitimation of an American pastime.* Pacific Grove, CA: Books/Cole Publishing Company.

Rosenhan, D. L. (1973). On being sane in insane places. *Science, 179,* 250–258.

Ross, L. (1977). The intuitive psychologist and his shortcomings: Distortions in the attribution process. In L. Berkowitz (Ed.), *Advances in experimental social psychology* (Vol. 10, pp. 173–220). New York: Academic Press.

Rowntree, L. G. (1923). Water intoxication. *Archives of Internal Medicine, 32*(2), 157–174.

Seager, C. P. (1970). Treatment of compulsive gamblers by electrical aversion. *British Journal of Psychiatry, 117,* 545–553.

Shaffer, H. J. (1986). Assessment of addictive disorders: The use of clinical reflection and hypotheses testing. *Psychiatric Clinics of North America, 9*(3), 385–398.

Shaffer, H. J. (1992). The psychology of stage change: The transition from addiction to recovery. In J. H. Lowinson, P. Ruiz, R. B. Millman, & J. G. Langrod (Eds.), *Substance abuse: A comprehensive textbook* (2nd ed., pp. 100–105). Baltimore: Williams & Wilkins.

Shaffer, H. J. (1994a). Considering two models of excessive sexual behaviors: Addiction and obsessive-compulsive disorder. *Sexual Addiction & Compulsivity, 1*(1), 6–18.

Shaffer, H. J. (1994b). Denial, ambivalence and countertransference hate. In J. D. Levin & R. Weiss (Eds.), *Alcoholism: Dynamics and treatment* (pp. 421–437). Northdale, NJ: Jason Aronson.

Shaffer, H. J. (1996). Understanding the means and objects of addiction: Technology, the Internet, and gambling. *Journal of Gambling Studies, 12*(4), 461–469.

Shaffer, H. J. (1997a). The most important unresolved issue in the addictions: Conceptual chaos. *Substance Use & Misuse, 32*(11), 1573–1580.

Shaffer, H. J. (1997b). The psychology of stage change. In J. H. Lowinson, P. Ruiz, R. B. Millman, & J. G. Langrod (Eds.), *Substance abuse: A comprehensive textbook* (3rd ed., pp. 100–106). Baltimore: Williams & Wilkins.

Shaffer, H. J. (1999). On the nature and meaning of addiction. *National Forum, 79*(4), 10–14.

Shaffer, H. J., & Burglass, M. E. (Eds.). (1981). *Classic contributions in the addictions.* New York: Brunner/Mazel.

Shaffer, H. J., Hall, M. N., & Vander Bilt, J. (2000). "Computer addiction": a critical consideration. *American Journal of Orthopsychiatry, 70*(2), 162–168.

Shaffer, H. J., & Jones, S. B. (1989). *Quitting cocaine: The struggle against impulse.* Lexington, MA: Lexington Books.

Shaffer, H. J., & Robbins, M. (1991). Manufacturing multiple meanings of addiction: Time-limited realities. *Contemporary Family Therapy, 13,* 387–404.

Shaffer, H. J., & Robbins, M. (1995). Psychotherapy for addictive behavior: A stage-change approach to meaning making. In A. M. Washton (Ed.), *Psychotherapy and substance abuse: A practitioner's handbook* (pp. 103–123). New York: Guilford Press.

Skinner, B. F. (1969). *Contingencies of reinforcement: A theoretical analysis.* Engelwood Cliffs, NJ: Prentice Hall.

Sobell, L. C., Cunningham, J. A., & Sobell, M. B. (1996). Recovery from alcohol problems with and without treatment: Prevalence in two population surveys. *American Journal of Public Health, 86*(7), 966–972.

Sobell, L. C., Ellingstad, T. P., & Sobell, M. B. (2000). Natural recovery from alcohol and drug problems: Methodological review of the research with suggestions for future directions. *Addiction, 95*(5), 749–764.

Svanum, S., & McAdoo, W. G. (1989). Predicting rapid relapse following treatment for chemical dependence: A matched-subjects design. *Journal of Consulting and Clinical Psychology, 57,* 222–226.

Szasz, T. (1987). *Insanity: The idea and its consequence.* New York: Wiley.

Szasz, T. (1991). Diagnoses are not diseases. *Lancet, 338,* 1574–1576.

Tucker, J. A., Donovan, D. M., & Marlatt, G. A. (Eds.). (1999). *Changing addictive behavior.* New York: Guilford Press.

Vaillant, G. E. (1982). On defining alcoholism. *British Journal of Addiction, 77,* 143–144.

Vaillant, G. E. (1988). What can long-term follow-up teach us about relapse and prevention of relapse in addiction? *British Journal of Addiction, 83,* 1147–1157.

Volberg, R. A. (1996). *Gambling and problem gambling in New York: A 10-year replication study, 1986 to 1996.* New York: New York Council on Problem Gambling.

Weems, M. L. (1812). *God's revenge against gambling: Exemplified in the miserable lives and untimely deaths of a number of persons from both sexes, who had sacrificed their health, wealth, and honor at the gaming tables* (2nd ed.). Philadelphia: Independent Press.

WEFA Group, ICR Survey Research Group, Lesieur, H., & Thompson, W. (1997). *A study concerning the effects of legalized gambling on the citizens of the state of Connecticut*: State of Connecticut Department of Revenue Services, Division of Special Revenue.

Weiner, I. B. (1975). *Principles of psychotherapy*. New York: Wiley.

Widiger, T. A., & Clark, L. A. (2000). Toward *DSM-V* and the classification of psychopathology. *Psychological Bulletin, 126*(6), 946–963.

Wise, R. A. (1996). Addictive drugs and brain stimulation reward. *Annual Review of Neuroscience, 19*, 319–340.

World Health Organization. (1992). *The ICD-10 classification of mental and behavioral disorders: Clinical descriptions and diagnostic guidelines*. Geneva: World Health Organization.

Wray, I., & Dickerson, M. (1981). Cessation of high frequency gambling and "withdrawal" symptoms. *British Journal of Addiction, 76*, 401–405.

Zinberg, N. E. (1975). Addiction and ego function. *Psychoanalytic Study of The Child, 30*, 567–588.

Zinberg, N. E. (1984). *Drug, set, and setting: The basis for controlled intoxicant use*. New Haven: Yale University Press.

Ziskin, J. (1970). *Coping with psychiatric and psychological testimony* (2nd ed.). Beverly Hills: Law and Psychology Press.

2

The Neurobiology of Addiction

Kyle J. Frantz
Georgia State University

George F. Koob
The Scripps Research Institute

TRUTH OR FICTION?

___ 1. Drugs of abuse affect natural reward circuitry in the brain with unnatural strength and persistence.

___ 2. The nervous system is specialized for communication in the body, with the goal of maintaining homeostatic balance.

___ 3. Sensitization *describes a decrease in drug effect, whereas* tolerance *describes an increase in drug effect.*

___ 4. All drugs of abuse exert their behavioral effects exclusively through mesocortico-limbic dopamine transmission.

___ 5. Drug withdrawal syndromes usually include dysphoria, anxiety, irritability, malaise, and sleep disturbance.

___ 6. Only those neural systems directly involved in drug reinforcement are implicated in protracted withdrawal syndromes.

___ 7. Negative reinforcement is a process through which presentation of an aversive stimulus decreases the probability that a behavior will be exhibited.

___ 8. Psychomotor stimulant drugs such as cocaine exert activating effects almost opposite the sedative-hypnotic effects of alcohol or barbiturates. Therefore, these different drugs cannot share common neurobiological mechanisms to maintain drug intake.

___ 9. Corticotropin releasing factor (CRF) acting as both a hormonal activator and neurotransmitter is integral to the acute and long-term detrimental effects of drug abuse.

___ 10. Peptide neurotransmitters are too large to be affected by chronic drug use.

___ 11. Semi-permanent changes in neuronal morphology can be induced after chronic drug use via transcription factor–regulated changes in gene expression.

___ 12. Drug-associated environmental cues are highly effective triggers of relapse to drug-seeking behavior.

___ 13. *An organism's hedonic set-point cannot change throughout a lifetime and is staunchly defended by neural subsystems.*

___ 14. Allostasis, *the process of maintaining stability through change, may prove costly to an organism and result in long-term physiological dysfunction.*

___ 15. *The most effective treatment for drug addiction is drug abuse prevention.*

As you prepare to counsel individuals with drug and alcohol abuse problems, you need to be aware of the biological events underlying the signs and symptoms of drug addiction. This chapter will aid in your professional development by describing the effects of short- (acute) and long-term (chronic) drug exposure on nervous system function and behavior. As you work within a treatment team, understanding the neurobiology of addiction will help you promote effective synergy between pharmacological, behavioral, and cognitive treatment strategies.

We start by reviewing nervous system function and its alteration by drugs. Then, we examine hypotheses about the neurobiological substrates critical to the development, maintenance, and persistence of drug dependence. Much of the research on the neurobiology of drug addiction has been conducted using animal models of human drug intake, so we emphasize them in this chapter. Finally, we summarize comprehensive theories that address the shift from controlled drug use to compulsive drug abuse, given that such a shift is a defining feature of drug dependence. One central hypothesis regarding this shift is that chronic drug abuse dysregulates the neural substrates mediating drug reward while also overactivating counteradaptive brain stress systems.

Reading this chapter should answer many questions you may have about the biological underpinnings of drug addiction. However, we cannot present all the available scientific data on drug abuse. For example, genetic predispositions and environmentally induced vulnerabilities to drug abuse are outside the scope of this chapter. Moreover, many areas in the neurobiology of addiction remain to be explored in the future by investigators like you.

HOW DO DRUGS AFFECT NERVOUS SYSTEM FUNCTION AND ANIMAL BEHAVIOR?

The Nervous System: What Is It Good For?

The nervous system is a complex of signaling pathways that transmit, sort, and process information between internal organs and the external environment. Parsed according to structure and function, the nervous system has two major divisions: the central nervous system and the peripheral nervous system. The *central nervous system* (CNS) includes the brain and spinal cord. Within the brain, major subdivisions include the hindbrain, midbrain, basal forebrain, and cortical structures. Outside the CNS, the *peripheral nervous system* (PNS) consists of the *autonomic* nervous system controlling the heart, intestines, and other organs, and the *somatic* nervous system controlling skeletal muscles and glands. Further partitioning of the autonomic nervous system designates the *sympathetic* division as engaging the body in "fight or flight" activational states and the *parasympathetic* division as maintaining "rest and digest" conservational functions. Drugs of abuse selectively affect various parts of the nervous system. For example, *sympathomimetic drugs* are stimulants that selectively activate the sympathetic division of the autonomic nervous system, thereby mimicking the body's own "fight or flight" response.

One of the most important roles of the nervous system is to maintain **homeostasis**, which is the stabilization of body variables within a fixed range for optimal processing. With regard to drug abuse, a major system to keep in balance is the reward or motivational system. Deviations from the **reward** or motivational set point can be caused by drug abuse. These deviations trigger *neuroadaptations*, which mediate attempts to return the body to normal homeostatic balance.

1. Which of the following structures is considered part of the central nervous system (CNS)?
   a. brain only
   b. brain and spinal cord
   c. sympathetic division
   d. parasympathetic division

2. One of the most important roles of the nervous system is to _____.
   a. maintain homeostasis
   b. inhibit sleep
   c. trigger perspiration
   d. mimic its own "fight or flight" system

Neurotransmission Involves Electrochemical Communication Between Neurons

Neurons are the communicating cells of the nervous system. Their structure is well-suited for receiving and transmitting information in two forms: 1) electrical potentials created by redistribution of charged atoms (ions), and 2) chemical signaling via release and binding of chemical messengers known as *neurotransmitters*. The classic conception of synaptic transmission is that a burst of electrical energy (action potential) traverses from the cell body down the axon to its terminal where neurotransmitters are released into the synaptic cleft (Fig. 2.1). In the cleft, neurotransmitters encounter *receptor proteins*, specialized structures bound in membranes of neighboring neurons. Neurotransmitter–receptor interactions form the basis of chemical communication.

3. Which of the following is the sending end of a neuron (nerve cell), containing the terminal(s) from which neurotransmitters are released to interact with another nerve cell?
   a. cell body
   b. dendrite
   c. axon
   d. synapse

Diverse chemical messages are sent using this system. Messages are encoded according to the types of neurotransmitters released, the number of neurotransmitter molecules, and the subtypes of receptor proteins encountered. Neurotransmitters integrally involved in drug abuse and dependence include dopamine, serotonin, norepinephrine, acetylcholine, γ-aminobutyric acid (GABA), and glutamate. Neuropeptide transmitters are also involved, such as met-enkephalin, dynorphin, neuropeptide Y (NPY), corticotropin releasing factor (CRF), and many more. (*Peptides* are short chains of amino acids.) Most students imagine the neurotransmitter–receptor interaction as a key–lock relationship. What happens when the key unlocks the door?

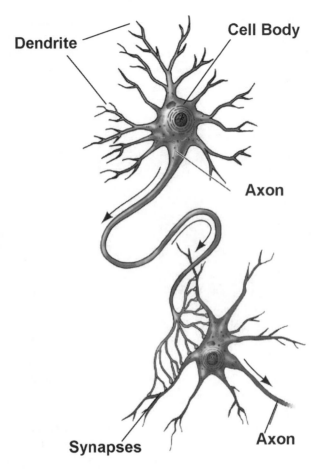

FIG. 2.1. Prototypical neurons have extensive dendritic branches and long axons. Dendrites usually receive electrochemical messages from other neurons, whereas axons with numerous terminal boutons send information via electrochemical neurotransmission to other neurons, or to glandular or muscle tissue. (From Purves, W. K., Sadava, D., Orians, G. H., and Heller, H. C. (2001). *Life: The Science of Biology,* 6th Ed. Reprinted with permission from Sinauer Associates, Sunderland, Massachusetts.)

Conformational changes in receptor proteins triggered by neurotransmitter binding alter membrane permeability, membrane potential, and a myriad of other cellular activities. Some receptors directly open or close membrane channels (ionotropic receptors), influencing ion flow across the membrane. Other receptors indirectly modulate ion flow by stimulating or inhibiting intracellular metabolic pathways, via enzymes activated by G-proteins attached on the intracellular side of the receptor proteins (metabotropic receptors). **Adenylyl cyclase** is one such activational enzyme; it activates cyclic adenosine monophosphate **(cAMP)**, a second messenger. *Second messengers* are regulatory proteins that amplify signals from "first" messengers (neurotransmitters), and trigger functions ranging from rearrangement of the cytoskeleton to regulation of gene expression. Whereas neurotransmitter release, receptor binding, and direct modulation of ion flow occur over several thousandths of a second, second messenger activation and subsequent effects endure much longer: several seconds or sometimes minutes to hours. Gene expression may be altered for days, or even permanently.

4. Choose the correct sequence for the steps of neurotransmission.
   a. arrival of action potential at terminal bouton, release of neurotransmitter into synapse, neurotransmitter inactivation, receptor binding, and second messenger activation
   b. receptor binding, second messenger activation, arrival of action potential at terminal bouton, release of neurotransmitter into synapse, neurotransmitter inactivation
   c. release of neurotransmitter into synapse, receptor binding, second messenger activation, neurotransmitter inactivation, arrival of action potential at terminal bouton
   d. arrival of action potential at terminal bouton, release of neurotransmitter into synapse, receptor binding, second messenger activation, and neurotransmitter inactivation

Drugs Interfere With Neurotransmission: Pharmacodynamics and Pharmacokinetics

The study of drug interactions with biological systems is known as *pharmacodynamics*. Most drugs of abuse exert their neurochemical and behavioral effects by modulating the pattern, intensity, or timing of neurotransmission. *Agonist* drugs mimic or enhance the effects of **endogenous** (naturally-occurring) transmitters. On the other hand, *antagonist* drugs attenuate or block the activity of endogenous neurotransmitters. However, individuals do not usually apply drugs directly to the brain or to neurons; drug molecules arrive at these sites via the bloodstream. As discussed in chapter 1, pharmacokinetic factors such as route of drug administration into the body, drug solubility, and drug metabolism influence the quality and quantity of drug effect.

5. The study of the ways in which drug molecules influence neurotransmission is _____?
   a. pharmacodynamics
   b. pharmacokinetics
   c. pharmacy
   d. pharmacology

6. Drugs often interfere with _____, meaning naturally-occurring, neurotransmitters.
   a. antagonistic
   b. agonistic
   c. endogenous
   d. chemical

HOW DO BASIC CONCEPTS IN PHARMACOLOGY APPLY TO DRUGS OF ABUSE?

Drug Dose and Response Are Integrally Related and Change With Repeated Drug Administration

Pharmacology is the study of drugs and their sources, appearance, chemistry, actions, and uses. Descriptive graphs in the field of pharmacology depict relationships between drug-dose and drug effects and are known as ***dose-response curves*** (see Fig. 2.3 for an example). Dose-response relationships can change after repeated drug exposure. Drug ***tolerance*** refers to a *decrease* in drug effect after repeated administration of the same drug dose. It reveals the body's drive toward homeostasis; metabolic, behavioral, or pharmacodynamic mechanisms counteract or minimize drug effects. Conversely, some drug effects *increase* in magnitude with repeated, intermittent administration of similar doses. This phenomenon is known as **sensitization** and involves the body's increasing sensitivity to drug effects. Sensitization is robust for some of the motor effects induced by psychomotor stimulant drugs and some withdrawal effects associated with sedative-hypnotic drugs. Tolerance to some effects can be coupled with sensitization to others, resulting in a complicated imbalance between physiological systems. Tolerance and sensitization are neuroadaptations that can persist long after the drug itself is cleared from the body.

7. After repeated administration of a pain-relieving medication, adequate pain-relief was no longer achieved with a stable dose of 1200 mg in patient PB. This demonstration of _____ may have resulted from an increased rate of drug metabolism.
   a. tolerance
   b. withdrawal
   c. sensitization
   d. dose-response

Cessation of Drug Intake Reveals Physiological and Behavioral Adaptations to the Drug

Drug *withdrawal* describes a constellation of signs and symptoms associated with cessation of drug use. Withdrawal syndromes can be physical or affective in nature and are generally opposite the high or intoxicated state. For example, **dysphoria,** irritability, anxiety, malaise, and sleep disturbance all comprise common drug withdrawal states. A withdrawal syndrome provides evidence of tolerance mechanisms counteracting acute drug intake, but then overshooting homeostatic balance when a drug is no longer acting on the nervous system. You can conceptualize the relationship between drug effect, tolerance, and withdrawal as a playground see-saw. Starting with the drug-free naïve state of the body in homeostasis, the see-saw is balanced. A drug presented at one end of the see-saw would tip that end down. Counteractive tolerance mechanisms exerted by the body on the other end would rebalance the see-saw. Once the drug is cleared from the body (or jumped off its end of the see-saw) the tolerance end would crash to the ground, representing the imbalance of withdrawal.

Behavioral Reinforcement Helps to Describe Drug-Related Behavior

Humans and other animals actually seek drug stimulation under a variety of conditions. We define *drug-seeking behavior* as any activity carried out toward approaching, obtaining, or consuming a drug. *Reinforcement* is a hypothetical construct used to describe the process through which a stimulus (drug or otherwise) increases the probability of a subject making a response (e.g., a drug-seeking response). **Positive reinforcement** is the process through which *presentation of a stimulus* increases the probability of a subject making a response that presents the stimulus again. The stimulus in positive reinforcement is often considered to be a pleasurable reward, such as drug-induced euphoria. Conversely, **negative reinforcement** is defined as a process through which *removal of a stimulus* increases the probability of a subject making a response that removes the stimulus again. The stimulus in negative reinforcement appears to be generally uncomfortable, depressing, or otherwise aversive, such as physical or emotional pain.

In a process akin to *classical conditioning* (Pavlovian conditioning), positive or negative reinforcing stimuli can be paired with previously neutral stimuli, such as drug-injection needles or drug-taking environments. After repeated pairings, conditioned positive reinforcement or conditioned negative reinforcement develops, such that encountering a stimulus previously paired with a positive or negative reinforcing stimulus increases the probability of a subject seeking the reinforcing stimulus itself. For example, an environment in which drugs had previously been used may trigger an individual's desire to experience drug-induced euphoria or drug-associated pain relief. Conditioned stimuli are often blamed in episodes of relapse.

8. Name the behavioral process whereby removal of an aversive stimulus increases the likelihood an organism will exhibit a particular behavior.
   a. drug withdrawal
   b. drug craving
   c. positive reinforcement
   d. negative reinforcement

ARE ANIMAL MODELS HELPFUL TO RESEARCH ON DRUGS OF ABUSE?

Due to similarities in nervous system function and behavioral repertoire across species, animal models of human drug-related behavior help define the neurobiology of drug reinforcement and have high predictive value for the addictive potential of drugs in humans. Research scientists carry out these methods with rodents or nonhuman primate species in controlled laboratory experiments. We briefly introduce three such methods here because they have contributed substantially to our knowledge of drug-related neural responses and adaptations. First, through mechanisms of behavioral reinforcement, if presentation of a drug is made contingent upon an animal pressing a lever in a specialized operant chamber, then rodents and nonhuman primates will press levers consistently to self-administer drugs of abuse intravenously or orally (Fig. 2.2). Generally, drugs that animals self-administer have high abuse potential for humans.

9. A rat associates lever-pressing in an operant chamber with intravenous infusions of morphine. Subsequently, the rat lever-presses repeatedly and self-administers morphine steadily. This sequence of events is an example of _____.
   a. negative reinforcement
   b. conditioned negative reinforcement
   c. positive reinforcement
   d. conditioned positive reinforcement

Electrical brain stimulation reward is another unique tool for analysis of reward-related brain circuitry and behavior. Humans and other animals readily self-stimulate their own neural circuitry by pressing a lever to activate an electrode implanted into the medial forebrain bundle, a tract of axons projecting from the midbrain into the basal forebrain, normally activated by conventional reinforcers such as food, water, and sex. Investigators can record the threshold, or minimum level, of electrical stimulation that will support behavioral responding. Pretreatment or simultaneous treatment with drugs of abuse decreases the minimum (threshold) level of electrical stimulation that will maintain responding (Fig. 2.3), presumably because the compound pharmacological and electrical stimulus is more rewarding than electrical stimulus alone. This procedure is known as *Intracranial self-stimulation* (ICSS).

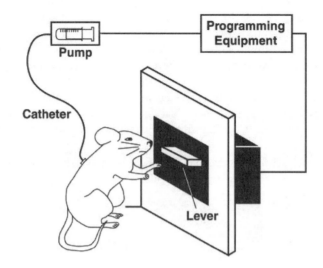

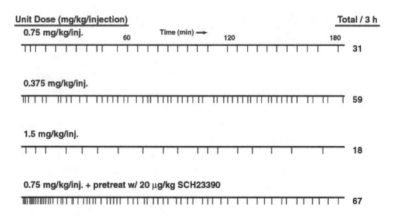

FIG. 2.2. Rats can be trained to self-administer drugs, such as cocaine. Rats implanted with intravenous catheters are trained to lever-press using intravenous infusions of drug solutions as reinforcing stimuli. Event records indicate the number and pattern of drug infusions earned per 3-hr sessions. On a fixed-ratio schedule of reinforcement (e.g., 5 lever-presses required for 1 drug infusion), different doses of cocaine maintain different rates of **drug self-administration**. Lowering the dose from 0.75 mg/kg/injection to 0.375 mg/kg/injection increases the number of injections received. Conversely, raising the dose to 1.5 mg/kg/injection decreases the number of injections. Pretreatment with a dopamine receptor antagonist (SCH23390) also increases the number of injections, presumably by competing with cocaine-stimulated dopamine for binding at receptors. (From Caine, S. B., Lintz, R., & Koob, G. F. (1993). Intravenous drug self-administration techniques in animals. In A. Sahgal (Ed.) *Behavioral Neuroscience: A Practical Approach,* vol. 2, pp. 117–143. Reprinted with permission of Oxford University Press.)

10. Predict the direction of change in the brain stimulation reward threshold during withdrawal from abused drugs.
    a. decrease, a reflection of the positive affect of withdrawal
    b. no change, due to absence of the abused drug in the body
    c. increase, a reflection of the negative affect of withdrawal
    d. decrease, followed by increase, due to the initially negative, then positive, affective states of withdrawal

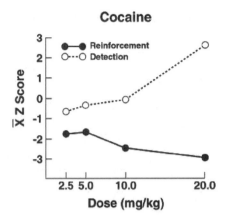

FIG. 2.3. Cocaine pretreatment enhances the reward value of brain stimulation, without decreasing the detection of brain stimulation. The first step in this analysis was to measure the threshold level of brain stimulation reward that supports operant behavior, with or without cocaine pretreatment. A *z-score* was then calculated as the difference between reinforcement threshold values with cocaine pretreatment divided by the standard deviation of thresholds without cocaine pretreatment. A *z-score* of 2 was considered significant. The 10 mg/kg and 20 mg/kg doses of cocaine decreased thresholds, probably by facilitating reward (*filled circles*). The second step was to measure threshold brain stimulation detectable by a rat. *Z-score* calculations indicate that cocaine alters detection thresholds only at the highest dose (*open circles*). (From Kornetsky, C., & Bain, G. (1982). Biobehavioral bases of the reinforcing properties of opiate drugs. In K. Verebey (Ed.) *Opioids in Mental Illness: Theories, Clinical Observations, and Treatment Possibilities* (series title: Annals of the New York Academy of Science, vol. 398, pp. 241–259). Reprinted with permission of the New York Academy of Sciences, New York.)

Finally, a classical conditioning procedure pairs an unconditioned stimulus with a conditioned stimulus, such that eventually the conditioned stimulus elicits a conditioned response almost identical to the unconditioned response elicited naturally by the unconditioned stimulus. With regard to the reinforcing effects of drugs of abuse, a drug state (unconditioned stimulus) can be paired with a distinctive environment (conditioned stimulus), such that eventually the drug-paired environment is preferred over a neutral site. This outcome, termed *conditioned place preference*, may be related to positive affective states associated with acute drug intake. The opposite can also occur: a paired environment may be avoided, as in a *conditioned place aversion*. Pairing a distinctive environment with the negative withdrawal state often conditions place aversions.

11. A mouse that received injections of morphine on the light side of a two-chambered apparatus would most likely do what when given the option to roam the apparatus freely a few days later?
    a. explore both chambers equally
    b. spend more time on the light side of the apparatus
    c. spend more time on the dark side of the apparatus
    d. become immobile

WHAT ARE THE NEUROBIOLOGICAL SUBSTRATES OF DRUG REWARD?

Reward-Related Messages Traverse the Medial Forebrain Bundle and Extended Amygdala

Although drugs of abuse affect nearly every major subdivision of the nervous system, one particular brain pathway is most relevant to drug abuse: the medial forebrain bundle (Fig. 6). Neuronal cell bodies in the hindbrain and midbrain send diffuse ascending projections to the forebrain in the medial forebrain bundle, whereas the basal forebrain sends major descending projections to the brainstem also in the bundle (Fig. 2.4). These projections are integral to motivated behavior, that is, they participate in the behavioral approach to naturally rewarding stimuli, as well as to drugs. One important subset of projections is the mesocorticolimbic dopamine pathway, with cell bodies in the midbrain ventral tegmental area (VTA) and axonal projections releasing dopamine in targeted basal forebrain nuclei including the nucleus accumbens, amygdala, frontal cortex, and limbic cortex. Nucleus accumbens dopamine transmission

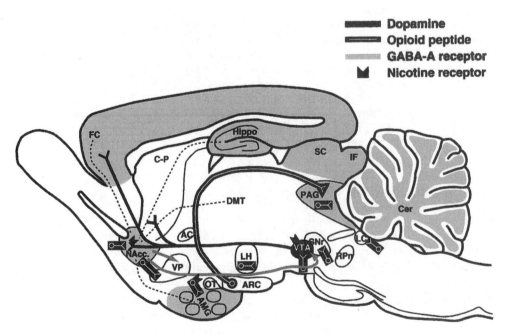

FIG. 2.4. A sagittal section through the brain of a rat. Neurochemical circuits implicated in the reinforcing effects of drugs of abuse are indicated. Dopamine projections from the ventral tegmental area (VTA) to the nucleus accumbens (NAcc), caudate-putamen (C-P), and frontal cortex (FC) are critical for psychomotor stimulant reward. Projections both toward and away from the NAcc modulate reward (*dotted lines*), as do GABAergic projections using GABA-A receptor subtypes. Opioid peptide systems include local circuits and longer loops. Projections converge in the medial forebrain bundle. Nicotine binds to receptors distributed in reward-related regions, indirectly activating opioid and dopaminergic systems. VP, ventral pallidum; LH, lateral hypothalamus; SNr, substantia nigra pars reticulate; DMT, dorsomedial thalamus; PAG, periaqueductal gray; OT, olfactory tract; AC, anterior commissure; LC, locus ceruleus; AMG, amygdala; Hippo, hippocampus; Cer, cerebellum; SC, superior colliculus; IF, inferior colliculus; ARC, arcuate nucleus; RPn, raphe pontis nucleus. (Reprinted from Koon, G. F. (1992). Drugs of abuse: Anatomy, pharmacology, and function of reward pathways. *Trends in Pharmacological Sciences 13*(5), 117–184 with permission from Elsevier.)

in particular is elevated by many drugs of abuse. Additionally, serotonin-releasing neurons with cell bodies in the dorsal and median raphe nuclei of the midbrain and pons send more diffuse projections to the basal forebrain to modulate drug reward and influence affective components of drug use. Also important are opioid peptides and amino acid neurotransmitters, such as GABA and glutamate. These systems interact extensively with a functional group of nuclei with similar cell morphology, protein expression, and extensive interconnectivity, termed the *extended amygdala* (Heimer & Alheid, 1991). Activation of the extended amygdala spans natural and drug reward, indicating common neural substrates for many types of reward.

12. In which of the following reward-related brain regions is dopamine elevated by several drugs of abuse?
    a. hypothalamus
    b. cerebellum
    c. nucleus accumbens
    d. none of the above

13. The brain reinforcement system has which of the following characteristics?
    a. It is comprised of many neurons distributed throughout the brainstem and projecting locally within the brainstem.
    b. It is comprised of neuronal circuits within the medial forebrain bundle that project in both directions between the forebrain and the midbrain, pons, and medulla.
    c. It is comprised of neuronal cell body groups in the cortex and hippocampus that project to several nuclei in the pons and medulla.
    d. It is comprised of many neurons distributed throughout the forebrain and projecting locally within the forebrain.

Cocaine and Other Indirect Sympathomimetics Directly Activate Dopamine Transmission

Amphetamine, methamphetamine, 3,4-methylenedioxymethamphetamine (MDMA, "ecstasy"), cocaine, and other related indirect sympathomimetics are known as *psychomotor stimulants* due to their robust activating effects. In humans, they produce euphoria, stimulate activity, decrease fatigue, and decrease hunger. In other animals, they produce motor activation and decrease food intake. In terms of behavioral reinforcement, they maintain operant behavior (e.g., lever-pressing in the self-administration paradigm), condition preferences for stimulant-paired environments, and decrease thresholds in brain ICSS reward paradigms. Withdrawal from psychostimulants results in an initial crash (loss of energy, sleep disturbance, irritability), followed by a sustained syndrome of craving, anxiety, apathy, and general dysphoria.

Stimulant drugs share structural and functional similarities with endogenous neurotransmitters and increase the synaptic availability of dopamine, serotonin, and norepinephrine. The acute reinforcing effects of psychomotor stimulants rely directly on increased dopamine transmission in mesolimbic circuits (see Koob & LeMoal, 2001, for review).

14. Indirect sympathomimetics exert their behaviorally reinforcing effects specifically by:
    a. activating the "fight or flight" division of the autonomic nervous system.
    b. increasing dopamine in synapses of the mesolimbic pathway.
    c. increasing dopamine, serotonin, and norepinephrine in synapses throughout the body.
    d. indirectly elevating rate of self-administration.

Opioid Drugs Interact With Endogenous Opioid System

Opioid drugs are a large class of pain-relieving (analgesic), cough-suppressing, euphoria-inducing compounds either naturally derived from the opium poppy (opiates including opium, morphine, and codeine) or synthesized in laboratories from other chemicals (opioids including methadone, meperidine, oxycodone, and many others). Heroin is a semi-synthetic opiate created by slightly altering the structure of morphine. Similar to psychomotor stimulant drugs, opiates and opioid drugs maintain stable intravenous self-administration, decrease thresholds in brain stimulation reward paradigms, and condition place preferences. In humans and other animals, opiate withdrawal involves flu-like symptoms, pain hypersensitivity, diarrhea, and dysphoria.

Both opioid and dopamine receptors play roles in opioid-related reward and reinforcement. Opioid receptor antagonists injected systemically or centrally into the nucleus accumbens or VTA decrease heroin self-administration, whereas disruption of mesolimbic dopamine transmission attenuates opiate conditioned place preference (see van Ree, Gerrits, & Vanderschuren, 1999, for review).

Opioid peptide neurotransmitters are endogenous agonists at the opiate receptors integral to opiate reward. Involved in pain perception and memory, along with feeding, sexual activity, body temperature, blood pressure, and immune function, endogenous opioid peptides are divided into two major classes, *enkephalins* and *endorphins*. Not only opioid drugs activate this endogenous opioid circuitry; nicotine, alcohol, and THC (tetrahydrocannabinol, the primary psychoactive constituent of marijuana) also access this system to exert their psychoactive effects.

15. Based on your reading in this chapter, evidence that opiate drugs bind to opioid receptors to induce their reinforcing effects on behavior might include which of the following?
    a. Mice genetically engineered to express high levels of opioid receptors do *not* demonstrate morphine reward or analgesia.
    b. Opioid drug injections into the brain decrease brain stimulation reward thresholds.
    c. Reinforcement associated with opioid drugs is, in part, mediated by dopamine-independent pathways.
    d. Specific opioid receptor antagonists block heroin self-administration.

Nicotine Indirectly Stimulates Both Dopamine and Opioid Peptide Systems

In humans and other animals, nicotine induces stimulant-like effects such as increased activity and decreased fatigue, as well as anxiolysis (anxiety reduction), improved cognitive performance (e.g., sustained visual attention), and behavioral reinforcement (e.g., intravenous self-administration). Nicotine dependence is characterized by tolerance, withdrawal, craving, and high rates of relapse even after protracted abstinence. Irritability, headache, craving for nicotine, and depressed mood are well-quantified components of nicotine withdrawal. Although a direct agonist at receptors for the endogenous neurotransmitter acetylcholine, nicotine indirectly activates mesolimbic dopamine transmission. Dopamine receptor antagonists block nicotine self-administration. Through other indirect mechanisms, nicotine also activates endogenous opioid peptide systems (see Mathieu-Kia, Kellogg, Butelman, & Kreek, 2002, for review).

16. Nicotine is a direct agonist at which receptors?
    a. acetylcholinergic
    b. GABAergic
    c. opioidergic
    d. dopaminergic

Alcohol, Barbiturates, and Benzodiazepines Have Multiple Neurochemical Substrates

The sedative-hypnotic drugs, such as alcohol, barbiturates, and benzodiazepines can induce mild euphoria, behavioral disinhibition, anxiolysis, sedation, and hypnosis. Withdrawal from alcohol results in "hangover" symptoms including headache, blurred vision, tremors, nausea, sleep disturbances, and dysphoria. Multiple neurotransmitter systems appear to mediate these effects. Antagonists at the GABA$_A$ receptor subtype attenuate the behavioral effects of alcohol and decrease alcohol-related behavioral reinforcement. Opioid peptides are also involved. Alcohol may further block glutamate receptors and increase serotonin transmission. Finally, a role for the mesolimbic dopamine pathway is indicated; dopamine receptor antagonists decrease oral self-administration of alcohol (see Weiss & Porrino, 2002, for review).

17. Which of the following endogenous neurotransmitter systems is implicated in the behavioral effects of alcohol?
    a. dopamine
    b. opioid peptides
    c. GABA
    d. all of the above are involved

THC Exerts Effects Similar to Other Drugs of Abuse

The pharmacologically active component of cannabis is THC. In humans, notable components of acute THC intoxication include mild euphoria, hunger, time distortions, and hallucinations. On the other hand, cannabis withdrawal results in restlessness, insomnia, reduced appetite, and depression. As is the case with many other drugs of abuse, THC decreases thresholds in brain stimulation reward paradigms, induces conditioned place preferences, and maintains self-administration in monkeys. A synthetic THC maintains self-administration in mice. THC binds with receptors that are normally activated by an endogenous fatty acid, anandamide. Indirectly, THC also activates mesolimbic dopamine transmission, as do many drugs of abuse (see Tanda & Goldberg, 2003, for review).

18. The reinforcing effects of THC are mediated at least in part through receptors normally activated by which molecule?
    a. glutamate
    b. GABA
    c. anandamide
    d. alcohol

IN WHAT WAYS DOES THE BRAIN CHANGE IN RESPONSE TO REPEATED OR PROLONGED DRUG EXPOSURE?

Drugs affect natural reward circuitry in the brain with unnatural strength and persistence, resulting in functional alterations in brain and behavior that can eventually become severely pathological. Animal models support the existence of changes in affective state that reflect neuroadaptations on multiple physiological levels, with the ability to change the brain's "internal landscape" dramatically (see Nestler, 2001, for review). Neuroadaptations occur not only in the circuits affected acutely by drugs, but also in systems recruited to counteract drug effects, such as stress circuitry. One of the defining behavioral features of addiction is relapse to drug-seeking, even after extended periods of abstinence. Investigators therefore seek to identify neuroadaptations that endure for months to years after cessation of drug use.

Brain Reward Circuitry is Compromised

The brain-stimulation-reward paradigm reveals compromised reward-related brain circuitry after repeated or prolonged drug exposure (see Table 2.1). For example, withdrawal from chronic stimulant administration increases the ICSS reward threshold. Opiate withdrawal, which can be precipitated by injection of an opiate receptor antagonist in opiate-dependent rodents, also increases the ICSS reward threshold. The same is true for spontaneous withdrawal from alcohol, and either precipitated or spontaneous withdrawal from chronic nicotine or THC. Insofar as an increase in brain stimulation threshold is a model of dysphoria in humans, this paradigm provides evidence that negative affect is a consistent consequence of acute withdrawal from abused drugs (see Koob & LeMoal, 2001, for review).

19. Intracranial self-stimulation studies conducted using animals in withdrawal from chronic drug exposure provide:
    a. a model of changes in reward systems.
    b. evidence for drug-induced euphoria.
    c. data quantifying receptor down-regulation.
    d. details on dopamine and serotonin neurotransmission.

TABLE 2.1

Drug Effects on Thresholds of Rewarding Brain Stimulation

Drug Class	Acute Administration	Withdrawal From Chronic Treatment
Psychostimulants (cocaine, amphetamines)	↓	↑
Opiates (morphine, heroin)	↓	↑
Nicotine	↓	↑
Sedative-hypnotics (ethanol)	↓	↑

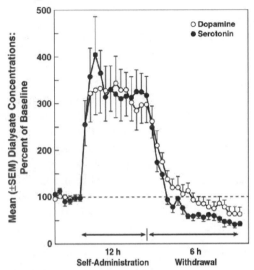

Extracellular DA and 5-HT in the Nucleus Accumbens During Cocaine Self-Administration and Withdrawal

FIG. 2.5. Dopamine and serotonin (5-HT) levels in the nucleus accumbens increase dramatically during a 12-hr binge of cocaine self-administration, but drop below baseline upon drug withdrawal. Data represent percent of baseline concentrations of dopamine (5.3±0.5 nM) or serotonin (1.0±0.1 nM). (From Parsons, L. H., Koob, G. F., & Weiss, F. (1995). Serotonin dysfunction in the nucleus accumbens of rats during withdrawal after unlimited access to intravenous cocaine. *Journal of Pharmacology and Experimental Therapeutics, 274*(3), 1182–1191. Reprinted with permission from the American Society for Pharmacology and Experimental Therapeutics, Bethesda, Maryland.)

Mesolimbic Neurochemistry Is Altered During Drug Intake and Withdrawal

As discussed previously, dopamine transmission in the mesolimbic pathway is involved to some degree in the reinforcing actions of many drugs. Extracellular levels of dopamine increase during drug intake, as do levels of serotonin and norepinephrine. A technique known as *in vivo* **microdialysis** reveals that drug-induced increases in neurotransmitters such as dopamine and serotonin are followed by abrupt decreases below pre-drug baselines upon cessation of drug intake (e.g., Fig. 2.5). Subnormal levels of dopamine are associated with inactivity, lack of reward, and depression. Low levels of serotonin are implicated in disorders of thought, unstable mood, impulsivity, sleep abnormalities, depression, and anxiety. These behavioral deficits should sound familiar; they are components of drug withdrawal syndromes.

20. *In vivo* microdialysis studies revealing drastic declines in extracellular levels of dopamine and serotonin during drug withdrawal imply that:
    a. these neurotransmitters contribute to the affective and motivational deficits of drug withdrawal.
    b. investigators cannot record significant drug-related changes in neurotransmission.
    c. chronic drug intake induces only temporary neuroadaptations.
    d. homeostasis occurs at the behavioral level.

Intracellular Signaling Pathways Are Upregulated by Chronic Drug Intake

Inside each neuron is the machinery that translates neurotransmitter–receptor binding into intracellular activities, using second messengers such as cAMP. Via dopamine receptors, acute drug intake inhibits cAMP, but chronic drug use eventually upregulates the cAMP signaling pathway. The cellular effects of cAMP are extensive, hinging in large part on a **transcription factor,** cAMP response element binding protein (**CREB**). CREB regulates transcription of genes that encode for enzymes, neurotransmitter precursors, other transcriptional regulators, and growth factors. High levels of CREB activated by high levels of cAMP may mediate some aspects of drug-related tolerance and withdrawal. ΔFosB is another transcription factor upregulated by cocaine, amphetamine, opiates, nicotine, and alcohol. It is activated at a low level with each drug administration but its stable protein increases gradually with repeated drug administration and remains elevated. However, CREB and ΔFosB activation endures only several days (CREB) or one to two months (ΔFosB), whereas drug-related vulnerability to drug relapse threatens throughout a lifetime (Fig. 2.6; see Nestler, 2001; Nestler, Barrott, & Self, 2001, for reviews).

Neuron Structure and Neurogenesis May Be Permanently Altered by Drugs

Permanent changes in synaptic structure are among the best current explanations for the long-term drug-induced behavioral adaptations. Repeated opiate exposure decreases the size of dendrites and cell bodies in dopaminergic neurons in the VTA. Repeated cocaine or amphetamine increases dendritic branching and dendritic spine outgrowth on neurons in the nucleus accumbens and pyramidal cells in the medial prefrontal cortex. Changes in neuronal morphology (shape) translate into changes in neurotransmission. Moreover, a process known as *neurogenesis* produces new neurons daily in the hippocampus. Drugs of abuse decrease neurogenesis. Studies to date have tracked the duration of these changes to approximately four months after cessation of drug exposure in rodents; these structural and functional changes in the nervous system fit logically into a sequence of increasingly long-lasting changes induced by drugs (see Nestler, 2001, for review).

21. Among the possibilities below, how can investigators best define the contributions of transcription factors such as CREB and ΔFosB to behavior?
    a. Use conditioned place preference.
    b. Block the activity of cAMP and record neurochemical as well as behavioral changes.
    c. Over- or under-express the transcription factors and record behavioral alterations in multiple behavioral paradigms.
    d. Ask subjects to estimate their own levels of endogenous CREB or ΔFosB, and correlate them with drug craving.

22. Which of the following is a feature of the ΔFosB protein that makes it promising as part of the molecular foundation of protracted drug withdrawal?
    a. ability to stimulate transcription regulator AP-1
    b. association with reduced cocaine reward
    c. eventual decline in tolerance-like manner with repeated drug exposure
    d. gradual accumulation over weeks to months due to protein stability

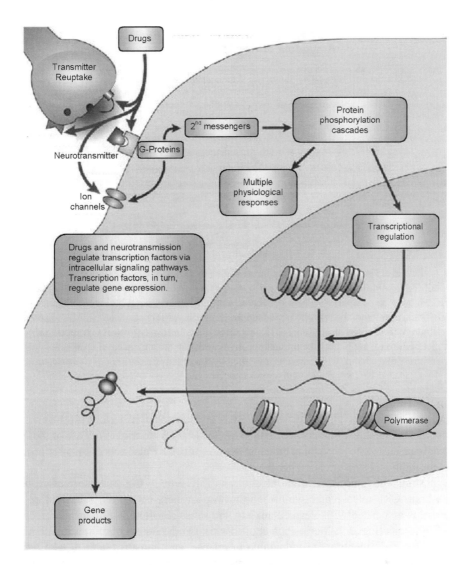

FIG. 2.6. Via their modulatory actions in synapses, drugs of abuse change transcription
factor-regulated gene expression. Transcription factors activated in the cytoplasm migrate to the
nucleus to bind with genes. Polymerases are then more likely to initiate gene transcription, translation,
and assembly of gene products. Conversely, some transcription factors repress gene expression.
(Modified from Nestler, E. J. (2001). Molecular basis of long-term plasticity underlying addiction.
Nature Reviews Neuroscience, 2, 119–128. Reprinted with permission from Nature Publishing Group.)

Corticotropin-Releasing Factor (CRF) Increases During Drug Intake and Withdrawal

Stress can be defined as any challenge to, or alteration in, homeostatic processing. Within
this conceptualization, both drug intake and drug withdrawal are stressors. As such, they
trigger stress responses (Koob & LeMoal, 2001), including acute activation of the sympathetic
nervous system, endocrine (hormonal) activation, and potentially long-term disruptions such
as decreased immune function or insulin insensitivity. Released from hypothalamic neurons

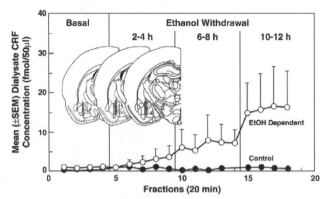

Extracellular CRF Levels in the Central Amygdala During Ethanol Withdrawal

FIG. 2.7. Levels of corticotropin releasing factor (CRF) in the amygdala rise during withdrawal from alcohol self-administration. Samples of extracellular fluid were collected over four 2-hr periods, separated by three 2-hr periods of noncollection. Coronal sections of rat brain reveal the location (*vertical lines*) of microdialysis probe implantation. (From Merlo-Pich, E., Lorang, M., Yeganeh, M., Rodriguez de Fonseca, F., Raber, J., Koob, G. F., et al. (1995). Increase of extracellular corticotropin-releasing factor-like immunoreactivity levels in the amygdala of awake rats during restraint stress and ethanol withdrawal as measured by microdialysis. *Journal of Neuroscience, 15,* 5439–5447. Reprinted with permission from the Society of Neuroscience.)

into the anterior pituitary gland, corticotropin-releasing factor (CRF) kicks off the endocrine response by stimulating adrenocorticotropic hormone (ACTH) to trigger release of the "stress hormone" corticosterone (cortisol in humans). In the brain, CRF also acts as a neurotransmitter to activate additional stress-related behaviors.

Psychostimulants, opioids, nicotine, alcohol, and THC actually trigger acute stress responses through brain CRF release and sympathetic nervous system activation. Furthermore, drug withdrawal is associated with elevated anxiety and stress reported by humans and increased brain CRF in rats (Fig. 2.7; Merlo-Pich et al., 1995). On the other hand, stressful conditions make humans and rodents more vulnerable to relapse, and humans claim to take drugs to alleviate stress. Thus, drug use and stress comprise a feed-forward loop in which stress leads to drug intake which leads to stress, and so on. With the aim of reducing the negative reinforcing effects of relapse to drug intake, novel therapeutic strategies are based on alleviating CRF-related anxiety during drug withdrawal (see Sarnyai, Shaham, & Heinrichs, 2001, for review).

23. Alleviation of CRF-related anxiety could benefit efforts to eliminate drug dependence by:
   a. decreasing the strength of negative reinforcement related to drug-induced relief of aversive withdrawal states.
   b. increasing the strength of negative reinforcement processes that terminate drug craving.
   c. decreasing positive reinforcement related to drug-induced relief of aversive withdrawal states.
   d. any of the above are possible.

Non-Stress, Anti-Reward Systems May Be Over-Activated After Chronic Drug Use

Additional neural systems indirectly related to acute drug effects and stress responses include (but are not limited to) NPY and dynorphin. Acute administration of NPY is anxiolytic, reducing stress and sedating activity. However, several drugs of abuse decrease NPY expression. Conversely, dynorphin expression increases after drug exposure. As part of a negative feedback circuit regulating activity in dopamine neurons, dynorphin inhibits dopamine activity in the VTA. Generally, the decrease in NPY and increase in dynorphin appear to be part of the counteractive, anti-reward circuitry set off to balance the intense drug-induced stimulation of reward circuitry. Abnormal regulation of these peptides may contribute to intense anxiety and dysphoria (see Koob & LeMoal, 2001, for review).

24. A(n) _____ in NPY, coupled with a(n) _____ in dynorphin may contribute to "anti-reward" circuitry in the brain.
    a. decrease . . . lack of change
    b. increase . . . lack of change
    c. decrease . . . increase
    d. increase . . . decrease

Sensitization Involves Dopamine, CRF, and Glutamate Activity

Time-dependent adaptations in dopamine, CRF, and glutamate systems mediate sensitized drug responses (Koob & LeMoal, 2001; Robinson & Berridge, 1993). First of all, sensitization involves increased activation of mesolimbic dopamine neurons. For example, opiates or amphetamines injected directly into the cell body region of the VTA sensitize behavioral responses to systemic drug injections. However, changes in dopamine sensitivity last only four to eight days, whereas behavioral sensitization continues perhaps a year (Robinson & Berridge, 1993). CRF may also sensitize dopaminergic responses via corticosterone circulation, a change which may endure longer. In terms of sociobiology, drug intake induces social problems that may also be stressful and long-lasting. (Consider compounding problems resultant from legal incarceration on drug-related charges.) Stress may promote drug intake both by increasing positive reinforcing effects of drugs via sensitization and by facilitating negative reinforcing effects. Thus, long-lasting psychosocial stressors may induce long-lasting sensitization. Whether considering sensitization via repeated presentation of the same stimulus, or **cross-sensitization** between external stressors and drugs, glutamate transmission is involved. For example, blockade of the N-methyl-D-aspartate (NMDA) subtype of glutamate receptor attenuates cellular and behavioral sensitization.

25. Sensitization to drug effects could contribute to drug dependence in which of the following way(s)?
    a. gradually decreasing cAMP responsivity
    b. increasing positive reinforcement
    c. decreasing the effectiveness of negative reinforcement
    d. blocking NMDA glutamate receptors upon reinstatement of drug intake

HOW CAN WE CONCEPTUALIZE COMPULSIVE DRUG USE IN TERMS OF NEUROADAPTATIONS?

Having reviewed some of the critical neurobiological substrates and neurotransmitters involved in drug use, abuse, and dependence, we address the challenge of constructing a framework in which to view addiction. We should recognize that addictions outside of drug categories could be included in an explanatory framework; uncontrollable gambling, food obsessions, sex addictions, compulsive exercise, drug abuse, and so forth all involve lapses of self-regulation. In every case, we must explain the radical shift from occasional, measured intake to chronic, unregulated intake.

Behavioral Reinforcement Mechanisms Shift During Chronic Drug Use

Complex interchanges between seeking pleasure, alleviating emotional or physical ailments, and forming habitual associations between stimuli are likely to underlie the progression from drug use to dependence. Positive reinforcement is heavily implicated in the initiation of drug intake, and it may actually increase early in drug use via sensitization processes. With time after continued drug use, however, tolerance may develop to the positive affective states of drug-related "highs" or intoxication. Simultaneously, negative reinforcement may rise, such that alleviation of an aversive withdrawal state drives further drug-seeking behavior. In some cases, negative reinforcement may have been influential from the outset, as individuals may self-medicate either preexisting or drug-induced affective disorders (Markou, Kosten, & Koob, 1998). Regardless of the force behind drug-seeking behavior, conditioned positive and negative reinforcement are likely to exacerbate existing drug-seeking drives. Environments, people, music, objects, and so forth that are repeatedly paired with either drugs or drug withdrawal serve as triggers to drug craving, drug-seeking, and relapse in addicted individuals.

26. Which of the following terms best describes the situation in which individuals take illicit drugs to alleviate affective disorders they diagnosed themselves?
    a. positive reinforcement
    b. negative reinforcement
    c. affective-centered pharmacotherapy
    d. self-medication

Opponent Process Theory Interprets Behavioral Shifts

Stimuli that challenge homeostasis trigger behaviors to restore balance, or induce physiological adaptations to cope with imbalance. **Opponent-process theory** (Solomon & Corbit, 1974) describes this chain of events. *A-processes* represent initial responses to a drug (e.g., activation of reward circuitry). *B-processes* represent the reaction against the initial response (e.g., recruitment of brain CRF pathways). In theory, repeated drug intake causes a-processes to decline in magnitude, while b-processes increase in magnitude. Declining a-processes are evidenced by findings such as decreased opiate-induced euphoria or analgesia, due to drug tolerance. Rising b-processes are evidenced by findings such as increased aversive symptoms or hyperalgesia during withdrawal. The shift from occasional "recreational" use to frequent compulsive use may be mediated by decreased drug reward, along with increased aversion in withdrawal.

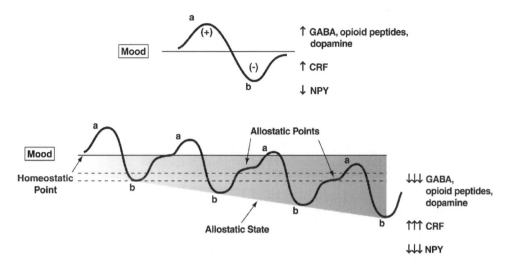

FIG. 2.8. A conceptualization of drug-related changes in hedonic set point. Affective responses to drugs include *a-processes* in the direction of positive hedonic states (mood states) and *b-processes* in the direction of negative hedonic states (derived from opponent-process theory in Solomon and Corbit, 1974). The top panel shows a- and b-processes during the initial experience of a drug with no prior drug history; ample time is provided for a- and b-processes to balance back to the normal range. The bottom panel shows hypothesized changes in the affective state for an individual with repeated, frequent drug use. Drug-taking reinitiated before the b-process returns to the homeostatic level results in progressively larger deviations from the former hedonic set point. Allostatic set points may eventually be defended by dysregulated reward systems involving GABA, opioid peptides, and dopamine, along with recruited counteradaptive systems including CRF and NPY. (From Koob, G. F. (2001). Drug addiction, dysregulation of reward, and allostasis. *Neuropsychopharmacology, 24,* 97–129. Reprinted with permission from Nature Publishing Group.)

Moreover, alleviating the negative affect of withdrawal may require escalated drug doses in the face of tolerance to their rewarding effects (Fig. 2.8).

27. In opponent-process theory, the basic opposing processes are _____ and _____?
    a. stimulants ... depressants
    b. sensitization ... tolerance
    c. acute drug responses ... organismic counteradaptations
    d. cAMP down-regulation ... CREB up-regulation

Allostasis Represents an Attempt to Maintain Homeostasis in the Face of Change

Drug intake challenges the *hedonic set point*, an individual's optimal or tolerable balance between pleasure and discomfort. If no opportunity to recover normal balance is granted between drug-taking episodes, then diminished a-processes coupled with strengthening b-processes could trigger the following compound responses: (a) gradually raising the hedonic level at which pleasure can be experienced; (b) lowering the level at which discomfort can be tolerated, and (c) on the whole, lowering the hedonic state experienced by the organism—that is, induce chronic negative affect.

Allostasis is the process through which bodily systems attempt to maintain stability through change. Applied to the hedonic set point, allostasis implies that the higher threshold for experiencing reward coupled with a lower hedonic state achievable by the organism constitutes a semi-permanent change in hedonic processing. An allostatic state could include malaise, irritability, dysphoria, or emotional instability—a protracted withdrawal syndrome. The change in hedonic processing may be induced by dysregulation in the same neural circuits implicated in drug reinforcement (mesocorticolimbic and extended amygdala), as well as other circuits (brain and hormonal CRF systems). Accumulating biological expense exerted over time to defend a new set point may result in the pathological state of compulsive drug-seeking and the severe physiological damage associated with substance dependence.

28. A hypothetical allostatic change in hedonic set point would result from which of the following events?
    a. acute elevations in hedonic state due to drug intake
    b. failure of the nervous system to counteract drug-induced euphoria
    c. lack of opportunity to recover normal hedonic balance between disruptive events
    d. heavy allostatic load

29. Which of the following neural subsystems is implicated in protracted withdrawal syndrome?
    a. extended amygdala
    b. medial forebrain bundle
    c. hypothalamic CRF-releasing neurons
    d. all of the above

HEDONIC DYSREGULATION IS A RISKY BUSINESS

No single neuroadaptation explains the full spectrum of long-term drug effects, yet researchers have made great strides in identifying likely influences in the addiction cycle. The adaptations outlined in this chapter suggest two key treatment approaches. First, it is crucial to decrease affective withdrawal. Second, it is necessary to decrease the need for excessive reward. These general ideas form the basis for many current attempts to identify pharmacological adjuncts to behavioral and cognitive therapies. Through effective rehabilitation with protracted abstinence, it may be possible to return the hedonic set point to a normal range of function (see Table 2.2). In sociobiological terms, one may consider the hedonic system as a limited resource throughout the lifetime. It appears possible to expend mass quantities of one's valuable reserve in a relatively short period of time. The risk associated with reckless expenditure is the costly downward spiral of addiction. For those of you working in the area of drug use prevention and drug abuse counseling, it is important to make this risk of drug experimentation clear to young people confronted with personal decisions regarding drug use. Similar risks of drug relapse must be made apparent to individuals in abstinence from chronic substance abuse. Both populations need to develop alternative approaches to maintaining a healthy hedonic set point. Research advances on the neurobiology of addiction substantiate the severe consequences of failing to do so.

TABLE 2.2

Affective and Neurochemical Components of Transitions From Drug-Taking Through Protracted Abstinence

Transitioning Component	Drug Reward in Nondependent Individuals	Transition to Drug Dependence (Addiction)	Drug Dependence (Addiction)	Protracted Abstinence
Positive Affective State	↑Reward Experiences	↑↑Reward Experiences	↓Reward Experiences	−Reward Experiences
Negative Affective State	−Negative Emotional State	↑↑Negative Emotional State	↑↑↑Negative Emotional State	↑Negative Emotional State
Sample Classic Neurotransmitter Systems	↑Dopamine ↑Serotonin	↑↑Dopamine ↑↑Serotonin	↓↓Dopamine ↓↓Serotonin	↓Dopamine ↓Serotonin
Peptide Neurotransmitters	↑CRF	↑↑CRF ↓↓NPY ↑↑Dynorphin	↑↑↑CRF ↓↓↓NPY ↑↑Dynorphin	↑CRF ↓NPY

30. A normal hedonic set point is likely to decrease drug abuse in which of the following ways?
    a. decrease likelihood of self-medication
    b. decrease risk of negative reinforcement associated with alleviation of the negative affective state of drug withdrawal
    c. provide reinforcement through nondrug means
    d. all of the above

KEY TERMS

adenylyl cyclase: Enzyme that converts ATP to cAMP when postsynaptic receptors with which it is associated are stimulated by appropriate substances; an enzymatic link between neurotransmitters (first messengers) and intracellular second messengers.

allostasis: The process of achieving stability of internal processes through change.

cAMP (cyclic adenosine monophosphate): An intracellular second messenger that activates kinases to regulate gene expression, neurotransmitter synthesis, cell morphology, membrane conductance, etc.

classical conditioning: A learning procedure in which a stimulus that naturally produces a defensive or appetitive response (*unconditioned stimulus*) is paired with a stimulus that initially elicits only an orienting response. After repeated pairings, the second stimulus (*conditioned stimulus*) eventually elicits a response (*conditioned response*) that is similar to the original defensive or appetitive response (*unconditioned response*). Also known as *Pavlovian conditioning*.

CREB (cAMP Response Element Binding protein): A transcription factor controlled by enzymes and in control of gene expression for peptides and proteins, including several involved in neurotransmission and drug effects.

cross-sensitization: Increased responsiveness to a drug after repeated exposure to a constant dose of a different drug, stressor, or other similar stimulus.

ΔFosB: A transcription factor controlled by enzymes and in control gene expression for peptides and proteins, including several involved in neurotransmission and drug effects.

dose-response curve: Graphic representation of the relationship between drug dose and organismic response; similar to dose-effect function.

drug self-administration: Operant paradigm in which a behavioral response results in presentation of a drug stimulus, such that behavioral responding is maintained by the drug.

dysphoria: A negative or aversive emotional state, often associated with drug withdrawal.

endogenous: Produced from within, naturally-occurring.

hedonic set point: Hypothesized optimal value of the hedonic system variable involved in regulating the balance between pleasure and discomfort.

homeostasis: The process of maintaining an organism's substances and characteristics at their optimal level.

in vivo **microdialysis:** Neurochemical method whereby components of extracellular fluids can be extracted from tissue in freely behaving animals and analyzed for chemical makeup such as neurotransmitter concentrations.

intracranial self-stimulation (ICSS): Operant paradigm in which a behavioral response results in an electrical stimulation of the medial forebrain bundle, such that behavioral responding is maintained by the electrical stimulation; brain stimulation reward.

negative reinforcement: Process through which removal of an aversive stimulus increases the probability of the behavior that resulted in the removal of the stimulus.

opponent-process theory: Conceptualization of the interaction between drug-induced *a-processes* and naturally-occurring, counteractive *b-processes*. The affective state of an organism would equal the sum of the a- and b-processes.

positive reinforcement: Process through which presentation of a rewarding stimulus increases the probability of the behavior that resulted in the stimulus presentation.

reward: A stimulus that is generally pleasurable or contributes to drive-reduction or satiation.

second messenger: An intracellular regulatory molecule that itself is regulated by a G-protein coupled to a receptor protein. Once activated, a second messenger distributes throughout the cytoplasm to alter cellular activity. (The first messenger is the neurotransmitter.)

sensitization: Increased drug responsiveness after repeated exposure to a constant dose of a drug.

tolerance: Reduced drug responsiveness after repeated exposure to a drug.

transcription factor: Regulatory molecule that binds to the control element of a gene, thereby enhancing or repressing gene expression.

DISCUSSION QUESTIONS

1. Why is it helpful to identify the neural substrates of drug dependence? List reasons in several categories, including at least the following: a) future therapeutic methodologies, b) sociopolitical implications, c) genetic screening.

2. Given the basic information about dendrites provided in Figure 2.1, generate a few hypotheses about the potential neurochemical and behavioral effects of changes in dendritic size, thickness, or branching in the VTA and/or nucleus accumbens.

3. From memory, draw a basic sketch of the major neural pathways involved in reinforcing drug effects. (Use Figure 2.4 as a detailed model.)

4. Compare and contrast tolerance and sensitization. Describe how each phenomenon might alter the effective dose of a drug of abuse.

5. For each major drug class, make two lists of drug effects. Place effects that might be considered *a-processes* in one list and those that might be considered *b-processes* in

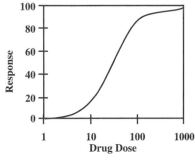

FIG. 2.9.

a second list. Conduct a literature search for increases or decreases of the effects with repeated drug exposure to substantiate or refute your placement of the effects on each list.

6. Discuss the ways in which homeostasis contributes to long-term drug effects. Compare and contrast homeostasis and allostasis.

7. List several different ways in which a drug could alleviate the negative affective components of drug withdrawal.

8. Design a series of experiments to test the hypothesis that a newly developed therapeutic drug decreases the negative affective components of withdrawal from drugs of abuse. Include a variety of behavioral paradigms and species of experimental subjects.

9. If Figure 2.9 represents the initial dose-response relationship between drug X and analgesia, redraw the graph to show how the relationship changes after tolerance to the drug's analgesic effects develops. How would the graph have changed if sensitization to the analgesic effects had developed instead?

10. What does it mean, in neural terms, to be addicted to a drug?

ACKNOWLEDGMENT

The authors would like to thank Mike Arends for his excellent editorial assistance.

SUGGESTED FURTHER READING

Ali, S. F. (Ed.). (2002). *Annals of the New York Academy of Science*: Vol. 965. *Cellular and molecular mechanisms of drugs of abuse II*. New York: New York Academy of Sciences.

A collection of advanced level papers from a 2001 conference.

Cooper, J. R., Bloom, F. E., & Roth, R. H. (2003). *The biochemical basis of neuropharmacology* (8th ed.). New York: Oxford University Press.

An excellent, readable primer on neurotransmitters and drugs that affect them.

McEwen, B. (2002). *The end of stress as we know it*. Washington DC: Joseph Henry Press.

For additional explorations of stress, including allostasis, written for the layman.

McGinty, J. (Ed.). (1999). *Annals of the New York Academy of Science*: Vol. 877. *Advancing from the ventral striatum to the extended amygdala*. New York: New York Academy of Sciences.

A collection of advanced level papers from a 1998 conference.

Nestler, E. J., Hyman, S. E., & Malenka, R. C. (2001). *Molecular basis of neuropharmacology: A foundation for clinical neuroscience.* New York: McGraw-Hill.

For in-depth explanations of intracellular signaling and its modulation by drugs.

Rosenzweig, M. F., Breedlove, S. M., & Leiman, A. L. (2002). *Biological psychology: An introduction to behavioral, cognitive, and clinical neuroscience* (3rd ed.). Sunderland, MA: Sinauer Associates.

An introductory text book covering material from basic neuroanatomy to emotions.

REFERENCES

Caine, S. B., & Koob, G. F. (1995). Pretreatment with the dopamine agonist 7-OH-DPAT shifts the cocaine self-administration dose-effect function to the left under different schedules in the rat. *Behavioural Pharmacology, 6,* 333–347.

Caine, S. B., Lintz, R., & Koob, G. F. (1993). Intravenous drug self-administration techniques in animals. In A. Sahgal (Ed.), *Behavioral Neuroscience: A Practical Approach,* vol. 2, pp. 117–143.

Heimer, L., & Alheid, G. (1991). Piecing together the puzzle of basal forebrain anatomy. In T. C. Napier, P. W. Kalivas, & I. Hanin (Eds.), *Advances in experimental medicine and biology*: Vol. 295. *The basal forebrain: Anatomy to function* (pp. 1–42). New York: Plenum Press.

Koob, G. F. (1992). Drugs of abuse: Anatomy, pharmacology and function of reward pathways. *Trends Pharmacological Sciences, 13*(5), 177–184.

Koob, G. F., & LeMoal, M. (2001). Drug addiction, dysregulation of reward, and allostasis. *Neuropsychopharmacology, 24,* 97–129.

Koon, G. F. (1992). Drugs of abuse: Anatomy, pharmacology, and function of reward pathways. *Trends in Pharmacological Sciences, 13*(5), 117–184.

Kornetsky, C., & Bain, G. (1982). Biobehavioral bases of the reinforcing properties of opiate drugs. In K. Verebey (Ed.), *Annals of the New York Academy of Sciences*: Vol. 398. *Opioids in mental illness: Theories, clinical observations, and treatment possibilities* (pp. 241–259). New York: New York Academy of Sciences.

Markou, A., Kosten, T. R., & Koob, G. F. (1998). Neurobiological similarities in depression and drug dependence: A self-medication hypothesis. *Neuropsychopharmacology, 18,* 135–174.

Mathieu-Kia, A. M., Kellogg, S. H., Butelman, E. R., & Kreek, M. J. (2002). Nicotine addiction: Insights from recent animal studies. *Psychopharmacology, 162,* 102–118.

Merlo-Pich, E., Lorang, M., Yeganeh, M., Rodriguez de Fonseca, F., Raber, J., Koob, G. F., et al. (1995). Increase of extracellular corticotropin-releasing factor-like immunoreactivity levels in the amygdala of awake rats during restraint stress and ethanol withdrawal as measured by microdialysis. *Journal of Neuroscience, 15,* 5439–5447.

Nestler, E. J. (2001). Molecular basis of long-term plasticity underlying addiction. *Nature Reviews Neuroscience, 2,* 119–128.

Nestler, E. J., Barrot, M., & Self, D. W. (2001). DeltaFosB: A sustained molecular switch for addiction. *Proceedings of the National Academy of Sciences USA, 98,* 11042–11046.

Parsons, L. H., Koob, G. F., & Weiss, F. (1995). Serotonin dysfunction in the nucleus accumbens of rats during withdrawal after unlimited access to intravenous cocaine. *Journal of Pharmacology and Experimental Therapeutics, 274,* 1182–1191.

Purves, W. K., Sadava, D., Orians, G. H., and Heller, H. C. (2001). *Life Science of Biology,* 6th Ed. Sunderland, MA: Sinauer Associates.

Robinson, T. E., & Berridge, K. C. (1993). The neural basis of drug craving: An incentive-sensitization theory of addiction. *Brain Research Reviews, 18,* 247–291.

Sarnyai, Z., Shaham, Y., & Heinrichs, S. C. (2001). The role of corticotropin-releasing factor in drug addiction. *Pharmacological Reviews, 53,* 209–243.

Solomon, R. L., & Corbit, J. D. (1974). An opponent-process theory of motivation: I. Temporal dynamics of affect. *Psychological Reviews, 81,* 119–145.

Tanda, G., & Goldberg, S. R. (2003). Cannabinoids: Reward, dependence, and underlying neurochemical mechanisms—a review of recent preclinical data. *Psychopharmacology, 169*(2), 115–134.

van Ree, J. M., Gerrits, M. A., & Vanderschuren, L. J. (1999). Opioids, reward and addiction: An encounter of biology, psychology, and medicine. *Pharmacological Reviews, 51,* 341–396.

Weiss, F., & Porrino, L. J. (2002). Behavioral neurobiology of alcohol addiction: Recent advances and challenges. *Journal of Neuroscience, 22,* 3303–3305.

3

Types of Addictive Drugs

Cynthia M. Kuhn
Wilkie A. Wilson
Duke University Medical Center

TRUTH OR FICTION?

___ 1. All addictive drugs increase synaptic levels of dopamine.

___ 2. Rates of alcoholism among Asians are lower because they tend to voluntarily limit alcohol use due to the bad reactions they have when they drink.

___ 3. Ethanol decreases the function of the inhibitory neurotransmitter GABA.

___ 4. All psychomotor stimulants improve attention, increase blood pressure, and are reinforcing.

___ 5. Smoking crack can be more addicting than snorting cocaine because cocaine enters the brain faster after smoking crack.

___ 6. Children who receive psychomotor stimulant treatment for attention deficit hyperactivity disorder are more likely to develop drug abuse problems than children who are not treated.

___ 7. Methylphenidate, amphetamine, and cocaine have similar mechanisms of action.

___ 8. Oxycodone delivered by sustained release is a safe and effective pain medication that is not addictive.

___ 9. Methadone acts on the same receptor system as heroin but is safe to use as therapy for addicts because of its extremely long half-life.

___ 10. Daily use of zolpidem for insomnia is likely to be effective for up to a year.

___ 11. Triazolam is a better medication for insomnia than secobarbital because there is a ceiling effect on benzodiazepine-like sedatives that make them safer than barbiturates.

___ 12. Physical dependence does not develop to marijuana.

___ 13. The psychoactive compounds in marijuana cause very little serious organ damage. Its main organ toxicities result from toxic byproducts that are formed because people smoke it.

___ *14. The most likely toxicity of using LSD is having a bad trip.*
___ *15. MDMA (methylenedioxymethamphetamine or Ecstasy) is never lethal. If someone*
       overdoses on Ecstasy it is because what he or she took was not MDMA.

This chapter provides a review of the pharmacology of the most common abused and addictive drugs. It serves as a complement for chapter 2, which describes the neurobiological processes of **addiction**, and chapter 11, which provides more information about behavioral and clinical issues related to drug abuse. It includes those issues that you will encounter in clinical practice. Nicotine is absent because it is legal for most Americans. Alcohol is present because, although it is legal, it frequently appears in addiction treatment contexts.

ADDICTIVE VERSUS ABUSED DRUGS

The definition of addiction is a behavioral/psychiatric one. Addictive drugs are those drugs that people use compulsively despite adverse consequences in their lives. Neurobiological changes underlie addiction. These changes likely derive from the repeated stimulation of the reinforcement circuits described in chapter 2. Changes in these neural circuits can produce long-lasting changes in behavior.

Not everyone who uses the potentially addictive drugs listed herein becomes addicted. Alcohol provides a good example: The great majority of people (probably 92%–95%) who drink alcohol control their alcohol use. However, a significant minority develop compulsive and uncontrolled patterns of use for the many reasons that are covered in other chapters. Genetics, family history, environment, and underlying psychiatric disease are all significant contributors. But the neurobiological actions of the drugs play a key role.

1. Which of the following are addictive drugs?
   a. MDMA and marijuana
   b. cocaine and alcohol
   c. ephedrine and heroin
   d. nicotine and LSD

The list of drugs that people use compulsively is surprisingly short: nicotine, alcohol, psychomotor **stimulants** including cocaine and amphetamines, **narcotic** analgesics, some **sedative-hypnotic** drugs, and marijuana. There are probably three characteristics that addictive drugs share: (1) the mechanisms by which they act, (2) their ability to cause adaptive changes in neural circuits that organize motivated behavior, and (3) the pattern with which people use them. Some drugs can be illegal or health damaging but not addictive. **Hallucinogens** and methylenedioxymethamphetamine (MDMA or Ecstasy) are both illegal and can cause serious health problems, but they are probably not addicting—they are rarely if ever used in this way.

2. Addiction results from:
   a. an addictive personality and early childhood abuse.
   b. repeated experience with an addictive drug leading to loss of control over the use of the substance.
   c. total cumulative alcohol intake, which leads eventually to brain changes that cause addiction.
   d. a preexisting state in the brain.

Addictive drugs have the unique ability to stimulate the reward circuits by increasing synaptic dopamine in mesolimbic projections. Addictive drugs can be identified in the following ways: (a) animals and people will voluntarily self-administer them, (b) they cause increases in dopamine release in mesolimbic projection systems, and (c) they lower the threshold for brain stimulation reward.

Simply increasing dopamine alone does not cause addiction. The repeated activation of dopaminergic circuits eventually leads to adaptive changes in the circuits regulating motivated behavior. Current research indicates that neural activity in the anterior and cingulate cortex, areas involved in motivation and planning of activities, is abnormal in addict brains. These changes may be more important for persistent drug taking than the increase in dopamine. Some scientists hypothesize that people continue to use drugs even when they no longer cause reinforcement.

Some patterns of drug delivery and removal seem to be more enjoyable, and tend to lead to compulsive use more easily. Routes that deliver drugs to the brain quickly combined with rapid metabolism are most likely to lead to patterns of compulsive use. This rapid rise and fall of brain levels leads to dramatic peaks and valleys in drug effects.

Slow-release formulations that maintain steady blood levels are less likely to lead to abuse, which is why clinical use of such formulations usually does not lead to abuse. Psychostimulants like methylphenidate, used to treat attention deficit hyperactivity disorder (ADHD), and the long-acting narcotic analgesic methadone provide examples: These drugs can increase synaptic dopamine but generally are not abused. The likely reason is that the onset and offset of drug action are so slow that the rapid change in occupation of dopamine receptors that seems to be necessary for the experience of reward happens much less intensely. Understanding this is important for clinicians who might fear prescribing needed medication to patients out of concern about abuse.

3. Which statement about the pattern of drug delivery that causes addiction is correct?
   a. Taking drugs orally is almost never addicting.
   b. Injecting heroin is more addicting than smoking heroin.
   c. Smoking cigarettes is less addictive than taking methadone.
   d. Injecting methamphetamine is more likely to be addicting than taking methylphenidate.

Although all addictive drugs share the final common effect of activating brain reward circuits and releasing dopamine, each activates reward circuits in different ways. Some (the psychostimulants) act directly on dopamine neurons. Others (narcotics) stimulate dopamine neurons indirectly through synaptic contacts, or by stimulating reward pathways downstream from dopamine neurons. Moreover, addictive drugs also have individually different effects that are related to other sites of action in the brain. Each addictive drug activates a particular and different target receptor with its own anatomical distribution. For example, psychostimulants are alerting, while ethanol and sedative-hypnotics are sedating. The total effect of a drug thus reflects the sum of the distribution of the receptors.

4. Addictive drugs share which of the following effects in the brain?
   a. decrease in inhibitions
   b. mimesis of the excitatory neurotransmitter glutamate
   c. increase in the neurotransmitter dopamine in reward circuits
   d. atrophic changes in the brain

ALCOHOL

Alcohol is the most widely used addictive drug. The reason is not that alcohol is so terribly addictive, but that its use is so prevalent. Almost half of Americans age 12 or older, 109 million people, used alcohol in 2001 (NIDA Household Survey). Of these, approximately 7 million (6%) are addicted to alcohol. In contrast, although almost 25% of Americans smoke, most smokers are addicted to nicotine. Alcohol is sedative, anxiolytic, and, at high doses, hypnotic (sleep-inducing). People use alcohol almost exclusively as an aqueous mixture of ethanol with other components. The concentration of ethanol in ingested beverages ranges from 3.5% to 9% in beer, 9% to 12% in wine, 40% to 50% in distilled spirits, and up to 80% in "fortified" beverages. Alcohol absorption occurs in the small intestine, and so the rate of ethanol absorption depends upon stomach contents: The presence of food will slow stomach emptying and somewhat delay absorption. Maximal blood alcohol levels occur about 40 minutes after ingestion. Blood alcohol concentration (BAC) is typically described in grams percent (g%), meaning grams of ethanol per 100 grams of blood. In most states, a level of 0.08% or higher is legally intoxicated. Death can occur at levels of 0.30% and above.

Alcohol is metabolized mainly in the liver by two enzymes. Alcohol dehydrogenase converts alcohol to acetaldehyde and acetaldehye dehydrogenase converts acetaldehyde to acetic acid. There is also a little alcohol dehydrogenase in the stomach that metabolizes a small percentage of ethanol before it enters the small intestine.

Women have higher blood alcohol levels than men after drinking equivalent doses for several reasons: They have more body fat and less body water, so alcohol distributes into a smaller volume. They also have less gastric alcohol dehydrogenase and so pass more alcohol along to the small intestine to be absorbed.

Many (50%) Asians have at least one inactive copy of acetaldehyde dehydrogenase that cannot degrade acetaldehyde. When they drink, their blood alcohol concentrations are not different (and they do not become more intoxicated), but their clearance of acetaldehyde is slower, and high levels of acetaldehyde cause nausea and flushing. Rates of alcoholism in people of Asian ethnic background tend to be lower in part because many Asians voluntarily limit alcohol use due to the bad reactions they have when they drink it.

Alcohol is metabolized at the constant rate of approximately $1/2$ to 1 ounce of absolute ethanol an hour (one half to one standard drink), regardless of how quickly a person drinks. If someone drinks much faster than their liver can eliminate alcohol, blood levels will rise in proportion to the difference. Blood levels are lower in larger than in smaller people who drink the same amount. However, even the largest person can drink fast enough to experience a fatal overdose.

5. Identify the correct statement about alcohol absorption and metabolism.
    a. Drinking on an empty stomach causes more rapid intoxication because alcohol is absorbed faster from the stomach.
    b. Native Americans are more likely to be alcoholic because they can't metabolize alcohol.
    c. Maximal blood alcohol levels occur about 40 minutes after drinking.
    d. If someone drinks five drinks in 2 hours, their BAC is the same as if they drank them all at once and then stopped for 2 hours.

Alcohol is a sedative-hypnotic drug that causes a dose-related inhibition of central nervous system (CNS) activity. It causes gross locomotor impairment, impairment of memory, and sedation that can lead to unconsciousness, coma, and death as blood levels rise. At a BAC of 0.06% to 0.09%, subtle impairment of fine motor skills and judgment occurs. When BACs in this range occur as blood levels are rising, people are disinhibited rather than sedated. At 0.10% to 0.15%, fine motor skills are substantially impaired, speech is slurred at higher levels, and people have trouble with balance and walking. As BAC approaches 0.25% to 0.30%, people will fall asleep, or "black out" (experience retrograde amnesia). They can have amnesia for the event. As BAC rises, CNS depression extends, and levels of 0.35% and above can be fatal due to inhibition of respiration. The euphoria associated with rising BAC is not recapitulated as BAC falls, perhaps due to acute tolerance.

6. A BAC of _____ can be lethal.
   a. .12%
   b. .24%
   c. .08%
   d. .36%

This pharmacology of ethanol explains why people like to drink on an empty stomach and why they continue to drink although they are quite intoxicated. An empty stomach allows a faster rise in alcohol level and thus a faster rise in brain dopamine. Then, so long as a person is experiencing a rising blood level, she is stimulating her reward circuit and "feeling the buzz."

Ethanol acts on receptors for the neurotransmitters gamma amino butyric acid (GABA) and glutamate, and also influences serotonin and adenosine function. How these actions combine to produce the behavioral effects of ethanol is still not completely understood. The ability of ethanol to enhance the actions of the major inhibitory neurotransmitter GABA is the best characterized action of ethanol. The sedation and anxiolytic effects of ethanol are thought to result from potentiation of GABA-mediated inhibition of the brain. At behaviorally relevant concentrations, ethanol binds to a some GABA-A receptors and increases GABA-mediated opening of the chloride channel. Ethanol does not affect all GABA receptors, but may affect a subpopulation that has a particular anatomical distribution. Ethanol also blocks the N-methyl-D-aspartate (NMDA) receptors for the excitatory neurotransmitter glutamate at behaviorally relevant concentrations. These actions may contribute to sedation and ataxia, and almost certainly contribute to impairment of learning and memory. Finally, ethanol may augment the actions of the neuromodulator adenosine. Because adenosine released into the extracellular space is associated with sedation and sleep, this action could contribute to its behavioral effects.

7. Ethanol is addictive because:
   a. it stimulates receptors for the inhibitory neurotransmitter GABA.
   b. it blocks receptors for the excitatory neurotransmitter glutamate.
   c. it increases dopamine indirectly through its GABA agonist effects.
   d. it increases the action of adenosine.

Dramatic tolerance to the sedative-hypnotic properties of ethanol develops in proportion to alcohol consumption. Tolerance develops to its sedating, anxiolytic, locomotor, and anticonvulsant effect, but unfortunately, tolerance does not develop to its lethal effects. This tolerance reflects mainly adaptation at the cellular sites of ethanol action in the brain, but also induction of metabolism in the liver. In general, tolerance leads to increased CNS excitability upon ethanol withdrawal. Heavy regular drinkers can experience mild withdrawal symptoms each day: anxiety, tremors, insomnia, and autonomic hyperactivity, and the intensity of withdrawal increases with daily consumption. At its most severe, alcohol withdrawal causes a severe syndrome called *delirium tremens* with tremors; severe agitation; marked increase in blood pressure, heart rate and respiration; delusions; and possibly seizures. Alcohol withdrawal peaks two to three days after the cessation of drinking, and wanes by four or five days. However, craving for alcohol use will last anywhere from weeks to years. This behavioral component is thought to be a very important factor in resumption of drinking.

Ethanol stimulates firing of dopamine neurons in the reward system and also may stimulate GABA mechanisms at other places in the reward circuitry. Evidence supports at least a strong role for ethanol's GABA-agonist properties but we do not know how its other neurochemical actions contribute to addiction. Tolerance clearly develops to its GABA-mimetic actions, and GABA receptor tolerance in reward pathways could contribute to alcohol addiction. Also, avoiding the unpleasant effects of withdrawal definitely motivates drinking. Although research has not yet shown definitely that changes in ethanol effects on reward systems contributes to addiction, some intriguing recent research does suggest that ethanol-induced changes in dopamine receptor populations may be functionally important.

8. Ethanol withdrawal:
   a. only occurs in severe alcoholics.
   b. subsides in treated alcoholics at the same time as craving for alcohol.
   c. results from decreased dopamine.
   d. results from increased CNS excitability due to adaptations in GABA and glutamate receptor function.

Genetics clearly plays a role in alcoholism, as do family history and rearing environment (see chapter 11). Genetics may play an especially strong role in the group of alcoholics who begin drinking as teens and progress rapidly to abusive drinking. The group of alcoholics who start in young adulthood often drink to self-medicate for anxiety and progress to alcoholism more slowly. The gene(s) involved are poorly understood. Although the dopamine system offers a number of logical targets (dopamine receptors, for example), abnormalities in these genes do not occur in alcoholic populations more often than in nonalcoholic populations according to the bulk of research studies.

Alcohol is more toxic to organ systems than other addictive drugs. Alcohol-related liver injury progressing from fatty liver up to cirrhosis occurs in direct proportion to the amount and duration of alcohol ingestion, regardless of pattern (binge or daily). Women are more sensitive to liver injury than men, with measurable changes occurring at levels of intake that exceed 2 to 3 drinks daily according to the most recent literature. Excessive use of alcohol is the leading cause of cardiomyopathy in the United States. Prolonged heavy drinking is associated with increased incidence of ulcers and gastrointestinal bleeding.

9. Alcohol-related liver damage:
   a. is typically worse in men than women.
   b. is related to total consumption regardless of pattern of drinking.
   c. is rarely reversible.
   d. doesn't happen in people who only drink beer.

Significant cognitive impairment and brain injury can result from long-term heavy drinking. The most common effect is a significant impairment of recent and remote memory, especially for drinking episodes when BAC was extremely high. Structural changes in the brain including increased size of brain ventricles correlate with these changes. However, some improvement in both memory and structural changes occurs if the drinking stops. Wernicke's syndrome is an alcohol-related encephalopathy associated with 6th nerve palsy and ataxia that results from thiamine deficiency. It typically can be reversed if thiamine deficiency is corrected. Korsakoff's syndrome represents a more severe and less reversible form of alcohol-related brain injury that results in profound amnesia for recent events, and impairment of visuospatial, abstract, and conceptual reasoning. Finally, in 5% to 10% of alcoholics, long-term ethanol use can lead to peripheral neuropathy, which causes numbness, tingling, and paresthesias.

10. Alcohol-related brain injury:
   a. is reversed easily by thiamine treatment.
   b. like liver injury, is related to total consumption regardless of pattern of drinking.
   c. is more common in people who drink regularly to high BAC.
   d. is usually irreversible after years of drinking.

STIMULANTS: AMPHETAMINES AND COCAINE

Cocaine, the amphetamines (including methamphetamine and amphetamine), and methylphenidate comprise the class of *psychomotor stimulants*. These drugs cause euphoria and sense of well-being and energy that users find pleasant. They also are arousing and increase attentiveness to relevant stimuli. All of the psychomotor stimulants also trigger a "flight or fight"–like activation of the sympathetic nervous system. Blood pressure and heart rate rise, pupils and bronchioles dilate, and blood glucose rises.

All the psychomotor stimulants have valid clinical uses as well as abuse liability. Cocaine is used for its vasconstrictive and local anesthetic properties in certain types of surgery. Amphetamine, methamphetamine, and methylphenidate are approved for treatment of ADHD. Although methamphetamine and amphetamine are approved for treatment of obesity, they are almost never used for this purpose because their abuse liability is too high.

11. Stimulants do all of the following *except*:
   a. raise blood pressure.
   b. increase arousal.
   c. cause bronchodilation and improve asthma.
   d. lead to overeating.

All of the psychomotor stimulants enter the brain easily, although methylphenidate enters more slowly than the others. The smoked (e.g., crack, ice) and intravenous routes deliver stimulants to the brain the fastest. Delivery is much slower after snorting because drugs must be absorbed through the nasal mucosa, and so enter the bloodstream more slowly than the same drug delivered intravenously. The practice of crushing methylphenidate pills and snorting them is becoming more common, although there has been little study of how reinforcing methylphenidate is after this route. The onset of action after ingestion is much slower than these other routes, and delayed release forms that are typically used for ADHD treatment deliver the drug even more gradually. *Nevertheless, stimulants are abused by all of these routes.* Although cocaine is not used orally in the United States because its bioavailability is so low, chewing leaves and preparation of teas represent common routes in South America, where the drug is still used as a mild stimulant.

While the onset of stimulant action is highly influenced by route, the duration of effect is related to the rate of metabolism and varies widely from stimulant to stimulant. Cocaine effects peak almost immediately after smoking or intravenous injection, and effects are over in about 20 to 30 minutes after smoking because cocaine is degraded quite quickly (the half-life is about 30–40 minutes). Smoked methamphetamine peaks just as quickly, but amphetamines remain in the circulation much longer (half-lives of amphetamine and methamphetamine are 8–10 hours). Methylphenidate enters the brain the most slowly and its effects last 3 to 6 hours in a regular formulation, and up to 8 hours with sustained release preparation. This combination of characteristics contributes to its much lower incidence of compulsive use.

12. The following are commonly abused routes of stimulant use *except*:
    a. oral cocaine.
    b. oral methamphetamine.
    c. smoked methamphetamine.
    d. injected cocaine.

The psychomotor stimulants increase synaptic levels of the monoamine neurotransmitters norepinephrine, dopamine, and serotonin by related mechanisms (Table 3.1). Cocaine does so by binding to and blocking the action of the transporter on the plasma membrane that recaptures released monoamine into the presynaptic terminals. Cocaine blocks the reuptake of norepinephrine, dopamine, and serotonin transporters equally. The amphetamines act by a related mechanism: They bind to the transporter and are transported into the terminals, where they displace monoamines, which exit by backward movement through the transporter. Methylphenidate has both uptake blocking and some releasing properties.

All of these psychostimulants increase dopamine, and so theoretically can be addicting. However, there are dramatic differences in the typical use patterns of these drugs. Forms of cocaine and methamphetamine that people smoke (crack and ice) or inject intravenously deliver the drug most rapidly to the brain, provide the fastest high and represent the greatest hazard. However, methamphetamine is highly addictive even though the high lasts for hours, and snorting amphetamine or taking it orally leads to addiction in many users.

13. Which of the following stimulants are highly addictive?
    a. cocaine and methylphenidate
    b. methamphetamine and ephedrine
    c. cocaine and methamphetamine
    d. cocaine and ephedrine

TABLE 3.1

Profile of Monoamine Uptake Inhibitor Action

Drug	Monoamine Uptake	Release?	Other Actions
Cocaine	NE = DA = 5HT	No	Local anesthetic
Amphetamine Methamphetamine	NE = DA > 5HT	Yes	
Methylphenidate	DA > NE > 5HT	Yes	

NE = norepinephrine; DA = dopamine; 5HT = serotonin.

The addiction liability of methylphenidate is controversial. Fears of its abuse represent one strong motivation of the anti-Ritalin, anti-ADHD activist community. While studies exist showing that animals will self-administer methylphenidate, these studies used intravenous delivery, a route that is extremely rare at best among human users. Intravenous administration to humans can also cause euphoria, but it is short-lasting and not intense. Methylphenidate enters the brain fairly slowly compared to other psychostimulants, even after intravenous administration. The best evidence shows that children who receive adequate therapy for ADHD, including treatment with methylphenidate, are actually less likely to become drug users.

14. Methylphenidate:
   a. is as addictive as methamphetamine.
   b. increases dopamine but enters the brain slowly so has less addiction potential.
   c. is not addictive.
   d. should to be used to treat children with ADHD who have a family history of drug abuse because it increases dopamine.

Tolerance develops to many effects of psychostimulants, especially to appetite suppression. This tolerance limits the usefulness of these drugs in long-term treatment of obesity. However, this tolerance represents a benefit in treatment of ADHD, as some of the troublesome side effects, including insomnia and slowed growth, wane with time.

People sometimes use cocaine or amphetamines in a binge-like pattern of hours to days of continuous use. With continued high dose use, distinct behavioral patterns emerge. While tolerance develops to some behavioral effects as described above, other effects actually become more exaggerated. People also can develop repetitive grooming behaviors that take the form of picking at imagined insects or objects under the skin. A psychotic state closely resembling paranoid schizophrenia can emerge that typically resolves when the user stops. A single binge or repeated binges can produce high-dose toxicities which can be life-threatening, including seizures (cocaine or amphetamines) and hyperthermia (amphetamines). Death can result from overdose with all the psychostimulants. It typically results from cardiovascular events and/or lethal hyperthermia. Death from cocaine use results typically from either cardiovascular events or seizures.

NARCOTICS

Narcotic drugs, or **opioid** drugs, are either products of the opium poppy or synthetic derivatives of these compounds. The term *narcotic* is often misused in some contexts to include any illegal drug or any addictive drug. Pharmacologically, the definition is far more specific: These drugs induce a state of dreamy sleep, analgesia, and euphoria associated with derivatives of the opium poppy. These drugs are among the first medicines used by man. They have also been widely abused by man. In the late 1800s in the United States, the prototypic narcotic addict was a middle-aged white woman who used a patent medicine. The invention of the hypodermic syringe permitted morphine injection during Civil War field surgeries and also led to the first generation of postwar opiate addicts.

There are many narcotic drugs that vary in their efficacy as analgesics and in their pharmacokinetics (Table 3.2). All of these drugs can stimulate the reward system, and all can be addictive. Like the psychomotor stimulants, forms that enter the brain more rapidly represent more abuse hazard. Appropriate clinical use, even on an outpatient basis, is acceptable with appropriate prescription practice. These drugs are sometimes the most effective treatment for pain, and should be used appropriately.

Narcotic drugs produce a unique array of effects. The two most clinically important effects are suppression of pain, the basis of their clinical use, and the dreamy, pleasant euphoria they cause, the reason for abuse. The feeling of pleasure from intravenous injection of narcotics is so intense users often compare it to orgasm. All narcotic drugs decrease breathing, which is the typical reason for death from overdose. They also decrease gastrointestinal motility, inducing constipation, cause constriction of the ciliary muscle of the eye, producing the diagnostic "pinpoint pupils," suppress coughing, and often cause itching.

15. Which of the following is *not* an effect of narcotic drugs?
    a. suppressed breathing
    b. diarrhea
    c. analgesia
    d. euphoria

Heroin is the prototypic abused narcotic because people buy it on the street for the sole intent of abuse. However, the only important pharmacological difference between morphine and heroin is that heroin enters the brain faster. The abuse potential of injected morphine is just as high as that of heroin. Another commonly used and abused agent, Fentanyl, exists in two formulations—an injectable form that is used with other agents during induction of anesthesia, and a skin patch that is used as a sustained-release form to treat pain. Methadone and buprenorphine are full and partial opiate agonists (respectively) that are used not only as analgesics but also to suppress withdrawal during treatment of opiate addiction. Codeine is a low efficacy analgesic that is used primarily for mild pain and to suppress cough. At the other end of the spectrum, two narcotic drugs, diphenoxylate and loperamide, do not enter the brain. This allows their over-the-counter use to combat traveler's diarrhea (see Table 3.2).

16. Which of the following is a nonaddictive opiate?
    a. diphenoxylate
    b. codeine
    c. morphine
    d. oxycodone

TABLE 3.2

Efficacy and Duration of Action of Narcotic Analgesic Drugs

Drug	Analgesic Efficacy	Duration of Action
Heroin	High	Medium
Morphine	High	Medium
Methadone	High	Long
Fentanyl, Sufentanil	High	Short
Oxycodone, Hydrocodone	Medium	Medium
Codeine	Low	Medium
Buprenorphine	Agonist/Antagonist	Medium
Propoxyphene (Darvon)	Negligible	Medium
Diphenoxylate, Loperamide	Absent	Medium

Like the psychomotor stimulants, the likelihood of abuse varies with the way that narcotics are delivered. Intravenous and smoked routes seem to present the greatest addiction liability. However, use of narcotics by any route including smoked, intravenous, snorted, or swallowed, can be and often is addictive. The recent epidemic of oxycodone abuse (see box) provides a good example. Use of snorted heroin provides another example. The purity of heroin available in the United States increased dramatically in the late 1980s and early 1990s from an annual average of about 6% to 8% to 40% to 50% in many cities. In the early 1990s the purity of heroin was so high (60%–75%) that people could get high (or dead) from just snorting the heroin—they did not need to inject it. At first, users seemed to stick to this route, and to less compulsive patterns of use. Soon enough, however, people started showing up in treatment facilities requesting treatment of heroin addiction associated with snorting or following progression from snorting to intravenous use.

Despite these cautions, medical use of narcotic drugs is often appropriate and drugs should not be withheld out of concern for abuse, especially during end-of-life care. Clinicians need to assess the likelihood that the patient will abuse drugs, maintain good prescribing practices, and prescribe drugs with less abuse liability. Methadone represents a good prototype. Methadone can only be used orally, has a slow onset of action, and has an extremely long duration of action (18–24 hours). It therefore represents an ideal treatment for opiate addiction, because its prolonged action can suppress withdrawal for hours, but it lacks the rapid delivery to the brain that causes a high. These same qualities have made it more popular in recent years as an analgesic drug for people with chronic pain.

Many studies show that in-hospital use of narcotic drugs to treat postsurgical pain (their main clinical use) rarely leads to abuse unless the patient is a former abuser. The reasons are not certain, but probably relate to the unpleasant circumstances in which the drug was delivered and the fact that the patient returns home and leaves the drug-using environment.

OXYCONTIN: DRUG OF ABUSE DU JOUR

The recent meteoric rise of the narcotic drug *oxycodone* in abuse circles represents a common tale of a wave of drug popularity. Oxycodone has been used medically for many years. In recent years, clinicians have used it more in place of the less efficacious codeine as part of a nationwide effort to control pain adequately. This may have played a minor role in its increased popularity. In 1996, Purdue Pharma introduced a novel sustained release formulation called *Oxycontin*. The gradual release was intended to decrease abuse liability, and should have, because the onset and offset of drug action was more gradual. Unfortunately, the particular formulation they chose was easily subverted to abuse: If users bit down on the capsule, they could release the entire drug dose immediately. Popularity of this drug shot up in abuse circles, and Oxycontin users started showing up in emergency rooms and treatment facilities at a skyrocketing rate (a 50% increase from 1994–2001). Addiction and overdose deaths increased, including some high-profile cases that led to lawsuits in which family members asserted that the drug was used within parameters prescribed by a physician. The drug has since been reformulated but it remains popular in abuse circles. Oxycodone is not a unique narcotic, but has achieved great notoriety perhaps because users included members of middle-class and affluent communities, not easily stigmatized inner city "junkies." Regardless of the demographics of use, oxycodone addiction is classical opiate addiction that is not particularly different from heroin addiction.

17. Which of the following is a correct statement about narcotic addiction?
   a. You don't get addicted to snorting heroin.
   b. Oral methadone is rarely associated with abuse because of its long half-life.
   c. It is inappropriate to use narcotics during end-of-life care because clients will become physically dependent.
   d. People rarely abuse narcotics that are prescribed on an "as needed" basis for chronic pain.

Narcotic addiction is perhaps the prototypic example of the relationships among tolerance, addiction, and physical dependence. These drugs clearly can be addictive, with users self-administering in a steady pattern of daily use whenever the drug is available, rather than in binges like stimulant users. Also, they produce dramatic tolerance and physical dependence. Physical dependence on narcotics begins to develop as soon as regular use begins. This occurs whether use results from appropriate clinical use or self-administration. As described in earlier chapters, physical dependence generally represents the converse of tolerance to drug effects. The withdrawal signs for narcotics are exactly what would be predicted based on their acute effects. People crave the drug. They also are restless, achy, and irritable and experience nausea, diarrhea, sweating, gooseflesh, and perhaps feel pain more easily. Pupils are dilated, and blood pressure and heart rate increase somewhat. After long-term, high dose regimens, narcotic withdrawal can be extremely uncomfortable. However, unlike alcohol withdrawal, it is not life threatening.

Addiction and physical dependence are not inextricably linked. *Physical dependence in the context of clinical use does not mean the patient is addicted.* It simply means that the patient is developing tolerance to narcotic effects. If the patient uses drugs according to an appropriate schedule and does not escalate use, then physical dependence should be regarded as a symptom to be managed. Gradual withdrawal from the drug and avoiding peaks and valleys in drug levels will help. Tolerance and dependence result from adaptation of opioid receptors

RUNNER'S HIGH, "ENDORPHINS," AND NARCOTIC EFFECTS

What is the relationship between narcotic drugs and the "endorphins" that supposedly account for every good feeling from runner's high to acupuncture? Narcotic drugs exert their physiologic and behavioral effects because they mimic the actions of three related peptide neurotransmitter families: the *enkephalins*, *dynorphins*, and *endorphins* that naturally occur in the body. The peptides exist in separate neurons and have distinct functions. The two most important are the endorphin system, which probably coordinates physiologic and behavioral responses to overwhelming stress, and the enkephalin neurons that control gastrointestinal motility in the enteric nervous system, as well as breathing and sensations of pain. Narcotics stimulate all these systems simultaneously. Popular mythology asserts that the decreased feeling of pain and overwhelming feeling of contentment that result at the end of extreme stress (like at the end of an intense run—the so-called runner's high) results from activity of endorphin neurons. There is some truth to this myth, however it is far more likely at the end of a marathon or other very intense stressor than at the end of a mild 2-mile jog.

and their signaling pathways in whatever parts of the body they appear. Withdrawal signs reflect these changes. Although opioids can induce the adaptive changes in reward circuitry associated with addiction, the conditions under which these changes develop are not certain, and people clearly can use narcotics for pain relief according to physician instructions and not be addicted but still develop physical dependence.

18. Narcotic withdrawal:
    a. is manifested as diarrhea, gooseflesh, and drug craving.
    b. can be life-threatening.
    c. is a sign of addiction.
    d. should be managed medically with small doses of methadone.

Overdose deaths from narcotics almost always result from suppression of respiration. This can be rapidly reversed if a patient receives treatment promptly. The opiate antagonist drug naloxone (Narcan) can displace the narcotic from its receptor sites and reverse the suppression of respiration.

CNS DEPRESSANTS: BARBITURATES AND BENZODIAZEPINES

Sedative-hypnotic drugs comprise a broad category of drugs that are used for anesthesia, treatment of insomnia, and anxiety-reduction. A *sedative* is a drug that decreases excitement and agitation, and calms the patient, and a *hypnotic* drug produces sleep. This distinction is somewhat artificial, as many drugs in this class are sedative at low doses and hypnotic at high doses. Many people who abuse these drugs first receive them as treatment and then progress to misuse and abuse.

There are two main classes of sedative-hypnotics. The most commonly used are the benzodiazepines and newly introduced imidazopyridine drugs that are widely used for anxiety reduction and treatment of insomnia. The barbiturates are the classic drugs of this class, but they are used much less often today because overdose hazard is much greater. Table 3.3 provides a list of the most commonly used drugs in this class.

TABLE 3.3

Major Clinically Used Anxiolytic and Sedative Drugs

Drug	Class	Use
Alprazolam (Xanax)	Benzodiazepine	Anxiolysis
Chlordiazepoxixe (Librium)	Benzodiazepine	Anxiolysis
Diazepam (Valium)	Benzodiazepine	Anxiolysis
Flurazepam (Dalmane)	Benzodiazepine	Anxiolysis
Lorazepam (Ativan)	Benzodiazepine	Anxiolysis
Triazolam (Halcion)	Benzodiazepine	Hypnosis
Midazolam (Versed)	Benzodiazepine	Hypnosis
Zolpidem (Ambien)	Imidazopyridine	Hypnosis
Pentobarbital (Nembutal)	Barbiturate	Hypnosis
Phenobarbital (Secobarbital)	Barbiturate	Hypnosis, epilepsy
Secobarbital (Seconal)	Barbiturate	Hypnosis

Sedative-hypnotic drugs have common effects that result from a shared mechanism of action. They all cause a dose-dependent inhibition of all brain functions. At low doses they reduce anxiety and cause mild sedation. Some (phenobarbital for example) are useful in treating epilepsy. At higher doses, they cause sleep. At higher doses still, some can gradually suppress vital brain functions and cause death due to suppression of respiration. The reason that all have the same broad profile of action is that they all activate the receptor for GABA, the main inhibitory neurotransmitter in the brain.

The benzodiazepine and imidazopyridine groups exhibit a very important and substantive difference from barbiturates: There is a ceiling on the effects they can cause, and, taken orally and alone, they present very little overdose hazard. They are so much safer that they have generally replaced barbiturate drugs in the treatment of anxiety and insomnia. The reason these drugs are so much safer is that their mechanism of action differs in a subtle but important way: Although barbiturates can mimic the actions of GABA by themselves, benzodiazepine and imidazopyridine drugs can only augment what GABA does by itself. This imposes a ceiling that is rarely fatal.

The introduction of these newer drug classes to treat anxiety has revolutionized treatment of these disorders. The drugs are safe and effective when used properly. However, they do present some challenges and a significant abuse potential. The behavioral problems they cause are manifestations of their major action. They can decrease coordination just like alcohol and therefore make activities like driving dangerous. They all can cause amnesia for the time that the drug was present. This is much more marked for some, like midazolam, than others.

19. Sedative-hypnotic effects:
    a. include decrease of anxiety, sedation, and hypnosis for all members of this class of drugs.
    b. are highly addictive.
    c. show a "ceiling" for benzodiazepines but not barbiturates.
    d. should never be used to treat insomnia.

Marked tolerance develops to these drugs. Tolerance is especially significant for the drug's hypnotic effects. None of these drugs was intended for chronic treatment of insomnia, and after long use, people who cease using them experience a significant withdrawal syndrome. Like alcohol, withdrawal manifests as a general CNS excitability. For the benzodiazepines, it emerges most commonly as insomnia and a return of anxiety symptoms (but it can include seizures). For barbiturates, withdrawal can be as life-threatening as it is for alcohol.

Compulsive use of these drugs occurs, but in a lower percentage of users than those who use narcotics or stimulants. Probably the percentage approximates that of alcohol abusers (5%–10%). Abuse occurs most often in the context of multi-drug abuse, especially alcohol and narcotics. Therefore, sedative-hypnotic tolerance and withdrawal will contribute to the global state of the patient, especially during withdrawal.

20. Barbiturates but not benzodiazepines:
    a. increase the action of the inhibitory neurotransmitter GABA.
    b. cause sedation.
    c. are widely used to treat anxiety and insomnia.
    d. are useful anesthetic agents.

CANNABIS

Marijuana is the most-used illegal drug in the United States. Approximately 40% of young adults have smoked marijuana at some point in their lives, and about 25% of high school seniors have smoked in the last month (National Household Survey on Drug Use and Health, 2002). Marijuana may also be the most controversial drug of abuse in America at the current time. Advocates lobby for decriminalization and promote medical use, and government agencies committed to reducing drug use have focused on marijuana use as their prime target. From a drug abuse treatment perspective, it is usually the first illegal drug that adolescents use. Most people who use other drugs also use marijuana, and so it is crucial to understand its effects because they are probably superimposed upon effects caused by other drugs.

Smoking is the most common route of marijuana use. People smoke marijuana cigarettes (joints), cigars that are emptied out and partially refilled with marijuana (blunts), or smoke the plant product directly in a water pipe (bong). Hashish is the resin from the flowering tops of Cannabis plants that contains the highest content of psychoactive components. It is smoked itself or rolled into a cigarette. Some people ingest marijuana, most often in brownies or other food. Absorption is very rapid after smoking, but much slower and less predictable after oral use. This unpredictability leads to more frequent "overdose" experiences, such as panic attacks or dissociative experiences, than after smoking. Marijuana remains in the body longer than any other psychoactive drug. The half-life (period of time it takes for the body to eliminate half a dose) of THC in the body is between 18 and 24 hours. *This long half-life means that people who use every day are chronically intoxicated.*

21. Which of the following are benzodiazepine-like drugs useful in treating anxiety?
    a. alprazolam and triazolam
    b. triazolam and secobarbital
    c. alprazolam and diazepam
    d. zolpidem and midazolam

Marijuana contains a number of psychoactive constituents, but delta-9 tetrahydrocannabinol (THC) is the most important. The amount of THC in smoked marijuana in the United States is a matter of much dispute but this arises more from the parts of the plant that are used, rather than from changes in the plants. The THC content of seized marijuana tested by the government has ranged from 3% to 5% since 1980. Rates of sinsemilla, the flowering tops of the plant that have the highest THC content, have ranged from 6% to 12% over that same time frame, but these numbers fluctuate. Hash oil contains the highest THC content, ranging from 9% to 20%.

Marijuana causes a highly individual and subjective experience, but most users report a pleasant sense of relaxation, increased attention to sensory experience, reduction in anxiety, and a sense of well-being. People can feel dissociated from their normal concerns and the immediate outside world, the feeling that may motivate its use as self-medication for PTSD and anxiety disorders. At high doses, marijuana can cause a marked dissociation that is enjoyable to some and anxiety-provoking to others.

Marijuana causes a marked disruption of memory function while the user is intoxicated. It also can impair coordination at high doses and so interfere with driving and other locomotor skills. It somewhat increases heart rate. Marijuana can impair fertility by interfering with the hypothalamic centers that regulate anterior pituitary function, although it certainly cannot be relied upon as a contraceptive.

Pharmacologically, marijuana is probably the least toxic drug of abuse. The most common adverse effect is marked anxiety (and even panic attacks) that can result from the dissociative state that marijuana can produce, especially after ingesting large amounts. Its effects on organ system function are mild, and it is basically impossible to die from an overdose of marijuana (because life-sustaining centers are not sensitive to THC). However, marijuana smoke is carcinogenic, and heavy (daily) users experience bronchitis and other adverse respiratory effects similar to those of cigarette smoking. Marijuana smoking may be associated with unique cancers of the oral cavity.

The biggest problem presented by daily marijuana use is caused by the long half-life of the drug. Daily users are chronically intoxicated. Memory, coordination, and cognitive functions are impaired as long as the THC is present. The so-called *amotivational syndrome* that was used for years to describe long-term effects of marijuana on behavior may represent mainly a state of chronic intoxication.

Marijuana also produces tolerance and dependence. Some tolerance develops to the effects of marijuana, although many people report that the psychoactive effects actually increase as they become more "experienced" users, perhaps because their expectation shapes the experience. Recent research has shown that heavy (daily) use can lead to a withdrawal syndrome when people stop. Prominent symptoms include restlessness, irritability, mild agitation, mild insomnia, and some nausea. Although this syndrome is mild in comparison to ethanol withdrawal, many users often refuse to stop, perhaps due to the combination of their perception that it is not particularly dangerous and the discomfort they experience when they stop. The best research suggests that marijuana is about as addicting as ethanol—roughly 5% to 9% of regular users progress to habitual use that they have difficulty stopping. Many treatment providers report that adolescents have more difficulty stopping, although there is not clear-cut research support for this speculation at this time.

MARIJUANA AS MEDICINE

Advocates tout marijuana as a treatment for everything from glaucoma to pain. Many users self-medicate with marijuana, especially for anxiety reduction, and users often justify use based on its purported medical efficacy. A 1999 report by the Institute of Medicine reviewed the evidence and provided a useful summary (Watson et al., 2000). Marijuana has been advocated most actively for suppression of nausea, stimulation of appetite, treatment of spasticity and analgesia, as well as for its obvious psychoactive properties. Claims of clinical effectiveness for treatment of glaucoma, spasticity, and epilepsy are either unsubstantiated, or the effects are so transient and mild that it is not a credible medicine. Marijuana can be an effective antiemetic and appetite stimulant. However, it is psychoactive at doses at which it has these effects. While some patients may find these effects acceptable or even welcome, others do not. Route of administration presents another problem. Smoking marijuana is really the best way to control dose, but then the user experiences all the toxicities of smoking.

22. Cannabis:
    a. is more addictive than alcohol.
    b. impairs memory for up to 24 hours after a large dose (several joints) because its half-life is so long.
    c. is more effective at decreasing nausea taken as a pill than if smoked.
    d. has no concerning side effects from regular use.

23. Cannabis withdrawal:
    a. is associated with irritability and insomnia.
    b. does not exist.
    c. lasts for months.
    d. occurs in 30% of people who smoke marijuana.

24. Marijuana is most likely to be useful as a medicine for which of the following purposes?
    a. analgesia
    b. appetite stimulation in AIDS patients
    c. anti-vomiting for cancer chemotherapy
    d. spasticity

HALLUCINOGENS

People take hallucinogens for different reasons than many of the other drugs, and they have different reasons for taking different drugs in this category. The main effect of these drugs is a gross distortion of sensation, dissociation from one's sense of self, and for some users, a sense of insight that is an important reason for use. Of course, recreation plays a big part as well, but few people take cocaine for spiritual enlightenment or to get along with people better, two common reasons for using hallucinogens.

Lysergic acid diethylamide (LSD), psilocybin-containing mushrooms, and dried cactus buds that contain mescaline are the main hallucinogens used in the United States. The entactogen MDMA (Ecstasy) has some similarity in effects and is now used by more people (mainly teenagers) than any other drug in this category. Although it is not, strictly speaking, a hallucinogen, it fits better in this category than in any other.

LSD is the prototypic hallucinogen used in the United States. Use of LSD is much less frequent than use of the other drugs listed in this chapter; the National Household Survey of Drug Use and Health reports that about 8% to 10% of the population has ever used LSD, and about 3% to 5% of young adults use it annually. LSD is so potent that it can be identified tentatively by the form in which it appears. People typically take LSD as a small piece of paper into which a few drops of LSD have been adsorbed or a mini-gelatin capsule or tiny pill. An average dose is 50 μg to 150 μg. If someone has taken a normal size pill or capsule, it probably did not contain just LSD.

A "typical" LSD experience begins within 30 to 60 minutes with a feeling of unreality, sometimes anxiety, and the feeling that sensations are becoming more vivid. Pupils dilate, and people can have a mild sympathetic responses with increased heart rate and blood pressure. These are usually mild. From 1 to 2 hours, the experience peaks. Users experience changes in visual images ranging from wavy-like distortions of peripheral vision to overt hallucinations, depending upon the dose. People can have other unusual sensations including facial flushing, goosebumps, and body twitches. A sense of separation from self and normal reality is strong, and time sense can be strongly distorted. People can have extremely positive feelings, including a sense of energy and a feeling of awareness and understanding, or negative feelings, ranging from anxiety to a sense of complete dissociation of self from reality. Over the next several hours these effects wane, and people report fatigue and perhaps a contemplative state the next day. The whole experience can last for 6 to 12 hours, which is much longer than any other hallucinogen. LSD can cause a range of experiences from illusions (sense of unreality) through pseudohallucinations (experiences the user knows to be unreal) to frank hallucinations (sensory experiences that are unreal).

25. An LSD experience can include which of the following?
    a. illusions, pseudohallucinations, or hallucinations
    b. pseudohallucinations and illusions
    c. analgesia
    d. hallucinations only

The most common adverse reaction to LSD is anxiety or panic resulting from a bad trip. Almost everyone who uses LSD frequently (more than ten times) reports at least one bad trip. Advocates argue that control of the environment of drug taking ("set and setting") minimizes this risk, but there is no scientific proof that this is true. The most effective strategy is to provide supportive talking and if necessary, anxiolytic medication. Although antipsychotic drugs have been used, they are often ineffective and can make things worse.

"Flashbacks" (posthallucinogen perceptual disorder) are the next most common adverse reaction to LSD. These take many forms, ranging from a feeling of unreality and wavering visual fields when someone is tired (mild) to a reemergence of overt hallucinations, or permanently distorted visual sensations like afterimages or patterns imposed upon the visual field (most intense). They tend to diminish over months to years after someone completely stops using LSD, but there are case reports of users who experience them for years, perhaps for life. They can happen after a single use, but usually do not. They do become more common as total number of LSD experiences increases.

The ability of hallucinogens to mimic or trigger psychotic states is still controversial. There are distinct differences between a hallucinogenic experience and typical psychotic symptoms. For example, the hallucinations triggered by drugs are typically visual rather than auditory. However, other aspects of the hallucinogenic experience, including dissociation and sense of unreality, resemble aspects of psychosis. It is almost impossible to know if LSD "triggers" psychosis in previously healthy people. The literature better supports the idea that hallucinogens can easily trigger a worsening of symptoms or an actively psychotic state in someone who is already psychotic or in the prodromal stage of the disease.

26. A "bad trip" typically manifests as:
    a. acute psychosis.
    b. anxiety and/or panic.
    c. dangerous elevation of blood pressure.
    d. loss of coordination.

Psilocybin-containing mushrooms and cactus buttons containing mescaline are the other two most commonly used hallucinogens. Although no two hallucinogens cause exactly the same experience, the LSD experience described above is a good starting point. Both of these drugs cause mild sympathetic responses similar to LSD. The experience is usually more focused on visual images and much shorter.

The only clue we have about the neurochemical trigger for hallucinations is that all of the hallucinogenic drugs are agonists at a particular serotonin receptor—the 5HT2 receptor. Many of them have additional effects, but they share this in common. The location of these receptors in the cortex gives us our best guess about how hallucinations of particularly visual content arise: they are highly localized in the dendrites of cortical neurons in the visual cortex. However, that is the limit of our mechanistic knowledge. None of these hallucinogens is addicting. People typically use them intermittently—monthly at most. Very rapid tolerance develops to all of these drugs, so taking a second dose a day after one dose will have much milder, if any, effects. These drugs probably are not addicting because their mechanism of action is quite distinct from the addictive drugs described above. None of these drugs releases dopamine, in keeping with their lack of addictiveness. Although LSD has some direct dopamine agonist properties, this does not lead to compulsive use.

27. The following are common risks of using LSD regularly *except*:
    a. "flashbacks."
    b. a bad trip.
    c. addiction.
    d. anxiety.

Ecstasy (MDMA) should really be in its own category—strictly speaking, it is not a hallucinogen. Use of this drug and its relative MDA (methylenedioxyamphetamine) has increased more rapidly in the last five years than any other drug in America. About 10% of high school seniors in the United States have used Ecstasy at some point. Teenagers and young adults use it in social settings, especially all-night dance parties (raves). MDMA causes a unique profile of effects that make it attractive for this purpose. It combines the increase of arousal and sense of energy of a stimulant with a unique feeling of warmth and empathy that increases sociability. Though MDMA increases attention to physical sensations, it typically does not cause hallucinations. MDMA also has amphetamine-like properties of increasing alertness, physical activity, as well as a typical "flight or fight" stimulation of the sympathetic nervous system. Heart rate and blood pressure increase, body temperature rises, people feel energetic, and want to move around in their environment.

28. MDMA is:
    a. a psychostimulant.
    b. a hallucinogen.
    c. an entactogen.
    d. an analgesic.

People typically take MDMA as a single pill on a weekend. Repeat users use about once a month, and may gradually increase their intake from one pill to several. MDMA has a fairly long half-life (4–6 hours). Experienced users often develop a pattern of taking a second or third dose several hours after the first, when the effects are starting to wane. The addictiveness of MDMA is controversial. Animals do not self-administer it the way they do psychomotor stimulants. However, a few users will use it daily in a compulsive pattern that typically defines addiction.

MDMA causes effects like psychomotor stimulants because it shares some of the same biochemical mechanisms. MDMA provokes release of the catecholamine neurotransmitters norepinephrine and dopamine, just like amphetamine. However, it also causes a marked release of serotonin as well. The combination of these effects leads to SNS stimulation and increased arousal (norepinephrine), a sense of well-being and desire to explore (dopamine), and a sense of warmth and empathy (serotonin). The high body temperature probably results from the combination of the two. People typically feel high for several hours, and have a low, depressed feeling 2 to 3 days after using.

29. The effects of MDMA include:
    a. elevated body temperature and analgesia.
    b. increased blood pressure, anorexia, and mild sensory dissociation.
    c. increased body temperature and increased appetite.
    d. analgesia, euphoria, and slowed respiration.

The potential dangers of MDMA are tremendously controversial. The following list high-light some of the myths and, in contrast, the facts as well as science can determine them at this time. It is critical to know these facts because clients will often present their own versions that are based on semi-scientific analyses of the literature.

1. Some users believe MDMA is not toxic or lethal—only contaminants are lethal. *False*. MDMA can be lethal at doses three to four times above a single dose. There are people with variants of drug metabolizing enzymes who may be particularly vulnerable to overdose hazards.

2. There is a myth that MDMA overdoses are all caused by water intoxication. *False*. However, some deaths at raves have resulted from people drinking so much water in an effort to "prevent" hyperthermia that they experience fatal hyponatremia (dilution of electrolytes in the blood).

3. Another belief is that reports that MDMA can damage serotonin or dopamine neurons in the brain are exaggerated and based on flawed experiments. This is a tough one. No animal model is perfect. However, there are now data from human users showing the loss of markers of serotonin nerve terminals that resemble those shown in animal studies. Assuming the animal research is wrong is a big gamble that is probably ill-advised.

4. There are no well-established long-term psychiatric toxicities. *True*. However, there are case reports of anxiety disorders and depression. Research literature shows increased impulsivity and hostility.

5. Some users blame other drugs, for example, supposed memory effects of MDMA are all caused by marijuana use. *False*. While it is extremely difficult to unravel effects in people who use both drugs (the majority of users), some research indicates that heavy use of MDMA is associated with a particular form of cognitive impairment that may be unique.

30. MDMA:
    a. is a hallucinogen.
    b. has stimulant-like properties.
    c. does not cause lethal overdoses if the drug is "pure."
    d. is never used compulsively.

Nicotine, alcohol, and some other sedative-hypnotics, narcotic analgesics, psychostimulants, and perhaps marijuana comprise the short list of abused drugs that are clearly addictive. Each addictive drug exerts a unique profile of physiologic and behavioral effects and act through specific mechanisms ranging from inhibition of dopamine uptake (psychostimulants), activation of GABA-A receptors (ethanol) to activation of opioid receptors (narcotic analgesics). However, these addictive drugs also have a common denominator—they all increase synaptic dopamine, either directly or indirectly through activation of afferent input to dopamine cell bodies. Chronic use of addictive drugs leads to adaptive changes in dopamine neurons and/or their targets that influence reward-based behavior. Other actions of these drugs (sedation or arousal, analgesia, sleep, etc.) depend upon the specific mechanism of drug action, ones that mediate the drug-specific toxicities unique for each drug.

If you follow some practical guidelines, these drugs can be used for the treatment of clinical conditions, including ADHD, pain, and sleep disorders. First, use good prescribing practice and avoid "as needed" when prescribing. And, of course, monitor the clinical condition for which you are using the drug and treat the condition only as long as it lasts. Finally, when appropriate, use drugs with delayed onset of action and long half-life to help minimize the rapid on/rapid off stimulation of the reward system that facilitates the development of addiction.

Other abused drugs have adverse effects on brain and behavior even though they may not be addictive. Ecstasy (MDMA), an entactogen, improves mood and causes a feeling of well-being, can be lethal in overdose, and may cause long-lasting dysfunction of serotonin neurons. Although LSD has few immediate toxicities, it can, with repeated use, cause hallucinogen perceptual disorder (HPDD). Above all else, be guided by the adverse consequences—social, legal, or biological—experienced by your clients as a result of using these drugs.

KEY TERMS

addiction: Compulsive drug use caused by adaptation in reward/motivation circuits following chronic use of alcohol, marijuana, nicotine, stimulants, or opioids.

cannabinoid: Drug that possesses the action of smoked marijuana.

hallucinogen: Drug that causes a state characterized by illusions, pseudohalluinations, or hallucinations.

narcotic: Drug that produces a state of drugged sleep, usually an opioid.

opioid: Drug that causes the characteristic effects of the opium poppy including analgesia, reward, constipation, and inhibition of respiration.

sedative-hypnotic: Drug that causes sedation, sleep, and anxiety reduction.

stimulant: Drug that causes a combination of CNS arousal and sympathetic activation. The class typically includes amphetamines, cocaine, and ephedrine.

DISCUSSION QUESTIONS

1. What part of addiction is neurochemical? How can you envision this interacting with genetics, family history, or underlying psychiatric disorder?
2. Who would you worry about more: a patient who smoked marijuana twice a week or a patient who drank two six packs of beer on the weekend? Why?
3. If addiction requires brain changes associated with the drug, why is it good idea to let patients in drug treatment keep smoking cigarettes?
4. What principles of pharmacology should clinicians consider when evaluating use of stimulants in treating ADHD?
5. Are there biologic "limits" on how well anxiolytic drugs can medicate anxious personality?
6. What criteria should a psychoactive drug like marijuana fulfill to be used as a medication?
7. What patterns of alcohol drinking should concern you?
8. How do you convince adolescents, who do not see future consequences, that heavy use of MDMA will cause trouble for them in the coming months or years?

9. Why would people keep taking cocaine even if they didn't feel the "rush" when they took it any more?
10. What drugs would you make illegal? Why?

SUGGESTED FURTHER READING

Description of Drug Effects: Drug users typically can describe drug effects better than nonusers. One of the most thorough and neutral encyclopedias of drug effects can be accessed on the Web at www.erowid.org. This is a drug advocacy use site and, as is typical of such sites, can minimize potential risks. However, descriptions of what drugs do are accurate and thorough and can provide a background for professionals who have less experience with drugs than do their clients.

DeVries, T. J., & Shippenberg, T. S. (2001). Neural systems underlying opiate addiction. *Journal of Neuroscience, 22,* 3321–3325.

Drug Use Statistics: The most up to date statistics are on the Web. The National Household Survey of Drug Abuse and Health (http://www.samhsa.gov/oas/nhsda.htm#NHSDAinfo) covers drug abuse for the whole population. The Monitoring the Future Study (http://monitoringthefuture.org/index.html) encompasses only high school students.

REFERENCES

Everitt, B. J., & Wolf, M. E. (2001). Psychomotor stimulant addiction: A neural systems perspective. *Journal of Neuroscience, 22,* 3312–3320.
Julien, R. M. (2001). *A primer of drug action.* New York: Worth Publishers.
Koob, G. F., & Le Moal, M. (2001). Drug addiction, dysregulation of reward and allostasis. *Neuropsychopharmacology, 24,* 97–129.
Kuhn, C., Swartzwelder, S., & Wilson, W. (2003). *Buzzed: The straight truth about drugs from alcohol to ecstasy,* (2nd ed.). New York: Norton Press.
Maldonado, R., & deFonseca, F. R. (2002). Cannabinoid addiction behavioral models and neural correlates. *Journal of Neuroscience, 22,* 3326–3331.
Roberts, A. J., & Koob, G. F. (1997). The neurobiology of addiction: An overview. *Alcohol Health and Research World, 21*(2).
Trends in Pharmacological Sciences, (1992). 15, 169–219.
Volkow, N. D., & Fowler, J. S. (2000). Addiction, a disease of compulsion and drive: involvement of the orbitofrontal cortex. *Cerebral Cortex, 10,* 318–325.
Watson, S. J., Benson, J. A., & Joy, J. E. (2000). Marijuana and medicine: Assessing the science base: A summary of the Institute of Medicine Report. *Archives of General Psychiatry, 57*(6), 547–552.

4

History of Drug Policy, Treatment, and Recovery

William L. White
Chestnut Health Systems

TRUTH OR FICTION?

___ 1. *Alcoholics Anonymous was the first and the fastest-growing alcoholic mutual aid society in the world.*

___ 2. *America's "discovery of addiction" in the early twentieth century led to the "noble experiment" of alcohol prohibition.*

___ 3. *Men, women, and children consumed alcohol every day in Colonial America.*

___ 4. *Most people addicted to narcotics in the nineteenth century were provided narcotics by physicians or ingested narcotics to self-treat medical conditions.*

___ 5. *Opiate addiction in America during the nineteenth century was primarily a problem experienced by the Chinese.*

___ 6. *The disease concept of alcoholism was first introduced by E. M. Jellinek.*

___ 7. *Maintaining opiate addicts on medically monitored, daily doses of narcotics was first introduced as a treatment for addiction in the 1960s.*

___ 8. *Methadone maintenance was pioneered by Drs. Dole, Nyswander, and Kreek.*

___ 9. *The only federally-funded treatment resources for narcotic addiction treatment in the 1930s and 1940s were the public health hospitals ("narcotics farms") in Lexington, Kentucky and Fort Worth, Texas.*

___ 10. *A major milestone in the history of addiction treatment was the birth of the thera-peutic community in the late 1950s.*

___ 11. *The anti-medication bias in the field of addiction treatment is historically rooted in the number of such medications that have later been found to have a high potential for misuse.*

___ 12. *The president most associated with pushing prevention and treatment as a national drug control policy was Richard Nixon.*

_____ 13. *The American Association for the Study and Cure of Inebriety was founded upon the belief that inebriety was a bad habit rather than a disease.*

_____ 14. *A major factor in the explosive growth of addiction treatment between 1975 and 1985 was the expansion of insurance benefits to treat alcoholism and other addictions.*

_____ 15. *The most influential document in the rise of the modern alcoholism treatment system was the 1967 report of the Cooperative Commission on the Study of Alcoholism.*

The purpose of this chapter is to offer you a brief overview of the history of: (a) alcohol and drug-related problems, (b) recovery mutual aid societies, (c) addiction treatment, and (d) addiction-related laws and social policies in America. The histories of mutual aid and treatment, unless otherwise noted, are drawn from *Slaying the Dragon: The History of Addiction Treatment and Recovery in America* (White, 1998). The history of alcohol, tobacco, and other drug-related laws and social policies is drawn primarily from the published works of Drs. David Musto (1973, 1974) and David Courtwright (1982, 1991).

History is about chronology and context; it is about how events influence one another to shape the present and future. The importance of studying the roots of our field is reflected in the words of Lily Tomlin who once noted, "Maybe if we listened, history wouldn't have to keep repeating itself" (quoted in White, 1998, p. 328).

WHEN DID ALCOHOL AND OTHER DRUG PROBLEMS BEGIN IN THE UNITED STATES?

Alcohol usage was pervasive in colonial America. Men, women, and children consumed alcoholic beverages every day and throughout the day. The tavern was the center of colonial life. America's first colleges had breweries on campus for the convenience of faculty and students. In spite of the ever-presence of alcohol, drunken comportment was highly stigmatized, and there was no recognition of alcoholism as we know it today. Isolated problems of chronic drunkenness were viewed as a moral or criminal matter rather than a medical or public health problem.

Dramatic changes in drinking patterns following the Revolutionary War changed the conception of alcohol from the "Good Creature of God" to "Demon Rum." Between 1780 and 1830, annual per capita alcohol consumption in America rose from $2^{1}/_{2}$ gallons to more than 7 gallons, and drinking preferences shifted from fermented beverages such as cider and beer to rum and whiskey (Rorabaugh, 1979). Rising alcohol-related problems during this period led to the "discovery of addiction" (Levine, 1978).

Alcohol was not the only drug generating public concern in the nineteenth century. Increased consumption of opium, morphine, cocaine, chloral, ether, and chloroform via medical treatment or liberal self-treatment with patent medicines generated new patterns of addiction and growing civic alarm. The dominant profile of the opiate addict during this period was an educated, affluent, middle-aged white woman (particularly in the South).

1. Most people addicted to opiates in the nineteenth century were:
   a. middle-aged white women.
   b. aging Chinese men.
   c. young African American men.
   d. young Italian immigrants.

TABLE 4.1

Technology and the Rise of American Drug Problems

Technological Innovation	Significance
Increased distillation	Increased alcohol addiction (shift from fermented beverages to distilled spirits)
Isolation of plant alkaloids	Increased morphine and cocaine addiction
Hypodermic syringe	Increased opiate and cocaine addiction
Newspaper advertising	Promotion of alcohol-, opiate-, and cocaine-based patent medicines
The wooden match; cigarette rolling machine	Increased nicotine addiction

New technologies that heightened drug potency, expanded the methods of drug ingestion, increased drug availability, and unleashed unprecedented promotional forces played a significant role in the rise of these new patterns of addiction (Table 4.1).

2. What technological achievement contributed to the rise of narcotic addiction in the nineteenth century?
   a. introduction of the hypodermic syringe
   b. packaging of morphine and cocaine together
   c. synthesis of demerol
   d. introduction of a morphine inhaler

3. What innovation contributed to the rise of nicotine addiction in the nineteenth century?
   a. pipe
   b. cigarette
   c. wooden match
   d. filtered cigarette

In 1800, America had no conception of addiction; in 1900, we had witnessed a growing psychoactive drug menu, experienced our first anti-drug campaigns, passed numerous local and state anti-drug laws, and generated a significant body of literature about addiction—all of which were about to culminate in the prohibition of alcohol, tobacco, and the nonmedical use of opiates and cocaine.

WHEN DID THE FIRST MEDICAL CONCEPTIONS AND RESPONSES TO ADDICTION BEGIN?

The revolution in consciousness about alcohol was engineered by America's most prominent social activist, most eminent physician, and a leading clergyman. In 1774, Anthony Benezet, a Quaker social reformer, published a stinging indictment of alcohol entitled *Mighty Destroyer Displayed.* He christened alcohol a "bewitching poison" and spoke of "unhappy dram drinkers . . . bound in slavery" who had lost voluntary control of their decision to drink or not drink (Benezet, 1774, p. 4). Dr. Benjamin Rush followed Benezet's writings with a series of pamphlets culminating in his 1784 *Inquiry into the Effects of Ardent Spirits on the Human Mind and Body.* Rush posited that chronic drunkenness was a "disease induced by a vice," described the progressive nature and medical consequences of the disease, and suggested that chronic drunkenness be viewed as a medical rather than a moral problem (Benezet, p. 6). Perhaps most importantly, Rush argued that it was the responsibility of physicians to treat the disorder, and suggested several methods (ranging from religious conversion to aversive conditioning) by which chronic drunkards could be cured. By 1790, Rush was calling for the creation of a special hospital for inebriates (a "Sober House"). The third influence on America's changing conception of alcohol and chronic drunkenness was the Reverend Lyman Beecher who in 1825 delivered his widely read *Six Sermons on the Nature, Occasion, Signs, and Remedy of Intemperance*. Beecher spoke of the drunkard as being "addicted to sin," (p. 3) characterized intemperance as an accelerating disease, meticulously detailed its early stages, and argued that complete and enduring abstinence was the only method of prevention and cure.

4. The pioneer physician who rightly deserves the title of the "Father of Addiction Medicine" and the "Father of the Addiction Disease Concept" is _____.
   a. David Smith
   b. E. M. Jellinek
   c. Benjamin Rush
   d. William Silkworth

By the late 1820s, the **American temperance movement** was underway, and there was a growing trend toward the medicalization of alcohol and other drug problems. Between 1828 and 1832, two prominent medical directors of state insane asylums—Drs. Eli Todd and Samuel Woodward—added their support for the creation of special institutions for the care of the inebriate.

In the transition from the eighteenth to the nineteenth century, a vanguard of American physicians and social reformers redefined drunkenness as a medical problem, encouraged physicians to treat inebriety in their medical practice, and called for the creation of specialized institutions. Inherent in this shift were the core elements of an addiction disease concept: hereditary predisposition, drug toxicity, morbid appetite (craving), pharmacological tolerance and progression, loss of volitional control of drug intake, and the pathophysiology of chronic alcohol, opiate, or cocaine consumption. This early movement reached fruition in the work of Swedish physician Magnus Huss, who in 1849 introduced the term *alcoholism* to characterize the cluster of symptoms "formed in such a particular way that they merit being designated and described as a definite disease" (quoted in White, 1998, p. 22). While many new terms were suggested for this phenomenon, *inebriety* was the preferred term whose meaning is analogous to the term *addiction*. Texts of the day included chapters on alcohol inebriety, opium inebriety, cocaine inebriety, and inebriety from coffee and tea. The term *alcoholism,* whose use is presently diminishing, did not achieve professional or cultural prominence until the early decades of the twentieth century (White, 2002b).

5. The person responsible for coining the term *alcoholism* was _____.
   a. Dr. Benjamin Rush
   b. Dr. Eli Todd
   c. Dr. Magnus Huss
   d. Dr. E. M. Jellinek

6. The preferred nineteenth century term to refer to the condition of chronic drunkenness was _____.
   a. inebriety
   b. dipsomania
   c. alcoholism
   d. methomania

WHEN DID ADDICTION TREATMENT BEGIN IN THE UNITED STATES AND WHAT TYPES OF TREATMENT WERE FIRST AVAILABLE?

By the 1830s, the growing Temperance Movement was experimenting with "rescue work" with inebriates. Several temperance societies concluded that inebriates needed more than pledge-signing and attendance at temperance meetings to sustain sobriety. To buttress such sobriety, **inebriate homes** were created that viewed recovery from alcoholism as a process of moral reformation and immersion in sober fellowship. The first of these homes—the Washingtonian Homes in Boston and Chicago—opened in 1857 and 1863. The inebriate homes utilized short, voluntary stays followed by affiliation with local recovery support groups.

The call for specialized medical facilities resulted in another institution—the medically-directed inebriate asylum that relied on legal coercion (multi-year legal commitments) and emphasized physical and psychological methods of treatment (e.g., drug therapies, hydrotherapy, hypnotherapy). The first of these facilities—the New York State Inebriate Asylum—opened in 1864 under the leadership of Dr. Joseph Edward Turner.

7. The first medically-oriented addiction treatment institution in the United States opened in _____.
   a. 1794
   b. 1864
   c. 1924
   d. 1964

8. Which of the following institutions were noted for prolonged periods of residential care *and* physical methods of treatment?
   a. inebriate homes
   b. inebriate penal colonies
   c. inebriate asylums
   d. urban missions

In 1870, the leaders of several inebriate homes and asylums met in New York City to found the American Association for the Study and Cure of Inebriety—the first professional association of addiction treatment providers (Table 4.2). In 1876, the Association began publishing the *Quarterly Journal of Inebriety,* the first addiction-themed specialty journal. It was edited by Dr. T. D. Crothers for the life of its publication (1876–1914).

As inebriate homes and asylums achieved greater visibility, they faced competition from several sources, including private, proprietary (profit-making) addiction cure institutes. The most famous of these, the **Keeley Institute,** was founded in 1879 with the proclamation by

TABLE 4.2

Bylaws of the American Association for the Study and Cure of Inebriety (1870)

1. Intemperance is a disease.
2. It is curable in the same sense that other diseases are.
3. Its primary cause is a constitutional susceptibility to the alcoholic impression.
4. This constitutional tendency may be either inherited or acquired.

Dr. Leslie Keeley that "Drunkenness is a disease and I can cure it." Dr. Keeley went on to franchise more than 120 Keeley Institutes that used his "Double Bi-Chloride of Gold Cures for Drunkenness and the Opium and Tobacco Habits."

There were also bottled home cures for the "alcohol, tobacco and drug habits." These aggressively promoted products were the brainchild of both the addiction cure institutes and the same patent medicine industry that was doping the nation. These alleged addiction cures continued until an exposé in 1905 revealed that most of these products contained high dosages of morphine, cocaine, alcohol, and cannabis. The morphine addiction cures that promised consumers a product containing no narcotic or narcotic substitute nearly all contained high dosages of morphine.

9. A 1906 exposé of the patent medicine addiction cures revealed that most of the cures for morphine addiction contained _____.
   a. morphine
   b. cocaine
   c. high proof alcohol
   d. cannabis

Institutional intervention into chronic alcoholism was also provided by religiously oriented urban rescue missions and rural inebriate colonies. The former were pioneered by Jerry McAuley who opened the Water Street Mission in 1872 after his own religiously inspired recovery from alcoholism. Such rescue work with late-stage alcoholics was later institutionalized within the programs of the Salvation Army.

The final institution that bore an increasing brunt of responsibility for the care of the chronic inebriate was the urban city hospital. Bellevue Hospital in New York City opened an inebriate ward in 1879 and saw its alcoholism admissions increase from 4,190 in 1895 to more than 11,000 in 1910. Table 4.3 summarizes some of the most influential institutions to provide treatment for addictions in the 1800s.

10. Which of the following branches of nineteenth century treatment was organized to make a profit for its owners/stockholders?
    a. inebriate homes
    b. addiction cure institutes
    c. inebriate asylums
    d. rural inebriate colonies

It should be noted that nearly all of these institutions—particularly the **inebriate asylums** and addiction cure institutes—treated addictions to all drug addictions, including cocaine addiction. There were facilities like Dr. Jansen Mattison's Brooklyn Home for Habitues (opened in 1891) which specialized in the treatment of morphine and cocaine addiction.

TABLE 4.3

Professionalized Treatment of Addiction in the Nineteenth Century

Treatment/Care of Inebriates	Representative Institution/Product	Founding Date
Inebriate homes	Washingtonian Home	
	—Boston	1857
	—Chicago	1863
	Martha Washington Home (first women's facility)	1869
Inebriate asylums	New York State Inebriate Asylum	1864
For-profit addiction cure institutes	Keeley Institutes	1879
	Gatlin Institutes	
	Neal Institutes	
Bottled/boxed addiction cures	Hay-Litchfield Antidote	1868
	Knight's Tonic for Inebriates	1870s
	Collin's Painless Opium Antidote	1880s
Urban missions and inebriate colonies	Water Street Mission	1872
	Keswick Colony of Mercy	1897
City hospital inebriate wards	Bellevue Hospital—New York City	1879

WHAT HAPPENED TO THE HUNDREDS OF TREATMENT PROGRAMS THAT EXISTED IN THE NINETEENTH CENTURY?

Between 1900 and 1920 most of the addiction treatment institutions that had been founded in the second half of the nineteenth century closed. This virtual collapse of America's first network of addiction treatment programs was caused by multiple factors: (a) exposés of ethical abuses related to the field's business and clinical practices, (b) ideological schisms within the field, (c) absence of scientific studies validating the effectiveness of treatment, (d) loss of the field's leadership via aging and death, (e) unexpected economic downturns that deprived the field of philanthropic and governmental support, and (f) growing cultural pessimism about the prospects of permanent recovery from alcohol and other drug problems.

The rise of therapeutic pessimism led to a bold new vision for resolving these problems: Let those currently addicted to alcohol and other drugs die off and prevent the creation of a new generation of addicts through temperance education, the legal prohibition of alcohol and tobacco, and legal control of the nonmedical use of opiates and cocaine.

On the heels of this change in public attitudes came a shift in cultural ownership of alcohol and other drug problems. As specialized addiction treatment programs closed, people with severe and prolonged alcohol and other drug problems were shuttled into the "foul wards" of urban community hospitals, the back wards of aging state insane asylums, and sentenced to rural inebriate penal colonies.

It was in this climate of disregard that those addicted to alcohol and other drugs suffered iatrogenic insults (treatment-caused injuries): mandatory sterilization, serum therapy (a procedure involving blistering the skin, withdrawing serum from the blisters and then re-injecting it as an alleged aid in withdrawal), and bromide therapy (anesthesia-aided detoxification that was lauded in spite of its high mortality rate). Over the years, alcoholics and addicts were subjected to whatever prevailing techniques dominated the field of psychiatry, from the indiscriminate application of chemical and electroconvulsive therapies, to psychosurgery and drug therapies that later proved to have significant potential for misuse, such as LSD, barbiturates, amphetamines, and a wide variety of tranquilizing and anti-anxiety agents. Much of the lingering anti-medication bias in the addiction treatment field stems from the shadow of this history.

11. Which of the following has *not* been used in the treatment of alcoholism?
    a. LSD
    b. amphetamines
    c. PCP
    d. barbiturates

The few pockets of hope for the addicted during the opening decades of the twentieth century were the remaining specialty programs, a new generation of private sanatoria and hospitals (e.g., the Charles B. Towns Hospital for the Treatment of Alcoholic and Drug Addictions in New York City that provided discrete drying out for the rich), and a clinic model of outpatient counseling. The clinic model was pioneered within the Emmanuel Church of Boston (1906) and utilized a unique program of lay therapy that brought individuals in recovery like Courtenay Baylor, Francis Chambers, and Richard Peabody into the role of lay alcoholism psychotherapists. These **lay therapists** were the precursors to today's addiction counselors. The Emmanuel Clinic also organized its own mutual aid fellowship (the Jacoby Club) for those it treated.

12. An outpatient clinic model of alcoholism psychotherapy provided by lay therapists (recovered alcoholics) was pioneered at _____.
    a. Hazelden
    b. the Emmanuel Church of Boston
    c. Towns Hospital
    d. Bellevue Hospital

WHEN WERE THE FIRST RECOVERY SUPPORT GROUPS FOUNDED IN THE UNITED STATES?

Recovery mutual aid societies have a very long history in the United States. The earliest of these societies grew out of Native American religious and cultural revitalization movements. Native American recovery "circles" date from the 1730s and were particularly vibrant during the nineteenth century. Some of the most prominent leaders of these movements included Wangomend, the Delaware Prophets (Papoonan, Neolin), the Kickapoo Prophet (Kenekuk), the Shawnee Prophet (Tenskwatawa) and Handsome Lake (Ganioda'yo).

By the 1830s, Euro-American alcoholics were seeking sober refuge within local temperance societies, but it wasn't until the Washingtonian Movement of 1840 that Euro-American alcoholics banded together in large numbers for sobriety-based mutual support. The Washingtonians rapidly grew to a membership of more than 400,000 and then collapsed, with many recently sobered alcoholics moving underground via the creation of sobriety-based Fraternal Temperance Societies. John Gough and John Hawkins were among the most prominent Washingtonian speakers and organizers of this period. They spent most of their adult lives organizing local recovery support groups, providing personal consultations to alcoholics and their family members, and maintaining a prolific correspondence with people seeking or in recovery. When

TABLE 4.4

Eighteenth to Nineteenth Century Recovery Mutual Aid Societies

Recovery group	Founding Year(s)
Native American Religious/Cultural Revitalization Movements	(1730s–present)
Washingtonian Movement	(1840)
Fraternal Temperance Societies	(mid-1840s)
Ribbon Reform Clubs	(1870s)
The Drunkard's Club	(early 1870s)
Institutional Support Groups	
—Ollapod Club	(1864–1868)
—Godwin Association	(1872)
—Keeley Leagues	(1891)
Business Men's Moderation Society	(1879)

the Fraternal Temperance Societies were torn with political conflict or lost their desire to help the still-suffering alcoholic, they were replaced by the Ribbon Reform Clubs and other local sobriety-based fellowships such as the Drunkard's Club in New York City. There were also alcoholic mutual aid societies that sprang up within the inebriate homes, asylums, and addiction cure institutes. The most prominent of the early recovery mutual aid societies are displayed in Table 4.4 (White, 2001a).

13. Which of the following recovery mutual aid societies was not birthed inside a treatment institution?
   a. Godwin Association
   b. Keeley Leagues
   c. Ollapod Club
   d. Washingtonian Temperance Society

The nineteenth century mutual aid societies collapsed in tandem with the inebriate homes and asylum. Only a few local recovery support fellowships (e.g., the Jacoby Club in Boston) filled the void between this collapse and the founding of Alcoholics Anonymous (AA) in 1935. AA is the standard by which all other mutual aid groups are evaluated due to its size (2.2 million members and more than 100,000 groups; 1.1 million members in the United States), its geographical dispersion (more than 175 countries) and its longevity (more than 65 years) (http://www.alcoholics-anonymous.org). The last half of the twentieth century witnessed growing varieties of AA experience reflected in the growth of specialty groups (e.g., women, young people, newcomers, old-timers, gay and lesbian meetings) as well as religious (the Calix Society; Jewish Alcoholics, Codependents and Significant Others [JACS]) and non-religious (AA for Atheists and Agnostics) adjuncts to AA. The AA program has been adapted for family members (Al-Anon), for persons addicted to drugs other than alcohol (Narcotics Anonymous, Cocaine Anonymous), for persons experiencing co-occurring disorders (Dual Disorders Anonymous, Dual Recovery Anonymous), and for nearly every other imaginable human problem. Also evident are a growing number of secular alternatives to AA (Women for Sobriety, Secular Organization for Sobriety, Rational Recovery, SMART Recovery, LifeRing Secular Recovery, and Moderation Management (White, 2003; Table 4.5).

TABLE 4.5

Twentieth to Twenty-First Century Recovery Mutual Aid Societies

Recovery group	Founding Year(s)
Jacoby Club	(1909)
United Order of Ex-Boozers	(1914)
Alcoholics Anonymous	(1935)
—Calix Society	(1949)
—JACS	(1979)
Alcoholics Victorious	(1948)
Narcotics Anonymous	(1947/1953)
Al-Anon	(1951)
Women for Sobriety	(1975)
Cocaine Anonymous	(1982)
Dual Disorders Anonymous	(1982)
Secular Organization for Sobriety	(1985)
Rational Recovery	(1986)
Dual Recovery Anonymous	(1989)
Moderation Management	(1993)
SMART Recovery	(1994)
LifeRing Secular Recovery	(1999)

14. Which of the following is not a secular alternative to Alcoholics Anonymous?
    a. Women for Sobriety
    b. Rational Recovery
    c. Secular Organization for Sobriety
    d. Alcoholics Victorious

15. The first major alternative to Alcoholics Anonymous was _____.
    a. Women for Sobriety
    b. Rational Recovery
    c. Secular Organization for Sobriety
    d. Moderation Management

16. Which acronym represents the first recovery mutual aid society developed specifically for alcoholic women?
    a. SOS
    b. WFS
    c. CA
    d. WAA

HOW HAVE POLICIES AND LAWS TOWARD ALCOHOL, TOBACCO, AND OTHER DRUGS EVOLVED OVER THE PAST CENTURY?

By 1850, the American temperance movement had shifted its strategy from promoting the moderate use of fermented alcohol to promoting total abstinence from all alcoholic beverages and advocating the legal prohibition of the sale of alcohol. Experiments with local and state prohibition led to a drive for national prohibition, ratification of the Eighteenth Amendment to the Constitution, and passage of the **Volstead Act** (the enforcement provisions of prohibition). National prohibition was inaugurated in 1919 and successfully reduced alcohol-related problems during the early twenties. Alcohol-related problems rose in the late twenties as the illicit alcohol trade increased. By the late 1920s, there was growing sentiment that the "noble experiment" of prohibition was failing. National prohibition came to an end in 1933 with the ratification of the Twenty-first Amendment to the Constitution.

17. National alcohol prohibition in America lasted from 1919 to _____.
    a. 1923
    b. 1933
    c. 1943
    d. 1953

The first anti-narcotics ordinance in the United States, a local ordinance passed in 1875 in San Francisco, was aimed at suppressing the Chinese opium dens. This was followed by other municipal ordinances and state laws aimed at the control of opium, morphine, and cocaine. What was emerging by the end of the nineteenth century was a policy of having physicians serve as gatekeepers for the legitimate distribution of these drugs (prescription laws) and the criminalization of the nonmedical sale of these substances.

18. The first anti-narcotics ordinance in the United States occurred in what city?
    a. San Francisco
    b. Chicago
    c. Philadelphia
    d. Jamestown

The first federal law addressing psychoactive drugs other than alcohol and tobacco was the Pure Food and Drug Act of 1906. This act, which required that all medicines containing alcohol, opiates, or cocaine be so labeled, had two effects. It quickly lowered rates of narcotic addiction and it banished most of the bottled addiction cure frauds. The most historically significant piece of drug legislation—the **Harrison Anti-Narcotic Act**—was passed by Congress in 1914. This federal act required that opiates and cocaine be sold only by a physician or a pharmacist authorized by a physician.

19. The Pure Food and Drug Act of 1906:
    a. required a physician prescription to obtain opium or morphine.
    b. required labeling of products containing alcohol, opium, and morphine.
    c. prohibited the growing of opium poppies in the United States.
    d. prohibited the manufacture of heroin.

Between 1914 and 1919, a series of Supreme Court decisions interpreted the Harrison Act. In the most important of these decisions (***Webb v. the United States***), the Supreme Court declared in 1919 that for a physician to maintain an addict on his or her customary dose was not in "good faith" medical practice under the Harrison Act and was an indictable offense. By one account, twenty-five thousand physicians were indicted for violation of the Harrison act between 1919 and 1935 and 2,500 went to jail.

20. The law that will mark the onset of the criminalization of the status of drug addiction in the United States (in effect if not intent) was the _____.
   a. Pure Food and Drug Act
   b. Marihuana Tax Act
   c. Harrison Anti-Narcotic Act
   d. France Bill

In 1912, Dr. Charles Terry, director of public health in Jacksonville, Florida, opened a clinic to treat opiate addicts. This marked the beginning of clinic-directed detoxification and maintenance of narcotic addicts. Following the *Webb v. United States* decision, physicians in forty-four communities established morphine maintenance clinics, all of which were closed by 1924 under threat of legal indictment. Many of these physicians become the harshest critics of the Harrison Act and this new era of drug repression and federal involvement in medical practice. In the same year of the *Webb v. United States* decision, the France Bill, which would have provided federal support for physician-directed, community-based treatment for addicts, came before Congress, but failed to pass. Between 1924 and 1935, treatment for narcotic addiction other than detoxification was almost nonexistent.

Cannabis (marijuana) was included in the first draft of the Harrison Act, but was deleted under pressure from physicians and pharmacists on the grounds that there were many legitimate medical uses for cannabis and that its nonmedical abuse was rare. An anti-marijuana campaign in the late 1920s and early 1930s led to passage of the Marihuana Tax Act of 1937, which designated cannabis a narcotic with penalties for its possession and sale similar to those for heroin.

21. Marijuana was first nationally prohibited under what law?
   a. The 1906 Pure Food and Drug Act
   b. The 1914 Harrison Anti-Narcotic Act
   c. The 1937 Marihuana Tax Act
   d. The Controlled Substances Act of 1970

There was also a well-organized anti-tobacco campaign of the late nineteenth and early twentieth centuries that successfully banned the sale of tobacco in many states. Following repeal of alcohol prohibition and the collapse of support for anti-tobacco legislation in the 1930s, alcohol and tobacco became highly promoted and celebrated drugs in American society, while the nonmedical use of opiates, cocaine, and cannabis became further stigmatized and criminalized via accelerating legal penalties. The harshness of new anti-drug measures in the 1950s set the stage for the reform movements in the 1960s and 1970s. For a summary of twentieth century narcotic control policies, see Table 4.6.

In 1966, Congress passed the **Narcotic Addicts Rehabilitation Act** (NARA), which provided treatment as an alternative to incarceration for narcotic addicts. This was followed by a further liberalization of drug laws in the 1970s, sparked primarily by concern with youthful drug experimentation and reports of heroin addiction among American soldiers in Vietnam. It was during the administration of President Richard Nixon that national drug policy shifted from an emphasis on law enforcement to one that placed a greater emphasis on prevention and treatment. This was followed in the 1980s by a backlash against what were perceived as "soft" approaches to the drug problem. This backlash was fueled by growing alarm about new patterns of cocaine addiction and drug-related violence. President Reagan re-allocated the national drug control budget, shifting two-thirds of the total budget into law enforcement with the remaining dollars devoted to prevention and treatment—exactly opposite the ratio established during the Nixon years.

TABLE 4.6

Early Milestones in American Narcotic Control Policy

Year	Event	Significance
1906	Pure Food and Drug Act	Requires labeling of medicines containing opium, cocaine, cannabis, and chloral
1909	Shanghai Opium Commission	First international discussion of drug control
1909	The Smoking Opium Exclusion Act	Prohibits importation of opium for smoking
1912	The Hague Opium Convention	Commits United States to pass drug control legislation
1914	Harrison Anti-Narcotic Act	Establishes physicians as gatekeepers of access to opiates and cocaine
1919	Webb v. United States Supreme Court decision	Threatens legal punishment for physicians medically maintaining addicts on opiates
1922	Narcotics Import and Export Act	Prohibits importation of processed morphine and cocaine into the United States
1924	Heroin Act	Prohibits importation of opium for use in manufacture of heroin
1937	Marihuana Tax Act	Prohibits sale and possession of cannabis
1942	Opium Poppy Control Act	Prohibits growth/harvesting of opium poppies without license
1951	Boggs amendment to the Harrison Act	Implements mandatory minimums in sentencing of drug offenders
1956	Narcotic Control Act	Increases penalties and introduces first death penalty provision within drug control legislation

Where earlier policy had focused resources on those drugs with greatest risks and social costs (e.g., heroin) Reagan's position of "zero tolerance" shifted the focus from treating addiction to discouraging casual drug use, particularly marijuana use. The representation of drug offenders among the state prison population jumped during the Reagan era from one in fifteen inmates to one in three inmates, with 85% of these offenders incarcerated on possession charges (Baum, 1996).

The explosive growth of prisons in the closing decades of the twentieth century was a product of increased incarceration of drug offenders. There are now more than 1.5 million drug-related arrests per year in the United States (up more than one million since 1980), and drug offenders now make up more than 60% of the federal prison population (Office of Applied Statistics, SAMHSA, 2000). The racial disparities reflected within these trends are glaring. Though African Americans represent only 15% of illicit drug consumers, they constitute 60% of those incarcerated in state prisons on felony drug convictions (U.S. Department of Justice, 2000). And whereas the rate of prenatal exposure of infants to drugs is the same for Caucasian and African American women, the latter are ten times more likely to be reported to child welfare authorities for prenatal drug exposure (Neuspeil, 1996).

22. What five-year period marked the most explosive growth of incarceration of drug offenders in American history?
   a. 1900–1905
   b. 1940–1945
   c. 1960–1965
   d. 1985–1990

TABLE 4.7

Drug Control Policy/Legislative Milestones: 1960–Present

Year	Event	Significance
1963	President's Advisory Commission on Narcotics and Drug Abuse	Recommends exploring option of treatment for drug offenders as an alternative to incarceration
1965	Drug Abuse Control Amendments	Provides strict controls on amphetamines, barbiturates, and LSD
1972	President's Commission on Marijuana and Drug Abuse	Recommends relaxation of marijuana laws; 12 states follow with decriminalization laws
1970	Controlled Substances Act	Replaces all previous drug legislation; introduces drug scheduling
1984	Crime Control Act	Increases mandatory minimum penalties for drug possession/sale; property forfeiture provisions
1977	President Carter advocates federal decriminalization of marijuana	Drug-related controversies among White House staff leads to abandonment of this initiative
1980	President Reagan introduces "zero tolerance" for drug use	Restigmatization, demedicalization, and recriminalization of alcohol and other drug problems
1986 1988	Anti-Drug Abuse Acts	Focus on discouraging casual drug use; two-thirds of funds go for law enforcement; one-third for prevention and treatment

There have been many influences that have shaped anti-drug campaigns (Table 4.7), but one glaring theme is the association of particular drugs with specific minority groups. The West Coast anti-opium campaign of the 1870s linked opium to the Chinese during a period of intense racial and class conflict. The first anti-cocaine laws in the South linked cocaine with violence by blacks at a time there is little evidence of widespread cocaine use among African Americans. This history continued: the drive toward alcohol prohibition tapped anti-Catholic and anti-German sentiment, the anti-heroin campaign tapped growing fears about crime and violence by immigrant youth, the anti-cannabis campaign heavily targeted Mexican immigrants, and the anti-cocaine laws of the 1980s were targeted primarily against poor communities of color.

23. The first anti-cocaine laws were associated with what group of people?
    a. Chinese immigrants
    b. African Americans
    c. Mexican immigrants
    d. Eastern European immigrants

WHAT LED TO THE REBIRTH OF TREATMENT BETWEEN 1940 AND 1970?

Two advancements were required to lay the foundation for the rise of a national network of community-based addiction treatment programs in the 1970s and 1980s: (1) a fundamental change in public attitudes and policies, and (2) the development of credible and replicable treatment models.

A number of institutions pioneered new approaches to alcohol-related problems in the 1940s and 1950s. Their collective efforts have been christened the ***modern alcoholism movement***.

- Alcoholics Anonymous and its professional friends reinstilled optimism about the prospects of long-term recovery.
- The Research Council on Problems of Alcohol promised a new scientific approach to the prevention and management of alcohol problems.
- The Yale Center of Studies on Alcohol conducted alcoholism-related research, educated professionals, established a clinic model of outpatient treatment, and promoted occupational alcoholism programs.
- The National Committee for Education on Alcoholism, founded by Mrs. Marty Mann in 1944, waged an unrelenting public education campaign about alcoholism and encouraged local communities to establish detoxification and treatment facilities.

There were five **kinetic ideas** (developed by Dwight Anderson and Marty Mann) that were at the center of this modern alcoholism movement's reengineering of public opinion and legislative policy (see Table 4.8).

24. The five kinetic ideas around which the modern alcoholism movement was organized were developed by _____.
    a. Bill W. and Dr. Bob
    b. Dr. E. M. Jellinek
    c. Senator Harold Hughes
    d. Dwight Anderson and Marty Mann

25. Which of the following is not one of the kinetic ideas of the modern alcoholism movement launched in the 1940s?
    a. Alcoholism is hereditary.
    b. Alcoholism is a disease.
    c. The alcoholic is a sick person.
    d. The alcoholic can be helped.

The modern alcoholism movement was actually many movements—each aimed at changing how particular institutions viewed alcoholism and the alcoholic. The targeted institutions were those of religion, law, business, medicine, and the media. The success of the movement was indicated by the increased percentage of American citizens who viewed alcoholism as a sickness from 6% in 1947 to 66% in 1967, and the number of professional organizations making public pronouncements about alcoholism in the 1950s and 1960s (see Table 4.9).

TABLE 4.8

Anderson and Mann's Five Kinetic Ideas

---

1. Alcoholism is a disease.
2. The alcoholic, therefore, is a sick person.
3. The alcoholic can be helped.
4. The alcoholic is worth helping.
5. Alcoholism is our No. 4 public health problem, and our public responsibility. (Mann, 1944)

TABLE 4.9

Key Policy Statements on Alcoholism (1950–1970)

Year	Organization	Position
1951	American Hospital Association (AHA)	Resolution on "Admission of Alcoholic Patients to the General Hospital" declares alcoholism a "serious health problem"
1952	American Medical Association (AMA)	Defines alcoholism
1956	AMA	Resolution calling on general hospitals to admit the alcoholic as a "sick individual"
1957	AHA	Resolution urging local hospitals to develop programs for the treatment of alcoholism
1963	American Public Health Association	Resolution declaring alcoholism a treatable illness
1965	American Psychiatric Association	Publishes a statement recognizing alcoholism as a disease
1967	AMA	Resolution that alcoholism is a "complex disease that merits the serious concern of all members of the health professions"

The shift in public attitude and professional policy were crystallized in the work of the Cooperative Commission on the Study of Alcoholism whose 1967 report called for a comprehensive, national approach to the prevention and treatment of alcohol problems as well as investments in alcoholism-related professional training and research. The Commission report provided a blueprint for the modern system of alcoholism treatment.

The first state alcoholism commissions were organized in the 1940s, and several alcoholism treatment modalities emerged between 1940 and 1965, including:

- Hospital-based detoxification and brief (5 day) treatment models via AA collaboration with hospitals in Akron, New York City, Cleveland, Philadelphia, and Chicago
- An outpatient clinic model pioneered in Connecticut and Georgia
- A residential model (the "Minnesota Model of Chemical Dependency Treatment") developed at Pioneer House, Hazelden and Willmar State Hospital
- A halfway house movement of the 1950s that championed the need for posttreatment recovery support services

26. The decade most associated with the rise of alcoholic halfway houses was the
_____.
    a. 1950s
    b. 1960s
    c. 1970s
    d. 1980s

Federal support for alcoholism services grew in the 1960s through funding from the National Institute of Mental Health and the Office of Economic Opportunity. The decades-long campaign of the modern alcoholism movement reached fruition with the passage of the Comprehensive Alcoholism Prevention and Treatment Act of 1970. This legislative milestone (often referred to as the "Hughes Act" for its champion, Senator Harold Hughes of Iowa), created the National Institute on Alcohol Abuse and Alcoholism (NIAAA) to lead a federal, state, and local partnership to build, staff, operate, and evaluate community-based alcoholism treatment programs across the United States. The number of alcoholism programs in the United States jumped from a few hundred in 1970 to more than 4,200 programs by 1980.

The growth of treatment programs for addiction to drugs other than alcohol went through a similar process. First, there were reform campaigns that called for the movement of addicts from systems of control and punishment to systems of medical and psychological care. The earliest of these efforts resulted in the creation of two federal **narcotics farms** designed to rehabilitate narcotic addicts entering the federal prison system. These were opened in Lexington, Kentucky in 1935 and Fort Worth, Texas in 1938. Evaluations of these programs showing exceptionally high relapse rates for addicts returning to their communities created pressure to create local, community-based treatment alternatives. The work of the American Medical Association and the American Bar Association in the 1950s and 1960s played an important role in calling for the shift from a criminal justice to a public health approach to the problem of addiction. Growing drug use by white youth in the 1960s tipped the scales toward a major investment in addiction treatment.

27. The absence of treatment for narcotic addiction changed in the 1930s with:
    a. the introduction of methadone maintenance.
    b. the opening to two federal narcotic "farms."
    c. passage of civil commitment laws.
    d. the introduction of narcotic antagonists.

To build a treatment system required replicable models of intervention and posttreatment recovery support. These came in four stages: (1) the founding of Narcotics Anonymous in 1953, (2) the birth of the therapeutic community via the founding of Synanon in 1958, (3) the development of methadone maintenance by Drs. Dole, Nyswander, and Kreek in the mid-1960s, and (4) the emergence of a variety of drug-free outpatient therapies for youth polydrug abuse during the late 1960s. These efforts came together in 1971 in an executive order by President Richard Nixon that created the Special Action Office for Drug Abuse Prevention and the passage of the Drug Abuse Treatment Act of 1972. This law created a counterpart to NIAAA—the National Institute on Drug Abuse (NIDA)—to support the development of a national network of addiction treatment programs. The number of such programs in the United States increased from less than one hundred in 1970 to more than eighteen hundred in 1975. The era of modern treatment had begun, with about two-thirds of the national drug control budget focused on demand reduction (prevention and treatment) through the Nixon, Ford, and Carter administrations (Baum, 1996; Massing, 1999).

WHAT WERE SOME OF THE MOST SIGNIFICANT MILESTONES IN THE MODERN HISTORY OF ADDICTION TREATMENT?

The modern field of addiction treatment has experienced three phases in its development. The focus of the first stage (1970–1980) was on the development of federal, state, and local organizational infrastructures through which treatment services could be planned, delivered, and evaluated. This required:

- Codification of treatment processes, for example the National Council on Alcoholism's development of diagnostic criteria for alcoholism (1972)

- The development of national (NIAAA and NIDA) and state training systems to educate and professionalize addiction treatment personnel
- The infusion of resources into research on addiction and treatment effectiveness
- The emergence of addiction counseling as a "new profession" via the founding of the National Association of Alcoholism Counselors and Trainers (the precursor to The National Association of Addiction Counselors; 1972) and state counselor associations
- Studies on core competencies of addiction counseling (the Littlejohn and Birch and Davis Reports of the mid-1970s) that formed the foundation of state counselor certification systems
- The development of national accreditation and state licensure standards for treatment programs (early 1970s)
- The highly controversial organizational integration of alcoholism and drug abuse treatment programs (1975–1985)

28. Most addiction counselor certification systems were organized in the _____.
   a. 1960s
   b. 1970s
   c. 1980s
   d. 1990s

This first phase resulted from hard-fought changes in public perception of alcoholism and the alcoholic created to a great extent by declarations of recovery from alcoholism by many prominent Americans, including First Lady Betty Ford. The National Council on Alcoholism played a significant role in this achievement via its Operation Understanding campaigns—press conferences held in 1976 and 1978 at which prominent people from diverse professions publicly announced their successful recovery from alcoholism.

The second phase in the development of modern treatment was characterized by an explosive growth of addiction treatment driven by the increase in inpatient hospital and for-profit residential treatment programs (and franchises). This initial trend was spurred by the decision of many insurance companies to begin offering alcoholism treatment benefits within their health policies. Rapidly rising costs of addiction treatment and exposure of ethical abuses related to aggressive marketing, inappropriate admissions, and lengths of stay led to a rapid curtailment of these benefits and the emergence of an aggressive program of managed behavioral health care during the late 1980s. Between 1988 and 1993, a large number of these programs were closed, and others shifted their emphasis from inpatient to outpatient services. This period of explosive growth and backlash lasted roughly from 1981 to 1993. There was also an ideological backlash during this period that challenged many of the foundational concepts of addiction treatment, for example the disease concept of alcoholism.

29. The most dramatic decline in the number of private and hospital-based addiction treatment programs occurred _____.
   a. 1969–1974
   b. 1975–1980
   c. 1981–1987
   d. 1988–1993

30. The financial backlash against addiction treatment in the late 1980s and early 1990s
    was in reaction to:
    a. an unexpected economic depression.
    b. financial exploitation of clients/families by addiction treatment providers.
    c. the perception that addiction counselors were being overpaid.
    d. a dramatic increase in public dollars allocated to addiction treatment.

The modern field of addiction treatment moved into a stage of maturity as it entered the twenty-first century. This maturation is evident in the aging and beginning exit of its first and second generation leaders, the expansion of programs for special populations, near universal interest in bridging the gap between research and front-line clinical practices, and the movement of treatment services into other social systems, for example the child welfare system, the criminal justice system, and public health agencies (particularly those involved in HIV/AIDS-related services). There is also evidence of the field's philosophical maturation via the shift from ideological intolerance (single-modality programs believing their approach was the only way to treat all addiction) to a growing recognition that substance use disorders spring from multiple etiological pathways, unfold in diverse patterns and needs, respond to a variety of treatments, and resolve themselves through multiple pathways and styles of long-term recovery.

Some of the most important technical achievements during this evolution of modern treatment include research-validated screening and assessment instruments and diagnostic and placement criteria; early intervention programs (EAP, SAP, Family Intervention); replicable treatment models that span multiple and linked levels of care; effective outreach and engagement techniques (e.g., motivational interviewing); an expanded menu of psychopharmacological adjuncts; evidence-based, manualized therapies; age, gender, and culturally informed treatment; relapse prevention tools; and an expansion of posttreatment recovery support services (see chapter 19 for a discussion of recovery tools). The most significant systems achievement during the modern era has been the resilience of the federal, state, and local partnership that has shared responsibility for building, staffing, operating, monitoring, and evaluating community-based addiction treatment programs.

As this book goes to press, there are two movements that promise, by their success or failure, to reshape the future of addiction treatment. The first is a treatment renewal movement that seeks to get the field of addiction treatment ethically recentered, move addiction treatment providers back into deep relationships with the communities out of which they were born, and relink treatment to the larger and more enduring process of addiction recovery (White, 2002a). The second is a new recovery advocacy movement led by recovering people and their families that is trying to counter the restigmatization, demedicalization, and recriminalization of alcohol and other drug problems. These grassroots organizations are putting a face and a voice to recovery, pushing prorecovery policies, and working to expand treatment and recovery support services within local communities (White, 2001b). The energy generated by these two movements makes it an exciting time to enter the world of addiction treatment.

SO WHAT DOES THIS HISTORY TELL US ABOUT HOW TO CONDUCT ONE'S LIFE IN THIS MOST UNUSUAL OF PROFESSIONS?

The lessons from those who have gone before you are very simple ones. Respect the struggles of those who have delivered the field into your hands. Respect yourself and your limits. Respect the individuals and family members who seek your help. Respect (with a hopeful but healthy skepticism) the evolving addiction science. And respect the power of forces you cannot fully understand to be present in the counseling process. Above all, recognize that what addiction professionals have done for more than a century and a half is to create a setting and an opening in which the addicted can transform their identity and redefine every relationship in their lives, including their relationship with alcohol and other drugs. What we are professionally responsible for is creating a milieu of opportunity, choice, and hope. What happens with that opportunity is up to the addict and his or her god. We can own neither the addiction nor the recovery, only the clarity of the presented choice, the best clinical technology we can muster, and our faith in the potential for human rebirth. The individuals, families, and communities impacted by alcohol and other drugs need and deserve a new generation of addiction counselors who are willing to dedicate their lives to carrying forth the movements chronicled in this chapter. For those willing to follow that calling, I bequeath you a field whose rewards are matched only by its challenges (adapted from White, 1998).

KEY TERMS

American temperance movement: A social movement arising in the early nineteenth century that, following a brief call for moderation of alcohol consumption, generated mandatory temperance education, drinking age laws and eventually the drive to legally prohibit the sale of alcohol.

habitues: A nineteenth-century term used most frequently to depict those who had become dependent upon opium or morphine, later expanded to encompass those addicted to any drug.

Harrison Anti-Narcotic Act: The 1914 act that set the stage for the criminalization of the status of narcotic addiction in the United States.

inebriate asylums: Medically-directed institutions for the long-term care of the inebriate.

inebriate homes: Residential homes for the care of inebriates that portrayed recovery as a sobriety decision (pledge signing), a process of moral reformation, and a process of mutual surveillance and support.

inebriety/inebriate: Inebriety was the term for what today would be called addiction; the person suffering from addiction was known as an inebriate.

Keeley Institutes: The largest chain of for-profit addiction cure institutes that flourished in the late nineteenth century.

kinetic ideas: Ideas and phrases thought to have power in galvanizing public opinion, e.g., "alcoholism is a disease."

lay therapists: Recovered alcoholics trained to serve as lay psychotherapists within the Emmanuel Clinic in Boston; later used to depict recovered counselors who lacked formal training in medicine, psychology, or social work.

modern alcoholism movement: Term applied to the post-Repeal efforts of multiple organizations to change American perceptions of alcoholism and the alcoholic.

Narcotic Addicts Rehabilitation Act (NARA): Expanded access to treatment for narcotic addiction in the 1960s.

narcotics farms: Term applied to the federal prisons in Lexington, KY, and Forth Worth, TX, that were designated for the treatment/containment of narcotic addicts within the federal prison system.

Volstead Act: The 1919 enforcement arm of federal prohibition of the sale of alcohol.

Webb v. United States: The 1919 Supreme Court decision that prohibited physicians from maintaining addicts on their "usual and customary dose"—the practical implication was the transfer of narcotic addicts from the medical community to the criminal justice community.

DISCUSSION QUESTIONS

1. What technological developments influenced the history of addiction in America? What future technological breakthroughs could influence the history of addiction in the twenty-first century?
2. As alcohol and other drug problems grew in the nineteenth century, there was a struggle to define whether these problems were the province of religion, law, or medicine. What institutions are competing for ownership of these problems today, and what is your perception of how these institutional interests affect social policy?
3. Evaluate the health or vulnerability of the modern field of addiction treatment using the six factors discussed in this chapter.
4. Given the demise of all of AA's predecessors, what factors contributed to AA's growth and endurance?
5. What is your perception of the current role of race, class, and generational conflict in recent anti-drug campaigns, the application of drug laws via arrest and sentencing, and access to treatment?
6. How have public opinions changed between 1944 and the present regarding Anderson and Mann's five kinetic ideas?
7. Cultural responses to addiction treatment modalities often have little to do with scientific studies of their relative effectiveness. There was great popular support for therapeutic communities long before their effectiveness was evaluated, and great public and professional criticism of methadone maintenance long after its effectiveness had been overwhelmingly documented. How do you account for such cultural, professional, and scientific disparities?
8. This chapter has reviewed the rise, fall, and rebirth of addiction treatment and recovery mutual aid societies in America. What are your predictions about the future of treatment and mutual aid movements? What do you think are the most important factors that will shape this future?
9. The history of addiction treatment is marked by cycles of *segregation* (organization of a specialized field of addiction treatment) and *integration* (absorption of alcoholics and addicts into other systems of care or control). The abuses within or inadequacies of the latter generally lead to a process of respecialization. What dangers, if any, do you think exist in the current integration of addiction treatment into broader conceptual (behavioral health) and service (merger of mental health and addiction treatment units) umbrellas?
10. Grassroots recovery advocacy organizations are again trying to counter the restigmatization, demedicalization, and recriminalization of addiction in America. What effects do you think such organizations will exert on the field of addiction treatment?

SUGGESTED FURTHER READING

Inciardi, J. (1986). *The war on drugs: Heroin, cocaine, crime and public policy.* Palo Alto, CA: Mayfield Publishing.

An excellent and highly readable account of modern drug trends and drug policies.

Kurtz, E. (1979). *Not God: A history of Alcoholics Anonymous.* Center City, MN: Hazelden.

The definitive history of Alcoholics Anonymous.

Morgan, H. (1981). *Drugs in America: A social history 1800–1980.* Syracuse, NY: Syracuse University Press.

Perhaps the best single history of illicit drug use in America.

Sinclair, A. (1962). *Era of excess: A social history of the prohibition movement.* New York: Harper & Row.

The book to read if you are interested in the social history of prohibition.

REFERENCES

Baum, D. (1996). *Smoke and mirrors: The war on drugs and the politics of failure.* Boston: Little, Brown and Company.

Benezet, A. (1774). Might destroyer displayed in some account of the dreadful havock made by the mistaken use as well as abuse of distilled spiritous liquors. In A lover of mankind. Philadelphia: Joseph Crukshank.

Courtwright, D. (1982). *Dark paradise: Opiate addiction in America before 1940.* Cambridge, MA: Harvard University Press.

Courtwright, D. (1991). Drug legalization, the drug war, and drug treatment in historical perspective. *Journal of Policy History, 3,* 393–414.

Levine, H. (1978). The discovery of addiction: Changing conceptions of habitual drunkenness in America. *Journal of Studies on Alcohol, 39*(2), 143–174.

Mann, M. (1944). Formation of a national committee for education on alcoholism. *Quarterly Journal of Studies on Alcohol, 5*(2), 354.

Massing, M. (1999). *The fix.* New York: Simon & Schuster.

Musto, D. (1973). *The American disease: Origins of narcotic controls.* New Haven: Yale University Press.

Musto, D. (1974). History of drug control. In P. Levin (Ed.), *Contemporary problems of drug abuse* (pp. 26–38). Acton, MA: Publishing Sciences Group.

Neuspeil, D. R. (1996). Racism and perinatal addiction. *Ethnicity and Disease, 6,* 47–55.

Office of Applied Statistics, Substance Abuse and Mental Health Services Administration, Department of Health and Human Services. (2000). *Substance abuse treatment in adult and juvenile correctional facilities: Findings from the 1997 survey of correctional facilities.* Rockville, MD: Author.

Rorabaugh, W. (1979). *The alcoholic republic: An American tradition.* Oxford: Oxford University Press.

U.S. Department of Justice, Bureau of Justice Statistics. (2000). *Prisoners and jail inmates at midyear 1999.* Washington, DC: Author.

White, W. (1998). *Slaying the dragon: The history of addiction treatment and recovery in America.* Bloomington, IL: Chestnut Health Systems.

White, W. (2001a). Pre-AA Alcoholic Mutual Aid Societies. *Alcoholism Treatment Quarterly, 19*(1), 1–21.

White, W. (2001b). The new recovery advocacy movement: A call to service. *Counselor, 2*(6), 64–67.

White, W. (2002a). The treatment renewal movement. *Counselor, 3*(1), 59–61.

White, W. (Ed). (2002b). *The addiction disease chronologies of William White, Ernest Kurtz, and Caroline Acker.* Retrieved from www.bhrm.org

White, W. (in press 2003). Alcoholic mutual aid societies. In J. Blocker and I. Tyrell (Eds.). *Alcohol and temperance in modern history* (pp. 24–27). Santa Barbara, CA: ABC-CLIO.

INDIVIDUALS, FAMILIES, AND DRUGS

5

Lifespan Development and Drugs

Robert J. Pandina
Valerie L. Johnson
Rutgers University

TRUTH OR FICTION?

___ 1. *The lifespan approach to drug-using behaviors includes examination of biological underpinnings.*

___ 2. *The definition of drug use has become commonly agreed upon in recent years.*

___ 3. *A biopsychosocial model of drug abuse has become a dominant theoretical view of drug use disorders.*

___ 4. *The DSM–IV focuses upon the entire continuum of substance use patterns and outcomes.*

___ 5. *The concept of* stages of use *is one that is not agreed upon by all researchers and practitioners.*

___ 6. *The gateway hypothesis is the most scientifically proven way of characterizing transitions in drug use.*

___ 7. *All drug dependent persons have followed the same pathway in this disorder.*

___ 8. *Early age of use onset has been a consistent predictor of all drug abuse behaviors.*

___ 9. *Not all risk factors linked with drug abuse are malleable.*

___ 10. *There is a general taxonomy of drug use development that captures outcomes for all drugs of concern.*

___ 11. *Measures of use intensity and use impact are essential as defining criteria of abuse or dependence.*

___ 12. *Movement along a continuum from drug abstinence to drug dependence is unidirectional.*

___ 13. *Studies have shown that, whereas the absolute levels of drug use vary by gender, both men and women display similar growth curves of use.*

___ 14. *Risk factors for drug use can vary by stage of use involvement.*

___ 15. *Once present, risk factors cannot be altered.*

The manner in which drug-using behavior develops and changes across the lifespan is one of the central questions in the field of addiction studies. This question is a central one not only because its answer will lead to an understanding of root causes of drug use, but also because a satisfactory answer can provide clues to the development and implementation of appropriate and effective intervention methods aimed at the prevention of use and the treatment of abuse and dependence.

WHAT DO WE MEAN BY LIFESPAN DEVELOPMENT IN THE CONTEXT OF DRUG ABUSE RESEARCH?

Lifespan research has been characterized as an approach that covers the full spectrum of growth from "cradle to grave." The lifespan approach recognizes that the development of any behavior, including drug use, should be placed within the broad context of biological, psychological, and social development, and change and transition (Magnusson, 1996; Staudinger & Lindenberger, 2003). In this regard, we believe that no single behavior, including drug use (or nonuse) develops in a vacuum. Hence, drug use, like other aspects of a person's behavioral repertoire is a product of fundamental processes such as learning and self-regulation. A lifespan perspective also acknowledges the dynamic nature of human behavior where ebb and flow in the behavioral repertoire is the norm. Drug use patterns themselves ebb and flow within the life of a given individual. For that matter, use patterns fluctuate within our society and within sub-populations as popularity of drugs change and as new drugs arrive on the use scene. These fluctuations become reflected in the individual **drug use trajectories** and the overall patterns we track in various population surveillance approaches. Within the last several decades, advances in genetic research have extended this lifespan perspective to include the biological underpinnings of human development beginning before a person is born, that is, biological characteristics (e.g., genes) passed on from parents to children. This view has been embedded in drug abuse research in one way or another long before modern research protocols were developed. Perhaps the best recognized example is the long-held view that alcoholism runs in families.

1. The lifespan approach to drug use postulates that:
   a. development, change, and transition within individuals are a given.
   b. use patterns ebb and flow over the life course.
   c. biological characteristics may affect use behavior.
   d. all of the above.

WHAT DO WE MEAN BY DRUG USE?

You're probably thinking that the question is simple and the answer is obvious! However, characterizing the topography of drug use "space" is rather complex. For example, do you consider alcohol, nicotine, and prescription medications the same way you do heroin and ecstasy? When would you consider use of a prescription medication illicit—that is, inappropriate, illegal, or harmful? Do you view underage drinking as a form of drug abuse? Does your view separate use patterns and consequences from type of drug? How do you blend traditional estimates of use intensity such as quantity and frequency in characterizing an individual's or a group's use profile? Further, how do you blend patterns of multiple drug use? And, how do you handle change in patterns over time? These are some of the many major challenges that face drug abuse researchers when we attempt to define drug use behavior patterns.

Several viable schemes for classifying drugs (e.g., chemical composition, biological targets, behavioral effects, legal status) are available, a discussion of which could occupy the remainder of the chapter. In some cases, these schema are even at odds with each other. For example, marijuana is both classified as a Schedule 1 controlled dangerous substance by the Food and Drug Administration system and often characterized as a *narcotic* in law enforcement circles, a category reserved for opioids by pharmacologists.

2. A viable scheme for classifying drugs use includes identifying:
   a. chemical composition.
   b. biological target.
   c. behavioral effects.
   d. all of the above.

WHAT IS IT ABOUT THE NATURE OF A DRUG THAT MAKES US CONCERNED ABOUT ITS USE?

Drugs and drug categories typically studied by researchers interested in understanding the development of use behavior in the general population include substances such as alcohol and tobacco, which are legally available; prescription medications, which may be obtained through both legitimate or illegitimate routes; and over-the-counter medications. It probably seems obvious that we as researchers, clinicians, and members of society are concerned about drugs because they have the potential to—and do—cause serious problems. How does this manifest itself in studying drug use? Exhibit 5.1 also provides a set of some of the major common dimensions or delineators that shape research about drug use development. Factors can be arranged on a rough continuum from those that are biological in nature to those that are more socioenvironmental in scope. Hence, a drug's chemical composition, mechanisms of action, potency, and toxicity fall on the more biological pole or dimension of the continuum. A drug's capacity to alter behavioral functioning, including its impact upon overt behaviors and upon brief and longer duration internal mental states, can be summarized broadly as a drug's impact on the individual. These concepts are often viewed categorically as a psychological

EXHIBIT 5.1

Common Harm Potential Delineators

Chemical Composition
Potency
Toxicity
Biologic Targets
Action Mechanisms
Motivations for Use
Methods of Use
Psychobehavioral Effects/Costs
Socioenvironmental Effects/Costs
Social Attitudes/Beliefs
Legal Status

---

or psychobehavioral dimension. Although these considerations are related to primary biological concepts, they are also heavily dependent upon the role played by a person as an active participant in use behavior. In a sense, this dimension reminds us that while drugs can and do cause changes in biological systems, it is not drugs that take people but people who take drugs. Finally, issues such as social norms and use practices, societal attitudes and beliefs about a drug or drug use pattern, real and perceived economic impact and cost of use, legal status and real and perceived impact on the sociogeopolitical environment form the other polar extreme or dimension of the continuum. These factors, though even more remote from a drug's biochemical profile, are also important factors that shape drug use trajectories and are included in the most sophisticated analyses of use trajectories.

The fact that drug use behavior and its development appear to have such a broad impact on, and themselves appear to be impacted by, biological psychobehavioral and sociogeopolitical environmental factors, has led most researchers and clinicians to the view that drug use is a multideterminant disorder and disease. Hence, the dominant theoretical view is that a given drug use disorder and, by implication, all drug use behaviors, are **biopsychosocial** in nature.

3. Clinicians are concerned about drugs because:
   a. of the potential of physical harm to the client.
   b. of the potential impact upon the mental state of the client.
   c. of the impact of the escalating cost on imports.
   d. a & b.

IS THERE A GENERAL TAXONOMY OF DRUG USE DEVELOPMENT THAT ADEQUATELY CAPTURES OUTCOMES, CONDITIONS, AND STATUSES FOR ALL DRUGS OF CONCERN?

What features would such a generic **taxonomy** need to display to be maximally useful for researchers and clinicians? Several questions would have to be addressed. For example, the formulation would have to take into account the multiplicity of biological, psychobehavioral, and socioenvironmental actions and impacts of a wide variety of drugs separately and in combinations. In a similar vein, a highly variable range of use patterns within and between drug categories would need to be incorporated. Individual differences would need to be considered. And, of course, the dynamic changes in use across developmental periods in the lifespan should also be reflected.

Unfortunately, there is no single formulation of use stages, statuses, or outcomes that would be accepted by all in the field as an adequate—let alone comprehensive—base for a general taxonomy of drug use behaviors suited for both research and clinical purposes. There are, however, a variety of approaches used to capture the complexity of developmental use patterns.

4. A very useful feature for determining problem use is:
   a. individual psychological profile.
   b. neighborhood safety.
   c. parental use.
   d. age of onset.

Perhaps, the most formal and systematic attempt at characterizing and standardizing important stages in use development is the *Diagnostic and Statistical Manual of Mental Disorders*, (*DSM–IV–TR*; American Psychiatric Association [APA], 2000). By design, the *DSM–IV* focuses upon the more severe end of the developmental spectrum, that is, disorders and diseases related to use of individual substances (e.g., alcohol, heroin). The *DSM–IV* also makes provisions for multiple drug use outcomes. Though an important and useful clinical standard, it has been challenged as having limited utility for many research purposes, including the development of comprehensive drug use trajectories that are suited to the full range of patterns and outcomes. Nonetheless, the *DSM–IV* is a reasonable clinical tool and we suggest you familiarize yourself with its formulations, particularly when preparing for licensure or in conducting and communicating in routine clinical practice. (The *International Classification of Diseases*, ICD–10, is another example of a categorical approach focusing on the extreme outcome end of the use continuum). These approaches have been operationalized by the development of several instruments (e.g., Diagnostic Interview Schedule) aimed at producing reliable and valid categorizations based on these systems. A major issue raised by researchers is the limitation of categorical approaches, such as that reflected in the *DSM–IV* and *ICD–10* taxonomies, in capturing the more dynamic features of use trajectories. Further, as mentioned above, this approach places emphasis on end state and other pathological outcomes. This is in contrast to taxonomies relying on more dimensional features of use and that include a more comprehensive range of signs and symptoms related to a full range of use statuses.

5. Instruments commonly used for drug use diagnoses, such as the *DSM–IV*:
   a. do not consider multiple drug use.
   b. place emphasis on pathological end states.
   c. are well suited to describing the full range of use outcomes.
   d. none of the above.

Exhibit 5.2 presents common terms often used in characterizing a broader range of stages, statuses, and outcomes. These are presented in order ranging from presumed "least" to presumed "most extensive" experience level or stage of use involvement. Terms at each level

EXHIBIT 5.2

Experimental Stage Model

Common Statuses, Stages, and Outcomes	Dimensions of Defining Criteria
Nonuse/Nonuser Use/User Misuse/Misuser Abuse/Abuser Problem Use/ Problem User Dependence/Dependent User Addiction/Addict Recovery/Recovering Addict	1. Use Intensity Typical Measurement = Quantity & Frequency/Unit Time, provides estimate of level/length of intoxication episodes 2. Use Impact Typical Measurement = Aggregated Problem Index, indicates cumulative short/long term consequences on behavioral competencies, physical functioning interpersonal interactions, systemic relationships

of involvement refer to both an **experiential stage** (e.g., use) and an individual's status (e.g., user). Even what would appear the most clear-cut consensus terms, *nonuse* and *nonuser*, are not always simple to operationally define. For example, nonuser may refer either to "not currently a user, but have used in the past" or to "never having used." You might also find it curious to consider nonuse as an active behavior pattern under either definition! However, consider a twenty-two- or twenty-three-year-old healthy male or female college student who does not and has never used alcohol. It is likely that sustaining this use pattern is effortful and has a very interesting dynamic.

The other end of the experiential spectrum—recovery and recovering addict (or dependent user, in remission)—represents a presumed level of involvement that includes movement through a series of steps or stages. These stages range from simple exposure through prolonged or extensive use, dependence, and then presumably return to the lowest level of use involvement, nonuse or abstinence. Given the generic nature of the steps along the spectrum, each step would seem to have the capacity to accommodate a wide range of drugs without the need for separate stage descriptors for different drugs. Superficially, at least, it would appear that similar criteria could be used to define steps for each drug. Two sets of criteria come to mind that capture two interrelated dimensions of various stages. *Criterion set one* can be viewed as capturing a use *intensity* dimension. Typically, assessing the quantity (q) of a drug used and the frequency (f) of its use define this dimension. To obtain a more complete picture, assessment often includes some estimate of the unit of time (ut) for which q/f estimates are obtained. In this way, we hope to capture a picture of how much time an individual spends under the influence of a particular drug and the level of that influence. *Criterion set two* attempts to capture the *impact* of a particular $q/f\,ut$ pattern. This dimension attempts to estimate the aggregated consequences upon an individual associated with a particular $q/f\,ut$ pattern. Impact assessments typically include effects on short- and long-term behaviors and behavioral capacity, biological organ systems, interpersonal interactions, and systemic relationships.

6. Critical dimensions of consumption to capture include all *except*:
   a. quantity–frequency.
   b. times ever used.
   c. beverage of choice.
   d. frequency of intoxications.

This experiential spectrum approach also presents some problems and limitations. An important consideration is the fact that experiential stages may vary considerably in one or both dimensions and may require combing information from both dimensions. Status as a *user* may encompass a very wide range of q/f use patterns that overlap with all other more intensive experiential stages. Hence, it may be difficult to determine acceptable quantitative boundaries that mark the transition between statuses. For example, at what point on the intensity dimension does a user transit to the problem use status? Of course, the issue of defining transition points between more severe statuses requires balancing intensity and impact dimensions. It is also sometimes the case that these two critical dimensions may carry differential weight in defining user status. Another set of problems focuses upon the issue of equivalency of criteria across drug categories. In other words, are intensity and impact criteria weighted in the same manner for all drugs or drug categories in determining statuses? For example, does twice weekly use of alcohol equate to twice weekly use of cocaine irrespective of impact? And, what status do you assign each use pattern?

7. It is difficult to determine boundaries that mark the transition from use to abuse to dependence due to:
   a. disparity about what constitutes "heavy use."
   b. dispute about current legal sanctions against use of drugs by certain groups and in certain circumstances.
   c. variation in the nature and extent of outcomes related to use.
   d. all of the above.

A related issue is the manner in which information about several drugs is blended at any point in time and across snapshots. This bears on an important question in the drug field that we will return to later in this chapter, that is, does use of one drug lead to use of another? This is the so called **gateway hypothesis**.

WHAT ARE SOME OF THE IMPORTANT ISSUES TO CONSIDER IN DETERMINING AND CHARACTERIZING TRANSITIONS BETWEEN DRUG USE STAGES?

The transitional period model, outlined in Exhibit 5.3, differentiates three primary **developmental processes** or periods. Each of these periods is further differentiated into more fluid or elastic phases that reflect the fact that transitions are, or at least appear, continuous or smooth in nature and that the boundaries between periods and phases are not always clearly demarcated. (For an in-depth discussion, we recommend Pandina & Johnson, 1999, as well as the other chapters in Glantz & Hartel, 1999). In these types of models, the emphasis is more upon describing the processes that occur, rather than on use identifying outcomes such as those represented in experiential stage models.

The *acquisition period* refers to the developmental period during which an individual initiates use behaviors and begins to experiment with various forms of use. Note that the earliest phase in the acquisition period occurs prior to actual use initiation. This phase is labeled *priming*. Inclusion of this phase is a way of acknowledging that individuals are exposed to many "facts" and "rules" (including accurate information, folklore, and myths) about drug use prior to any actual experiences involving drugs. Thus, parental and peer models, media representations, and other potential behavior-shaping influences may set up, incline, or prime the individual toward use. *Initiation* is defined as an individual's first set of actual experiences of use. Much attention is now being focused upon this phase by some researchers to

EXHIBIT 5.3

Developmental/Transitional Process Model

I. *Acquisition Period*	III. *Control Period*
A. Priming Phase	A. Problem Awareness Phase
B. Initiation Phase	B. Interruption/Suspension Phase
C. Experimentation Phase	C. Cessation Phase
II. *Maintenance Period*	
A. Habit Formation Phase	
B. Dependence Phase	
C. Obsessive-Compulsive Phase	

determine whether initial reactions to things like first drinking experience or first reaction to cigarette smoke may signal later risk for escalation to, or protection from, more intensive use experiences. Such indicators are being developed for a wide range of investigations including those seeking to identify specific genetic links for addiction liability. Finally, the later phase of acquisition is designated *experimentation*. Here, the individual learns by doing. The "new" behavior may be viewed as a unique behavior or featured event. In this phase, a particular form of use behavior is becoming a more regular feature of the general behavioral repertoire as the individual gains in more experiences involving a substance.

8. Priming:
   a. is a positive result of the individual's first use of a drug.
   b. is bias not related to genetic links for addiction.
   c. occurs upon actual use.
   d. refers to an individual's expectations about drug use.

The *maintenance period* is marked by the transition to regularized use. In this period, use behaviors become more clearly integrated into the general response. The period is characterized by a sequence of phases ranging from habit formation to dependence to obsessive-compulsive use. The *habit formation* phase is characterized by the increased integration of the use behavior from one viewed as a novel event to one viewed as routine—a habit. The behavior is viewed as being under the choice and control of the individual and not one leading to significant or chronic negative consequences. The *dependence* phase is marked by signs and symptoms typically associated with clinical manifestations and diagnoses of use-related disorders. In this phase, users employ drugs to maintain behavioral (and often physical) homeostasis; cessation of the drug causes serious dysfunction for the user. What we have identified as the *obsessive-compulsive* phase recognizes that drug dependence, as defined in clinical schema such as the *DSM–IV*, may not be a homogeneous entity. A subset of users meeting such criteria may be more seriously affected to the extent, for example, that they are no longer able to maintain dynamic homeostatic control even when they continue to use the drug. Arguably, this phase may mark the most severe end stage outcome of dependence and may not be a truly separate phase.

9. In the maintenance phase:
   a. use is not yet habitual.
   b. the user regards consumption as a choice.
   c. use does not have negative consequences.
   d. cessation causes problems for the user.

Of course, it is not inevitable that individuals who enter the acquisition or maintenance period for a particular substance automatically transit to the next period or phase within a period. It does appear, however, that transitions to more "advanced" locations in the cycle require passing through earlier phases. A key aspect of trajectory research is the determination of factors that foster or inhibit transition to more advanced use patterns as well as the manner in which these factors serve to escalate or limit use development. We add a third developmental period to the developmental process model, which we identify as the *control period*. While other researchers often describe only acquisition and maintenance, we believe it is important to consider control or limitation of use to a particular period or phase as an active transitional process. In the control period, the individual begins to recognize that use at the level of development they are experiencing has created, or has the potential of creating, problems in an important life domain.

Alternatively, control may be marked by the recognition that moving to the next phase in a period would create a serious risk to important life functioning. Hence, control begins with a *problem awareness* phase that results from actual or anticipated consequences related to a particular use pattern. This phase is followed by an *interruption* or *suspension* phase in which a particular use behavior is either limited to its current form (in the case that it is anticipated that escalation to the next period would result in harm) or regressed to an earlier form or phase (in the case that actual harm has occurred or harm is anticipated). In the final phase—*cessation*—an individual may abandon a particular use behavior for short or longer periods of time.

10. In the control phase, the individual contemplates:
    a. that the drug isn't causing problems.
    b. moving to the next phase of use may solve problems.
    c. abandoning the substance use.
    d. all of the above.

What is unique about control processes is that they are superimposed upon, and operate parallel to, other developmental processes during acquisition and maintenance. Control processes result in limiting use to a particular use phase. Interestingly, control processes may and do result in limitations as early as the priming phase of acquisition for many people and for many drugs. For example, most individuals acquire information about heroin use that invokes control processes limiting even use initiation. Hence, these processes actively block exposure and nonuse becomes an automatic feature of the drug use repertoire. We view nonuse of a drug as an actively maintained pattern.

11. In the developmental process model, transitions of drug use include all *except*:
    a. control.
    b. contemplation.
    c. acquisition.
    d. maintenance.

12. The maintenance phase of drug abuse goes from:
    a. habit formation to obsessive-compulsive use.
    b. binge use to dependence.
    c. dependence to despair.
    d. none of the above.

13. All of the following are associated with drug acquisition stage, *except*:
    a. observation of parental use.
    b. experiencing physical craving for drugs.
    c. positive reaction to initial use.
    d. forms positive attitudes toward use by viewing media.

14. Which of the following are associated with drug maintenance stage?
    a. the need to preserve system homeostasis
    b. cessation of use causing serious system dysfunction
    c. a & b
    d. neither a nor b

15. The characteristic that is unique about the control phase of drug use is:
    a. the processes here operate in tandem to processes found in acquisition and mainte-
       nance.
    b. the individual never recognizes the potential problems of drug use.
    c. there can be regression to a former phase.
    d. none of the above.

Stage and developmental transition models are neither incompatible nor mutually exclusive. They are, in fact, complementary, capturing different features of drug use trajectory characteristics. Transition models, like stage models, can be used as templates to capture repeated snapshots of individuals' use of the many substances. Taken together, these snapshots can yield informative use profiles of an individual or group. The problems of establishing quantitative and qualitative standards and other indicators that may mark the boundaries of transitions between periods and phases remain a challenge for researchers as they did in the case of the stage model. To some extent, the problems of equivalences of criteria are eased in that this model focuses upon identifying common processes and may avoid more value-laden comparisons such as equating problem use with varying and sometimes arbitrary levels of exposure for different drugs. Such models may also help in trying to capture the blend of various use behaviors as well as the fluctuations in various patterns across time.

Next, we turn to the question of whether drug use "causes" further drug use and, if so, why and how this happens.

DOES DRUG USE BEGET DRUG USE? IF SO, ARE THERE PROTOTYPE DRUGS OR USE BEHAVIORS THAT TRIGGER DRUG USE ESCALATION?

One of the consistent results of many studies of the past several decades was that one of the best predictors of future drug use was drug use itself! That is, drug use tended to persist over time especially when use behavior occurred at an early age. This view, although greatly elaborated upon, continues today and is reflected in such recent controversial observations that early onset of alcohol use may be a potent predictor of alcohol dependence in adulthood. Perhaps more important for the study of trajectories was the observation that drug use behaviors appeared to have an orderly sequence of expression, at least in regard to onset of involvement. Kandel and colleagues (Kandel & Yamaguchi, 2002) were among the first researchers to demonstrate a prototypical sequence in the development of drug use in a sample of young people followed across time. A typical sequence of drug use onset described by Kandel and colleagues and often replicated by other research teams (including our own) uses a three-stage model to describe the general sequence of onset development. First, a three stage mode tends to describe the general sequence of onset development. The legal substances (alcohol and cigarettes) appear to be initiated in a first stage of use, followed by a second stage in which marijuana is initiated, and finally in a third stage, cocaine and subsequently heroin are initiated after marijuana. In stage one, the dominant sequence is movement from alcohol to marijuana initiation. In a variant of this stage, cigarette use is initiated prior to alcohol use and a large proportion of those who initiate both go on to begin marijuana use. In some cases in stage three, heroin use precedes cocaine use. Second, "progression" is not always the rule, nor is it inevitable. Individuals who are operating in an earlier development stage do not necessarily move on to the next stage. Third, individuals who do move on to other stages may not remain in those stages; that is, they may regress to earlier sequences (see also Bates & Labouvie, 1997; Labouvie, Bates, & Pandina, 1997; Labouvie & White, 2002). Finally, the model does not include a major pathway for other drugs such as hallucinogens or prescription medications. However, in other work, researchers (including Kandel) have identified a sequence in which marijuana use (preceded by alcohol and/or cigarettes) precedes other drugs such as hallucinogens and prescription medications. Further, subpathways from alcohol directly to prescription medications have been identified.

16. In the three-stage model:
    a. stage one is usually the movement from tobacco to alcohol.
    b. individuals usually move on to the next stage of use.
    c. marijuana use comes in the second stage.
    d. heroin and then cocaine comprise stage three.

Does this mean that cigarettes, alcohol, and marijuana can act like "gateway" drugs to stimulate or cause greater drug involvement? The notion of progression along the use continuum is one of the more difficult and complex issues encountered in discussing drug use trajectories. (For a thorough discussion you are referred to an excellent book edited by Denise Kandel, 2002.) In the 1970s and 1980s, it became popular to interpret results regarding use pathways like those discussed to mean that marijuana use "caused" progression to use of other more "dangerous" forms of drug use behavior (e.g., cocaine and heroin). This interpretation, however, was an oversimplification of a very complex phenomenon and, in fact, was not the interpretation intended or favored by researchers. Nonetheless, the notion of gateway drugs (where gateway is equated with causation) has remained a popular characterization. Of course, delaying onset of use is a significant outcome in and of itself but it is far from certain that drug use of any kind sustains or causes drug use in the absence of consideration of a host of other **risk factors** (Pandina, 1998).

17. Which of the following is *not* applicable to the gateway hypothesis?
    a. "Gateway" is equated with causation.
    b. It demonstrates prototypical sequencing in the development of drug use.
    c. Progression from one to stage to another is inevitable.
    d. Use of legal substances typically precedes use of illegal substances.

18. All of the following are hypothesized to be gateway drugs *except*:
    a. ecstasy.
    b. marijuana.
    c. alcohol.
    d. cigarettes.

WHAT ARE SOME OF THE OTHER USE-RELATED FACTORS THAT INFLUENCE THE DEVELOPMENT OF DRUG USE TRAJECTORIES?

The initial research on sequencing of drug use involvement focused upon a relatively narrow aspect of use—onset or initiation. Subsequent research broadened the scope of the gateway question by looking at other aspects of use that might improve our understanding of use progression. An important and consistent finding was the relationship between intensity of use of an "early" sequence substance and likelihood of advancing in the use sequence. By and large, individuals experiencing more intensive use involvement with a drug at a given stage are considerably more likely to become involved in substances at later stages. Other "soft" use-related factors appear to influence the development of use. For example, beliefs about the perceived benefits and potential risks of use are related to the intention or inclination to use and to actual use behaviors among both individuals who may have some exposure to a drug and, significantly, to those who have not yet initiated use. Hence, expectancies may act to sustain, and possibly escalate, use among those who have initiated use and may be a stimulating factor acting to prime use among those who may not have initiated. It is worth noting that experiences with one drug may set the tone for expectancies about other drugs, at least to the extent that generic experiential learning about use itself may transfer between drugs. The learning transfer may be affected by a number of variables. For example, upper middle class youths for whom cigarette, alcohol, and marijuana use are all illegal may be willing to experiment with these substances partly because of a view that these are "soft" drugs whose use is part of their adolescent social scene. However, these same youth may draw the line at heroin use because of social stigmas related to the heroin user among adults and peers in their social networks.

19. Expectancies:
    a. sustain use.
    b. escalate use.
    c. stimulate use for those who haven't initiated.
    d. all of the above.

20. Which of the following is *not* related to intention to use drugs?
    a. beliefs about perceived benefits
    b. beliefs about perceived risks
    c. beliefs about generic learning
    d. beliefs about population usage

   A host of other factors influence the development of drug use trajectories that are related to biological, psychological, and social characteristics. Before we turn attention to these risk factors we need to explore another fundamental issue of use trajectories having to do with their stability.

ARE THERE PRIMARY OR PROTOTYPIC TRAJECTORIES? HOW DO DRUG USE TRAJECTORIES CHANGE ACROSS TIME?

Thus far, we have discussed definitions of use behaviors, identified various models for characterizing use development, and explored problems in tracking sequences in use of various substances. We turn attention now to looking at examples of various use trajectories. It would not be possible in the space allotted to present a detailed summary of all the research conducted in this area. We refer those of you who wish to dig deeper to several excellent sources (e.g., Bachman et al., 2002; Glantz & Hartel, 1999; Glantz & Pickens, 1992; Kandel, 2002; Lettieri, Sayers, & Pearson, 1980). In attempting to give you a cross-sectional glimpse at prototypic use trajectories and the manner in which researchers study them, we draw upon work conducted in our own research group, the Health and Human Development Laboratory. The trajectories we discuss are derived from a longitudinal study we have been conducting for more than twenty years (Pandina, Labouvie, & White, 1984). In this study, begun in 1978, we tracked the use

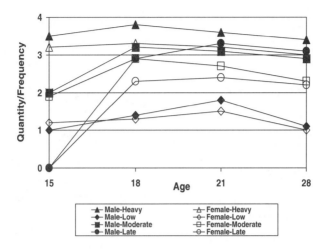

EXHIBIT 5.4. Trajectories based on quantity/frequency of alcohol use.

behaviors and outcomes as well as related etiologic factors among about 1300 individuals drawn from a representative community sample. We began observing them as early as age twelve and have repeatedly assessed their use behavior. All of these subjects are now well into their thirties. By using these examples we hope to give you a flavor for representative types of trajectories you can expect to see in the general population.

First, we examined "simple" use trajectories for the substance most commonly used in our society, alcohol. The developmental trajectories were based on reports of the quantity and frequency of alcohol use, thus representing the intensity dimension of use. We have found that for both males and females, alcohol use escalates dramatically between ages 15 and 20, well before individuals reach the legal drinking age.

Using growth curve analyses applied to these data, we were able to discern significant subtrajectories or drinking profiles for both men and women. Exhibit 5.4 identifies four dynamic drinking profiles. We characterize these profiles as *low level drinking* through the period of observation, *late onset drinking* (individuals lagging behind the group norm, eventually settling into a moderate drinking profile), *consistently moderate drinking* from mid-adolescence into adulthood, and, *consistently heavy drinking* from mid-adolescence into adulthood.

21. Which statement best characterizes the development of drinking profiles?
    a. Drinking does not become a well-established behavior in most people until adulthood.
    b. There are a variety of drinking profiles characterizing several prototypical trajectories.
    c. Drinking profiles established during early adulthood remain stable across the remainder of the lifespan.
    d. Drinking profiles are the same for both men and women.

These same caveats apply in attempts to characterize problematic outcomes related to use. Specifically, there are several subtypes of drinking outcome profiles, each with very distinctive characteristics. It has long been observed that drinking intensity and negative drinking outcomes are not perfectly correlated (e.g., White & Labouvie, 1989)—thus, the importance of considering impact as a separate profiling dimension. Exhibit 5.5 illustrates major prototypes of "problem" trajectory profiles related to alcohol use for the same individuals whose

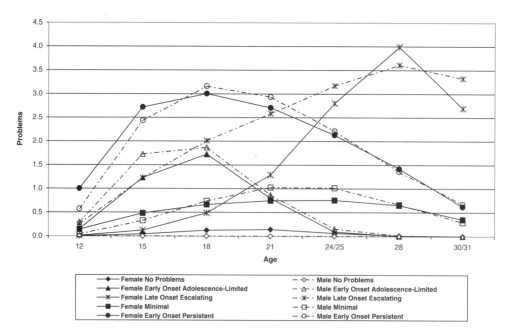

EXHIBIT 5.5. Trajectories based on alcohol related problems.

drinking profiles are described above. Six prototype problem profiles are identified: no problem (NP); moderate problem, with deceleration in adulthood (MP); adolescent limited problem (AP); chronic problem, with deceleration in adulthood (CP); and late onset, rapid escalation (LEP).

> 22. Which statement most accurately describes the development of problem drinking?
>   a. There is a direct correspondence between drinking intensity and problem drinking.
>   b. Problem drinking in adolescence inevitably predicts problem drinking in adulthood.
>   c. Drinking related problems may emerge and subside across the lifespan.
>   d. People who postpone drinking until adulthood do not develop drinking problems.

A number of important points are illustrated by these trajectories. First, a distinction can be made between problematic outcomes that are limited primarily to adolescence (APs) and those that are persistent and extend into mid-adulthood (CPs). The CP trajectories are more serious in that they are more intensive and continue for relatively long periods in the lifespan, hence, increasing the likelihood of longer term accumulation of negative consequences. AP trajectories suggest a more time-limited set of problems spiking in early- to mid-adolescence and "maturing" out over time. Second, there is a tendency for problem intensities to diminish even in the CP grouping; however, it is likely that the impact on other areas of life will continue even after drinking-related problems abate. The AP/CP distinction has been noted for other forms of problem behaviors (e.g., Moffit, 1993; White, Bates, & Buyske, 2001; White, Johnson, & Buyske, 2000). Third, our research has identified another very important trajectory, namely, late onset of use-related problems that escalate, achieve a very high impact rating, and appear to maintain at a very high level into mid-adulthood (LEP). This pattern appears to emerge at an earlier age and developmental stage for men than for women but a significant number of women are represented in this potentially dangerous trajectory.

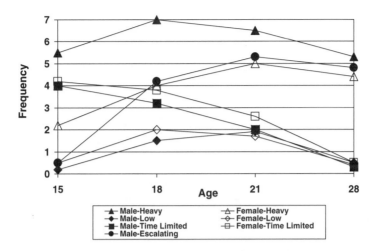

EXHIBIT 5.6.   Trajectories based on frequency of marijuana use.

23. In comparing the development of drinking and drug use patterns, which statement is most accurate?
   a. Drinking and drug use profiles differ significantly in general trajectory characteristics.
   b. Drinking and drug use trajectories share similar characteristics.
   c. Drug use results in more severe outcomes.
   d. Drug use, once established, tends to remain constant across time whereas alcohol use patterns show greater fluctuation.

We have been using examples of trajectories drawn from alcohol use. Do the general principles discussed for drinking apply to use of other substances? We have found that rates of use are much lower for any substance other than alcohol at every developmental stage of growth. In addition, women are slightly less drug involved than are men across the lifespan. Finally, as with alcohol, drug use involvement tends to peak in late adolescence and early adulthood and declines sharply thereafter. As we learned with alcohol, however, closer inspection of a given drug reveals more complex patterns. We will use data about marijuana use intensity and problems in our community sample to illustrate this point.

Exhibit 5.6 provides information about frequency of marijuana use over time. Four distinctive "growth curves" or involvement trajectories paralleling those observed for alcohol are discernable: trajectory 1, low level use diminishing during early adulthood; trajectory 2, more intensive use beginning in adolescence limited primarily to that period of development; trajectory 3, relatively late onset of use continuing into adulthood and escalating to heavier use; and trajectory 4, persistent or chronic heavy use that appears to be well established during adolescence. Both genders are represented in most trajectories with the exception of the heaviest persistent pattern, which is dominated by men. More intensive use by women appears to emerge somewhat later and does reach levels as high as males by the time of adulthood. As was the case with alcohol use, the largest proportion of cases falls within the trajectories characterized by the more moderate levels of involvement.

Exhibit 5.7 presents significant trajectories for problem marijuana use. In general, some of the same key features we noted for alcohol are observed for marijuana. At the extreme ends, patterns representing chronic, more intensive problems (trajectories 5, 6, and 7) and low level problem involvement (1, 2, and 3) are similar to those observed for major alcohol trajectories.

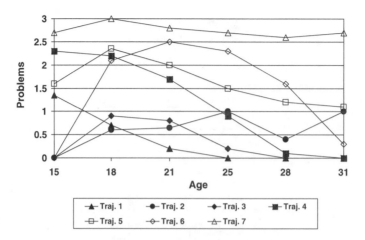

EXHIBIT 5.7. Trajectories based on marijuana related problems.

There are some notable differences. In trajectory 6, problem levels increase dramatically in late adolescence and persist through young adulthood and then decline. To some extent, this pattern mirrors the late onset rapid escalation (LEP) alcohol trajectory. Low level problem trajectory 2 appears to have an intermittent characteristic that suggests recurrent problem emergence, though at lower intensity levels. Trajectory 4 appears to be a variant of adolescent limited patterns where relatively intensive problems diminish during adulthood.

Although there are interesting and subtle differences and variations in trajectory character-istics, the broader features identified for alcohol use patterns are also apparent for marijuana. These broader features may be summarized in four general patterns: chronic, more intensive problems; low level problems that diminish with age; developmental stage limited problems; and late onset, relatively intensive, and persistent problems.

24. Which one of the following is *not* a general pattern found for marijuana related prob-
    lems?
    a. high level of persistent patterns across the lifespan
    b. high levels of problems found at adolescence and older adulthood only
    c. persistent low levels, associated with experimental use
    d. the numbers of problems spiking in adolescence followed by nonuse

Can these broad features be applied to other drugs such as cocaine, heroin, and nicotine? For most other drug categories, with the exception of nicotine, exposure to drugs among the general population is fairly limited. It is probably fair to say that for most drugs, the domi-nant use patterns are: low level intermittent or transient use tending to diminish during the transition to adulthood; adolescence/early adulthood, limited with (somewhat more intensive use); and persistent use emerging in late adolescence characterized by heavier use involvement. Low level intermittent and developmentally limited patterns are accompanied by few persistent problems. This does not mean that these patterns are not without potentially serious risks, how-ever. There are clearly limited instances of harmful, sometimes life-threatening consequences given the toxicity potential of many of these substances. For the most part, chronic heavier drug use trajectories, such as would be indicative of dependence, contain relatively fewer cases. As we noted, the exception is probably nicotine, where a significant portion of individuals fall into persistent heavier use trajectories indicative of dependence.

25. Which is true?
    a. Except for nicotine, exposure to drugs is fairly limited among the general population.
    b. A significant portion of individuals fall into heavy persistent nicotine use.
    c. Low-level intermittent drug use is without serious risk.
    d. a and b

26. Why is even limited use of so-called hard drugs considered harmful?
    a. toxicity potential is high
    b. legal sanctions are harsh
    c. dependence potential is great
    d. all of the above

ARE THERE OTHER FACTORS THAT ACCOMPANY, INFLUENCE, OR "PREDICT" THE DEVELOPMENT OF DRUG USE?

Perhaps the "holy grail" of drug abuse etiological research is the quest to identify the quintessential "factor" that triggers a use or problem trajectory resulting in the more serious pathological end states (e.g., dependence). In spite of the extensive efforts of a large cadre of researchers, as of this writing, no single factor or set of factors has emerged as a leading candidate (Clayton, 1992; Glantz & Hartel, 1999; Glantz & Pickens, 1992; Hawkins, Catalano, & Miller, 1992; Leshner, 1998; Pandina, 1998; Petraitis, Flay, & Miller, 1995). In fact, several recent attempts to catalogue potential risk factors have identified considerably more than one hundred apparently different ones that seem to have sufficient "explanatory" power over important aspects of drug use development to warrant serious consideration.

Mrazek and Haggerty (1994, p.127) define *risk factors* as "those characteristics, variables, or hazards that, if present for a given individual, make it more likely that this individual, rather than someone selected at random from the general population, will develop a disorder." The presence of potential *protective factors*, conversely, reduces the likelihood that such outcomes will occur. Many researchers (e.g., Anthony & Cohler, 1987; Campos, Hinden, & Gerhardt, 1995) consider protective factors important buffers that may build resilience in otherwise susceptible individuals. Exhibit 5.8 presents important characteristics of such risk and protective factors. Many identified risk and protective factors have not been definitively causally linked to specific use outcomes. Often, such factors have secondary or moderating influence in shaping use

EXHIBIT 5.8

General Characteristics of Risk and Protective Factors

- *markers*—surface indicators
- *modifiers*—secondary influences
- *mediators*—primary mechanisms
- can be cumulative or synergistic
- risk and protective factors may differ qualitatively and quantitatively
- variations in importance across individuals or groups
- variations in influence at different times during life cycle
- variations in significance for the emergence of drug use stages and outcomes
- are subject to change and can be significantly reduced or induced

outcomes; that is, they may play only a partial, though significant, role in outcomes. Still other factors may be surface indicators of more fundamental processes or a set of processes marked by the indicator. Life events may not "cause" a change in drug use behavior in and of themselves but these may signify or mark many life course processes that summate to produce change.

27. Which of the following does *not* characterize a risk factor?
    a. They can be mediators of use behavior.
    b. They can be moderators of risk behavior.
    c. They are associated with only high levels of use.
    d. They can be indicators of use behavior.

Researchers in our laboratory (e.g., Bry, 1983; Bry, McKeon, & Pandina, 1982) using data from the longitudinal study we described previously in this chapter, were among the first to note a significant association between the number of risk factors present in a given individual and the likelihood that the individual would experience an extreme use outcome. Further, we demonstrated that the early presence of larger numbers of risk factors predicted more extreme outcomes in subsequent developmental stages. Since this initial work, a number of investigators have replicated these findings and have methodologically refined the risk factor approach (Newcomb & Felix-Ortiz, 1992; Newcomb, Maddahian, & Bentler, 1986).

Exhibit 5.9 presents a relatively broad example of what such a taxonomy of risk factors might look like. Note that we identify three major domains of factors—biological, psychobehavioral, and socioenvironmental—and included in these domains are specific factor categories that serve to illustrate the kinds of factors to be considered under each subheading.

28. Which of the following statements about risk factors is most accurate?
    a. The number of risk factors exhibited is the most potent predictor of subsequent problem use.
    b. Specific risk factors are related to specific types of use behavior.
    c. Only more extreme forms of use (such as dependence) are related to risk factors.
    d. None of the above.

In clinical practice, appreciation of the risk factor approach can be useful in assessing and intervening with clients. Exhibit 5.10 (adopted from Newcomb et al., 1986) indicates the relationship between number of risk factors and frequency of use for five different substance categories. Subsequent research by Newcomb & Felix-Ortiz (1992) demonstrated that these risk factor estimates were potent predictors of use outcomes many years after initial assessment. That follow-up work also examined protective factors and determined that such factors may buffer individuals against adverse outcomes. These relationships emphasize the importance of assessing risk and protective factors in attempting to understand the development of use intensity and related problematic trajectories.

29. Assessing risk factors in individuals or groups is most useful for:
    a. scientists attempting to understand drug use etiology.
    b. clinicians treating clients.
    c. public health officials estimating intervention needs of a community.
    d. all of the above.

EXHIBIT 5.9

Classification Schema for Risk and Protective Factors

Major Biological Factors
- genetic profile
- sensory processing disturbances
- neurocognitive alterations
- personal history of affective disorders, impulse disorders
- family history of alcoholism, drug abuse
- family history of impulse disorders (e.g., conduct disorder, antisocial personality)
- family history of affective disorders and emotional disturbance (e.g., depression, anxiety)

Major Psychological/Behavioral Factors
- personality styles (e.g., sensation seeking, harm avoidance, reinforcement sensitivity)
- emotional profile
- self-regulation style (e.g., coping repertoire)
- behavioral competence
- positive and negative life events/experiences
- attitudes, values, beliefs regarding drug use

Major Social/Environmental Factors
- structure/function of family supports
- parenting styles
- opportunities for development of basic competencies
- peer affiliations
- economic and social (including educational) opportunities
- general social support structure
- availability of prosocial activities in relevant environments (e.g., schools, communities, workplace)
- strength and influence of the faith community
- social norms, attitudes, and beliefs related to drug use
- availability and projected attractiveness of drugs and drug use

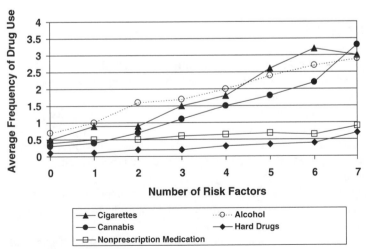

Note. From Newcomb, Maddahian, & Bentler, 1986.

EXHIBIT 5.10. Frequency of substance use by number of risk factors.

FINAL COMMENTARY

We believe that in order to understand fully the development and expression of drug use behavior it is essential to consider characteristics and dynamics of normative changes and transitions in human maturation and development. Interventions may require adjustments in their application to account for the considerable variability that characterizes differences in the trajectories of development throughout the entire lifespan.

In this same vein, drug use itself needs to be viewed as a dynamic developmental process consisting of distinctive phases and stages although arguably the boundaries between phases and stages may be somewhat difficult to gauge. Nonetheless, we believe that intervention opportunities need to incorporate knowledge about the development and staging of drug use behaviors including the manner in which individuals acquire and integrate information about substance use into their behavioral repertoire.

Finally, etiological research, to date, has identified and linked a myriad of putative moderating and mediating influences (currently characterized in the literature as risk and protective factors) to differing degrees, with varying aspects of substance use behaviors. Important challenges in the intervention process include: identifying the impact that different etiological factors have in affecting drug use trajectories; understanding how these factors may vary in influencing transitions between various use stages as a function of differences in human developmental stages; and, applying such knowledge in developing and implementing interventions.

30. In what ways are risks associated with the frequency of drug use?
    a. the particular type of risk factor
    b. the total number of risk factors
    c. the balance of risk and protective factors
    d. all of the above

KEY TERMS

biopsychosocial model of drug use behaviors: The view that drug use does not occur in a vacuum and, in fact, can be explained only by the interplay of biological, intrapersonal, interpersonal, and environmental influences.

developmental process model of drug use: Model that outlines three phases of drug use, namely acquisition, maintenance, and control.

drug use trajectories: Longitudinal sequencing of drug use behaviors. Also referred to as drug use pathways; typically measured using drug type, drug use intensity, and drug use–related consequences.

experiential stage model: Method of describing the common stages of drug use beginning with abstainer and transiting to user, misuser, abuser, problem user, dependent user, addict, and recovering addict.

gateway hypothesis: Controversial model that postulates that use of one substance causes progression to use of other more dangerous forms of drug use behavior.

lifespan development: This perspective acknowledges the dynamic nature of human behavior, including drug-using behaviors. Drug use patterns fluctuate within a given individual and within subpopulations.

risk and protective factors: Factors found to be related to initiation of and escalation in drug use behaviors. These have been described to be biological, psychological, and social in nature.

taxonomy: Systematic classification scheme organizing concepts according to meaningful or functional categories.

DISCUSSION QUESTIONS

1. Why is it important for a clinician to consider the equivalency of criteria across drug groups in their assessments using the *DSM–IV*?
2. Why is it important for a clinician to deliver interventions that are developmentally appropriate considering both the specific drug of abuse, as well as for the stage of the individual's problem?
3. What are some of the important factors in defining the transitions from use to abuse?
4. Under what circumstances would you consider use of a prescription medication inappropriate?
5. How would you determine ways to place weight onto a variety of drug use consequences, ranging from those affecting cognitive functioning to legal status?
6. What degree of increase or decrease in drug use intensity should be considered clinically significant?
7. What level of change in drug use consequences should be considered clinically significant?
8. How might the set of risk factors for drug use and escalation change for an individual over his or her life course?
9. Do you consider the use of multiple drugs to have an additive, synergetic, or exponential effect? Why?
10. How can knowledge about drug use trajectories help you to assess and plan for your client?

ACKNOWLEDGMENT

We would like to acknowledge the support provided by the National Institute on Drug Abuse (DA 03395 and DA 17552), the National Institute on Alcohol Abuse and Alcoholism (AA 11699) and by the Peter F. McManus Charitable Trust.

SUGGESTED FURTHER READING

Broderick, P. C., & Blewitt, P. (2002). *The lifespan: Human development for helping professionals*. Upper Saddle River, NJ: Prentice Hall.

This book will help practitioners to have a working knowledge of developmental research. The book introduces theoretical models and issues and explores physical, social, and cognitive development from infancy to later life.

Chassin, L., Collins, R. L., Ritter, J., & Shirley, M. C. (2001). Vulnerability to substance use disorders across the lifespan. In R. E. Ingram & J. M. Price (Eds.), *Vulnerability to psychopathology: Risk across the lifespan* (pp. 165–172). New York: Guilford Press.

This book reviews concepts of vulnerability in psychopathology. The Chassin chapter examines alcohol and substance abuse in terms of adolescents and adults.

Juntunen, C. L., & Atkinson, D. R. (Eds.). (2002). *Counseling across the lifespan: Prevention and treatment.* Thousand Oaks, CA: Sage.

This book focuses on counseling intervention strategies from the perspective of an individual's lifespan.

Ray, O. S., & Ksir, C. J. (2004). *Drugs, society and human behavior with PowerWeb: Drugs and HealthQuest 3.0.* New York: McGraw-Hill.

This book provides current facts and information about drugs from a variety of perspectives, including behavioral, pharmacological, historical, social, legal, and clinical.

REFERENCES

American Psychiatric Association. (2000). *Diagnostic and statistical manual of mental disorders* (text rev.). (4th ed.). Washington, DC: Author.

Anthony, E. J., & Cohler, B. J. (Eds.).(1987). *The invulnerable child.* New York: Guilford Press.

Bachman, J. G., O'Malley, P. M., Schulenberg, J. E., Johnston, L. D., Bryant, A. L., & Merline, A. C. (2002). *The decline of substance use in young adulthood: Changes in social activities, roles, and beliefs.* Mahwah, NJ: Lawerence Erlbaum Associates.

Bates, M. E., & Labouvie, E. W. (1997). Adolescent risk factors and the prediction of persistent alcohol and drug use into adulthood. *Alcoholism: Clinical and Experimental Research, 21*(5), 944–950.

Bry, B. (1983). Predicting drug abuse: Review and reformulation. *International Journal of Addiction, 18,* 223–233.

Bry, B. H., McKeon, P., & Pandina, R. J. (1982). Extent of drug use as a function of number of risk factors. *Journal of Abnormal Psychology, 91*(4), 273–279.

Campos, B. E., Hinden, B. R., & Gerhardt, C. A. (1995). Adolescent development: Pathways and processes of risk and resilience. *Annual Review of Psychology, 46,* 265–293.

Clayton, R. (1992). Transitions in drug use: Risk and protective factors. In M. Glantz & R. Pickens (Eds.), *Vulnerability to drug abuse* (pp. 15–51). Washington, DC: American Psychological Association.

Glantz, M. D., & Hartel, C. R. (Eds.). (1999). *Drug abuse: Origins and interventions.* Washington DC: American Psychological Association.

Glantz, M. D., & Pickens, R. (Eds.). (1992). *Vulnerability to drug abuse.* Washington, DC: American Psychological Association.

Hawkins, J. D., Catalano, R. F., & Miller, J. Y. (1992). Risk and protective factors for alcohol and other drug problems in adolescence and early adulthood: Implications for substance abuse prevention. *Psychological Bulletin, 112*(1), 64–105.

Kandel, D. B. (Ed.). (2002). *Stages and pathways of drug involvement: Examining the gateway hypothesis.* New York: Cambridge University Press.

Kandel, D. B., & Yamaguchi, K. (2002). Stages of drug involvement in the U.S. population. In D. B. Kandel (Ed.), *Stages and pathways of drug involvement: Examining the gateway hypothesis.* New York: Cambridge University Press.

Labouvie, E., Bates, M. E., & Pandina, R. J. (1997). Age of first use: Its reliability and predictive utility. *Journal of Studies on Alcohol, 58,* 638–643.

Labouvie, E. W., & White, H. R. (2002). Drug sequences, age of onset, and use trajectories as predictors of drug abuse/dependence in young adulthood. In D. B. Kandel (Ed.), *Stages and pathways of involvement in drug use: Examining the gateway hypothesis.* New York: Cambridge University Press.

Leshner, A. I. (1998). From the prevention lab to the community. In *National conference on drug abuse prevention research: Presentations, papers, and recommendations* (NIH Publication No. 98-4293, pp. 1–16). Rockville, MD: National Institute on Drug Abuse.

Lettieri, D. J., Sayers, M., & Pearson, H. W. (1980). *Theories on drug abuse: Selected contemporary perspectives* (NIDA Research Monograph No. 30). Rockville, MD.

Magnusson, D. (1996). *The lifespan development of individuals: Behavioral, neurobiological, and psychosocial perspectives.* New York: Cambridge University Press.

Moffitt, T. E. (1993). Adolescent-limited and life-course-persistent antisocial behavior: A developmental taxonomy. *Psychological Review, 100,* 674–701.

Mrazek, P. J., & Haggerty, R. J. (Eds.). (1994). *Reducing the risk for mental disorders: Frontiers for preventive intervention research.* Washington, DC: National Academy Press for the Institute of Medicine, Committee on Prevention of Mental Disorders.

Newcomb, M. D., & Felix-Ortiz, M. (1992). Multiple protective and risk factors for drug use and abuse: Cross-sectional and prospective findings. *Journal of Personality and Social Psychology, 63*(2), 280–296.

Newcomb, M. D., Maddahian, E., & Bentler, P. M. (1986). Risk factors for drug use among adolescents: Concurrent and longitudinal analyses. *American Journal for Public Health, 76*, 525–531.

Pandina, R. J. (1998). Risk and protective factor models in adolescent drug use: Putting them to work for prevention. In *National conference on drug abuse prevention research: Presentations, papers, and recommendations* (NIH Publication No. 98-4293, pp. 17–26). Rockville, MD: National Institute on Drug Abuse.

Pandina, R. J., & Johnson, V. (1999). Why do people use, abuse and become dependent on drugs? Progress toward a heuristic model. In M. Glantz & C. R. Hartel (Eds.), *Drug abuse: Origins and preventions* (pp. 119–148). Washington, DC: American Psychological Association.

Pandina, R. J., Labouvie, E. W., & White, H. R. (1984). Potential contributions of the lifespan developmental approach to the study of adolescent alcohol and drug use: The Rutgers Health and Human Development Project, a working model. *Journal of Drug Issues, 14*, 950–973.

Petraitis, J., Flay, B. R., & Miller, T. Q. (1995). Reviewing theories of adolescent substance use: Organizing pieces in the puzzle. *Psychological Bulletin, 117*(1), 67–86.

Staudinger, U. M., & Lindenberger, U. (Eds.). (2003). *Understanding human development: Dialogues with lifespan psychology.* Norwell, MA: Kluwer Academic Publishers.

White, H. R., Bates, M. E., & Buyske, S. (2000). Adolescence-limited versus persistent delinquency: Extending Moffitt's hypothesis into adulthood. *Journal of Abnormal Psychology, 110*, 600–609.

White, H. R., Johnson, V., & Buyske, S. (2000). Parental modeling and parenting behavior effects on offspring alcohol and cigarette use: A growth curve analysis. *Journal of Substance Abuse, 12*, 287–310.

White, H. R., & Labouvie, E. W. (1989). Towards the assessment of adolescent problem drinking. *Journal of Studies on Alcohol, 50*(1), 30–37.

6

Diverse Drug Abusing Populations

Rodolfo R. Vega
JSI Research and Training Institute, Inc.

Dharma E. Cortés
Cambridge Health Alliance Harvard Medical School

TRUTH OR FICTION?

___ 1. *The use of terms such as* special populations *or* diverse populations *may result in overgeneralizations.*

___ 2. *About one in five people has a diagnosable mental disorder during the course of a given year.*

___ 3. *The 2000 U.S. Census asked questions about sexual orientation.*

___ 4. *Drug use has a stronger impact in the African American population because they tend to use more drugs.*

___ 5. *Same-sex partners are less likely to use drugs than different sex partners.*

___ 6. *Hispanics tend to drink more alcohol than Whites.*

___ 7. *Specific drug abuse counseling techniques developed for diverse populations are scarce.*

___ 8. *Hispanics and African Americans are less likely to have health insurance than Whites.*

___ 9. *Cultural competency is an easier skill to acquire than cultural humility.*

___ 10. *As a counselor working with diverse populations, you will have to deal with the issue of trust.*

___ 11. *It might be important to make reference to the client's family during a counseling session.*

___ 12. *The cultural value of* machismo *could play a negative as well as a positive role in the life of clients.*

___ 13. *When counseling Hispanic families, you may have to address the issue of shame before approaching the topic of drug use.*

___ 14. *Poverty is more likely to influence foreign-born Hispanics.*

___ 15. *Migrant status is associated with higher drug use.*

In this chapter we provide tools and a frame of reference to understand the complex issues related to substance abuse treatment among diverse populations. The term *diverse populations* as it is used throughout this chapter may include African Americans; Alaska Natives; American Indians; Asian Americans; Pacific Islanders; Hispanics; lesbians, gays, bisexuals, transsexuals (LGBT); women; and the mentally ill, as well as those groups of individuals that may experience disproportionate use of substance abuse and are underserved in terms of substance abuse prevention and treatment programs.

We also provide basic demographics of these diverse groups, discuss the extent of their substance abuse problems, and address contextual factors that might be related to their substance abuse problems as well as their treatment. These contextual factors include **culture, acculturation, migration** and poverty, as well as issues related to treatment. Although research addressing these issues for all these groups is scant, we provide information derived from scientifically sound and rigorous studies and clinical consensuses that are most relevant to practitioners.

WHAT ARE THE DEMOGRAPHIC CHARACTERISTICS OF DIVERSE POPULATIONS?

Minority populations are the fastest growing segments of the U.S. population. United States Census figures showed that between April 2000 and July 2001, the Hispanic population grew to 37 million, up 4.7%. The African American population increased about 2% to 36.1 million during the same period (United States Census Bureau, 2003). The U.S. Census Bureau projects that by year 2050 almost half of the American population will be minority: 16% Black, 24% Latino/Hispanic, and 10% Asian (United States Census Bureau, 2001). The Hispanic population, already the predominant minority group in California, has also already become the largest minority group in the United States. Substance abuse treatment providers will need to make significant modifications to their practices in order to accommodate these demographic changes.

1. The largest segment of the minority population in the United States is comprised of
_____.

   a. Blacks
   b. Asians
   c. Hispanics
   d. None of the above

About How Many People Experience a Mental Health Disorder in the United States in a Given Year?

According to the United States Surgeon General's report *Mental Health: Culture and Ethnicity* (2001b) about one in five people has a diagnosable mental disorder during the course of a year (i.e., one-year prevalence). The same report indicates that about 3% have both mental and addictive disorders and 6% have addictive disorders alone. Thus 28% to 30% of the population has either a mental *or* an addictive disorder. Also, about 20% of children are estimated to experience mental disorders and at least 5% to 9% experience serious emotional disturbances (Friedman Katz-Leavy, Manderscheid, & Sandheimer, 1996).

2. What proportion of the American population will experience a mental health condition during the course of a year?
   a. 10%
   b. 30%
   c. 20%
   d. 5%

Because poverty is associated with substance use and access to health care, it is important to acknowledge the number and identity of those people that live in poverty in the United States. According to the U.S. Census (*Poverty in the United States*, 2000), poverty rates for both Blacks and Hispanics declined between 1999 and 2000. However, poverty rates among non-Hispanic Whites, Asians, Pacific Islanders, American Indians, and Alaska Natives did not experience any declines. In terms of percentages, the vast majority of poor individuals in the United States are Blacks (22.7%) and Hispanics (21.4%) followed by non-Hispanic Whites (9.9%).

3. Which segment of the United States population represents the largest proportion of those living in poverty?
   a. Whites
   b. Blacks
   c. Hispanics
   d. Non-Hispanic Whites

What Is the Proportion of the LGBT Population in the United States?

There are no reliable estimates of the LGBT population in the United States. For example, the 2000 U.S. Census did not ask questions about sexual orientation. However, it asked about "same sex partners living together" which yielded an estimate of LGBT couples but not of the LGBT population at large. The conventional figure that 10% of the male population and 5% to 6% of the female population are homosexual is based on the now dated Kinsey Report (Kinsey, Pomeroy, & Gephard, 1953). More recent studies estimate that in the United States, 9.8% of men, and 5% of women report same-gender sexual behavior since puberty; about 8% of both male and female report same gender sexual desire; and 2.8% of men and 1.4% of women report homosexual or bisexual identity (Michaels, 1996, as cited in USDHHS, 2001a).

4. About what percentage of the American population experiences same-gender sexual desire?
   a. At least 8%
   b. About 10%
   c. 3% to 4%
   d. We all experience same-gender sexual desire at one time or another.

PREVALENCE RATES

What Is the Prevalence of Drug and Alcohol Groups Among Diverse Populations?

The National Household Survey on Drug Abuse (NHSDA), sponsored on a yearly basis by the Substance Abuse and Mental Health Services Administration (SAMHSA), is the most reliable source of information on the prevalence of drug use in the United States. The latest version (SAMHSA, 2002) estimates that 7.1% of the United States population used an illicit drug during the month prior to the survey. This figure represents an increase of 0.8% from 1999 to 2000 (6.3% to 7.1%). The term *illicit drug* includes marijuana, cocaine, heroin, hallucinogens, inhalants, and nonmedical use of tranquilizers, sedatives, and stimulants.

5. About what percentage of the American public has consumed illegal drugs in the last month?
   a. 10%
   b. .01%
   c. 25%
   d. 7%

Are There Racial and Ethnic Differences in the Prevalence of Drug Use?

Table 6.1 shows past month use of illicit drugs for all the major racial/ethnic groups as well as the Hispanic and Asian subgroups. Although the rate of current drug use among Blacks and Whites is fairly similar, the impact of drug use in terms of criminal justice involvement, family disruption, and health consequences (e.g., HIV/AIDS) is stronger for Blacks. A review of the statistics for Asian and Hispanic subgroups reveals that Chinese reported the lowest rate of drug use at 1.3%, and Koreans reported the highest at 5.5%. Among Hispanics, Puerto Ricans reported the highest rate of current drug use at 9.9% and Central/South Americans the lowest at 3.6%. These figures demonstrate the importance of taking into account the diversity that exists within racial and ethnic groups.

6. Which of these ethnic groups reports the lowest consumption of drugs?
   a. Filipinos
   b. Puerto Ricans
   c. Blacks
   d. Chinese

Are There Gender Differences in the Prevalence of Drug Use?

In 2001, the NHSDA reported that men were more likely to use drugs than women (8.7% vs. 5.5%; SAMHSA, 2002). Gender differences in current drug use among youths age 12 to 17 are less evident. About 11.4% of boys and 10.2% of girls reported drug use in the last month. Finally, current drug use rates for pregnant women age 15 to 44 years were 3.7% but for those 15 to 17 years of age the rates were much higher (15.1%).

TABLE 6.1

Past Month Illicit Drug Use Among Persons Age 12 or Older,
by Race/Ethnicity: 2000–2001 Averages

Race/Ethnicity	Percent Using in Past Month
White	6.8
Black	6.9
Am. Indian/Alaskan Native	11.2
Asian Subgroups	
Chinese	1.3
Filipino	2.2
Japanese	4.5
Asian Indian	2.2
Korean	5.5
Vietnamese	3.0
Pacific Islander	5.1
Hispanic Subgroups	
Mexican	5.8
Puerto Rican	9.9
Central/South American	3.6
Cuban	3.7

Source: SAMHSA. (2002). Results from the 2001 NHS on drug abuse: Volume I. Summary of national findings (OAS, NHSDA Series H-17, DHHS Publication No. SMA 02-3758). Rockville, MD: Author.

7. Are there gender differences in drug use?
    a. Yes, men consume more drugs than women.
    b. Yes, there are gender differences among adults but not among teenagers.
    c. Yes, women consume more drugs than men.
    d. No, men and women use drugs at similar rates.

What Do We Know About Drug Use of LGBT Populations?

There is no conclusive evidence on the actual rates of substance abuse among LGBT populations. This is partly due to the lack of sexual orientation identifiers in national surveys. However, there is ample anecdotal evidence suggesting that LGBT individuals experience higher rates of substance abuse than the mainstream population (Freese, Obert, Dickow, Cohen, & Lord, 2000). For example, the *Healthy People 2010 Companion Document for LGBT Health* reports an analysis of the NHSDA data concluding that same-sex partners were more likely to use illicit drugs than were different sex partners (Gay and Lesbian Medical Association, 2001). The Department of Health and Human Services Web site (www.health.org/ features/lgbt/default.aspx) highlights three main issues contributing to the lack of knowledge on the prevalence of drug use among LGBT populations:

1. The number of individuals who are LGBT has not been determined.
2. Drug use among LGBT has only recently been identified as a significant social problem.
3. Denial and secrecy commonly characterize alcoholism and drug abuse in all populations.

8. Which of the following explains our scant knowledge of substance use among LGBT populations?
   a. We do not know the exact number of the LGBT population.
   b. We just recently found out about the seriousness of the problem among LGBT populations.
   c. Secrecy and denial interfere with disclosure and help-seeking behavior among the LGBT population
   d. All of the above.

About How Many People Both Experience Mental Illness and Consume Drugs?

The **National Comorbidity Study** (Kessler et al., 1996), the largest epidemiological study on comorbidity ever conducted in the United States, estimates the rate of substance abuse disorders accompanied by mental illness at 29% (as cited in Laudet, Magura, Vogel, & Knight, 2000). The same study found that the current prevalence of alcohol dependency and mental illness is 7.2% (Petrakis, González, Rosenheck, & Krystal, 2002).

9. Which of the statements below is true?
   a. About three out of ten people experience both substance abuse and mental health problems.
   b. The comorbidity of drug abuse and mental illness is larger than the comorbidity of alcohol abuse and mental illness.
   c. Comorbidity of mental disorders and drugs or alcohol abuse is a serious problem in the United States.
   d. All of the above.

What Are the Alcohol Use Rates of Diverse Populations?

In 2001, according to the NHSDA, of Americans who reported using alcohol in the last month, Whites had the highest rate (52.7%). Asians reported the lowest rates at 31.9%; for Blacks the rate was 35.1%. The rate for American Indians/Alaskan Natives was also 35.1%.

10. Which ethnic/racial group reports the highest use of alcohol?
    a. American Indians
    b. Hispanics
    c. Blacks
    d. Whites

Although the NHSDA does not report data on the current drug use of Hispanics, some other studies do provide estimates. For example, differences in drinking patterns have been found across Hispanic subgroups. Mexican Americans reported drinking more heavily than Puerto Ricans and Cubans (Caetano & Medina-Mora, 1988). Other differences have been highlighted regarding the consequences of abusing alcohol such as alcohol-related and marital problems. In this regard Mexican American and Puerto Rican men reported these problems more frequently than did their Cuban counterparts (Caetano & Medina-Mora).

SALIENT ISSUES

Which Substance Abuse Treatment Modalities Are Available for Special Populations?

Addressing the substance abuse treatment needs of diverse populations will challenge your skills as a counselor. First, there is a scarcity of specific treatment techniques created specifically for diverse populations. One exception is the work of José Szapocznik and his colleagues (1980, 1994) who have developed structural family therapy treatment models and techniques to address substance abuse–related issues among Hispanics. Second, you will have to choose among the techniques developed for the mainstream population and apply them to diverse populations. Finally, you may opt to tailor those generic counseling techniques to the specific needs of diverse populations. In this section we limit the discussion to issues related to treatment.

Who Receives Substance Abuse Treatment?

The NHSDA (SAMHSA, 2002) estimated that 2.6% of Whites, 3.1% of Blacks, and 3.3% of Hispanics were in need of substance abuse treatment. However, of those in need of treatment, only 15% of Whites, 28.7% of Blacks, and 15.9% of Hispanics received treatment. Thus, Blacks were more likely than Whites and Hispanics to receive treatment. There is no consensus as to whether or not race and ethnicity play a role in treatment entry. Some researchers have found that being male, under 40 years of age, and of Hispanic ethnicity in California are predictors of treatment entry in a wide variety of treatment programs (Kaskutas, Weisner, & Caetano, 1997). Others have observed that being African American is associated with higher treatment entry when compared to Whites (Farabee, Leukefeld, & Hays, 1998). Still others have found no differences (Hser, Anglin, & Fletcher, 1998).

11. Which of the following statements is true?
    a. Race and ethnicity play important roles in treatment entry.
    b. Ethnicity, but not race, hampers the process of getting treatment.
    c. There is no consensus among scientists as to whether or not race and ethnicity play important roles in treatment entry.
    d. Researchers have observed that Whites are more likely to obtain treatment than African Americans.

There are a number of factors that may affect treatment entry among diverse populations. Chief among them are cultural value differences between the health care system and diverse populations, language differences, the fact that treatment interventions have been developed for and from a white American perspective and experiences, as well as practical issues such as lack of health insurance. In fact, Hispanics and African Americans are less likely to have health insurance than Whites, and that might have an impact on their access to treatment.

What Is the Role of Gender in Substance Abuse Treatment?

The relation between treatment entry and gender is inconclusive. Some researchers have highlighted that gender has not been found to be related to entry in substance abuse treatment programs (Tsogia, Copello, & Orford, 2001). Others observe that women are less likely to get into treatment mainly because they experience greater barriers such as child rearing and family obligations (Westermeyer & Boedicker, 2000). In fact, there is a lack of treatment programs that specifically address gender issues such as childcare and traumatic life experiences (e.g., domestic and sexual violence), which are more prevalent among women.

12. Some researchers have indicated that:
   a. women experience more barriers to treatment than men.
   b. there is a lack of treatment programs that are sensitive to gender issues.
   c. women experience more traumatic experiences than men.
   d. all of the above.

Does the Seriously Mentally Ill Individual Get a Share of Substance Abuse Treatment?

Less than half of those individuals suffering a serious mental illness (47%) have received treatment or counseling during the past year (USDHHS, 2001c). Adults 26 and older are more likely to receive treatment than those in the 18 to 25 age bracket. Women (52%) are more likely to receive treatment than men (38%). Also, Whites with a serious mental illness are more likely to receive treatment than Blacks or Hispanics.

13. Which of the following groups is more likely to receive mental health services?
   a. women
   b. Whites
   c. older people
   d. all of the above

What Is the Role of Sexual Orientation in Substance Abuse Treatment?

Although in practice, substance abuse treatment approaches with LGBT clients should be no different from those used with mainstream populations, in reality, the LGBT client needs to confront issues of homophobia, stigma, and discrimination that may preclude them from entering treatment. Treatment modalities and facilities specifically designed for LGBT populations are scarce. Until now, the approach taken to treat this diverse group has been to make clinicians aware of LGBT issues, some of which are discussed in following sections.

14. Which of the following statements is true?
   a. We know very little about LGBT populations and substance abuse treatment.
   b. The literature on gender issues and substance abuse treatment is abundant.
   c. Treatment modalities specifically designed for LGBT populations are not science-based.
   d. All of the above.

The rest of this chapter is devoted to discussing two main issues: (1) how we should approach cultural issues as drug counselors, and (2) contextual factors that may affect the effectiveness and delivery of drug counseling to special populations.

HOW DO WE APPROACH CULTURAL ISSUES?

What Are Some of the Best Practices for Substance Abuse Treatment Interventions With Diverse Populations?

Research on science-based best practices for substance abuse treatment with diverse populations is scarce. A recent survey focusing on outpatient substance abuse treatment and three culturally competent treatment strategies (i.e., racial/ethnic matching between staff and client, linguistic capacity, and cultural competency training) found no consistent relation between these strategies and service utilization (Campbell & Alexander, 2002). The findings suggest that more specific strategies applied to the particular needs of the client may be more appropriate. We consider that specifying needs for each of the diverse groups and subgroups is beyond the scope of this chapter. Thus, in the spirit of the concept of "cultural humility" discussed in Tervalon and Murray-Garcia (1998), we limit our discussion to those cultural approaches that are applicable to all diverse groups; and we recommend some basic processes that can be applied to all diverse populations.

15. Some of the culturally competent strategies that have been used in outpatient substance abuse treatment include _____.
    a. culturally competent training
    b. client–counselor ethnic/racial matching
    c. linguistic capacity
    d. all of the above

Cultural Competency or Cultural Humility: How Should We Address the Needs of Special Populations?

The approach that we endorse is that of *cultural humility*, defined by Tervalon and her colleagues as "a lifelong process that individuals enter into on an ongoing basis with patients, communities, colleagues, and with themselves" (p. 118). In order to practice cultural humility, a counselor needs to: (a) view the client as an expert of his or her own culture, (b) use self-reflection and self-critique in his or her interaction with the client, (c) practice mutual respect, (d) continually search for knowledge of other cultures, and (e) be flexible and humble to recognize what he or she does not know. In other words, you need to become a student of the client's culture and actively pursue its understanding in order to become a true partner in the **therapeutic alliance** (Tervelon & Murray-García, 1998).

16. A basic tenet of cultural humility is that:
    a. the client is the expert.
    b. the counselor is knowledgeable about the client's culture.
    c. the counselor needs to pursue active understanding of the client's culture.
    d. the client is encouraged to engage in reflection and self-critique.

Strategies That Can Be Adopted When Counseling Special Populations

An approach to counseling diverse groups in substance abuse settings that is congruent with the concept of cultural humility is the framework developed by Finn (1996). He anchors his framework on the following four core tenets.

Individualize the Treatment Approach.   Although there is a wide array of treatment and intervention techniques in the field, obviously some approaches are more effective for some clients than for others. Researchers have tried to ascertain which approaches are better for different groups; the reality is that there is no agreement on this issue. We cannot make the statement, for example, that a specific intervention is better for Asian Americans because they have difficulties expressing their emotions. Also, you cannot simply use the same approach with a particular group because of the existing differences within that cultural group. Therefore, it is important to understand your clients' worldviews in order to tailor your approach to their needs.

Avoid Assumptions.   As a counselor you need to be sensitive to your client's behavior. You may interpret as lack of assertiveness the fact that your client makes no eye contact with you. However, that could be a sign of respect toward authority figures in many other cultures. The search for knowledge about other cultures and the practice of humility, which asserts that we do not know, are never ending (Finn, 1996). Therefore, we should never make assumptions regarding our client's culture.

17. What should we assume when the client shows "yeah-saying" or acquiescent behavior?
    a. that the counselor is obviously correct
    b. that the client views the counselor as an authority figure
    c. we should not make any assumptions
    d. lack of assertiveness

Act to Build Trust.   There is well-documented evidence (Durso, 1997) that some members of diverse groups such as African Americans and Hispanics distrust professionals or institutions. In the eyes of the client, you, as a counselor, are a representative of the institution for which you work. Your institution may or may not be trusted by members of diverse groups. Finn (1996) suggests that to gain the client trust you need to: (a) discuss some of your personal experiences with the client, (b) be able to express your feelings, and (c) let the client know how confidentiality will be maintained.

Identify and Address Cultural Issues That May Affect Clients' Drug Problems.   According to Finn (1996), counselors may have reasons to not discuss cultural issues with a client. They may not believe that culture plays a role in recovery, they may feel that all clients need to be treated the same, they may be concerned about exposing their own ignorance about the client's culture, or they may feel that the client will use cultural differences as a way to justify drug use behavior. Other counselors may fear that discussing these issues may unnecessarily heighten awareness of cultural differences between themselves and the client (Finn). All these reasons are valid, but they do not supersede the reality that "counselors are less likely to succeed with a client from another ethnic or racial background unless the cultural issues affecting the client's recovery are openly and objectively addressed" (Finn, 1996, p. 331).

18. Some counselors may not believe that culture plays an important role in the client's recovery because:
    a. they want to treat all clients the same way.
    b. they do not want to be perceived as ignorant.
    c. they do not want to encourage the client to use culture as an excuse for her substance abuse.
    d. all of the above.

Later in the chapter we provide examples of specific cultural issues you may want to address with your clients. Meanwhile, we point out specific issues raised by Sue and Sue (1990, quoted by Finn, 1996). These counselors offer the following strategies to raising cultural issues during a counseling session:

1. Resolve any cultural discrepancies you may encounter.
2. Explore how the client feels toward a counselor of a different race or ethnicity.
3. Assess whether the client has difficulties in disclosing personal matters.
4. Make reference to the client's family and identify to what extent the family serves as a source of support.
5. Gauge the expectations and perceptions clients have toward the counseling process.

Exploring Issues Around Racial Identity

Racial identity, or the way that a client uses his or her perceived race or ethnicity as a cultural referent, is a salient issue for many clients. For example, often Hispanics of African descent feel excluded from both the African American population and the Hispanic population. This is an issue that you may want to explore as it may contribute to the social network that supports their drug use behavior. Finally, you should assess the role of contextual and environmental factors that may be related to the client's drug use. Later, we discuss the contextual factors of migration, racial discrimination, the HIV/AIDS epidemic, and homophobia.

19. Why does racial identity may become an issue to consider when counseling a Hispanic client of African American descent?
    a. It may contribute to a client's association with drug using peers.
    b. It is a crucial issue for all Afro-Hispanic clients.
    c. It plays a central role in the client's behavior.
    d. It helps to gain the client's trust.

What we have described can be applied to any individual seeking counseling. But when we are dealing with members of diverse populations, these strategies become more relevant and salient. We now move to specific cultural values that have been well documented in the literature.

What Are Some of the Specific Cultural Values of Diverse Populations?

We begin this section by defining the term *culture*. Culture refers to the values, beliefs, and worldviews that a particular group uses to express meaning and organize strategies to interact with their environment (Swidler, 1986). This definition allows us to think of culture as a set of tools or strategies that individuals employ to deal with environmental demands. We focus on the cultural ingredients individuals use that are directly relevant to substance abuse treatment interventions.

20. Culture could be seen as _____ that a client uses to deal with her environment.
    a. values
    b. beliefs
    c. worldviews
    d. all of the above

Castro and Hernández Alarcón (2002) suggested that counselors cannot be oblivious or "culturally blind" to the role played by culture in the recovery process and points out how specific cultural factors may affect the treatment process. For example, **machismo** among Hispanics could have a negative impact in the sense that their attitude of dominance and abuse of others and irresponsibility in meeting social obligations may hamper the treatment engagement process. However, *machismo* can also have a positive impact on the recovery process. For example, *machismo* may be characterized by responsible behavior personified in someone as caretaker and family provider, protector of the family, or simply as a tough individual that can face and win over addiction with very little help.

21. Which of the following statements is true?
    a. Cultural values may be positive or negative depending on the context in which they are expressed.
    b. Some cultural values are categorically negative.
    c. Inclusion of cultural values is not essential in treatment of diverse populations.
    d. Cultural values do not influence the recovery process.

As Castro and Hernández Alarcón (2002) pointed out, the relation between cultural factors and substance abuse treatment is complex. For example, the counselor may foster a sense of strong ethnic pride in the client, but having strong identification with one's ethnicity may work only if the individual's family upholds traditional family values.

A traditional value that might be universal is *familism*, or reliance on the family for emotional and social support. However, this core value of diverse populations places a great burden on, for example, the process of "coming out" for LGBT African American and Hispanics. Combined with the value of *machismo* which places the gay man at the center of the family, coming out becomes a difficult process for Hispanic LGBTs because of their fear of being shunned and rejected by the family.

22. Which of the following cultural values does not relate to substance abuse treatment?
    a. food preference
    b. familism
    c. coming out
    d. shame

Another example is the shame that drug use brings to Hispanic families in the light of their strong feelings toward the family unit. Counselors often have difficulties approaching or discussing the problem of drug use directly. Thus in a family counseling session the counselor needs to work on engagement and go around the topic before bringing up the issue of drug use directly.

The challenge for you as a counselor is to be aware of the cultural tools and strategies that are available to individuals of diverse populations and how they might be relevant to the treatment of minority populations.

CONTEXTUAL FACTORS

We end this chapter by discussing important contexts specific to diverse populations and substance abuse treatment. We discuss the topics of acculturation, migration, poverty, gender issues, racial discrimination, stigma, and HIV/AIDS.

Acculturation

In recent years *acculturation*, the process whereby immigrants change their behavior, attitudes, and values toward those of the host society's culture (Rogler, Cortés, & Malgady, 1991), has been linked to substance abuse and HIV risk studies focusing on culturally diverse populations (Carmona, Romero, & Loeb, 1999; De La Rosa, Vega, & Radish, 2000; Zule, Desmond, Medrano, & Hatch, 2001). The rationale for examining the role of acculturation in substance abuse among members of diverse groups is twofold. Firstly, it is argued that the process of adopting the elements of a new culture—usually more permissive about substance use than the culture of origin—might lead to an increase in substance use. Secondly, acculturation might be related to substance abuse via the stresses that accompany the process of adaptation to a different sociocultural system. Within this paradigm, substance abuse emerges as a coping mechanism to mitigate the stresses that immigrants encounter in the host society.

23. Acculturation is closely related to _____.
    a. adaptation to the host culture
    b. racial pride
    c. ethnic identification
    d. all of the above

Regardless of how acculturation is measured, findings indicate that there is a significant relationship between acculturation, substance abuse, and alcohol use (Amaro, Whitaker, Coffman, & Heeren, 1990). The relationship among these three variables, however, is very complex and multidimensional. For example, the effect of acculturation on illicit drug use and alcohol use and abuse is stronger among women than men, a finding that has been somewhat consistent throughout the literature for more than a decade (Black & Markides, 1993).

Migration

The migration process has impacted the lives of African Americans, Hispanics, and other minority groups. For example, a large number of African Americans moved from the rural South to the urban North of the United States between 1910 and 1970, whereas Puerto Ricans and Dominicans have been migrating to the United States since the 1930s and late 1970s, respectively). Cubans and Mexicans have also migrated in large numbers to the United States.

As mentioned earlier, acculturation—a byproduct of migration—seems to play a role in substance abuse. Thus we need to be cognizant of the ways in which being an immigrant might impact the need for counseling services among diverse populations. We do know, for example, that migrants have less access to health care and that migrant status is associated with higher drug use. As a counselor, you need to be aware that migration may exercise its influence on substance abuse and help-seeking behavior in three significant ways:

1. Migration ruptures the natural sources of support and forces the individual to seek new ones in the context of a different culture.
2. Migration usually entails downward social mobility.
3. Migration often forces individuals to adapt to a new cultural system (Rogler, 1994).

24. Migration may influence drug involvement by:
    a. disrupting the natural sources of support and forcing the individual to seek new ones
       in the context of a different culture.
    b. changing the person's socioeconomic context, often in a downward direction.
    c. forcing the individual to adapt to a new cultural system.
    d. all of the above.

Poverty

Poverty has also been highlighted as an important factor contributing to high incidence of substance abuse among American-born highly acculturated Hispanics, but not among Hispanics born elsewhere (Burnam, Hough, Karno, Escobar, & Telles, 1987; Vega & Gil, 1998). According to Gil and Vega (2001), attachment to the culture of origin seems to protect poor recent immigrants against drug use. Other contextual factors such as living in inner-city neighborhoods or urban areas, combined with length of residence in the United States, augments the chances of illicit drug use among Mexicans (Vega, Alderete, Kolody, & Aguilar-Gaxiola, 1998).

25. Poverty contributes to the drug-use behavior of which of the following individuals?
    a. those living in the inner city
    b. those highly acculturated
    c. those with no racial/ethnic identification
    d. all of the above

Heterosexism and Homophobia

The Center for Substance Abuse Treatment (CSAT) defines *heterosexism* as a "prejudice similar to racism and sexism" (USDHHS, 2001a, p. 7). Heterosexism obviates, denigrates, and stigmatizes any form of nonheterosexual behavior. Heterosexism is the failure to acknowledge any type of social or emotional behavior of LGBT in individuals. *Homophobia*, in turn, is antigay bias, fear, and hatred of the LGBT community.

These prejudices may push some LGBT individuals to cope with shame through the use of drugs thereby lowering their self-esteem. CSAT outlines five specific ways heterosexism and homophobia directly affect drug counseling and substance abuse treatment (USDHHS, 2001a, p. 8). Such attitudes can cause or contribute to:

1. Self-blame
2. A negative self-concept
3. Internalized anger resulting in substance abuse
4. Feelings of inadequacy, hopelessness, and despair
5. Self-victimization that may affect self-growth

From the standpoint of cultural humility we need to understand how these prejudices impact our LGBT clients. Because we were socialized in a heterosexual culture, as counselors we need to carefully examine the extent to which we may be heterosexist or homophobic.

26. Heterosexism:
    a. ignores any form of nonheterosexual behavior as a way to show one's gender identity.
    b. is more common among Hispanics.
    c. provides social support to the community.
    d. none of the above.

27. Homophobia may lead to _____.
    a. self-blame
    b. negative self-concept
    c. self-victimization
    d. all of the above

Racial Discrimination

The Institute of Medicine (IOM; 2002) in one of its latest published studies acknowledged the following:

"Racial and ethnic disparities in healthcare occur in the context of broader historic and contemporary social and economic inequality, and evidence of persistent racial and ethnic discrimination in many sectors of American life" (p. 123).

According to the IOM, **disparities in healthcare** stem from "an historic context in which healthcare has been differentially allocated on the basis of social class, race, and ethnicity" (IOM, 2002, p. 123). The February 2003 issue of the *American Journal of Public Health* is entirely devoted to racism and health. One of the contributors concluded, "The subjective experience of racial bias may be a neglected determinant of health and a contributor to racial disparities in health" (Williams, Neighbors, & Jackson 2003, p. 206).

Stigma

Stigma is defined as a mark of shame or discredit. It applies to many forms of exclusionary speech or behavior; in this case, it refers specifically to the use of negative labels used to define those people with HIV/AIDS. Stigma often deters individuals from seeking mental health, substance abuse, and HIV/AIDS services. Stigmas are fueled by misconceptions, half-truths, and inaccuracies. Individuals that experience stigma are reluctant to seek help and often become isolated.

28. Stigma may affect _____.
    a. mental health services
    b. substance abuse services
    c. HIV/AIDS services
    d. all of the above

Drug Use and HIV/AIDS

Drug use is related to the HIV/AIDS epidemic in a number of ways. Injection drug use plays a large role in the spread of HIV/AIDS and when injection drug users share their "works" or drug equipment such as syringes. Drug use also impairs decision making which may lead to unsafe and unprotected sex. Drug users may also exchange sex for drugs or money to maintain their habit, and drug users are more likely to have sex with other drug users (NIDA, 1998).

29. Some of the ways in which substance abuse is related to the spread of HIV/AIDS include
_____.
    a. sharing syringes
    b. exchanging sex for money or drugs
    c. impaired decision making
    d. all of the above

As a counselor, you need to be fully aware of the devastation that HIV/AIDS has had among diverse populations. It is estimated that one in fifty Black men are infected with HIV (all figures cited in this section stem from the Centers for Disease Control, 2001). The figure among Black women amounts to 1 in 160. Black men comprise more than half of all new cases. Black women, in turn, account for 64% of all new cases. Among Hispanics, HIV/AIDS is the second leading cause of death for Hispanic men ages 35 to 44 and for Hispanic women in the same age group.

30. Which of the following statements is true?
    a. HIV/AIDS is the fourth leading cause of death among Hispanic males.
    b. Over 50% of new HIV/AIDS cases occur among African American women.
    c. One in one hundred cases of HIV/AIDS cases occurs among African American men.
    d. Drug use plays a stronger role in HIV/AIDS among Whites than among Hispanics.

AIDS cases among White men are mostly due to men having sex with men (74%). Drug use among Whites men accounts for a relatively small proportion of AIDS causes. Among Black and Hispanic men, drug use is a major factor contributing to AIDS. Among women, 58% of cumulative AIDS cases is accounted for by Black women and 20% by Hispanic women.

We bring to your attention these findings so that on the road to cultural humility you can reexamine your beliefs and perceptions toward your clients and become aware of how racism can lead to health disparities.

KEY TERMS

acculturation: The process by which a culture is transformed due to the massive adoption of cultural traits from another society.

culture: Refers to the values, beliefs, and worldviews that a particular group uses to express meaning and organize strategies to interact with their environment.

disparities in healthcare: Differences in the incidence, prevalence, mortality, and burden of disease and other adverse health conditions that exist among specific population groups in the United States.

diverse populations: A term that refers to African Americans, Alaska Natives, American Indians, Pacific Islanders Hispanics, gays, bisexual, and transsexuals.

machismo: Belief that males are superior to females—commonly found in undeveloped or developing nations.

migration: The movement of a group of people from one country or locality to another.

National Comorbidity Study: the largest epidemiological study on comorbidity ever conducted in the United States.

prevalence rates: The total number of cases of a disease in a given population at a specific time.

therapeutic alliance: The special bond that exists between therapist and client.

unequal access to care: Disparities in the way members of a special population receive treatment.

DISCUSSION QUESTIONS

1. To what extent does the fact that minority populations have become a significant segment of the United States impact the drug counseling practice?
2. Discuss the impact that poverty has on diverse populations in the United States.
3. Most state and national population surveys do not ask about sexual orientation. What are some of the implications that this lack of reporting has on research and funding of substance abuse treatment in the United States?
4. What, in your opinion, is the demographic characteristics of special populations that impact your counseling practice?
5. Discuss some of the factors contributing to the lack of knowledge about drug use patterns among LGBT populations.
6. Discuss some of the current limitations of the literature addressing the substance abuse treatment needs of diverse populations.
7. Discuss how race and ethnicity may or may not play a role in treatment entry.
8. What are some of the gender-specific factors that make it difficult for drug-involved women to enter treatment?
9. Discuss ways you would apply the concept of *cultural humility* in your counseling practice.
10. Why do you think that some treatment approaches work well for some ethnic/racial groups but not for others?

SUGGESTED FURTHER READING

Harwood, A. (Ed.), (1991). *Ethnicity and medical care*. Cambridge, MA: Harvard University Press.

A classic text in the overall relation of ethnicity and healthcare.

Cultural issues in substance Abuse Treatment. (1999).

A publication from U.S. DHHS, SAMHSA, and CSAT that provides substance abuse treatment information for all racial and ethnic groups in the United States. A free copy can be obtained by calling the NCHAD Information (NCADI) at 1.800.729.6686.

U.S. Department of Health and Human Services. (2001a). *A provider's introduction to substance abuse treatment for lesbian, gay, bisexual, and transgender individuals*. Rockville, MD: Author.

Deals with the various issues related to drug abuse counseling and LGBT populations.

U.S. Department of Health and Human Services. (2001b). *Mental health: Culture, race, and ethnicity—A supplement to mental health report: A report of the surgeon general*. Rockville, MD: Author.

Provides an overview of mental health issues among diverse populations. This report was published by DHHS, SAMHSA, and CMHS.

REFERENCES

Amaro, H., Whitaker, R., Coffman, G., & Heeren, T. (1990). Acculturation and marijuana and cocaine use: Findings from HHANES 1982–1984. *American Journal of Public Health, 80*(Suppl.), 54–60.

Black, S. A., & Markides, K. S. (1993). Acculturation and alcohol consumption in Puerto Rican, Cuban-American, and Mexican-American women in the United States. *American Journal of Public Health, 83*, 890–893.

Burnam, A., Hough, R., Karno, M., Escobar, J. L., & Telles, C. (1987). Acculturation and life time prevalence of psychiatric disorders among Mexican Americans in Los Angeles. *Journal of Health and Social Behavior, 88* 89–102.

Caetano, R., & Medina-Mora, M. E. (1988). Acculturation and drinking among people of Mexican descent in Mexico and the United States. *Journal of Studies on Alcohol, 49*, 462–471.

Campbell, C. I., & Alexander J. A. (2002). Culturally-competent treatment practices and ancillary service use in outpatient substance abuse treatment. *Journal of Substance Abuse Treatment, 22*, 109–119.

Carmona, J. V., Romero, G. J., & Loeb, T. B. (1999). The impact of HIV status and acculturation on Latinas' sexual risk taking. *Cultural Diversity and Ethnic Minority Psychology, 5*(3), 209–221.

Castro, F., & Hernández Alarcón, E. (2002). Integrating cultural variables into drug abuse prevention and treatment with racial/ethnic minorities. *Journal of Drug Issues, 3*, 783–810.

Centers for Disease Control and Prevention. (2001). HIV and AIDS cases Surveillance Report, *13*, 2.

De La Rosa, M., Vega, R., & Radish, M. A. (2000). The role of acculturation in the substance abuse behavior of African American and Latino adolescents: Advances, issues, and recommendations. *Journal of Psychoactive Drugs, 32*(1), 33–42.

Durso, T. W. (1997). Scientist, health care inequities lead to a mistrust of research, *Scientist, 11*(4), 1.

Farabee, D., Leukefeld, C. J., & Hays, L. (1998). Accessing drug abuse treatment: Perceptions of out-of-patient injectors. *Journal of Drug Issues, 28*, 381–394.

Finn, P. (1996). Cultural responsiveness of drug user treatment programs: Approaches to improvement. *Substance Use and Misuse, 31*, 493–518.

Freese,T. E., Obert, J., Dickow, A., Cohen, J., & Lord, R. H. (2000). Metamphetamine Abuse: Issues for Special Populations. *Journal of Psychoactive Drugs, 32*, 177–182.

Friedman, R. M., Katz-Leavy, J. W., Manderscheid, R. W., & Sandheimer, D. L. (1996). Prevalence of serious emotional disturbance in children and adolescents. In R. W. Manderschied & M. A. Sonnerschein (Eds.), *Mental Health, United States* (pp. 71–89). Washington, DC: U.S. Department of Health and Human Services, Substance Abuse and Mental Health Services Administration, Center for Mental Health Services.

Gay and Lesbian Medical Association. (2001). *Healthy People 2010 Companion Document for LGBT Health.* San Francisco: Gay and Lesbian Medical Association.

Gil, A. G., & Vega, W. A. (2001). Latino drug use: Scope, risk factors, and reduction strategies. In M. Aguirre-Molina, C. W. Molina, & R. E. Zambrana (Eds.), *Health issues in the Latino community* (pp. 435–458). San Francisco: Jossey-Bass.

Hser, Y., Anglin, M. D., & Fletcher, B. (1998). Comparative treatment effectiveness: Effects of program modality and client drug dependence history on drug use reduction. *Journal of Substance Abuse Treatment, 15*, 513–523.

Institute of Medicine. (2002). *Unequal treatment: Confronting reacial and ethnic disparities in health care.* Washington DC: National Academy Press.

Kaskutas, L. A., Weisner, C., & Caetano, R. (1997). Predictors of help seeking among a longitudinal sample of the general population. *Journal of Studies on Alcohol, 58*(2), 155–161.

Kessler, R. C., Berglund, P. A., Zhao, S., Leaf, P. J., Kouzis, A. C., et al. (1996). The 12-month prevalence and correlates of serious mental illness. In R. W. Manderscheid, & M. A. Sonnenschein (Eds.), *Mental health, United States, 1996* (DHHS Publication No. SMA 96-3098, pp. 59–70). Washington, DC: U.S. Government Printing Office.

Kinsey, A. C., Pomeroy, C. E., & Gephard, P. (1953). *Sexual Behavior in the Human Female.* Philadelphia: W.B. Saunders.

Laudet, A. B., Magura, S., Vogel, H. S., & Knight, E. (2000). Support, mutual aid and recovery from dual diagnosis. *Community Mental Health Journal, 36*(5), 457–476.

National Institute of Drug Abuse. (1998). HIV prevention with drug-using populations: Current status and future prospects. *Public Health Reports, 113* (Supplement 1), 1–3.

Petrakis, I. P., González, G., Rosenheck R., & Krystal, J. H. (2002). Comorbidity of alcoholism and psychiatric disorders: An overview. *Alcohol Research and Health, 26*, 81–89.

Rogler, L. H. (1994). International migrations: A framework for directing research. *American Psychologist, 49*, 701–708.

Rogler, L. H., Cortés, D. E., & Malgady, R. G. (1991). Acculturation and mental health status among Hispanics: Convergence and new directions for research. *American Psychologist, 46*(6), 585–597.

Substance Abuse and Mental Health Services Administration. (2002). *Results from the 2001 National Household Survey on Drug Abuse: Volume I. Summary of National Findings* (Office of Applied Studies, NHSDA Series H-17, DHHS Publication No. SMA 02-3758). Rockville, MD: Author.

Swidler, A. (1986). Culture in action: Symbols and strategies. *American Sociological Review, 51*, 273–286.

Szapocznik, J., & Fein, S. (1994). Issues in preventing alcohol and other drug abuse among Hispanic/Latino families. In J. Szapocznik (Ed.), *A Hispanic/Latino family approach to substance abuse prevention* (pp. 1–18). Rockville, MD: U.S. Center for Substance Abuse Prevention.

Szapocznik, J., Kurtines, W. M., & Fernández, T. (1980). Bicultural involvement and adjustment in Hispanic-American youths. *International Journal of Intercultural Relations, 4*, 353–365.

Tervalon, M., & Murray-García, J. (1998). Cultural humility versus cultural competence: A critical distinction in defining physician training outcomes in multicultural education. *Journal of Health Care for the Poor and Underserved, 9*, 117–125.

Tsogia, D., Copello A., & Orford, J. (2001). Entering treatment for substance misuse: A review of the literature. *Journal of Mental Health, 10*, 481–499.

U.S. Census Bureau. (2001). United States Statistical Abstracts. Retrieved December 21, 2002, from http://www.census.gov/prod/2001pubs/statab/sec20.pdf

U.S. Department of Health and Human Services. (2001a). *A provider's introduction to substance abuse treatment for lesbian, gay, bisexual, and transgender individuals.* Rockville, MD: Author.

U.S. Department of Health and Human Services. (2001b). *Mental health: Culture, race, and ethnicity—A supplement to mental health report: A report of the surgeon general.* Rockville, MD: Author.

U.S. Department of Health and Human Services. (2001c). *Summary of findings from the 2000 National Household Survey on Drug Abuse.* Rockville, MD: Author.

United States Census. (2003). Press release. Public Information Bureau. January 21, 2003.

United States Census. (2000). Poverty in the United States. Retrieved December 21, 2002, from http://www.census.gov/hhes/www/poverty.html.

Vega, W. A., Alderete. E., Kolody, B., & Aguilar-Gaxiola, S. (1998). Illicit drug use among Mexicans and Mexican Americans in California: The effects of gender and acculturation. *Addiction, 93*, 839–1850.

Vega, W. A., & Gil, A. G. (1998). *Drug use and ethnicity in early adolescence.* New York: Plenum.

Westermeyer, J., & Boedicker, A. E. (2000). Course, severity, and treatment of substance abuse among women versus men. *American Journal of Drug and Alcohol Abuse, 26*, 523–535.

Williams, D. R., Neighbors H. W., & Jackson J. S. (2003). Racial/Ethnic Discrimination and Health: Findings from Community Studies. *American Journal of Public Health, 93*, 200–208.

Zule, W. A., Desmond, D. P., Medrano, M. A., & Hatch, H. P. (2001). Acculturation and risky injection practices among Hispanic injectors. *Evaluation and Program Planning, 24*, 207–214.

7

Psychopathology

Lynn F. Field
Linda Seligman
Private Practice

TRUTH OR FICTION?

___ 1. *Understanding the* Diagnostic and Statistical Manual of Mental Disorders *is not important for counselors who focus their work on the treatment of people with substance use disorders.*

___ 2. *People with substance use disorders rarely have an accompanying mental disorder because the use of drugs or alcohol reduces their depression and anxiety.*

___ 3. *Nearly everyone with a substance use disorder also has a comorbid mental disorder.*

___ 4. *When treating someone with a substance use disorder and another mental disorder, always treat the substance use disorder first; treat the other mental disorder after the person is well into recovery from the substance use disorder.*

___ 5. *Counselors in treatment facilities focused on the treatment of people with substance use disorders also should be prepared to treat any other mental disorders that the clients present.*

___ 6. *The use of alcohol to self-medicate is common.*

___ 7. *Twelve-step programs provide effective treatment for people with the combination of an eating disorder and a substance use disorder.*

___ 8. *Psychotic disorders accompanied by alcohol dependence are caused by the alcohol and will almost always improve when the person stops using alcohol.*

___ 9. *People with personality disorders are comfortable with their personality styles and so rarely turn to drugs or alcohol to help them feel better.*

___ 10. *Even skilled counselors often have difficulty determining whether a mental disorder preceded or resulted from a substance use disorder.*

___ 11. *In the United States, the* DSM *is the most widely used manual to diagnose mental disorders.*

___ 12. *Substance-related disorders do not include alcohol abuse or alcohol dependence.*

___ 13. *Panic disorder is a type of anxiety disorder.*
___ 14. *Dissociative disorders are all characterized by out-of-body experiences.*
___ 15. *Inhalants are the only substance commonly abused by adolescents also diagnosed with conduct disorders.*

This chapter provides pertinent information for the addictions counselor on accurate diagnosis and effective treatment planning for mental disorders. An overview of the *Diagnostic and Statistical Manual of Mental Disorders.* (*DSM–IV–TR*; American Psychiatric Association [APA], 2000) is presented along with mental disorders that most often co-occur with substance use disorders. A broad description of these disorders is provided along with their relationship to drug and alcohol use and abuse. Additionally, substance-induced disorders are discussed and a section on when and how to refer a client will provide readers with useful information.

1. The letters *DSM* stand for
   a. Directory of Scientific Methodology.
   b. Diagnostic and Statistical Manual.
   c. Degrees and Standards of Measurement.
   d. The Development of Subjective Meaning.

USING THE *DSM–IV–TR*

The Diagnostic and Statistical Manual of Mental Disorders, now in its fourth edition with a text revision (APA, 2000) is an important tool for addictions counselors. The ***DSM–IV–TR*** is the most widely used and accepted diagnostic system in the United States. Understanding how to diagnose and use the *DSM–IV–TR* provides counselors with a consistent framework and a set of criteria for naming and describing mental disorders as well as treatment planning and collaboration (Seligman, 1996). Additionally, an accurate diagnosis aids counselors in determining whether they have the appropriate skills and knowledge needed to work with a client and to determine whether a referral for medication or other services is needed.

CATEGORIES OF MENTAL DISORDERS

The *DSM–IV–TR* (APA, 2000) includes seventeen broad categories of mental disorders with multiple diagnoses included in each category. Later, this chapter focuses on the specific disorders that most frequently co-occur with substance use disorders. However, here we provide a broad overview of the seventeen categories in the *DSM*.

2. How many broad categories are included in the *DSM*?
   a. twenty-four
   b. fifty
   c. ten
   d. seventeen

Disorders Usually First Diagnosed in Infancy, Childhood, or Adolescence

This first section of the *DSM* provides information on disorders that typically begin before the age of 18. However, many of these disorders often continue into adulthood, and it is not unusual for them to be first identified at that time. The disorders in this category that co-occur most frequently with substance use disorders include: conduct disorder, which is characterized by behavior that violates others' rights, social norms, or rules; oppositional defiant disorder, which is evidenced in defiant and often hostile behavior; and attention deficit/hyperactivity disorder (ADHD), which includes **symptoms** such as inattention and/or hyperactivity/impulsivity.

3. Which one of the following is a mental disorder that is often found in young people who misuse substances?
   a. mental retardation
   b. conduct disorder
   c. separation anxiety disorder
   d. cyclothymic disorder

Delirium, Dementia, and Amnestic and Other Cognitive Disorders

Disorders addressed in this section of the *DSM* are due to brain damage or dysfunction and are treated primarily by psychiatrists or neurologists so specific details are not provided. It is, however, important for counselors to be aware of and able to identify signs of these disorders so that appropriate referrals can be made. Of particular interest to readers are substance-induced delirium, substance-induced persisting **dementia**, and substance-induced persisting amnestic disorder covered later in this chapter.

Substance-Related Disorders

In general, disorders included in this section include those "related to the taking of a drug of abuse (including alcohol), to the side effects of a medication, and to toxin exposure" (APA, p. 191). The two groups of substance-related disorders include *substance-use disorders* (substance abuse and substance dependence), covered in more detail later in this chapter, and *substance-induced disorders*. Substance-induced disorders typically result from behaviors associated with substance use disorders.

4. The relationship of substance use disorders and substance-induced disorders is that:
   a. substance-induced disorders cause substance use disorders.
   b. they are unrelated.
   c. substance use disorders cause substance-induced disorders.
   d. each one causes the other in equal proportion.

Schizophrenia and Other Psychotic Disorders

Disorders covered in this section of the *DSM* are characterized by psychotic symptoms and are not caused by a medical condition. The symptoms of schizophrenia, one of the most severe of the mental disorders, are **delusions**, hallucinations, disorganized speech or behavior and/or catatonic behavior lasting at least six months. The other psychotic disorders are schizophreniform disorder, a disorder similar to schizophrenia with the exception of duration (one to six months) and decline in functioning; schizoaffective disorder, a mix of symptoms of schizophrenia and a mood disorder; delusional disorder, characterized by nonbizarre delusions; brief psychotic disorder in which symptoms of **psychosis** last less than one month; and shared psychotic disorder in which psychotic symptoms develop in an individual who is associated with someone currently experiencing psychosis.

5. The duration of a schizophreniform disorder is:
   a. at least one year.
   b. one to six months.
   c. lifelong.
   d. at least two weeks.

Mood Disorders

Mood disorders are characterized by depressed **mood** and/or elevated mood. Major depressive disorder includes symptoms of severe depressed mood lasting for at least two weeks. Dysthymic disorder can be diagnosed when criteria for major depression are not met and symptoms of depressed mood occur more days than not for at least two-years. Bipolar disorder involves episodes of dysfunctional mood, might include major depressive episodes, must include either manic episodes or hypomanic episodes, and may include mixed episodes. The hallmark of manic episodes is elevated mood. Hypomania is similar to mania but is less severe. A diminished need for sleep is a common symptom of both mania and hypomania. Mixed episodes include symptoms of both depression and mania.

6. Which of the following is a common symptom of hypomania?
   a. severe depression
   b. severe anxiety
   c. infidelity
   d. sleeping much less than usual

Anxiety Disorders

Disorders covered in this section of the *DSM* are characterized by the physical and emotional symptoms of **anxiety**. Of the many anxiety disorders the ones covered in this chapter include panic disorder, generalized anxiety disorder, and posttraumatic stress disorder. Panic disorder is characterized by very brief periods of unexpected panic. Generalized anxiety disorder includes persistent and excessive worry and anxiety lasting at least six months. Posttraumatic stress disorder is characterized by the reexperiencing of a trauma (e.g., nightmares, flashbacks) with symptoms of increased arousal and/or avoidance of stimuli associated with the event.

Somatoform Disorders

The common feature of these disorders, sometimes referred to as psychosomatic disorders, is the belief that one has a physical or medical condition when the presence of that condition cannot be verified. Important somatoform disorders include: somatization disorder, indicated by a long history of multiple physical complaints; conversion disorder, manifested by motor or neurological symptoms or deficits; pain disorder, where pain without a medical basis is reported; hypochondriasis, evidenced by extreme concern about having a serious illness; and body dysmorphic disorder, characterized by a preoccupation with an imagined or exaggerated physical deficit.

7. Another term for a somatoform disorder is:
   a. a psychosomatic disorder.
   b. a psychotic disorder.
   c. an impulse-control disorder.
   d. agoraphobia.

Factitious Disorders

Disorders included in this category are described as occurring with predominantly psychological signs and symptoms, with predominantly physical signs and symptoms, or a combined type. What characterizes factitious disorder is the intentional feigning of symptoms for the purpose of assuming the role of a sick person and receiving sympathy and attention.

8. The usual goal of a person with a factitious disorder is to:
   a. obtain financial gains such as disability payments.
   b. confuse their physicians.
   c. impress their family and physicians.
   d. receive sympathy and attention.

Dissociative Disorders

Dissociative disorders are characterized by a disruption in memory, identity, or awareness not caused by a physical illness. These disorders include: dissociative amnesia, an inability to recall information about one's identity or past; dissociative fugue, sudden travel away from home accompanied by memory loss; dissociative identity disorder, the presence of two or more distinct personalities as well as significant memory loss; and depersonalization disorder, the persistent feeling of being detached or outside one's body.

Sexual and Gender Identity Disorders

The groups of disorders included in this category include sexual dysfunctions, paraphilias, and gender identity disorders. Sexual dysfunctions are characterized by difficulties in sexual desire, arousal, comfort, and functioning. Paraphilias involve at least six months in which a person's primary source of sexual arousal is unhealthy and/or illegal (e.g., sexual attraction to children, voyeurism). Gender identity disorders are indicated by an intense identification with the opposite gender and significant distress with one's assigned sex.

Eating Disorders

Eating disorders include anorexia nervosa and bulimia nervosa. Anorexia nervosa is characterized by low body weight, food restriction, or purging, and poor body image. Bulimia entails frequent bingeing and compensatory behaviors such as purging and/or over-exercising as well as poor body image. People with this disorder are generally at an appropriate weight or overweight.

9. An important difference between people with anorexia nervosa and those with bulimia nervosa is:
   a. their pattern of bingeing.
   b. their weight.
   c. early attachment patterns.
   d. their excessive use of laxatives and diuretics.

Sleep Disorders

The sleep disorders such as insomnia, hypersomnia, and breathing-related sleep disorder may be an additional focus of treatment for people engaged in substance use. Insomnia is characterized by difficulty falling asleep or staying asleep. Hypersomnia is diagnosed when the person experiences excessive sleepiness and difficulty awakening. Breathing-related sleep disorder involves a breathing condition that interferes with sleep and is characterized by loud, sudden snoring.

Impulse-Control Disorders Not Elsewhere Classified

This section of the *DSM* focuses on disorders not covered elsewhere that are characterized by episodes of failure to resist potentially harmful impulses. Intermittent explosive disorder is evidenced by violent and aggressive behavior which results in assault or destruction of property. The remaining disorders in this section of the *DSM* include kleptomania (theft of unneeded objects), pyromania (recurrent fire setting), pathological gambling, and trichotillomania (pulling out hair on one's own body or head).

Adjustment Disorders

Adjustment disorders entail clinically significant symptoms of depressed mood, anxiety, mixed anxiety and depression, or conduct problems. Mild to moderate distress develops within three months of a psychosocial stressor, and this diagnosis can be maintained for six months subsequent to the end of the stressor and its consequences.

10. What is the maximum duration of an adjustment disorder that developed in response to a stressor?
    a. one year
    b. the disorder has no maximum duration
    c. two months after the end of the stressor
    d. six months after the end of the stressor

Personality Disorders

Personality disorders are pervasive and deeply ingrained patterns of behavior and inner experience that lead to impaired functioning. They typically develop by late adolescence or early

11. By definition, a personality disorder is:
    a. longstanding.
    b. severely incapacitating.
    c. very responsive to treatment.
    d. due to physical or sexual abuse.

12. How many personality disorders are described in the *DSM*?
    a. six
    b. seventeen
    c. ten
    d. Four for men and seven for women.

adulthood, are stable over time, and are most likely evidenced by poor social skills, impulse control difficulties, and distress in most or all areas of life. There are ten personality disorders. Patterns evidenced in each of these personality disorders are:

- Paranoid personality disorder—distrust and suspiciousness
- Schizoid personality disorder—disinterest in social relationships and restricted range of emotion
- Schizotypal personality disorder—significant discomfort with relationships, cognitive or perceptual distortions, and eccentric behavior
- Antisocial personality disorder—disregard for the law or rights of others in addition to impulsivity and irresponsibility
- Borderline personality disorder—self-destructive and impulsive behavior, unstable relationships, and low self-esteem
- Histrionic personality disorder—high emotionality and attention-seeking
- Narcissistic personality disorder—egocentrism, a sense of entitlement, and a considerable need for admiration.
- Avoidant personality disorder—social discomfort and concern with negative judgment
- Dependent personality disorder—submissiveness and low self-esteem.
- Obsessive-compulsive personality disorder—perfectionism, inflexibility, and a need for control.

Other Conditions That May Be a Focus of Clinical Attention

Conditions described in this section of the *DSM* are not considered mental disorders, but they often are the focus of attention in counseling. Relational problems and problems related to abuse or neglect are examples of conditions found in this category.

13. Conditions, as described in the *DSM*, are:
    a. a person's environment.
    b. medical illnesses.
    c. characterized by clear symptoms.
    d. not mental disorders.

MULTIAXIAL ASSESSMENT

For a broad understanding of clients, the *DSM–IV–TR* (APA, 2001) suggests that a multiaxial diagnosis be made using five axes. Axis I is used for reporting all mental disorders or conditions, with the exception of personality disorders, borderline intellectual functioning, and mental retardation which are reported on Axis II. Axis III includes any medical conditions that are relevant to the client's emotional condition. On Axis IV, any current or recent psychosocial or environmental factors or stressors that may be causing the client difficulty is reported. Finally, Axis V, or global assessment of functioning, is a 1 to 100 scale on which clinicians can rate their client's level of functioning.

14. On what axis would schizoid personality disorder be listed?
    a. I
    b. II
    c. III
    d. IV

15. What is listed on axis III of the *DSM*?
    a. intelligence level
    b. vegetative symptoms
    c. medical conditions
    d. psychosocial stressors

16. What is listed on axis IV of the *DSM*?
    a. intelligence level
    b. vegetative symptoms
    c. medical disorders
    d. psychosocial stressors

17. What is reflected on axis V of the *DSM*?
    a. the client's overall level of functioning
    b. the treatment prognosis
    c. the client's treatment history
    d. any substance use problems the client might have

COMORBID DISORDERS

Research bolstered by clinical experience suggests that there are many disorders that often co-occur with substance use disorders. The following are especially common:

• Disruptive behavior disorders including attention-deficit/hyperactivity disorder (ADHD); conduct disorder (CD), and oppositional defiant disorder (ODD)
• Mood disorders including primarily major depressive disorder (MDD) and bipolar disorders (BD)
• Psychotic disorders
• Anxiety disorders including posttraumatic stress disorder (PTSD), panic disorder, and social phobia
• Eating disorders, including anorexia nervosa and bulimia nervosa

- The impulse control disorders, particularly intermittent explosive disorder and pathological gambling
- The personality disorders, particularly borderline and antisocial personality disorders

Disruptive Behavior Disorders

Disruptive behavior disorders including ADHD, ODD, and CD are the most common comorbid disorders in adolescents with drug or alcohol misuse (Bukstein, Brent, & Kaminer, 1989). In a large-scale study, Kandel et al. (1999) found that 68% of adolescents diagnosed with a substance use disorder also had a comorbid disruptive behavior disorder. The incidence of ADHD among adolescents with substance use disorders has been found to range from 30% to 50% (Horner & Scheibe, 1997; Riggs, 1998; Wilens, Biederman, & Spencer, 1996). The incidence of CD among adolescents with substance use disorders has been found to range from 40% to 57% (Brown, Gleghorn, Schuckit, Myers, & Mott, 1996; DeMilio, 1989; McKay & Buka, 1994). Studies by Stowell and Estroff (1992) and Wilens, Biederman, and Spencer (1992) have documented rates of ODD ranging from 30% to 68% in substance using adolescents.

18. Approximately what percentage of adolescents with substance use disorders can also be diagnosed with attention-deficit/hyperactivity disorder?
    a. 10%–20%
    b. 20%–40%
    c. 30%–50%
    d. 70%–85%

In a more current study of 395 adolescents with an alcohol use disorder, Molina, Bukstein, and Lynch (2002) determined that as many as 30% had a significant number of ADHD symptoms and 73% had three or more CD symptoms. Additionally, they found that while fewer girls than boys were diagnosed with ADHD, rates of ADHD in girls were still higher than in the general population.

Another recent study (Grella, Hser, Joshi, & Rounds-Bryant, 2001) of about one thousand adolescents from twenty-three drug treatment programs determined that more than half had a comorbid disorder. Of that half, a majority had CD, and these adolescents were more likely to be dependent on marijuana and about twice as likely to be treated in the hospital rather than in an outpatient program than the others in the study.

There are considerable implications resulting from comorbidity of substance disorders and disruptive behavior disorders. Adolescents in treatment for substance misuse who also have ADHD were found to use drugs at an earlier age, have more severe substance problems (Horner & Scheibe, 1997), use more drugs, and have more substance dependence diagnoses than adolescents in treatment for drug use without ADHD (Thompson, Riggs, Milulich, & Crowley, 1996).

Cognitive-behavioral techniques used with adults, such as relapse prevention, may be helpful for adolescents with comorbid substance use and disruptive behavior disorders (Bukstein & Van Hasselt, 1993). Attention to the substance use is important; however, counselors need to target the factors underlying unacceptable social behaviors or risk factors for effective treatment (Bukstein, 1994; Bukstein & Van Hasselt, 1993).

According to Bukstein (2000), alcohol and drug misuse may increase intentional or unintentional prescribed medication overdoses, and some of the psychotropic medications may have inherent abuse potential. For example, pharmacologic treatment of ADHD involves the use of certain nervous system stimulants, such as Ritalin, which offer a potential for abuse. Some preliminarily evidence suggests that treatment of ADHD with medication may help prevent development of substance use disorders (Biederman, Wilens, Mick, Spencer, & Faraone, 1999; Molina, Pelham, & Roth, 1999).

Psychotic Disorders

Substance use among those with psychotic disorders, including schizophrenia, is common. For example, statistics from the Epidemiological Catchment Area study indicated that the lifetime prevalence of substance abuse is about 50% among individuals with schizophrenia (Regier et al., 1990). Unfortunately, comorbidity of psychotic disorders and substance misuse has been associated with a high risk of suicide, self-harm, and homicide (Appleby et al., 1999). It is therefore important that substance abuse counselors are prepared to assess psychotic disorders in the substance abusing population and assess substance abuse in those with comorbid psychotic disorders.

19. The risk level for people diagnosed with both a substance use disorder and a psychotic disorder is _____.
    a. minimal
    b. moderate
    c. very high
    d. extremely variable

In a study of ninety-six hospitalized patients with psychotic symptoms, Cassano, Pini, Saettoni, Rucci, and Dell'Osso (1998) diagnosed alcohol dependence in about 45% of the patients and drug dependence in about 38%. Their research suggested that substance misuse in psychotic patients seemed to help lessen their expression of psychopathology.

People with psychotic disorders, as well as mood disorders, may actually use various substances to self-medicate and alleviate symptoms (Test, Wallisch, & Allness, 1989; Leibenluft, Fiero, Bartko, Moul, & Rosenthal, 1993) such as side effects of neuroleptic drugs which are often used to treat psychosis (Schneier & Siris, 1997). Finally, comorbid psychosis and substance misuse have been associated with poor prognosis (Drake & Wallach, 1989), poor treatment compliance (Pristach & Smith, 1990), high admission rates to inpatient programs (Haywood, Kravitz, & Grossman, 1995), increased risk of breaking the law (Tessler & Dennis, 1989), and violent behavior (Bartel, Drake, Wallach, & Freeman, 1991; Scott et al., 1998; Swartz et al., 1998).

Mood Disorders

Franken and Hendriks (2001) assert that mood disorders in the substance using population are high. In their study of 116 participants in a substance abuse treatment program, almost half had either a current mood or anxiety disorder and more than half had a lifetime history of a mood or anxiety disorder. Mood disorders among adolescents with substance problems have been found to range from 18% to 35% for major depressive disorder, 5% to 34% for dysthymic disorder, and 8% to 11% for bipolar disorder (Bukstein, Glancy, & Kaminer, 1992; DeMilio, 1989; Deykin, Buka, & Zeena, 1992; Schiff & Cavaiola, 1990; Stowell & Estroff, 1992; Wilens, Biederman, & Spencer, 1996). Multiple studies have indicated that approximately 40% to 50% of people who are cocaine abusers meet the criteria for a mood disorder (Gawin & Kleber, 1986; Wallace, 1987, 1991).

Major Depressive Disorder

Major depressive disorder can have a significant impact on the lives of people and, when co-occurring with substance misuse, complicates treatment. Studies of adults indicate that people who are disagnosed with substance use disorders with comorbid depression tend to have distinct clinical features, personality characteristics, clinical course, adaptive functioning, and family psychopathology (Epstein, Ginsburg, Hesselbrock, & Schwarz, 1994; Grant, Hasin, & Dawson, 1996; Powell, Read, Penick, Miller, & Bingham, 1987). Lin, Bai, Hu, and Yeh (1998) examined substance use disorders among inpatients with mood disorders and determined that the prevalence of misuse of sedatives, hypnotics, and anxiolytics was high in those who were diagnosed with major depressive disorder.

Factors associated with the development of substance misuse in depressed adolescents were explored by Rao et al. (1999). The progression from alcohol or drug initiation to the onset of a substance use disorder occurred more rapidly in adolescents who were depressed, and comorbidity was associated with serious psychosocial impairment.

Suicide. With comorbid depression, suicide becomes an issue. Most studies support the view that misuse of alcohol or psychoactive substances is strongly associated with suicide risk (Harris & Barraclough, 1997; Moscicki, 1997). Specifically, alcohol use is a significant risk factor for suicidal behavior; completed suicides were seven to twenty times higher in people who misused substances than in the general population (Galanter & Castaneda, 1985).

20. The suicide risk for people who have a substance use disorder, compared to the general population, is _____.
    a. much lower
    b. much higher
    c. about the same
    d. unknown

Bipolar Disorder

A significant amount of research has focused on the co-occurrence of bipolar disorder and substance use. According to the National Institute of Mental Health Epidemiologic Catchment Area study (Kessler et al., 1994), bipolar disorder was the Axis I disorder most likely to co-occur with some form of substance dependence. A study by Brady, Casto, Lydiard, Malcolm, and Arana (1991) found that 30% of those diagnosed with bipolar disorder also met criteria for drug or alcohol misuse. In a study of sixty bipolar patients, Miller, Busch, and Tanenbaum (1989) found that 25% misused one or more drugs. A rationale provided for the high rate of comorbidity in this population is that substances may be used to manage the symptoms associated with mania (Sonne, Brady, & Morton, 1994) or to enhance the euphoria associated with mania (Goodwin & Jamison, 1990).

Dysthymic Disorder

Few studies have examined comorbid dysthymic disorder and substance use disorders. Very little is known about substance abuse in this population (Kell, 1995). Eames, Westermeyer, and Crosby (1998), however, did examine people with comorbid dysthymia and substance use disorder and found no significant difference in substance use among those with substance use disorder only and those with comorbid dysthymia.

21. Which of the following disorders is least likely to be associated with a substance use disorder?
    a. major depressive disorder
    b. bipolar disorder
    c. oppositional defiant disorder
    d. dysthymic disorder

Treatment Implications

Studies indicate that comorbid depression and substance abuse in adults is associated with poor treatment compliance (Ravndal & Vaglum, 1994; Wolpe, Gorton, Serota, & Sanford, 1995), increased use of treatment services (Helzer & Przybeck, 1988; Kessler et al., 1996; Westermeyer, Eames, & Nugent, 1998), and poorer response to treatment and long term outcome (O'Sullivan et al., 1988; Rounsavelle, Dolinsky, Babor, & Meyer, 1987). However, an accurate clinical assessment of clients who misuse substances may offer a more favorable treatment outcome (Milby & Stainback, 1991).

22. People diagnosed with both a substance use disorder and a depressive disorder are likely to be:
    a. more compliant with treatment.
    b. less compliant with treatment.
    c. very unpredictable in their compliance with treatment.
    d. prone to sabotage treatment.

Anxiety Disorders

There are many studies which examine comorbid substance abuse and anxiety disorders. According to the Epidemiologic Catchment Area survey (Regier et al., 1990), people with anxiety were 50% more likely to be diagnosed with an alcohol use disorder. Kessler et al. (1996) determined that the lifetime prevalence rate for substance use disorders is three times greater for individuals with generalized anxiety disorder and two times greater for people with panic disorder when compared to the general population. In a series of studies, Stewart, Samoluk, and MacDonald (1999) established that the more sensitive people are to being anxious the more they use alcohol to cope with these feelings.

23. Which anxiety disorder has an especially strong likelihood of being accompanied by a substance use disorder?
    a. adjustment disorder with anxious mood
    b. specific phobia
    c. generalized anxiety disorder
    d. pervasive anxiety reaction

Posttraumatic Stress

The incidence of substance misuse among those diagnosed with PTSD has been investigated extensively. Estimates of alcohol dependence in combat veterans with PTSD have ranged from 41% to 85% (Stewart, 1996). Also, rates of PTSD occurring in persons identified with or in treatment for substance misuse vary from 20% to 59% (Triffleman, 1998).

Panic Disorder

Higher rates of alcohol and drug abuse have also been noted in people who suffer from panic disorder (Klerman, Weissman, Ouellette, Johnson, & Greenwalk, 1991). Jensen, Cowley, and Walker (1990) found that those with subsyndromal panic, or panic that does not meet the criteria for panic disorder, misuse opiates more often but cocaine less often than patients with full blown panic disorder.

Katerndahl and Realini (1999) found no significant difference in the prevalence of substance misuse between those with subsyndromal panic and panic disorder. They did, however, determine that the onset of **panic attacks** seemed to occur most commonly after the substance was misused. Only 10% of people in their study used alcohol, specifically, to self-medicate, and Katerndahl and Realini found that abuse of alcohol, barbiturates, stimulants, and cocaine was significantly associated with panic.

Social Phobia

The onset of social phobia precedes the onset of alcohol abuse in 66% to 85% of those affected by both (Kushner, Sher, & Beitman, 1990; Ross, Glaser, & Germanson, 1988; Schneier, Johnson, Horig, Liebowitz, & Weissman, 1992). Schneier et al. (1992) suggested that people who misuse alcohol with social phobia have a higher incidence of depression than those without social phobia.

24. In people diagnosed with both social phobia and an alcohol use disorder, the order of onset of these disorders is most likely to be:
    a. social phobia followed by the alcohol use disorder.
    b. the alcohol use disorder followed by the social phobia.
    c. simultaneous.
    d. unpredictable.

Thomas, Thevos, and Randall (1999) found that people who misuse alcohol and who have a comorbid social phobia showed greater severity of alcohol dependence than those without social phobia. These people did not drink more often nor did they drink greater amounts of alcohol, but they reported greater dependence on alcohol than people without social phobia. Those with social phobia may depend on alcohol to improve their social abilities and overall functioning. Furthermore, they may enter treatment with more severe psychological problems, including depression.

Treatment

Treatment literature for comorbid anxiety disorders and substance abuse has focused on PTSD. Long-term treatment outcome is poorer among those with comorbid PTSD and substance use disorders than among those with substance use disorders alone (Ouimette, Finney,

& Moos, 1999). Additionally, substance use relapse has been found to occur more quickly following treatment among substance abusers with PTSD (Brown, Stout, & Mueller, 1996) than those without.

Abueg and Fairbank (1992) developed a phased-treatment approach for Vietnam veterans with PTSD and a substance use disorder, based on Prochaska and DiClemente's (1983) stages of change. Following detoxification and initial stabilization, a brief period of psychoeducation occurs. This stage is followed by direct therapeutic exposure for the PTSD in addition to self-control training for addiction and relapse prevention for both substance misuse and PTSD.

Eating Disorders

Much discussion has occurred surrounding the topic of eating disorders and substance use. Whether one disorder precedes the other or whether they occur concurrently is information that is helpful for the mental health professional to assess. High rates of alcohol use disorders have been observed in people with eating disorders (e.g., Mitchel, Hatuskami, Eckert, & Pyle, 1985) and high rates of eating disorders have been documented in people with alcohol use disorders (e.g., Grilo, Levy, Becker, Edell, & McGlashan, 1995). It has been reported that 35% to 70% of women with an alcohol use disorder admitted to inpatient alcoholism treatment have a history of a prior eating disorder (Beary, Lacey, & Merry, 1986; Higuchi, Suzuki, Yamada, Parrish, & Kono, 1993; Lacey & Mourelli, 1986).

25. People with the restricting type of anorexia nervosa:
    a. almost never use either drugs or alcohol.
    b. are at high risk for inhalant abuse.
    c. are at high risk for alcohol use disorders.
    d. are at relatively low risk for alcohol use disorders.

The literature on both eating disorders and substance use disorders indicates the frequent co-occurrence of both disorders. However, bulimia and purging type anorexia are much more commonly associated with alcohol use disorders than restricting type anorexia (Lilenfeld & Kaye, 1996).

Holderness, Brooks-Gunn, and Warren (1994) reviewed fifty-one studies which addressed comorbid eating disorders and substance use disorders. They concluded that the prevalence of alcohol and other drug use disorders differs significantly among people diagnosed with restricting anorexia, binge-eating/purging anorexia, and bulimia. Rates of alcohol abuse or dependence among those with restricting anorexia ranged from 0% to 6% and rates of other drug abuse or dependence, including amphetamines, ranged from 5% to 19%. In contrast, the corresponding rates in those diagnosed with bulimia were significantly higher, ranging from 14% to 49% for alcohol abuse or dependence and from 8% to 36% for other types of drug abuse or dependence.

Often, women with a comorbid eating disorder and substance use disorder have been diagnosed with additional mental disorders. A study of young women with and young women without an eating disorder who misused alcohol, reported that women with alcohol disorders and eating disturbances had significantly higher rates of depression and borderline personality disorder.

Controversies exist on approaches to treating comorbid substance use disorders and eating disorders. Sinha and O'Malley (2000) have recommended an integrated approach that targets alcohol use and pathological eating. They suggest using interventions such as using self-monitoring records, identifying high-risk situations, and teaching coping skills to manage feelings or social situations that may lead to loss of control.

Lilenfeld and Kaye (1996) suggest that effective treatments for alcohol misuse and eating disorders differ because distinctive behaviors must be addressed for both types of disorders. The primary focus when treating alcohol misuse is to avoid consuming the substance whereas with eating disorders, particularly bulimia, the focus is to change the manner in which the substance is consumed. Treatment needs to take into account both consumption patterns as well as disturbed body image.

Perhaps the most controversial approach to treating eating disorders is the 12-step approach. The addiction model of eating disorders (Wilson, 1991) has contributed to the notion that eating disorders and alcohol or drug abuse may respond to similar treatment approaches. However, no rigorous, scientifically designed studies have demonstrated the benefits of a 12-step approach for treating bulimia.

Impulse Control Disorders

Assuming an elevated co-occurrence of substance use disorders and impulse control disorders seems logical. However, little research is available which addresses the overlap.

McElroy, Soutillo, Beckman, Taylor, and Keck (1998) evaluated twenty-seven individuals who had been diagnosed with intermittent explosive disorder. They reported that they all demonstrated substantial additional psychopathology which included substance use disorders as well as mood, anxiety, eating, and other impulse control disorders.

Up to 50% of people with severe gambling problems have been found to have a substance use disorder (Lesieur & Blume, 1993), and up to 30% of those with substance use disorders have been found to have problems with gambling (Feigelman, Kleinman, & Leiseur, 1995). Petry (2001) explored the co-occurrence of substance use in problem gamblers and suggested that both disorders may be manifestations of an underlying impulse control disorder. Of the sixty gamblers that were assessed, 35% had a history of substance use disorders with alcohol use disorders being the most common (71%), followed by marijuana (62%) and cocaine (33%) use disorders. The majority of those interviewed in the study had received professional treatment for the substance use disorder.

26. The most common substance use disorder found in people diagnosed with pathological gambling is:
    a. an alcohol use disorder.
    b. a cannabis use disorder.
    c. a cocaine use disorder.
    d. a caffeine use disorder.

PERSONALITY DISORDERS

Among people with substance use disorders, prevalence of any personality disorder ranges from 30% to 70% (Verheul, van den Brink, & Hartgers, 1995). Driessen, Veltrup, Wetterling, John, & Dilling (1998) recently found that 34% to 38% of people who misused alcohol also suffered from personality disorders. Estimates of personality disorders in those abusing cocaine specifically range from 30% to 75% among inpatient samples (Kleiman et al., 1990; Kranzler, Satel, & Apter, 1994; Weiss, Mirin, Griffin, Gunderson, & Hufford, 1993). For people with opiate or benzodiazepine use disorders, a majority (88% and 91% respectively) were found to have an axis II diagnosis (Busto, Romach, & Sellers, 1996; DeJong, van den Brink, Hartevedt, & van der Wilen, 1993). Approximately 90% of people who misuse multiple substances typically meet the criteria for a personality disorder diagnosis (DeJong, van den Brink, Hartevedt, & van der Wielen, 1993; Lewis, Rice, & Helzer, 1983).

27. The percentage of people who misuse multiple substances and who also meet the diagnostic criteria for a personality disorder is approximately _____.
    a. 15%
    b. 40%
    c. 60%
    d. 90%

Cluster A personality disorders are characterized by odd, eccentric, and guarded behavior and include paranoid, schizoid, and schizotypal personality disorders. Cluster B personality disorders are characterized by emotional, unpredictable, and egocentric behavior and include antisocial, borderline, histrionic, and narcissistic personality disorders. Cluster C personality disorders are characterized by anxiety, fearfulness, and self-doubt and include avoidant, dependent, and obsessive-compulsive personality disorders. A study by Verheul et al. (2000) determined that a majority of inpatient substance abusers (57%) met the criteria for at least one personality disorder. In their study, cluster B (27%) disorders were the most prevalent, particularly antisocial (27%) and borderline personality disorders (18%). The most common comorbid diagnosis in cluster A was paranoid personality disorder (13%), and the most common comorbid diagnosis in cluster C was avoidant personality disorder (18%).

28. One of the personality disorders that is most likely to be associated with a substance use disorder is _____.
    a. schizoid personality disorder
    b. antisocial personality disorder
    c. obsessive-compulsive personality disorder
    d. dependent personality disorder

29. Another one of the personality disorders that is most likely to be associated with a substance use disorder is _____.
    a. borderline personality disorder
    b. dependent personality disorder
    c. histrionic personality disorder
    d. narcissistic personality disorder

The prevalence of antisocial personality disorder seems to stand out among the axis II diagnoses in those who abuse various substances. It has been consistently linked to alcohol use disorders (Schuckit, 1985), with comorbidity estimates ranging from 15% to 50% (DeJong et al., 1993; Malow, West, Williams, & Sutker, 1989; Nace, Davis, & Gaspari, 1991). Antisocial personality disorder in those with alcohol use disorders has been associated with early onset problem drinking, chronicity of abuse/dependence and a greater number of alcohol-related disorders (Cooke, Winokur, Fowler, & Liskow, 1994; Hesselbrock, Hesselbrock, & Stabenau, 1985). Hatzitaskos, Soldatos, Kokkevi, and Stefanis (1999) examined substance use patterns and their association with antisocial and borderline personality disorder. Ninety-five percent of those diagnosed with antisocial personality disorder also met criteria for substance abuse.

In addition to antisocial personality disorder, borderline personality disorder is more common in those who misuse substances. It has been identified in approximately 13% to 18% of those with alcohol dependence (Mirin & Weiss, 1988; Nace, Davis, & Gaspari, 1991; Nurnberg, Rifkin, & Doddi, 1993). Higher estimates have been reported—from 28% to 34% (Jonsdottir-Baldursson & Horvath, 1987; Kranzler et al., 1994). People who misuse substances who also have a borderline personality disorder tend to be younger, have more suicide attempts, demonstrate more pathology and tend to be at a greater risk for misusing other substances (Bunt, Galanter, Lifshutz, & Castaneda, 1990; Jonsdottir-Baldursson & Horvath, 1987; Skinstad, 1994).

As with any axis I diagnosis, a diagnosis of a personality disorder increases the complexity of the treatment process. In fact, personality disorders have been associated with poorer treatment response in people who are alcohol dependent (Booth, Cook, & Blow, 1992; Nace & Davis, 1993; Nurnberg, et al., 1993) and drug dependent (Andreoli, Gressot, Aapro, Tricot, & Gognalons, 1989; el-Guebaly, 1995) patients.

SUBSTANCE-INDUCED DISORDERS

The two diagnoses that are used to describe the behavior of misusing drugs and alcohol are *substance abuse* and the more severe *substance dependence*. Substance abuse and substance dependence can lead to secondary mental disorders, reflecting the direct negative impact of the substances. The *DSM* refers to these as *substance-induced disorders*. Included in the *DSM* are the following substance-induced disorders:

- Substance intoxication
- Substance withdrawal
- Substance-induced delirium
- Substance-induced persisting dementia
- Substance-induced persisting amnestic disorder
- Substance-induced psychotic disorder
- Substance-induced mood disorder
- Substance-induced anxiety disorder
- Substance-induced sexual dysfunction
- Substance-induced sleep disorder
- Hallucinogen persisting perception disorder (flashbacks)

The possible substance-induced disorders associated with a particular substance vary, depending on the impact of that substance on people's physical and emotional functioning. Alcohol abuse or dependence, for example, can cause every one of the substance-induced disorders listed above while caffeine dependence is associated with only three of the substance-induced disorders (caffeine intoxication, caffeine induced anxiety disorder, and caffeine-induced sleep disorder). The *DSM* includes a list of possible induced disorders associated with the misuse of each of the eleven substances it addresses (discussed elsewhere in this book).

Of course, even though a particular substance has the potential of inducing a lengthy list of secondary disorders, this certainly does not mean that everyone diagnosed with abuse or dependence on that substance will develop all of those disorders. Some people diagnosed with substance abuse or dependence will have no induced disorders, some will have one induced disorder, and a small percentage will have more than one induced disorder. People who have made heavy and prolonged use of harmful substances are more likely to have developed induced disorders but intoxication and withdrawal, as well as many of the other induced disorders, can occur without either prolonged or heavy use, depending on the substance. Clinicians should familiarize themselves with the induced disorders associated with each of the eleven substances and then assess carefully whether the symptoms of those induced disorders are, indeed, present.

Induced or Preexisting?

Most people who misuse substances have other symptoms. Particularly common are depression, anxiety, and problems with sleep and sexual functioning. These symptoms often worsen when people are dealing with the difficult and stressful experience of halting their unhealthy use of drugs or alcohol.

Determining which came first, the misuse of a substance or the mental disorder, is often difficult, yet it has important treatment implications. Several guidelines can help clinicians determine whether symptoms reflect an induced or preexisting condition or disorder:

• *Obtain a detailed history.* Through an intake interview and subsequent conversations with clients and, if possible, their family and close friends, clinicians can try to determine whether the emotional symptoms preceded or followed the onset of the substance use disorder.

• *Wait at least a month after the person has stopped using substances to make a decision.* For at least a month after a person has stopped using drugs and alcohol, that person's symptom picture is likely to be clouded by withdrawal symptoms, cravings for the once-gratifying substance, and the challenge of adjusting to life without substances. However, after about a month, clinicians can begin to assess symptoms to determine what comorbid mental disorders, if any, were present before and during the time the person was misusing substances.

• *Consider the possibility that drugs or alcohol were used to self-medicate.* For example, alcohol often reduces the severity of hallucinations in people who meet the criteria for a psychotic disorder while stimulant drugs can ameliorate depression.

If all three criteria are present (reported emotional difficulties prior to the inception of the substance misuse, the emergence or continuation of symptoms at least one month after the cessation of drug and alcohol misuse, and the probability of a short-term beneficial impact of the substance on the symptoms), then the person probably has another, preexisting mental disorder in addition to any diagnosed substance use and substance-induced disorders. If emotional symptoms are clearly linked to the substance use disorder and only occur in conjuction with that disorder, then the person probably has both a substance use disorder and a substance-induced disorder. If the person has no symptoms of emotional dysfunction that are not directly linked to the substance use, then the person probably has neither a preexisting mental disorder nor a substance-related disorder.

MAKING A REFERRAL

Determining whether or not clients have another mental disorder, in addition to a substance use disorder, is essential in determining effective treatment. If clinicians treat only the substance use disorder and ignore the comorbid disorder, treatment is not likely to be effective. This is especially true if the substance had been ameliorating the symptoms of the comorbid disorder and those symptoms worsen when the use of drugs or alcohol stops. The exacerbation of the underlying comorbid disorder may well interfere with people's efforts to stop misusing substances and may lead them to question whether it is really beneficial for them to cease their unhealthy use of drugs or alcohol.

If clinicians determine that a comorbid disorder is present, it is essential that they help their clients obtain treatment for that disorder as well as for their substance use disorder. If the clinician has the experience and skills needed to treat both disorders, that is ideal and a comprehensive treatment plan can easily be developed, addressing both disorders. Often, however, the clinician does not have the expertise to treat the comorbid disorder and needs to make a referral to a psychiatrist or another mental health therapist for treatment of the underlying disorder. Several principles should guide the nature of this referral:

- If possible, identify a referral source who is knowledgeable about both the comorbid disorder and the substance use disorder.
- Explain to the client the need for a referral and obtain the client's written authorization to contact and share information with the referral source.
- Contact the referral source and provide information on the client's background, diagnoses, and need for collaborative treatment, emphasizing the presence of the substance use disorder.
- Work closely with the referral source to develop a treatment plan for the client that targets all diagnosed disorders.
- Monitor the client closely, especially if psychotropic medication is prescribed, in an effort to maintain treatment compliance and prevent misuse of the prescribed medications.

30. Which of the following should *not* be done when you are referring someone with a substance use disorder to another clinician for treatment of a comorbid mental disorder?
    a. Obtain the client's written permission before contacting the referral source.
    b. Inform the referral source of the client's substance use disorder.
    c. Discuss the referral with the client, both before and after the referral is made.
    d. Protect your client by not disclosing information on the substance use disorder.

By following these guidelines, clinicians can offer their clients a powerful treatment package that maximizes the likelihood of ameliorating not only the substance use disorder but also the comorbid disorder.

KEY TERMS

affect: How an individual's mood appears to others.

anxiety: Sense of general discomfort (typically including apprehension, hypervigilance, and physical symptoms such as muscle tension, fatigue, and sleep disturbance) that does not have a well-defined cause.

delusion: A belief held despite evidence that it is not true.

dementia: Development of multiple cognitive deficits, including memory impairment.

DSM–IV–TR: Current diagnostic manual of the American Psychiatric Association.

mood: A person's emotional state.

panic attack: Sudden onset of physiological symptoms such as sweating, trembling, chest pain, and shortness of breath. This may or may not have an apparent precipitant.

personality: Distinctive pattern of emotional, interpersonal, and behavioral traits that characterizes an individual.

phobia: Marked fear that is disproportionate or unreasonable, brought about by the presence or anticipation of a specific object or situation.

psychosis: A condition that involves the loss of contact with reality including the presence of delusions, hallucinations, disorganized speech, or grossly disorganized or catatonic behavior.

symptom: Apparent manifestation of a physical or a mental disorder.

DISCUSSION QUESTIONS

1. What are the three most important things that substance use disorder counselors need to know about diagnosis of mental disorders?
2. How does treatment of a person with both a substance use disorder and a mental disorder differ from treatment of a person who has only a substance use disorder?
3. Why do you think young people with either a conduct disorder or an attention deficit/hyperactivity disorder so often also have a substance use disorder?
4. How would you go about determining whether the mental disorder or the substance use disorder came first? Why is this important?
5. How should referrals of people with substance use disorders be made?
6. Why is bulimia usually not effectively treated using the 12-step recovery approach?
7. How do Cluster A, Cluster B, and Cluster C personality disorders differ and why is this important to understand?
8. How does substance abuse differ from substance dependence?
9. Explain the use and importance of a multiaxial diagnosis in client assessment.
10. Comorbid psychosis and substance misuse have poor prognoses: Why?

SUGGESTED FURTHER READING

American Psychiatric Association. (2000). *The diagnostic and statistical manual of mental disorders* (4th ed., text rev.). Washington, DC: Author.

This manual is essential for clinicians making diagnoses of mental disorders. It provides specific criteria for mental disorders as well as information on typical course of disorder and comorbid disorders.

Seligman, L. (1996). *Diagnosis and treatment planning in counseling.* New York: Plenum.

This book provides an overview of the processes of diagnosis and treatment planning. Charts facilitate accurate diagnosis.

Seligman, L. (1998). *Selecting effective treatments.* San Francisco: Jossey-Bass.

This book synthesizes the research on effective treatments of the major mental disorders. A chapter on diagnosis and treatment of substance-related disorders should be particularly useful to people treating clients with those disorders.

REFERENCES

Abueg, F. R., & Fairbank, J. A. (1992). Behavioral treatment of the PTSD-substance abuser: A multidimensional stage model. In P. Saigh (Ed.), *Posttraumatic stress disorder: A behavioral approach to assessment and treatment* (pp. 111–147). New York: Pergammon Press.

American Psychiatric Association. (2000). *Diagnostic and statistical manual of mental disorders* (4th ed., text rev.). Washington, DC: Author.

Andreoli, A., Gressot, G., Aapro, N., Tricot, L., & Gognalons, M. Y. (1989). Personality disorders as a predictor of outcome. *Journal of Personality Disorders, 3,* 2–3.

Appleby, L., Shaw, J., Amos, T., McDonnell, R., Kierman, K., Davies, S., et al. (1999). *Safer services: Report of the National Confidential Inquiry into Suicide and Homicide by People with Mental Illness.* London: Stationary Office.

Bartel, S. J., Drake, R. E., Wallach, M. A., & Freeman, D. H. (1991). Characteristic hostility in schizophrenic outpatients. *Schizophrenic Bulletin, 17*(1), 163–171.

Beary, M. D., Lacey, J. H., & Merry, J. (1986). Alcoholism and eating disorders in women of fertile age. *British Journal of Addictions, 81,* 685–689.

Biederman, J., Wilens, T., Mick, E., Spencer, T., & Faraone, S. V. (1999). Pharmacotherapy of attention deficit/hyperactivity disorder reduces the risk for substance use disorder. *Pediatrics, 104,* 20.

Booth, B. M., Cook, C. L., & Blow, F. C. (1992). Comorbid mental disorders in patients with AMA discharges from alcohol treatment. *Hospital Community Psychiatry, 43,* 730–731.

Brady, K. T., Casto, S., Lydiard, R. B., Malcolm, R., & Arana, G. (1991). Substance abuse in an inpatient psychiatric sample. *American Journal of Drug and Alcohol Abuse, 17,* 389–397.

Brown, P. J., Stout, R. L., & Mueller, T. (1996). Posttraumatic stress disorder and substance use relapse among women: A pilot study. *Psychology of Addictive Behavior, 10.* 124–128.

Brown, S. A., Gleghorn, A., Schuckit, M. A., Myers, M. G., & Mott, M. A. (1996). Conduct disorder among adolescent alcohol and drug abusers. *Journal of Studies on Alcohol, 57,* 314–324.

Bukstein, O. G. (1994). Substance abuse. In M. Hersen, R. T. Ammerman, & L. A. Sisson (Eds.), *Handbook of aggressive and destructive behavior in psychiatric patients.* New York: Plenum Press.

Bukstein, O. G. (2000). Disruptive behavior disorders and substance use in adolescents. *Journal of Psychoactive Drugs, 32,* 67–79.

Bukstein, O. G., Brent, D. A., & Kaminer, Y. (1989). Comorbidity of substance abuse and other psychiatric disorders in adolescents. *American Journal of Psychiatry, 46,* 1131–1141.

Bukstein, O. G., Glancy, L. J., & Kaminer, Y. (1992). Patterns of affective comorbidity in a clinical population of dually diagnosed adolescent substance abusers. *Journal of the American Academy of Child and Adolescent Psychiatry, 31,* 1041–1045.

Bukstein, O. G., & VanHasselt, V. B. (1993). Alcohol and drug abuse. In A. S. Bellack, & M. Hersen (Eds.), *Handbook of behavior therapy in the psychiatry setting* (pp. 453–476). New York: Plenum Press.

Bunt, G., Galanter, M., Lifshutz, H., & Castaneda, R. (1990). Cocaine "Crack" dependence among psychiatric inpatients. *American Journal of Psychiatry, 147,* 1542–1546.

Busto, U. E., Romach, M. K., & Sellers, E. M. (1996). Multiple drug use and psychiatric comorbidity in patients admitted to the hospital with severe benzodiazepine dependence. *Journal of Clinical Psychopharmacology, 16,* 51–57.

Cassano, G. B., Pini, S., Saettoni, M., Rucci, P., & Dell'Osso, L. (1998). Occurrence and clinical correlates of psychiatric comorbidity in patients with psychotic disorders. *Journal of Clinical Psychiatry, 59,* 60–68.

Cooke, B. L., Winokur, G., Fowler, R. C., & Liskow B. J. (1994). Classification of alcoholism with reference to comorbidity. *Comprehensive Psychiatry, 35,* 165–170.

DeJong, C. A., van den Brink, W., Hartevedt, F. M., & van der Wielen, E. G. (1993). Personality disorders in alcoholics and drug addicts. *Comprehensive Psychiatry, 37,* 87–94.

DeMilio, L. (1989). Psychiatric syndromes in adolescent substance abusers. *American Journal of Psychiatry, 146,* 1212–1214.

Deykin, E. Y., Buka, S. L., & Zeena, T. H. (1992). Depressive illness among chemically dependent adolescents. *American Journal of Psychiatry, 149,* 1341–1347.

Drake, R. E., & Wallach, M. A. (1989). Alcohol use and abuse in schizophrenia: A prospective community study. *Hospital Community Psychiatry, 40,* 1041–1045.

Driessen, M., Veltrup, C., Wetterling, T., John, U., & Dilling, H. (1998). Axis I and axis II comorbidity in alcohol dependence and the two types of alcoholism. *Alcoholism: Clinical & Experimental Research, 22,* 77–86.

Eames, S. L., Westermeyer, J., & Crosby, R. D. (1998). Substance use and abuse among patients with co-morbid dysthymia and substance disorder. *American Journal of Drug and Alcohol Abuse, 24,* 541–550.

el-Guebaly, N. (1995). Substance use disorders and mental illness: The relevance of comorbidity. *Canadian Journal of Psychiatry, 40,* 2–3.

Epstein, E. E., Ginsburg, B. E., Hesselbrock, V. M., & Schwarz, J. C. (1994). Alcohol and drug abusers subtypes by antisocial personality and primary or secondary depressive disorder. *Annual New York Academy of Science, 708,* 187–201.

Feigelman, W., Kleinman, P. H., & Lesieur, H. R. (1995). Pathological gambling among methadone patients. *Drug and Alcohol Dependence, 39,* 75–81.

Franken, I. H. A., & Hendriks, V. M. (2001). Screening and diagnosis of anxiety and mood disorders in substance abuse patients. *The American Journal on Addictions, 10*, 30–39.

Galanter, M., & Castaneda, R. (1985). Self-destructive behavior in substance abusers. *Psychiatric Clinics of North America, 8*, 251–261.

Gawin, F. H., & Kleber, H. D. (1986). Abstinence symptomatology and psychiatric diagnosis in cocaine abusers. *Archives in General Psychiatry, 43*, 107–113.

Goodwin, F. K., & Jamison, K. R. (1990). *Manic depressive illness.* NY: Oxford University Press.

Grant, B. F., Hasin, D. S., & Dawson, D. A. (1996). The relationship between *DSM–IV* alcohol use disorders and *DSM–IV* major depression: Examination of the primary-secondary distinction in a general population sample. *Journal of Affective Disorders, 38*, 113–128.

Grella, C. E., Hser, Y., Joshi, V., & Rounds-Bryant, J. (2001). Drug treatment outcomes for adolescents and comorbid mental and substance use disorders. *The Journal of Nervous and Mental Disease, 186*, 384–392.

Grilo, C. M., Levy, K. N., Becker, D. F., Edell, W. S., & McGlashan, T. H. (1995). Eating disorders in female inpatients with versus without substance use disorders. *Addictive Behaviors, 20*, 255–260.

Harris, E. C., & Barraclough, B. (1997). Suicide as an outcome for mental disorders. *British Journal of Psychiatry, 170*, 205–228.

Hatzitaskos, P., Soldatos, C. R., Kokkevi, A., & Stefanis, C. N. (1999). Substance abuse patterns and their association with psychopathology and type of hostility in male patients with borderline and antisocial personality disorder. *Comprehensive Psychiatry, 40*, 1542–1546.

Haywood, T. W., Kravitz, H. M., Grossman, L. S., et al. (1995). Predicting the revolving door phenomenon among patients with schizophrenic, schizoaffective and affective disorders. *American Journal of Psychiatry, 152*, 856–861.

Helzer, J. E., & Przybeck, T. R. (1988). The co-occurrence of alcoholism with other psychiatric disorders in the general population and its impact on treatment. *Journal of Studies on Alcohol, 49*, 219–224.

Hesselbrock, V. N., Hesselbrock, M. N., & Stabenau, J. R. (1985). Alcoholism in men patients subtypes by family history and antisocial personality. *Journal of Studies on Alcohol, 46*, 59–64.

Higuchi, S., Suzuki, K., Yamada, K., Parrish, K., & Kono, H. (1993). Alcoholics with eating disorders: Prevalence and clinical course, a study from Japan. *British Journal of Psychiatry, 162*, 403–406.

Holderness, C. C., Brooks-Gunn, J., & Warren, W. P. (1994). Comorbidity of eating disorders and substance abuse: Review of the literature. *International Journal of Eating Disorders, 16*, 1–34.

Horner, B. R., & Scheibe, K. E. (1997). Prevalence and implications of attention-deficit hyperactivity disorder among adolescents in treatment for substance abuse. *Journal of the American Academy of Child and Adolescent Psychiatry, 36*, 30–36.

Jensen, C. E., Cowley, D. S., & Walker, R. D. (1990). Drug preferences of alcoholic polydrug abusers with and without panic. *Journal of Clinical Psychiatry, 51*, 189–191.

Jonsdottir-Baldursson, T., & Hovarth, P. (1987). Borderline personality disordered alcoholics in Iceland: Descriptions on demographic, clinical and MMPI variables. *Journal of Consulting and Clinical Psychology, 55*, 738–741.

Kandel, D. B., Johnson, J. G., Bird, H. R., Weissman, M. M., Goodman, S. H., Lahey, B. B., et al. (1999). Psychiatric comorbidity among adolescents with substance use disorders. Finding from the MECA study. *Journal of the American Academy of Child and Adolescent Psychiatry, 38*, 693–699.

Katerndahl, D., & Realini, J. P. (1999). Relationship between substance abuse and panic attacks. *Addictive Behaviors, 24*, 731–736.

Kell, M. J. (1995). Opiate dependence, comorbidity and seasonality of birth. *Journal of Addictive Disease, 14*, 19–34.

Kessler, R. C., McGonagle, K. A., Zhao, S., Nelson, C. B., Hughes, M., Eschleman, S., et al. (1994). Lifetime and 12-month prevalence of *DSM–III–R* psychiatric disorders in the United States: Results from the National Comorbidity Survey. *Archives of General Psychiatry, 51*, 8–19.

Kessler, R. C., Nelson, C. B., McGonagle, K. A., Edlund, M. J., Frank, R. G., & Leaf, P. J. (1996). The epidemiology of co-occurring addictive and mental disorders: Implications for prevention and service utilization. *American Journal of Orthopsychiatry, 66*, 17–31.

Kleiman, P. H., Miller, A. B., Millman, R. B., Woody, G. E., Todd, T., Kemp, J., et al. (1990). Psychopathology among cocaine abusers entering treatment. *Journal of Nervous and Mental Disease, 178*, 442–447.

Klerman, G. L., Weissman, M. M., Ouellette, R., Johnson, J., & Greenwalk, S. (1991). Panic attacks in the community. *Journal of the American Medical Association, 265*, 742–746.

Kranzler, H. R., Satel, S., & Apter, A. (1994). Personality disorders and associated features in cocaine-dependent inpatients. *Comprehensive Psychiatry, 35*, 335–340.

Kushner, M. G., Sher, K. J., & Beitman, B. D. (1990). The relation between alcohol problems ad anxiety disorders. *American Journal of Psychiatry, 147*, 685–695.

Lacey, J. H., & Mourelli, E. (1986). Bulimic alcoholics: Some features of a clinical sub-group. *British Journal of Addiction, 81*, 389–393.

Leibenluft, E., Fiero, P. L., Bartko, J. J., Moul, D. E., & Rosenthal, N. E. (1993). Depressive symptoms and the self-reported use of alcohol, caffeine and carbohydrates in normal volunteers and four groups of psychiatric outpatients. *American Journal of Psychiatry, 150*, 294–301.

Lesieur, H. R., & Blume, S. B. (1993). Pathological gambling, eating disorders, and the psychoactive substance use disorders. *Journal of Addictive Diseases, 12*, 89–102.

Lewis, C. E., Rice, J., & Helzer, J. E. (1983). Diagnostic interactions: Alcoholism and antisocial personality. *Journal of Nervous and Mental Disease, 171*, 105–113.

Lilenfeld, L. R., & Kaye, W. H. (1996). The link between alcoholism and eating disorders. *Alcohol Health & Research World, 20*, 94–99.

Lin, C., Bai, Y., Hu, P., & Yeh, H. (1998). Substance use disorders among inpatients with bipolar disorder and major depressive disorder in a general hospital. *General Hospital Psychiatry, 20*, 98–101.

Malow, R. M., West, J. A., Williams, J. I., & Sutker, P. B. (1989). Personality disorders classification and symptoms in cocaine and opioid addicts. *Journal of Consulting and Clinical Psychology, 57*, 765–767.

McElroy, S. L., Soutullo, C. A., Beckman, D. A., Taylor, P. Jr., & Keck, P. E. Jr. (1998). *DSM–IV* intermittent explosive disorder: A report of 27 cases. *Journal of Clinical Psychiatry, 59*, 203–211.

McKay, J. R., & Buka, S. L. (1994). Issues in the treatment of antisocial adolescent substance abusers. *Journal of Child and Adolescent Substance Abuse, 3*, 59–81.

Milby, J. B., & Stainback, R. D. (1991). Psychoactive substance use disoders. In Hersen and Turner (Eds.), *Adult psychopathology and diagnosis* (pp. 110–148). New York: Wiley.

Miller, F. T., Busch, F., & Tanenbaum, J. H. (1989). Drug abuse in schizophrenia and bipolar disorder. *American Journal of Drug and Alcohol Abuse, 15*, 291–295.

Mirin, S. M., & Weiss, R. S. (1988, May). *Character pathology in substance abusers.* Presented at the American Psychiatric Association Annual Meeting, Montreal.

Mitchell, J. E., Hatsukami, D., Eckert, E. D., & Pyle, R. I. (1985). Characteristics of 275 patients with bulimia. *American Journal of Psychiatry, 142*, 482–485.

Molina, B. S. G., Bukstein, O. G., & Lynch, K. G. (2002). Attention-deficit/hyperactivity disorder and conduct disorder symptomatology in adolescents with alcohol use disorder. *Psychology of Addictive Behaviors, 16*, 161–164.

Molina, B., Pelham, W., & Roth, J. (1999, June). *Stimulant medication and substance use by adolescents with childhood history of ADHD.* Paper presented at the Biennial Meeting of the International Society for Child and Adolescent Psychopathology, Barcelona, Spain.

Moscicki, E. K. (1997). Identification of suicide risk factors using epidemiological studies. *Psychiatric Clinics of North America, 20*, 499–517.

Nace, E. P., & Davis, C. W. (1993). Treatment outcome in substance-abusing patients with a personality disorder. *American Journal of Addiction, 2*, 26–33.

Nace, E. P., Davis, C. W., & Gaspari, J. P. (1991). Axis II comorbidity in substance abusers. *American Journal of Psychiatry, 148*, 118–120.

Nurnberg, H. G., Rifkin, A., & Doddi, S. (1993). A systematic assessment of the comorbidity of *DSM–III–R* personality disorders in alcoholic outpatients. *Comprehensive Psychiatry, 34*, 447–454.

O'Sullivan, K., Rynne, C., Miller, J., O'Sullivan, S., Fitzpatrick, V., Hux, M., et al. (1988). A follow-up study on alcoholics with and without co-existing affective disorder. *British Journal of Psychiatry, 152*, 813–819.

Ouimette, P. C., Finney, J. W., & Moos, R. H. (1999). Two-year posttreatment functioning and coping of substance abuse patients with posttraumatic stress disorder. *Psychology of Addictive Behaviors, 13*, 105–114.

Petry, N. M. (2001). Pathological gamblers, with and without substance abuse disorders, discount delayed rewards at high rates. *Journal of Abnormal Psychology, 110*, 482–484.

Powell, B. J., Read, M. R., Penick, E. C., Miller, N. S., & Bingham, S. F. (1987). Primary and secondary depression in alcoholic men: An important distinction? *Journal of Clinical Psychiatry, 16*, 98–101.

Pristach, C., & Smith, C. (1990). Medication compliance and substance abuse among schizophrenic patients. *Hospital Community Psychiatry, 41*, 1345–1348.

Prochaska, J. O., & DiClemente, C. C. (1983). Stages and processes of self-change of smoking: Toward an integrative model of change. *Journal of Consulting Psychology, 51*, 390–395.

Rao, U., Ryan, N. D., Dahl, R. E., Birmaher, B., Rao, R., Williamson, D. E., et al. (1999). Factors associated with the development of substance use disorder in depressed adolescents. *Journal of the American Academy of Child and Adolescent Psychiatry, 38*, 1109–1117.

Ravndal, E., & Vaglum, P. (1994). Self-reported depression as a predictor of dropout in a hierarchical therapeutic community. *Journal of Substance Abuse Treatment, 11*, 471–479.

Regier, D. A., Farmer, M. E., Rae, D. S., Locke, B. Z., Keith, S. J., Judd, L. L., et al. (1990). Co-morbidity of mental disorder with alcohol and other drug abuse: Results from an epidemiological catchment area (ECA) study. *Journal of the American Medical Association, 264*, 2511–2518.

Riggs, P. D. (1998). Clinical approach to treatment of ADHD in adolescents with substance use disorders and conduct disorder. *Journal of the American Academy of Child and Adolescent Psychiatry, 37*, 331–332.

Ross, H. E., Glaser, F. B., & Germanson, T. (1988). The prevalence of psychiatric disorders in patients with alcohol and other drug problems. *Archives of General Psychiatry, 45*, 1023–1031.

Rounsaville, B. J., Dolinsky, Z. S., Babor, T. F., & Meyer, R. E. (1987). Psychopathology as a predictor of treatment outcome in alcoholics. *Archives of General Psychiatry, 44*, 505–513.

Schiff, M. M., & Cavaiola, A. A. (1990). Teenage chemical dependence of psychiatric disorders: Issues for prevention. *Journal of Adolescent Chemical Dependency, 1*, 35–46.

Schneier, F. R., Johnson, J., Horig, C. D., Liebowitz, M. R., & Weissman, M. M. (1992). Social phobia: Comorbidity and morbidity in an epidemiologic sample. *Archives of General Psychiatry, 49*, 282–288.

Schneier, F. R., & Siris, S. G. (1997). A review of psychoactive substance use and abuse in schizophrenia: Patterns of drug choice. *Journal of Nervous and Mental Disease, 175*, 641–652.

Schuckit, M. (1985). The clinical implications of primary diagnostic groups among alcoholics. *Archives of General Psychiatry, 42*, 1043–1049.

Scott, H., Johnson, P., Menezes, P., Thornicroft, G., Marshall, J., Bindman, J., et al. (1998). Substance misuse and risk of aggression and offending among the severely mentally ill. *British Journal of Psychiatry, 172*, 345–350.

Seligman, L. (1996). *Diagnosis and treatment planning in counseling.* New York: Plenum Press.

Sinha, R., & O'Malley, S. S. (2000). Alcohol and eating disorders: Implications for alcohol treatment and health services research. *Alcoholism: Clinical and Experimental Research, 24*, 1312–1319.

Skinstad, A. H. (1994). MMPI characteristics of alcoholics with borderline personality disorder. *European Journal of Psychological Assessment, 10*, 34–42.

Sonne, S. C., Brady, K. T., & Morton, W. A. (1994). Substance abuse and bipolar affective disorder. *Journal of Nervous and Mental Disease, 182*, 349–352.

Stewart, S. H. (1996). Alcohol abuse in individuals exposed to trauma: A critical review. *Psychological Bulletin, 120*, 83–112.

Stewart, S. H., Samoluk, S. B., & MacDonald, A. B. (1999). Anxiety sensitivity and substance use and abuse. In S. Taylor (Ed.), *Anxiety sensitivity: Theory, research, and treatment of the fear of anxiety.* Mahwah, NJ: Erlbaum.

Stowell, R., & Estroff, T. (1992). Psychiatric disorders in substance abusing adolescent inpatients: A pilot study. *Journal of the American Academy of Child and Adolescent Psychiatry, 31*, 1036–1040.

Swartz, M. S., Swanson, J. W., Hiday, V. A., Borum, R., Wagner, H. R., & Burns, B. J. (1998). Violence and severe mental illness: The effects of substance abuse and non-adherence to medication. *American Journal of Psychiatry, 155*, 226–231.

Tessler, R. C., & Dennis, D. L. (1989). A synthesis of NIMH-funded research concerning persons who are homeless and mentally ill. NIMH Division of Education and Service Systems Liaison, Washington, DC.

Test, M. A., Wallisch, L. S., & Allness, D. J. (1989). Substance abuse in young adults with schizophrenia. *Schizophrenia Bulletin, 15*, 465–476.

Thomas, S. E., Thevos, A. K., & Randall, C. L. (1999). Alcoholics with and without social phobia: A comparision of substance use and psychiatric variables. *Journal of Studies on Alcohol, 60*, 472–479.

Thompson, L. L., Riggs, P. D., Milulich, S. K., & Crowley, T. J. (1996). Contribution of ADHD symptoms to substance use problems and delinquency in conduct disordered adolescents. *Journal of Abnormal Child Psychology, 24*, 325–347.

Triffleman, E. (1998). An overview of trauma, PTSD and substance abuse. In H. Kranzler & B. Rounsaville (Eds.), *Dual diagnosis and treatment* (2nd ed., pp. 263–316). New York: Marcel Dekker.

Verheul, R., van den Brink, W., & Hartgers, C. (1995). Prevalence of personality disorders among alcoholics and drug addicts: An overview. *European Addiction Research, 1*, 166–177.

Verheul, R., Kranzler, H. R., Poling, J., Tennen, H., Ball, S., & Raunsaville, B. J. (2000). Axis I and axis II disorders in alcoholics and drug addicts: Fact or artifact? *Journal of Studies on Alcohol, 61*, 101–110.

Wallace, B. C. (1987). Crack addiction: Treatment and recovery issues. *Contemporary Drug Problems,* Spring, 1990.

Wallace, B. C. (1991). *DSM–III–R:* Diagnosing cocaine dependence and other psychopathology. In Crack cocaine (pp. 15–36). New York: Brunner/Mazel.

Weiss, R. D., Mirin, S. M., Griffin, M. L., Gunderson, J. G., & Hufford, C. (1993). Personality disorders in cocaine dependence. *Comprehensive Psychiatry, 34*, 145–149.

Westermeyer, J., Eames, S. L., & Nugent, S. (1998). Comorbid dysthymia and substance disorder: Treatment history and cost. *American Journal of Psychiatry, 155*, 1556–1560.

Wilens, T. E., Biederman, J., & Spencer, T. J. (1996). Attention-deficit hyperactivity disorder and the psychoactive substance use disorders. *Child and Adolescent Psychiatric Clinics of North America, 5*, 73–91.

Wilson, G. T. (1991). The addiction model of eating disorders: A critical analysis. *Advances in Behavior Research and Therapy, 13*, 27–72.

Wolpe, P. R., Gorton, G., Serota, R., & Sanford, B. (1995). Predicting compliance of dual diagnosis in patients with aftercare treatment. *Hospital Community Psychiatry, 44*, 45–49.

8

Families and Drugs

Ann W. Lawson
Gary W. Lawson
California School of Professional Psychology
Alliant International University

TRUTH OR FICTION?

___ 1. Biology and environment both play a part in the etiology of alcoholism.

___ 2. Systems thinking is not concerned with what causes addiction.

___ 3. Bowen theory was influenced by biology.

___ 4. There is no research evidence that family therapy is successful in treating adolescent drug abuse.

___ 5. Birth order affects the roles children play in families.

___ 6. Healthy boundaries in families that allow closeness and independence are referred to as disengaged.

___ 7. Coalitions involve three people.

___ 8. Family rituals are important in reducing the intergenerational transmission of addictions in families.

___ 9. Having an alcoholic parent increases a person's risk for developing alcoholism.

___ 10. Personality factors have been shown to have no effect on a person's risk for alcoholism.

___ 11. Cultural factors can affect physiological reactions to mind-altering substances.

___ 12. Once a parent achieves sobriety the problems of the children go away.

___ 13. Children of alcoholics often have developmental delays.

___ 14. Adult children of alcoholics continue to experience problems after they leave home.

___ 15. Fifty percent of children raised in substance abusing homes become alcoholics in their lifetime.

The goals of this chapter are to: (a) introduce you to systems thinking, (b) give you a history of systems thinking in the substance abuse field, (c) define family therapy terminology and help you apply this thinking to family dynamics that foster and maintain addictive behaviors, (d) provide you with a biopsychosocial model of the effects of substance abuse on the family, and (e) increase your understanding of the effects of addiction on children of alcoholics and adult children of alcoholics.

Although you may not be trained as a family therapist, understanding how substance abuse in one family member affects the entire family system is essential in understanding how to treat a substance abuser. There are still many questions to be answered in the field of substance abuse. It is ever evolving with new theories and treatment modalities. However, there is one thing we know. Substance abuse and addictive behaviors tend to run in families generation after generation.

Systems thinking differs from *linear* cause and effect thinking (A causes B). From a systems perspective, A causes B that causes C that affects D and interacts with E, which affects A and B, and so on. There is no real beginning or ending and family members' behaviors are bidirectional. Behavior is understood in a context, and problems are seen as symptoms of a stuck system that may be maintaining the problem.

This chapter provides a systems model of thinking about addictions and a biopsychosocial model that looks at risk factors in the physical, social or environmental, and psychological areas. Although this can be used as a way to view an individual's risk factors for addiction, there are important family factors that can be assessed with this model. We first provide some history of systems thinking and how this has influenced the substance abuse field. Then we introduce the family factors found in the biopsychosocial model and conclude with a discussion of problems and resiliencies of children of alcoholics.

ROOTS OF FAMILY THERAPY

Family therapists have borrowed a notion from anthropology's approach to *functionalism*—that deviant behavior may serve a protective function for a social group—and then applied it to the symptoms of family members (Nichols & Schwartz, 1995). Functionalists believed that families needed to adapt to their environments and if they developed symptoms they were not adapting and were unable to meet their needs.

Ludwig von Bertalanffy, a biologist, developed a model of general **systems theory** that related to any system, whether physical like a machine, biological like a dog, psychological like a personality, or sociological like a labor union. These systems had properties or rules, such as *a system is more than the sum of its parts*—or *wholeness*. For example, a watch is made up of wheels and parts, but when put together it can also tell time (Davidson, 1983).

1. Bertalanffy's theory that systems are more than the sum of their parts is _____.
   a. wholeness
   b. empathy
   c. equifinality
   d. circular causality

Cybernetics was another major influence on family therapy that was developed by Norbert Weiner, a mathematician studying machines. The central principle of his theory was the *feedback loop*—a process of getting self-correction information to maintain a balance or make progress toward a goal (Nichols & Schwartz, 1995). These can be *positive* feedback loops, which amplify deviation from a state or direction, or *negative* feedback loops, which reduce deviation. The classic example is the regulation of the temperature in a house by a thermostat. As the outside temperature increases, it creates a negative feedback loop and the thermostat activates the air conditioner to cool off the house. This brings it back to its original state.

2. The concept of *feedback loops* comes from _____.
   a. general systems theory
   b. cybernetics
   c. Bowen theory
   d. behavioral therapy

3. In the example of the thermostat, the outside temperature is _____.
   a. negative feedback loop
   b. positive feedback loop
   c. a conduit
   d. a reinforcer

Gregory Bateson, an anthropologist, brought the concept of cybernetics to family therapy with his notion of **circular causality.** He believed that symptoms or psychopathologies were caused by ongoing circular feedback loops (Nichols & Schwartz, 1995). Family therapists apply these concepts to families by studying: (a) rules that govern behavior, (b) negative feedback loops, (c) the sequence of events around a problem and how a pattern evolves, and (d) the outcome of negative feedback loops that do not solve the problem or positive feedback loops that do not push for new solutions. These responses can be viewed in the alcoholic family system that has a set pattern in response to the intoxicated behavior of a family member. The family springs into action to try to solve the problem. Rules get established as the mother says, "Stop making noise. It'll upset your father." The nonalcoholic parent may become overresponsible and take on the management of the family. The children learn it is better not to talk about the problem. Secrets are kept and rigid role behaviors are developed to try to solve the problem. This all leads to a static state to keep the family together, but the sequences of behavior become part of the problem. Instead of the drinking behavior being a *deviation*, it becomes the *expected* and family members learn to adapt, creating a stuck system. Often negative feedback, such as nagging or complaining, has failed to correct the deviation. The classic example of a negative feedback loop that fails is, "If you didn't nag, I wouldn't drink."—to which is responded, "If you didn't drink, I wouldn't nag!" This can lead to an increase in the drinking behavior or a continuation of the current pattern.

Another theorist, Murray Bowen, was strongly influenced by the biological sciences that govern living organisms. His most important concept, *differentiation of self*, was taken from cell biology and is based on the process in which cells differentiate from each other or are fused together. Thus, differentiation of self is a metaphor representing the emotional process people experience when they differentiate themselves from others or when they choose to "fuse" with others. He referred to a high level of emotional reactivity as an *undifferentiated family ego mass* (Nichols & Schwartz, 1995). The influence of the theory of evolution can be seen in Bowen's premise of the **multigenerational transmission** *process* whereby low levels of differentiation and high levels of reactivity are passed down through generations, creating symptoms in family members. This concept helps explain the multigenerational processes in substance abusing families that transmit alcoholism and other drug addiction across generations. Bowen describes the transmission of alcoholism in families in the only paper he wrote about a particular symptom (Bowen, 1974).

The History of Family Therapy and Substance Abuse

The early 1950s saw the beginning of the paradigm shift from viewing substance abuse as an individual problem to a symptom of family dysfunction or multigenerational processes. In one of the first articles, four types of wives of alcoholics were identified: the sufferer, who needs to punish herself by living with an alcoholic; the *controller,* who tries to change her mate; the *waverer,* who needs to be needed and is fearful and insecure yet competent; and the *punisher,* who demonstrates her superiority to her mate and drives him to drink. Although this is not a systemic understanding of the relationship between an alcoholic and his wife, it was the beginning of trying to understand how systems can become stuck and harmful to all those involved.

A review of the family and substance abuse literature reveals four distinct areas of research: 1) biological influences, 2) environmental influences, 3) risk factors for children of alcoholics, and 4) treatment outcome studies. The first two areas are covered in the section on the biopsychosocial model, and the children's issues are reviewed in the last section of the chapter.

Obviously, treatment outcome research is needed to establish the efficacy of using a family therapy model to treat addictive disorders. Studies have usually found that including the spouse or other family members improves treatment outcome. Many studies evaluating behavioral marital therapy have shown good treatment outcomes when using spouse involvement as opposed to not involving the spouse in treatment (McCrady et al., 1986; O'Farrell, Cutter, & Floyd, 1985; O'Farrell & Choquette, 1991). The National Institute of Drug Abuse (NIDA) funded several treatment outcome studies to evaluate the usefulness of family therapy with adolescent substance abuser. Most, if not all, found family therapy to be superior to other modalities (Friedman, Tomko, & Utada, 1991; Joanning, Quinn, Thomas, & Mullen, 1992; Liddle & Diamond, 1991; Piercy & Frankel, 1989; Quinn, Kuehl, Thomas, & Joanning, 1988; Szapocznik, Kurtines, Foot, Perez-Vidal, & Hervis, 1986). In 1995, the *Journal of Marital and Family Therapy* published meta-analyses of treatment outcome studies of the effectiveness of treating alcoholism and drug abuse with a marital or family therapy approach (Edwards & Steinglass, 1995; Liddle & Dakof, 1995). Both reported positive findings for the effectiveness of a family approach. These reviews have recently been brought up to date. Rowe and Liddle (2003) reported significant progress in the treatment of drug abuse problems, particularly with adolescents. They concluded, "Family-based treatments are currently recognized as among the most effective approaches for adolescent drug abuse" (p. 97). With regard to adult drug abusers, they reported that recent systematic application and testing of engagement techniques and behavioral couples therapy approaches have produced better outcomes. O'Farrell and Fals-Stewart (2003) reported that if the alcoholic was willing to seek help, MFT helped the family cope better and motivated the alcoholic to enter treatment. They also found Al-Anon helped families, Community Reinforcement and Family Training encouraged treatment entry, and behavioral couples therapy (BCT) was more effective than individual treatment in increasing abstinence and improving the marital relationship. BCT reduced social costs, domestic violence, and emotional problems for the children in the family.

The early contributions from various fields led to the development of some key concepts common to several theoretical models of family therapy. However, each theory has unique concepts and terminology to explain how problems are created and maintained in families. The next section of this chapter overviews some core ideas common to systems thinking.

KEY CONCEPTS IN VIEWING THE FAMILY AS THE CLIENT

The following are terms and ideas that will help you view and assess families in which one or more people are addicted to alcohol and/or other drugs. Structural family therapy and strategic family therapy adhere to the majority of these concepts. Intergenerational family therapists see symptom formation and maintenance from a different perspective. The intergenerational approach to viewing substance abuse is covered the next section.

Homeostasis

Gregory Bateson, an anthropologist, was interested in communication in families, particularly in families with schizophrenic children. Don Jackson, working with Bateson's research group in Palo Alto, CA, coined the term *homeostasis* to define balancing behavior in families. This balance shifts in response to changes in the family system and pressures from without. If you can imagine the family being like a mobile (the art form), with each family member being a piece of the mobile connected with wires and strings, you can see how the pieces move about and return to a balance—homeostasis (Wegscheider, 1981).

Ewing and Fox (1968) applied this theory to the alcoholic marriage that is "established . . . to resist change over long periods of time. The behavior of each spouse is rigidly controlled by the other. As a result an effort by one person to alter typical role behavior threatens the family equilibrium and provides renewed efforts by the spouse to maintain status quo" (p. 87).

Alcohol and other drugs often become a part of the family homeostasis. Family members adapt to the presence of drug abuse and it becomes familiar. If the addicted person stops using the drug, the family is thrown into turmoil as if it were a mobile in a windstorm. This can increase the risk for relapse or posttreatment divorces.

> 4. Jackson coined the term *homeostasis* which refers to:
>   a. the structure of the family.
>   b. the intergenerational transmission process.
>   c. the balance of equilibrium of the family.
>   d. the members of the family.

Family Roles

The principles of homeostasis include predictable roles that family members play and the rules that govern them, both overt and covert. Birth order often plays an important role in determining the behavior of children. Firstborn children are only children until the second children are born. They are born into a family of adults who may have high expectations for these children. Older daughters often become caretakers for younger children. If the oldest child is a high achiever, the second born may not wish to compete. He or she might excel in other areas, such as sports or the arts, or may develop problems to take the focus off of a strained marriage or symptomatic parent. With the birth of the third child, the second born becomes the middle child, who may be concerned with fairness and equal treatment. Youngest children are born into an established family that may have rigid rules about how to deal with addiction in the family. They may feel left out and have a high need for attention. These birth orders can change with blended families. For instance, when parents remarry, the oldest child in one family may be younger than a stepsibling from the other family.

All families have roles that the members play. However, in families with addictions or other problems, these roles become rigid. Children often blame themselves for the pain in the family and try to fix it by rigidly playing out their role in the system, for example, the oldest making better grades. Virginia Satir, a pioneer in the family therapy field, identified role behaviors that people play when they are under stress (Bandler, Grender, & Satir, 1976). She labeled the roles the *blamer,* the *placater,* the *irrelevant* and the *superreasonable.*

5. Which birth order is most likely to produce a high achiever?
   a. oldest
   b. second born
   c. youngest
   d. middle child

When addiction is present in the family, children know that something is wrong and frequently blame themselves. It gives them a false sense of control to think that if they caused the problem, then they can work harder at fixing themselves and, in turn, fix the parent with the problem or the troubled family system. Family members work hard at their roles to save the family, even at the expense of their own emotional or physical health.

Two of the early pioneers in the promotion of treatment for children of alcoholics, Sharon Wegscheider and Claudia Black, developed typologies of role behaviors. Wegscheider (1981), a student of Virginia Satir's, gave titles to family roles played in the alcoholic family. The children's roles included: (a) the *family hero,* usually the oldest, who provides self worth for the family with hard work, achievement, and success, but feels lonely, hurt, and inadequate; (b) the *scapegoat,* the child who acts out, abuses alcohol and drugs, and takes the focus off the seemingly unsolvable family problem of alcoholism, but feels lonely, rejected, hurt, and angry; (c) the *lost child*, who offers relief by not being a problem, but withdraws, is quiet, and feels lonely, hurt, and inadequate; and (d) the *mascot,* often the youngest, who distracts family members by, providing fun and humor senses tension, and feels insecure, frightened, and lonely.

These role behaviors become rigid in stressful times and serve as attempts as survival. If these children don't receive help through counseling or family therapy, they are likely to repeat them as adults. However, if they receive help they can modify these roles and expand the positive attributes of the roles.

6. In Wegscheider's roles of the alcoholic family, which role is taken by the child who acts out, abuses alcohol and drugs, and takes the focus off the family problem of alcoholism?
   a. the family hero
   b. the scapegoat
   c. the lost child
   d. the mascot

Black (1981) defined the role behavior of children of alcoholics in two categories: (a) the misbehaving, obviously troubled children, and (b) the mature, stable, overachieving, behaving children, who Black believed are the majority. She divided these young children of alcoholics into three types:

1. *responsible* ones, usually the oldest who feel responsible for everyone; are adult-like, serious, rigid, and inflexible; have little time for play or fun; and whose self-reliance leads to loneliness
2. *adjusters*, who follow directions are flexible to adjust to the fighting, separations, and life changes of the alcoholic family; and feel they have no power over their own lives
3. *placaters*, who are emotionally sensitive children; take care of others first to reduce their own pain and make life easier; feel they don't deserve to have their own needs met; sooth conflicts; are rewarded for their help; work too hard at taking care of others; and neglect their own feelings and needs.
   (See Table 8.1 for a summary of these role behaviors.)

7. What is Black's corresponding role to Wegscheider's "family hero"?
   a. adjuster
   b. placater
   c. mascot
   d. responsible one

Family Rules

Although it is difficult to separate rules from roles, the rules are more a part of the homeostasis and boundaries in families. Some of these rules are spoken or *overt*, such as bedtime, or *covert*, such as an unspoken deal made at the time of the marriage: I will teach you to have fun if you will be the responsible one and won't expect much from me. Everyone in the family knows the rules and these rules govern family members' behavior. Rules may include who can express feelings, what feelings are appropriate, and when it is "dangerous" to express them. Rules are often created about levels of independence, conflict, or closeness in families. Typical rules in alcoholic or addict families concern the best way to deal with the intoxicated or high person and secret keeping to protect the alcoholic or addict or to preserve the family.

Black (1981) listed three rules that may occur for children of alcoholics: Don't talk. Don't trust. Don't feel. Children come to believe that commenting on or noticing the intoxication could make it worse. They may have experienced this more than once. They also learn that an alcoholic's promise is soon forgotten in favor of drinking. Feelings are usually too painful to

TABLE 8.1

Role Behaviors of Children of Alcoholics

Wegscheider	*Black*	*Characteristics*
Family hero	Responsible one	loneliness, overachievment, parentified
Scapegoat	Misbehaving	hurt, anger, rejection, takes focus off alcoholic
Lost child	Adjuster	loneliness, isolation, escapes, no problem to the family
Mascot	Placater	provides relief, makes others feel better, emotionally isolated

acknowledge and certainly might cause too much family disruption. These children learn to deny their feelings and thoughts in favor of trying to make things better in the family.

Boundaries

Boundaries in this context are not the rules for behavior of children, nor are they processes of limit setting or punishment. *Boundaries* include rules about how people relate to each other, how much closeness or distance can be tolerated, and how the family connects with the larger society. This concept of structural family therapy is defined on a continuum with very rigid (disengaged) boundaries on one end and very diffuse (enmeshed) boundaries on the other. Health is defined as being closer to the middle of the continuum or having clear boundaries.

8. Which type of boundary is considered the most healthy for families?
   a. enmeshed
   b. disengaged
   c. rigid
   d. clear

Enmeshed or diffuse boundaries leave no room for flexibility or differences. Sameness or belonging is stressed in these relationships, resulting in a sense of closeness or cohesion. Ethnic and cultural factors dictate how much closeness a family can tolerate. Many families with a cultural background that expects family closeness can tolerate a great deal of closeness without creating symptoms in a family member.

Disengaged or rigid boundaries are frequently seen in alcoholic families with the result of isolation of family members from each other and isolation of the family from the community. The disengagement of family members is perpetuated by family rules such as: it is not safe to comment on alcoholism or drug addiction, it is not wise to confront the alcoholic or addict, and it is essential to the survival of the family to protect the alcoholic or addict so things don't get worse. The lack of social contact sets up a rigid boundary around the family, especially during active substance use. Children may feel a lack of cohesion or connectedness to the family and may not be receiving the kind of parenting that helps them develop a solid sense of themselves. As these children reach adolescence, they find it difficult to leave home in a healthy manner. They may be using drugs and unable to keep a steady job. Researchers have reported that young adults and adolescents with drug problems often describe their families as chaotic and disengaged (Friedman et al., 1991; Olson & Killorin, 1987).

9. Which type of boundary had the least tolerance for independence?
   a. clear
   b. disengaged
   c. rigid
   d. enmeshed

Alliances and Coalitions

Alliances are connections between two people in the family about some issue or a position they are taking. Parents can have an alliance with one another about how to parent the children. Two sisters may create an alliance to deal with a pesky brother. However, families usually operate in triangles to create a sense of stability. This could be two against one, two for one, one pulled between two, one as a go-between for two others, and so forth. Drugs and alcohol can be the third point of a triangle, as well.

10. An *alliance* involves how many people?
    a. two
    b. three
    c. two adults and one child
    d. two children and one adult

Coalitions are created in a family when two people ally against a third. When a wife is afraid to confront her husband for fear of a violent response, she may create an alliance with her son to fight her battle. Coalitions often create cross-generational boundaries. For instance, if a wife has not successfully individuated from her **family of origin** before she gets married, she may continue an enmeshed relationship with her mother that is stronger than her marriage. If this relationship creates conflict in her marriage, a coalition of mother and daughter against the daughter's husband could be very damaging to the marriage.

11. The definition of a *coalition* is:
    a. two people involved with an issue.
    b. the purpose of a subsystem.
    c. the siblings in a family.
    d. two people in an alliance against a third.

In healthy families, alliances are within the generations. There is an alliance between the husband and wife, between grandfather and grandmother, and among the siblings. When cross-generation alliances are created between a spouse and a parent or between a parent and a child, this often substitutes for marital closeness. "Whenever generational boundaries are consistently violated and members of one generation supply what should be received in another generation, pathology can be expected" (Haley, 1976, p. 39).

12. An example of a *cross-generational alliance* would be:
    a. between husband and wife.
    b. between siblings.
    c. between a wife and her mother.
    d. between grandparents.

Symptoms

Symptoms, as defined by family systems thinking, are the problems that are created when a system becomes stagnant and unable to move through the family life cycle. The family roles, rules, boundaries, alliances, and coalitions combine to establish a family homeostasis. In the substance abusing family, the substance of abuse (alcohol or other drugs) becomes part of the balance. Family members learn to adapt to the presence of the abuse. Although alcohol and other drug abuse can be viewed as a symptom of a problematic system, it is difficult to determine if the addiction caused the system to be stuck or the system produced the symptom. This is not important if you are conceptualizing the problem using circular causality, which is more interested in what is *maintaining* the symptom. This does not necessarily mean that if the system is changed through family therapy that the alcoholic or addict will immediately stop abusing drugs. However, it may allow the person with the addiction to seek treatment.

Bowen (1974) defined three areas within the **nuclear family** in which symptoms are expressed: marital conflict; dysfunction in a spouse, such as addiction; and projection to one or more children. Bowen called the third area the family projection process. In this process, families project their problems onto their children, who become symptom bearers for the family. This child is referred to as the identified patient (IP) who carries the symptoms of the problematic family. Family therapy sees the symptom bearer as the person who expresses the pain of the whole family.

13. What is *not* an area where symptoms occur in the nuclear family according to Bowen Theory?
    a. marital conflict
    b. dysfunction in a spouse
    c. cross-generational alliance
    d. projection to one or more children

Although the symptoms of alcoholism and drug addiction are extremely disruptive to families, they often become part of the systemic balance and serve a function in the family. Davis, Berenson, Steinglass, and Davis (1974) observed that families tend to maintain alcoholic behaviors. They videotaped couples in therapy when the alcoholic husband was drinking (wet state) and when he was not (dry state). They found the couple to be more relaxed and talkative when the husband was intoxicated and more rigid and closed when he was not. These observations led them to believe that patterns of behavior were set up around the wet and dry states and created **adaptive consequences** that, in turn, maintained the symptom. They reported that these adaptive consequences of alcohol abuse "are reinforcing enough to maintain the drinking behavior regardless of its causative factors. These adaptive consequences may operate on different levels including intrapsychic, intracouple, or to maintain family homeostasis" (Davis, Berenson, Steinglass, & Davis, 1974, p. 210).

14. A concept defined by Davis, Berenson, Steinglass, and Davis that explains why drinking behavior is maintained by its positive attributes that are either intrapsychic, intracouple, or used to maintain family homeostasis is _____.
    a. the reinforcing principle
    b. the adaptive consequences
    c. the negative consequences
    d. cohesion

INTERGENERATIONAL TRANSMISSION OF ADDICTIONS

One of the most important concepts in the field of families and addictions is the transmission of addictive behaviors in families, generation after generation. Bowen (1974) developed a theory of multigenerational transmission. While working with schizophrenic families he saw a distinction between affective states and cognitive processes and that led to his scale of differentiation. *Differentiation* is the ability to maintain a nonanxious presence in the face of anxious others and saying "I" when others are demanding "we" (Friedman, 1991). He found that the more people could connect with their families of origin without losing their positions and were able to regulate their reactivity, the more they were differentiated.

Low levels of differentiation are often found in substance abusing families in which family members are highly reactive to the addiction and often sacrifice their needs for the sake of protecting the alcoholic or addict and the family system. "Basically, the concept states that emotional responses, both their nature and the degree of their intensity, are passed down from generation to generation" (Friedman, 1991, p. 147). Thus, the lower the levels of differentiation in the family, the higher the chances become for transmitting addictive behaviors from one generation to another.

15. The concept of self-differentiation is part of what theory?
    a. Bowen theory
    b. structural family theory
    c. experiential family theory
    d. behavioral theory

Wolin and associates were interested in this multigenerational process in alcoholic families and how the family environment may be a transmitter of alcoholism (Bennett, Wolin, Reiss, & Teitelbaum, 1987; Steinglass, Bennett, Wolin, & Reiss, 1987; Wolin & Bennett, 1984). They investigated *family rituals*, which they defined as repetitive patterns that are stable over time, such as dinnertime, holidays, evenings, weekends, vacations, visitors in the home, and discipline. They believed that these patterns were important because they "stabilize ongoing family life by clarifying expectable roles, delineating boundaries within and without the family, and defining rules so that all family members know that 'this is the way our family is'" (Wolin, Bennett, & Noonan, 1979, p. 590). Steinglass et al. (1987) stated, "family rituals are, in effect, condensed, prepackaged training modules intended to convey to all family members the important facts about family identity" (p. 309). The researchers found that families whose rituals were disrupted or changed during the period of heaviest drinking by the alcoholic parent were more likely to transmit alcoholism to the younger generation than were families whose rituals remained intact.

In another study of married children of alcoholics, these researchers found that couples that were the most resistant to transmission lived two hundred miles away from their families of origin and visited them two times per year (Bennett, Wolin, & Reiss, 1988). This process was referred to as *selective disengagement.*

Another concept, *deliberateness,* was coined from a study of spouse selection (Bennett, Wolin, & Reiss, 1988). Children of alcoholics who deliberately selected healthy mates and took control of their own lives communicated important messages to their children. Spouse selection in a deliberate way, establishment by the couple of their own family rituals and heritage, participation in institutions of the community, and selective disengagement from the families of origin are strategies proposed by this group of researchers to reduce the transmission of alcoholism across generations. In summation of their ritual studies, Steinglass et al. (1987) said:

We believe that the transmission of alcoholism from one generation to the next involves the whole family system over time. The context for transmission is the sum total of interactions, attitudes, and beliefs that define the family. The process is ongoing and dynamic and has no particular beginning, end, or pivotal event. And it often goes on outside the awareness of the participants involved, the "senders" as well as the "receivers." (p. 304)

The importance of studying the intergenerational transmission of alcoholism and drug addiction in families lies in the potential to stop this transmission and reduce the risk for the children. This is an important concept for prevention of this high-risk group (children of alcoholics). This is further explored in the last section of this chapter.

16. What did Wolin and his associates find that reduced the transmission of alcoholism to the next generation?
   a. adaptive consequences
   b. maintaining family rituals
   c. independence of the spouse
   d. family cohesion

A BIOPSYCHOSOCIAL MODEL OF RISKS FOR ADDICTIONS

When we closely examine addictive behavior it seems clear that there are multiple factors involved in why one person becomes addicted and another person does not. For convenience we can divide these factors into three areas. In this case, the *physiological* (also called the *biological*), the *psychological*, and the *sociological* areas all seem to play a part in the likelihood of a person becoming or not becoming addicted to something during his or her lifetime. The family is indeed influential in the majority of factors in each of these areas. From the makeup of your DNA to the cultural values you hold, the customs you practice to the development of your personality, your family has a major impact on your development. However, none of these factors alone is entirely predictive of addiction in any individual. One individual who has many high-risk factors may not become addicted whereas another person, from the same family, seemingly with the same risk factors, does. All risk factors must be examined in combination.

How does one child in a family become an addict and another child, in the same family, remain addiction free? The answer to this and many other questions about addictions can be examined using what we envision as the dynamics of addictions, in this case the *family* dynamics of addiction. Let us first examine each of the three areas individually and then how all of the factors come together to produce an addictive family dynamic.

Physiological Risk Factors

Would you like to know through genetic profiling if you are at high risk for an addictive disorder? What would you do if you were? We currently have a much better understanding of the functions of different genes in our chromosomes than we did just a few years ago. Addiction is such a complicated process involving so many variables it is unlikely that any one gene will ever be identified as the "addiction gene." However, we do know from a great deal of research that there are genetic and biological factors that run in families that increase the risk of addictions in members of certain families. More than 20 years ago Cotton (1979) reviewed thirty-nine studies of the incidence of family alcoholism. She found that regardless of the population studied, an alcoholic was more likely to have a father, mother, or more distant relative who was an alcoholic than nonalcoholic comparisons. Two-thirds of the studies found that at least 25% of the alcoholics had fathers who were alcoholics. Family studies, twin studies, adoption studies, half-sibling studies and animal studies have all shown a tendency for addiction to run in families. (Lawson & Lawson, 1998). However, so does speaking English, French, or Japanese. That does not necessarily mean they are genetic or even biological in nature.

17. A research method used to separate nature from nuture would be
    a. adoption studies
    b. twin studies
    c. half-sibling studies
    d. all of the above

The primary point here is that if you come from a family where addiction has been a problem you are likely to be at a higher risk than someone who does not. Here are some questions to determine if you or someone you are working with in therapy is a physiological risk for becoming addicted to alcohol:

1. Do you have a parent or grandparent who was alcoholic?
2. If you have started drinking, are you able to drink larger amounts of alcohol than most of your friends with fewer physical consequences (e.g., hangover)?
3. Did you drink large amounts of alcohol from the first time you started drinking?

If the answer to one or more of the questions above is yes, there is a good chance that you are at risk for an alcohol problem, unless of course, you choose not to drink alcohol. Biological risk is more complicated with other addictions such as addictions to behaviors, like gambling or shopping, or addiction to other related things we routinely do like eating or having sex. With these disorders the line between compulsion and addiction becomes blurred, but the dynamics are often the same in both addictions and compulsions. However, we can conclude that addictive behavior may have a biological component and be transmitted genetically.

18. Which would be more likely to increase your physiological risk for alcoholism?
    a. having a parent who is alcoholic
    b. having a friend who is alcoholic
    c. living in a culture where there are alcoholics
    d. none of the above

Psychological Risk Factors

What makes a person psychologically at risk for addictive behaviors and what does the family have to do with it? There is sufficient research to indicate that one's psychological makeup is a factor in the dynamics of addiction and that the family plays a role in how we develop our personalities. There does not seem to be a specific typology of the "addictive personality." However, characteristics such as dependency, denial, depression, superficial sociability, emotional instability, suspiciousness, low tolerance for frustration, impulsivity, self-devaluation, and chronic anxiety occur with high frequency (Kaufman, 1994).

19. Which is *not* a personality trait that is likely to increase the risk for alcoholism?
    a. independent
    b. impulsive
    c. low tolerance for frustration
    d. emotional instability

There are several issues to consider regarding personality. Can one change his or her basic personality? What role does the family play in the development of personality? Do these psychological risk factors result from the addiction and will they go away if the addictive behavior is stopped?

If personality is defined as the approach one takes when interacting with the world around them, then certainly one can change. There appear to be three primary things individuals can change: their behavior, their thinking, and their feelings. The environment, and thus the family, impacts all these and can also be instrumental in eliciting change in these areas.

Clinical experience and research has taught us there are three common psychological themes found in treating addicted persons, which are closely related to family issues. They are attachment, control, and self-concept. We develop our ideas regarding *attachment* early in our family of origin depending on how connected we feel to our parents or primary care taker. The risk of addictive behaviors increases if we do not develop an appropriate attitude regarding attachment to others. Coombs and Landsverk (1988) found that lack of closeness to father was highly predictive of drug use among adolescents. The closer they reported they were to their father, the less likely they were to use drugs. Closeness to mothers was also highly predictive but not as much as with fathers.

Control, meaning the number of parentally defined conduct norms was also a predictor in the Coombs and Landsverk (1988) study. The more conduct norms, the less likelihood of substance abuse. Control is also important in reducing anxiety levels. The more anxious we are, the more likely we are to develop addictive behaviors in an attempt to control the anxiety.

Attachment and control are both directly related to *self-image*. How we see ourselves has a great deal to do with how we behave, think, and feel. Our family is where we develop our ideas about control and attachment. It is also where we begin to develop our concept of self. Messages we get from our family have a profound effect on our sense of self and our ability to deal with the environment.

Parenting and Risk

We suggest four types of parents who, by the nature of their interaction within families (family dynamics), are likely to produce children who are at high risk for addiction. These include: the addict or alcoholic parent, the teetotaler parent, the overly demanding parent, and the overly protective parent (Lawson & Lawson, 1998).

The *alcoholic or addict parent* increases risk in their children by modeling substance abuse, which increases the chances their children will follow their lead. Also, alcoholic or addict parents often provide an environment for their children that seems out of control or unpredictable. The family dynamics listed above cause anxiety and feelings of negative self-worth. We must, however, recognize that in some cases, this seemingly unhealthy environment produces children who thrive and develop survival skills that serve them well as adults.

The *teetotaler parent* is defined as someone who has a moral or religious objection to the use of mind-altering substances like alcohol. Often they object to such use by anyone. Teetotalers may set up a dynamic where children are feeling too controlled, which may lead to rebellion through substance abuse. However, this leaves adolescents with a sense of guilt and betrayal of their family beliefs. It is true that children from these structured situations are less likely to use drugs or alcohol, however, if they do use, they are more likely to have problems related to their use (Stolnick, 1958).

The *overly demanding parent* is one who never gives the child an opportunity to reach a level of self-worth that is necessary for a life without mental anguish. But we believe that this overdemanding is most often covert: parents who achieve at a level well above most others in society set the bar so high that their children feel unable to ever match or exceed what their parents have done. These children may develop poor self-image, frustration, and a higher risk for substance abuse or addiction.

In the case of the *overly protective parent,* the parent never gives the child a chance to develop a sense of self-sufficiency because they do everything for the child or protect them from natural negative consequences.

This leads to a poor sense of self and an inability to make decesions, which can lead to the child mediating these problems with alcohal and/or drugs. These four parent types are not mutually exclusive and it is possible for a child to have parents who are all of the above. An example would be a teetotaling, overly protective mother and an overly demanding alcoholic father. Poor child!

20. Which is *not* one of the parent types listed as high risk in this chapter?
    a. overdependent
    b. overprotective
    c. overdemanding
    d. teetotaler

THE POOR CHILD

When Josh was young he was consistently anxious. His father was an alcoholic who would often come home drunk and fight with his mother. She did not approve of her husbandi's drinking. She had been taught as a child that drinking alcohol was morally wrong and she still believed this. When she married Josh's dad she knew he drank, but she believed she would be able to change him as her mother had changed her father, from a drunk to a nondrinker. She remembered her dad coming home drunk and fighting with her mother. She promised herself she would not let her children suffer the same anguish she had as a child. Although she had not been able to stop her husband from drinking as she had hoped, she was able to be very protective of Josh in most areas of his life. She was unaware Josh was upset by his parents' fighting because most of the time he was in bed before the fighting started.

Josh's father was a very successful attorney who did not believe his drinking was a problem. He set very high standards for Josh. In academics, sports, and other competitive endeavors, Josh was expected to excel just as his father had. Often he was unable to do this and would turn to his mother for support when his father would chide him for failing to do better. She was happy to provide this support as it made her feel needed and she was in some way getting back at her husband for his drinking behavior.

What are some of the dynamics of this family? What are some risk factors for Josh? What would you do if the wife came to see you for therapy? What would you do if you were a school counselor and Josh's teacher referred him to you for sadness and depression? How could you change the dynamics of this family?

PSYCHOLOGICAL CHARACTERISTICS OF PEOPLE WHO ARE AT HIGH RISK FOR ADDICTIONS

1. Low identification with viable role models that refer to a person's self-concept and reference group (family)
2. Low identification with and responsibility for family process
3. High faith in miracle solutions to problems
4. Inadequate intrapersonal skills
5. Inadequate interpersonal skills
6. Inadequate systemic skills
7. Inadequate judgment skills

Note. Adapted from Glenn (1981).

Sociocultural Risk Factors

Just as control, attachment, and self-image are interlinked, psychological and sociocultural risk factors are closely connected. A behavior that would make someone proud in one social or cultural group might make them ashamed in another social group or culture. Such behavior in each case would, of course, have a direct impact on self-concept.

There are both cultural and social groups whose members are at high risk for substance abuse and addictions compared to other social or cultural groups. For example, Native Americans have an exceedingly high rate of addiction to alcohol as compared to the population in general. However, there are some tribes with low rates of alcoholism. Orthodox Jews have an exceedingly low rate, as do Mormons and other groups with strong communal sanctions against the use of mind-altering substances. Culture might even be a factor in how one reacts to a drug. In a fascinating study of two distinct groups of Mayan Indians, the Chichicastenango of Guatemala and the Chamula of Mexico, Bunzel (1940) reported that although both tribes were hard-drinking and drinking was sanctioned by the culture, the Chichicastenango experienced guilt and hangovers after each binge while the Chamula did not. The cultural aspects of addictive behavior are important to consider when trying understanding addiction especially as they relate to family dynamics.

Cultural aspects can act as a protective factor in the risk of addiction and abuse of substances. In terms of the family, O'Connor (1975) identified eight characteristics that correlate with a low incidence of alcoholism:

1. Children are exposed early to alcohol in family or religious situations.
2. The parents present an example of moderate drinking.
3. The beverages most commonly used contain large amounts of nonalcoholic components.
4. The beverages are viewed as food and are usually served with meals.
5. No moral importance is attached to drinking.
6. Drinking is not viewed as proof of adulthood or virility.
7. Abstinence, but not excessive drinking or intoxication, is considered socially acceptable.
8. There is virtually complete agreement among group members on standards of drinking behavior.

21. Which would be a cultural aspect that would be likely to affect an individual's decision to start, continue, or stop drinking?
    a. beverages are viewed as food
    b. no moral importance is attached to drinking
    c. parents model appropriate drinking
    d. all of the above

Family environments, parenting styles, family structure, and other sociological factors contribute to family dynamics of addictions. Most recently, a review of the research regarding effectiveness of the use of family-based treatment models for both substance abuse (Rowe & Liddle, 2003) and alcohol abuse (O'Farrell & Fals-Stewart, 2003) was published. Family models seem to be effective and in some cases better than individual models. Understanding the dynamics of both functional and dysfunctional families and how the cultural and social factors increase and decrease the risk of addictions is an important aspect in developing family treatment and prevention models.

The purpose of this section was to identify some of the risk factors in each of the three areas and to present a biopsychosocial model of the etiology of addiction. Risk factors are important in the etiology, the prevention, and the treatment of addictive disorders and their accompanying problems.

EFFECTS OF ADDICTION ON CHILDREN

Children of alcoholics are at a higher risk for developing alcoholism and other additions, including eating disorders and compulsive behaviors. As covered in the preceding section on the biopsychosocial model, these risk factors are increased when a child has first-degree relatives with addictive disorders, comes from an environment that is nonsupportive, violent, models alcohol and drug abuse, or comes from a culture that tolerates the abuse. From a developmental perspective, these children may lack the family stability and close loving relationships in their families that promote normal child development. These problems often do not go away when the child leaves home or when the alcoholic or addict is in recovery. In a study of families in Pennsylvania, Booz-Allen and Hamilton (1974) found that "the treatment and recovery of the alcoholic parent does not appear to reduce the problems experienced by the children" (p. 63). The children with the highest risk for developing alcoholism were from a low socioeconomic group, witnessed or experienced violence, were 6 years old or younger at the time of parental alcohol abuse, and lived in a nonsupportive family. The sober family may continue to operate with a poor marital relationship and a parent and child with reversed roles. Family members may have learned dysfunctional communication patterns, lack parenting skills, and be left with many losses. Relapse is all too common. Generally, the problems found in alcoholic families can be put into three categories: marital problems, parental problems, and cross-boundary or child–parent relationship problems (Lawson & Lawson, 1998).

22. In a study of children of alcoholics by Booz-Allen and Hamilton, they concluded what about the effect of treatment and recovery of parents on the problems experienced by children of alcoholics?
    a. it reduced the children's problems dramatically
    b. it did not appear to reduce the problems experienced by the children
    c. it reduced the children's depression
    d. the children developed different problems after their parents' treatment

23. Which was *not* a factor of increased risk for children developing problems in the Booz-Allen and Hamilton study?
    a. lower socioeconomic group
    b. witnessed or experienced physical abuse
    c. six years old or older at the onset of the parental alcohol abuse
    d. lived in a nonsupportive family situation

Marital instability, fighting, and divorce are common in alcoholic families, which can have long-term effects on children. In an early study, Cork (1969) interviewed 115 children living with alcoholic parents. These children reported that their main concerns about their families were parental fighting and quarreling and a lack of interest in them (the children) by both parents. Drinking was sixth on the list of concerns and was only a primary concern for one child compared to ninety-eight children worrying about parental fighting.

These marital problems can be further complicated by spouse abuse, loss of a spouse through a drunk driving death, imprisonment, or death from physical complications of alcoholism. Perhaps the most damaging effects of addiction in the family environment are the lack of structure, inconsistencies in parenting, or lack of parenting altogether. With the preoccupation of the alcoholic with their addiction, the obsession of the spouse with the alcoholic, and the marital disruption of the family, it is no wonder that very little energy is available to the parents for the difficult job of parenting (Lawson, 1990). Inconsistencies in discipline make it hard for children to learn cause and effect connections. Family rules are often not clear and can be contradictory, frequently changing through the wet and dry cycling. When the parent subsystem is overly involved with alcohol or other drugs, it is difficult for them to understand their children's dilemmas.

24. What was the number one concern of children of alcoholics in the Cork study?
    a. parental drinking
    b. parental drunkenness
    c. unhappiness of a parent
    d. parental fighting and quarreling

Children of Alcoholics

There is no single profile of a typical child of an alcoholic. They are valedictorians, school dropouts, class presidents, juvenile delinquents, or invisible children that nobody knows. Not all children of alcoholics develop symptoms, but those who do frequently have problems that are physical, social, or psychological (Lawson, 1990).

25. What are the four categories of problems of children who live in alcoholic families?
    a. physical neglect or abuse, acting out behaviors, emotional reactions, and social and interpersonal difficulties
    b. abuse, aggression, emotional problems, and isolation
    c. developmental problems, emotional reactions, social problems, and academic problems
    d. social problems, academic problems, family problems, and responsibility problems

PROBLEMS OF CHILDREN WHO LIVE IN ALCOHOLIC FAMILIES

Physical Neglect or Abuse
Serious illness
Frequent accidents
Psychosomatic illness

Externalizing Behaviors
Aggression
Justice system involvement
Drug and alcohol abuse

Internalizing Behaviors and Emotional Problems
Depression
Repressed emotions
Suicidal tendencies
Lack of self-confidence
Lack of life direction
Fear of abandonment
Fear of the future
Perfectionism

Social and Interpersonal Difficulties
Family relational problems
Peer problems
Adjustment problems
Developmental lags
Over-responsibility
Feeling different from the norm
Embarrassment about parental behavior
Feeling unloved
Unable to trust

26. Which child is at the most risk for intergenerational transmission of alcoholism?
    a. Susie, who was born to two alcoholic parents, is an only child, has witnessed violence between her parents, lives in a low socioeconomic neighborhood, and is a good student
    b. John, whose father developed alcoholism when John was in high school, has three other siblings, and is an athlete
    c. Mary, whose father is alcoholic and whose parents divorced when she was in junior high, is second born, and eats dinner with her family every evening
    d. Bob, whose mother is a recovering alcoholic, is second born, and has no alcoholic grandparents

Adult Children of Alcoholics

As the substance abuse field moved away from believing that addiction was a problem only for the individual affected, it turned to viewing the other family members as needing help in the recovery process. There was one group, however, who was ignored until the 1980s. Jacobson (1991) chronicled the Adult Children of Alcoholics (ACOA) movement and claimed the term was not used until 1979. It was first coined by Stephanie Brown (1979) in *Newsweek* magazine. This article launched a national frenzy of adults who connected the problems they had in their alcoholic families with their struggles in adulthood.

Depending on the time of onset and the severity of the alcoholism in the family, children may arrive in adulthood having missed out on normal childhood development. However, there is great variability in the problems of ACAs. Researchers report the similarities of ACAs with other people in therapy and the differences between the types and severities of problems ACAs brought into therapy (Vannicelli, 1989). Lawson and Lawson (1998) found differences between clinical and nonclinical populations and other predictors of problems including:

1. Whether one or both parents were alcoholic
2. Age of the child at the onset of parental alcoholism
3. Economic stability of the family
4. Availability and use of external support
5. Duration and severity of the alcoholism
6. Number of generations of alcoholism
7. Recovery status of alcoholic
8. Psychiatric illness in the family
9. Physical or sexual abuse
10. Abilities of the nonalcoholic spouse

The next wave of criticism of the pathologizing of all ACAs came from research on resilient children from alcoholic families (Wolin & Wolin, 1993). These researchers pointed out that although children of alcoholics are a high risk group, only 25% to 30% became alcoholic in their lifetimes—70% to 75% did not.

27. What percentage of children of alcoholics will become alcoholic themselves?
    a. 25%–30%
    b. 40%–45%
    c. 70%–75%
    d. 50%–55%

The Challenge Model of Resiliency

It is clear that not all children of alcoholics are the same. However, even children who have struggled with their parents' alcoholism from birth can rise above adversity and be successful. Wolin and Wolin (1993) identified those children who are less affected as *resilient*, as defined by living, working, and playing well. They call their model the *challenge model* because the children see the challenge of their childhood and rise above adversity. It is in contrast to the medical model or what they call the *damage model* that says a troubled family damages the child, who then has childhood pathologies and succumbs to have only pathology in adolescence and adulthood. The challenge model suggests that the troubled family creates damages and challenges, which, in turn, create child pathologies and resiliencies. They have identified the following seven resiliencies:

1. **Insight**—psychological sophistication, and early *sensing* that something is wrong; in adolescence, sensing becomes *knowing*; and as an adult, sensing becomes *understanding* about themselves and others.

2. **Independence**—the ability to live apart yet relate to others with pressures or demands; an early sign of independence is *straying* away from the family; as an adolescent, *disengaging* feels better; and as adults, they are *separating* from their families in a freely chosen, rational way.

3. **Relationships**—*connecting*; a selective process by which children can bond with parents or others; early on they are *interacting* with healthy parts of their families; later they are *connecting* with others, such as neighbors, coaches, or teachers; and as adults they are *bonding* with friends, spouses, children, and siblings.

4. **Initiative**—the ability to recover from adversity; having a deep sense of self-trust and personal control—survivor's pride; they love a challenge; early on they are *exploring*, in adolescence they are *working*; and in adulthood initiative becomes *generating*.

5./6. **Creativity and Humor**—these are linked and share a common process. *Creativity* is the ability to express and resolve issues through the arts. *Humor* is the ability to laugh at oneself and play to heal. Young children are *playing* with imagination; adolescents are *shaping* this play to add discipline. The adult version of creativity is *composing* and the adult version of humor is *laughing*.

7. **Morality**—the activity of an informed conscience; young children begin *judging* the rights and wrongs of life and their parents; adolescents change this to *valuing* decency, compassion, honesty, and fair play; adults are *serving* others even though they did not receive what they deserved in their families—restore themselves by helping others.

28. In Wolin and Wolin's study on resilient children of alcoholics, which resilience is defined as the ability to recover from adversity, having a deep sense of self-trust and personal control—survior's pride?
    a. morality
    b. insight
    c. initiative
    d. independence

29. Which two resiliencies are linked and share common processes?
    a. initiative and insight
    b. independence and initiative
    c. humor and creativity
    d. relationship and independence

PREVENTION ISSUES

Because children of alcoholics are at high risk for developing alcoholism and other addictive behaviors, it is important to understand what makes them more or less high risk. The biopsychosocial model and the systems model are compatible when the psychological and social areas of risk consider the family dynamics that are set up in the face of active addiction. In order to do a complete risk analysis that leads to a prevention plan, therapists need to consider physical risk factors; sociocultural risk factors—family problems, such as divorce, physical abuse, sexual abuse, and family systems dynamics; and psychological risk factors that may have developed as a result of some of the family factors. The other part of the assessment needs to consider family strengths and individual resiliencies of the family members. Prevention efforts and treatment processes that take all of these areas into consideration will have a better chance of succeeding.

30. When planning a prevention program or a treatment plan it is important to assess _____.
    a. physicial risk factors
    b. social cultural factors and family dynamics
    c. psychological problems and resiliencies
    d. all of the above

KEY TERMS

adaptive consequences: A concept that implies that there is a function of the symptom of alcoholism that maintains drinking in a system.

boundary: A concept of structural family therapy that describes the emotional distance between individuals, subsystems, families, and the larger society.

circular causality: The notion that events are related through interacting loops and repeating cycles

deliberateness: A term that Wolin and his associates gave to ACAs who were aware of whom they were picking as mates. They made deliberate healthy choices.

differentiation: A Bowen concept which is the opposite of fusion; the availability of both cognitive and emotional processes; the ability to relate without loss of self.

disengaged: A type of boundary defined by structural family therapy that creates isolation in the family; also called *rigid* boundaries.

enmeshed: A type of boundary defined by structural family therapy that blurs boundaries and reduces individuality; also called *diffuse* boundaries.

family of origin: A person's parents and siblings.

feedback: A return of the output of the system to maintain the output at predetermined limits or to modify the system.

homeostasis: A balance of the family's equilibrium; a tendency to resist change.

multigenerational transmission: A process that Bowen described in which chronic anxiety in families transports symptoms from generation to generation; can be through the family projection process.

nuclear family: The family of the parents and children.

selective disengagement: A term that Wolin and his associates gave to the type of relationship that ACAs who are doing well have with their families of origin.

systems theory: A term for the study of related elements that operate as a whole; influenced by general systems theory and cybernetics.

DISCUSSION QUESTIONS

1. Why is it important to examine family history of substance abuse and current family dynamics when treating addiction?

2. How is systems thinking different from linear thinking?
3. What are some family dynamics that promote the intergenerational transmission of substance abuse in families?
4. What increases the risk for the transmission of alcoholism in families? What is caused by biology and what is caused by the environment?
5. Describe a family that is high risk in all three biopsychosocial categories.
6. How do the three biosychosocial categories interact? How does this happen over time?
7. Why is the concept of *adapative consequences* of alcoholism important?
8. How can the concept of *resilience* be used to stop the intergenerational transmission of alcoholism?
9. Explain how families with disengaged boundaries and rigid rules create problems for children in these families.
10. In what ways are children's development interrupted by addiction?

SUGGESTED FURTHER READING

Bowen, M. (1974). Alcoholism as viewed through family systems theory and family psychotherapy. *Annals of the New York Academy of Science, 233*, 115–22.

This is an application of Bowen Theory applied to the etiology of alcoholism in a system. It is the only paper he wrote about a particular symptom and is a classic in the field.

Lawson, A., & Lawson, G. (1998). *Alcoholism and the family: A guide to treatment and prevention*. Austin, TX: ProEd Publishers.

This book is an expansion of the topics covered in this chapter. It goes into depth on each of the sections and reviews the literature in the field.

Lawson, G., & Lawson, A. (Eds.). (1992). Adolescent substance abuse: Etiology, treatment, and prevention. Austin, TX: ProEd Publishers.

This is an edited book with chapters that cover all the unique issues in the treatment if adolescent substance abuse.

Steinglass, P., Bennett, L. A., Wolin, S. J., & Reiss, D. (1987). *The alcoholic family*. New York: Basic Books.

This book reviews the important research done in the field of the treatment of alcoholism in the family. It includes research on family rituals, selective disengagement, adaptative consequences, and deliberateness.

Treadway, D. (1989). *Before it's too late*. New York: W.W. Norton.

This book describes a treatment model that the author refers to as a Minuchin/Bowen model of working with couples in which one spouse has an alcohol problem. It has an excellent chapter on treatment with an adolescent.

Wolin, S. J., & Wolin, S. (1993). *The resilient self: How survivors of troubled families rise above adversity*. New York: Villard Books.

This is a book written for clinicians and clients. It describes resilient ACAs and reviews the resiliencies that lead to ACAs living, loving, and working well.

REFERENCES

Bandler, R., Grender, J., & Satir, V. (1976). *Changing with families*. Palo Alto, CA: Science & Behavior Books.
Bennett, L. A., Wolin, S. J., Reiss, D., & Teitelbaum, M. A. (1987). Couples at risk for transmission of alcoholism: Protective influences. *Family Process, 26*, 111–29.
Bennett, L. A., Wolin, S. J., & Reiss, D. (1988). Deliberate family process: A strategy for protecting children of alcoholics. *British Journal of Addiction, 83*, 821–829.
Black, C. (1981). *It will never happen to me*. Denver: M.A.C. Publishers.

Booz-Allen & Hamilton, Inc. (1974). *An assessment of the needs of and resources for children of alcoholic parents.* Prepared for the National Institute on Alcohol Abuse and Alcoholism, Rockville, MD.

Bowen, M. (1974). Alcoholism as viewed through family systems theory and family psychotherapy. *Annuals of the New York Academy of Science, 233,* 115–122.

Brown, S. (1979, May 28). Kids of alcoholics, *Newsweek,* 82.

Bunzel, A. (1940). The role of alcoholism in two Central American Cultures. *Psychriatry, 3,* 361–387.

Coombs, R., & Landsverk, J. (1988). Parenting styles and substance use during childhood and adolescents. *Journal of Marriage and the Family, 50,* 473–482.

Cork, M. (1969). *The forgotten children.* Toronto: Alcoholism and Drug Addiction Research Foundation.

Cotton, N. S. (1979). The familial incidence of alcoholism: A review. *Journal of Studies on Alcohol, 46,* 89–113.

Davis, D. J., Berenson, D., Steinglass, P., & Davis, S. (1974). The adaptive consequences of drinking. *Psychiatry, 37,* 209–215.

Davidson, M. (1983). *Uncommon sense: The life and thought of Ludwig von Bertalanffy.* Los Angeles. J. P. Tarcher.

Edwards, M. E., & Steinglass, P. (1995). Family therapy treatment outcomes for alcoholism. *Journal of Marital and Family Therapy, 21*(4), 475–509.

Ewing, I. A., & Fox, R. E. (1968). Family therapy of alcoholism. In S. Messerman (Ed.), *Current psychiatric therapies* (pp. 104–119). New York: Grune & Stratson.

Friedman, A. S., Tomko, I. A., & Utada, A. (1991). Client and family characteristics that predict better family therapy outcome for adolescent drug abusers. *Family Dynamics of Addiction Quarterly, 1*(1), 77–93.

Friedman, E. (1991). Bowen theory and therapy. In A. S. Gurman & D. P. Kniskern (Eds.), *Handbook of family therapy, Vol. II* (pp. 134–170). New York: Brunner/Mazel.

Glenn, S. (1981, February). *Directions for the 80s.* Paper presented at the Nebraska Prevention Center, Omaha.

Haley, J. (1976). *Problem solving therapy.* New York: Harper & Row.

Jacobson, S. B. (1991, October). *The recovery movement: From children of alcoholics to codependency.* Paper presented at the National Consensus Symposium on Children of Alcoholics and Co-Dependence, Warrenton, VA.

Joanning, H., Quinn, W., Thomas, F., & Mullen, R. (1992). Treating adolescent drug abuse: A comparison of family systems therapy, group therapy, and family drug education. *Journal of Marital and Family Therapy, 18*(4), 345–356.

Kaufman, E. (1994). *Psychotherapy with addicted persons.* New York: Guilford Press.

Lawson, A. (1990). Group therapy for adult children of alcoholics. In D. A. Ward (Ed.), *Alcoholism: Introduction to theory and treatment* (3rd ed., pp. 477–493). Dubuque, Iowa: Kendall-Hunt.

Lawson, A., & Lawson, G. (1998). *Alcoholism and the family: A guide to treatment and prevention.* Austin, TX: ProEd Publishers.

Liddle, H. A., & Dakof, G. A. (1995). Efficacy of family therapy for drug abuse: Promising but not definitive. *Journal of Marital and Family Therapy, 21*(4), 511–544.

Liddle, H., & Diamond, G. (1991). Adolescent substance abusers in family therapy: The critical initial phase of treatment. *Family Dynamics of Addiction Quarterly, 1*(1), 55–68.

McCrady, B. S., Noel, N. E., Abrams, D. B., Stout, R. I., Nelson, H. F., & Hay, W. M. (1986). Comparative effectiveness of three types of spouse involvement in outpatient behavioral alcoholism treatment. *Journal of Studies on Alcohol, 47*(67), 459–466.

Nichols, M. P., & Schwartz, R. C. (1995). *Family therapy: Concepts and methods.* Boston: Allyn & Bacon.

O'Connor, J. (1975). Social and cultural factors influencing drinking. *Irish Journal of Medical Science, June,* 65–71.

O'Farrell, T. J., & Choquette, K. (1991). Marital violence in the year before and after spouse involved alcoholism treatment. *Family Dynamics of Addiction Quarterly, 1*(1), 32–40.

O'Farrell, T. J., Cutter, H. S. G., & Floyd, F. J. (1985). Evaluating behavioral marital therapy for male alcoholics: Effects on marital adjustment and communication from before to after therapy. *Behavior Therapy, 16,* 147–167.

O'Farrell, T. J., & Fals-Stewart, W. (2003). Alcohol abuse. *Journal of Marital and Family Therapy, 29*(1), 121–146.

Olson, D. H., & Killorin, E. A. (1987). *Chemically dependent famiies and the circumplex model.* Unpublished research report, Univeristy of Minnesota, St. Paul, MN.

Piercy, F. F., & Frankel, B. R. (1989). The evolution of an integrative family therapy for substance-abusing adolescents: Toward the mutual enhancement of research and practice. *Journal of Family Psychology, 3*(1), 5–25.

Quinn, W. H., Kuehl, B. P., Thomas, F. N., & Joanning, H. (1988). Families of adolescent drug abusers. Systemic interventions to attain drug-free behavior. *American Journal of Drug and Alcohol Abuse, 14*(1), 65–87.

Rowe, C. L., & Liddle, H. A. (2003). Substance Abuse. *Journal of Marital and Family Therapy, 29*(1), 97–120.

Steinglass, P., Bennett, L. A., Wolin, S. J., & Reiss, D. (1987). *The alcoholic family.* New York: Basic Books.

Stolnick, J. H. (1958). Religious affiliation and drinking behavior. *Quarterly Journal of Studies on Alcohol, 19,* 452–470.

Szapocznik, J., Kurtines, W. M., Foot, F., Perez-Vidal, A., & Hervis, O. (1986). Conjoint versus one-person family therapy: Further evidence for the effectiveness of conducting family therapy through one person with drug-abusing adolescents. *Journal of Consulting and Clinical Psychology, 54*(3), 395–97.

Vannicelli, M. (1989). *Group psychotherapy with adult children of alcoholics*. New York: Guilford Press.

Wegscheider, S. (1981). *Another chance: Hope and help for the alcoholic family*. Palo Alto, CA: Science & Behavior Books.

Wolin, S. J., Bennett, L. A., & Noonan, D. L. (1979). Family rituals and recurrence of alcoholism over generations. *American Journal of Psychiatry, 136*, 589–593.

Wolin, S. J., & Bennett, L. A. (1984). Family rituals. *Family Process, 23*, 401–20.

Wolin, S. J., & Wolin, S. (1993). *The resilient self: How survivors of troubled families rise above adversity*. New York: Villard Books.

COMMON CLIENT PROBLEMS

Tobacco Use

Steve Y. Sussman
*Keck School of Medicine
University of Southern
California*

Christi A. Patten
*Mayo Clinic College
of Medicine*

Bernice Order-Connors
*School of Public Health,
University of Medicine and
Dentistry of New Jersey*

TRUTH OR FICTION?

__ 1. *A majority of drug abusers also use tobacco products.*

__ 2. *A greater percentage of alcoholics than heroin addicts smoke cigarettes.*

__ 3. *In general, recovery practice over the last ten years supports smoking cessation.*

__ 4. *Cigarette smoking is second only to alcohol as the leading behavioral cause of death.*

__ 5. *The tobacco use quit rate tends to be higher the longer a person is clean and sober.*

__ 6. *One should only consider having their clients quit smoking after they achieve sobriety from other substances.*

__ 7. *Smokers in recovery tend to smoke at equal levels with smokers who do not suffer another addiction.*

__ 8. *One good approach to counseling your clients to quit smoking to use the 5As heuristic—Ask, Advise, Assess, Assist, and Arrange for follow-up.*

__ 9. *If your client is not interested in quitting tobacco use, you should just stop talking about it.*

__ 10. *Abrupt withdrawal is the preferred method to stop smoking among those persons in recovery.*

__ 11. *Environmental changes may be needed to help clients quit tobacco use early in recovery.*

__ 12. *Pharmacological adjuncts and mood management approaches are not recommended quit-strategies to use with smokers in recovery.*

__ 13. *Time of first cigarette is predictive of how dependent a tobacco user is on nicotine.*

_____ 14. *Relapse rates are higher earlier in recovery rather than later among persons who make a serious attempt to quit smoking.*

_____ 15. *A 12-step approach to recovery is intrinsically incompatible with effective smoking cessation.*

Tobacco use is the leading behavioral cause of death. Combining tobacco use with alcohol use exerts a synergistic effect (even more deadly than use of either substance alone) on the occurrence of cardiovascular and lung diseases and cancers of the mouth, throat, and esophagus. Individuals treated for alcoholism are more likely to die of tobacco-related diseases than of alcohol-related causes. Combining cigarette smoking with marijuana use most likely exerts a synergic effect on the occurrence of lung diseases and lung cancer. Thus, treatment for tobacco use is imperative among patients suffering alcohol or drug abuse or dependence disorders.

1. Clients treated for alcoholism are more likely to die from:
   a. alcohol-related causes.
   b. tobacco-related causes.
   c. forest fires.
   d. cirrhosis.

Development of effective integrated tobacco dependence treatment programs for persons recovering from alcohol or another drug abuse or dependence problem is ongoing. This work has begun for at least four reasons (Sussman, 2002). First, there is a high prevalence of cigarette smoking among drug abusers ranging from 60% (typical of alcoholics) to nearly 100% (typical of heroin users). High prevalence of smoking is reported across many different categories of drug use; heavier users of drugs are more likely to smoke cigarettes, smoke more efficiently (i.e., obtain more nicotine per cigarette smoked), and smoke greater numbers of cigarettes per day (Shiffman & Balabanis, 1996).

2. The percentage of drug users who also smoke cigarettes is:
   a. less than 5%.
   b. about 25%.
   c. about 50%.
   d. more than 60%.

Second, smokers in drug recovery generally live in a social climate composed of many other smokers. Even part of the recovery process itself (e.g., attendance at 12-step meetings where smoking is often permitted) may reinforce continued smoking. These smokers are often part of a community of people who will continue to smoke without the introduction of outside policies, clinical treatments, or other smoking cessation programming.

Third, as already mentioned, there are several negative health consequences of combining cigarette smoking with other drugs use (e.g., oral cancer and cardiovascular diseases). Considering the probable long duration of using both cigarettes and other substances together, to permit better overall recovery, it is wise for individuals to quit cigarette smoking and the other substances together. Research has shown that continued tobacco use may act as a cue for alcohol and other drug use (Frosch, Shoptaw, Nahom, & Jarvik, 2000; Stuyt,

1997). Moreover, by quitting all substances, one may gain an increased sense of mastery over self.

Fourth, considering the moderate **association** among the addictions, it may be best for addiction treatment providers to provide a consistent message to patients by addressing all substances of misuse (Little, 2000). Quitting cigarette smoking concurrently with use of other substances more clearly directs a positive overall change in lifestyle as a goal.

3. Treatment for tobacco use should be addressed among individuals in recovery from alcohol and drugs because:
   a. the prevalence of tobacco use is very low in this group.
   b. these individuals smoke fewer cigarettes per day and thus require less intensive treatment.
   c. there are several negative health consequences from combining tobacco use with other drug use.
   d. the social climate of drug users generally supports abstinence from tobacco.

Primary Assertion to the Counselor

The main point that you should be clear about is that tobacco use is not "the lesser of two evils" or a safe alternative to other drug use (Sussman & Ames, 2001). *Nicotine*, the addictive substance in all tobacco products, is as addictive as heroin or alcohol and shows similar relapse rates (Hughes, Higgins, & Bickel, 1994; U.S. Department of Health and Human Services [USDHHS] 1988). Unlike those who use other substances, tobacco users do not tend to engage in the same type of dramatically impairing activities while using tobacco, however, tobacco use is still responsible for a number of negative life consequences (USDHHS, 1989). It accounts for approximately half of all forest and house fires; half of all people who continue to smoke will die of tobacco-caused illnesses; it is a known cause of Sudden Infant Death Syndrome (SIDS) (DiFranza & Lew, 1995); it is responsible for over 53,000 passive smoking deaths in the U.S. annually; (i.e., due to new exposure to smokers' tobacco smoke by nonsmokers, including lung cancers and lung diseases; see U.S. DHHS, 1986); and is a contributing cause of accidents because of a focus on using tobacco rather than the activity at hand (e.g., driving). Tobacco use has become less socially acceptable and may interfere with one's role as a co-worker through effecting a greater number of sick days and time away from the desk. As use becomes more restricted, there is a greater likelihood of significant job impairment due to workplace **smoke-free** policy violations associated with tobacco use. *Substance abuse disorder* is defined by recurrent social, role (e.g., as a co-worker or parent) physical danger, and legal consequences (American Psychiatric Association [APA], 1994). Hence, the signs of an APA-defined *tobacco use disorder* are in the workings.

This being said, many persons in recovery use tobacco and have long viewed its use as an acceptable crutch. For example, while many nonsmoking recovery group meetings are in process, smokers are still permitted to smoke outside the doors of the meeting by using ashtrays provided for them. Although **12-step programs** such as Alcoholics Anonymous (AA) do not have official opinions about tobacco use (in keeping with their traditions), the culture of many such programs is of implicit acceptance of tobacco use. This, however, is slowly changing as more people, including those in recovery, are quitting smoking. One may legitimately ponder whether ashtrays should be provided or whether smokers should be encouraged to wait to smoke until the meeting is over and they have left the premises.

4. Why should recovery facilities become tobacco free?
   a. Tobacco use is an addictive drug like alcohol or heroin.
   b. Tobacco use is the number one behavioral killer.
   c. A consistent recovery message needs to apply to tobacco use as well as to other drugs.
   d. All of the above.

As an addiction counselor, you have a major challenge ahead to try to facilitate tobacco dependence treatment among your clients. We hope that when you have finished reading this chapter, you will appreciate the importance of assisting your clients in quitting smoking or other forms of tobacco use concurrently with their other addiction treatment. In addition, we hope you will understand and gain clues on how to surmount the barriers to providing effective tobacco cessation treatment. Further, we hope you will learn ways to approach your clients regarding their tobacco use and know some tobacco cessation tools including best practices for treating tobacco dependence.

BARRIERS TO TOBACCO CESSATION TREATMENT FOR PERSONS IN RECOVERY

At least five arguments have been employed against addressing smoking cessation treatment for drug abusers already in treatment (Sussman, 2002). First, among those new in recovery there is a notable low success rate. For example, while those new in recovery make the same number of quit attempts as nonabusers, they are 30% to 65% less likely to quit. Second, there is a cultural belief that quitting smoking may be detrimental to drug abuse treatment for some users (Kalman, 1998). In particular, the heavier poly-drug users may tend toward drug substitution. However, for most poly-substance abusers, attempting to quit smoking does not interfere with recovery from the other substance abuse and may in fact enhance recovery from other addictions (Bobo, McIlvain, Lando, Walker, & Leed-Kelly, 1998; Frosch et al., 2000; Hurt et al., 1994; Lemon, Friedmann, & Stein, 2003; Sees & Clark, 1993). For example, among individuals in recovery from alcoholism, quitting smoking may actually enhance recovery success (Massachusetts Medical Society, 1997).

Third, smoking has relatively fewer immediate negative consequences compared to other drugs, even though tobacco is the number one behavioral killer. The tragedy of successfully recovering from alcoholism, only to die of tobacco dependence, has its roots in the very foundation of the 12-step treatment movement. Bill Wilson who began his successful recovery from alcoholism in the 1930s and became a co-founder of AA, died of emphysema, and Dr. Bob Smith, another cofounder of AA, died of pharyngeal cancer. Unfortunately, Bill and Dr. Bob's stories are often repeated today, even though we now have treatments to improve a substance abuser's chances of becoming and staying abstinent from tobacco (Toft, 2002).

Fourth, cigarette smoking can be a means of bonding drug users with one another in the beginning stages of their recovery. In social situations, the very behavior of using a cigarette as a social tool mimics the use of other substances. For example, social activities that are often encouraged, and that may assist in recovery, such as participation in 12-step groups and sober clubs or having a 12-step sponsor, may actually be strong social-environmental obstacles to quitting smoking. This is especially the case when the groups permit smoking or the sponsor is also a smoker. For successful cessation of co-occurring substance and tobacco use, other means of bonding would need to be developed.

Finally, some persons argue that one needs to treat cessation of different substances separately hence (hence the development of different **12-step programs** for support of the cessation of different drugs). A related belief promulgated by members of the 12-step community is that clients in drug recovery should wait a year or more before attempting to stop smoking. This, however, is not in keeping with our approach to treating other drugs of abuse. "Although the dogma has been that it is too difficult to give up all the addictions at the same time, the reality is that the only addiction not addressed when a patient initially presents for substance abuse treatment is nicotine addiction" (Sees & Clark, 1993).

Though these arguments against treating smoking co-occuring with another addiction have been accepted in the past, they are now increasingly recognized as generally dysfunctional beliefs rather than as helpful guidelines. For example, individuals in early alcohol and drug recovery (i.e., three–six months) have been able to successfully stop smoking without jeopardizing their alcohol/drug abstinence (Stotts, Schmitz, & Grabowski, 2003). Thus, there is reason to believe that, for most persons in drug abuse treatment, concurrent exposure to tobacco dependence treatment will assist with recovery.

5. What has been the recovery movement's perspective on tobacco use cessation?
   a. Tobacco use is a fine behavior to engage in.
   b. Tobacco use is a bad behavior.
   c. One could consider quitting tobacco use or other unhealthy behaviors after first things are considered first.
   d. Tobacco use is a core feature of recovery.

6. Barriers or arguments against addressing smoking cessation among individuals in recovery from alcohol and other drugs include:
   a. the low success rate of smoking cessation, especially during early recovery.
   b. there are fewer immediate consequences of smoking compared with other drugs.
   c. cigarette smoking can be a means of bonding drug users with one another in the beginning of recovery.
   d. all of the above.

Indeed, the underlying treatment message should be that it is better to simultaneously quit *all* dangerous substances of misuse or abuse. More and more, tobacco use is being viewed as a dangerous "half measure." If tobacco use is not addressed as part of the recovery process, that would be akin to ignoring another devastating illness or disease, such as uncontrolled hypertension or diabetes, or ignoring substances other than the one that brings the client to treatment. However, to discern helpful strategies of smoking cessation for persons in recovery, you should carefully investigate the characteristics of individuals who both smoke and use other substances.

CONSIDERING YOUR CLIENTS WHO USE TOBACCO: HOW DO THEY DIFFER FROM SMOKERS WHO DO NOT REPORT DRUG PROBLEMS?

It is important to know that 15% of smokers have current, and 40% have past, alcohol problems. Also, greater than 40% of alcoholics have had problems with using other drugs. Thus, current smoking cessation knowledge is likely to apply to many alcoholics and drug abusers (Hughes, 1996). Of course, precisely how generalizable this body of knowledge is to those in recovery is unknown.

Drug abusers who smoke differ in at least six ways from non–drug abusers who smoke (Sussman, 2002). First, drug abusers who smoke often begin smoking at a younger age. Second, drug abusers who smoke are comparatively more addicted to nicotine. In fact, they smoke an average of ten cigarettes more per day than non–drug abusers among adults. Also, the prevalence of heavy smoking (e.g., two or more packs per day) is 72% among drug abusers versus 9% among non–drug abusers. Abusers with a severe drug problem smoke more (two packs to up to four packs per day) than those with a moderate (around one and half packs), or a mild (around one-fourth of a pack) problem. They may report worse withdrawal symptoms (see **nicotine withdrawal** in "key terms"). Third, these smokers generally have more cognitive deficits, perhaps due to the effects of using drugs. Fourth, they have relatively more psychological problems, including depression, anxiety disorders, and personality disorders. Fifth, they have more medical problems, including upper digestive and respiratory cancers, heart disease, pancreatitis, and cirrhosis. Finally, they report relatively low levels of smoking cessation self-efficacy. Although it is impressive to note that 50% to 75% do want to quit smoking, and about 60% want to quit all substances if offered in cessation programming, this is still less than the 80% to 90% of non–drug abusers who want to quit. Also, these clients do show more reticence about taking action to quit—about 65% to 70% are not considering quitting in the next six months (40% among non–drug abusers). This may be due in part to fear–about 5% to 30% believe quitting smoking may impact negatively on the drug use cessation process (Kalman, 1998). Fortunately, though, of those in recovery for several years, 45% to 65% eventually quit smoking, equivalent to that rate for the general population of smokers (around 45%). In summary, drug users who smoke have more life obstacles that may make it more difficult to quit. Later in recovery they seem better able to master more obstacles on their own and successfully quit. However, it is important to note that historically this group has not been offered assistance or encouragement to address their tobacco use. It would be interesting to study quit-rates of people in recovery as treatment providers begin to include tobacco dependence treatment within the addiction treatment milieu. The following sections provide a review of the treatment work that has been completed on this population of smokers.

7. Why are tobacco use rates higher among drug abusers than non–drug abusers?
   a. Both tobacco use and other drug use may have similar effects on the brain.
   b. Drug abusers need many crutches to survive.
   c. Tobacco takes off the edge on all other drugs of misuse.
   d. Tobacco use is fun among long-time users.

8. Smokers who use other drugs differ from those who do not report drug problems in which of the following ways?
   a. They are less likely to want to quit.
   b. They start smoking at a later age.
   c. They are less addicted to nicotine.
   d. They have fewer psychological and medical problems.

TREATMENT IMPLICATIONS: STAGES OF RECOVERY

Therapists need to consider whether the smoker is still using drugs and wants to stop all use concurrently (initial cessation), has just quit drug use (early recovery, stabilization), or has been off other drugs awhile (middle or later recovery). These phases reflect the potential force of drug withdrawal or interaction effects, attributions regarding use of different substances, acute and postacute withdrawal symptoms, adequacy of coping, and social influences. No more than 12% of teen or adult inpatient groups (initial cessation) are able to quit tobacco use or stay tobacco-free when measured approximately 6 months after inpatient treatment. During a cessation attempt, the drug user may experience additional symptoms if he or she quits cigarettes (two-week withdrawal) as well as a drug such as alcohol (one-week withdrawal). On the other hand, the effects of smoking may serve to cue use of another drug such as alcohol to enhance overall psychoactive effects (e.g., awake but relaxed). Thus, cessation may be difficult whether or not one tries to quit both smoking and another drug concurrently (Cooney, Cooney, Pilkey, Kranzler, & Oncken, 2003).

9. When encouraging your client to stop tobacco use, you should consider which of the following factors in relation to your client's stage of recovery?
   a. potential for additional withdrawal symptoms
   b. coping resources
   c. social influences
   d. all of the above

10. Inpatient drug abusers receiving a variety of smoking cessation intervention approaches achieve smoking cessation rates at six months of about.
   a. 50%
   b. 12% or less
   c. more than 90%
   d. 5%

The optimal timing of tobacco use interventions in relation to duration of recovery is currently not well known and needs further study. Early recovery may be an ideal time to engage patients who use tobacco because they are usually well connected to a treatment system for alcohol/drug use (e.g., inpatient treatment) rather than delaying tobacco cessation interventions to a time when the client may not be connected to treatment and professional support. The development of skills for managing high-risk situations for quitting and maintaining abstinence from tobacco use may generalize to other behaviors such as successful maintenance of alcohol and drug abstinence. The National Institute on Alcohol Abuse and Alcoholism (NIAAA) has endorsed the treatment of tobacco in alcoholism treatment and there is increasing reporting that patients who address their tobacco use in treatment fare better (NIAAA, 1998). These patients are better able to focus on the issues central to their recovery and are more likely to complete treatment (Rustin, 1998; Stuyt 2000). During early recovery, clients are likely to experience confusion and urges to use alcohol and/or drugs and may lack effective alternative ways to deal with daily stresses. Smoking may ease urges temporarily and improve affect and thus help the client refrain from using alcohol or drugs. Of course, if one runs short on cigarettes, the urges and confusion may be greater, potentially leading to a greater chance of drug use relapse. Furthermore, others the person meets early in recovery (e.g., at a recovery home) are also likely to be smoking cigarettes. Findings from the Mayo Clinic have suggested that allowing tobacco use in the treatment program, even in a controlled manner had many negative effects including clients reporting difficulties in abstaining from tobacco use due to the daily exposure to smoking as an accepted behavior in the treatment setting (Hurt et al., 1994). Thus, unless policies in treatment programs change, access and social pressures to smoke cigarettes are likely to be great, at least until leaving the recovery placement—which is a tragic loss of opportunity to intervene with clients regarding their tobacco use.

Unfortunately, the first three months of recovery reveal the highest rates of smoking (and drug use) relapse. Generally there are many salient, issues to address, such as DUI, school and license suspension, monetary debt, acute stress, hospitalization, strong urges, school or work issues, relationship damage, and recovery from injuries. Thus, the need for social support is great. Quitting smoking during this time is one more stress, unless smokers quit within a **tobacco-free** environment among people who strongly support recovery from **nicotine dependence**, get through the drug abuse consequences "fall-out" promptly and appropriately (i.e., are able to cope with the reality of their wreckage) and are entrenched with others in an ongoing nonsmoking milieu. This may require large social environmental changes in the recovery community. Contingency management might be pursued for those chemical dependence patients with little other support (Shoptaw, Jarvik, Ling, & Rawson, 1996).

11. The highest rates of relapse occur within the first three months for which of the following drugs?
    a. heroin
    b. alcohol
    c. tobacco
    d. all of the above

Regarding abusers of most drugs, those in very early recovery quit smoking at about one-third the rate of those with more than three months of recovery (e.g., 25% versus 60%; Sussman, 2002). Only 12% of those heroin addicts who are placed on methadone quit smoking successfully while in early recovery (Richter, Gibson, Ahluwalia, & Schmelzle, 2001; Shoptaw et al., 1996). One study did find that more than 40% of drug abusers in very early recovery reported that they had quit for one week; however, 80% of them relapsed rapidly thereafter (Joseph, 1993). On the other hand, there is good news for those persons in early recovery that quit tobacco use for one month or more. They relapse at about the same rate as those who quit later in recovery (e.g., down to 10% versus 25% at one-year follow-up). Thus, the key is to get more people in early recovery to quit smoking for at least two to four weeks (Sussman, 2002).

After three to six months in recovery, smoking cessation rates begin to approach those of non–drug abusers (Kalman, 1998). For those who have been sober for several years, cessation rates are as high as 46% at one year, particularly if **mood management** approaches are included. Because tobacco use cessation rates tend to increase with length of sobriety, some counselors delay encouragement of smoking cessation until some stability in recovery from other drug or alcohol use has been achieved. Later in recovery, once the many sources of stress are addressed, and once the person no longer experiences strong urges to use drugs, smoking cessation may be achieved more successfully.

12. Smoking cessation rates among drug abusers in recovery begin to approach that of non–drug abusers after _____.
    a. three to six months of recovery
    b. two weeks of recovery
    c. one month of recovery
    d. twelve years of recovery

We encourage counselors to encourage their patients to quit smoking as soon as they reach treatment. You, as a counselor, should not be a tobacco user if you are to do this successfully. Your treatment context would need to be smoke-free. You would need to encourage attendance at smoke-free meetings and begin to embed your clients into a smoke-free milieu. At minimum, your clients may fail to quit tobacco use, while not affecting their life negatively otherwise. At maximum, you help them gain a more stable recovery and lengthen the duration of their lives. We believe that large social environmental change in attitudes about tobacco use is the key that opens the door into successful cessation in early recovery.

BEST PRACTICES IN TREATMENT OF TOBACCO USE

In counseling clients on their tobacco use, you can use a very basic approach known as the *5 As* (ask, advise, assess, assist, arrange). The 5 As are recommended by a recent guideline on the best clinical practices for treating tobacco use (Fiori et al., 2000; Rohsenow, Colby, & Martin, 2002; The Smoking Cessation Practice Guidelines Panel and Staff, 1996). These steps are as follows:

1. *Ask* the client about their tobacco use.
2. *Advise* your client to quit using tobacco in a clear, strong, and personalized manner. This includes discussing the health risks of continued tobacco use and emphasizing that quitting tobacco use is one of the most important actions the client can take to improve his or her health.
3. *Assess* whether or not the client is willing to make a quit attempt within the next thirty days and provide the client with self-help tobacco cessation materials.
4. *Assist* your client in quitting and refer for pharmacotherapy if indicated. Provide support and encourage your client to arrange for social support. Suggest and encourage the use of problem-solving methods and skills for cessation and implementing a tobacco-free household.
5. *Arrange* for follow-up assessment of your client's tobacco use.

13. The 5 As recommended as part of best practices for treating tobacco use include:
    a. *advocating* for your client to continue use of tobacco to deal with the stress of sobriety.
    b. *advising* your client to wait to stop smoking at least two years after successful recovery.
    c. *admonishing* your client for using tobacco.
    d. *advising* your client to quit smoking in a clear, strong, and personalized manner.

Important behavioral strategies to assist your clients in quitting tobacco use include skills training, problem solving, and provision of social support as part of treatment. Social support comes from you as a counselor and other tobacco users in group treatment, and from helping your client to secure social support outside of treatment (from a spouse, other family member, or friend). These behavioral strategies also are fundamental to the best practices of treating alcohol and drug use and thus could be readily applied to your tobacco cessation counseling.

14. Effective approaches for assisting your client with stopping tobacco use include.
    a. multiple counseling sessions
    b. skills training and problem solving
    c. providing social support
    d. all of the above

A MODEL OF SMOKING CESSATION BEST PRACTICES AS APPLIED TO PERSONS IN RECOVERY

1. Establish rapport, and ask your client about their attitudes toward their use of drugs now that they are in recovery. (Questions that follow assume that the client has been fully screened for use of other drugs, mental status, and medical status.) Assess how long your client has been in recovery. Also, ask your client about the intensity and components of their recovery program (including 12-step approaches, spiritual program) and other tools currently used to remain alcohol and drug free. Further, ask the extent of smoking permitted at recovery-related social functions and meetings, whether they have a 12-step sponsor, whether the sponsor smokes and is supportive of your client quitting smoking, and what other social support is present.

2. Ask the client about their use of tobacco. Ask them how long they have been smoking or using other tobacco products, their reasons for smoking, and how much they currently smoke per day. Ask whether they use any other tobacco products such as smokeless tobacco (chewing tobacco or snuff), cigars, tobacco pipes, or *bidis* (Indian cigarettes). (These are NOT safe alternatives to smoking.) Ask them when they first smoke after waking up in the morning and previous experiences and successes with quitting smoking. As rules of thumb, a strong addiction to tobacco is indicated if the client smokes a pack or more per day (a half a canister or more of snuff, several cigars or pipes), uses tobacco within 30 minutes of waking up, or reports bad withdrawal experiences in past quit attempts. (Use of pharmacological agents is then recommended.)

3. Ask the client if they would like to quit immediately or sometime during their current treatment for recovery from another drug of abuse. If not right now, ask the client if and when they are planning to quit. (It is best to have a protocol in place for screening and assessing all clients for their tobacco use and to include tobacco in all aspects of their alcohol and other drug treatment.)

4. Assist the client in identifying the negative impact of tobacco use on his or her current life. Reinforce the concept of tobacco as an addictive drug and tobacco use as an addictive behavior. Advise your client of the added health risks of combining alcohol, drugs, and tobacco. Generally, it is best to provide a direct statement that the client quit use of all tobacco products. For example, you might say, "As your counselor, I strongly advise you to quit tobacco use in addition to your other drugs of choice" or "Tobacco use is a dangerous half measure. I advise you to quit its use," or "Quitting now greatly enhances your recovery from alcohol and other drugs." (See also Bobo & Gilchrist, 1983.)

5. If your client does not want to quit, use **motivational interviewing** approaches, which include a supportive, nonconfrontational style when talking with the client. Your goal here is to have the client talk about the benefits and drawbacks to quitting in a supportive environment. Encourage their consideration of quitting and reinforce their ability to do so. Provide self-help materials and arrange for a follow-up assessment of the client's tobacco use. Encourage clients to learn about some potential tools and resources they can use when they are ready (decide) to quit, and to learn about the benefits of abstinence.

6. If your client is not ready to quit, other behavioral strategies include requesting that the client keep a log of their tobacco use. Also, request that they write down

the pros and cons of quitting as well as their personal reasons both for continued tobacco use and for quitting. Further, request that they make attempts to delay use or cut down on amount used, and become familiar with (listen to) stories and experiences of former smokers or chewing tobacco users. From a chemical dependence perspective, you can help your client to recognize their defenses (e.g., denial, rationalization), identify the importance of their tobacco use, and identify powerlessness in controlling use. For example, clients in drug recovery attempting to stop smoking may say "I have enough to deal with already," or "I've tried to quit before but failed," as a rationale for not attempting to quit. You can teach your clients that quitting smoking may actually help them cope better, and that most smokers make several attempts at quitting before experiencing success. Moreover, you can encourage your client to identify their fears in quitting, accept the need for recovery of tobacco use, and to use the 12 steps (Stotts et al., 2003).

7. Strategies for those clients interested in quitting are described in the text. These include both behavioral and pharmacological strategies.

Moreover, the effectiveness of your counseling will increase with its intensity (i.e., more sessions, and longer duration of sessions). Thus, patients should be provided with multiple sessions, and, arguably, should attend at least four sessions to enhance probability of quitting successfully. You should also make use of follow-up sessions, including counseling phone calls and visits. More details on the 5 A's are provided in the box.

15. Which of the following is a safe alternative to alcohol or other drugs of abuse?
   a. cigarettes
   b. chewing tobacco
   c. snuff
   d. none of the above

16. If a client is not ready to quit tobacco use, you should:
   a. confront the client about their tobacco use.
   b. provide the client with self-help materials on quitting tobacco.
   c. encourage the client to listen to stories of people who decided not to quit.
   d. acknowledge that the client has enough to deal with already in treatment.

17. Chemical dependence or 12-step approaches to addressing tobacco use include:
   a. advising the client to keep a log of their tobacco use.
   b. referring the client for pharmacotherapy.
   c. helping the client to accept the need for recovery and to identify their powerlessness in controlling their tobacco use.
   d. encouraging the client to substitute chewing gum or fruit when experiencing urges to smoke.

18. Which of the following would be an indicator of a client's strong dependence on tobacco?
   a. smoking within twenty minutes of waking up
   b. few withdrawal symptoms experienced during prior quit attempts but the client fears it would be worse this time
   c. smoking five cigarettes a day
   d. enjoys a cigar with friends when celebrating holidays

19. If a client rationalizes their continued tobacco use by pointing out the stress they are
    already experiencing with becoming alcohol/drug free, you could:
    a. empathize with your client that quitting tobacco use may be difficult for them.
    b. build their confidence to quit (e.g., by pointing out previous successes in quitting
       tobacco or their current ability to maintain successful recovery).
    c. reinforce tobacco use as an addictive drug/behavior.
    d. all of the above.

TREATMENT IMPLICATIONS: STRATEGIES FOR QUITTING

Much progress is now being made in the treatment of tobacco use among individuals with
alcohol and/or drug abuse disorders (Bobo, Anderson, & Bowman, 1997). Tobacco cessation
education or counseling can be delivered through a variety of settings (e.g., drug offender
education, residential care, outpatient group counseling, telephone counseling; Leed-Kelly,
Russell, Bobo, & McIlvain, 1996; Stuyt, Order-Connors, & Ziedonis, 2003). Aside from obtaining the best practices book (Fiori et al., 2000), quit programming material can be acquired
from the National Cancer Institute (www.nci.nih.gov), your local American Heart Association (www.americanheart.org), American Lung Association (www.lungusa.org), or American
Cancer Society (www.cancer.org), as examples. Some of this material can be downloaded after
a cursory Web search.

Programming specifically for persons in recovery is now beginning development. As an
example, there is assistance available from the American Academy of Family Physicians
(www.aafp.org/afp/980415ap/mcilvain.html). Written quit programing material literature now
exists (e.g., see Hoffman et al., 2004; JSI Research and Training Institute, Inc., 2002
Massachusetts Tobacco Education Clearinghouse, e.g., www.mteccatalogue.com; [www.
familydoctor.org/269.xml]). Also, there are chat rooms for persons who want to share
their experiences with quitting tobacco addiction (e.g., www.QuitSmokingChat.com). There
also are policy guidelines for recovery facilities (e.g., "Drug-Free is Nicotine-Free: A
Manual for Chemical Dependency Treatment Programs," www.tobaccoprogram.org and
www.BHCS.co.alameda.ca.us; see also Stuyt et al., 2003), and Web pages from experts on
smoking cessation for those in recovery (e.g., Rustin (1998); www.QuitAndStayQuit.com).
There is even an organization to promote tobacco use cessation among persons in recovery
(CENAR or Council to End Nicotine Addiction in Recovery; see www.healthrecovery.org/proj/
tobpro/tobpro.html).

Because drug abusers who smoke are likely to incur medical problems, a *medical screening*
and exam should be completed prior to initiating a treatment program. This is also useful in
assessing for any contraindications to using pharmacological aids in cessation, if appropriate.
Numerous strategies have been shown to be effective in smoking cessation. These are not
presented in any particular order and counselors should consider using these strategies in
combinations that will best aid their clients.

Environmental Strategies

Treatment in a tobacco-free setting provides tremendous environmental support. Here, patients
are free from exposure to tobacco use both indoors and on the facility's grounds, and tobacco

cessation assistance is fully integrated into the treatment milieu, which can assist at least short-term cessation and provision of tobacco and nicotine education. Education and ongoing options for smoking cessation should also be provided to drug abuse treatment providers, as 30% to 40% of these treatment providers smoke, and 50% to 60% of recovering providers smoke. It is possible to achieve attitudes more favorable toward smoking cessation treatment among staff once they understand the rationale for integrating tobacco treatment. As a policy, a more favorable nontobacco environment may be achieved by persuading staff to not only refrain from tobacco use on site, but to also not be identifiable as a tobacco user during work hours. It is also possible to instruct staff on counseling patients regarding smoking cessation (e.g., see box). However, enforcement of the practice is needed so that a majority of patients would be counseled. While some treatment agents may be afraid that one will lose clients if one pushes tobacco use cessation along with initial cessation of other drugs at the facility, such an effect has only been observed briefly in facilities that have changed their policies on tobacco use, not in the long-run (Hoffman et al., 2004).

A good example of developing tobacco-free recovery facilities is provided in the "12 steps to becoming tobacco-free for addictions treatment programs" (Hoffman & Slade, 1993). This is a blueprint for a systematic policy approach to developing a tobacco-free program. The most challenging component of this approach is that staff persons are required to not be identifiable as tobacco users. It is implicit in providing tobacco use treatment on par with alcohol and drug abuse treatment that staff role model a tobacco-free lifestyle. Realistically, those who have quit tobacco use are better able to help clients be successful in quitting than staff who continue to smoke. One may need to spend at least twelve months in converting a facility from one that allows smoking to one that does not. Initially, resistance from patients and staff is expected, but resistance vanishes after several months with little loss of income for the facility. Once the tobacco-free facility goal is accomplished, clients have the advantage of not being tempted by the sight of tobacco paraphernalia or the smell of cigarette smoke. It is of note that in 1999, the state of New Jersey adopted the Residential Substance Abuse Treatment Facilities Licensure Standards giving tobacco parity with alcohol and other drugs of abuse and requiring a paradigm shift necessitating tobacco-free residential treatment. This type of action helps to level the playing field and support clients receiving addiction treatment in getting optimal comprehensive treatment for their tobacco addiction.

During or after leaving the recovery facility, the drug abuser's home environment also needs consideration. Drug abusers who smoke have relatively more family, friends, and peers who are smokers (e.g., 53% of drug abusers versus 40% of non–drug abusers who smoke live with a smoker). Thus, there is a need to provide significant-other education or provide material on how to cope with smokers. For example, given *a priori* agreement with others in the household, smokers can be asked to move all smoking outside. Alternatively, it can be expected that the nonsmoker will remove him- or herself from a location where smoking is occurring (Hurt, Croghan, Offord, Eberman, & Morse, 1995; Joseph, 1993; Patten et al., 1999; Patten, Martin, & Owen, 1996).

20. Which of the following are environmental factors to consider in planning your client's treatment for tobacco use?
   a. the client's medical problems
   b. your own tobacco use and tobacco use among other treatment staff
   c. the client's cognitive abilities
   d. the client's psychological problems (e.g., depression)

21. Significant others can assist your client with stopping tobacco use by:
    a. smoking near the client.
    b. stealing the client's cigarettes.
    c. limiting the client's smoking to only one room of the house or outside.
    d. encouraging the client to smoke in the morning but not the evening.

22. Information to help persons in recovery quit tobacco use is provided by _____.
    a. the AAFP
    b. CENAR
    c. Hazelden
    d. all of the above

23. Tobacco cessation programming is most effective in recovery facilities if:
    a. treatment staff smoke only on the grounds.
    b. all tobacco use is limited to outside the facility buildings.
    c. tobacco use is limited to tobacco use sections of the facility.
    d. tobacco is not used anywhere in the facility or on the grounds.

Cognitive Strategies

One may need to use various motivation strategies to recruit smokers to treatment and facilitate quit-attempts. In particular, one might use **stages of change**–related approaches to assist smokers in deciding to quit (e.g., self-reevaluation, consideration of costs versus benefits of smoking; Prochaska & DiClemente, 1983). Further, mnemonics and other memory devices can help when teaching techniques for quitting and remaining tobacco-free. These kinds of mental strategies can also help to accommodate cognitive deficits as well as assist in commiting material to memory.

Belief System/Language Strategies

Tailoring interventions to the needs of your clients using this strategy, popularly used in many recovery facilities, may enhance success, especially if your client is actively engaged in such a program. The group support provided in a traditional chemical dependence program could be easily expanded to deal with nicotine use issues. While some counselors prefer to have a group dedicated to tobacco use and cessation, it is best to incorporate nicotine as "just another drug of abuse/addiction" into *all* regular groups addressing other drug and alcohol use.

Because many of your smoking clients will have experienced or participated in 12-step approaches to recovery, the same approach can be transferred to stopping and maintaining tobacco abstinence. The basis for the 12-step philosophy is for individual clients to recognize their powerlessness over the drugs of abuse followed by working through specific steps of personal growth to achieve recovery. For example, the counselor can present each component of the intervention for stopping tobacco (e.g., cutting down on cigarettes, creating a smoke-free home, attending only nonsmoking AA meetings, getting a nonsmoking sponsor, and seeking out support) as "steps" in the process. Maintenance of a tobacco-free lifestyle can include such steps as writing out a tobacco use inventory, sharing this inventory with a sponsor, and making amends to others for the worry that may have been produced by the client's tobacco use or by passive exposure to tobacco smoke. In addition, the client could serve as a sponsor or pathfinder for others who wish to quit tobacco use (e.g., Toft, 2002). Referral to Nicotine Anonymous (www.nicotine-anonymous.org) or Smokers Anonymous (www.realfriendsandfamily.org/sa.html) could be considered, as well. Also, some books and other resources that use a 12-step approach are available to help patients recovering from nicotine. For example, the book, *If Only I Could Quit* presents the personal stories of twenty-three people who grappled with nicotine addiction as well as ninety daily meditations readers can use for their own recovery (Casey, 1987). Another source is the "Twelve steps for tobacco users: For recovering people addicted to nicotine" (Jeanne, 1984).

Related to this, it is helpful for clients to think about quitting tobacco use as a process that requires continued vigilance for a prolonged period, similar to their recovery from alcohol and drugs. Thus, encourage your clients to actively engage in their program for stopping tobacco use much like they would for their alcohol/drug recovery. Moreover, the same philosophy used in 12-step approaches to alcohol/drug recovery highlighted by phrases such as "One day/moment at a time," and "This too shall pass," and focusing on progress made can also be very helpful in tobacco use cessation. Build on the clients' *success* in their alcohol/drug recovery—the same methods by which the client became sober/drug free can be applied to stopping tobacco. For example, if your client experiences urges to smoke or is dealing with negative mood, ask the client what they have done or are currently are doing when they experience alcohol/drug urges or when they felt depressed or anxious when stopping alcohol/drug use, and reinforce those same methods with tobacco. This will also allow you to provide a consistent message regarding all drugs of abuse. Other chemical dependence-based strategies that you could suggest to the client include developing an emergency list of persons and actions to use in relapse-risk situations or when experiencing urges to use tobacco. You might also help your client in recognizing the loss and related feelings in stopping tobacco, finding or seeking out support from a 12-step sponsor, attending an AA, 12-step, or other group meeting, and talking with a friend or seeking professional help (see Stuyt et al., 2003).

Because it may be difficult for your clients to try to stop tobacco use at the same time as other substances, frequently a client who has made unsuccessful attempts to stop tobacco use or who has relapsed may state, "At least I'm not using [drugs/alcohol]." It will be helpful for you to reinforce their alcohol/drug abstinence (focus on the progress made), remind them of the importance of quitting tobacco, and encourage them to try again and to apply the same tools that have been successful in their recovery from other drugs of abuse.

24. Tobacco use is a safe alternative to the use of other drugs if:
    a. one considers use of heroin or other intravenous drugs.
    b. one considers that tobacco use can help people bond together in fellowship.
    c. one smokes outdoors.
    d. none of the above.

25. Will one lose clients if one begins to push tobacco use cessation along with cessation of other drugs at the facility?
    a. yes, in the short run
    b. yes, in the long run
    c. no, not in the short run or the long run
    d. yes, in the short run, but not in the long run

26. For clients ready to quit tobacco, you can suggest which of the following strategies?
    a. 12-step approaches
    b. aversion therapy
    c. hypnosis
    d. none of the above

Mood Management Training Strategies

Many drug abusers may smoke as a mood elevator, and some other means of coping with negative affect may be needed. Moreover, the majority of clients in alcohol or drug recovery have experienced clinical depression or high levels of depressive symptoms, and there also is a high rate of current or past depression among tobacco users. Cognitive-behavioral strategies to assist in mood regulation can be applied to both tobacco use and alcohol and drug recovery. These include increasing awareness of the relationships among negative thoughts (e.g., "I will never be able to quit smoking"), mood (e.g., anxiety), and tobacco use by having clients increase their attention to or even write down their negative thoughts and mood each time they use tobacco. In other words, they may realize that tobacco use causes stress. Other strategies include increasing enjoyable, pleasant activities and social contacts; relaxation training; and assertiveness and social skills training. Mood management strategies may also include antidepressant medications or other pharmacotherapy. (See Patten, Martin, Myers, Calfas, & Williams, 1998, for a review of mood management training.)

27. Mood management strategies:
    a. assist clients in using the 12 steps.
    b. help clients in overcoming cognitive deficits.
    c. assist clients in coping with stressful situations.
    d. help clients recognize the relationship between drug use and medical problems.

28. Mood management strategies for tobacco cessation include:
    a. antidepressant medication or other pharmacotherapy.
    b. quitting cold turkey.
    c. attendance at 12-step meetings.
    d. creating a smoke-free home.

Abrupt Withdrawal

Regarding specific quit method, naturally occurring successful quitting behavior among this group tends to be *abrupt withdrawal*. One should consider "cold turkey" over tapering. You can prepare your clients by capitalizing on their prior experiences in quitting and build on any previous successes. You could set up a quit date with your client. Ways to prepare your client for their quit date include encouraging them to attend only nonsmoking meetings and removing all ashtrays and tobacco products from their residence. If they are residing in a recovery home or halfway house it is best for the facility to have tobacco-free policies which would remove or reduce cues to smoke in their environment by having both indoor and outdoor smoke-free policies. For the individual, it is helpful to limit all smoking to the outdoors and to refrain from socializing with others when using tobacco (all tobacco use is done alone). It is important to have a plan for coping with withdrawal symptoms; have candies, gum, fruit, water, and other substitutes available to deal with smoking urges.

Pharmacologic Adjuncts

Because drug abusers tend to be heavier smokers, effective treatment for tobacco use generally combines pharmacologic and behavioral approaches. Guidelines on best practices for treatment of tobacco use recently recognized five first-line medications (nicotine gum, nicotine patches, nicotine nasal spray, nicotine vapor inhaler, and bupropion) and two second-line medications (nortriptyline and clonidine; Fiore et al., 2000). Many people in drug recovery have medical contraindications to using some of these therapies. For example, if a client reports a history of seizures or current alcohol dependence placing them at risk for withdrawal seizures, use of bupropion would be contraindicated. Except in the presence of contraindications, clients attempting to stop smoking should use one or more effective pharmacotherapies (Dale, Ebbert, Hays, Hurt, 2000). Individuals in alcohol or drug recovery show high initial rates of smoking abstinence with nicotine patch therapy, but also a high rate of relapse to smoking. The nicotine patch is usually associated with higher rates of compliance than other forms of **nicotine replacement therapy** (NRT). Aside from contraindications, the choice of pharmacotherapy should be guided by client preferences, tolerability of potential side effects, and cost.

Clients who smoke more than a pack a day may benefit from medically supervised use of multiple patches and ad lib use of another nicotine replacement product such as gum, lozenge or an inhaler with gradual tapering (Dale et al., 2000). Bupropion has been shown to be even more effective when combined with the nicotine patch (Hurt et al., 1997), however this combination is associated with more hypertension so blood pressure needs to be monitored. Because of the high prevalence of a past history of depression in smokers with alcohol/drug abuse or dependence, you may encounter a client who wants to stop smoking but is already receiving treatment with an antidepressant. There is no drug/drug interaction to preclude the use of bupropion with either selective serotonin reuptake inhibitors (SSRIs) or tricyclic antidepressants. Thus, it is preferable to add bupropion to an SSRI rather than discontinue that medication and use only bupropion (Hurt & Patten, 2003). Details on the use of buproprion, clonidine, nortriptyline, and nicotine (patch, gum, inhaler, or spray) can be found in the Fiore et al. (2000) USDHHS *Treating Tobacco Use and Dependence* reference guide for clinicians (ISSN-1530-6402; Available by calling 1-800-CDC-1311).

29. Pharmacologic adjuncts for treating tobacco use include _____.
    a. bupropion
    b. nicotine inhaler
    c. clonodine
    d. all of the above

30. When considering options for pharmacotherapy you should consider:
    a. clonidine as a first-choice medication.
    b. results of the client's medical screening.
    c. whether or not the client's home is smoke-free.
    d. frequency of client attendance at 12-step meetings.

Though this doesn't really need to be said, some clients might suggest that they quit smoking by engaging in "marijuana maintenance." A good source of marijuana consequence information is available from the British Lung Foundation (2002). As an addictive drug with numerous consequences, you could say, "Marijuana is not a safe alternative to tobacco use."

———

There is still much to learn regarding smoking cessation for those who also have a current or past history of drug abuse. Recruiting large numbers of smokers to treatment early in recovery (e.g., greater than 20% of those smokers at a facility) demands that a strong and consistent anti-smoking message needs to be provided at these organizations. The use of cigarettes as a means of sharing and bonding, or as a means of self-identification as being one in recovery, demands counteraction; "waiting time" alternatives (e.g., computer games, sharing of sugar free candies or recovery tip cards, small "gossip" rooms) might be offered instead. The nostalgic look at smoking portrayed in personal stories told at meetings or in some recovery literature now are being at least tempered with a recognition that tobacco use is dangerous (e.g., non-smoking recovery meetings are increasing in popularity). Although other substances incur more dramatic immediate effects on behavior, handing out posters that both inform about the harms of tobacco use and encourage recovery from nicotine dependence at treatment facilities should be considered. Staff not being identifiable as tobacco users and an ultimate goal of 100% cessation by staff should be encouraged (as is being realized at present among physicians, who now serve as good role models for their general practice patients).

Treatment needs to be supportive for quitting multiple substances, and structured so as to support sustained quitting—up to a full month—perhaps after which time the client may be better able to maintain smoking cessation. Of course, maintenance strategies (coping, vigilance) need thorough instruction. Finally, for those who do not quit early in recovery, after six-months of abstinence, promotion of tobacco cessation should be revisited in aftercare programs, drug diversion facilities, and at locations of recovery meetings. Eventually, with continued research and practice, and use of tailored program development strategies, cessation rates will improve among the many smokers in recovery.

NOTES

Correspondence regarding this chapter should be addressed to Steve Sussman, Ph.D., Institute for Health Promotion and Disease Prevention Research and Department of Preventive Medicine, University of Southern California, 1000 S. Fremont Ave., Unit 8, Alhambra, CA, 91803 (e-mail: ssussma@hsc.usc.edu). This chapter was supported by grants from the National Institute on Drug Abuse (#DA13814, #P50 DA16094), the California Tobacco-Related Disease Research Program (#6RT-0182), and from the National Institute on Alcohol Abuse and Alcoholism (#AA11890, #P50 AA11999). We would like to thank Janet Smeltz, M.Ed., and Cathy McDonald, M.D., M.P.H., for their very helpful comments and great strides to furthering tobacco use cessation among persons in recovery.

KEY TERMS

5 As: A basic approach to use in counseling clients on their tobacco use (ask, advise, assess, assist, arrange) recommended by a recent guideline on the best clinical practices for treating tobacco use.

12-step program: The basis for the 12-step philosophy is that clients recognize their powerlessness over the drugs of abuse, followed by working through specific steps of personal growth to achieve recovery. Alcoholics Anonymous and Nicotine Anonymous are two examples of a 12-step program.

association: Co-variation; the observation that two specific things occur together more often than by chance alone.

mood management: Strategies to assist clients in regulating and coping with negative affect and depression. Includes antidepressant medication and cognitive-behavioral strategies (e.g., identifying negative thoughts, increasing pleasant activities, and training in relaxation and assertiveness).

motivational interviewing: A directive, client-centered counseling style for eliciting behavior change by helping clients explore and resolve ambivalence.

nicotine dependence: A diagnosis based on the criterion that the client exhibits at least three of the following symptoms: a) tobacco used in larger amounts and over a longer period of time than intended, b) persistent desire or unsuccessful efforts to cut down, c) a great deal of time is spent in activities necessary to obtain tobacco or recover from its effects, d) important social, occupational, or recreational activities are given up or reduced related to tobacco use, e) continued use despite social, psychological, or physical problems, f) marked tolerance or markedly diminished ability to achieve effect, and g) tobacco is used to avoid withdrawal symptoms.

nicotine replacement therapy: Pharmacological treatment for nicotine dependence involving nicotine replacement in the form of the patch, nasal spray, gum, or inhaler. These products vary as to their dosages, their availability over the counter (patch, gum) or by prescription (inhaler, nasal spray), and their speed of administration and nicotine absorption (steady state levels of nicotine obtained with the nicotine patch versus more rapid administration with the nasal spray).

nicotine withdrawal: Syndrome including the following symptoms, which occur within 24 to 48 hours of stopping or cutting down on tobacco use: a) irritability, frustration, or anger; b) dysphoria or depressed mood; c) anxiety; d) restlessness; e) difficulty concentrating; f) sleep disturbance; and g) increased appetite or weight gain (APA, 1994).

smoke-free: When a treatment program does not permit smoking indoors or on the grounds. Although a smoke-free program protects nonsmokers from the hazardous effects of environmental tobacco smoke, it does not address either the addiction to nicotine for the patient or the incongruence of staff and volunteer use of tobacco products within the setting of chemical dependency treatment (Hoffman et al., 2004).

stages of change: The stages identified by Prochaska, DiClemente and colleagues (e.g., Prochaska, & DiClemente, 1983) that people tend to go through as they change their tobacco use. The stages include precontemplation (not considering stopping), contemplation (thinking about stopping), preparation (planing to quit in the next thirty days), action (stopping for less than six months), and maintenance (stopping for six months or more).

tobacco-free: When tobacco use is not permitted in any form indoors or on the grounds. Tobacco-free programs understand that use of any tobacco products is incongruent with a lifestyle free of addictive drugs and recognize the need to assist patients, employees, and volunteers at the facility in addressing their own tobacco and nicotine issues (Hoffman et al., 2004). Utilizing a tobacco-free program does not preclude the use of pharmacological adjuncts in the treatment of tobacco and nicotine dependence.

tobacco use: Cigarette, cigar, or pipe smoking; using chewing tobacco or snuff.

tobacco use disorder: A diagnosis based on the following criteria: (a) individual demonstrates an inability to control his or her use of tobacco products despite cognitive, behavioral, or physiological symptoms, and b) the symptoms have been present for at least one month.

DISCUSSION QUESTIONS

1. Do you think that recovery facilities will all become smoke free in the future? Should they be tobacco free?
2. What accounts for the association one finds between tobacco use and other drug use?
3. Why would a counselor try to promote tobacco use cessation when entering recovery, even though tobacco use cessation rates increase the longer a client has abstained from use of other drugs?

4. What are the benefits and costs of advising your clients to quit smoking? Why might the benefits outweigh the costs?
5. What changes does the 12-step movement need to make, if any, to accommodate smoking cessation as a treatment goal?
6. What are some useful tobacco cessation preparation strategies (e.g., remove all tobacco products from one's locker, car, or home)?
7. Why might abrupt withdrawal be preferred to gradual withdrawal as a quit strategy?
8. What are the costs and benefits of using pharmacological adjuncts for clients in recovery who are trying to quit tobacco use?
9. What are some other strategies that might help your clients follow through with a tobacco use quit attempt (e.g., prayer, waiting out urges, call a friend)?
10. What are some strategies that might help your client maintain sobriety from tobacco use (e.g., aftercare, Nicotine Anonymous meetings).

SUGGESTED FURTHER READING

1. The 12 Questions About Smoking from People in Recovery can be located on the Massachusetts Tobacco Education Clearinghouse Web site (www.mteccatalogue.com). More guidelines from the Massachusetts Bureau of Substance Abuse Services can be found at www.state.ma.us/dph/bsas. A manual on smoking cessation for persons in recovery was published in 2004 by the Massachusetts Department of Public Health (Hoffman et al., 2004).
2. A manual on smoking cessation and information on becoming a tobacco-free facility can be obtained from the School of Public Health at the University of Medicine Dentistry of New Jersy (DUMDNJ; www.tobaccoprogram.org)
3. More information on the Council to End Nicotine Addiction in Recovery (CENAR), which began in 1994, can be obtained from Janet Smeltz at the Tobacco, Addictions, Policy, and Education Project of the Institute for Health and Recovery at 617-661-3991, or e-mail her at tape@healthrecovery.org.
4. For smokers in recovery that wish to quit smoking in the context of other addictions but who do not desire a 12-step approach, you can consider referring them to other approaches, all of which would handle nicotine addiction similarly to other substances of abuse (Sussman & Ames, 2001). Rational recovery (R.R.) was originally based on the principles of Rational Emotive Therapy. R.R. is a learning process based on rational self-empowerment, whereby the person "licks" the addiction and gains self-esteem in the process (also see www.rationalrecovery.org). Alternatively, you might consider referring your client to Self Management and Recovery Training (SMART Recovery), which sponsors about 250 weekly support groups in North America for individuals who desire to abstain from any type of addictive behavior. Its Four Point Program involves enhancing and maintaining motivation (e.g., considering the costs and benefits of using and quitting, increasing self-awareness), coping with urges (not acting on temptation, developing alternative behaviors), solving other problems (e.g., identifying and resolving conflict), and balancing momentary and enduring satisfactions (see www.smartrecovery.org). Similarly, Secular Organizations for Sobriety/Save Our Selves (SOS) was formed in 1986 as a nonspiritual program specifically for those alcoholics or addicts who were uncomfortable with the spiritual nature of 12-step programs (see www.secularhumanism.org/sos/index.htm). This nonreligious program encourages self-empowerment, self-determination, self-affirmation, and free thought. It is believed that sobriety can be successfully achieved through personal responsibility and self-reliance.

REFERENCES

American Psychiatric Association. (1994). *Diagnostic and statistical manual of mental disorders* (4th ed.). Washington, DC: Author.

Bobo, J. K., Anderson, J. R., & Bowman, A. (1997). Training chemical dependency counselors to treat nicotine dependence. *Addictive Behaviors, 22*, 23–30.

Bobo, J. K., & Gilchrist, L. D. (1983). Urging the alcoholic client to quit smoking cigarettes. *Addictive Behaviors, 8*, 197–305.

Bobo, J. K., McIlvain, H. E., Lando, H. A., Walker, R. D., & Leed-Kelly, A. (1998). Effect of smoking cessation counseling on recovery from alcoholism: Findings from a randomized community intervention trial. *Addiction, 93*, 977–887.

British Lung Foundation. (2002). *A smoking gun? The impact of cannabis smoking on respiratory health.* Retrieved October, 2002, from www.britishlungfoundation.com

Casey, K. (1987). *If only I could quit: Recovering from nicotine addiction.* Minneapolis, MN: Hazelden Foundation.

Cooney, J. L., Cooney, N. L., Pilkey, D. T., Kranzler, H. R., & Oncken, C. A. (2003). Effects of nicotine deprivation on urges to drink and smoke in alcoholic smokers. *Addiction, 98*, 913–921.

Dale, L. C., Ebbert, J. O., Hays, J. T., & Hurt, R. D. & (2000). Treatment of nicotine dependence. *Mayo Clinic Proceedings, 75*, 1311–1316.

DiFranza, J. R., & Lew, R. A. (1995). Effect of maternal cigarette smoking on pregnancy complications and Sudden Infant Death Syndrome. *Journal of Family Practice, 40*, 385–394.

Fiore, M. C., Bailey, W. C., Cohen, S. J., Dorfman, S. F., Gildstein, M. G., Girtz, E. R., et al. (2000). *Clinical Practice Guideline. Treating tobacco use and dependence.* Rockvill, MD: USDHHS.

Frosch, D. L., Shoptaw, S., Nahom, D., & Jarvik, M. (2000). Associations between tobacco smoking and illicit drug use among methadone-maintained opiate-dependent individuals. *Experimental and Clinical Psychopharmacology, 8*, 97–103.

Hoffman, A. L., Kantor, B., Leech, T., Lindberg, D., Order-Connors, B., Schreiber, J., et al. (2004). *Drug-free is nicotine-free: A manual for chemical dependency treatment programs.* New Brunswick, NJ: School of Public Health at the University of Medicine & Dentistry of New Jersey. (See also www.tobaccoprogram.org.)

Hoffman A. L., & Slade J. (1993). Following the pioneers: Addressing tobacco in chemical dependency treatment. *Journal of Substance Abuse Treatment, 10*, 153–160.

Hughes, J. R. (1996). Treating smokers with current or past alcohol dependence. *American Journal of Health Behavior, 20*, 286–290.

Hughes, J. R., Higgins, S. T., & Bickel, W. K. (1994). Nicotine withdrawal versus other drug withdrawal syndromes: Similarities and dissimilarities. *Addiction, 89*, 1461–1470.

Hurt, R. D., Croghan, I. T., Offord, K. P., Eberman, K. M., & Morse, R. M. (1995). Attitudes toward nicotine dependence among chemical dependency unit staff: Before and after a smoking cessation trial. *Journal of Substance Abuse Treatment, 12*, 247–252.

Hurt, R. D., Eberman, K. P., Croghan, I. T., Offord, K. M., Davis, L. J., Jr., Morse, R. M., et al. (1994). Nicotine dependence treatment during inpatient treatment for other addictions: A prospective intervention trial. *Alcoholism: Clinical and Experimental Research, 18*, 867–872.

Hurt, R. D., & Patten, C. A. (2003). Treatment of tobacco dependence in alcoholics. *Recent Developments in Alcoholism, 16*, 335–359.

Hurt, R. D., Sachs, D. P., Glover, E. D., Offord, K. P., Johnston, J. A., Dale, L. C., et al. (1997). A comparison of sustained-release buproprion and placebo for smoking cessation. *New England Journal of Medicine, 337*, 1195–1202.

Jeanne, E. (1984). Twelve steps for tobacco users: For recovering people addicted to nicotine. Minneapolis, MN: Hazelden Foundation.

Joseph, A. M. (1993). Nicotine treatment of the Drug Dependency Program of the Minneapolis VA Medical Center. A researcher's perspective. *Journal of Substance Abuse Treatment, 10*, 147–152.

JSI Research and Training Institute, Inc. (2002). *Twelve questions about smoking from people in recovery.* Cambridge, MA: Massachusetts Tobacco Education Clearinghouse. (See also www.mteccatalogue.com.)

Kalman, D. (1998). Smoking cessation treatment for substance misusers in early recovery: A review of the literature and recommendations for practice. *Substance Use & Misuse, 33*, 2021–2047.

Leed-Kelly, A., Russell, K. S., Bobo, J. K., & McIlvain, H. (1996). Feasibility of smoking cessation counseling by phone with alcohol treatment center graduates. *Journal of Substance Abuse Treatment, 13*, 203–210.

Lemon, S. C., Friedmann, P. D., & Stein, M. D. (2003). The impact of smoking cessation on drug abuse treatment outcome. *Addictive Behavior, 28*, 1323–1331.

Little, H. J. (2000). Behavioral mechanisms underlying the link between smoking and drinking. *Alcohol Research & Health, 24*, 215–224.

Massachusetts Medical Society. (1997). Efforts to quit smoking among persons with a history of alcohol problems—Iowa, Kansas, and Nebraska, 1995–1996. *MMWR, 46*, 1144–1148.

National Institute on Alcohol Abuse and Alcoholism. (1998). Alcohol and Tobacco. *Alcohol Alert, 39.* Morbidity and Mortality Weekly Reports.

Patten, C. A., Martin, J. E., Hofstetter, C. R., Brown, S. A., Kim, N., & Williams, C. (1999). Smoking cessation following treatment in a smoke-free navy alcohol rehabilitation program. *Journal of Substance Abuse Treatment, 16*, 61–69.

Patten, C. A., Martin, J. E., Myers, M. G., Calfas, K. J., & Williams C. D. (1998). Effectiveness of cognitive-behavioral therapy for smokers with histories of alcohol dependence and depression. *Journal of Studies on Alcohol, 59*, 327–335.

Patten, C. A., Martin, J. E., & Owen, N. (1996). Can psychiatric and chemical dependency treatment units be smoke free? *Journal of Substance Abuse Treatment, 13*, 107–118.

Prochaska, J. O., & DiClemente, C. C. (1993). Stages and processes of self-change of smoking; toward an integrative model of change. *Journal of Consulting and Clinical Psychology, 51*, 390–395.

Richter, K. P., Gibson, C. A., Ahluwalia, J. S., & Schmelzle, K. H. (2001). Tobacco use and quit attempts among methadone maintenance clients. *American Journal of Public Health, 91*, 296–299.

Rohsenow, D. J., Colby, S. M., & Martin, R. A. (2002). Brief interventions for smoking cessation in alcoholic smokers. *Alcoholism: Clinical and Experimental Research, 26*, 1950–1951.

Rustin, T. (1998). Incorporating nicotine dependence into addiction treatment. *Journal of Addictive Diseases, 17*, 83–108.

Sees, K. L., & Clark, H. W. (1993). When to begin smoking cessation in substance abusers. *Journal of Substance Abuse Treatment, 10*, 189–95.

Shiffman, S., & Balabanis, M. (1996). Do drinking and smoking go together? *Alcohol Health & Research World, 20*, 107–110.

Shoptaw, S., Jarvik, M. E., Ling, W., & Rawson, R. A. (1996). Contingency management for tobacco smoking in methadone-maintained opiate addicts. *Addictive Behaviors, 21*, 409–412.

The Smoking Cessation Practice Guidelines Panel and Staff. (1996). The Agency for Health Care Policy and Research smoking cessation clinical practice guideline. *Journal of the American Medical Association, 275*, 1270–1280.

Stotts, A. L., Schmitz, J. M., & Grabowski, J. (2003). Concurrent treatment for alcohol and tobacco dependence: Are patients ready to quit both? *Drug and Alcohol Dependence, 69*, 1–7.

Stuyt, E. B. (1997). Recovery rates after treatment for alcohol/drug dependence: Tobacco users vs. non-tobacco users. *The American Journal on Addictions, 6*, 159–167.

Stuyt, E. B. (2000, February). *Effect of insisting some patients stop tobacco use as a condition of remaining in treatment.* Presented at the sixth SRNT Annual meeting, Alexandria, Virginia.

Stuyt, E. B., Order-Connors, B., & Ziedonis, D. M. (2003). Addressing tobacco through program and system change in mental health and addiction settings. *Psychiatric Annals, 33*, 447–456.

Sussman, S. (2002). Smoking cessation among persons in recovery. *Substance Use & Misuse, 37*, 1275–1298.

Sussman, S., & Ames, S. L. (2001). *The Social Psychology of drug abuse.* Maidenhead, Berkshire, UK: Open University Press, McGraw-Hill House.

Toft, D. (2002, Winter). Snuffing out tobacco in the recovery community. *Hazelden Voice, 7*, 1–2, 16.

U.S. Department of Health and Human Services. (1988). *The health consequences of smoking: Nicotine addiction* (DHHS Publication No. CDC 88-8406. Rockville, MD: Office on Smoking and Health.

U.S. Department of Health and Human Services. (1989). *Reducing the health consequences of smoking: Twenty-five years of progress. A report of the surgeon general* (DHHS Publication No. CDC 89-8411). Rockville, MD: Office on Smoking and Health.

U.S. Department of Health and Human Services. (1986). *The health consequences of involuntary smoking* (DHHS Publication No. CDC 87-8398). Rockville, MD: Office on Smoking and Health.

10

Problem Drinking

Christopher Barrick
Kimberly S. Walitzer
Research Institute on Addictions
University at Buffalo

TRUTH OR FICTION?

___ 1. *A 5-ounce glass of wine has the same alcohol content as a 1.5-ounce glass of 80-proof whiskey.*

___ 2. *Alcohol addiction is a purely biological disorder.*

___ 3. *The meaning and specific criteria of a diagnosis of alcohol abuse has remained constant over time.*

___ 4. *A thorough diagnostic assessment for an individual about to enter alcohol treatment should include coverage of areas at risk for negative consequences, even if no negative consequences have yet occurred.*

___ 5. *A functional analysis of alcohol use means gauging how well a person is able to work while under the influence of alcohol.*

___ 6. *Heavy alcohol use increases the risk of developing certain cancers.*

___ 7. *Alcoholics are at great risk for diabetes strictly because of the sugars contained in alcohol.*

___ 8. *Neurological damage in Wernicke-Korsakoff syndrome is the result of alcohol's damaging effect on the brain's neurons.*

___ 9. *Most individuals arrested for driving while intoxicated (DWI) are later arrested again for DWI.*

___ 10. *If alcohol is used, sexual assaults are more likely to occur between individuals who do not know each other well.*

___ 11. *The goal of motivational therapy is to encourage an individual to not drink alcohol again.*

___ 12. *Coping skills training helps an individual learn positive ways to manage stressors instead of using alcohol.*

_ 13. *Alcoholics Anonymous (AA) is often most helpful to individuals who adopt the philosophy and tenets of the organization.*
_ 14. *Pharmacological treatments are designed to prevent an individual from developing an alcohol problem.*
_ 15. *Some pharmacological interventions work by reducing alcohol's reinforcing stimuli.*

This chapter offers an overview of problem drinking, its effects, and its treatment. The alcoholism research field is broad, and this chapter can only offer a brief overview of some of the key issues. To supplement your study, suggestions for further reading are offered at the end of the chapter.

WHAT IS MEANT BY "A DRINK," WHO DRINKS, AND WHY?

What Is Meant by "A Drink"?

Alcohol is often a pleasant part of a variety of social activities. Moderate alcohol use, typically defined as up to two drinks per day for men and one drink per day for women and older people, is not harmful for the majority of adults (Table 10.1). However, 60% of males and 30% of females report having had one or more alcohol-related adverse life events resulting from an episode of consuming too much alcohol (American Psychiatric Association, 2000).

1. What is the typical definition of *moderate* alcohol use; the daily amount of alcohol the majority of adults can safely consume?
   a. no amount of alcohol consumption is considered "moderate use"
   b. two drinks per day for males, one drink per day for females and older adults
   c. an average of fourteen to twenty-one drinks per week
   d. any amount of wine, but two hard liquor or beer drinks per day for males, one liquor or beer drink per day for females and older adults

Negative Consequences of Alcohol Use

A substantial minority of Americans abuse alcohol, with best estimates suggesting nearly 14 million, or one in every thirteen, adults have a drinking problem. Heavy drinking can

TABLE 10.1

What Is a Drink?

Defining the size of a drink is important, and it isn't simply one glass. When discussing alcohol consumption, the term drink usually refers to a **standard drink**.

A standard drink is:
• One 12-ounce bottle of beer* or wine cooler
• One 5-ounce glass of wine
• 1.5 ounces of 80-proof distilled spirits

Different beers have different alcohol content. Malt liquor has a higher alcohol content than most other brewed beverages.

increase the risk for certain cancers, exacerbate symptoms of diabetes, negatively impact the functioning of the body and organs, and can cause harm to a fetus during pregnancy. In addition, drinking increases the risk of fatality in automobile crashes and of harm from physical abuse and sexual assault.

2. Which contains the most alcohol?
   a. one 15-oz. glass of red wine
   b. three 12-oz. bottles of beer (not malt liquor)
   c. one 16-oz. glass of 80-proof scotch
   d. two 12-oz. bottles of wine cooler

Epidemiology of Alcohol Use

Problem alcohol use cuts across age, culture, gender, and ethnic background. The National Comorbidity Survey (Anthony, Warner, & Kessler, 1994) found that 14.1% of the respondents (or one person in seven) reported a history of alcohol dependence. According to the survey, men were more likely to be problem drinkers than were women, and alcohol problems were highest among those age 18 to 29 and lowest in those age 65 and above. In terms of ethnic background, studies have found that alcohol use problems are most common among Native Americans, followed by people of Hispanic origin, White Americans, African Americans, and Asian Americans/Pacific Islanders. There is an age and ethnicity interaction, with African American adolescents reporting the lowest prevalence of lifetime drinking, whereas Hispanic adolescents report the highest, followed by White Americans.

3. Which of the following statements best describes epidemiological findings on alcohol use?
   a. There are no patterns to how people use alcohol by age, ethnic background, or gender.
   b. Patterns to how people use alcohol exist only with gender.
   c. Patterns of alcohol use are consistent with age cohorts, but decline as people age.
   d. There is an interaction between some key demographic variables (i.e., age and ethnic background) when examining patterns of problem drinking.

What Causes Alcohol Addiction?

There is no simple explanation to the cause of problem alcohol use; however, most researchers currently subscribe to a biopsychosocial model of the behavior. This means that there are likely to be multiple determinants, including biological factors, psychological factors, and sociocultural factors.

Biological Factors

Biological factors include genetic predisposition to alcohol problems, physiological and neurological effects of alcohol on the brain and brain activity, and biological mechanisms in alcohol **tolerance** and **withdrawal**. Although research suggests that having a family member who is a problem drinker increases the risk that an individual will have an alcohol use problem, there is not an unconditional relationship. Clearly, biological factors alone do not explain alcohol addiction.

Psychological Factors

Problem drinking can be viewed as a learned behavior that is reinforced both positively and negatively. It is hypothesized that deficits in coping behaviors and the skills necessary to manage stressful life events may lead to problem drinking. From this viewpoint, heavy drinking has been adopted as an ineffective generalized coping response.

Sociocultural Factors

Social influences may have either a *protective* (e.g., strong familial and social support) or a *predisposing* (e.g., childhood trauma) effect. Social norms and peer influences may also affect a person's drinking habits and even how easy it is to obtain alcohol. Membership in particular groups (i.e., ethnic background, age, gender) also can influence vulnerability to alcohol problems.

4. The traditional "medical" model of alcoholism suggests that it is a disease. Which category of factors would the medical model fall under?
   a. psychological factors
   b. biological factors
   c. sociocultural factors
   d. biopsychosocial model

WHAT DEFINES PROBLEM DRINKING?

Psychological Diagnosis and Assessment

Diagnosis of Alcohol Abuse Versus Alcohol Dependence

Diagnostic criteria for problem alcohol use reflect a consensus of researchers and clinicians describing circumscribed constellations of behavior and physiological characteristics. These criteria assist in treatment planning and administration, insurance reimbursement, and allowing access to medical insurance coverage (e.g., Valliant, 1995). The *Diagnostic and Statistical Manual of Mental Disorders*, 4th edition, text revision (*DSM–IV–TR*; American Psychiatric Association [APA], 2000) offers the diagnostic criteria for most common mental disorders and includes the disorder's description, diagnosis, treatment, and an overview of research findings. The most recent edition, *DSM–IV–TR*, offers two diagnostic categories for alcohol use disorders: alcohol abuse and alcohol dependence.

Alcohol Dependence. Alcohol *dependence* is characterized by a cluster of behavioral, cognitive, and physiological symptoms that indicate continued use of alcohol despite significant alcohol-related problems. Three or more criteria must be met for a period of 1 year for a diagnosis (APA, 2000). There is a pattern of repeated self-administration that usually results in tolerance, withdrawal, and compulsive alcohol use. Criteria for a diagnosis of alcohol dependence are listed in Table 10.2.

Alcohol Abuse. Alcohol *abuse* is a maladaptive pattern of alcohol use, manifested by recurring and significant adverse consequences related to repeated use. There may be failure to fulfill major role obligations, use of alcohol in situations where it is physically

TABLE 10.2

Alcohol Dependence

Three or more of the following:
- Tolerance
- Withdrawal
- Large amounts over a long period
- Unsuccessful efforts to cut down
- Time spent in obtaining the substance replaces social, occupational, or recreational activities
- Continued use despite adverse consequences

TABLE 10.3

Alcohol Abuse

One or more of the following:
- Failure to fulfill major obligations
- Use when physically hazardous
- Recurrent legal problems
- Recurrent social or interpersonal problems
- With alcohol abuse, the user has a choice: he or she uses in spite of illegal, unsafe consequences or inappropriateness of the drinking experience.

hazardous, multiple legal problems, and recurrent social and interpersonal problems which occur in the same 12-month period (APA, 2000). Unlike alcohol dependence, alcohol abuse does not include tolerance, withdrawal, or a pattern of compulsive use. Criteria for a diagnosis of alcohol abuse are listed in Table 10.3.

5. What distinguishes a diagnosis of alcohol *dependence* from alcohol *abuse*?
   a. Alcohol abuse includes tolerance, withdrawal, or a pattern of compulsive use.
   b. Alcohol dependence includes tolerance, withdrawal, or a pattern of compulsive use.
   c. Alcohol abuse only includes a pattern of compulsive use.
   d. They are considered essentially same, but are distinguished only by the total number of expressed symptoms.

6. A client reports problematic relationships with his family and friends, mostly related to his alcohol use. Occasionally, he misses work and reports losing a contract for his business because of an alcohol-related absence. He denies binge drinking or being in financial difficulty. Finally, he reports an arrest and being charged with driving while intoxicated (DWI). He states that he has not had a drink for a week, feels fine, and has had no other distressing physical symptoms. Given the above information , what would be the most likely diagnosis for the person described above?
   a. alcohol dependence
   b. alcohol intoxication
   c. alcohol abuse
   d. alcohol withdrawal

Assessment Issues in Alcohol Treatment

A thorough assessment of an individual's alcohol use is necessary to properly diagnose problem drinking and ongoing assessment is an important component of the treatment process. Therefore, a complete and nonjudgmental survey of factors contributing to the patient's alcohol use and life consequences resulting from such use should occur prior to and during treatment.

Assessment of Alcohol Use

An assessment of current alcohol use should include an identification of the types of alcohol used, the quantity and frequency of alcohol use, and information, when appropriate, on other drug intake. Frequency of use is straightforward and usually references the number of times a particular substance is used in a typical day, week, or month. Quantity of use is more complex, and care must be taken to account for different "proofs," or ethanol content, of various alcoholic beverages (see box entitled, "What Is a Drink?"). In addition to amount, the style of alcohol use is also important to assess. Pathological styles, or methods of ingestion highly associated with abuse, include morning drinking, binges, and use to counteract withdrawal symptoms.

7. What is *not* a part of a thorough assessment of alcohol use?
   a. preferred type of alcohol used
   b. other substances used
   c. urine and blood toxicology reports
   d. tolerance test of alcohol use

Assessment of Negative Consequences

The majority of *DSM–IV–TR* diagnostic criteria are based on consequences of alcohol use. Current and lifetime assessment of negative consequences from use should cover a variety of areas including social, legal, financial, marital, family, work, health, and dependence symptoms. Although in practice the majority of this information may be gathered simply from a patient's spontaneous report, it is worthwhile to inquire into areas not mentioned by the individual. The assessment should also include areas in which the individual is at risk for consequences that have not yet occurred. For instance, while an individual who drinks and drives may not have experienced negative consequences as a result of driving while intoxicated, the risk for physical, legal, and financial consequences is great.

Assessment of Contributing Factors

Various factors contributing to the development and maintenance of alcohol problems should also be assessed. The individual's family history of alcohol and drug problems is important, both in terms of the possible genetic contribution as well as social learning and modeling effects. Beliefs and cognitions regarding alcohol's effects, such as alcohol/drug expectancies, are important factors in maintaining alcohol use and in **relapse**. Assessment of social and lifestyle factors that may encourage or promote alcohol use is also important.

Functional Analysis of Alcohol and Substance Use

Functional analysis of substance use seeks to identify how substance use "functions" within the patient's life and specific factors that serve to maintain or reinforce substance use. Identifying emotions, activities, environments, and people that are strongly associated with substance ingestion will begin to illustrate the manner in which the substance use is functioning. Although the majority of the functional analysis can be performed during the pretreatment assessment, it is worthwhile to continue to consider and reassess the functional analysis during and after treatment as additional issues become apparent.

Collateral Reports

While research has found the self-reports of alcohol and drug users generally are reliable and valid, valuable insights can be obtained from the perspective of a spouse or significant other of the patient. Most individuals will permit collateral interviews when the contacts are presented to the patient as a way of obtaining an alternate perspective on the patient's functioning. Important information can be obtained from collaterals concerning home, family, work, and social life in regards to substance use and factors that maintain or encourage use.

Physiological Assessment

Measures of physiological alcohol use assess use within a limited time frame and are not necessarily diagnostic, as many test results may be elevated for physiological reasons not associated with alcohol or drug use. The most common physiological assessment for the presence of alcohol is the breath test, which is noninvasive, accurate, and quick and easy to administer. Urinalysis can be used to test for the presence of other drugs. Biochemical measures derived from blood samples provide an indication of longer-term alcohol use. These and other laboratory tests can be especially useful when posttreatment results are compared to pretreatment values, since readings generally return to normal levels following cessation of heavy drinking.

> 8. Which of the following is *not* a commonly assessed domain in the assessment of problem drinking?
>   a. report of collateral's own current negative consequences from alcohol use
>   b. lifetime negative consequences from alcohol use
>   c. current negative consequences from alcohol use
>   d. future risks from alcohol use negative consequences

CHRONIC PHYSICAL EFFECTS OF HEAVY ALCOHOL USE

Certain health problems develop gradually and may become evident only after many years of heavy drinking. Because alcohol affects nearly every organ in the body, long-term heavy drinking increases the risk for many serious health problems.

Cancer

Long-term heavy drinking increases the risk of certain forms of cancer. Individuals who excessively consume hard liquors are at greater risk for cancers of the mouth, pharynx, esophagus, larynx, liver, and pancreas; those who excessively consume beer are at greater risk for colon and bladder cancers. Alcohol is considered a co-carcinogen because it is a cellular irritant, harming cell membranes and facilitating damage to the cells' genetic material. Individuals who both smoke and drink heavily are at thirty-five times greater risk for mouth, tracheal, and esophageal cancers compared to nonsmokers and drinkers (Corrao, Bagnardi, Zambon, & Arico, 1999).

9. Which of the following is true regarding cancers and problem alcohol use?
    a. Problem alcohol use alone puts individuals at thirty-five times greater risk for mouth, tracheal, and esophageal cancers.
    b. Development of specific cancers cannot be precisely attributed to problem alcohol use.
    c. Problem alcohol use damages the cell membranes and makes cells more susceptible to damage to the genetic material.
    d. Problem alcohol use is responsible for the majority of cancers.

Diabetes

Alcohol intake can hamper the regulation of the body's blood sugar levels, and in diabetics, alcohol use can worsen blood sugar control. Heavy drinking can also cause the accumulation of certain acids in the blood and worsen diabetes-related medical complications. If not prevented or treated, this damage can lead to coma or death (Emanuele, Swade, & Emanuele, 1998).

10. Individuals who have problem alcohol use may be at risk for:
    a. excessively high blood sugar levels.
    b. dangerously low blood sugar levels.
    c. both excessively high blood sugar levels and dangerously low blood sugar levels.
    d. neither excessively high blood sugar levels nor dangerously low blood sugar levels.

Fetal Alcohol Syndrome

Fetal alcohol syndrome (FAS) is a pattern of birth defects found in children whose mothers consumed alcohol during the course of their pregnancy. FAS, the leading preventable cause of mental retardation, is evidenced by academic, employment, and legal difficulties. It is defined by four criteria: maternal drinking during pregnancy, a characteristic pattern of facial anomalies, growth retardation, and brain damage (Stratton, Howe, & Battaglia, 1996). Although damage can occur at any time, research has suggested that the first and third trimesters are considered particularly sensitive.

11. Which is the correct set of criteria for fetal alcohol syndrome (FAS)?
    a. maternal drinking during pregnancy, a characteristic pattern of facial anomalies, growth retardation, and brain damage
    b. maternal drinking during pregnancy, a characteristic pattern of facial anomalies, and growth retardation
    c. maternal drinking during pregnancy, a characteristic pattern of facial anomalies, growth retardation, brain damage, and alcohol use occurs only during the first trimester
    d. maternal drinking during pregnancy, a characteristic pattern of facial anomalies, growth retardation, brain damage, and alcohol use occurs only during the first and third trimesters

Heart Disease

Heavy drinking over a long period of time increases the risk for heart disease, high blood pressure, and some kinds of stroke. Alcohol consumption raises the levels of fibrinolytic protein tissue-type plasminogen activator (t-PA), which increases the risk of heart disease (Rimm, Williams, Fosher, Criqui, & Stampfer, 1999).

12. Why does heavy drinking promote heart disease?
    a. Alcohol promotes changes to high-density lipoprotein cholesterol (HDL-C) levels in the blood.
    b. Alcohol promotes changes to triglyceride levels in the blood.
    c. Alcohol promotes changes to fibrinolytic protein tissue-type plasminogen activator (t-PA) levels in the blood.
    d. Alcohol promotes changes to fibrinogen levels in the blood.

Interactions With Medications

There are more than 150 medications that should not be mixed with alcohol with a varying range of effects. For example, if you are taking antihistamines for a cold or allergy and drink alcohol, the alcohol will increase the drowsiness that the medicine alone can cause, making driving or operating machinery even more dangerous. Drinking alcohol while consuming high doses of the painkiller acetaminophen (Tylenol) risks serious liver damage.

Liver Disease

Heavy, long-term drinking can cause *alcoholic hepatitis*, or inflammation of the liver. Symptoms include fever, jaundice (abnormal yellowing of the skin, eyeballs, and urine), and abdominal pain. If drinking continues, hepatitis can cause death, whereas if drinking ceases, the condition may be reversible. About 10% to 20% of heavy drinkers develop *alcoholic cirrhosis*, or scarring of the liver. Cirrhosis can be fatal and is not reversible, but if a person with cirrhosis stops drinking, the chances of survival improve considerably (National Institute on Alcohol Abuse and Alcoholism [NIAAA], 1993).

13. Regarding liver damage and heavy alcohol use, which statement is true?
    a. Liver damage from *neither* hepatitis nor cirrhosis of the liver is reversible.
    b. Liver damage from *both* hepatitis and cirrhosis of the liver is reversible.
    c. Liver damage from hepatitis *is not* reversible, but damage from cirrhosis of the liver *is* reversible.
    d. Liver damage from hepatitis *is* reversible, but damage from cirrhosis of the liver *is not* reversible.

Nutrition

Alcohol inhibits the normal absorption of nutrients from food primarily by decreasing the secretion of digestive enzymes, damaging the small intestine's cell lining that transports nutrients to the blood, and impairing utilization. Chronic heavy drinking is associated with deficiencies in many vitamins (vitamins A, C, D, E, K, and the B family) and minerals (calcium, magnesium, iron, and zinc; Lieber, 1989).

14. Which of the following digestive problems is *not* caused by heavy alcohol use?
    a. a decrease in the secretion of digestive enzymes
    b. damage to the small intestine's cell lining that transports nutrients to the blood
    c. a decreased level of food ingestion
    d. an increased metabolic rate

Pancreatitis

Long-term heavy drinking can lead to *pancreatitis*, or inflammation of the pancreas. Acute pancreatitis can cause severe abdominal pain and can be fatal. Chronic pancreatitis is associated with chronic pain, diarrhea, and weight loss. Individuals who use alcohol heavily can exacerbate damage to the pancreas if they have a protein-deficient diet (Korsten, 1989).

Wernicke-Korsakoff Syndrome

Wernicke-Korsakoff syndrome is an impairment of motor, memory, and cognitive functioning caused by malnutrition, especially vitamin B1 (thiamine) deficiency, related to heavy alcohol consumption. Symptoms include changes in vision, loss of muscle coordination, loss of memory, confusion, inability to form new memories, **confabulation,** and hallucinations. Intellectual functioning and verbal memory remain generally intact. Left untreated, Wernicke-Korsakoff syndrome is fatal. Treatment includes total abstinence and, increased thiamine to potentially improve muscle coordination and confusion. However, memory loss and cognitive deficits are typically permanent (Snyder & Nussbaum, 1999).

15. Which of the following is true regarding Wernicke-Korsakoff syndrome?
    a. Wernicke-Korsakoff syndrome symptoms may include confabulation.
    b. Wernicke-Korsakoff syndrome is not life-threatening.
    c. Wernicke-Korsakoff syndrome causes a marked decline in intellectual functioning and verbal memory.
    d. Wernicke-Korsakoff syndrome causes vitamin B1 (thiamine) deficiency.

OTHER ALCOHOL-RELATED PROBLEMS

Drunk Driving

Although most states set the blood alcohol concentration (BAC) limit for adults who drive after drinking at 0.08 or 0.10, driving skills are affected with BACs as low as 0.02 percent. A 160-pound man will have a BAC of about 0.04 percent 1 hour after drinking two 12-ounce beers or two other standard drinks on an empty stomach (see the box entitled, "What Is a Drink?"). Data collected on drunk driving arrests suggest that the **recidivism** rate is around one-third, meaning that approximately one-third of individuals arrested for DWI will commit a second offense (Michigan Office of Public Safety, 1998).

16. What is the blood alcohol content (BAC) level that most states use as a cutoff for DWI?
    a. 0.008–0.010
    b. 0.08–0.10
    c. 8.0–10.0
    d. 0.02–0.04

Crime and Violence

Crime statistics gathered by the Arrestee Drug Abuse Monitoring (ADAM) program show that approximately one-half of the arrestees had recently consumed alcohol, and 21% were under its influence at the time of the crime. Men were more likely to have recently used alcohol or to be under its influence than were women. ADAM data suggest that, except for robbery, alcohol intoxication is as likely as cocaine use to precede violent crimes and is more likely than cocaine use to precede family violence (U.S. Department of Justice, 1999).

Sexual Assault

Alcohol consumption by the perpetrator, victim, or both, is involved in approximately one-half of sexual assault cases. Alcohol contributes to sexual assault through multiple pathways, including beliefs about alcohol's effects on sexual and aggressive behavior, stereotypes about women who drink, and alcohol's effect on cognitive and motor skills. Although alcohol and non–alcohol related sexual assaults share many characteristics, important differences exist. For example, sexual assaults involving alcohol are more likely to occur between people who do not know each other well (Abbey, Ross, McDuffie, & McAuslan, 1996).

17. Which of the following beliefs contribute to the elevated risk of sexual assault following alcohol use?
    a. beliefs about alcohol's effects on sexual and aggressive behavior
    b. beliefs about stereotypes about women who drink
    c. beliefs about alcohol's effect on cognitive and motor skills
    d. All of the above

Child Abuse

Alcohol and child abuse share a two-fold relationship. First, some research suggests that parental problem alcohol use may be associated with physical and sexual abuse of children. Findings are inconsistent, but several studies suggest that parental alcohol abuse may increase a child's chance of physical or sexual abuse by either a family member or another person (e.g., Ammerman, Kolko, Kirisci, Blackson, & Dawes, 1999). Second, there appears to be a link between childhood abuse and the development of alcohol-related problems as an adult. Several studies have suggested that women who had experienced childhood abuse were more likely to have alcohol-related problems as an adult than those who had not experienced abuse (e.g., Wisdom, Ireland, & Glynn, 1995).

18. What best describes the relationship between alcohol and child abuse?
    a. Parental alcohol abuse may increase a child's chance of physical or sexual abuse by either a family member or another person.
    b. There appears to be a link between childhood abuse and the development of alcohol-related problems as an adult.
    c. There appears to be a two-fold relationship that includes both increased risk of child abuse because of parental alcohol use and a link between childhood abuse and the development of alcohol-related problems as an adult.
    d. Too few studies have investigated the link of childhood abuse and alcohol problems.

TREATING PROBLEM DRINKING AND ALCOHOLISM

Psychosocial Treatments

Empirical outcome studies have examined the efficacy of a variety of treatment strategies for alcohol and drug problems. What follows is a description of the more frequently used and most promising treatment modalities. Recent reviews of the alcoholism treatment outcome literature conclude that a variety of treatment strategies may be used effectively alone or in combination, depending on the needs of an individual client.

Motivational Enhancement Therapy

A framework for understanding behavior change and motivation has been provided by Prochaska and DiClemente (1982). They identify five *stages of change* that are relevant to alcohol treatment: precontemplation, contemplation, preparation, action, and maintenance. *Precontemplation* is the stage prior to recognizing or identifying a drinking problem. As the individual begins to identify the problem and weigh the costs and benefits of change, he or she enters the *contemplation* stage. *Preparation* is the stage at which the individual decides that he or she intends to change, but has as yet taken only initial steps toward change. *Action* represents the point at which the individual takes significant concrete steps toward change, such as attending a self-help group meeting or beginning alcohol treatment. *Maintenance* occurs when the desired change has been accomplished, and the individual focuses on consolidating gains made. This model is a dynamic, not linear, process in which the individual's placement along the stages, and hence his or her motivation for change, can fluctuate from week to week, day to day, and even minute to minute. When a *relapse* occurs, it represents the individual's cycling back to an earlier stage.

The goal of motivational enhancement therapy, or motivational interviewing, is to move an individual from one stage (e.g., precontemplation or contemplation) to a further stage (e.g., action or maintenance). Miller and Rollnick (2002) provide a full description, background, and multiple applications for this intriguing therapeutic method. Briefly, motivational interviewing utilizes six specific elements to increase clients' motivation to change their drinking behavior, summarized by the acronym FRAMES. They include personalized *feedback* of information from assessment, emphasis on client *responsibility* for change and freedom of choice, *advice* as to how to change, providing a *menu* of therapeutic alternatives from which to choose, therapist *empathy*, and facilitation of client *self-efficacy*. In a motivational interview, the therapist uses specific listening and questioning strategies to help the client work through his or her ambivalence about making a change. The therapist's goal is to have the client, rather than the therapist, voice the reasons for change, thereby building the client's motivation for change. If the client already appears committed to change, the therapist's role is to facilitate the strengthening of that commitment.

19. What are the five stages of change that are a part of the motivational enhancement model described by Prochaska and DiClemente?
    a. precontemplation, contemplation, preparation, action, and maintenance
    b. contemplation, preparation, action, relapse and maintenance
    c. precontemplation, contemplation, preparation, action, and reflection
    d. contemplation, preparation, action, reflection, and maintenance

Coping Skills Training

The coping skills training approach to alcoholism treatment is based on the foundation that individuals with alcohol problems have skills deficits that make it difficult for them to respond to and adapt to major and minor life stressors. Lacking positive alternative coping responses, increasingly heavier drinking becomes the alcoholic's response to stress. Coping skills training for alcoholism focuses on teaching and enhancing a variety of general life coping skills and alcohol-specific coping skills, specifically in the realms of interpersonal skills, intrapersonal skills, and responding to alcohol-related cues. As with other behavioral treatment approaches, the client is first presented with a rationale for each coping skill. The therapist then models these skills. Finally, the client does in-session role plays and practices the skill outside of the session.

Interpersonal coping skills include assertiveness skills, speaking skills, listening skills, giving and receiving positive feedback, and drink refusal. Monti, Kadden, Rohsenow, Cooney, and Abrams (2002) suggest that these skills improve both the client's ability to obtain positive social support as well as skill in coping with situations that may lead to relapse. The *intrapersonal* skills in the Monti et al. manual primarily focus on coping with negative affect and cognitions, managing craving, anger management, increasing positive activities, managing negative or irrelevant thinking, and problem solving skills. Finally, the rationale underlying cue exposure training is to help clients develop coping skills for dealing with the internal reactions to exposure to *alcohol-related cues* in their environment. Cues can include the sight and smell of a favored alcoholic beverage, as well as people, places, times, and emotions that have been previously associated with drinking. The client is exposed to their salient, alcohol-related cues in a safe environment and learns and practices alternative strategies such as relaxation, nondrinking behaviors, and recalling the benefits of sobriety.

20. Which are considered *interpersonal coping skills* as described in the coping skills training model?
    a. coping with negative affect and cognitions, managing craving, anger management, increasing positive activities, managing negative or irrelevant thinking, and problem solving skills
    b. internal reactions to exposure to alcohol-related cues in their environment
    c. assertiveness skills, speaking skills, listening skills, giving and receiving positive feedback, and drink refusal
    d. all of the above

Marriage and Family Approaches

There are two primary rationales underlying the variety of marital and family therapies for alcoholism treatment. First, improving and strengthening the significant relationships in the client's life may both reduce marital and family stress and improve motivation for a positive sober life. Second, a spouse's reactions and responses to past and future alcohol-related situations may play an important role in supporting the client's sobriety. Thus, these approaches emphasize the importance of the spouse and additional family members playing an active role in treatment.

Of the several approaches to marital and family therapy, behavioral couples therapy (BCT) has the strongest empirical support for efficacy. In addition to the alcohol-specific content for the client, behavioral couples therapy incorporates two major therapeutic components: (1) increasing positive joint activities and behavioral exchanges between the spouses, and (2) enhancing communication and negotiation skills. The first component is designed to increase positive affect and marital satisfaction and usually comprises the first four to five therapy sessions. The second component, presented and practiced during the remaining five to six therapy sessions, is designed to improve the couple's ability to communicate effectively with one another, especially with respect to areas of conflict. Behavioral couples therapy has been administered both in conjoint settings as well as in couples' groups (O'Farrell & Fals-Stewart, 2003).

Reviews of BCT efficacy studies with alcoholics indicate that BCT, relative to individual-based treatment, reliably produces better alcohol outcome and marital functioning. Studies have also indicated that BCT, relative to individual-based treatment, reduces domestic violence and improves the psychosocial functioning of the couple's children (Kelley & Fals-Stewart, 2002).

21. Which of the following statements best summarizes the rationales for employing any of the variety of marital and family therapies for alcoholism treatment?
    a. These approaches emphasize the importance of the spouse and additional family members in treatment after other treatments have not been successful.
    b. These approaches emphasize the importance of the spouse and additional family members playing an active role in treatment.
    c. These approaches emphasize that treatment cannot be successful without the intervention of the spouse or additional family members in treatment.
    d. None of the above.

Self-Help Groups

Alcoholics Anonymous (AA) has been in existence since 1935 and is one of the oldest structured approaches to alcohol problems. The program, led by AA members rather than mental health professionals, combines a spiritual orientation with insight, confrontation, and social support. Members are encouraged to attend meetings daily, work the Twelve Steps of AA, and regularly interact with other members. Studies (e.g., McCrady, Horvath, & Delaney, 2003) have yielded the unsurprising, but nevertheless important, conclusion that AA-oriented programs and groups are generally most helpful and effective for individuals who adopt the philosophy and tenets of the organization. The strengths of AA include social support, structure, and widespread availability of meetings. A potential disadvantage is a rigid adherence to ideology that makes it an unacceptable option for some alcoholics who disagree with one or more of its tenets.

Other self-help organizations have developed over the years for persons with substance use disorders. These include Secular Organizations for Sobriety (SOS), an organization geared predominantly toward alcohol abusers; Narcotics Anonymous (NA) and Cocaine Anonymous (CA), geared toward drug problems and following tenets similar to those of AA; and Rational Recovery (RR), geared toward both alcohol and other drug abusers.

Reviews of the efficacy and effectiveness of self-help groups and, in particular, AA, suggest a positive, if modest, benefit (e.g., McCrady, Horvath, & Delaney, 2003). A meta-analysis of controlled clinical trials of AA indicates that whereas individuals who are coerced to attend AA (e.g., court-mandated attendance) may experience poor outcomes, clients who willingly attend AA reap benefits from the self-help involvement.

22. Research suggests that self-help groups are most effective when:
    a. clients willingly attend self-help groups.
    b. individuals' attendance is closely monitored by a court or other legal mandate.
    c. no mention is made of self-help group attendance during treatment (to maintain anonymity).
    d. individuals pick and choose the philosophy and tenets of the self-help organization that best suits them.

23. Which psychosocial treatment for alcoholism does not rely on working with a mental health professional?
    a. motivational enhancement therapy
    b. coping skills training
    c. self-help groups
    d. marital and family approaches

Pharmacological Approaches

While psychosocial treatment interventions have a positive impact on achieving abstinence and preventing relapse with alcohol dependent patients, between 40% and 70% of patients resume alcohol consumption following treatment (Swift, 1999). Because of this problem, pharmacological adjuncts that aid in relapse prevention have long been of interest to clinicians and researchers. Table 10.4 offers an overview of the pharmacological adjuncts discussed in this section and their proposed mechanisms of action.

TABLE 10.4

Current Pharmacological Adjuncts for Alcohol Dependence and Relapse Prevention

Drug Name (trade)	Brand Name	Type	Proposed Mechanism of Action in Alcohol Dependence
Acamprosate	Campral Aotal (France)	NMDA and GABA receptor modulator	Reduces craving, pleasant effects of alcohol, unpleasant effect of alcohol abstinence.
Disulfiram	Antabuse	Aversive agent	Increases aversive effects of alcohol ingestion by increasing acetaldehyde.
Naltrexone	ReVia	Opioid antagonist	Reduces craving and pleasurable, stimulating effects of alcohol.

24. What is the approximate relapse rate for individuals following psychosocial alcoholism treatment?
   a. Between 4% and 7% of patients resume alcohol consumption following treatment.
   b. Between 10% and 20% of patients resume alcohol consumption following treatment.
   c. Between 7% and 40% of patients resume alcohol consumption following treatment.
   d. Between 40% and 70% of patients resume alcohol consumption following treatment.

Deterrent Medications (Disulfiram)

Deterrent medications alter the body's response to alcohol, making ingestion of even small amounts unpleasant. Disulfiram, the most widely used deterrent medication, inhibits aldehyde dehydrogenase (ALDH), the enzyme that catalyzes the oxidation of acetaldehyde to acetic acid. Alcohol consumption following the inhibition of this enzyme causes blood acetaldehyde levels to rise, causing a disulfiram–ethanol reaction (DER). Patients' physical reactions to the DER include nausea, vomiting, and facial flushing, with variations in intensity depending on the dose of medication and amount of alcohol consumed (Kranzler, 2000). Strict compliance and closely linked behavioral reinforcers (e.g. cue extinction, skills training, behavioral contracts, and taking the medication under observation) have been reported to be key elements in its efficacy. Contracting with a significant other to promote compliance, offering regular reminders, and providing additional relevant information to patients have also been suggested as vehicles to improve disulfiram's effectiveness.

25. By what means does a deterrent medication aid in relapse prevention?
   a. It alters the body's response to alcohol, making ingestion of even small amounts unpleasant.
   b. It prevents alcohol's reinforcing stimuli from occurring, or occurring at the same level, thereby reducing their impact.
   c. It reduces craving symptoms, the pleasant effects of alcohol, and the unpleasant effects of alcohol abstinence.
   d. All of the above.

26. Symptoms of the disulfiram–ethanol reaction (DER) include nausea, vomiting, and facial flushing. What causes these symptoms?
   a. decreasing blood levels of acetaldehyde
   b. the increased production of aldehyde dehydrogenase (ALDH), the enzyme that catalyzes the oxidation of acetaldehyde to acetic acid
   c. the inhibition of aldehyde dehydrogenase (ALDH), the enzyme that catalyzes the oxidation of acetaldehyde to acetic acid
   d. consistent blood levels of acetaldehyde

Opioid Antagonists (Naltrexone)

Unlike deterrent medications, opioid antagonists attempt to prevent alcohol's reinforcing stimuli from occurring, or occurring at the same level, thereby reducing their impact. Naltrexone has been found to be effective with both social and problem drinkers. Social drinkers taking naltrexone report less positive and more sedative and unpleasant effects with alcohol (King, Volpicelli, Frazer, & O'Brien, 1997). Problem drinkers reported less of an "alcohol high" and were less likely to progress to heavy drinking with naltrexone. Craving for alcohol is also reduced among patients who have problems with alcohol as well as among social drinkers. However, as with disulfiram, compliance is a key component in naltrexone's effectiveness.

27. By what means does an opioid antagonist aid in relapse prevention?
    a. It alters the body's response to alcohol, making ingestion of even small amounts unpleasant.
    b. It prevents alcohol's reinforcing stimuli (notably emotional) from occurring, or occurring at the same level, thereby reducing their impact.
    c. It reduces craving symptoms, the pleasant effects of alcohol, and the unpleasant effects of alcohol abstinence.
    d. All of the above.

28. Which of the following statements is true regarding the opioid antagonist Naltrexone?
    a. The medication enhances the alcohol-induced release of dopamine.
    b. The medication is only effective with social drinkers.
    c. The medication causes problem drinkers to feel no negative effects from alcohol consumption.
    d. The medication's primary effect appears to be its ability to reduce the patient's emotional response to alcohol consumption.

Acamprosate

Although its exact action is still under investigation, it is clear that acamprosate interacts with different neurological pathways than the opioid antagonists. The drug is believed to restore normal activity to two neurotransmitter systems that are disrupted by chronic alcohol use. Like naltrexone, acamprosate's primary effect is to reduce the "high" from alcohol use as well as craving associated with conditioned alcohol withdrawal.

There is consistent evidence that acamprosate is an effective drug in alcohol treatment. Because acamprosate has a benign profile of side effects, and it is not substantially metabolized in the liver, but rather eliminated from the body, it may be employed for use even in patients with liver disease. Not yet approved for use in the United States, acamprosate has been widely used to treat alcohol-dependent patients in Europe. Patients taking acamprosate achieved higher abstinence rates, and those who resumed drinking experienced a significantly longer time to relapse (Tempesta, Janiri, Bignamini, Chabac, & Potgreter, 2000).

29. By what means does acamprosate aid in relapse prevention?
    a. It alters the body's response to alcohol, making ingestion of even small amounts unpleasant.
    b. It prevents alcohol's reinforcing stimuli (notably emotional) from occurring, or occurring at the same level, thereby reducing their impact.
    c. It reduces craving symptoms, the pleasant effects of alcohol, and the unpleasant effects of alcohol abstinence.
    d. All of the above.

30. Which of the following statements is true regarding acamprosate?
    a. Acamprosate may be safely employed for use in patients with liver disease.
    b. Acamprosate may not be safely employed for use in patients with liver disease.
    c. Acamprosate is not primarily metabolized in the liver.
    d. Acamprosate is believed to restore normal activity to the liver.

KEY TERMS

confabulation: Explaining nonrecalled behaviors by making up stories that have little relation to reality.

functional analysis: A specialized assessment procedure useful in treatment planning for individuals in alcohol use treatment.

recidivism: The relapse of a behavior pattern, often associated with recurrent DWIs.

relapse: The return of problem alcohol use.

standard drink: A standard measurement of alcohol content across a variety of alcohols (defined as one 12-ounce bottle of beer or wine cooler, one 5-ounce glass of wine, or 1.5 ounces of 80-proof distilled spirits).

tolerance: The need for greatly increased amounts of alcohol to achieve intoxication, or a diminished effect with continued alcohol use.

withdrawal: Physiological and cognitive consequences that occur when the blood or tissue concentrations of alcohol decline after prolonged heavy use of alcohol.

DISCUSSION QUESTIONS

1. Describe the biopsychosocial model of problem drinking behavior. What strengths and weaknesses do you see when comparing it to the traditional "medical" model of addiction (which suggests that alcoholism is a disease)? What are the treatment implications of these two models?

2. Discuss the key differences in the diagnostic criteria for alcohol abuse and alcohol dependence. Which is the more serious diagnosis and why?

3. Describe the steps and key issues you would examine as part of a thorough assessment for an individual entering alcoholism treatment. What would be challenges you could encounter in obtaining this information? Describe a potential strategy to deal with each of the challenges you list.

4. What are the strengths and weaknesses of self-report of alcohol use? What are the strengths and weaknesses of obtaining collateral reports? List two potential pitfalls of both, and why you would or would not use either or both in an assessment.

5. Name *five* physical conditions caused directly or indirectly by excessive alcohol use. Detail the role that alcohol plays in each of the conditions.

6. What evidence is there that a large proportion of motorists who drive under the influence of alcohol go undetected? What is the relationship of that evidence with the driving while intoxicated (DWI) recidivism rate? What are the implications for alcohol treatment professionals if the recidivism rate for DWI is approximately one-third?

7. Discuss alcohol's role in crime and violence, with a specific focus on sexual assault and child abuse. Why do you think there is such a relationship? What do you think treatment providers can do to help with this problem?

8. Discuss the four psychosocial treatments for problem drinking described in the chapter. What do you think are the strengths and weaknesses of each approach? How could these treatment approaches be modified to meet the needs of individual clients? On what bases would you modify or choose treatment components for individual clients?

9. Discuss the three pharmacological treatments for problem drinking described in the chapter. Which do you think would be the most effective and why?

10. Discuss the merits of the psychosocial versus pharmacological treatments for problem drinking described in the chapter. What combination of treatments do you think would

be the most effective and why? How do these approaches fit with the biopsychosocial model of problem drinking behavior discussed at the beginning of the chapter?

SUGGESTED FURTHER READING

The field of problem drinking treatment is broad, and this chapter can only offer a brief overview of some of the key issues. While some of the important issues in the field were discussed in this chapter, further reading can offer a fuller picture. We recommend the following texts:

DiClemente, C. (2003). *Addiction and change: How addictions develop and addicted people recover*. New York: Guilford Press.

This text offers discussion of addictions from the stages of change perspective. It covers issues of multiple areas of life functioning, including relationships, beliefs and attitudes, enduring personal characteristics, and social systems, and how they interact with change processes in addiction and recovery.

Leonard, K., & Blane, H. (Eds.). (1999). *Psychological theories of drinking and alcoholism* (2nd ed.). New York: Guilford Press.

Chapters in this text review established and emerging approaches that guide research into the psychological processes influencing drinking and alcoholism. The book takes a multidisciplinary approach as well as taking into account biological, pharmacological, and social factors, offering insights into the development and escalation of drinking problems and the various approaches to treatment.

Marlatt, G., & VandenBos, G. (Eds.). (1997). *Addictive behaviors: Readings on etiology, prevention, and treatment*. Washington, DC, American Psychological Association.

This volume offers a collection of reprinted articles from American Psychological Association journals, providing a current view of psychological research on addictive behaviors. Research in the fields of the effects of drug action, epidemiology and etiology of drug and alcohol abuse, developing and evaluating prevention and treatment programs, and studying the effects of drug policies on human behavior are discussed.

REFERENCES

Abbey, A., Ross, L. T., McDuffie, D., & McAuslan, P. (1996). Alcohol and dating risk factors for sexual assault among college women. *Psychology of Women Quarterly, 20*, 147–169.

American Psychiatric Association. (2000). *Diagnostic and statistical manual of mental disorders* (4th ed., text revision). Washington, DC: Author.

Ammerman, R. T., Kolko, D. J., Kirisci, L., Blackson, T. C., & Dawes, M. A. (1999). Child abuse potential in parents with histories of substance use disorder. *Child Abuse & Neglect, 23*, 1225–1238.

Anthony, J., Warner, L., & Kessler, R. (1994). Comparative epidemiology of dependence on tobacco, alcohol, controlled substances, and inhalants: Basic findings from the National Comorbidity Survey. *Experimental and Clinical Psychopharmacology, 2*, 244–268.

Corrao, G., Bagnardi, V., Zambon, A., & Arico, S. (1999). Exploring the dose-response relationship between alcohol consumption and the risk of several alcohol-related conditions: A meta-analysis. *Addiction, 94*, 1551–1573.

Emanuele, N., Swade, T., & Emanuele, M. (1998). Consequences of alcohol use in diabetics. *Alcohol Health & Research World, 22*(3), 211–219.

Kelley, M. L., & Fals-Stewart, W. (2002). Couples versus individual-based therapy for alcoholism and drug abuse: Effects on children's psychosocial functioning. *Journal of Consulting and Clinical Psychology, 70*, 417–427.

King, A., Volpicelli, J., Frazer, A., & O'Brien, C. (1997). Effect of naltrexone on subjective alcohol response in subjects at high and low risk for future alcohol dependence. *Psychopharmacology, 129*, 15–22.

Korsten, M. (1989). Alcoholism and pancreatitis: Does nutrition play a role? *Alcohol Health & Research World, 13*, 232–237.

Kranzler, H. (2000). Pharmacotherapy of alcoholism: Gaps in knowledge and opportunities for research. *Alcohol & Alcoholism, 35*, 537–547.

Lieber, C. S. (1989). Alcohol and nutrition: An overview. *Alcohol Health & Research World, 13*(3), 197–205.

McCrady, B. S., Horvath, A. T., & Delaney, S. I. (2003). Self-help groups. In R. K. Hester & W. R. Miller (Eds.), *Handbook of alcoholism treatment approaches: Effective alternatives* (3rd ed.), pp. 165–187). Boston: Allyn & Bacon.

Michigan Office of Public Safety (1998). *1998 drunk driving audit.* Lansing, MI: Michigan Office of Public Safety.

Miller, W. R., & Rollnick, S. (Ed.). (2002). *Motivational interviewing: Preparing people for Change* (2nd ed.). New York: Guilford Press.

Monti, P. M., Kadden, R. M., Rohsenow, D. J., Cooney, N. L., & Abrams, D. B. (2002). *Treating alcohol dependence: A coping skills training guide* (2nd ed.). New York: Guilford Press.

National Institute on Alcohol Abuse and Alcoholism (NIAAA). (1993). *Alcohol alert No. 19: Alcohol and the liver.* Rockville, MD: Author.

O'Farrell, T. J., & Fals-Stewart, W. (2003). Marital and family therapy. In R. K. Hester & W. R. Miller (Eds.), *Handbook of alcoholism treatment approaches: Effective alternatives* (3rd ed., pp. 188–212). Boston: Allyn & Bacon.

Prochaska, J. O., & DiClemente, C. C. (1982). *Stages of change in the modification of problem behaviors.* Newbury Park, CA: Sage.

Rimm, E. B., Williams, P., Fosher, K., Criqui, M., & Stampfer, M. J. (1999). Moderate alcohol intake and lower risk of coronary heart disease: Meta-analysis of effects on lipids and haemostatic factors. *British Medical Journal, 319,* 1523–1528.

Snyder, P., & Nussbaum, P. (1999). *Clinical neuropsychology.* Washington, DC: American Psychological Association.

Stratton, K., Howe, C., & Battaglia, F. (Eds.). (1996). Fetal alcohol syndrome: Diagnosis, epidemiology, prevention, and treatment. Washington, DC: National Academy Press.

Swift, R. M. (1999). Drug therapy for alcohol dependence. *New England Journal of Medicine, 340,* 1482–1490.

Tempesta, E., Janiri, L., Bignamini, A., Chabac, S., & Potgreter, A., et. al. (2000). Acamprosate and relapse prevention in the treatment of alcohol dependence: A placebo-controlled study. *Alcohol and Alcoholism, 35,* 202–209.

U.S. Department of Justice (1999). *Arrestee drug abuse monitoring (ADAM) program in the United States.* Washington, DC: Author.

Valliant, P. M. (1995). Personality, peer influence, and use of alcohol and drugs by first-year university students. *Psychological Reports, 77,* 401–402.

Wisdom, C. S., Ireland, T., & Glynn, P. J. (1995). Alcohol abuse in abused and neglected children followed-up: Are they at increased risk? *Journal of Studies on Alcohol, 56,* 207–217.

11

Illicit Drug Use and Prescription Drug Abuse

Delinda E. Mercer
Region West Medical Center
Panhandle Health Services

Robert F. Forman
Treatment Research Institute
University of Pennsylvania

TRUTH OR FICTION?

___ 1. Anxiolytics *are medications that tend to produce anxiety even if taken as prescribed.*

___ 2. A *synergistic effect is the healing that occurs when someone has successfully completed withdrawal from any drug.*

___ 3. The *rebound effect is when a person withdrawing from a drug experiences symptoms that are opposite to the effects of the drug they had been dependent on.*

___ 4. *Smoking marijuana increases a person's risk for heart disease, cancer, and lung disease.*

___ 5. *People who smoke marijuana are more likely to test positive on a urine drug screen than individuals who use other drugs because THC is fat soluble and as a result remains in the body longer.*

___ 6. *Flashbacks are a commonly occurring phenomenon following hallucinogen use.*

___ 7. *There is evidence that ecstasy (MDMA) can damage nerve cells in the brain.*

___ 8. *Inhalants are most commonly used by young people because these substances are easily accessible and inexpensive.*

___ 9. *Opioids are effective analgesics (pain killers).*

___ 10. *Heroin is a Schedule I drug in the United States, which means that it is not legal to prescribe it and there is no legal use for it.*

___ 11. *All drugs in the opioid category are illegal in the United States.*

___ 12. *Tolerance to a drug has occurred when one becomes increasingly sensitive to the effects of the drug and can no longer tolerate the same amount as they used to.*

___ 13. *Cocaine and amphetamines both stimulate the central nervous system.*

___ 14. *Amphetamine use tends to increase one's self-confidence unrealistically, which is sometimes referred to as the "Superman Syndrome."*

_____ 15. *Ingesting crack cocaine by smoking is very inefficient because much of the drug is rendered chemically inactive by the process of burning.*

This chapter discusses the commonly abused illicit (illegal) and prescription drugs and the clinical problems that may occur as a result. Commonly abused drugs include: opioids, stimulants, **central nervous system** (CNS) depressants, cannabis, hallucinogens, dissociatives, inhalants, and steroids. We will discuss the scope of use, desired and harmful effects, and common clinical problems within each drug category, and will point out commonalities across categories.

HOW WIDESPREAD IS ILLICIT DRUG USE IN THE UNITED STATES?

According to the 2001 National Household Survey on Drug Abuse (NHSDA), approximately 15.9 million Americans aged 12 or older (7.1% of the population) were current users of illicit drugs. Approximately 94.1 million Americans aged 12 or older (41.7%) reported ever using illicit drugs, an estimated 4.8 million Americans (2.1%) were misusing prescription drugs, and 36 million (16%) reported ever misusing prescription drugs (Office of Applied Studies, 2002).

1. What percentage of Americans, aged 12 and older, have ever used illicit drugs?
   a. 25.5%
   b. 35.7%
   c. 41.7%
   d. 50.2%

WHO USES ILLICIT DRUGS OR MISUSES PRESCRIPTION MEDICATIONS?

The general trends show that men are more likely to report current (in the past month) illicit drug use than women (8.7% vs. 5.5%) as reported in the 2001 NHSDA. Women are about equal to men (2.0% vs. 2.2%) in nonmedical use of prescription drugs (Office of Applied Studies, 2002).

Among the major racial and ethnic groups, rates of current illicit drug use are 7.4% for African Americans, 7.2% for Whites, and 6.4% for Hispanics. The rate of use is highest among American Indians/Alaskan Natives at 9.9% and lowest among Asians at 2.8% (Office of Applied Studies, 2002).

Rates of drug use vary by age, with the highest use among those aged 16 to 25 years (Fig. 11.1). The age distribution of users also varies a great deal by type of drug.

2. Which statement is *not* correct about gender differences in drug use?
   a. IV drug use is more common among women than men.
   b. There is more reported illicit drug use among men.
   c. For most age groups, men and women are about equal in nonmedical use of prescription drugs.
   d. Among adolescents 12 to 17 years old, girls are more likely to misuse prescription drugs than boys.

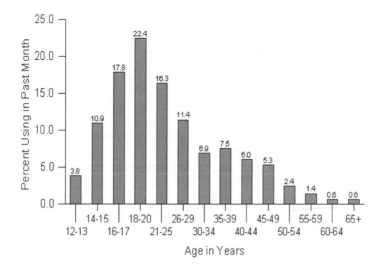

FIG. 11.1. Current (past month) Illicit Drug Use by Age. [Reprinted from the 2001 National Household Survey on Drug Abuse (NHSDA)].

3. Overall, the age group associated with the highest rate of drug use is _____.
   a. 12–15
   b. 16–25
   c. 26–34
   d. 35 and older

HOW ARE PRESCRIPTION AND ILLICIT DRUGS CATEGORIZED?

The Comprehensive Drug Abuse Prevention and Control Act of 1970 (also called the Controlled Substances Act) established new legislation in a number of areas related to drug abuse and prevention. It established a classification system for categorizing drugs based on their abuse potential and their clinical usefulness (see Table 11.1). These classifications, which are called schedules, go from I to V.

4 . Which of the following is true of the Controlled Substances Act?
   a. It is also referred to as the Drug Abuse Prevention and Control Act.
   b. It was enacted in 1970.
   c. It established a five-schedule classification system.
   d. All of the above.

5. Which of the following is *not* true about Schedule I drugs in the United States?
   a. They have a high abuse potential.
   b. Doctors need a special DEA number to prescribe them.
   c. They include heroin and LSD.
   d. There is no current medical use for them.

TABLE 11.1

Drug Schedules

Schedule	Criteria	Examples
I	High potential for abuse No current medical use in U.S. Lack of accepted safety for use	heroin, marijuana, LSD, psilocybin
II	High potential for abuse Currently accepted medical use Abuse may lead to severe dependence	morphine, cocaine, Demerol, methadone, injectable methamphetamine
III	Moderate potential for abuse Currently accepted medical use Abuse may lead to moderate dependence	opium, Vicodan, some amphetamines and barbiturates
IV	Lower potential for abuse Currently accepted medical use Abuse may lead to limited dependence	Darvocet, Xanax, Valium, and some barbiturates
V	Low potential for abuse Currently accepted medical use Abuse may rarely lead to limited dependence	Lomotil, Phenergan and liquid suspensions

WHAT ARE THE MOST COMMONLY ABUSED DRUGS?

Commonly abused drugs at present include: cannibis, opioids, cocaine, amphetamines, benzo-diazepines, sedatives, hallucinogens, dissociative drugs, "club" drugs, inhalants, and anabolic steroids (Table 11.2). Some of these drugs are *illicit* like heroin and marijuana, while others, such as amphetamines and **benzodiazepines**, are legally used as prescription medications but can be abused.

Cannibis

What Is the Scope of Use?

Marijuana is the most commonly used illegal drug in America with approximately 37% of Americans age 12 and older having tried it at least once, and about 9% having used it the past year (Office of Applied Studies, 2002). According to the White House Office of National Drug Control in 2000, Americans spent about $10 billion on marijuana and consumed approximately 1000 metric tons of it (Office of National Drug Control Policy).

6. What is the most commonly used illegal drug in the United States?
   a. cocaine
   b. Valium
   c. marijuana
   d. Ecstasy

What Are the Desired Effects?

The effects of smoking marijuana typically last 2 to 4 hours and vary somewhat depending on the user's experience. Effects may include a feeling of lightness; heightened sensitivity to

TABLE 11.2

Common Drugs of Abuse

Category	Drug	Mode(s) of Ingestion	Desired Effects	Common Harmful Effects
Cannibis	marijuana, hashish	smoked, eaten	euphoria, mild alterations of perception	cognitive impairment, respiratory illness
Opioids	heroin	injected, sniffed, smoked	Euphoria, relaxation, drowsiness	injection risks, respiratory or cardiac arrest
	prescription opioids (Demerol, OxyContin, Vicodin)	injected, swallowed		
Stimulants	cocaine	sniffed, smoked, injected	rush of energy, alertness and excitation, sense of confidence and power	injection risks, heart attack, stroke, depression, psychosis (tactile hallucinations and paranoia)
	amphetamines	swallowed, sniffed, smoked, injected		
Depressants	sedatives (barbiturates) anti-anxiety agents (benzodiazepines)	swallowed, injected	intoxification, relaxation, sleep	respiratory depression, withdrawal syndrome (may include seizures, delirium)
	alcohol	drunk		
Hallucinogens	LSD	swallowed	alterations in perception including increased emotionality and sense of connection	bad trips, depression, psychosis, flashbacks
	psilocybin, peyote, mescaline	eaten		
Inhalants	glue, gasoline solvents, nitrous oxide	Inhaled	excitation, lightheadedness, disinhibition, disorientation	cognitive impairment, asphyxia, cardiac arrest, brain damage

music, food, and sights; and an altered sense of time. Marijuana is considered a mild hallucinogen, though it is not nearly as potent as drugs such as LSD.

What Are the Harmful Effects?

Marijuana can produce various adverse consequences, particularly for those who use the drug heavily over a protracted period of time. These effects include: respiratory illness, cancer, compromised immune system, accidental injuries, cardiovascular disease, and cognitive impairment. In addition, contrary to popular belief, chronic marijuana smokers can experience

withdrawal symptoms such as irritability, depressed mood, and craving (Budney, Hughes, Moore, & Novy, 2001) and people do become addicted to it.

---

7. Marijuana is considered a mild _____.
    a. stimulant
    b. hallucinogen
    c. herbal remedy for depression
    d. tranquilizer

8. The harmful effects of marijuana include all of the following *except* _____.
    a. respiratory illness
    b. cancer
    c. compromised immune system
    d. blood-borne infections

9. Dependence on marijuana.
    a. is associated with withdrawal symptoms including depression, irritability, and craving.
    b. is not possible.
    c. decreases the appetite.
    d. happens only to glaucoma patients.

What Are the Common Treatment Challenges?

"Low Bottom" Snobbery.   Individuals who are dependent on marijuana are often not treated as seriously by counselors and other clients as individuals who are dependent on the "harder" drugs such as crack cocaine or heroin. A minimizing attitude on the part of counselors, fellow clients, or other recovering people at 12-step meetings will undermine the prospects of marijuana dependent individuals being able to recover. The perception of marijuana as a "soft drug" is one of the factors that may keep people from seeking help in the first place.

Recommendation—It is important to recognize that marijuana dependence can be severely destructive to individuals and their families. Marijuana dependence increases risks for injury, cancer, and heart diseases and like all other dependent individuals, their **addiction** can have serious consequences on their work, education, and social relations.

Tested Positive But Has No Symptoms.   THC can be detected in the urine for several weeks after last use and as a consequence the chances that an occasional marijuana user will test positive are fairly high. Consequently, a substantial number of marijuana users are referred for counseling whose only problem is "they got caught." While marijuana dependent individuals are likely to be among those who test positive, there may also be individuals who do not have any other symptoms of dependence or abuse. The inclusion of nondependent individuals in a *recovery* group is a misuse of treatment resources and can undermine the progress of group members who can benefit from treatment.

Recommendation—The motivational interviewing (MI) approach described by Miller and Rollnick (2002) can be extremely valuable with clients in this category. Even if they do not meet the diagnostic criteria for dependence or abuse, they still could benefit from a brief intervention in which they step back and examine what they like—and don't like—about their drug use. Also, some clinics have initiated separate groups for clients referred through driving under the influence (DUI) and workplace drug testing: these groups combine MI with basic education about addiction and recovery, "just in case" the group participants eventually develop an addiction.

The Pro-Marijuana Drug Culture.

More than any other drug of abuse, there is an active and vocal marijuana subculture that advocates its use. Hundreds of Web sites sell marijuana seeds and paraphernalia, and marijuana use is in popular movies and music. Efforts to make medical marijuana available by prescription also contribute to the impression that marijuana is a harmless substance. These sociocultural factors can undermine the commitment of individuals trying to recover from marijuana dependence.

Recommendations—Individuals who are in treatment for marijuana dependence are faced with a dilemma that is similar to people recovering from alcoholism. Specifically, although *most* people who drink alcohol do not become alcoholic, if a person does develop alcoholism, then they need to recognize that this is best treated with complete abstinence. Similarly, individuals for whom marijuana use becomes a problem (whether it meets criteria for dependence or not), need to abstain.

Opioids: Heroin and Prescription Opioids[1]

Drugs in the **opioid**, or **narcotic**, category include both illicit and prescription drugs. Heroin is the most abused and the most rapidly acting of the opiates. It is a Schedule I drug which means it is illegal in the United States.

Prescription opioids are drugs, either natural or synthetic, that are related to opium. They are similar to heroin in the way they affect the body, but there is a range of potency (how powerful they are). Opioids are commonly prescribed because of their **analgesic** properties, especially for relatively severe pain like broken bones, cancers, and severe headaches. Some of these drugs—for example, codeine—can be used to relieve coughs and diarrhea. Medications that fall within this class—sometimes referred to as *narcotics*—include: morphine, codeine, oxycodone (OxyContin), propoxyphene (Darvon), hydrocodone (Vicodin), hydromorphone (Dilaudid), and others. Opioids which are more potent and more rapidly acting have greater abuse potentials.

10. Opioid drugs include all of the following *except* _____C_____.
    a. codeine
    b. heroin
    c. barbital
    d. oxycodone

11. Prescription opioids are used to treat all of the following problems *except* _____C_____.
    a. pain
    b. cough
    c. respiratory arrest
    d. diarrhea

---

[1] The more broad term "opioids" is used here instead of "opiates" because the latter refers specifically to those drugs that are derived from opium, whereas opioids include opium-derived drugs as well as other synthetic, opiate-like substances.

Heroin

What Is the Scope of Use?

An estimated 3.1 million people have used heroin at some point in their lives; 123,000 of them reported using it within the last month. This represents a lifetime prevalence (at least one use in a person's lifetime) of heroin use by people age 12 and older of 1.4% (Office of Applied Studies, 2002). Adults over age 30 have typically been the largest user group, but there is a strong trend toward younger people starting to use heroin (National Institute on Drug Abuse [NIDA], 2000).

Heroin is typically sold as a white or brownish powder or as the black sticky substance known as *black tar heroin*. Although purer heroin is becoming more common, most street heroin is "cut" with other drugs or with substances such as sugar, starch, powdered milk, or quinine. Heroin is usually injected, sniffed/snorted, or smoked. Intravenous injection provides the greatest intensity and most rapid onset of euphoria (7–8 seconds). When heroin is sniffed or smoked, peak effects are usually felt within 10 to 15 minutes. Although smoking and sniffing heroin do not produce a "rush" as quickly or as intensely as intravenous injection, all three forms of heroin administration can be addictive.

Injection is the predominant method of heroin use. However, as more potent heroin has become available, making it possible for users to get a powerful high with a less direct route of ingestion, there is a shift in use patterns, away from injection to sniffing and smoking. This shift is associated with increased diversity of users. Older users, over 30, mostly use via injection. However, new, younger users are lured by inexpensive, high-purity heroin that can be sniffed or smoked instead of injected. These younger users appear to want to avoid the stigma and the disease risks associated with injecting (NIDA, 2000).

12. Younger heroin users are ingesting heroin more by smoking and sniffing rather than injecting for all of the following reasons *except*:
    a. avoidance of the stigma of injecting.
    b. it is less expensive to get the desired effects via sniffing.
    c. reducing risk of HIV and Hepatitis B and C.
    d. the high quality of the heroin enables users to get the desired effects via sniffing or smoking.

Prescription Opioids

What Is the Scope of Use?

In 1999, approximately 2.6 million people in the United States were reported to have misused prescription opioids within the past month (NIDA, 2001b). The most dramatic increase in **prescription drug misuse** occurs among adolescents (aged 12–17) and young adults (aged 18–25). Men and women have similar rates of misuse of prescription drugs, except among those aged 12 to 17 where young women are more likely to misuse prescription drugs (Simoni-Wastilla, 2000). Hydrocodone and oxycodone are associated with significantly increased emergency department visits from 1999 to 2001 (Office of Applied Studies, 2003).

The higher potency prescription opioids (morphine, fentanyl, and meperidine [Demerol]) usually appear in legally prepared injection forms that have been diverted from medical use. They may be injected either intravenously (IV) or subcutaneously (skin popping). The lower potency prescription opioids (codeine, propoxyphene) usually come in pill form and are taken orally.

The following sections refer to heroin and prescription opioids.

What Are the Desired Effects?

Soon after ingestion, opioids cross the blood–brain barrier which typically produces a "rush" and a feeling of euphoria. The intensity of the experience is a function of how much drug is taken and how rapidly the drug enters the brain and binds to the natural opioid receptors, which depend on the particular drug and how it is ingested. After the initial effects, abusers usually will be drowsy for several hours.

What Are the Harmful Effects?

Opioid injection presents the following risks: scarred or collapsed veins, bacterial infections due to unsanitary injection practices, and blood-borne infections due to sharing needles. Contaminants found in street drugs (as opposed to pharmaceutical drugs that have been diverted) may also lead to blocked or clogged blood vessels, arthritis, and other rheumatologic problems. Regardless of how ingested, opioid use can cause respiratory complications, and overdose death through respiratory and cardiac depression.

13. The risks associated with injection include all of the following *except*:
    a. scarred or collapsed veins.
    b. endocarditis and other bacterial infections.
    c. arthritis and other rheumatologic conditions.
    d. several forms of cancer.

What Are the Common Treatment Challenges?

Relapse Risk.   Many opioid addicts in recovery struggle with relapse; the risk of relapse is associated with a significant danger of death by overdose. **Detoxifying** from opioids reduces one's **tolerance**, thus it becomes easy for the relapsing individual to overestimate the amount of drug they can handle and to overdose.

Recommendation—While treatment should focus on relapse prevention, it should also adopt a harm reduction perspective in advising patients of the increased risk of death from overdose due to decreased tolerance.

Feeling Manipulated.   Opioid addicts may enter drug treatment to get a brief respite after which they can get a better high because of their decreased tolerance. This can be frustrating to treatment providers and insurance companies alike, who feel that they are being used.

Recommendation—No one can predict when an addicted individual will turn the corner and begin a healthy recovery. There are many serious health and social consequences associated with opioid addiction. Regardless of the patient's motives, treatment does some good for both patients and their communities.

Management of Chronic Pain.   Opioids are effective drugs for managing acute pain. When opioids are prescribed for a relatively short time, most patients will be able to use the medication appropriately and then stop using the drug when the pain remits. However, prolonged use of opioids for chronic conditions can lead to tolerance and physiological dependence, and about 5% percent of patients will seek increasing amounts of the drug.

Recommendation—Because of the subjective nature of chronic pain, counselors should make referrals when indicated to a qualified pain management specialist, knowledgeable about addiction.

Withdrawal. Withdrawal is the addicted individual's body reacting to the absence of the drug. In regular users, withdrawal may occur as early as a few hours after the last administration, and produce drug craving, restlessness, muscle and bone pain, insomnia, diarrhea and vomiting, cold flashes with goose bumps ("cold turkey"), kicking movements ("kicking the habit"), and other symptoms. Major withdrawal symptoms peak between 48 and 72 hours after the last dose and subside after about a week. Opiate dependent individuals refer to withdrawal as "drug sickness" and they will typically go to great lengths to avoid it. The withdrawal experience is usually described to nonusers as akin to a bad flu, with aches, nausea, diarrhea, and overall discomfort. Opiate dependent individuals in withdrawal are notorious for leaving detox programs AMA (against medical advice).

Recommendations—During detox, medications such as methadone, clonidine, or buprenorphine may be used to manage withdrawal; without these medications, AMA rates can be as high as 50%. It is helpful for the clinician to offer as much support as is reasonable to aid the patient through the discomfort and to educate about withdrawal, particularly highlighting its temporary nature. Although opioid withdrawal is usually uncomfortable, it is not medically dangerous unless complicated by other health problems. Heroin withdrawal is generally less dangerous than alcohol or barbiturate withdrawal.

Heightened Sensitivity to Pain. Following cessation of opioid use, some patients experience heightened sensitivity to pain; it is unclear whether this is a consequence of opioid dependence or a preexisting condition. This low tolerance to pain can be a relapse trigger.

Recommendations—The clinician may offer support and encouragement to remind the recovering person that his sensitivity is most likely a temporary phenomenon that will self-correct over time as the body's natural endorphins readjust.

Maintenance or Withdrawal? Should the patient detoxify and go into "drug-free" treatment, or to go onto methadone or buprenorphine maintenance treatment? There are pros and cons to either choice. Some people are opposed to replacing one drug of abuse (e.g., heroin) with another safer, but similar, drug (e.g., methadone). However, research consistently shows that methadone maintenance treatment is associated with decreased social, legal, and health problems. Patients in maintenance treatment are less likely than untreated heroin addicts to resort to criminal activity, more likely to retain a job and be a functional member of a family, and less likely to contract HIV and other infectious diseases.

Recommendation—Methadone maintenance has limited availability based upon location and is prohibited in some states. However, when there are options, the clinician should take into consideration the motivation of the patient, the chronicity of the problem, and the patient's life circumstances. Ideally, the patient should become drug free and only use methadone or other opiate agonist therapies as a last resort. Yet, the bulk of the evidence suggests that it is very difficult to abstain from opioids once addicted. The relapse rate is high and the consequences potentially fatal. Consequently, buprenorphine or methadone replacement therapy should be considered after a patient's first *re*admission into treatment (their second treatment episode). Ultimately, it is the patient's decision which approach to recovery to pursue.

HIV Risk Reduction. Opioid addicts are at increased risk for contracting HIV and other infectious diseases, primarily through risky injection procedures but also through unsafe sexual behaviors.

Recommendation—Research has shown that drug treatment reduces risk for HIV infection for heroin addicts (Metzger, Navaline, & Woody, 1998). The same is likely true for other blood-borne infections. Drug treatment reduces disease risk in three main ways. First, treatment hopefully reduces, if not eliminates, drug use. Second, treatment programs can be a resource for risk reduction information and even supplies (condoms, bleach kits, etc.). Finally, the ongoing contact with a counselor who cares about how the patient is doing—and who will not judge the patient for not being completely risk-free—helps the patient make an effort to reduce his or her risks. Counselors should be aware of their role in helping clients reduce their risks.

14. Drug treatment impacts HIV risks in which of the following ways?
    a. reduces or eliminates drug use
    b. gives the drug user access to resources like condoms, bleach kits, clean needles, and education
    c. gives the user ongoing contact with a counselor who cares and is interested in supporting positive efforts
    d. all of the above

Stimulants: Cocaine and Amphetamines

Cocaine and amphetamines are both stimulants. They act on the central nervous (CNS) by increasing alertness, excitation, and euphoria. Stimulants cause a sense of energy and feeling of well-being and confidence that users find pleasurable. The sympathetic nervous system is stimulated as well, causing increased pulse rate and blood pressure and dilation of the bronchioles in the lungs.

15. Which of the drugs listed below is *not* a stimulant?
    a. buspirone
    b. methamphetamine
    c. Ecstasy
    d. Cocaine

Cocaine

Cocaine is an addictive stimulant with local anesthetic properties. *Coca leaves*, the source of cocaine, have been ingested for thousands of years and the pure chemical, cocaine hydrochloride, has been used for more than 100 years. Today, cocaine is a Schedule II drug, meaning that it has high potential for abuse, but can be used for medical purposes (for example, as a local anesthetic).

What Is the Scope of Use?

Cocaine use peaked in the 1980s, with 5.7 million current cocaine users (3% of the population) in 1985 and approximately 1.0 to 1.5 million new users each year. Cocaine use fell to a low point in the early 1990s, then leveled off, with small changes from year to year (NIDA, 1999b). Recent statistics indicate 1.7 million current users, and 27.8 million lifetime (meaning have ever used) users (Office of Applied Studies, 2002).

Adults aged 18 to 25 years have a higher rate of current cocaine use than any other age group. Men have a higher rate of current cocaine use than women. According to the 1997 NHSDA, rates of current cocaine use were 1.4% for African Americans, 0.8% for Hispanics, and 0.6% for Caucasians (NIDA 1999b).

Cocaine exists in two chemical forms: the hydrochloride salt and the "freebase." The hydrochloride salt, or powdered form of cocaine, dissolves in water and can be taken intravenously (by vein) or intranasally (in the nose). *Freebase* refers to a compound that has not been neutralized by an acid to make the hydrochloride salt. The freebase form of cocaine, which is crystalline, is smokable.

Street cocaine is a fine, white, crystalline powder and may be diluted with other substances such as cornstarch, talcum powder, or with active drugs such as procaine (a chemically-related local anesthetic). *Crack* is freebase cocaine that has been processed from the powdered cocaine hydrochloride form to a smokable form that causes the user to experience a high in fewer than 10 seconds. This immediate euphoric effect is one of the reasons crack became enormously popular in the mid 1980s.

What Are the Desired Effects?

Users generally seek the euphoria, the feeling of energy and the sense of power, or invincibility associated with the cocaine "rush." This rush occurs almost immediately and lasts a relatively short time, usually less than an hour.

What Are the Harmful Effects?

Cocaine causes stimulation of the sympathetic nervous system, which increases levels of adrenaline and causes vasoconstriction. This vasoconstriction has harmful effects on the heart, respiratory system, and other systems in the body. Cocaine use has been linked to heart disease and it can trigger chaotic heart rhythms (ventricular fibrillation), strokes, chest pain (angina), and in some cases, lead to cardiac arrest. It is associated with rapid breathing and respiratory failure, neurological conditions like seizures and headaches, and gastrointestinal problems including pain and nausea. Snorting cocaine can lead to nasal damage. Injecting cocaine is associated with increase risk for HIV and other infectious diseases, collapsed veins, blocked or clogged blood vessels, and arthritis and rheumatologic problems. Taking cocaine with alcohol, which is a common combination, results in the two drugs being converted in the body to cocaethylene. Cocaethylene has a longer duration of action in the brain, is more toxic than either drug alone, and is a very common drug combination that can result in death.

16. Stimulants do all of the following *except*:
    a. cause feelings of energy and confidence.
    b. increase alertness and purposeful movement.
    c. increase pulse rate and blood pressure.
    d. increase appetite.

What Are the Common Treatment Challenges?

Craving.   Cocaine users describe a powerful desire to binge on the drug, then have a period of time in which to recover, then use again. Addicts report feeling strong cravings or urges which lead to drug use unless a concerted effort is made to prevent relapse.

Recommendation—Help the client to recognize drug cravings and plan in advance what they will do when craving hits. Such a relapse prevention plan could include: attending a 12-step meeting, talking to a support person or doing an activity with nonusers, for instance, one's children. It is also helpful to remind the person struggling with craving that feelings, even strong ones, don't have to control one's actions. If not acted upon, craving will recede—just as it came on.

Relapse Triggers.   Relapse triggers are stimuli that can set off craving and lead to use. Frequently reported triggers among cocaine users are money and getting paid, paraphernalia like a crack pipe, places where one used or bought drugs, and people like a dealer or a sexual partner with whom one used. Feelings, which are called *internal triggers*, can be positive, celebratory feelings or dysphoric feelings like disappointment or loneliness.

Recommendation—Help the client to become aware of his or her drug triggers and learn how to either avoid them altogether or cope with them without using. Strategies should be developed collaboratively with the client and may include not keeping money on one's person, not going to locations where one bought or used drugs, and not spending time with drug-using associates.

Cocaine and Sex.   For some addicts, there seems to be a cocaine–sex connection. This tends to be manifested in two ways. Cocaine use becomes a trigger for sex and visa-versa. Also many people in active addiction will exchange sex for drugs or for money to buy drugs—in other words, prostitute themselves.

Recommendation—There are emotional and physical sequelae to these experiences which are important to address in counseling. If sex and cocaine become triggers for one another, this can be handled by strategizing how to avoid the trigger, or if that is not realistic, how to manage one's exposure to the trigger without using, similar to other relapse triggers. If one traded sex for drugs, one may have enduring feelings of shame, questions about sexual identity, worries about HIV and other STDs.

HIV Risk Reduction.   Cocaine addicts are at increased risk for contracting HIV and other blood-borne diseases.

Recommendation—Drug treatment reduces risk for HIV infection and other blood-borne infections for cocaine addicts (Shoptaw, Frosch, Rawson, & Ling, 1997), as it does for opiate addicts (see previous section).

Amphetamines

Amphetamines are powerful stimulants. Amphetamines may be legally prescribed for attention deficit hyperactivity disorder (ADHD), obesity, and narcolepsy (a disorder in which persons are overcome by sudden attacks of deep sleep).

Stimulant abuse became more prevalent in the United States in the 1960s with intravenous injection, although abuse of it in pill form was also common. The Controlled Substances Act reclassified amphetamines as a Schedule II drug placing tighter controls on manufacturing and prescribing them. Many doctors began to prescribe "pseudo-amphetamines" (such as methylphenidate, or Ritalin) instead of amphetamines.

17. Which of the following conditions would *not* be treated with amphetamines?
  a. liver disease
  b. narcolepsy
  c. attention deficit hyperactivity disorder (ADHD)
  d. obesity

What Is the Scope of Use?

An estimated 16 million people have used amphetamines in their lifetime, with 1 million reporting current use (Office of Applied Studies, 2002). For methamphetamine, 8.8 million people have tried it at some time in their lives, and 576,000 people report current use (Office of Applied Studies). Methamphetamine, the most potent form of amphetamine readily available, is the leading drug of abuse among treatment clients in the San Diego area and Hawaii and it is becoming a substantial problem in the West and Southwest (NIDA, 2001a). Because of the availability of agricultural chemicals used to manufacture methamphetamine in home labs, its availability and production are increasing in rural areas. The use of *ice*, a very potent, smokable form of methamphetamine, began in Hawaii and has spread to California and beyond, to Florida and Texas.

Amphetamines, or *speed*, can be taken by mouth in capsule form, snorted, smoked, or injected. *Crystal meth* is sold as a powder that is injected, inhaled, or taken orally. *Ice or glass* is a concentrated form of methamphetamine that resembles tiny chunks of translucent glass that can be smoked rather than injected.

What Are the Desired Effects?

The physical effects of amphetamines include euphoria, heightened alertness, loss of appetite, and greater energy.

What Are the Harmful Effects?

High doses of amphetamines, especially if repeated over several days or with regular use, can lead to delusions, hallucinations, and feelings of paranoia (sometimes called *amphetamine psychosis*). Psychotic reactions will usually be short-lived, but may develop into paranoid psychosis which may persist for months or more. The user may develop repetitive and compulsive behaviors while under the influence which may be acceptable (like cleaning) or may be bizarre. Amphetamine use can also lead to cardiac and respiratory problems, physical depletion including malnutrition, dehydration, rapid development of tolerance, and injection risks (if injected).

What Are the Common Treatment Challenges?

Depression.   After an amphetamine binge, users are likely to experience a "crash" in which they sleep for 24 hours or more, then wake feeling depressed, lethargic, tired, and hungry. This depression can be severe to the point of suicidality and usually lasts for days or longer. These withdrawal symptoms may tempt the user to take more amphetamines to relieve the unpleasant "crash."

Recommendation—The entire treatment team should be aware of the co-occurrence of addiction, depression, and suicidality. For severe or prolonged depression, the client should be referred for evaluation and medication if appropriate. Brief hospitalization, supportive counseling, medication, and contracting for safety are often required.

The "Superman Syndrome." Because amphetamine use unrealistically increases self-confidence, users tend to ignore the reality of personal limitations. Amphetamines can make a user feel powerful, violent, and sexually aggressive. When users attempt to perform tasks they are incapable of performing, this is referred to as the "Superman Syndrome."

Recommendation—Because the aggressive behavior may cause serious legal and personal problems, clinicians should clearly point out that amphetamine use leads to out-of-control behavior. Help the client recognize the role played by amphetamines (e.g., "Superman Syndrome") and help the client develop healthy strategies for feeling empowered.

Depressants

Sedatives and anti-anxiety agents are CNS *depressants* because they depress, or sedate, the activity of the brain. They are appropriately prescribed for treatment of anxiety and sleep disorders, but have been misused as intoxicants, date rape drugs, and in suicides and homicides. These medications do not produce the disorder known as *depression*; this is a common confusion due to the similar terminology.

Sedatives, also known as *sedative-hypnotics*, are typically prescribed for the treatment of sleep disorders. Many sedatives belong to the chemical family known as *barbiturates*.

Anti-Anxiety Agents (or **anxiolytics** and *tranquilizers*) include all drugs that belong to the chemical category known as *benzodiazepines* as well as a few other medications that are not related chemically to benzodiazepines. Examples of anxiolytics include diazepam (Valium), chlordiazepoxide (Librium), alprazolam (Xanax) and lorazepam (Ativan).

NONADDICTIVE ANTI-ANXIETY MEDICATION

One anti-anxiety medication, *buspirone* (trade name: BuSpar), appears to not produce dependence and does not appear to have abuse potential. This anti-anxiety medication is not a benzodiazepine.

---

18. All of the following are true of CNS depressants *except*:
    a. they include anxiolytics, sedatives, and alcohol.
    b. they can cause clinical depression.
    c. the depress the activity of the brain.
    d. they are used to treat anxiety and sleep disorders.

What Is the Scope of Use?

About 1.4 million Americans have used an anti-anxiety or sedative medication for non-medical purposes (Office of Applied Studies, 2002). These drugs are more frequently used by older adults than by younger people, and are used by women as often as men. Anxiolytics and sedatives are typically taken as pills.

What Are the Desired Effects?

People use anxiolytics and sedatives to reduce anxiety, produce sleep, and in some cases, create a state of intoxication. Individuals who have become dependent on them need to take larger doses in order to avoid withdrawal. Some individuals take anxiolytics or sedatives with alcohol to produce an extreme state of intoxication, which may lead to intentional or unintentional overdose death.

What Are the Harmful Effects?

Dependence and Withdrawal.   Anxiolytics and sedatives can produce physical dependence after as little as a month of heavy use, or several months of use at therapeutic levels. Withdrawal from these drugs must be medically managed because there is a risk for seizures and other serious medical complications including hallucinations, disorientation, vomiting, and sleep disorders.

Overdose.   Sedative overdose risk is increased when sedatives are taken in combination with other drugs including opioids, alcohol, or anxiolytics. Overdose risk is increased when barbiturates are taken with allergy medications that contain antihistamines. The relatively low risk for overdose of anxiolytics seriously increases if they are taken with alcohol, sedatives, or opioids. Taking anxiolytics or sedatives with alcohol produces a *synergistic effect*. These combinations lead to a disproportionately stronger effect than what might normally be expected and may result in death.

19. Suddenly discontinuing anxiolytics may cause withdrawal symptoms, including all of the following *except* _____.
    a. seizures
    b. sleep disorders
    c. watery eyes and runny nose
    d. hallucinations

20. Which of the following is *not* true of *synergistic effects*?
    a. They can lead to death.
    b. Cutting cocaine powder with lactose will produce them.
    c. Using alcohol with sedatives or anxiolytics will produce them.
    d. They are when a combination of drugs causes greater impairment than would be expected based on the amount used.

What Are the Common Treatment Challenges?

Not Like Other Addicts.   Anxiolytic and sedative abusers often view themselves as being different than people who use "street drugs" like cocaine and heroin. This perception may lead them to avoid participating in treatment and support groups.

Recommendation—Anxiolytic and sedative users need to find 12-step meetings where they will fit in. Similarly, they need to make an extra effort to apply what they are learning in treatment to their own situation. Some individuals who are dependent on prescription drugs are healthcare professionals; in many areas there are recovery support groups specifically for healthcare professionals.

Rebound Effect. Clients who have become dependent on anti-anxiety and/or sedative medications will experience a significant *rebound effect* if they stop using, which is associated with increased anxiety, irritability, and sleeplessness. These symptoms present a significant threat to recovery because they may be the same symptoms, but now more severe, that led the client to start misusing these drugs in the first place.

Recommendation—Communicate to the client that these symptoms are largely a result of the drug dependence and with extended abstinence they will lessen. Recovery is a process—it is important to provide encouragement and support to clients while their nervous systems re-adjust. Referral to a knowledgeable addiction psychiatrist may be appropriate since alternative, nonaddictive, prescribed medications might reduce the rebound symptoms. Alternative anxiety, stress, and insomnia interventions should also be pursued.

> 21. *Rebound effects* from anxiolytic dependence can involve all but which of the following?
>   a. anxiety
>   b. sleeplessness
>   c. unrealistic feelings of power
>   d. irritability

Physician Awareness. Because anxiolytic and sedative-dependent patients often receive their prescriptions legally from physicians, it is critical that physicians understand when dependence has developed and how to help their patient become abstinent.

Recommendation—With the client's signed consent, the clinician should communicate with their physician to discuss the client's treatment plan. In some cases, a referral to another physician knowledgeable about addiction recovery may be necessary.

Web-Based Pharmacies. Numerous Internet sites sell prescription drugs including anxiolytics and sedatives *with or without* a prescription. Web sites maintained outside the United States do not need to comply with federal laws. The existence of these Web sites presents a threat to individuals recovering from anxiolytic and sedative dependence because they provide easy access to drugs without any medical oversight.

Recommendation—You do not want to bring the existence of these Web sites to the attention of a patient who is not already aware of them. Consequently, their existence should not be routinely discussed with patients. On the other hand, if patients indicate that they have been receiving their medications through the Internet, then you should explore whether the Internet is a trigger and, if so, recommend that your patient cancel his or her current e-mail account or, if possible, stay off the Internet altogether for a period of time.

Hallucinogens

The most commonly used hallucinogens are as follows:

- Lysergic acid diethylamide (LSD)
- Psilocybin
- Peyote and mescaline

22. Hallucinogens include all of the following drugs, *except* _____.
   a. rohypnol
   b. mescaline
   c. psilocybin
   d. LSD

What Is the Scope of Use?

Hallucinogen use peaked in the 1970s, then receded steadily for the next two decades until 1992 when the use of LSD and other hallucinogens began to increase again. In 2001, approximately 6.6% of twelfth graders reported that they had tried LSD at least once in the previous year but this declined to 3.5% in 2002. (Johnston, O'Malley, & Bachman, 2002). *LSD*, sometimes called *acid,* is usually sold as very small tablets, called *microdots,* on thin squares of gelatin, called *windowpane,* or more commonly, on squares of paper, called *blotter acid.* LSD begins to take effect 60 to 90 minutes after ingestion and a using experience, referred to as a *trip,* typically lasts 8 to 10 hours.

No prevalence data are available for psilocybin, peyote, or mescaline. *Psilocybin* is a mushroom that is typically eaten, though it can be smoked. *Peyote* is a small cactus that is usually eaten. *Mescaline* is the active ingredient in peyote that can be extracted from peyote and certain other cacti. *Peyote* is used legally in religious ceremonies by members of the Native American Church.

23. Which is *not* true of hallucinogens?
   a. The effects of LSD will typically last about 24 hours.
   b. Use of hallucinogens peaked in the 1970s, then declined for two decades, then rose again.
   c. Peyote is legally used in Native American religious ceremonies.
   d. Psilocybin is a mushroom.

What Are the Desired Effects?

Individuals use hallucinogenic drugs to alter their consciousness, and in some cases, to have a mystical or spiritual experience. For this reason, the term *entheogen* (meaning "god within") has been proposed for this class of drugs. Generally, lower doses produce alterations in emotion, thought, and sensation that the user recognizes as being caused by the drug. The boundary between self and others begins to disappear and a connectedness with others and the universe may be experienced. Users report feelings of elation, awe, and bliss. At higher doses, "normal" consciousness is lost altogether, and hallucinations or visions are indistinguishable from reality.

What Are the Harmful Effects?

The immediate and short-term risks associated with hallucinogen use come from the powerful effect these drugs have on consciousness: instead of bliss and calm, a trip may produce panic attacks and paranoia. Individuals who take high doses of hallucinogens are at increased risk for accidental injury because they are out of touch with reality. The potential for having a *bad trip* is not predictable, although one's environment and mental set may be influential.

Flashbacks. Flashbacks are also known as *hallucinogen persisting perception disorder* (American Psychiatric Association [APA], 2000), and are a relatively rare phenomena in which a person who has used a hallucinogen reexperiences some of the same effects several weeks or in some cases, years later. People experiencing flashbacks realize that what they are seeing is not real.

Drug-Induced Psychosis. The effects of hallucinogens can be described as a drug-induced psychosis. This means that the user's ability to recognize reality and think rationally is distorted. Although psychotic reactions are usually temporary, they can persist long after the trip has ended.

24. The harmful effects of hallucinogens include all of the following *except* _____.
   a. flashbacks
   b. increased physical strength
   c. bad trips
   d. prolonged psychotic reactions

What Are the Common Treatment Challenges?

Acute Dysphoric Reaction (also known as **Bad Trips***).* Even individuals who have had several positive experiences using a hallucinogen can experience a bad trip, typically involving extreme anxiety and paranoia. Clients may be brought to your treatment center while they are having a bad trip.

Recommendation—These acute negative reactions can best be handled with calm reassurance, in a quiet, pleasant environment, until the effects of the drug wear off. The patient should be reminded that their experiences are due to the drug, and gently encouraged to keep their eyes open (closed eyes may intensify the drug effects) and sit up or walk around slowly (Ungerleider & Pechnick, 1997).

Prolonged Psychotic Reaction. Individuals who have used a hallucinogenic substance may experience a prolonged psychotic reaction that persists for weeks or even years after the trip has ended. The symptoms may include dramatic mood swings from mania to profound depression, paranoia, vivid visual disturbances, and hallucinations. Prolonged psychotic reactions are more likely to occur in individuals with prior histories of psychiatric illness.

Recommendation—Individuals experiencing prolonged psychotic reactions after using a hallucinogen should be referred to a psychiatrist familiar with this reaction for treatment with an psychotropic medication if appropriate. Generally, the prognosis for these individuals is good although there is some evidence that individuals who have a family history of mental illness have a poorer prognosis.

Flashbacks. Individuals who experience flashbacks may become anxious over whether this symptom will worsen or concerned that they are "losing their minds."

Recommendation—This relatively rare phenomenon typically disappears over time and is best addressed with supportive counseling that reassures the patient that the flashbacks are likely to become less frequent and less intense. If the flashbacks do persist for a prolonged period of time (more than 1 year), referral to a psychiatrist for medication evaluation should be considered.

Dissociative Drugs and Club Drugs

These two categories of drugs are discussed together because dissociative drugs, like so called club drugs, are often used in the social context of "Raves" or parties.

Dissociative Drugs

The most commonly used dissociative drugs are as follows:

- Phencyclidine (PCP)
- Ketamine
- Dextromethorphan (DXM)

Dissociative drugs produce changes in body sensations and a sense of being detached from reality.

Phencyclidine, known as *PCP*, *angel dust*, and *superweed* was originally developed as an anesthetic that produced a trance-like, out-of-body experience. It was never approved for use with humans but is used in veterinary medicine. PCP is usually combined with marijuana, tobacco, or dried parsley so that it can be smoked. When smoked, its desired effects appear almost immediately and last 3 to 5 hours. PCP use has been associated with increased violence, paranoia, memory and cognitive impairments, and **psychosis**. At high doses, users become unresponsive to pain, and may develop seizures and become comatose (Schnoll & Weaver, 1999).

Ketamine, also known as *Special K* and *cat Valium*, is legally used as a human and animal anesthetic and produces effects similar to PCP and DXM. Because it is odorless and relatively tasteless, it has been added to beverages and used as a date rape drug (NIDA, 1999a). Ketamine is used by some to produce spiritual experiences and has also been used in the "club drug" scene (see following section).

Dextromethorphan (DXM) is a common ingredient in over-the-counter cough suppressants. When used as recommended DXM is safe, but at higher doses it can produce effects similar to PCP and ketamine. Many of the cough suppressant medications that are abused by DXM-users also contain significant amounts of alcohol and antihistamines. Like PCP, seizures have been associated with the use of DXM.

Club Drugs

The most commonly used club drugs are as follows:

- Ecstasy
- GHB (gamma-hydroxbutyrate)
- Rohypnol

The term *"club drugs"* has been applied to several chemically distinct drugs, all of which have become associated with the "raves" and "circuit parties." *Raves* are all-night dance parties that are typically held in unregulated settings; primarily gay men attend *circuit parties*. In both of these social events, drugs including LSD, marijuana, Ecstasy, GHB, rohypnol, and ketamine are often used.

Ecstasy (MDMA)

Ecstasy, or E, (chemical name: methylenedioxymethamphetamine, or MDMA), is usually taken in pill form, though it can also be snorted or smoked; its effects usually peak in about 1 hour and begin to taper off after about 2 hours. In 2002, an estimated 676,000 people in the U.S., age 12 and over were current users of MDMA, while over 10 million reported trying the drug at least once (NIDA, 2004). People use Ecstasy because it creates feelings of euphoria and emotional connectedness. Ecstasy increases blood pressure, decreases the pumping efficiency of the heart, and unhearts the body's ability to regulate internal temperature. When used in association with sustained, strenuous activity, like dancing, severe dehydration and heart damage can occur and deaths have been documented.

25. Which is *not* true about Ecstasy?
    a. It produces euphoria.
    b. It causes a sense of emotional connectedness.
    c. It hydrates the body.
    d. It increases blood pressure.

GHB

GHB produces euphoria, reduced inhibitions, and sedative effects. When this drug is used with alcohol it's sedative effects are significantly increased and have resulted in hospitalizations for respiratory depression and overdose deaths. Because it reduces inhibitions (also known as *disinhibition*), this drug has been used as a date-rape drug.

Rohypnol

"Roofies" (pharmaceutical name: flunitrazepam) is a potent sedative used for treating insomnia and as a preanesthesia medication. It is not sold legally in the United States but can be purchased illegally for about $5 per pill. In combination with alcohol, it is reported to produce blackouts and disinhibition; it has also been used as a date-rape drug.

26. Which is *not* true about rohypnol?
    a. It is available by prescription in the United States.
    b. It is called the "date-rape" drug.
    c. It is a potent sedative.
    d. It can produce blackouts in combination with alcohol.

What Are the Common Treatment Challenges?

Poly-Drug Abuse/Dependence. Quite often, individuals who use dissociative and club drugs also use other substances, particularly hallucinogens, marijuana, and alcohol. Consequently, individuals in treatment might identify other substances as their drug of choice, and not mention their periodic use of dissociative or club drugs. Because of treatment implications, it is important that you know whether these drugs are being used.

Recommendation—In conducting clinical assessments, you should be sure to determine whether any of these substances are being used. Use of these drugs may indicate that your client is part of a particular drug subculture (e.g., circuit parties); this can have important implications in treatment planning and relapse prevention efforts.

   Club Drug Culture.   Club drugs are quite different from each other chemically but are grouped together because of where they are used—in raves and circuit parties. Because clients who participate in these parties belong to a social network, breaking free from the use of these substances typically means cutting off participation in the parties. Announcements of parties are often sent by e-mail.
   Recommendation—Because attendance at raves or circuit parties are likely to be strong relapse triggers, you should discuss with your client plans for distancing themselves from the club scene. Current e-mail addresses may need to be canceled so that your client no longer receives announcements about raves or circuit parties. Alternative social networks need to be pursued.

   Date Rape and PTSD.   Men and women have been raped while under the influence of these drugs. These sexual assaults may result in the development of posttraumatic stress disorder (PTSD)—a serious anxiety disorder that should be treated.
   Recommendation—Individuals who use these drugs should be screened for PTSD and, if indicated, a thorough PTSD assessment should be conducted and treatment provided.

Inhalants

What Is the Scope of Use?

   Inhalants tend to be inexpensive, legal substances that are inhaled in order to produce a high. These substances include: glue, gasoline, solvents, butane, typing correction fluid, spray paint aerosols, and the gas propellant in whip cream cans. Because of the ease with which inhalants may be obtained, they are commonly used by young people who might otherwise have restricted access to drugs. In 2002, 9.1% of eighth graders, 6.6% of tenth graders, and 4.5% of twelfth graders were found to have used an inhalant in the prior year (Johnston et al.).

What Are the Desired Effects?

   Inhalants typically produce their effects rapidly and for relatively brief duration. Because of the variety of inhalants, it is not possible to characterize all their effects but they tend to produce excitation, loss of inhibitions, lightheadedness, drowsiness, and disorientation.

What Are the Harmful Effects?

   In the short term, use of inhalants can produce cognitive impairment, accidents resulting from impaired judgment, and in some cases, death from asphyxia or cardiac arrest. Long-term use of inhalants has been shown to damage the brain, kidneys, liver, and lungs. Cognitive deficits affecting memory, social judgment, and, in some cases, coordination increase the risk for injury and accidental death. These cognitive deficits may also impede client progress in treatment.

27. All of the following are true of inhalants, *except*:
    a. They are often used by young people.
    b. They are legal substances, like glue and solvents.
    c. They are not associated with any lasting harmful effects.
    d. They are all inhaled.

28. The harmful effects of inhalants, that we know of, do *not* include:
    a. damage to the brain, liver, kidneys, and lungs.
    b. cognitive and memory deficits.
    c. death from asphyxia cardiac arrest.
    d. several forms of cancer.

What Are the Common Treatment Challenges?

Not Fitting In. Individuals who abuse inhalants may not fit in well with traditional substance abuse treatment programs. Inhalant abusers may not readily identify with other clients in treatment because they believe their drug use is different. Only a small number of individuals enter treatment for inhalant abuse so clinicians tend to not develop expertise in working with this group.

Recommendation—Education about inhalant abuse should be incorporated into staff training so that they are knowledgeable about the effects of these substances and how they are used. Little is known about specific counseling approaches that are particularly effective with inhalant abusers; counselors should use counseling approaches generally effective for drug treatment and adapt their treatment to address the special issues of this group of clients.

Inhalants in the Facility. Gasoline, whip cream can propellant, butane in cigarette lighters, and typing correction fluid may be readily available in treatment facilities and, as a consequence, may be used by inhalant abusers that are in treatment. The drug screens that are typically administered in clinics will not detect the use of inhalants.

Recommendation—Providers need to be vigilant in ensuring that inhalants are not accessible to patients. Specific drug screens enable monitoring of the major metabolites of certain inhalants such as toluene. Clinics will need to check with toxicology labs to determine whether these specific screens are available.

Anabolic-Androgenic Steroids

What Is the Scope of Use?

Estimates suggest that there are several hundred thousand users of anabolic-androgenic steroids (AASs) in the United States. Estimates of use among high schooler students indicate that about 2% to 3% of high school students used AASs in the past year (Johnston et al., 2002). Use of steroids is several times more common in males than females.

Some AASs are taken orally, others are injected into the muscle tissue or applied as gels or creams. Individuals taking steroids for nonmedical purposes (abusers) often take several different AASs at one time (called *stacking*). Another practice of AAS abusers is to "pyramid" their doses: low doses are used for several weeks, then dosage is increased for several more weeks, then doses are reduced until no AASs are being taken for several weeks. This cycle is then repeated.

What Are the Desired Effects?

AAS abusers use these drugs to enhance athletic performance and build muscle mass. Some individuals with distorted body images (also known as *"body dysmorphic disorder"*) use AASs because they think they are fat, small, or weak even if they are large and muscular. Some AAS users experience euphoria, increased energy, and sexual arousal.

What Are the Harmful Effects?

Steroid abuse interferes with normal production of hormones and may cause both reversible and irreversible damage. AASs can lead to serious medical problems including cardiovascular disease (including heart attacks and strokes) and liver tumors. Effects on the appearance of males include: acne, breast development (in men only), shrunken testicles, and baldness; women will experience *masculinization*: reduced breasts, coarse skin, enlarged clitoris and deepened voice. When taken as an adolescent, AASs can stop growth prematurely resulting in reduced height. AASs can contribute to increased aggressiveness and irritability.

29. Which is *not* true of AASs?
    a. AASs are used to enhance athletic performance and build muscle mass.
    b. AAS dependence is associated with physiological tolerance and a withdrawal syndrome.
    c. Their use is several times more prevalent among men than women.
    d. Some AAS users also have body dysmorphic disorder.

30. Use of anabolic-androgenic steroids is associated with all of the following, *except*:
    a. decreased testicular size and development of breasts (in males).
    b. cardiovascular disease, including heart attacks and strokes.
    c. excessive growth and taller stature.
    d. liver tumors.

What Are the Common Treatment Challenges?

AASs and Addiction.   AAS abuse and dependence are not currently listed as disorders in the *DSM–IV.* So, is it appropriate to consider AASs addictive substances?

Recommendation—AAS abusers meet many of the criteria for substance dependence including withdrawal (e.g., mood swings, fatigue, depression), continued use despite physical problems, and disturbed social relations. Although AAS dependence is not formally recognized as an addictive disorder, a physician knowledgeable about steroid abuse should medically supervise withdrawal from AASs. The NIDA has established a Web site (www.steroidabuse.org) because of the potential for AAS abuse and dependence.

Knowledgeable AAS Users.   Individuals who use AASs often become knowledgeable about their use. There are Web sites and other Internet-based information sources that are used by AAS abusers seeking information about how to use these substances. AAS users may challenge you because you do not know as much as they do about AASs.

Recommendation—It is appropriate to acknowledge that you might not know as much about AASs as they do; your specialty is helping people recover from addiction. Avoid the temptation of having the client educate you about these substances because the focus of treatment should be on their recovery—not on you! Resources for learning more about AASs can be found on the NIDA Web site (www.steroidabuse.org).

KEY TERMS

abuse: Refers to a maladaptive pattern of drug use that causes social or behavioral problems (e.g., getting a DWI, having hangovers resulting in lateness for school or work), but the use does not meet the criteria for dependence.

addiction: A chronic, relapsing disease characterized by compulsive drug seeking and use and by neurochemical changes in the brain.

analgesic: A drug that reduces or eliminates pain.

anxiolytic: Also called an Anti-anxiety agent, a drug that reduces anxiety, typically a benzodiazepine.

benzodiazepine: A type of CNS depressant usually prescribed to relieve anxiety or as a sedatives, trade names include Valium, Xanax, and Ativan.

central nervous system (CNS): The brain and spinal cord.

dependence: The diagnostic term for addiction. This refers to substance use that is compulsive and out of control, results in the reduction or elimination of other activites in the person's life, and may involve physiological dependence (tolerance and withdrawal).

detoxification: The process of allowing the body to rid itself of a drug, often done with medical management of the withdrawal symptoms.

flashback: A perceptual disorder where one reexperiences some of the effects of some previous (in this context, hallucinogen-induced) experience.

prescription drug misuse: Taking a prescription drug in a manner other than that prescribed or for a different condition than prescribed.

narcotic: Originally used to refer to many psychoactive drugs that were thought to reduce pain or dull the senses, including cocaine and heroin. Now the term is synonymous with opioids.

opioids: Drugs most often prescribed to manage pain; composed of natural or synthetic substances based on morphine, the active ingredient in opium.

psychosis: A mental disorder involving symptoms, such as hallucinations and delusions, that indicate an impaired perception of reality.

sedatives (also called *sedative-hypnotics*): Drugs prescribed for their calming or sleep-inducing effect; includes barbiturates.

stimulants: Drugs that enhance (or stimulate) the activity of the brain and lead to increased heart rate, blood pressure, and respiration.

tolerance: When increasing doses of a drug are required to produce the same effect as was experienced initially.

withdrawal: Symptoms that occur after the use of a psychoactive drug is reduced or stopped.

DISCUSSION QUESTIONS

1. At what point do you think recreational drug use among young people becomes a problem? What signs might indicate that it has become a problem for someone who thinks they are using drugs recreationally?

2. What factors might contribute to gender differences in drug use?

3. How dangerous is occasional marijuana use?

4. Should marijuana be legalized? If it was legalized, what do you think would happen with regard to use of it and the associated legal and social problems?

5. Why do you think methadone maintenance treatment (that is, treating heroin addiction by substituting another legally prescribed opioid, methadone) is controversial? Where do you stand on this issue?

6. Under what circumstances and with what controls (if any) do you think opioid drugs should be prescribed for pain control?
7. How does cocaine use contribute to HIV risk? How can users reduce their risks?
8. Why do you suppose amphetamines are currently more popular on the West Coast and in the Southwest?
9. What might influence regional differences in popularity of particular drugs?
10. As a counselor, how might one deal with a client who was obtaining drugs via the Web and teaching other clients in the program how to purchase drugs on the Web?
11. Can a person truly consent to sexual intimacy if he or she is "high" or intoxicated? And where should we draw the line—is one drink okay? Two drinks? One joint shared with a few people? Several joints?
12. If a college student sought advice because she was using drugs at a party, got very intoxicated, and thinks several people coerced her to have sex, but she doesn't remember what happened, what would you recommend?
13. Knowing that inhalants are very toxic to the brain, and that they are used mostly by young people, what elements would you include in a prevention intervention to point out the dangers to this audience?
14. Should compulsive anabolic-androgenic steroid use be treated as an addiction?
15. How might a counselor impress upon a young athlete using stimulants or AASs that although these drugs may temporarily enhance performance, the negatives outweigh the positives?

SUGGESTED FURTHER READING

The following are excellent resources for additional information about the substances described in this section.

Two of the Best Web sites

The National Institute on Drug Abuse (NIDA)—www.nida.nih.gov

The NIDA Web site is the starting point for scientific information about drugs of abuse. Their "Research Reports" are particularly useful. The NIDA Web site also provides access to the most up-to-date information available.

The National Clearinghouse for Alcohol and Drug Information (NCADI)—www.health.org (phone: 800-729-6686)

The NCADI Web site is a tremendous resource for drug information as well as other resources such as videotapes, posters, and treatment manuals.

Several Excellent Books in This Field

Hanson, G., & Venturelli, P. (1998). *Drugs and society* (5th ed.). Sudbury, MA: Jones & Bartlett.

This text presents an excellent overview of common drugs of abuse as well as useful information about theories of addiction and treatments.

Kuhn, C., Swartzwelder, S., & Wilson, W. (1998). *Buzzed: The straight facts about the most used and abused drugs from alcohol to Ecstasy*. New York: W. W. Norton & Company.

This resource, provides good information particularly for young adults and clients in treatment, in a straightforward, easy-to-understand format.

Ray, O., & Ksir, C. (1996). *Drugs, society and human Behavior* (7th ed.). St. Louis, MO: Mosby Year Book, Inc.

This comprehensive textbook presents an overview of drugs of abuse, provides a historical and sociocultural context for the development of abuse and addiction to different drugs, discusses addiction theories and treatment, and reviews some of the neurochemistry and pharmacology behind how drugs work.

REFERENCES

American Psychiatric Association. (2000). *Diagnostic and statistical manual of mental disorders* (4th ed., text revision). Washington, DC: Author.

Budney, A. J., Hughes, J. R., Moore, B. A., & Novy, P. L. (2001). Marijuana abstinence effects in marijuana smokers maintained in their home environment. *Archives of General Psychiatry, 58*(10), 917–924.

Johnston, L. D., O'Malley, P. M., & Bachman, J. G. (2002). *Monitoring the future: National results on adolescent drug use: Overview of key findings, 2001.* (NIH Publication No. 02-5105). Bethesda, MD: National Institute on Drug Abuse.

Metzger, D. S., Navaline, H., & Woody, G. E. (1998). Drug abuse treatment as AIDS prevention. *Public Health Reports, 113*(Suppl. 1), 97–106.

Miller, W. R., & Rollnick, S. (2002). *Motivational interviewing* (2nd ed.) New York: Guilford Press.

National Institute on Drug Abuse. (1999a). *Community drug alert bulletin: Club drugs,* (Sma) 00-4723.

National Institute on Drug Abuse. (1999b). *Research report series: Cocaine abuse and addiction*, NIH Publication No. 99-4342.

National Institute on Drug Abuse. (2000). *Research report series: Heroin abuse and addiction.* NIH Publication No. 00-4165.

National Institute on Drug Abuse. (2004). Research Report Series: MOMA Abuse (Ecstasy) Rockville, MD.

National Institute on Drug Abuse. (2001a) *Epidemiologic trends in drug abuse: Vol. II. Proceedings of the Community Epidemiology Work Group* (NIH Publication No. 01-4917A). Rockville, MD.

National Institute on Drug Abuse. (2001b). *Research report series: Prescription drugs/abuse and addiction.* NIH Publication No. 01-4881.

Office of Applied Studies. (2002). *Results from the 2001 National Household Survey on Drug Abuse: Volume II. Technical appendices and selected data tables.* NHSDA Series H-18. (DHHS Publication No. SMA 02-3759). Rockville, MD: Substance Abuse and Mental Health Services Administration (SAMHSA).

Office of Applied Studies. (2003). *The DAWN report: Narcotic analgesics in brief* (DHHS Publication No.–). Rockville, MD: Substance Abuse and Mental Health Services Administration (SAMHSA).

Office of National Drug Control Policy. (2000). *What america's users spend on illegal drugs, 1988–1998,* December. Under HHS contract no. 282-98-0006 prepared by Abt Associates, Inc., Cambridge: Mass.

Schnoll, S. H., & Weaver, M. F. (1999). Phencyclidine. In M. Galanter and H. D. Kleber, (Eds.), *Textbook of substance abuse treatment* (2nd ed. Chapter 20, pp. 205–214). Washington, DC: American Psychiatric Press.

Shoptaw, S., Frosch, D., Rawson, R. A., & Ling, W. (1997). Cocaine abuse counseling as HIV prevention. *AIDS Education and Prevention, 9*, 511–520.

Simoni-Wastilla, L. (2000). The use of abusable prescription drugs: The role of gender. *Journal of Women's Health and Gender-Based Medicine, 9*, 289–297.

Ungerleider, J. T., & Pechnick, R. N. (1997). Hallucinogens. In J. H. Lowinson, P. Ruiz, R. B. Millman, & J. G. Langrod (Eds.), *Substance abuse: A comprehensive textbook* (3rd ed., pp. 230–237). Baltimore, MD: Williams & Williams.

12

HIV/AIDS

Melvin I. Pohl
Las Vegas Recovery Center

TRUTH OR FICTION?

___ 1. The rate of new cases of AIDS is increasing in the United States.
___ 2. Sub-Saharan Africa has the most cases of AIDS.
___ 3. Worldwide, there are more cases of AIDS in men than women.
___ 4. In the United States over the past few years, most cases of AIDS have occurred in men who have sex with men (MSM).
___ 5. Use of alcohol and crack cocaine is associated with increased risk of HIV infection primarily via sexual transmission.
___ 6. HIV replicates at a rate of billions of copies of viral particles per day.
___ 7. A diagnosis of AIDS is based on a T-cell count below 500.
___ 8. A positive ELISA test for HIV should always be confirmed by a Western Blot Test.
___ 9. HIV antibody is more predictive of positive outcome than viral load.
___ 10. Treatment for HIV should be started for all clients as soon as they test positive for HIV.
___ 11. Zidovudine (AZT, or retrovir) was the first reverse transcriptase inhibitor used to combat HIV.
___ 12. Triple therapy is most appropriate to begin treatment for HIV/AIDS.
___ 13. Lipidodystrophy is an abnormality of fat metabolism and is a side effect of many antiretroviral medications used to treat HIV/AIDS.
___ 14. Methadone levels increase when a client is being treated for HIV with ritonovir.
___ 15. Lack of adherence to HIV treatment regimens is not a problem because missed doses do not affect viral progression.

The purpose of this chapter is to review information about Acquired Immune Deficiency Syndrome (AIDS). AIDS is an epidemic that was identified in 1981 with the first reported case of a young gay man who developed a fulminant terminal illness characterized by failure of the immune system and development of an unusual case of pneumonia heretofore seen in people with suppressed immune systems.

Soon after, a syndrome was defined called *GRID*, or "gay related immune deficiency," because the cases occurred mysteriously in previously healthy gay men and resulted in unusual malignancies, infections, and immune system abnormalities.

Since that time, millions of people have become infected worldwide with what has been found to be a virus, Human Immunodeficiency Virus (HIV; formerly called HTLV-3), which has resulted in more than thirty million cases of AIDS and more than twenty million deaths worldwide. A substantial number of people with AIDS and HIV infection have problems with addiction as well.

In the United States, in some regions of the country, over 42% of clients entering treatment for methadone maintenance are HIV positive. HIV also has a significant impact on morbidity and mortality among injection drug users in treatment settings. Furthermore, there is increased risk of HIV infection in alcohol and drug abusers who do not inject drugs, related to sexual behaviors while under the influence. Women may not be aware of their male partner's HIV status and may not suspect their partner of risky behavior; therefore they may unwittingly be exposed to HIV by sexual activity. Women who use alcohol and drugs often have sexual partners who are also at risk of infection. Stimulants, especially crack cocaine, and alcohol are associated with an increase of risky sexual behaviors associated with transmission of HIV infection.

The goals of this chapter are to: (a) review the epidemiology of AIDS and see the evolution over time of the epidemic as it has spread worldwide over the past twenty years; (b) explore the disease progression from infection, viral multiplication, effects on the immune system, worsening symptoms, and possible death; (c) identify the synergism between HIV/AIDS and addictive diseases; (d) explain treatments used for HIV and AIDS and their complications; and (e) help you see the role of the counselor in diagnosis, prevention, and treatment of HIV in clients who also have addiction.

1. The AIDS epidemic:
   a. is over.
   b. affects only gay men and IV drug addicts.
   c. has affected most countries in the world.
   d. only affects people in major cities.

EPIDEMIOLOGY

The face of the AIDS epidemic has changed dramatically over the past twenty years. Nearly 1 million North Americans, 1.4 million Latin Americans, and 7 million Asians are living with HIV.[1] It is estimated that 42 million people were living with HIV/AIDS by 2002, 70% of whom live in sub-Saharan Africa. Each year, 4.2 million adults are newly infected.

AIDS is the leading cause of death in Africa. Heterosexual transmission is the predominant mode of transmission with a rising incidence in women. In 1998, of the 54 million people who died worldwide, AIDS was responsible for 2.3 million of those deaths—more than malaria, TB (tuberculosis), or lung cancer. Another alarming trend is an increase in cases in Eastern Europe and Central Asia, primarily driven by injection drug use.

---

[1] All statistics in this section are from the CDC (1997, 1998).

In contrast to developing countries, during the mid-1990s in the United States, the number of people who were diagnosed with and died from AIDS dropped dramatically. This was due, in great part, to the development of new combination drug therapies (see "Treatment" section). Since 1998, a considerable drop-off in the rate of death has occurred. However, recent data suggest that there might be an upsurge of new infections among some segments of the population.

The Centers for Disease Control (CDC) estimates approximately 40,000 new cases each year in the United States—a substantial decrease from the 150,000 infections occurring annually in the late 1980s. In just the past ten years, AIDS deaths dropped 68% and new AIDS cases fell almost 30% between 1995 and 1997. In the United States alone, there have been more than one million cases of HIV/AIDS with more than 400,000 deaths.

HIV continues to affect large numbers of gay and bisexual men, and in some areas of this population, may be increasing. This is, in part, related to a marked decrease in the practice of safer sex.

Since the epidemic began, injection drug use has directly or indirectly accounted for approximately 36% of AIDS cases in the United States. Racial and ethnic minority populations and women are most heavily affected; in 1998, intravenous drug users (IVDUs) accounted for 36% of AIDS cases among African American and Hispanic adults and adolescents compared with 22% of cases among White adults and adolescents. Among women, 59% of AIDS cases have been attributed to injection drug use or sex with partners who inject drugs, compared with 31% of cases among men.

Noninjection drugs (e.g., crack cocaine, methamphetamine, and alcohol) also contribute to the spread of the epidemic when users trade sex for drugs or money, or when they engage in risky sexual behaviors that they might not engage in when not under the influence of these drugs.

AIDS and HIV have become chronic, manageable, and less likely than ever before to be fatal. This has led to new optimism about prognosis, which ironically, may be one reason for the resurgence in risky sexual behaviors.

Among African Americans, the death and disease rates are almost ten times higher than that of Whites, accounting for half of all new HIV infections. Over half of all new infections are occurring among people younger than age 25. Every hour of every day, a young person is infected with HIV in the United States. Half of those new cases in people younger than 25 are in women and half of the cases of AIDS worldwide are in women. Among adults, cases due to heterosexual exposure equal the rate for injection drug users. Among women, 75% of cases are caused by heterosexual contact.

2. HIV in women:
   a. represents one-half of the cases worldwide.
   b. has nothing to do with IV drug use.
   c. occurs only in White prostitutes.
   d. is declining in incidence.

3. There are a disproportionate number of AIDS cases in African Americans and Hispanics in which of the following groups?
   a. women
   b. all cases of AIDS
   c. children
   d. Hemophiliacs
   e. a, b, and c
   f. b and d

4. There is high incidence of HIV infection in _____.
    a. IV drug addicts
    b. clients in methadone maintenance programs
    c. crack users
    d. all of the above

PATHOPHYSIOLOGY

Transmission of HIV/AIDS

AIDS is caused by infection with HIV, which passes from person to person by the introduction from the first person of fluid containing the virus into the blood stream of a second person. The fluids that contain enough virus to transmit infection are limited to blood and semen. Virus is also present in saliva, urine, vaginal fluid, and tears, however in significantly lower concentrations not capable of transmitting infection.

Infection is more likely to occur with a greater amount of virus from one person and with deeper penetration into a second person's blood stream; in other words, an injection drug–using person who backdraws a quantity of his or her own blood into a syringe can pass a large quantity of virus to another person when injecting the drug from the shared syringe. Likewise, with sexual intercourse, trauma to the vagina, cervix, or rectum can permit virus present in semen to infect the recipient of this semen.

Precautions and recommendations for prevention of HIV transmission are based on minimizing the risk of transmitting infectious fluids from one person to another. Obviously, the safest thing would be to not have sex or any contact with an infected person and to not use a needle already used by someone who is infected (needle-sharing). If someone chooses to have sex, it is safest to avoid exposure to semen and blood; use of latex condoms is an effective way to accomplish this. Avoiding practices that result in trauma may decrease the susceptibility of infection through mucous membranes (Kamb, 1998).

You should become familiar with harm reduction principles as part of addiction counseling. Obviously abstaining from all mood-altering drugs is the safest in this hierarchy of risk. If your client continues to use, however, you can encourage him or her to reduce risk of infection by discontinuing injections (methadone is useful in decreasing intravenous (IV) heroin use but does not impact IV stimulant use). In clients who insist on continuing to use injectable drugs, providing needles (e.g., decriminalizing or needle exchange programs) will lower the risk of spreading HIV infection. Bleaching needles may help disinfect HIV but this procedure has been much less effective in preventing infection than believed earlier.

5. The cause of AIDS is _____.
    a. unknown
    b. infection with HIV
    c. multiple traumas
    d. psychiatric illness

6. Harm reduction models:
    a. are totally ineffective in decreasing the incidence of HIV.
    b. include needle exchange, methadone, and abstinence.
    c. lock people up to prevent them from hurting others.
    d. are just theory and have never been tried.

CDC Guidelines to Preventing Infection

- Gloves should be worn during contact with blood or other body fluids that could contain visible blood, such as urine, feces, or vomit.
- Cuts, sores, or breaks on both the care giver's and client's exposed skin should be covered with bandages.
- Hands and other parts of the body should be washed immediately after contact with blood or other body fluids, and surfaces soiled with blood should be disinfected appropriately.
- Practices that increase the likelihood of blood contact, such as sharing of razors and toothbrushes, should be avoided.
- Needles and other sharp instruments should be used only when medically necessary and handled according to recommendations for health-care settings. (Do not put caps back on needles by hand or remove needles from syringes. Dispose of needles in puncture-proof containers.)

Initial Infection

Initially, symptoms occur in about 50% of those who become infected and last two to four weeks. The other 50% are asymptomatic, so many have no inkling that they are infected. The symptoms are quite similar to those of acute infectious mononucleosis with fever, fatigue, swollen glands, and muscle and joint aches. Actually, it is at the time of acute infection that those with early infection may be most infectious.

Progression of Disease

The primary target of HIV is the CD4+ lymphocyte (also called T-helper cell or T-4 cell), although HIV has also been shown to infect nerve cells, other immune system cells called *macrophages*, brain cells, and others. The CD4+ lymphocyte is a crucial manager of the immune system, functioning much like an orchestra leader. As more CD4+ cells become infected, they eventually die, and the immune system function gradually becomes impaired.

It has recently been learned that upon infection, the body's immune system responds vigorously in an attempt to clear itself of this infectious agent, namely HIV. As a result, billions of HIV particles are killed while billions more are formed. This turnover lasts about 24 hours. A steady state system develops at a certain "set point" with the number of viral particles produced balanced by the amount of virus destroyed. Eventually, the immune system wears itself out, with the number of viral particles (*viral load*) rising exponentially over a period. This phase may last decades.

Some people are infected and remain asymptomatic for long periods of time (ten years or longer). Others become symptomatic over time with mild infections, swollen glands, weight loss, fatigue, shortness of breath, diarrhea, and night sweats. With progressive infection, the CD4+ cell population becomes depleted, leading to the development of opportunistic infections.

7. After initial infection with HIV, the virus is:
    a. dormant for six months, then starts replication.
    b. immediately replicating billions of copies.
    c. inactive for five years, then starts replicating.
    d. active in every cell of the body.

8. HIV is transmitted:
   a. by sexual contact with an infected person.
   b. by kissing with a closed mouth.
   c. between food-servers and diners, if hands are not washed.
   d. by someone crying on a person's shoulder.

9. CDC guidelines to prevent household transmission include:
   a. wearing gloves when in contact with blood.
   b. covering cuts and sores with bandages.
   c. washing hands after contact with blood or body fluids.
   d. not sharing razors and toothbrushes.
   e. all of the above.

AIDS DEFINITION

AIDS is defined by the occurrence of infections with microorganisms that usually do not cause illness in people with normally functioning immune systems (Table 12.1). These bacteria, viruses, fungi, and others, as well as various cancers, take the opportunity (hence, the name *opportunistic infections*) to invade the immune system, which has been rendered vulnerable to attack. Infections characteristic of AIDS include Pneumocystis pneumonia, Toxoplasmosis, Cytomegalovirus, Herpes, Tuberculosis, Cryptococcosis, Cryptosporidiosis, Candidiasis, and other unusual infections. Others with AIDS develop unusual forms of cancer such as Kaposi's sarcoma (KS) or lymphoma.

AIDS is also diagnosed if a person has HIV combined with evidence of infection of the brain (encephalopathy). HIV encephalopathy or dementia presents as problems with thinking, judgment, memory, mood, and other brain functions, including seizures. Finally, AIDS can be diagnosed in HIV-positive people with *wasting syndrome*, a condition characterized by severe weight loss, fever, and diarrhea.

HIV also has the ability to directly affect various systems leading to malfunctions of the lymphatic system, lungs, kidneys, and nervous system.

Normal CD4+ cell counts range from 500 to 1200. As will be discussed in the section on treatment, 500 and 200 are key cutoffs for treatment interventions. People with fewer than

TABLE 12.1

AIDS Definition

I. Opportunistic infections
   A. viral (e.g., herpes or cytomegalovirus)
   B. fungal (e.g., cryptococcosis or candidiasis)
   C. protozoal (e.g., pneumocystis or toxoplasmosis)
   D. tuberculosis
II. Cancers
   A. Kaposi's sarcoma
   B. lymphoma
III. Encephalopathy
IV. Wasting syndrome
V. T-cell count less than 200

200 CD4+ cells are also officially categorized as having AIDS and are subject to increasing problems with infections and cancers.

> 10. AIDS is diagnosed when the client has:
>   a. a CD4 count of 500 or less.
>   b. an IQ that drops below 60.
>   c. a CD4+ count of 200 or less.
>   d. had three or more opportunistic infections.

DIAGNOSIS

Testing for HIV is an important component in the process of reducing HIV transmission. If someone finds out that he or she is infected, then that person can make special effort to not infect others. This is essential in reducing the number of people exposed to this potentially debilitating or life-threatening disease.

Because a large number of HIV-infected individuals are unaware of their infection, it is critical that you are able to assess the risk for HIV and offer information and resources for testing, when appropriate. In the early years of the AIDS epidemic, surveillance focused on members of high-risk groups (gay and bisexual men, injection drug users, and hemophiliacs), but that approach is much less useful than thinking in terms of *risk behaviors*. A comprehensive addiction history includes thorough nonjudgmental questioning about sexual activity, which would contain information about possible risky behaviors. It is important for you to become comfortable in taking a sexual history so that you can encourage your client to speak openly and honestly. Disclosing information regarding sexual behavior is anxiety provoking; therefore, your task is to help the client feel comfortable, heard, and trusting.

> 11. When taking a sexual history:
>   a. tell the client not to have sex.
>   b. inform the client that they should not worry about HIV if they have only one sexual partner.
>   c. ask questions nonjudgmentally.
>   d. only ask about risky behaviors in clients who are gay.

HIV testing should be performed for any client who requests it. Any client with a history of alcohol abuse/dependence or drug abuse/dependence is prone to behaviors that could potentially transmit infection, including those done while under the influence or during a period of impaired memory (e.g., blackout), so that history may not be entirely reliable.

The diagnosis of HIV may still lead to social stigmatization, loss of health insurance, and discrimination in employment and housing. Furthermore, such a diagnosis inevitably leads to emotional trauma that will certainly have an impact on addiction treatment. In addition, HIV testing should be accompanied by pre- and posttest counseling, which should include a discussion of the purpose of the test, prognosis and progression of HIV-infection, transmission of HIV and risk reduction, partner notification, and other medical and social issues related to the diagnosis. If you are not familiar and comfortable with these issues, then the client must be referred for counseling and testing to an appropriate facility. Your facility must be prepared to deal with the "fallout" of an HIV-positive diagnosis. You can be helpful by offering but not insisting on providing counseling for sexual partners as well.

> 12. Pretest counseling should include all of the following *except*:
>   a. a discussion of the purpose of the test.
>   b. information about HIV and its progression.
>   c. mandatory informing of *all* sexual partners.
>   d. a discussion of treatment options if the results are positive.

TESTING

The most common screening test is the enzyme-linked immunosorbent assay (**ELISA**). The ELISA is used for initial screening because of its high sensitivity and its ease of handling. The ELISA must always be followed by a confirmatory test called the Western blot. This combination of tests is extremely accurate, though can be negative if someone has recently been infected but has not yet **seroconverted** (become positive with antibodies to HIV). This *window period* lasts from ten days to three or four weeks, and rarely exceeds six months. Thus, if someone has a history of risky behaviors but has a negative HIV test, you should recommend a repeat test in three to six months for confirmation.

The current test that is most accurate is a blood test; although a saliva test has recently been approved for use. The new test is rapid and can be performed at home but is somewhat less accurate than a blood test. The risk of such testing is that, if not associated with proper counseling and support, a positive result may lead to self-destructive or unhealthy behaviors.

Tests for *viral load* (the amount of viral particles in a person's bloodstream) can be done to assess disease progression and to get a sense of the client's clinical condition. Viral load tests are expensive and are routinely also used to assess the effectiveness of treatment.

> 13. The viral load test:
>   a. accurately measures the presence of "hidden" virus in cells.
>   b. is a cheap screening test and should be done on all clients.
>   c. is experimental and should not be ordered.
>   d. can be used to help guide treatment decisions.
>
> 14. The HIV antibody test:
>   a. should be mandatory in all addicted clients prior to entering treatment.
>   b. gives accurate information about prognosis.
>   c. is useless and outdated and should not be ordered.
>   d. should be offered to all addicted clients after providing proper counseling.

TESTING POSITIVE—ISSUES FOR ADDICTION COUNSELORS

Clients who test positive for HIV have a tendency to focus on their HIV illness and may have difficulty doing the work required as part of addiction treatment. Both HIV disease and addiction are associated with stigma—and your clients with these two conditions are likely to experience guilt and shame, not to mention be subject to significant discrimination. Addicted clients who are HIV positive present with a sense of uniqueness from other clients, and may have different issues than others in a population that is primarily negative for HIV. They will benefit from and should be referred to groups of HIV-positive addicts if such groups exist in your community (see http://www.hivanonymous.com).

Receiving a diagnosis of HIV/AIDS is associated with grief and loss. There are multiplicities of losses that are both real and anticipated such as loss of health, longevity, and family, social, and financial security. People with HIV/AIDS may become disabled while you are treating them, so active grief work is in order.

Many still associate AIDS with a death sentence despite the remarkable progress made in treating the disease. Clients and families may tend to feel pessimistic, which may result in wanting to "give up." These pessimistic feelings are often associated with a tendency to "give up" on recovery, with or without relapse to drug and alcohol use, so you must anticipate the possibility and be ready to deal with such behaviors.

People with HIV/AIDS may exhibit psychological symptoms common in addicted clients such as anxiety, fear, depression, insomnia, fatigue, and pain. Your job is to facilitate dealing with such feelings and conditions, preferably without the use of addicting mood-altering drugs. A clinical challenge may be when a recovering client is offered medications to relieve such conditions (e.g., **benzodiazepines** for anxiety, **opiates** for pain, THC for nausea, and appetite disturbance). This may be the biggest hurdle for a client with addiction who is suffering with intercurrent problems from their HIV infection; you can play an important role in deciding whether or not to use such medications (Batki, 1996).

In summary, clients with HIV/AIDS and addictive diseases are not run-of-the-mill clients. Psychosocial issues related to HIV are often synergistic with addiction issues and need to be addressed comprehensively in treatment. These clients present unique situations that require creative and solid approaches from you. It is common to suffer burnout when dealing with such clients, so stay aware of your own process and make sure you are receiving adequate supervision with these challenges. It is helpful to have linkages between your programs and HIV/AIDS treatment providers. Include such providers in the treatment planning process whenever possible.

15. Counseling clients who have a positive HIV test result and addiction may include all but the following:
    a. dealing with grief and loss issues.
    b. anticipating relapse and teaching prevention techniques.
    c. facilitating social work referrals for financial assistance
    d. forcing the client to prepare for death and read about dying.

16. Clients with HIV and addictions:
    a. are unique and can only be helped by others with both HIV and addictions.
    b. are all dying, so may as well use drugs until they die.
    c. cannot benefit from treatment.
    d. present with complicated and unique issues that must be dealt with during treatment.

HIV AND ADDICTION—OTHER ISSUES

Research has shown that cocaine use accelerates the progression of HIV in mice. Cocaine caused a 200-fold increase in viral load and a drop in CD4+ counts. Other studies have shown that in people who drank two beers, the infection rate of CD4+ cells was 25 to 250 times greater if beer was present in the serum. Heroin added to CD4+ cells in a test tube caused increased rate of viral replication.

Furthermore, as mentioned earlier in this chapter, multiple studies have shown that those who are under the influence of alcohol and other mood-altering drugs are more at risk of not practicing safer sex techniques, even though they are informed about them. Many drugs stimulate dopamine, causing increased libido and increased sexual activity. Crack cocaine and other stimulants are associated with "drugs for sex" with multiple partners; often those under the influence of stimulants do not use condoms or practice other safer sex practices. Counseling clients with addiction should always include a nonjudgmental discussion of safer sex techniques and recommendations to reduce possible transmission of HIV.

17. HIV replication has been found to be stimulated by _____.
    a. alcohol
    b. cocaine
    c. LSD
    d. GHB

TREATMENT

New developments in therapies against HIV have profoundly changed the way clients, their families, their physicians, and society now view the virus. New medicines and combinations of these medications have the potential to slow or stop the growth and multiplication of HIV and to slow the progression of the disease. AIDS has become a chronic manageable disease, much like addiction, requiring consistent interventions. Consequently there is reduced mortality and enhanced quality of life for people with AIDS.

Treatment of HIV and AIDS is complicated and subject to some controversy. In this section, I review management strategies for you to consider, as well as specific drug classes and medications in each class.

Those who treat people with HIV and AIDS are challenged to provide helpful guidance and the most effective therapies. The mainstay of treatment is comprised of the following:

- **Antiretroviral** treatments—those that kill or arrest the virus
- Prevention of opportunistic infections, or *prophylaxis*
- Treatment of major complications of AIDS, opportunistic infections, and cancers
- Providing comprehensive holistic care of the client and his or her family

You may participate in all four areas as they involve behavior changes that may be challenging for your clients.

Making Decisions About Medications

Since the introduction of new and improved medications for HIV treatment (e.g., HAART, or highly active antiretroviral therapy), complex regimens have been created to attack the virus. Often difficult and controversial decisions need to be made about when to start medication and which medications to take. Though you are not an expert in this area, you may be called upon to help clients decide on which course of treatment to accept.

Physicians generally agree that persons *with symptoms of HIV* should immediately start antiretroviral medication regardless of their T-cell count or viral load. There is quite a bit of controversy, however, about treating asymptomatic individuals. In these cases, decisions about when to treat are usually based on T-cell counts and viral load values. Some clinicians recommend starting treatment when T-cell count drops below 500; other experts recommend waiting until symptoms develop or T-cell count drops below 350 or even 200, especially if the viral load is lower than 10,000. Even others treat asymptomatic clients with T-cell counts higher than 500 if their viral loads are above 30,000.

Decisions about starting antiretroviral therapy must be individualized; your client's attitude is key in deciding when and how to embark on a treatment regimen. These medications will probably need to be taken for life, often have side effects, are expensive, and are complicated to take. Experts feel that once started, it is important to stay on these medications and to take them consistently as directed, missing not even one dose. Missed doses can result in the virus becoming resistant to medications, especially with protease inhibitors & nonnucleoside resistant inhibitors. This can be a daunting task, so many will prefer to hold off taking medication until they are having more problems with symptoms of the illness.

Long-term efficacy and safety of antiretroviral therapies are not known with any certainty, so no specific strategy is absolutely correct. Some promote the theory of "hit hard, hit early" in an attempt to control the viral replication before damage is done, whereas others prefer to wait to initiate medications, believing that there is no clear proof that early treatment prevents disease progression. Further, early therapy increases the likelihood of side effects and may increase resistance to the medications used, thereby making them inactive against the virus (Celentano, 1998). You may be called upon to help clients sort through this complicated decision process, so being informed about these treatments is helpful. Of course, you are not expected to become an expert in HIV treatment, but rather a facilitator in the decision-making process (Wong, 1997).

Medication regimens need to be changed when there are toxic side effects or disease progression (falling T-cell counts, rising viral load, or development of infections or cancer heralding worsening of the immune system). Blood tests can now measure patterns of drug resistance, so decisions can be made as to whether the drug regimen needs to be changed (Gulick, 1997).

Antiretroviral Drugs

There are four main classes of antiretroviral drugs:

Nucleoside Reverse Transcriptase Inhibitors (NRTIs)

- AZT or zidovudine (Retrovir)
- DDI or didanosine (Videx)
- DDC or zalcitabine (HIVID)
- D4T or stavudine (Zerit)

Combinations of these medications are commonly prescribed but caution must be used when combining DDI, DDC, and D4T because all have the potential for similar side effects. Other NRTIs include:

- 3TC or lamivudine (Epivir)
- Abacavir (Ziagen); commonly used in combination with AZT and lamivudine (Trizivir)

Nucleotides

- Tenofavir DF (Viread)

NonNucleoside Reverse Transcriptase Inhibitors (NNRTIs)

- Delaviridine (Rescriptor)
- Efavirenz (Sustiva) is taken once at night and is a very strong medication against HIV. It can cause a rash, sleepiness, confusion, insomnia, and abnormal dreams, which may be troublesome for a person in recovery from addictions.
- Nevirapine (Viramune)

Resistance to this class of drugs has been shown to develop rapidly, showing how important it is to take all doses properly.

Protease Inhibitors

This class of medications is strong and is associated with many problematic side effects.

- Indinavir (Crixivan)
- Ritonavir (Norvir); can be combined with other drugs to help boost their effectiveness
- Saquinavir (Fortovase and Invirase); often combined with ritonavir (Norvir)
- Nelfinavir (Viracept)
- Amprenavir (Agenerase)
- Lopinivir/ritonavir (Kaletra)
- Atazanivir (brand name not yet selected); a once daily medication due to be released soon

It appears that protease inhibitors cause problems with fat metabolism, resulting in a condition known as *lipidodystrophy*. This syndrome involves changes in the blood fats as well as changes in the distribution of fat on the body, causing disturbing cosmetic problems for many clients.

Several new medications have been released including: FTC (emtricitabine, Coviracil); T-20 (enfuviritide, Fuzeon), a new class of drug which is only available by injection twice daily and has some troublesome side effects; D4T extended-release (Zerit XR; FDA approval pending); and Fosamprenavir (908), which may get into the bloodstream better than currently available amprenavir (Agenerase).

The availability of increasing number of antiretroviral agents that have countless potential side effects and interactions with each other and with other medications (e.g., methadone) requires that medical care of clients be supervised by an expert, though you can be very helpful with issues related to side effects, proper taking of medications (adherence), and emotional issues that arise when taking strong medications such as these (Smith, 2000).

Vaccine trials are underway but none show promise for development of a useful preventive agent in the near future. Therefore, the most effective prevention efforts are towards behavior change and education (safer sex and discontinuing unsafe injection practices).

18. The oldest and among the most effective drugs against HIV:
    a. prevent HIV binding to CD4+ cells.
    b. inhibit reverse transcriptase.
    c. prevent activation of the virus.
    d. stop the virus from "budding" off from one CD4+ cell to another.

19. Resistance to which of the following class of drugs develops rapidly and requires not missing any doses?
    a. nonnucleoside reverse transcriptase inhibitors
    b. all nucleoside reverse transcriptase inhibitors
    c. protease inhibitors
    d. all of the above
    e. a and c

20. Protease inhibitors:
    a. cure AIDS in all clients.
    b. are totally ineffective in most clients.
    c. have the potential to cause troublesome side effects including problems with fat metabolism.
    d. are cheap and easy to take.

21. Vaccines for HIV:
    a. exist and will eradicate AIDS in the next five years.
    b. are still being developed.
    c. have replaced the need to practice safe sex.
    d. must be administered weekly.

ADHERENCE

As with treatment of other chronic conditions, therapeutic decisions require mutual understanding between the client and the healthcare provider regarding the benefits and risks of treatment. Antiretroviral regimens are complex, have major side effects, pose difficulty with adherence and carry serious potential consequences with the risk of resistance from nonadherence to the drug regimen. Client education and involvement in therapeutic decisions is critical for HIV treatment and you can help immeasurably as you work with clients and incorporate these goals.

Adherence with antiretroviral therapy has never been so important. Strict adherence to these new multi-drug regimens is essential to obtaining full and lasting benefit of therapy, maintaining suppression of viral replication, and preventing the development of drug resistance.

With respect to adherence, research shows a direct association between poor adherence and the complexity of drug regimens, the number of specific medications prescribed, and the extent to which assigned regimen interferes with daily life. Many clients with AIDS take multiple complicated regimens of antiretroviral medications in addition to medications to prevent or treat AIDS-related opportunistic infections, to stimulate appetite and/or libido, to relieve pain, to supplement suspected nutritional insufficiencies, and to combat depression, fatigue, nausea, diarrhea, and insomnia (Sherer, 1998).

Add to this a host of herbs, alternative, or complementary therapies, multivitamins, dietary supplements and other substances that many clients elect to take as part of their daily lives.

Clearly, there is a high complexity to a client's daily dosing regimen that makes compliance nothing short of miraculous. You can be helpful in promoting compliance with antiretroviral regimens by devising dosing schedules that can be integrated into a client's daily routine. You can also stress the importance of not missing even a single drug dose and of remaining compliant with these complex regimens (for the long haul), and you can help clients deal with problems with their treatment regimens.

There are predictors of poor adherence, which should be modified or acknowledged if possible. Here are several hindrances that you might help clients modify to enhance adherence:

- Number of medications: more medications mean greater problems adhering
- Complexity of regimens: number of daily doses, changing doses, special restrictions (e.g., with or without food or fluids)
- Special storage requirements (e.g., refrigeration)
- Medication interferes with lifestyle (pill-taking influences timing of activities such as meals, limits activities, requires time for preparation, or must be concealed from others)
- Poor communication with primary-care providers and other healthcare professionals

Strategies that you can employ to help clients maintain optimal adherence to these regimens require a partnership between clients and healthcare workers. These include the following (Friedland, 1997):

- Clarify the regimen
- Encourage clients to use a medication diary
- Tailor the regimen to the client's lifestyle on an individualized basis
- Establish a set time for pill taking
- Establish a set place for pill taking
- Plan any changes in routine well in advance
- Recognize that weekends and holidays are times when compliance may falter
- Lower the barriers to accessing care
- Provide adequate and regular follow-up

Though you will not be initiating medications, you can use your counseling skills to influence behavior, enhance motivation, and increase adherence.

Clearly, adherence to therapy is an additional challenge to those healthcare workers involved with people with HIV and AIDS. Here is a perfect opportunity for you to work closely with your clients as "partners in care" to achieve high levels of adherence, prevent the development of resistance, and obtain optimal benefits from these new therapies—with the ultimate result of slowing progression of HIV and improving quality of life for people with HIV and AIDS.

22. Predictors of poor adherence to HIV treatment protocols include:
    a. high number of medications.
    b. complex medication regimens.
    c. special storage requirements.
    d. poor communication with primary care providers.
    e. all of the above.

23. Strategies to establish and help clients adhere to treatment include:
    a. using a medication diary.
    b. individualize medication protocols.
    c. yell at the client to make them realize the seriousness of their drug program.
    d. let them gradually get used to the medication regimen, missing a few doses at the beginning.
    e. a and b.

HIV/AIDS AND PAIN

HIV and AIDS frequently are associated with painful conditions comparable to cancer pain, requiring prompt and adequate treatment. Because of new therapies (e.g., HAART), clients with AIDS are living longer. The longer people live, the more likely they are to develop painful conditions. Pain occurs in up to 75% of clients with AIDS. In clients who also have addictions, one study showed that there was no difference in pain nature or intensity or in effectiveness of pain relievers when comparing groups of clients with and without a history of addiction. Despite this, clients with AIDS receive in adequate doses of opioid medications. See Table 12.2 for a list of painful conditions in clients with HIV/AIDS.

The principles of pain assessment and treatment in the client who is HIV positive or has AIDS are not fundamentally different from those in the client with cancer. In addition to nonsteroidal anti-inflammatory drugs (NSAIDs) such as ibuprofen, aspirin, and others and opioids (e.g., codeine, hydrocodone, oxycodone, morphine, and others), adjuvant analgesics (antidepressants, **anticonvulsants**, and corticosteroids) have important applications in the treatment of AIDS-related pain, especially neuropathy. Tricyclic antidepressants, especially amitriptyline (Elavil), nortrptyline (Pamelor) and doxepin (Sinequan) in doses up to 150mg at bedtime may be helpful without causing addiction. Some serotonin reuptake inhibitors such as paroxetine (Paxil) in fairly high doses may also be useful for the treatment of neuropathy. Anticonvulsants like carbamazepine (Tegretol) and gabapentin (Neurontin), as well as newer anti-seizure drugs like lamotrigine (Lamictal) and tiagabine (Gabitril) have been shown to be effective in the treatment of neuropathy and are also appropriate for clients with histories of addiction (Anand, 1994).

You may be called upon to help addicted or recovering clients sort their way through decisions about selecting nonaddicting forms of treatment for pain but also with the difficult challenge of taking necessary opioid medications and not relapsing to other mood-altering drugs. Helping such clients integrate their HIV treatment with their addiction treatment is difficult at best. These clients may have significant problems engaging in 12-step programs

TABLE 12.2

Causes of Pain in HIV/AIDS

I. HIV INFECTION
    A. **Neuropathy** (40% of clients with AIDS)—direct irritation of nerve cell membranes by HIV
    B. Myelopathy—inflammation and swelling of muscle fibers
    C. Infections
        1. Herpes—pain at site of infection (e.g., skin, eye, brain, and other organs)
        2. Cytomegalovirus—pain at site of infection (stomach, skin, lungs)
    D. Arthritis—swelling of joints
    E. Wasting—loss of weight with discomfort secondary to decreased muscle mass and protective fat
    F. Cancers—local and distant invasion of nerves and other tissues
II. HIV TREATMENT
    A. Antiretrovirals (especially NRTIs)—can cause neuropathy, abdominal pain, chest pains, and other side effects
    B. TB treatments—headaches, neuropathy, and others
    C. Anti-cancer drugs—many different painful conditions depending on drug including abdominal pain, chest pain, cramps, headaches, and others

---

and recovery groups and may be best served in a special group or therapeutic setting with others with similar issues.

Some antiretroviral agents may increase or decrease the pain-relieving effects of opioids and tramadol (Ultram). Prescribers may not realize that such changes may occur, and you can be helpful in tracking pain relief and pain complaints and advocating for clients whose pain is not adequately controlled.

It is important to recognize that people with addictions and AIDS are quite likely to have comorbid psychiatric symptoms such as anxiety, insomnia, fear, and depression, as well as other physical symptoms such as nausea, vomiting, muscle cramps, and others, that can contribute to an increase in pain and suffering. Helping clients access care for these symptoms is something with which you can assist. Furthermore, assisting clients in dealing with symptoms through relaxation techniques in addition to exploring non–medication-based treatments such as cognitive-behavioral interventions will serve your clients greatly. You can assist clients in self-empowerment, possibly allowing them to avoid or minimize medications.

In summary, painful conditions present with HIV/AIDS are known to be undertreated when a history of addiction exists. Treatment of pain when there is a history of addiction complicates an already complex treatment course, often requiring the chronic use of opioid medications. If this occurs, strict enforcement of a set of rules understood by the client, the clinician, and the treatment team is essential to diminish the possibility of misusing these drugs. After adequate assessment of pain and the possible underlying causes, a multidisciplinary team approach to pain control is most appropriate. You can be extremely helpful in facilitating dialogue among clients, HIV care providers, treatment center staff, and other clinicians.

24. Pain in clients with HIV is caused by all of the following *except* _____.
    a. neuropathy
    b. cancer
    c. weight gain
    d. medication side effects

25. The appropriate treatment of pain in a person with HIV includes:
    a. opioids if necessary.
    b. never using opioids.
    c. antipsychotics like Thorazine.
    d. benzodiazepines like Valium.

26. Pain is properly treated in people with AIDS with _____.
    a. Anti-inflamatories
    b. opioids if necessary
    c. anticonvulsants
    d. antidepressants
    e. all of the above

INTERACTION OF HAART AND ADDICTING DRUGS

There are many potential reactions between prescription medications and addicting drugs, even when used "recreationally." There is little data about these interactions. It is advisable to consider these interactions whenever an increase or decrease in effects is noted.

Methadone and HIV/AIDS

Methadone is an effective treatment of opioid addiction. Many clients who are maintained on methadone are HIV positive and it is helpful to remember that methadone can interact with medications used to treat HIV/AIDS. For example, if amprenavir (Agenerase) and/or ritonavir (Norvir) are prescribed, either methadone levels or levels of amprenavir may can decrease. This might suggest increasing the dose of methadone in clients who are on amprenavir (you may witness the onset of methadone withdrawal in these clients prior to increasing their methadone dose). These reactions are extremely unpredictable, so it pays for you to be on alert to their potential occurrence, because AIDS specialists may not be aware of what is happening (Gourevitch & Friedland, 2000).

Stimulants

Ritonavir and delavirdine can inhibit the metabolism of amphetamines and Ecstasy (MDMA), causing potential increased stimulant effects and possible toxic levels. Two deaths have been reported from the combination of ritonavir and Ecstasy.

THC

Protease inhibitors and delavirdine may increase THC levels, whereas nevirapine and efavirenz may decrease THC effects.

27. When methadone-maintained clients start with HIV treatments:
    a. always stop methadone when starting antiretrovirals.
    b. encourage all clients on AIDS drugs to take methadone to reduce side effects.
    c. be aware that antiretrovirals may increase or decrease methadone levels and doses may need to be adjusted.
    d. methadone has no effect on antiretroviral therapies.

28. Ritonavir and delaviridine have potentially dangerous interaction with which drugs of abuse?
    a. hallucinogens like LSD
    b. alcohol
    c. benzodiazepines like Valium
    d. stimulants such as Ecstasy and methamphetamine

HEPATITIS, HIV, AND ADDICTION

A majority of people with Hepatitis C became infected by injection drug use, through sharing of injection equipment (needles, syringes, "cookers," cotton swabs, and rinse water). Hepatitis C is common in IVDU's and other addicted persons, as is HIV, because they are transmitted by similar modes.

Most with Hepatitis C are asymptomatic, with 85% developing chronic infection, 20% of whom subsequently can develop cirrhosis or liver cancer. When infected with both HIV and Hepatitis C, the course of disease and treatment is definitely more complex. Treatment for Hepatitis C includes injections of *interferon*, a potent antiretroviral medication that causes multiple troublesome side effects including flu-like symptoms, insomnia, irritability, and depression.

Obviously, in a client who is infected with both Hepatitis C and HIV, additional difficult decisions need to be made and you again can be helpful in decision-making and adherence to treatment protocols, as well as dealing with side effects. It is even more crucial for clients with Hepatitis C to abstain from alcohol to avoid further damage to the liver and you can help clients achieve this goal.

If a client is being tested for HIV, it is a good idea to encourage him or her to also be tested for Hepatitis C at the same time. The presence of Hepatitis C makes harm reduction more important, especially the discontinuation of sharing needles and drug paraphernalia.

29. Hepatitis C:
   a. is always fatal.
   b. is present in many intravenous drug users.
   c. treatment is a simple short course of oral medications.
   d. is always symptomatic.

30. When testing for HIV:
   a. never test for Hepatitis C at the same time because the tests counteract each other.
   b. always encourage your client to be tested for Hepatitis C at the same time because coinfection with HIV and Hepatitis C are common in addicts.
   c. don't bother to test for Hepatitis C because treatment is ineffective.
   d. test for Hepatitis C only if the client is symptomatic.

HIV/AIDS is caused by a virus known to cause a serious illness. Incidence of HIV/AIDS in addicted clients is significant, so you will be involved in caring for these people. This chapter summarizes clinical issues that you may face with infected clients including testing, transmission, treatment, adherence, and counseling needs. This is difficult but important work for all addiction counselors. It is important for you to familiarize yourself with these issues so that you may be effective with this population.

KEY TERMS

anticonvulsants: Medications used to prevent seizures.

antiretroviral therapy: Treatments to fight against HIV, a retrovirus.

benzodiazepines: Drug class used to treat anxiety and insomnia. Includes medications such as diazepam (Valium), chlordiazepoxide (Librium), alprazolam (Xanax), clonazepam (Klonipen), temazepam (Restoril), and many others.

ELISA (enzyme-linked immunosorbent assay): A common initial screening test for the presence of antibodies to HIV.

lipidodystrophy: A condition of abnormal fat metabolism with resulting redistribution of body fat and possible abnormalities of blood cholesterol and other blood fats.

neuropathy: Irritation or inflammation of a nerve fiber or fibers with symptoms including pain, numbness, and decreased function.

opiates: Drug class used to treat pain. Includes medications such as hydrocodone (Lortabs, Vicodin), oxycodone (Percodan, Tylox), codeine (many preparations), propoxyphene (Darvon), morphine (MSIR), and many others.

seroconverted: Changing from HIV negative to HIV positive indicating that a person has become infected.

DISCUSSION QUESTIONS

1. Discuss the issues related to an alcoholic client regarding abstinence from alcohol in order to begin taking Interferon to treat her hepatits C. She has AIDS, has been on three different drug regimens, and seems to be losing heart about surviving the two diseases. Alcohol is the only relief she finds these days.
2. Describe a relaxation exercise you might employ in a group of clients with pain who also have addiction and AIDS. Highlight the common themes you might underscore to enable clients to deal with both AIDS and addiction and how to integrate treatment for both.
3. You receive a call from your client's physician stating that he has received notification of multiple prescriptions for opioids and benzodiazepines, many of which are prescribed by other physicians. What would you say to the doctor and describe your approach to the client regarding possible abuse of his medications.
4. A client with AIDS you've been seeing in counseling sessions comes in to see you on a crisis appointment. She is in tears because her HIV specialist told her if she misses one more dose, he would stop seeing her in his practice. Describe how you would approach her lack of adherence and how you might help her relate to her HIV specialist in a positive manner.
5. Explain your approach with a client who has been given three prescriptions for medication and who is still uncertain about whether or not he wants to start medication for his asymptomatic case of HIV. He has a CD4+ count of 250 and a viral load of 35,000.
6. Describe a treatment setting you have worked in and outline a treatment approach when admitting a new client diagnosed with AIDS who also has cocaine addiction.
7. Discuss your approach to posttest counseling when the result of an HIV test is positive.
8. Describe the life cycle of HIV from infection to progression of disease and characterize how you would approach a counseling session with a client about these topics.
9. Review, compare, and contrast harm reduction principles with respect to drug use and sexual behaviors as you would explain them in a counseling session.
10. Describe the epidemiological trends worldwide in terms of increases and decreases in various populations.
11. Discuss the components of a thorough sexual history as it is relevant to someone at risk for HIV/AIDS.
12. Prepare a script for a pretest counseling session.

SUGGESTED FURTHER READING

Caulkins, G. (2001). The HIV anonymous positive attitudes workbook. San Clement, CA: HIV Anonymous.

This is a helpful guide to implementing specific techniques using 12-step methodology to deal with HIV (see www.hivanonymous.com).

Garfield, C., Spring, C., & Ober, D. (1995). *Sometimes my heart goes numb: Loving and caring in a time of AIDS.* San Francisco, CA: Jossey-Bass Publishers.

Thoughtful book describing the lives of people with AIDS and their caregivers.

Kubler-Ross, E. (1987). *AIDS—The ultimate challenge*. New York: Macmillan.

Description of the author's work with death, dying, and people with AIDS.

Pohl, M., Kay, D., & Toft, D. (1991). *The caregiver's journey: When you love someone with AIDS*. Sanfrancisco, CA: HarperCollins.

Narrative and descriptive book about what it is like to care for someone with AIDS.

Sontag, S. (1988). *AIDS and its metaphors*. New York: Farrar, Straus and Giroux.

This is a series of thoughtful essays about AIDS and disease in general.

Tilleraas, P. (1988). *The color of light: Daily meditations for all of us living with AIDS*. Center City, MN: Hazelden.

Useful daily reminders of spiritual principles in coping with AIDS.

REFERENCES

Anand, A. (1994). Evaluation of recalcitrant pain in HIV-infected hospitalized clients. *Journal of AIDS, 7*, 52–56.

Batki, S. (1996). Psychiatric disorders, drug use and medical status in injection drug users with HIV disease. *American Journal on Addictions, 5*, 249–258.

Celentano, D. (1998). The case for conservative management of early HIV disease. *Journal of the American Medical Association, 280*, 93–95.

Centers for Disease Control. (1997). Update: Trends in AIDS incidence. *Morbidity and Mortality Weekly Report, 46*, 861–867.

Centers for Disease Control. (1998). Recommendations for prevention and control of hepatitis C virus (HCV) infection and HCV-related chronic disease. *Morbidity and Mortality Weekly Report, 47*(No. RR-19).

Friedland, G. (1997). Adherence: The Achilles heel of highly active antiretroviral therapy. *Improving management in HIV Dis., 5*, 13–15.

Gourevitch, M., & Friedland, G. (2000). Interactions between methadone and medications used to treat HIV infection: A review. *The Mount Sinai Journal of Medicine, 67*, 429–439.

Gulick, R. M. (1997). Treatment with indinavir, zidovudine, and lamivudine in adults with human immunodeficiency virus infection and prior antiretroviral therapy. *New England Journal of Medicine, 337*(11), 734–739.

Kamb, M. (1998). Efficacy of risk-reduction counseling to prevent human immunodeficiency virus and sexually transmitted diseases. *Journal of the American Medical Association, 280*, 1161–1167.

Sherer, R. (1998). Adherence and antiretroviral therapy in injection drug users. *Journal of the American Medical Association, 280*, 567–568.

Smith, J. (2000). HIV/AIDS theme issue. *Journal of the American Medical Association, 284*, 145–240.

Wong, J. K. (1997). Identification of a reservoir for HIV-1 in clients on highly active antiretroviral therapy. *Science, 278*, 1295–1300.

13

Coexisting Disorders

Jennifer P. Schneider
Arizona Community Physicians

TRUTH OR FICTION?

___ 1. *Every new alcohol and other drug-dependent (AOD) client should be screened early on for the presence of a concurrent psychiatric disorder or other addiction.*

___ 2. *About one-half of people who are chemically dependent also have a psychiatric disorder.*

___ 3. *A person who has more than one type of addiction (e.g., alcohol and gambling) is said to have a dual diagnosis.*

___ 4. *Alcoholics have a significantly higher prevalence of other drug dependencies than do nonalcoholics.*

___ 5. *People who have one type of addiction (e.g., alcohol) have a significantly higher prevalence of other types of addictions (e.g., sex).*

___ 6. *In most alcoholics who have antisocial personality traits, the antisocial behavior preceded their alcoholism.*

___ 7. *Diagnosing underlying depression in an alcoholic is usually not difficult once the client has completed medical detoxification.*

___ 8. *Mentally ill patients have a very high rate of nicotine addiction.*

___ 9. *Newly clean and sober AOD clients who also have depression or anxiety should generally have early medication treatment of their mood disorder whether it is primary or secondary.*

___ 10. *Postalcohol withdrawal symptoms are psychiatric symptoms which can recur for months or even years.*

___ 11. *People who have a history of drug addiction should never be treated for pain with opioids (narcotics).*

___ 12. *Most cocaine and amphetamine addicts are also compulsive in their sexual behavior.*

_____ 13. *Unrecognized and untreated addictive behaviors are a significant risk factor for relapse to alcohol and drug dependency.*
_____ 14. *A man who has had eight sexual partners within the past year is most likely a sex addict.*
_____ 15. *A client who has two or more addictions should have the primary addiction identified and that addiction should be treated first.*

When you first see a client for treatment of an apparently straightforward chemical dependency problem, it may not be obvious to you that the client may also have a coexisting psychiatric disorder, another addictive disorder, or both. The presence of a second problem is likely to complicate your client's addiction treatment. If you suspect your client might also have a psychiatric disorder, refer him or her for psychiatric evaluation. This chapter will describe the various interactions of psychiatric and addiction problems and will explain how multiple addictions interact. I will separate the discussion of **coexisting addictions** and psychiatric disorders from the section on multiple addictions, but be aware that some clients have one or more type of addiction *as well as* one or more type of psychiatric disorder.

PART I: COEXISTING ADDICTIONS AND PSYCHIATRIC PROBLEMS

Because all drugs of abuse affect the brain, drug-dependent clients often present with depression, anxiety, confusion, and even psychotic thinking. Use or withdrawal of a drug can mimic various psychiatric diagnoses. To make the best treatment decisions, you must understand the underlying problem. This section describes people who have a ***dual diagnosis***, meaning that they have both an addiction and a psychiatric problem.

Prevalence of Coexisting Addiction and Psychiatric Problems

The Epidemiological Catchment Area (ECA) study of representative population samples in five cities in the United States (Regier et al., 1990) reported the lifetime prevalence of drug abuse and dependence and of various psychiatric disorders. One-third (34%) of the total sample had a diagnosis of alcohol abuse or dependency. Of this group, 37% had a comorbid psychiatric disorder. Among persons with a substance use disorder other than alcohol, an even larger percentage (53%) also had a mental disorder. Conversely, there was a 2.7-fold increase in the prevalence of a substance use disorder among persons with a mental disorder. This shows that having *either* a mental disorder or a substance use disorder significantly increases the likelihood of having *both*.

Also among alcoholics in the ECA study, 18% had a second drug dependency, compared with only 3.5% of the total persons surveyed. Now, more than twenty years later, it is likely that the prevalence of other drug dependencies among alcoholics is well above 18%. In the ECA study, the most common coexisting psychiatric diagnosis was antisocial personality disorder. But remember that antisocial behavior is overly represented among substance abusers because of a) the **disinhibiting effects** of some mood-altering drugs, and b) the illegal aspects of drug possession, use, and trafficking.

The ECA study unfortunately did not ask about tobacco use. The addicted mentally ill population has a very high rate of nicotine dependence. Smoking, the most common cause of lung cancer world-wide, increases the risk of several other cancers, as well as of heart disease, stroke, and emphysema. Smoking cessation deserves more attention by addiction counselors.

1. The prevalence of dual diagnosis among alcoholics is about _____.
   a. 10%
   b. 25%
   c. 37%
   d. 62%

2. All the following help account for why substance abusers may show antisocial behavior *except for*:
   a. the coexisting genetic predisposition to alcoholism and antisocial personality disorder.
   b. the tendency of some addicts to sell drugs.
   c. the disinhibiting effects of some drugs.
   d. the illegal effects of drug possession and use.

Why Is It Important to Identify the Presence of Dual Diagnoses?

First, persons with dual diagnoses sometimes cannot fully participate in addiction treatment because the cognitive complications of both disorders combine. For example, long-term drinkers often have problems with memory. Major depression can prevent a person from focusing. Schizophrenia can result in competing signals for the person's attention. Combine the alcohol and other drug (AOD) and mental disorders and the client may be just "not there." When it comes to attending Alcoholics Anonymous (AA) or other self-help groups, a depressed client simply might not have the energy to get to the meeting. A paranoid client may avoid groups because of belief that the group members might talk about him.

A second reason identifying dual diagnoses as important is that the intensity of the mental problem may require initial stabilization before the client can even begin to benefit from addiction treatment.

Third, addiction treatment may need to be modified for dually diagnosed clients. As Evans and Sullivan (2001) have pointed out, the confrontations often used in addiction treatment sometimes increase the psychotic symptoms or suicidal thinking of dually diagnosed clients.

Finally, untreated mental disorders are often responsible for relapse into the addiction problem. In fact, if an AOD client keeps relapsing, a very likely reason is the presence of an unrecognized mental disorder or **behavioral addiction**.

Unfortunately, it is not easy to assess psychiatric symptoms in an active substance abuser. The next section expands on how AOD & psychiatric disorders interact.

3. To make appropriate treatment decisions for a client who presents with a substance use problem, you need to identify the presence of a coexisting mental disorder. Which reason is *false*?
   a. The combined cognitive difficulties caused by both disorders may make the client unable to benefit from treatment for either disorder.
   b. A dual diagnosis may change the treatment plan for the addiction.
   c. An untreated Axis I or II disorder may predispose to relapse from addiction.
   d. An AOD client can't be treated until the psychiatric problem is resolved.

How Alcohol and Drug Dependency and Psychiatric Disorders Can Interact

AOD and psychiatric problems can interact in various ways:

- AOD initiates or exacerbates psychiatric symptoms.
- AOD masks, or is used to medicate, psychiatric symptoms.
- AOD withdrawal mimics psychiatric symptoms.
- The psychiatric problem initiates or exacerbates AOD.

Let's look at each in turn:

AOD Initiates or Exacerbates Psychiatric Symptoms

The biological effects of drugs can cause unintended psychiatric side effects. For example, alcohol has a depressive effect on the brain, so that many alcoholics are depressed. Alcohol also disinhibits behavior, which may explain why in the past many alcoholics were diagnosed with antisocial personality disorder, and why alcohol use is often part of domestic violence behavior. Stimulants (e.g., amphetamines, cocaine) "rev up" the body and often produce anxiety, sometimes even psychotic behavior. Phencyclidine can produce confusion and psychosis. A "bad trip" with marijuana can create panic in the user. As long as clients are using these drugs, you may have difficulty differentiating whether they indeed have a dual diagnosis or else a transient drug effect. It may take weeks of being off the drug before the psychiatric drug effects fade.

AOD Masks, or Is Used to Medicate, Psychiatric Symptoms

Many social drinkers use alcohol to relax and to "lubricate" conversations, easing shyness and social phobia. The sedative effect of alcohol is used by other people to "medicate" their anxiety. Some 80% of women alcoholics were sexually abused in childhood (Carnes, 1991); some of them drink so they can have sex without experiencing symptoms of posttraumatic stress disorder.

AOD Withdrawal Mimics Psychiatric Problems

It is no coincidence that the withdrawal symptoms of drugs seem to be the opposite of the effects of using them. When certain drugs are repeatedly used, the body adapts to functioning in the presence of those drugs. This is called *tolerance*. For example, alcohol depresses body functions. A large dose of alcohol in a body that is not used to it will produce sedation, sleep, or even death. An alcohol-tolerant body will increase its excitatory chemical messengers in order to compensate for the effects of the alcohol, so that the person can function relatively normally despite a high alcohol blood level.

When the person who has developed tolerance to alcohol stops drinking, it takes much longer for those compensatory mechanisms to go away than for the alcohol itself to be cleared from the body. The result is withdrawal symptoms of excitation—increased blood pressure and heart rate, fever, anxiety, insomnia, seizures, and hallucinations. Anxiety and insomnia can last for many weeks. Barbiturates (such as phenobarbital and pentobarbital) and benzodiazepines (Valium, Librium, Xanax, Ativan, and others) also have sedative effects and in fact can be used to alleviate alcohol's withdrawal symptoms, but if tolerance has developed, they too have excitatory withdrawal symptoms.

Cocaine and amphetamine have the opposite effect to alcohol—they are stimulants. Withdrawal from cocaine does not have as well defined a syndrome as does alcohol, but it can cause a real "downer"—sedation, no energy, and depression. The usual solution that stimulant addicts find is to use more of the same drug.

All substances that are abused act as emotional anesthetics. They are frequently abused for relief of insomnia, hurt, sadness, and painful memories. When stopped after tolerance develops, the emotional anesthesia wears off. This means that with the autonomic and physiological symptoms of withdrawal come poor sleep, unhappiness, irritability, and a flood of painful dreams and memories.

Another word about depression: the AOD addict's drug of choice is his or her best friend. Even in the absence of a specific **withdrawal syndrome**, many addicts go through a transient depression when they stop using, because they have lost their best friend. Newly clean and sober clients have another problem: because many of them have for so long avoided dealing with life's problems, they simply don't have the requisite coping skills. Moreover, their addiction has probably increased the number of problems they face—medical, relational, financial, perhaps legal. No wonder they get depressed, irritable, and anxious. They are feeling again for the first time. Unless your client has a prior history of depression, don't give him a dual diagnosis label on the basis of symptoms early after withdrawal.

A final word about withdrawal symptoms: People who have developed a high level of tolerance to their drug of abuse may experience a syndrome called *post acute withdrawal* (PAW), in which physical and emotional symptoms may reappear at intervals for up to several years. Geller (1991) notes that "An appreciation on the part of health care professionals of the genuine distress being experienced by the newly abstinent addict and an appropriate education of the patient can do much to mitigate the consequences" (p. 907).

The Psychiatric Problem Initiates or Exacerbates AOD

In clients with bipolar disorder, you have probably noted that in the upswing of their disease (that is, in the hypomanic phase), they are likely to use to excess anything available—alcohol, other drugs, sex, whatever. If they are being prescribed any mood-altering drugs, such as narcotics (opioids) or benzodiazepines, they will probably overuse these as well. With this type of client, successful treatment of an addictive disorder is unlikely until their underlying manic-depressive illness is controlled.

Women with borderline personality disorder frequently have a history of childhood abuse (in particular, sexual), which predisposes them to compulsive sexual acting out. Women alcoholics have a high prevalence of childhood sexual abuse, which also increases the risk of addictive disorders, including chemical addictions.

Children with attention deficit hyperactivity disorder (ADHD) have an increased risk of substance abuse in adolescence and adulthood. The standard treatment for ADHD is stimulants such as methylphenidate (Ritalin and others) and dextroamphetamine (Dexedrine). A recent meta-analytic review of the literature was performed to answer the question *Does stimulant therapy of ADHD beget later substance abuse?* (Wilens et al., 2003). Surprisingly, the answer was that compared with children with ADHD who were *not* treated with stimulants, those who were treated had a significant (1.9-fold) *decrease* in the likelihood of developing alcohol and drug disorders in later years. Possible reasons include the likelihood that treating the symptoms of ADHD reduces the risk or that treated children are monitored more closely.

4. Each of the following is a commonly seen way that AOD affects a psychiatric disorder *except*:
   a. AOD initiates or worsens psychiatric symptoms.
   b. AOD masks, or is used to medicate, psychiatric symptoms.
   c. AOD withdrawal improves psychiatric symptoms.
   d. AOD withdrawal mimics psychiatric symptoms.

5. Alcohol frequently interacts with psychiatric disorders in all of the following ways *except*:
   a. Alcohol may be used by the drinker to lessen anxiety.
   b. Alcohol withdrawal may lead to antisocial behavior.
   c. Alcohol use may disinhibit behavior.
   d. Alcohol withdrawal may lead to depression and insomnia.

6. Which of the following statements is true?
   a. Depression is a nonspecific effect of withdrawal from any drug dependency.
   b. Childhood sexual abuse is a common precursor of alcoholism, bipolar illness, and borderline personality disorder in women.
   c. The depressive phase of bipolar illness frequently initiates or worsens drug abuse or dependency.
   d. Anxiety and hallucinations are frequent symptoms of withdrawal from cocaine and amphetamine addiction.

7. Which one of the following statements is *false*?
   a. Undiagnosed primary depression is a risk factor for addiction relapse.
   b. Generally, primary depression should be treated before the client is asked to stop drinking or drugging.
   c. Secondary mood disorders are likely to resolve without medication treatment after a few weeks of sobriety.
   d. Secondary antisocial personality traits have a better prognosis than does primary antisocial personality disorder.

Treatment Issues for Concurrent AOD and Psychiatric Disorders

Primary Versus Secondary Disorders

Because the same psychiatric symptoms can either be a result of chemical dependency or might be a separate problem in their own right, how can you distinguish the two and why is this important? The answer is that symptoms (such as depression and anxiety) resulting from the addiction are usually temporary (*secondary*) and remit with addiction treatment once your client is clean and sober; but symptoms that reflect an underlying problem separate from the addiction (*primary*) require treatment. In a client with both a mental and a substance use disorder, the disorder that came first is usually the primary one. A detailed psychiatric and addiction history will help sort this out. Be sure to ask about psychiatric treatment preceding addiction, any family history of addiction and mental illness, and any family or personal history of suicide attempts or successfully completed suicide.

Untreated primary (underlying) psychiatric disorders are important risk factors for relapse to the addiction. On the other hand, secondary mood disorders seen in the first few weeks of sobriety usually remit with continued recovery work. You can help your client cope with drug-related mood changes by explaining that they are temporary and that staying sober is the best solution.

Alcohol and other drug use affect not only mood disorders (such as anxiety and depression), termed Axis I disorders in the DSM, but also Axis II personality traits. For example, during the active addiction, an individual may demonstrate antisocial behaviors such as lying and stealing and may fit the diagnosis of Antisocial Personality Disorder (listed under Axis II disorders in the *DSM–IV*) (APA, 2000). It is accepted that personality disorders are difficult to treat and unlikely to change. Yet the same individual, after some time in addiction treatment and a genuine commitment to 12-step recovery, may seem "like a new person."

Which Problem Do I Treat First?

When your client has both a drug dependency and a psychiatric disorder, it is important to determine which to treat first. Treatment decisions should ideally be made by psychiatrists with addiction training and qualifications. It is generally accepted that regardless of the primary disorder, clients who are currently drinking or drugging need first to be stabilized by detoxification. Depending on the client's case and the available resources, this can take place in a detox center or a psychiatric hospital.

8. The first step in treating an addicted client is:
   a. obtaining a signed consent form.
   b. getting agreement from family members to become actively involved.
   c. stabilization by detoxification.
   d. determining which is the primary addiction.

As Evans and Sullivan (2001, p. 5) argued, it is often not easy to sort out the primary diagnosis at intake. To determine whether a psychiatric hospital or a detox center is the best setting for stabilization, one needs a good psychiatric and AOD history. The intoxicated client with a psychiatric disorder may be too confused to present a coherent history, and may exhibit the classic denial of the addict. They therefore recommend that the initial treatment be based on the patient's immediate needs. For example, if the client is suicidal, then a safe environment and suicide treatment needs to be the first priority, regardless of the primary diagnosis. Optimally, this is done in an integrated addiction and psychiatric facility, but these are often not available. In addition, many clients don't have the insurance coverage or funds to pay even for stabilization.

Concurrent with detox, the psychiatrically unstable client may need urgent psychotropic medications as part of the stabilization process. Once the client is stabilized, you can the reassess the priority of treatment goals.

Dishonesty About Drug and Alcohol Use

Dealing with addicts can be very frustrating because of their denial, dishonesty, and outright lying about their addictions. Clients with dual diagnoses may tell you all about their mood disorder while saying nothing about their drug use. For this reason, it is very helpful at the time of intake to obtain the client's permission to speak with family members, which can be very informative.

Inpatient or Outpatient Treatment?

When you evaluate a new client for treatment, how do you decide whether he or she needs inpatient or outpatient treatment? Fortunately, there are now guidelines to help you make the decision. The American Society of Addiction Medicine (ASAM) has published a book called

Patient Placement Criteria for the Treatment of Psychoactive Substance Use Disorders (1996). The authors recommend that "the preferred level of care [be] the least intensive level that could accomplish the treatment objectives while providing safety and security for the patient" (p. 6). For example, their criteria for Level IV treatment, which constitutes inpatient care with 24-hour supervision, include at least one of the following:

1. Severe alcohol and/or other drug intoxication and/or potential withdrawal,
2. Medical conditions or medical complications of addiction that require medical management and skilled nursing care and observation, or
3. Emotional/behavioral conditions and complications.

9. When evaluating a client for the most appropriate level of treatment, first consult:
   a. the Hazelden Center.
   b. the Physician's Desk Reference.
   c. the *DSM–IV*.
   d. ASAM's *Patient Placement Criteria* (1996).

A client with both AOD and an emotional/behavioral problem is more likely to require initial inpatient admission than if only one disorder were present. However, each client needs to be evaluated individually. Some clients may need psychiatric hospitalization for initial stabilization, and then residential treatment because they are still at high risk for relapse or self-harm, but not to the extent that they continue to require inpatient care at a psychiatric hospital.

Medications

Clients with a dual diagnosis often require medications for their psychiatric disorder. Depression, anxiety, bipolar disorder, schizophrenia, and other Axis I disorders usually benefit from medication treatment. Tradition 10 of Alcoholics Anonymous (AA) states, "AA has no opinion on outside issues." This surely includes medical and psychiatric diagnosis and treatment. Nonetheless, the need to take pills that affect mood sometimes causes clients difficulty in their 12-step meetings. Some old-timers take a hard line, insisting that the definition of "clean and sober" precludes taking *any* mood-altering drugs, even if prescribed. As a counselor, you need to realize that for the last twenty years this has been contrary to the official position of AA, which states: "Just as it is wrong to enable or support any alcoholic to become readdicted to any drug, it's equally wrong to deprive any alcoholic of medication which can alleviate or control other disabling physical and/or emotional problems" (AA World Services, 1984, p. 13).

10. Prescription medication use:
    a. is never allowed in 12-step recovery prgrams.
    b. is only allowed for the program "old-timers."
    c. constitutes a break in sobriety.
    d. none of the above.

Nonetheless, some counselors and some recovering addicts believe that taking any mood-altering drugs, such as antidepressants or anti-anxiety agents constitutes a break in sobriety. This is particularly true of pain medications. Even in cases where pain is severe and the reason for the pain all too obvious, recovering addicts might decide, or be expected by their 12-step peers or sponsor, to suffer rather than take effective pain medications. There is no reason for this. A solution that has proven effective, when it is unclear how reliable the patient is, is to provide sufficient pain medication to the patient in the hospital, office, or other controlled setting (as an injection or supervised swallowing of a pill), but to not give the person a take-home prescription for opioids (e.g., Percocet, Vicodin, Tylenol 3). Careful follow-up is mandatory, including supervision of weaning off the medication when the pain problem has resolved.

As for medications for various ongoing physical diseases such as high blood pressure, diabetes, heart disease, and asthma, there is usually no problem either from AOD treatment centers or 12-step program members with continuing to take them during treatment and recovery. The same is not true for chronic pain. It is increasingly accepted that some patients with chronic noncancer pain, for whom surgery, injections, and "everything else" has been tried, can benefit from treatment with strong painkilling drugs such as morphine and oxycodone. Regulatory organizations and major medical associations have recently published position papers supporting the use of opioids (narcotics) for patients who have intractable pain, but many physicians—and other professionals—still have a very cautious attitude toward such treatment.

What happens, then, if an individual has both an addiction and a chronic pain problem? Most of the time their pain goes untreated, even if they have been in recovery from chemical dependency for years. In a 1995 study, twenty-four chronic pain patients who had a history of AOD (but not current use) were treated with opioids and were then followed up (Dunbar & Katz, 1996). Patients with a history of alcohol dependency, AA attendance, and family support, generally did well with opioid treatment, whereas half of those with a history of narcotic addiction relapsed. The lesson is that using opioids to treat a patient with a history of narcotic addiction has a significant risk of relapse, but the recovering alcoholic is at much less risk. On the other hand, untreated pain is a major risk factor for relapse to narcotic addiction, especially because the sufferer already knows how to get narcotics on the street.

Another difficult drug class is benzodiazepines (such as Valium, Librium, Xanax, and Ativan), which are overused (without good evidence) for insomnia and anxiety. Although they may have a legitimate use in treating panic disorder, many physicians prescribe them liberally for many indications. These drugs affect the brain like alcohol, and are a frequent factor in relapse, especially in relapse to alcohol use. They should generally be avoided in recovering addicts, and prescribed only after consultation with a physician knowledgeable about addictions.

11. Benzodiazepines usually should not be prescribed to a recovering addict because these drugs:
    a. act like alcohol on the brain.
    b. cause insomnia and increase anxiety.
    c. can precipitate a panic attack.
    d. none of the above.

If your client has a chronic pain problem, get a pain management physician involved, optimally one who also has knowledge of addiction medicine. Ideally, the pain specialist can evaluate whether the client is a candidate for prescription pain medication and, if so, can help create a treatment plan with sufficient structure to make it safe for the client. In some cases, it may be best to have another person dispense the medication. This may be a family member, friend, or business associate—someone who is reliable, has the best interests of the client at heart, and is not a drug abuser. The client has to agree not to pressure the dispenser for additional medication.

Remember that loss of control is the major characteristic of addiction; therefore an *actively using* alcoholic or drug addict cannot be expected to reliably follow instructions with regard to the use of pain medication. The treatment plan for their pain problem has to *begin with* sobriety.

12. Which one of the following statements is *false*?
    a. AOD addicts who are given mood-altering drugs have an increased risk of relapse.
    b. AOD addicts who have severe pain need effective pain medication even if it's an opioid (narcotic).
    c. Undertreated chronic pain is a risk factor for addiction relapse.
    d. AOD addicts should not be treated with opioids (narcotics) for chronic pain.

PART II: MULTIPLE ADDICTIONS AND THEIR INTERACTIONS

In the 1930s, when AA was founded, chemical dependency was synonymous with alcoholism. It was unusual to find other drug dependencies among alcoholics. Currently, however, alcoholics are frequently addicted to other drugs—and to other behaviors. Unrecognized and untreated addictions are a significant contributing factor to relapse to the addiction for which a client was initially treated. Knowledgeable addiction counselors and treatment centers now routinely screen incoming clients for the presence of other addictions. Chapter 11 discussed illicit drug use and prescription drug abuse. This chapter describes the main features of various behavioral addictions and how they interact with drug addictions.

In the *DSM–IV*, all substance dependencies have a similar set of criteria for diagnosis. These criteria consist of two physical features—tolerance and withdrawal—and five behavioral descriptors; only three of the seven must be present to make the diagnosis. The five behavioral criteria can be condensed to the three below:

1. Loss of control (i.e., compulsive use)
2. Continuation despite significant adverse consequences
3. Preoccupation or obsession with obtaining or using the drug or behavior

Loss of Control

The first criterion involves loss of choice about whether to stop or continue. The more a person is involved with the behavior, the less able he is to stop. Examples of loss of control include the following:

- Having six beers when you intended to have only one or two
- Spending all night on computer pornography when you planned on spending a half hour before bedtime
- Eating an entire box of cookies at one sitting when it was supposed to last a week
- Promising yourself that you're through gambling, and the next day betting on yet another horse race

Continuation Despite Adverse Consequences

An addict's life becomes focused on the addictive behavior, and even when the resultant problems are evident to everyone else, the addict continues the self-destructive behavior. Examples of continuation despite significant adverse consequences are as follows:

- Continuing to drink after the doctor tells you to stop because of liver damage, high blood pressure, or a serious gastrointestinal bleeding episode
- Continuing to gamble after losing a month's wages ("chasing your losses")

- Continuing to smoke even when you're on oxygen because of smoking-related severe lung damage, or, if you have asthma, using an inhaled bronchodilator to enable yourself to continue smoking.
- Returning to the red light district after being arrested for soliciting a prostitute

Obsession With Obtaining Addicting Substance or Behavior

Addicts' thinking is impaired. They have cognitive distortions, irrational justifications for using, fantasy, and preoccupation. Examples of preoccupation or obsession are as follows:

- Going out in bad weather in the middle of the night to buy a pack of cigarettes when you've run out of them because you can't concentrate on anything else
- Spending hours cruising the neighborhood looking for a promising window in which to peep
- Repeatedly ignoring your family's dinner conversation because all you can think about is your latest work project

When all three criteria are met in someone's relationship to a drug or behavior, that person has an addiction. What counts is not the quantity of the substance consumed, the amount of money lost or spent, or the number of sexual encounters a person has, but rather the *consequences* to the person. Understanding this distinction will help you recognize when an addictive disorder is present. The next section describes the features of several behavioral addictions and compulsions.

13. Which of the following is NOT a major criterion for an addictive disorder?
    a. loss of control
    b. large expenditures for the drug or behavior
    c. continuation despite significant adverse consequences
    d. preoccupation or obsession with the drug or behavior

Overview

Most clients suffering from behavioral addictions—sex, gambling, or eating disorders—come from families in which alcohol and other drug dependencies are found. Many sex addicts and gamblers also have AOD dependency. Profound shame, unconscious denial, secrets, and rationalization abound within the family. Family members find behaviors that help them escape from the obvious problems at home. One behavior addiction—sex—is discussed in greater detail than the two others—compulsive gambling and compulsive overeating—because there is already a wide literature on gambling and food. Remember, however, that many other behaviors, including work and spending, can be used compulsively.

14. Which statement below about addiction is true?
    a. The quantity of an addictive substance or behavior used is the best indicator that the user is addicted.
    b. It is unusual for families to have a multigenerational pattern of more than one addiction.
    c. Addictions often have both an environmental and a genetic component.
    d. A true addiction by definition involves putting a mood-altering drug into the body.

Addictive Sexual Disorders

Sex addiction is present when a person meets all of the following criteria:

1. Loss of control over a sexual behavior,
2. Continued sexual behavior despite significant adverse consequences, *and*
3. Obsession or preoccupation with sexual fantasies, urges, or behavior.

Sex addicts have an average of three out-of-control sexual behaviors, so you need to get a thorough sexual history. Some of the behaviors are "normal" ones taken to excess (e.g., masturbation, multiple sex partners), whereas others are listed in the *DSM–IV* as **paraphilias** (e.g., sadomasochism, pedophilia, exhibitionism) (APA, 2000). Table 13.1 lists ten sexual behavior patterns (Carnes & Schneider, 2000).

Women sex addicts, who comprise perhaps one-third of all sex addicts, are relatively more likely than male addicts to engage in exhibitionism (in particular in the way they dress) and in fantasy sex, and less likely than men to participate in voyeurism, anonymous sex, and paying for sex.

TABLE 13.1

Addictive Sexual Behavior Patterns

1. *Fantasy sex*: An obsessive sexual fantasy life; arousal depends on sexual possibility; neglecting responsibilities to engage in fantasy and/or prepare for the next sexual episode. Examples: Reading romance novels, spending significant amounts of time on computer e-mails and chat rooms corresponding on romantic or sexual themes. Often associated with masturbation.
2. *Seductive role sex*: Seductive behavior for conquest; arousal depends on conquest and diminishes rapidly after initial contact; arousal can be heightened by increasing risk and/or number of partners; much time spent on making yet another conquest. Examples: Multiple relationships, affairs, flirtation.
3. *Voyeuristic sex*: Visual arousal; the use of visual stimulation to escape into an obsessive trance; arousal may be heightened by masturbation or risk (e.g., peeping). Examples: pornography, window peeping, secret observation with cameras or telescopes; associated with excessive masturbation, even to the point of injury.
4. *Exhibitionistic sex*: Attracting attention to body or sexual parts of the body; sexual arousal stems from reaction of viewer shock or interest. Examples: exposing oneself in public, wearing clothes designed to expose.
5. *Anonymous sex*: High-risk sex with unknown persons; arousal involves no seduction or cost, no entanglements or obligations, and is immediate; arousal is often accelerated by unsafe or high-risk environments. Examples: one-night stands, sex with strangers in restrooms, beaches, bars or parks.
6. *Paying for sex*: Purchase of sexual services; arousal is connected to payment for sex and, with time, arousal becomes connected to money itself. Examples: prostitutes, phone sex, Internet sex sites.
7. *Trading sex*: Selling or bartering sex for power; arousal is based on gaining control of others by using sex as leverage. Example: being a sex worker.
8. *Intrusive sex*: Boundary violation without discovery; arousal occurs by violating boundaries with no repercussions. Example: touching others without permission (*frotteurism*).
9. *Pain exchange*: Causing or receiving pain or humiliation to enhance sexual pleasure; arousal is built around specific scenarios or narratives of humiliation and shame. Animals may be used sexually.
10. *Exploitative sex*: Exploitation of the vulnerable; arousal is based on particular targets of vulnerability. Use of force or partner vulnerability to gain sexual access. Examples: using professional position of power (physician, psychologist, priest, teacher) for sex, child molestation, incest, rape.

15. Which of the following statements about sex addiction is *false*?
    a. Some types of addictive sexual behaviors are called *paraphilias* in the *DSM–IV*.
    b. Normal sexual behaviors can be used addictively.
    c. The prevalence of AOD among sex addicts is similar to the prevalence of AOD in the general population.
    d. Because sex addicts usually have three types of addictive sexual behaviors, not identifying all of them during the workup can lead to relapse.

16. Carnes' ten patterns of addictive sexual behaviors include all of the following *except*
    _____.
    a. cybersex
    b. voyeuristic sex
    c. anonymous sex
    d. pain exchange

17. Compared to male sex addicts, women sex addicts are relatively less likely to participate in all of the following *except* _____.
    a. voyeurism
    b. pain exchange
    c. anonymous sex
    d. paying for sex

The sex addict may initially present to you in one of the following ways:

1. In the course of evaluating an client for AOD, you learn of a sexual history consistent with sex addiction.
2. The client has a pattern of several relapses to AOD. Your review of the relapse factors shows addictive sexual behavior associated with the relapse.
3. The client is in crisis precipitated by disclosure or discovery of some secret sexual behavior outside the relationship, especially when it has been recurrent.
4. The client or his sexual partner was unexpectedly diagnosed with an STD.
5. The client has been arrested for some sexual behavior: solicitation of a prostitute, exhibitionism or voyeurism, or exchanging child pornography.
6. The client has lost his or her job because of some sexual behavior: sexual harassment, viewing Internet pornography or other computer-related sexual activities during work time, or professional sexual misconduct.
7. The client is in financial difficulty because of sexually-related expenditures such as prostitutes, pornography, gifts to an affair partner, or payments (blackmail) made to keep sexual secrets from becoming known to others.

Treatment of sex addiction, like other addictions, involves a combination of addiction education, group and individual therapy, 12-step groups, healthy coping skills, shame reduction, and cognitive-behavioral relapse prevention strategies. The goal of sex addiction treatment, like the goal of treating eating disorders, is not abstinence. Rather, it is to develop a pattern of healthy sexuality and avoid sexual activities that serve as triggers for relapse. Family involvement in education and in their own recovery is strongly recommended. Couple therapy is usually needed.

You can obtain a basic understanding of diagnosis and treatment of sex addiction by consulting the resources listed at the end of the chapter.

18. Treatment of sex addictions should include all of the following *except* _____.
   a. education
   b. prolonged abstinence from sex
   c. shame reduction
   d. group and individual therapy

Pathologic Gambling

Pathologic gambling has very obvious addictive features. Pathologic gamblers indicate that what they seek is "action." The term refers to an aroused, euphoric state comparable to the euphoria or "high" obtained from use of cocaine or other drugs. They also describe a "rush" commonly associated with rapid heart rate, often experienced while anticipating winning or are preparing for gambling. Blood tests of compulsive gamblers have shown elevated levels of norepinephrine (noradrenaline), consistent with their aroused state (See Schneider & Irons, 1997). Recovering gamblers have described their disorder as "being hooked on their own adrenaline." Clients with a gambling disorder commonly have a pattern of multiple financial crises and unexplained disappearance of significant sums of money or valuable possessions. They engage in repetitive "bailout" behavior, turning to family and friends for financial help. They may have acute relationship crises precipitated by disclosure of secret squandering of family assets.

Diagnostic criteria for pathologic gambling can be found in the *DSM–IV*, where the resemblance to the criteria for substance use disorders is self-evident (APA, 2000). The standard screening test for pathologic gambling is the South Oaks Gambling Screen (Lesieur & Blume, 1987). Resources about compulsive gambling are listed at the end of the chapter.

19. Features of pathological gambling include all of the following *except*:
   a. an aroused euphoric state comparable to the "high" of drug use
   b. decreased levels of norepinephrine (noradrenaline) in the blood
   c. unexplained financial losses
   d. much time spent in gambling

Eating Disorders

The *DSM–IV* describes only two specific eating disorders: anorexia nervosa and bulimia nervosa. It also describes a proposed new diagnosis: binge-eating disorder. However, eating disorders can also be considered within an addiction framework. Eating disorders occur on a continuum, from rigid control over intake at one end, to loss of control on the other. In all cases, there is marked preoccupation with food and weight, and continuation of the behavior despite significant adverse consequences. Like substance abuse, eating disorders have very high rates of chronicity, relapse, recurrence, and psychosocial morbidity.

Eating disorders are commonly found together with substance use disorders. In one study, women undergoing AOD treatment had a 15% lifetime prevalence of anorexia or bulimia, which is significantly higher than expected (Hudson, Weiss, Pope, McElroy, & Mirin, 1992). Some patients tend to binge eat while intoxicated; others tend to substitute binge eating for AOD use. During treatment of one of these disorders, the other commonly worsens. Resources on eating disorders can be found at the end of the chapter.

20. The *DSM–IV* does *not* mention which of the following eating disorders?
    a. compulsive overeating
    b. bulimia
    c. anorexia nervosa
    d. binge-eating disorder

How Addictions Interact

There are several ways multiple addictions can interact. These include:

- Reinforcement and ritualization
- Substitution
- Masking
- Disinhibiting
- "Medicating"
- Bartering

Reinforcement and Ritualization

Cigarettes, sex, and food are often intertwined. Cigarette commercials for women emphasize how you can stay thin and more attractive by smoking. These ads set up psychological **reinforcement** for multiple addictions.

Addictions are driven by reinforcement. With drugs, the neurochemical effect of the substance is directly reinforcing to the brain. With gambling, it's the "big win." With sex, it can be the "big score." *Euphoric recall*—remembering how good it felt—additionally reinforces the behavior. The ritual behavior leading to the payoff becomes reinforcing in itself. All these actions result in the release of endogenous brain chemicals which enhance pleasure. More than one addictive behavior can become a part of the addict's ritual or pattern. The addict may become unable to act out his addiction without having every ingredient of the ritual recipe. Even if he can participate in only one addiction, that participation serves as a powerful trigger for the other. Some examples are as follows:

Cocaine and Sex.   Washton (1986) reported that 70% of cocaine addicts (both male and female) seeking outpatient treatment are compulsively sexual. This extremely high percentage was confirmed by Washton at the American Society of Addiction Medicine Annual Conference (May 2, 1999, New York, NY) and a similar prevalence of sexual compulsivity was reported among methamphetamine addicts by Dr. Richard Rawson in the same presentation.

21. Multiple addictions can interact by all of the following mechanisms *except* _____.
    a. substitution
    b. fear
    c. reinforcement
    d. masking

Edlin et al. (1992) studied the sexual behaviors and cocaine use among young women 18 to 29 years old, recruited in urban neighborhoods by street outreach workers. Among the 289 current regular crack cocaine smokers, 70.5% had sold sex, versus 4.3% of 236 who never smoked cocaine; 37% of the crack smokers had had more than one hundred lifetime male sex partners, compared with 3% of the nonsmokers. Crack cocaine smokers are at equal or greater risk for contracting HIV disease and other sexually transmitted diseases (STDs) than are intravenous drug users.

Alcohol and Sex.   Up to 80% of women alcoholics were sexually abused in childhood. The factors that predispose an individual to addictive behaviors, such as childhood sexual abuse, result in impairment of the self that predisposes to addictive behaviors (Young, 1990). Women may use alcohol and other drugs to numb their feelings.

Cybersex is the most common solo addictive sexual behavior that an addiction counselor will encounter. It is sometimes associated with smoking or alcoholic drinking. When a client says, "Yes, I do drink a lot by myself," you should also ask, "What else are you doing—are you on the Internet, are you masturbating?"

22. What percentage of cocaine addicts are also sexually compulsive?
   a. 10%
   b. 25%
   c. 40%
   d. 70%

Cigarette Smoking and Drinking.   Smoking and drinking are significantly correlated. About 14% of all smokers are currently alcoholic, and 28% of smokers have a lifetime history of alcoholism. Heavy smokers have a 21% prevalence of alcoholism (Evans, 2003).[1] Clients who smoke more than one pack per day should be screened for alcoholism.

Although most alcoholics in treatment want to quit smoking (77%), half (54%) prefer to wait until they've first quit drinking (Evans, 2003). Unfortunately, smoking and drinking reinforce each other. This is why many chemical dependency treatment centers strongly encourage their clients to quit smoking while in AOD treatment. In support of this, Stuyt (1997) found that there are higher rates of alcohol and drug abstinence among those who stopped smoking in treatment than among those who continued to smoke.

Cigarette Smoking and Gambling.   Cigarette smoking is associated with increased severity of gambling problems. A study of more than two hundred pathologic gamblers seeking treatment found that about two-thirds were also daily cigarette smokers (Petry & Oncken, 2002). Compared to nondaily smokers, the daily smokers gambled on more days and spent more money gambling; they also craved gambling more and had lower perceived control over their gambling. Additionally, they had psychiatric symptoms, especially anxiety, on more days than the nonsmokers, and were taking more psychiatric medications.

Substitution

When an addict ceases one behavior, he or she can find great comfort in turning to another addiction rather than experiencing the negative feelings that are unmasked. For example, smokers who quit drinking are likely to escalate their consumption of cigarettes. Smokers who quit smoking also tend to gain weight, and drinkers who quit drinking often consume more sugar.

Among women sex addicts, some are slender when they are acting out their sex addiction, but gain many pounds when they stop the sexual acting out. When they resume their compulsive

---

[1] Quoting Dr. John R. Hughes of the University of Vermont, speaking at the Annual Conference of the Association for Medical Education and Research in Substance Abuse.

sexual activities, they stop overeating and lose weight. They may spend years yo-yoing between sexual acting out and overeating.

Masking

One addiction can be used to cover up for another. For example, "I had multiple sex partners only because I was drinking." Or, "My domestic violence problems are a result of my drinking. When I'm sober, I'm always nice to her."

Disinhibiting

Drugs that diminish a person's ability to think about the consequences of their behavior, or that relieve tension and anxiety, may be used to allow that person to act in ways they would not when sober. A common example is alcohol and sex.

Medicating

Most commonly, one drug is used to counteract the unwanted physical effects of another. For example, a cocaine addict who is so revved up that he can't sleep might drink alcohol at the end of the day to counteract the insomnia. An addict may use one mood-altering drug or behavior to deal with emotions created by another drug or behavior—for example, to diminish the shame he feels about ongoing acting out with a different drug or behavior. A case example is given in the box below:

Leo, a forty-year-old physician with six years of unbroken recovery from alcoholism, was absent from work without explanation one Monday morning. When he did not answer his pager or his home phone, his colleague Ralph went to Leo's house to investigate. There he found Leo, drunk and depressed, and talking of suicide. Leo agreed to immediately enter a psychiatric hospital, while plans were made for where to send him for addiction treatment. That evening, after Leo had had some hours to sober up, Ralph visited him at the hospital. Leo, shaken and frightened, admitted to Ralph that in recent months he'd been getting increasingly involved in Internet sex chat rooms for gay men, and that in the past few weeks he had repeatedly arranged to meet men offline for unprotected sexual encounters. Despite his fears of health consequences and his shame about the possibility of being found out by his colleagues (from whom he'd concealed his sexual orientation all these years), he was unable to resist the lure of the Internet and the resultant clandestine anonymous sexual encounters.

"I finally got to where my only options were suicide or drinking, so I chose drinking," he explained to Ralph. During his earlier inpatient alcoholism treatment six years earlier, no one had asked him about his sexual activities. Back then he was occasionally meeting strangers in the park for sex, and after treatment had been able to limit this behavior to just a few times a year, but the advent of the Internet with its powerful drawing power had intensified his involvement in anonymous sex.

The next day Leo flew to a distant addiction treatment program, which he successfully completed after disclosing and dealing with *all* his addictive behaviors, not just the drinking.

Bartering

Two people can each fulfill the other's addictive needs. The most common example is trading sex for drugs. This may be done directly, or through the medium of money. For example, a physician may provide someone with a prescription for a narcotic or other desired drug, in exchange for sex. A pimp may give a prostitute cocaine or heroin, in exchange for money, which she obtains by selling sex, often to men who are addicted to purchasing sex.

23. A cocaine addict's pattern involves visiting a prostitute and smoking cocaine with her. This pattern is an example of which type of addiction interaction?
    a. "medicating"
    b. ritualization and reinforcement
    c. masking
    d. disinhibiting

24. Which of the following statements about the relationship between drug use and smoking is *false*?
    a. About 21% of heavy smokers are also addicted to alcohol.
    b. Among smoking alcoholics in treatment, those who stopped smoking during alcohol treatment have a higher rate of alcohol and drug abstinence than those who continued to smoke.
    c. The way smoking and drinking interact is an example of ritualization and reinforcement.
    d. Because it is so difficult to stop smoking, it's better for alcoholics in treatment to defer efforts to quit smoking.

25. Which statement about the relationship between smoking and pathological gambling is *false*?
    a. About one-third of compulsive gamblers are daily smokers.
    b. Compared with nonsmokers, daily smokers gambled more days, spent more money, and felt less control over their gambling.
    c. Casinos have a financial incentive to permit smoking.
    d. Gamblers who smoke have more anxiety than nonsmoking gamblers.

26. Which statement about primary versus secondary addiction is *false*?
    a. The primary addiction is likely to be the one that came first.
    b. When a client is addicted to both sex and drugs, the sex addiction often began later than the AOD addiction.
    c. No matter which is the primary addiction, detoxification from drug use is the first priority.
    d. Treating only one addiction is likely to make success in treating the other less likely.

Treatment Issues for Dual or Multiple Addictions

Treatment of all addictions follows the same basic principles, which include:

- Education about addiction in general and about the particular client's addiction
- A combination of group and individual therapy
- Introduction to 12-step programs

- Life skills training
- If possible, involvement of family members in education and treatment

Inpatient or Outpatient Treatment?

The key issue here is safety. The ASAM Patient Placement Criteria (see p. 300 in this chapter) can be used to determine the level of intensity needed to treat a client who has one or more addictions.

Primary Versus Secondary Addiction

As with dual diagnoses, the primary addiction is most likely to be the one that came first. Get a detailed history of both (or all) addictive behaviors. Patients with both sex and drug addiction often report that the sex addiction began around the time of puberty, whereas the AOD use started a little later. It is often easier for clients to stop the secondary than the primary addiction.

Order of Treatment

Because many sex addicts are also chemically dependent, you must decide which addiction to address first. By the time many sex addicts seek help, they are already in recovery from their AOD. If not, regardless of which addiction is primary, stopping the AOD use is the first priority. Detoxification is the first step. However, this is not to say that ongoing addictive behaviors can be ignored. It is very tempting for addicts who are restricted from one addictive substance or behavior to intensify one that is allowed. When they do this, they are still avoiding the feelings and problems they numbed with the addiction that brought them to treatment.

Once the client is stabilized, there are several options for addiction treatment. One option is *sequential* treatment: education, group therapy, 12-step work focused on the addiction that is considered the most problematic for that client. Work on the other addictive disorder is deferred. The client might later be referred for inpatient or outpatient treatment for the other addiction. This path is appropriate if you have very little knowledge about treating the other addiction.

Although there are common features to all addictive disorders, each one has its own specific features. Treatment is most effective if you, the counselor, are knowledgeable about the particular client's addiction and its issues. You need to be familiar with the vocabulary of the addiction, its tools and technology, the most common ways it is expressed, and the various consequences of the particular addiction.

Another treatment approach is the *concurrent* approach. This means that both addictions are addressed at the same time, but separately. For example, you might be doing individual counseling with a client about her AOD. She might attend a therapy group for drug addicts, and another for people with eating disorders. In addition, she would go to both AA and Overeaters Anonymous (OA) meetings.

A third approach—the *combined* strategy—is based on the principle that an addiction is an addiction and that basic addiction treatment requirements are similar for everyone. The client is part of a mixed group which receives education primarily about chemical dependency, with additional information about behavioral addictions, and goes to group therapy with a mixed addiction group. Individual counseling is tailored to the particular client, who also goes to separate 12-step meetings for the two addictions.

It's no secret that the most effective support groups are those in which people share a common problem. Therapy groups ideally also consist of clients with the same addiction.

In these groups, addicts receive the most support and the most specific confrontation. They share a common vocabulary and common issues. In sex addiction groups, for example, shame reduction is one major issue; another is fear about disclosing sexual behaviors to one's spouse or partner. In eating disorders groups, it's about the stigma of obesity or the constant need to make appropriate food choices. In compulsive gambling groups, the consequences of large financial losses is a key subject. AOD groups may be less focused on these particular issues, although stigma, disclosing secrets, and financial problems are relevant to all of them.

However, all addictions share dynamics and psychodynamic issues, so that much of education and discussion about addictive disorders is applicable to all addictions. The client with two or more addictions would certainly fit well into a combined educational class and a combined therapy group. The ideal treatment approach would include combined elements that apply to all addictions, plus individual groups for the particular addiction. There would also be attendance at 12-step meetings for each addiction.

The ideal treatment of clients with multiple addictions, just as of clients with a dual diagnosis, is integrated: The treatment center or agency has the expertise to treat all the various addictive and psychiatric disorders, and tailors an integrated program with combined, sequential, and concurrent elements that is individualized for each client.

In reality, the approach that is followed is often determined by the expertise of the counselors in your agency, the stated goals of your treatment center (whether focused on one type of addiction, or else to provide comprehensive treatment), the available manpower to run therapy groups, the number and mix of clients you have, and the local availability of different types of 12-step meetings. What you as an individual counselor can do in this situation is recognize where your expertise lies, know where to refer clients who have addictions and/or psychological problems outside your scope, and learn as much as you can about these other areas so that you will increase your competence in asking the right questions.

27. Which one of the following models of multiple addiction treatment is described *incorrectly*?
   a. Sequential—treating the most problematic addiction first
   b. Concurrent—treating both addictions in the same time period, but separately.
   c. Stabilization—getting the client stable enough to get back to work.
   d. Combined—treating both addictions in mixed groups

28. According to the ASAM Patient Placement Criteria, all but which are indications for level IV inpatient treatment?
   a. Severe alcohol and/or other drug intoxication and/or potential withdrawal is present.
   b. The patient's medical insurance permits inpatient treatment for addictions.
   c. The patient has medical conditions or medical complications of addiction which require medical management, skilled nursing care, and observation.
   d. Emotional or behavioral conditions and complications are found.

Medications

As with dually diagnosed clients, people with multiple addictions sometimes benefit from medications for one or another of the addictions or for concurrent depression. The same guidelines that are described earlier in this chapter (beginning on p. 302) apply.

As our understanding of the interrelatedness of addictions and psychiatric disorders increases, counseling AOD addicts is becoming increasingly complex. As in my own field—medicine—counselors are by necessity becoming specialized because the total body of knowledge relevant to the mental health needs of clients is ever growing. As you train for addiction counseling certification, you will need to have a basic body of knowledge. Beyond that, it behooves you to find some specific areas of interest and then carve out a niche for yourself which allows you to develop and exercise your expertise and recognize the client's other needs.

KEY TERMS

behavioral addiction: A disorder in which a behavior (e.g., gambling or sexual activity) takes place compulsively, is continued despite significant adverse consequences, and takes up a great deal of the person's mental life.

coexisting (or concurrent) addictions: The presence in one person of two or more addictions.

cybersex: Any type of sexual activity involving the computer. Examples are viewing and downloading pornography, sexual chat rooms, one-on-one real-time sexual exchanges.

disinhibiting effects: The effect of a drug which allows a person to act in ways he or she would not if not under the influence of the drug.

dual diagnosis: The presence in a person of both an addictive disorder and a psychiatric disorder.

paraphilia: A category of sexual disorder that is defined in the *DSM–IV* as "recurrent, intense sexually arousing fantasies, sexual urges, or behaviors generally involving (1) nonhuman objects, (2) the suffering or humiliation of oneself or one's partner, or (3) children or other nonconsenting persons, that occur over a period of at least 6 months." Examples are fetishism, exhibitionism, voyeurism, sadism, masochism, and pedophilia.

reinforcement: One drug or behavior intensifies the effects of another drug or behavior and makes it more likely that the person will continue in the first behavior.

ritualization: The use of a particular pattern of behavior that precedes and accompanies the acting out of some addiction. Addicts generally have their own rituals in connection with their addiction.

tolerance: The need for more of a drug or behavior to get the same effect as previously experienced or significantly diminished effect when the same amount of the substance or behavior is continued.

withdrawal syndrome: The development of a substance-specific set of symptoms that results when a drug is suddenly stopped or the dose decreased after prolonged and heavy use.

DISCUSSION QUESTIONS

1. Describe how AOD initiates or exacerbates psychiatric symptoms and vice versa.
2. How does a counselor determine whether a client's psychiatric problem is the result of chemical dependency or is a separate problem in its own right?
3. Which should be treated first, a chemical dependency or a psychiatric disorder? Why?
4. Why and how should you seek information about an addicted client from family members?
5. When should you refer an addicted client to inpatient or outpatient treatment?
6. Evaluate this advice: To help your client overcome his addiction and become completely clean and sober, encourage him to never take any mood-altering drug, at any time, for any reason.

7. How similar/different are behavioral addictions from chemical addictions?
8. What are the core therapies commonly used to treat addicted clients, regardless of whether chemically or behaviorally addicted.
9. Give some examples of how multiple addictions interact.
10. Evaluate this advice: As an addiction counselor it is better for you to be a generalist who can help all addicted clients, rather than focus your expertise on a more narrow niche.

ACKNOWLEDGMENT

Thanks to Reid Finlayson, M.D., Sandra Kline, M.A., and M. Deborah Corley, Ph.D. for reviewing this manuscript.

SUGGESTED FURTHER READING ON SEX ADDICTION

Books

Carnes, P. J. (1983). *Out of the shadows: Understanding sexual addiction.* Center City, MN: Hazelden.

The groundbreaking book that explains sex addiction in easily understood terms.

Carnes, P. J., & Adams, K. M. (Eds.). (2002). *Clinical management of sex addiction.* New York: Brunner/Mazel.

For clinicians, the latest on assessment and treatment.

Carnes, P. J., Delmonico, D. L., & Griffin, E. (2001). *In the shadows of the net: Breaking free of compulsive online sexual behavior.* Center City, MN: Hazelden.

About cybersex addiction.

Corley, M. D., & Schneider, J. P. (2002). *Disclosing secrets: When, to whom, and how much to reveal.* Wickenburg, AZ: Gentle Path Press.

A guide for professionals and clients about the process of disclosing sensitive addiction secrets to one's partner and others.

Earle, R., & Earle, M. (1995). *Sex addiction: Case studies and management.* New York: Brunner/Mazel.

For clinicians; deals with many aspects of counseling sex addicts.

Hope and recovery: A twelve-step guide for healing from compulsive sexual behavior. Center City, MN: Hazelden.

The "Big Book" for sex addicts.

Kasl, C. (1989). *Women, sex, and addiction: A search for love and power.* New York: Ticknor & Fields.

About women sex addicts and coaddicts.

Schneider, J. (2001). *Back from betrayal: Recovering from his affairs* (2nd ed.). Tucson, AZ: Recovery Resources Press.

The classic guide for women involved with sex-addicted men.

Schneider, J., & Schneider, B. (2004). *Sex, lies, and forgiveness: Couples speak on healing from sex addiction* (3rd ed.). Tucson, AZ: Recovery Resources Press.

A guide for couples who seek to rebuild their relationship.

Schneider, J., & Weiss, R. (2001). *Cybersex exposed: Simple fantasy or obsession?* Center City, MN: Hazelden.

Understanding and recovering from cybersex addiction—for addicts and their partners.

Web Sites

www.ncsac.org

> The Web site of the National Council on Sexual Addiction and Compulsivity. Definitions, lists of relevant 12-step programs, position papers, and list of sex addiction therapists by state.

www.sexhelp.com

> Dr. Patrick Carnes's Web site. Online sex addiction tests and information about books and articles by Dr. Carnes.

www.cybersexualaddiction.com

> For information on cybersex addiction.

www.jenniferschneider.com

> My Web Site contains articles I wrote explaining various aspects of sex addiction and information about my books.

SUGGESTED FURTHER READING ON COMPULSIVE GAMBLING

Books

Ciarrocchi, J. W. (2002). *Counseling problem gamblers*. San Diego: Academic Press.
Gamblers anonymous. (1986) Los Angeles: Gamblers Anonymous Publishing.

> The "Big Book" for compulsive gamblers.

LeSieur, H. R. (1984). *The chase: Career of the compulsive gambler*. Cambridge, MA: Schenkman.

Web Sites

www.gamblersanonymous.org

> The 12-step program for compulsive gambling.

www.ncpgambling.org

> The Web site of the National Council on Problem Gambling. Lists books, resources, 12-step group contacts. Helpline: 800-522-4700.

SUGGESTED FURTHER READING ON EATING DISORDERS

Books

Overeaters anonymous. (1984). Torrance, CA: Overeaters Anonymous World Services.

> The "Big Book" for compulsive overeating.

Roth, G. (1991). *When food is love*. New York: Penguin Books.

> Good explanation and suggestions for recovery from overeating.

Web Sites

www.overeatersanonymous.org

> The Web site of the 12-step program for compulsive overeaters.

REFERENCES

Alcoholics Anonymous World Services. (1984). *The AA member: Medications and other drugs.* New York: Author.

American Psychiatric Association. (2000). *Diagnostic and statistical manual of mental disorders* (4th ed., text rev.). Washington, DC.

American Society of Addiction Medicine. (1996). *Patient placement criteria for the treatment of psychoactive substance user disorders* (2nd ed.). Chevy Chase, MD: Author.

Carnes, P. J. (1991). *Don't call it love: Recovery from sexual addiction.* Center City, MN: Hazelden.

Carnes, P., & Schneider, J. P. (2000). Recognition and management of addictive sexual disorders: Guide for the primary care clinician. *Lippincott's Primary Care Practice, 4,* 302–318.

Dunbar, S. A., & Katz, N. P. (1996). Chronic opioid therapy for nonmalignant pain in patients with a history of substance abuse: Report of 20 cases. *Journal of Pain and Symptom Management, 11,* 163–171.

Edlin, B. R., Irwin, K. L., Ludwig, D. D., McCoy, H. V., Serrano, V., Word, C., et al. (1992). The multicenter crack cocaine and HIV infection study team. *Journal of Psychoactive Drugs, 24,* 363–371.

Evans, J. (2003, January 1). Recovering alcoholics can use help with smoking cessation. *Internal Medicine News,* p. 13.

Evans, K., & Sullivan, J. M. (2001). *Dual diagnosis: Counseling the mentally ill substance abuser* (2nd ed.). New York: Guilford Press.

Geller, A. (1991). Protracted abstinence. In N. S. Miller (Ed.), *Comprehensive handbook of drug and alcohol addiction* (pp. 905–913). New York: Marcel Dekker.

Hudson, J. I., Weiss, R. D., Pope, H. G., McElroy, S. K., & Mirin, S. M. (1992). Eating disorders in hospitalized substance abusers. *American Journal of Drug and Alcohol Abuse, 18,* 75–85.

Lesieur, H. R., & Blume, S. B. (1984). The South Oaks Gambling Screen: A new instrument for the identification of pathological gamblers. *American Journal of Psychiatry, 144,* 1184–1188.

Petry N. M., & Oncken, C. (2002). Cigarette smoking is associated with increased severity of gambling problems in treatment-seeking gamblers. *Addiction, 97,* 745–753.

Regier, D. A., Farmer, M. E., Rae, D. S., Locke, B. Z., Keith, S. J., Judd, L. J. et al. (1990). Comorbidity of mental disorders with alcohol and other drug abuse: Results from the Epidemiologic Catchment Area (ECA) Study. *Journal of the American Medical Association, 264,* 2511–2518.

Schneider, J., & Irons, R. (1997). Treatment of gambling, eating, and sex addictions. In N. S. Miller, M. S. Gold, & D. E. Smith (Eds.). *Manual of Therapeutics for Addictions* (pp. 225–245). New York: Wiley.

Stuyt, E. B. (1997). Recovery rates after treatment for alcohol/drug dependence: Tobacco users versus nonusers. *American Journal of Addictions, 6,* 159–167.

Washton, A. M. (1986). Special report: Women and cocaine. *Medical Aspects of Human Sexuality, 20,* 128–132.

Wilens, T. E., Faraone S. V., Biederman, J., & Gunawardene, S. (2003). Does stimulant therapy of attention-deficit/hyperactivity disorder beget later substance abuse? *Pediatrics III,* 179–185.

Young, E. B. (1990). The role of incest issues in relapse. *Journal of Psychoactive Drugs, 22*(2), 249–258.

COUNSELING THEORIES
AND SKILLS

14

Classical Counseling Models

William A. Howatt
Nova Scotia Community College

TRUTH OR FICTION?

___ *1. Rogers was a cognitive theorist.*
___ *2. Adler's model promoted spirituality.*
___ *3. Existential psychology has its roots in philosophy.*
___ *4. Jung's theory had three core conditions.*
___ *5. Rogers promoted self-actualization.*
___ *6. Adler believed in exploring the family constellation.*
___ *7. Existential therapy addressed life anxiety.*
___ *8. Jung was interested in spirituality.*
___ *9. Adler believed clients were discouraged, not mentally ill.*
___ *10. Rogers changed the name of his theory to client-centered.*
___ *11. Jung explored both the conscious and unconscious mind.*
___ *12. Jung believed there was a universal collective conscious mind.*
___ *13. Adler believed each client created his own life goals.*
___ *14. Existential therapy is based on a phenomenological orientation.*
___ *15. Existential therapy helps clients live more authentically.*

Of critical significance is the client's increasing capacity to be congruent, for it is this charge which makes it possible for him or her to be more open to experience and to take in more data more accurately (Rogers & Sardford, 1989, p. 1493).

One's counseling orientation is built upon a foundation of theory. The melding of theory, therapy, and technique is unique to the counselor's orientation. Chapters 14 and 15 provide an overview of eight counseling theories that provide the basis for many of the most popular present day counseling strategies. Both chapters have been written to address the 3 T's for each theory to keep sections congruent (theory, therapy, and technique).

This chapter provides an overview of four classical theories: Carl Rogers' person-centered therapy, existential therapy, Carl Jung's analytical psychoanalysis; and Alfred Adler's individual psychology.

PERSON-CENTERED THERAPY: CARL ROGERS

The person-centered approach focuses on the client's responsibility and capacity to discover ways to more fully encounter reality. (Corey, 2001, p. 173)

Carl Rogers graduated with a degree in psychology in 1931, starting a journey leading to him becoming one of the most influential figures in psychotherapy. In 1945, Rogers was invited to start the counseling center at the University of Chicago. While in this post in 1951, he published his seminal work, *Client-Centered Therapy*, outlining the core of his theory (later called person-centered therapy). Rogers was a prolific writer who contributed to many journals and authored forty-six books. When Rogers died, his theory was hailed as an effective **humanistic philosophy** for world peace—a powerful testament to the impact of his work (Corey, 2001). For more information on Rogers' work, visit: http://www.centerfortheperson.org/organizations.html.

Theory Overview

Person-centered therapy postulates that clients will change when they are willing to learn from their actions. Clients, through human evolution, know what is good for themselves. Rogers referred to this innate ability as *organismic valuing*. Person-centered therapy points out the need for clients to define for themselves what they need to achieve positive mental health. Rogers wanted clients to learn to not be misled by *social conditions of worth*; Rogers felt that too many people wait for society (e.g., parents) to fulfill their needs instead of learning how to responsibly satisfy their own individual needs.

The core of Rogers' theory is the concept of an internal life force called ***actualizing tendency***, a person's inner potential to solve his or her own problems (Howatt, 2000). Rogers asserted that the purpose of therapy is to engage in a process that reconciles the gap between the real self (the "I am") and the ideal self (the "I should"), which Rogers called *incongruity*. His belief was that the larger this gap of incongruity, the more pain a person would experience. Person-centered therapy purports that *neurosis* (psychological pain) originates in this incongruity.

Rogers suggested that many psychological problems can be observed by exploring the client's *interpersonal matrix*, or the range of one's ability and effectiveness in interacting with others (Todd & Bohart, 1994). For example, a client who has been exposed to an abusive relationship may be untrusting. To cope, the client develops an internal anxiety as a protection against further threats. However, this anxiety often becomes overbearing and inhibits the client's quality of life. Person-centered therapy takes the stance that each client's problems must be addressed in a safe and nonjudgmental treatment environment, created by the counselor to assist the client in lowering her anxiety. When the client's anxiety is lowered and she feels safe, the stage is set for her to tune into her potential to solve her own life challenges.

The clinical approach of person-centered therapy is nondirective, supportive, and nonconfrontational. This theory can be summarized by the *if–then* principle, a mathematical theorem that says that *if* P occurs (e.g., safe environment) *then* Q has an opportunity to occur (e.g., self-actualization). The *if–then* principle contextualizes the importance of the counselor's responsibility in setting the foundation for a safe counseling environment. Rogers believed that safe therapeutic environments ignited the client's ability to discover his full potential. Fully aware of the need to support the client, the counselor's interaction must be completely focused on assisting him in addressing his present life challenge.

In person-centered therapy, a client can discover how her introspection of present experiences impacts her self-perception both positively and negatively. This internal insight is the first step in building the client's positive self-regard by encouraging trust in her ability to succeed. This first step opens the door to nonjudgmental (of self and others) living. This new positive thinking fuels healthier choices and motivates the client to take action to improve her present situation. Self-regard is directly influenced by the reactions and responses of the counselor.

Therapy Overview

Rogers' main goal in therapy was for clients to learn to "focus attention on the doing of things rather than outcomes" (Rogers, 1961, p. 171). Person-centered therapy in action is clearly a self-directed process whereby the client is supported—not led—by the counselor. Because the client is the center of her own world, logically she is the most effective determinant of the behaviors that are limiting her potential. This introspection encourages the client to participate in a world that is constantly changing and to appreciate the benefits of understanding this reality.

Thorn (1992) pointed out the need for the counselor to be real and genuine. This assists in demystifying the counseling process so that it becomes an encounter between two equals. All willingness to understand the client's perceived struggle is centered on a counselor, who is fully present, focused, and authentically interested in the client's efforts. Person-centered therapy considers the mindset and present actions of the counselor to be of the utmost importance in helping the client progress positively down the road of self-change.

1. Rogers' therapeutic approach suggests the counselor:
    a. be present with the client and adhere to the three core conditions authentically. The process of therapy occurs as a natural byproduct of these actions.
    b. develop a list of structured questions that pace the client to his own discovery.
    c. develop a hierarchy of needs to teach the client to self-actualize.
    d. discover what is going on in the unconscious mind of the client, using a strategy such as dream analysis.

The core conditions of effective person-centered therapy are the concepts of empathy, congruence, and warm regard on the part of the therapist.

1. *Empathy*—the skill of being authentically interested in the client's view of the world and his ability to overcome present life challenges. Rogers (1951) explained how counselor empathy can unlock the client's inner ability to discover his full potential. Rogers believed that the power of empathy is not only helpful but is absolutely essential to the therapeutic process.

2. *Congruence*—when the counselor's actions are fully harmonious with her thoughts and behavior. Rogers (1980) referred to this act as being genuine, real, and truthful to the client's needs. In order to achieve congruence to the client's needs, Rogers was convinced the counselor also needs to be congruent and genuine to herself.

3. *Warm regard* (also known as *unconditional positive regard*)—when the counselor's support and observations are never negatively influenced by the client's particular behavioral choices. Rogers (1961) taught that every action or nonaction is seen as a valued choice, as long as it does not directly put the client or others in immediate danger.

Person-centered therapy is regarded as nondirective—the client's thinking determines the direction of counseling (Barrett-Lennard, 1999). However, Rogers encouraged asking "safe" questions to gain an understanding of the client's actions and choices.

2. What are Rogers' three core conditions of effective therapy?
   a. warm regard, empathy, and congruency
   b. warm regard, empathy, and active listening
   c. compassion, respect, and empathy
   d. congruency, empathy, and active listening

3. Person-centered theory was originally called:
   a. how to make friends and influence others.
   b. client-centered theory.
   c. humanistic oriented theory.
   d. none of the above.

4. *Incongruence* can be defined as:
   a. the gap between the real self and the ideal self.
   b. the counselor's commitment to being nonjudgmental.
   c. the counselor's willingness to explore the client's past.
   d. both a and b.

5. *Warm regard* can be defined as:
   a. when the counselor asks permission before asking questions.
   b. when the counselor in a kind voice challenges the client's present behavior.
   c. when the counselor's regard and support are never impacted negatively by the client's particular behavioral choices.
   d. when the counselor pays attention to the client's nonverbal cues.

6. *Actualizing tendency* can be defined as:
   a. awareness of one's deficits in problem solving.
   b. one's awareness of questions that explore life balance.
   c. the awareness gained from self-forgiving.
   d. the awareness of potential in a person to solve his problems.

Techniques Overview

Person-centered therapy emphasizes the tone and temperament of the counseling process more than specific techniques (Rogers, 1997). There are a few strategies, not necessarily person-centered therapy techniques, that clearly support Rogers' three core conditions:

1. The counselor creates an *aesthetic counseling* environment, by paying attention to lighting, sound, smell, space, comfort, color, and temperature.
2. The counselor develops his *micro-communication skills*, that is, nonverbal cues, active listening, reflection, paraphrasing, and open-ended questioning (Howatt, 2000).
3. The counselor develops his awareness of *multicultural* and *diversity* issues.
4. The counselor *stays engaged* in the three core conditions throughout the counseling process.
5. The counselor supports the client in developing her action plan by being a *nonjudgmental* sounding board.
6. The counselor *refrains from dictating* his agenda to the client and *stays focused* on the agenda developed by the client.

7. The counselor who works with high-risk populations must *monitor potential risk factors* that may put others or the client in danger. When necessary, the counselor will intervene to preserve safety in a supporting and caring manner.

EXISTENTIAL THERAPY

Everything can be taken from a man but one thing; the last human freedom is to choose one's attitude in any given set of circumstances, to choose one's own way. (Frankl, 1962, p. 109)

A number of individual theorists, two of the most prominent being Victor Frankl and Rollo May, developed a clinical orientation based upon existential philosophy. Existential therapy can be defined as being focused on solving current life challenges, in a cooperative, nondirective, and flexible way. This approach avoids labeling problems, addresses a wide range of human emotions, and is open-ended and phenomenological. *Phenomenology* refers to exploring one's model of the world and experience as a human being. In existential therapy, the client investigates her present set of circumstances to determine the appropriate action needed to live a more fulfilling and authentic life. The goal of this therapy is for the client to live with less fear and fewer questions (e.g., what does it means to be a human being?). Existential therapy addresses core life themes such as feelings of love, anxiety, anomie (loss of one's identity), loneliness, grief, despair, freedom, and creativity. For more information on existential therapy, visit: http://members.aol.com/timlebon/extherapy.htm.

7. Existential counseling's roots come from the study of _____.
   a. religion
   b. psychology
   c. philosophy
   d. sports

Theory Overview

Two guiding principles define existential theory: (1) identification of the client's life anxieties, and (2) development of therapeutic solutions to overcome these anxieties. Existential theory explores *neurotic anxiety*—anxiety that becomes all-controlling and not consistent to a particular situation (e.g., paranoid and worried about work and home to the point that anxiety completely disrupts one's life). At the core of neurotic anxiety lies existential neurosis. Frankl (1962) defined this as a chronic source of anxiety that drives despair within one's sense of self. He believed that neurotic anxiety stems from inauthentic living—the client is unable to manage her anxiety, because she avoids taking responsibility for herself and her actions.

Existential theory addresses three interrelated components that make up the client's view of the world. The first, *Unwelt*, or biological world (environment), is one's internal drives, instincts, and needs. The second, *Mitwelt*, or personal community, focuses on interpersonal relationships. The third, *Eigenwelt*, focuses on the relationship with one's self, such as self-awareness and self-relatedness. In existential theory, promoting personal insight into these different components prompts the client to discover the root cause of her life anxiety.

May and Yalom (2001) defined six themes that, unaddressed, create anxiety and inauthentic living:

1. *Responsibility*—all human beings are responsible for their own choices. This self-awareness frees the client from perceived external controls.

2. *Freedom*—all human beings have the choice to define who they are. Not making this choice is an inauthentic action that denies the client's ability to take responsibility for his own self.

3. *Isolation*—one major struggle for human beings is the knowledge that they will die alone. In the end, to be free from isolation, it is important to accept death and not fear it.

4. *Self-Awareness*—all human beings, to be fully alive, must live in the present. The past and the future are not real, and living there will prevent self-awareness in the now and limit the potential to live authentically in the present.

5. *Personal meaning*—the majority of human beings struggle to find their life purpose and meaning in this world. For a rewarding life, the client must learn to define his own meaning of life, and come to peace with this choice.

6. *Angst* (anxiety or apprehension often accompanied by depression)—many clients will spend a lifetime coping with anxiety associated with being a human being. The existential solution is to not hide from it but to challenge it. When the client accepts anxiety as a part of his life, he will be better prepared to move on and deal with other existential core themes such as guilt and self-awareness.

8. Existential psychology is the study of:
   a. the meaning of being a human being.
   b. the meaning of human religion.
   c. the meaning of evolution.
   d. the meaning of human choice.

9. Which is not an existential core life theme?
   a. freedom
   b. death
   c. money
   d. responsibilities

Therapy Overview

Existential therapy provides the client with a forum to identify maladaptive defenses and unconscious anxieties that originate from a personal struggle to cope with core life themes. Existential therapy by design is intended to help the client escape from a mental state defined as a condition of meaninglessness (*existential vacuum*) and internal guilt arising from a belief that one isn't able to live up to one's full potential (*existential guilt*). The counselor's objective is to assist the client in transcending significant past life events, become alive, and live in the present. When the client lives in the moment he is better prepared to make the daily choices needed to move toward authentic living (May, 1983). Van Deurzen-Smith (1987) explained that existential therapy is not a method or model for fixing the sick, like the traditional medical model; rather, it is a therapeutic approach to help the client find his own solutions. May (1983) taught that existential therapy is a powerful tool to help clients grasp reality.

The following model, adapted from Mahrer's (1996) 4-Step Existential Helping Process, illustrates how to implement existential therapy:

1. *Being in the moment*—the counselor tunes into her own feelings and thoughts. Once this is accomplished, she can better assist the client. In this process, both counselor and client identify emotions that come up in therapy, and put names to both emotions and thoughts. The

goal is to reach the deepest emotions, because the deeper the emotion, the closer the client is to being authentic.

2. *Integrating the felt experience into primary relationships*—the counselor helps the client explore his present emotions to relate to them and ultimately see the impact emotions have on present life and relationships.

3. *Making connections to the past*—the client organizes his internal resources (learned life skills) as the counselor cautiously coaches him through past situations that caused difficulty. Together, the client and counselor explore how the contemporary situation could be different using newfound coping skills. The client then focuses on the future as being pure, developing awareness of the choices being made in the moment.

4. *Integrating what has been learned*—in this stage, client and counselor together format a clear action plan of what choices the client will make to become more authentic and establish life meaning.

10. The *existential vacuum* can be defined as:
    a. a condition of being trapped in anger.
    b. a condition of meaninglessness due to not being able to find meaning in life.
    c. a condition of being trapped in guilt based on past choices.
    d. a condition of helplessness.

11. *Phenomenology* can be explained as the study of:
    a. a person's beliefs about the past.
    b. a person's perception of the future.
    c. a person's motivation for finding the meaning of life.
    d. a person's subjective reality and experience as a human being.

12. Which is not an existential technique?
    a. presence
    b. deflection of problem
    c. identification of core life themes
    d. hypnosis

Techniques Overview

Because many authors have contributed to the development of existential therapy, several different techniques have developed within the field. Here are five examples of contemporary existential techniques:

1. *Existential elucidation*—This strategy first surveys existential issues (e.g., guilt and anxiety) that are the primary sources of the client's anxiety (Frankl, 1962). The counselor uses core listening skills to look for opportunities to support and challenge the presenting existential themes, such as: death awareness, freedom, choice, and the quest for meaning. When a theme is found, it is explored and discussed fully in the context of the choices available.

2. *Identification of core life theme*—The counselor asks the client: "What is the hardest thing about living?" This starts the exploration of present life challenges. The counselor then asks the client to write her ten most important life challenges (e.g., balancing home and work). The desired outcome is to help the client become aware of her present internal fears and anxiety, while simultaneously defining what is important to her. This often becomes a definable place for therapy to begin since it has outlined both ends of the continuum of fears and desires for the client.

3. *Present state description*—The client defines his present thinking and then verbally explores the consequences of that mindset. It is important that this verbalizing occur with a trusted person (May, 1983). This activity helps the client be aware of his true state of mind, thus creating the opportunity for him to determine which core life themes to address to achieve life fulfillment.

4. *Deflection of problems*—The client is asked to look beyond her present problems (e.g., fear of the opposite sex) and consider the healthy choices and actions of a person who is not fearful of the opposite sex (e.g., the counselor). This activity prompts the client to identify skills that would add value to her life. For the client who can look to the future and see success, this introspection can help her move beyond her present fear (Frankl, 1962). Unless the client can see a future, it will be challenging for her to make healthy choices in the present. The counselor asks open-ended questions that help pace the client out of her present thinking to a future point where her problem is no more. When the client can create a future, she has a greater chance to map out an effective set of steps to get to where she wants to be.

5. *Presence*—This is when the counselor makes the commitment to be both authentic and in the moment with the client. The counselor does this by being an active participant in the therapeutic process and engaging the client with meaningful questions and dialogue. This is an excellent tool in improving the counseling process (Yalom, 1980).

13. Responsibility can be defined from an existential therapy point of view as:
    a. human beings are responsible when they learn to be honest with themselves.
    b. human beings are not responsible for their own choices; it is the responsibility of the counselor to make choices for the client.
    c. human beings are responsible for their own choices, and this self-awareness, when fully understood, is a key to freeing them from perceived controls.
    d. both b and d.

14. A *restrictive* existence can be defined as:
    a. when a person consciously discovers the magnitude and impact of her action or participation in her own life challenges.
    b. when a person makes the choice to give up on defining the meaning of life.
    c. when a person is not consciously aware of the magnitude and impact of his action or participation in his own life challenges.
    d. when a person avoids taking responsibility for her life.

ANALYTICAL PSYCHOANALYSIS: CARL JUNG

Dear Mr. Wilson,

. . . . I am strongly convinced that the evil principle prevailing in this world leads the unrecognized spiritual need into perdition, if it is not counteracted either by real religious insight or by the protective wall of human community . . . .

Yours sincerely,
C. G. Jung[1]

---

[1] From http://www.thejaywalker.com/pages/jung_ltr.html

Carl G. Jung was interested not only in the mind and body; he was also fascinated with spirituality. Jung started out as a student of Freud but later separated from Freud to establish his non-directive, holistic analytical psychoanalysis, which stresses the importance of finding life balance amongst three areas: physical, mental, and spiritual. An active, thought-provoking writer, Jung published extensively. Rich in content, his body of work includes his correspondence with Freud and an eighteen-volume series of his collective works. Jung's writing and research are the platform for the development of the modern day **Myers-Briggs Type Personality Indicator** (to experience this assessment go to http://www.humanmetrics.com/cgi-win/JTypes1.htm). For more information on Jung, visit: http://www.cgjungpage.org/.

Theory Overview

Analytical psychoanalysis posits that a client will grow personally when he finds a healthy balance between his *conscious mind* (external world) and his *unconscious mind* (internal world). Instincts such as hunger, thirst, sex, aggression, and individualization consciously and unconsciously impact the sense of self. Jung promoted the idea that these two subsystems, working in tandem to compensate for one another make up the *psyche* (Howatt, 2000).

In analytical psychoanalysis, the human psyche is the self-regulating system that influences human behavior. For example, if a client were to develop a strong belief about something consciously, this belief would simultaneously become highly ingrained in his unconscious (Jung, 1964). Analytical psychoanalysis explores present behavior at a conscious level, however Jung postulated that to get to the root problem, one must understand the client's unconscious mind (Corey, 2001).

Jung (1956) believed that the unconscious mind was made up of two parts: the *collective* unconscious mind (a pool of knowledge and wisdom) and the *individual* unconscious mind (unique to each individual). Jung taught that the collective unconscious mind was shared and universal, meaning that all human beings posses the same mental pool of energy, thoughts, and awareness. Furthermore, Jung (1964) determined that the client's unconscious mind was made up of three interconnected components: (1) *ego*—the center of conscious thinking, (2) *personal unconscious*—representing every experience forgotten that may be easily available if needed at a conscious level, and (3) *nonpersonal unconscious*—the database of archetypes. Instead of developing a formal theory of personality, analytical psychoanalysis uses the division of the unconscious mind to discover how to best work with the client to achieve life balance.

The challenge for Jung was to develop a platform that assisted both the client and the counselor in communicating with the unconscious mind. Jung did so by identifying various *archetypes* that acted as the primary communication medium with the unconscious mind. Archetypes are inborn psychic perceptions, emotions, and behaviors that are universal to all human beings (Corey, 2001). Jung (1964) developed a universal set of symbols to identify core archetypes chosen from folklore, myths and art. Each symbol represented a particular archetype and was given an assigned meaning. Some of Jung's most common archetypes were:

> *Shadow archetype*—identifies in the conscious mind concepts that the client does not like, or want to acknowledge about herself
>
> *Persona archetype*—bridges the real world and the inner self; it is the adapter, and is why each client may interact with the real world somewhat differently in similar circumstances
>
> *Animus and Anima*—the animus is the personification of all male tendencies in a woman's psyche, and the anima is the personification of all female tendencies in a man's psyche

Self—represents the greatness that is within each human being and which defines the mean-
ingfulness in life.

Jung used his list of archetypes as his core strategy for processing and interpreting the insights
from the client's unconscious mind in therapy. Jung called this process **guiding messages**
(Howatt, 2000).

15. Jung influenced the creation of what personality assessment?
    a. Myers-Briggs Type Indicator
    b. DISC
    c. MMPI
    d. SASSI

16. Jung determined the unconscious mind included both:
    a. the collective unconscious mind and the individual unconscious mind.
    b. the present collective unconscious mind and the past collective unconscious mind.
    c. the collective unconscious mind and the shared unconscious mind.
    d. none of the above.

17. Core *archetypes* help define:
    a. individual spirituality.
    b. a universal bridge of commonality among all people.
    c. a mapping system to explain conscious thinking.
    d. both b and c.

18. Jung's identified five core themes included:
    a. individualism.
    b. career.
    c. relationships.
    d. both a and c.

Therapy Overview

Analytical psychoanalysis, for the most part, involved dream analysis (Hackney & Cormier,
2001). In this process Jung would provide the client with an interpretation by first tracking
the occurrence of various archetypes that occurred in the dreams. Jung would then interpret
the meaning of the archetypes to provid insight into the client's present behaviors, motivations,
and actions (Jung, 1964). The actual process of dream analysis and the application of Jung's
archetypes are beyond the scope of this chapter. To effectively work with the unconscious
mind through dream analysis takes a great deal of training and experience (Kaufmann, 2001).
However, these components of analytical psychoanalysis can be used by an addiction counselor.

Jung (1956) identified five core themes essential in achieving life balance:

1. *Relationships*—to learn there are minimal differences between the sexes. Men and women
   are more alike than different.
2. *Spirituality*—for each client, the understanding of God is a very individualistic experience. Jung thought that without spirituality a client was incomplete, and would be
   challenged to achieve a meaningful life.

3. *Mid-life Crisis*—Jung worked with many clients in their forties who were experiencing a "mid-life crisis." It appeared to Jung that this age group first needed to accept who they were before they could enjoy the rest of their lives. Some of the issues commonly associated with a mid-life crisis were marriage, career, money, spirituality, and health.

4. *Death*—Jung believed each soul continued after death. Jung further believed it was important for clients to come to terms with death, and to understand that life is a journey.

5. *Individualism*—Jung coined the term *individualism instinct*, which he defined as a client's attempt to find his individual place in the world. Jung believed that internal forces motivated each client to define who he was as an individual.

Techniques Overview

The following two techniques are congruent with Jung's work for addressing the five core life themes:

1. *Spirituality*—The encouragement of exploring one's spirituality may open a door to finding meaning and purpose in life (Chopra, 1994). This can be done in the form of a suggestion such as, "Some people find spiritual exploration as a strategy for finding more meaning in life. Would you be interested in exploring this option?" The client will then need to define his actions to undertake such an exploration. Assigning reading such as Deepak Chopra's *Ageless Body, Timeless Mind: The Quantum Alternative to Growing* can help the client to process the connection between the mind, body, and spirituality.

2. *Life Coaching*—Life coaching helps a client find personal balance both at home and at work. Coaching provides a process for guiding a client in determining her life goals and what she can do to achieve them (Whitworth, House, Sandahl, & Kimsey-House, 1998). For more information on coaching, visit: http://www. coachinc.com/CoachU/default.asp?s=1.

19. Which of the following best explains Jung's argument for promoting spirituality?
    a. a safe task and focus to help a client learn about life
    b. the missing link for mental health
    c. both a and b
    d. a component critical to achieving life balance

20. Jung believed that each human being had both:
    a. the female (animus) and male (anima).
    b. the parent (anima) and child (animus).
    c. the male (anima) and female (animus).
    d. the male (animus) and female (anima).

21. Which of the following statements best represents Jung's view on spirituality?
    a. Without spirituality a person could be complete, though the path to life balance would be more difficult.
    b. Without spirituality a person was incomplete, and would not be able to truly find the full meaning of life.
    c. Spirituality was something for people to strive for throughout life.
    d. Without spirituality a person is doomed to have a painful life.

INDIVIDUAL PSYCHOLOGY: ALFRED ADLER

"We must be able to see with his eyes and listen with his ears" (Adler, 1958, p. 72).

Alfred Adler, like Jung, began his career as a student of Freud but later withdrew from Freud's Psychoanalytic Society in Vienna. Adler's orientation evolved to the opposite end of Freud's psychoanalysis. His theory of individual psychology can be described as goal-directed, cognitive-behavioral oriented, phenomenological, and holistic. Adler believed that human experiences such as interacting with others and societal influences impacted behavior. He referred to all human beings as being **mitmenschen** (equal fellows), who want to fit into society. During the next twenty-six years after leaving Freud until his death in 1937, Adler wrote eleven books on this theory, all translated into English. Today his theory continues to receive strong support in academic and therapeutic circles. For example, the University of Texas publishes *Journal of Individual Psychology: The Journal of Adlerian Theory, Research & Practice* (http://www.utexas.edu/utpress/journals/jip.html). For more information on Adler, visit: International Association of Individual Psychology: http://www.iaiponline.org/

Theory Overview

Individual psychology operates under the core assumption that a client defines life goals based on internal beliefs. Corey (2001, p. 109) reports that one of Adler's key themes was, "It is not what you are born with; it is what you do with what you are born with." Individual psychology focuses on the here and now. Adler believed that all human beings desire to fit into society, meaning an inclusive system called *society as a whole* or the *social interest*. Because of this thinking, Adler determined that a client's life challenges could not be studied in therapeutic isolation but needed to be within the context of her interaction with various external stimuli. This insight inspired Adler to take the time to learn about each client's social context (e.g., his role within the family), so as to better understand the motivations for his present behavior.

Adler noted that most clients who request the help of a counselor are generally more discouraged than mentally ill. Individual psychology is committed to helping clients achieve a profound insight and awareness of current life circumstances—an "Ah-ha" experience. Adler (1969) believed that this "self-actualizing experience" would fuel new healthy lifestyle choices needed to solve life challenges. Grounded in the core concept that every individual has the power of self-determination to choose his own goals, Adler (1958) explained that all humans are internally motivated and internally programmed at birth to strive for life mastery and superiority (over self, not others). Adler (1969) refers to this internal program as *the road to becoming*. Discouragement puts one at risk for developing life problems (e.g., an addictive disorder to compensate for discouragement). Hence, a principal goal of Adler's counseling strategy is to help the client gain personal insight, so that he can move from discouragement to encouragement. Adler believed that for a client to live a healthy life he needs to be able to compensate and adjust to the challenges of life (Kottler, 2002).

Individual psychology posits that each person traveling the road to becoming, is faced with five important life tasks. Success in each life task reduces feelings of inferiority and supports fulfilling life goals. Adler identified these five life tasks as:

1. *Friendship*—the need to have a circle of friends who are interested in the person's well-being, as well as having others to care about. All of these relationships must be supportive, nonjudgmental, and never at the expense of another human being.
2. *Work*—the need for meaningful work, to be a contributing part of society.
3. *Love*—the need to know that one is loved, to be able to receive and return love.
4. *Self-acceptance*—the need to feel accepted as a valuable and important person.
5. *Spiritual dimension*—a connection with one's spiritual being, to feel grounded and fulfilled.

Adler was interested in the family constellation (members of the nuclear family) because in this primary unit children develop socially (Howatt, 2000). Individual psychology is structured around five family positions: oldest, second of only two, middle, youngest, and only. All family members take one of these roles that are not necessarily determined by chronological age, and each position has a common set of challenges. Adler believed it essential for a therapist to seek to understand, from the client's model of the world, how his family unit may have positively or negatively impacted his development. He believed that study of the family constellation assisted the counselor in identifying the linkage between the client's childhood experiences and his present perception of his interaction with the world.

22. What statement best represents Adler's theory?
    a. All human beings define their own life goals, based on their internal beliefs.
    b. Human beings are searching to better understand their unconscious mind.
    c. All human beings are looking for the meaning of life.
    d. None of the above.

23. Which was *not* one of Adler's family positions?
    a. oldest
    b. second of two
    c. second of three
    d. only

Individual psychology has several core concepts:

Person—every client has his own personality, views, beliefs, and goals. Every person wants the same outcome: to be a part of the social interest and be an individual.

Life Purpose—every client defines his life purpose. This occurs from an internal set of rules called *fictional finalism.*

Fictional Finalism—rules that are the driving forces. They are often rigid, inaccurate, and as a result, negatively impact daily lifestyle choices.

Fear of Inferiority—fear of not being good enough. When this fear becomes dominant, it increases anxiety. This can breed faulty assumptions about the client's potential to succeed.

Discouragement—when a client feels that she is inferior and not good enough, she may be at risk of developing compensating behaviors (e.g., addiction) to feel a sense of superiority (control). Paradoxically, the more the client engages in these at-risk behaviors, the further they will move away from the social interest.

Private Logic—is the way a client see themselves and the world. Exploring private logic helps the client discover and create the internal "Ah-ha" experience.

Social Interest—the desire to become accepted and a contributing member of society. Individual psychology works to guide a client to becoming a part of the social interest.

24. Adler's five life tasks included which of the following?
    a. physical health
    b. education
    c. spiritual dimension
    d. parenting

25. What is the core driving force for all human beings, according to Adler?
    a. to feel they are a part of the social interest
    b. to discover one's private logic
    c. to define a meaningful life purpose
    d. to grow old in a loving relationship

26. What are the four stages of Adler's therapy?
    a. rapport, assessment, awareness/insight, and action planning
    b. rapport, dream analysis, awareness/insight, and action planning
    c. rapport, assessment, awareness/insight, and reassessment
    d. rapport, assessment, action planning, and follow up

27. *Fictional finalism* can best be defined as:
    a. rules that are the driving forces behind our life goals that define potential.
    b. rules that come from the social interest that define a person's potential.
    c. the frame of reference for individual life goals.
    d. all of the above.

Therapy Overview

Adler's therapy provides a structured process to help the client learn how to make new choices. Adler has four incremental stages of therapy:

1. *Rapport*—the first role of the counselor is to build a trusting relationship with the client. Corey (2001, p. 117) explains, "Adlerian counselors seek to first make person-to-person contact with clients, rather than starting with the problem."

2. *Assessment*—individual psychology uses a prescribed initial assessment format, a designed questionnaire, somewhat similar to what most addictions agencies use (e.g., intake assessment questionnaire). The assessment guides the counselor along a structured process for the purpose of discovering a clear hypothesis of the core issues that will be addressed in counseling.

3. *Awareness of Commitment*—the insight and comment stage. In this step the client and counselor evaluate the findings of the initial assessment, with the goal of obtaining an "Ah-ha" experience for the client. Often the counselor will use a technique Adler called *sharing a hunch*—the counselor takes a stab at what the core issue may be (Howatt, 2000). The counselor may say, "Could it be . . .?" and fills in the blanks. The counselor may need to make several attempts to get the client to discover his "Ah-ha" experience. Once the insight is obtained, the counselor will determine the client's level of motivation and ownership.

4. *Action Plan*—in the final stage, the client and the counselor take the insights the client has discovered to develop the appropriate action plan, provided the client is motivated.

Techniques Overview

In addition to the virtually hundreds of individual psychology techniques that come from Alder and his followers, Adler made it clear that a counselor must also draw on her own creativity and passion to move the counseling process forward. In other words, if the counselor has a technique that is legal and moral and helps the client learn consciously, Adler would be supportive of the strategy.

Below are seven examples of individual psychology techniques:

1. *Acting "as if"*—The goal of this technique is to help the client form a mindset of success. The expression "fake it until you make it" is the basis for this technique. The client is encouraged to act in a manner that would represent the desired thinking or behavior (e.g., happy at work). Adler believed it was important for a client to become aware of core competencies quickly. This technique was intended to get a client moving forward to feeling encouraged as quickly as possible.

2. *Catching oneself*—The counselor helps the client become aware of self-destructive or irrational thoughts. For example, the client may express how dumb he is. The counselor points this out, and then encourages the client to monitor this thinking in his daily activities. The goal is to teach the connection of internal beliefs and life fulfilment.

3. *Encouragement*—One of the counselor's core responsibilities is to recognize and point out positive qualities whenever the client presents the opportunity.

4. *"Magic wand"*—This is a straightforward metaphor in which the client is asked to pretend that she has a magic wand and to wish for what she would like to have in her life right now, regardless of her present situation.

5. *Offering Advice*—A directive approach, when the counselor determines there is an opportunity to make a suggestion, she first asks for permission.

---

28. Adlerian techniques relied on:
    a. counselor creativity and willingness to help the client grow.
    b. counselor's ability to adhere to set Adlerian techniques.
    c. counselor's ability to use behavioral techniques.
    d. none of the above.

29. Adler defined faulty thinking as:
    a. thinking that can negatively impact how a person interacts with the world.
    b. thinking that is judgmental and holds a person in the past.
    c. when a person thinks he is perfect.
    d. both a and b.

30. Adler offered the client advice when:
    a. the client was being disruptive.
    b. the counselor saw an opportunity to make a positive suggestion.
    c. the client did not know what to do.
    d. never.

TABLE 14.1

Summary of the 3 Ts

Criteria 3 Ts	Person-Centered Therapy (Carl Rogers)	Existential Therapy	Analytical Psychoanalysis (Carl Jung)	Individual Psychology (Alfred Adler)
Theory—highlights from an addiction counselor's perspective.	All clients have the potential from within to heal themselves. The counselor's main function is to support the client to help her discover her own potential, with the goal of self-actualizing.	Most clients are looking to define the meaning of life. Existential psychology helps teach the client how to live life authentically by overcoming core life anxieties (e.g., death).	Jung taught clients how to normalize their life challenges. His model promotes the commonality among all human beings. It also promotes the value of life balance: spirituality, body, and mind.	All clients are driven by an internal conscious need to fit in and be accepted by society. Adler's theory helps clients find a new path to do so. Clients are viewed as discouraged, not sick.
Therapy—highlights from an addiction counselor's perspective.	The process of therapy is fundamentally grounded in the attention and the engagement of the counselor with the client, who practices the three core conditions.	Core life themes are often the main source of life anxiety and meaninglessness. The goal of therapy is to move beyond anxiety and define meaning.	All of us have the ability to tap into universal solutions. The core action for the counselor is to help the client overcome the five common life challenges.	Adlerian therapy has four steps: 1. Rapport 2. Assessment 3. Awareness/Insight 4. Action Planning This process focuses on helping the client develop personal insight and motivation.
Techniques—highlights from an addiction counselor's perspective.	Empathy, warm regard, and Congruency are the core processes for building trust and a safe environment.	Exploration of core life themes, using techniques such as deflection (see techniques in existential section).	Exploring the meaning of life by exploring spirituality and life coaching.	Adlerian therapy is not so much focused on techniques as it is on the client. However, Adler had many techniques such as "the magic wand."

KEY TERMS

actualizing tendency: The internal drive to achieve personal fulfillment, persevere, and improve.

archetypes: Inborn psychic perceptions, emotions, and behaviors that are universal to all human beings.

guiding messages: The processing and interpreting of the client's insights from the unconscious mind.

humanistic philosophy: A way of treating and empowering people with respect and dignity.

mitmenschen: Equal fellows.

Myers-Briggs Type Indicator: An instrument developed by Isabel Briggs Myers and her mother, Katherine Cook Briggs. This instrument was developed out of their study of the various psychological types Carl Jung created to explain human behavior.

phenomenology: The study of discovering the client's conscious view of the world, with the outcome of learning and understanding how he experiences and sees the world.

psyche: Interaction of the conscious and unconscious mind.

psychoanalysis: A form of therapy that helps individuals overcome personal challenges through working with both the conscious and unconscious mind. This form of therapy requires expert training as well as years of supervision.

social interest: The area of social interaction Adler defined for all human beings.

DISCUSSION QUESTIONS

1. What are Rogers' core conditions and how could an addiction counselor use them in practice?
2. How could an addiction counselor use existential therapy with addictive disorder clients?
3. How could Adler's theory be used to help a client design life goals?
4. What core themes from Jung's work have applications for addictions counseling?
5. What are five techniques from this chapter that could be used effectively in addictions counseling?
6. From an Adlerian perspective, what are some core considerations as to why clients may not be successful in life?
7. Explain which of the four theories in this chapter best suits your counseling orientation.
8. How do the classical theories assist in addiction counseling?
9. Why can Rogers' work be used in any counseling orientation?
10. To assist a client in addressing a spiritual issue, which of the four classic theories would you use and why?

SUGGESTED FURTHER READING

Corey, G. (2001). *Theory and practice of counseling and psychotherapy* (6th ed.). Pacific Grove, CA: Brooks/Cole.

Corey provides an excellent overview of classical theories, as well as an effective process for developing one's own integrated counseling orientation.

Corsini, R. J., & Wedding, D. (Eds.). (2001). *Current psychotherapist* (6th ed.). Itasca, IL: F. E. Peacock.

This is probably the most technically detailed book on theory on the market today. for those who want to study counseling theory in detail, this is a must.

Howatt, W. A. (2000). *The Human services counseling toolbox: Theory, development, techniques, and resources.* Belmont, CA: Brooks/Cole.

Developed with students who were learning how to become addiction counselors. It is a reference tool containing information on theory, techniques, and strategies for working with persons with addictive disorders.

REFERENCES

Adler, A. (1958). *What life should mean to you.* New York: Capricorn.
Adler, A. (1969). *The science of living.* New York: Doubleday Anchor.

Barrett-Lennard, G. (1999). *Carl Rogers helping systems: Journey and substance.* London: Sage.

Chopra, D. (1994). *Ageless body, timeless mind: The quantum alternative to growing old.* New York: Random House.

Corey, G. (2001). *Theory and practice of counseling and psychotherapy* (6th ed.). Pacific Grove, CA: Brooks/Cole.

Frankl, V. (1962). *Man's search for meaning.* New York: Washington Square.

Hackney, H. L., & Cormier, L. S. (2001). *The professional counselor: A process guide to helping.* Needham Heights, MA: Pearson.

Howatt, W. A. (2000). *The human services counseling toolbox: Theory, development, techniques, and resources.* Belmont, CA: Brooks/Cole.

Jung, C. G. (1956). *Two essays on analytical psychology.* New York: Meridien.

Jung, C. G. (1964). *Man and his symbols.* Garden City, NY: Doubleday.

Kaufmann, Y. (2001). Analytical psychotherapy. In R. J. Corsini & D. Wedding (Eds.), *Current psychotherapist* (6th ed.). (pp. 99–131). Itasca, IL: F. E. Peacock.

Kottler, J. A. (2002). *Theories in counseling and therapy: An experiential approach.* Boston: Allyn & Bacon.

Mahrer, A. (1996). *The complete guide to experiential psychotherapy.* New York: Wiley.

May, R. (1983). *The discovery of being.* New York: W. W. Norton.

May, R., & Yalom, I. (2001). Existential psychotherapy. In R. J. Corsini & D. Wedding (Eds.), *Current psychotherapist* (6th ed.) (pp. 273–302). Itasca, IL: F. E. Peacock.

Rogers, C. (1942). *Counseling and psychotherapy.* Boston: Mifflin.

Rogers, C. (1951). *Client-centered counseling.* Boston: Mifflin.

Rogers, C. (1961). *On becoming a person: A therapist's view of psychotherapy.* Boston: Mifflin.

Rogers, C. (1980). *A way of being.* Boston: Mifflin.

Rogers, C. R., & Sardford, R. C. (1989). Clients-center psychotherapy. In H. I. Kaplan & B. J. Sadock (Eds.), *Comprehensive Text book of Psychiatry* (pp. 1482–1502). Baltimore, MD: Williams & Williams.

Rogers, C. (1997). *Carl Rogers on personal power: Inner Strength and its revolutionary impact.* New York: Delacorte Press.

Thorne, B. (1992). *Carl Rogers.* Newbury Park, CA: Sage.

Todd, J., & Bohart, C. B. (1994). *Foundations of clinical and counseling psychology.* New York: HarperCollins.

Van Deurzen-Smith, E. (1987). *Existential counseling in practice.* London: Sage.

Whitworth, L., House, H., Sandahl, P., & Kimsey-House, H. (1998). *Co-active coaching: New skills for coaching people toward success in work and life.* Boston: MeansBusiness Inc.

Yalom, I. (1980). *Existential psychotherapy.* New York: Basic Books.

15

Cognitive-Behavioral Models

William A. Howatt
Nova Scotia Community College

TRUTH OR FICTION?

___ *1. William Glasser is the author of REBT.*
___ *2. There is one dominant behavioral therapy.*
___ *3. Aaron Beck is known for the treatment of depression.*
___ *4. Albert Ellis' model helps clients overcome their irrational beliefs.*
___ *5. Reality therapy is the counseling process for choice theory.*
___ *6. Behavioral strategies are incorporated in Ellis, Beck, and Glasser orientations.*
___ *7. Choice theory was developed before reality therapy.*
___ *8. Beck developed his therapy based solely on the work of Albert Ellis.*
___ *9. Choice theory teaches clients how to develop an internal locus of control.*
___ *10. Ellis' theory is based on his ADC model.*
___ *11. Beck explored cognitive distortions with the client.*
___ *12. Empathy is a core element of behavioral therapy.*
___ *13. Glasser determined that all behavior is total.*
___ *14. Beck developed the cognitive triad.*
___ *15. Both Ellis and Glasser discussed basic needs.*

Cognitive-behavioral approaches all stress the importance of accepting responsibility for one's choice and behavior. (Kottler, 2002, p. 101)

Cognitive-behavioral theory emphasizes teaching the client how to take charge of his thinking and behavior. This chapter provides an overview of three major cognitive-behavioral theories that have influenced current counseling theories: William Glasser's choice theory and reality therapy, Albert Ellis' rational emotive behavior therapy (REBT) and Aaron Beck's cognitive-behavioral therapy (CBT). In addition, under the umbrella of behavioral therapy, this chapter will discuss Ivan Pavlov's classical conditioning, B. F. Skinner's operant conditioning, Albert Bandura's social cognitive learning strategy, and ten popular behavioral techniques (Table 15.1).

CHOICE THEORY AND REALITY THERAPY: WILLIAM GLASSER

Choice theory explains that, for all practical purposes, we choose everything we do, including the misery we feel. (William Glasser, 1998, p. 3)

William Glasser was training to be a psychiatrist in the late 1950s when he first observed that positive mental health occurred more frequently in clients who took responsibility for their actions and decisions than in those clients treated principally with psychotropic drugs (Glasser, 1965). And he rejected the general therapeutic trend of reliance on medication as a treatment strategy except in extreme cases such as schizophrenia. Glasser expands upon this logic in his groundbreaking book *Warning: Psychiatry Can Be Hazardous to Your Mental Health* (Glasser, 2003).

During his psychiatric training, Glasser also rejected Freud's work (Glasser, 1965), because he could not accept Freud's thinking that human behavior was controlled by the unconscious mind and early childhood experiences. For the past forty years, Glasser has been committed to developing alternative mental health treatments. The result of this commitment was the development of choice theory and reality therapy. Both choice theory (theory of human behavior) and reality therapy (model of counseling) are phenomenological and cognitive-behavioral in design. Over the course of his career, Glasser founded the William Glasser Institute (http://www.wglasser.com), developed the *Journal for Reality Therapy*, and published twenty books on choice theory and reality therapy.

Theory Overview

Choice theory hinges on the idea of an internal locus of control, which purports that a client can manage his choices internally (Rotter, 1982). Glasser (1984) argues that the majority of the population operates on the premise that an external locus of control, or their external environment, controls them (Howatt, 2000). Because of this perception, many clients think they are trapped and have few choices. Glasser (2000) explains that this manifestation of stimulus–response thinking is at the root of most mental health challenges. For a client to take control of his life, he needs to understand that he manages his own success by internalizing the perception of choice. Glasser (1998) explains that when a client achieves this insight he becomes empowered to make choices. These new choices then motivate the client to change his present behavior. Glasser (1965) taught that a client becomes motivated to change when he determines present behavior is not achieving desired wants, or he learns that he has the ability to make new choices. When the client obtains either frame of reference he has the opportunity to learn how to live a more fulfilling life.

Choice theory begins by teaching that all human beings are motivated by genetically driven basic needs: four conscious and one unconscious. The five basic needs are: (1) *Fun*—enjoyment and pleasure, (2) *Freedom*—ability to move freely and choose activities, (3) *Recognition and self-accomplishment*—acknowledgment and self-worth, (4) *Love and belonging*—supportive relationships, and (5) *Survival* (unconscious need)—food, shelter, and reproduction. Choice theory postulates that every client creates her own internal "photo album" for fulfilling these basic needs (referred to as the client's quality world) and has the choice of what to put in it—meaning that all humans have the same five basic needs, but each will choose different pictures (wants).

Glasser (1998) explains that clients filter the external world through their basic needs. When a client receives external stimuli different from what he wants, he will experience a brief and involuntary sensation of frustration. The purpose of this frustration is to alert the client that his needs are not being met (e.g., child not listening). Choice theory teaches that this signal occurs in the comparing of places, when the client compares what he wants with what he has. This sensation of frustration only occurs when the client perceives that his needs are not being met, and will last only a few microseconds; after that, he makes a choice.

Choice theory postulates that the client's menu of behavioral choices is stored in a cognitive database called *organized behavior*. Glasser (1998) argues that all a client can choose is what he knows or what he creates. Because of potential limitations in these stored learned behaviors, the client can get trapped in ineffective behavior. For example, if a client learns that alcohol reduces stress, he may rely on drinking to deal with stress to the point that alcohol use becomes problematic. Glasser believes that each client has the ability to create new behaviors. In the above instance, for example, if alcohol no longer appears to meet the client's needs, he may choose to use exercise to replace alcohol.

Glasser (1984) explains that all behavior can be described as *total behavior*. Hence, when a client changes her behavior and thinking—her feelings and physiology will change as well. Glasser employs a car metaphor to underscore the interconnected nature of behavior. The car in question is front wheel drive. The front wheels symbolize behavior and thinking, while the rear wheels represent feelings and physiology. The engine corresponds to the five basic client needs (universal to all, but each client will determine what meets his needs) and the steering wheel represents the choice each client has to direct his care. This metaphor promotes the concept that a client can take control of her life by controlling her actions and thinking. Because all behavior is total, any actions a client takes using her front wheels (action and thinking) directly impact her rear wheels (feelings and physiology). Wherever the front wheels go, the rear wheels will follow. Applying this metaphor to real life, a depressed client can change her emotions and get symptomatic relief from depression by choosing a positive, healthy behavior (e.g., playing golf with a friend). Glasser (2000) emphasizes that the healthy actions will positively impact emotions. He believes self-control starts by accepting responsibility for present behavior and thinking.

1. Glasser's five basic needs are:
   a. fun, freedom, passion, survival, and relationships.
   b. fun, freedom, survival, relationships, and achievement.
   c. fun, freedom, survival, recognition, and love.
   d. love, freedom, survival, relationships, and recognition.

2. Choice theory total behavior includes:
   a. behavior, thinking, wants, and physiology.
   b. behavior, thinking, pictures, and physiology.
   c. behavior, needs, feeling, and physiology.
   d. behavior, thinking, feeling, and physiology.

Therapy Overview

Reality therapy is the clinical application of choice theory. Glasser first developed reality therapy in the early 1960s. Then he authored choice theory (formerly called *control theory*) in 1984 because he realized that in order for his counseling process to be accepted in the mainstream, it needed to be grounded in an effective theory explaining the "whys" and "hows" of human behavior.

Reality therapy is taught in a linear process that weaves among three components. The first component is called *setting the counseling environment*. Glasser (2000) insists that a comfortable therapeutic environment creates an opportunity for the client to learn that you can be of value and not a threat. This trust is critical for counseling rapport and is the foundation for successful counseling. The second component is called the *procedures that lead to change*.

> 3. Reality therapy includes:
>   a. setting the environment, procedures that lead to change, and planning.
>   b. client assessment, procedures that lead to change, and planning.
>   c. setting the environment, procedures that lead to change, and relapse prevention.
>   d. none of the above.

This phase of therapy represents the main body of counseling and consists of four strategic questioning areas that you use to understand the client's present situation:

1. Ask the client how she is presently meeting her five needs. How is she determining those needs are not being fulfilled?
2. Ask the client what her wants are to learn what she believes will improve her present situation.
3. Dialogue with the client to define what she is presently doing to get what she wants and how these choices are impacting her total behavior. The goal of this questioning is to increase the client's awareness of the effectiveness of her actions or inactions.
4. Evaluate the client's choices and how she perceives those choices are helping her get what she wants. Then determine what she is willing to do to get what she wants. In this section of questioning, the counselor usually explores concepts from choice theory.

The final component of reality theory is *planning, measuring, and follow-up*. In this straightforward process, the counselor helps the client develop a client-centered action plan; that is, a plan based on what the client can control and realistically do on his own. It is important that the client determine clear measures of progress. Glasser (2000) believes that after a plan is developed, it is important to spend time challenging it to ensure that the client and the counselor have effectively explored potential risks, determined needed core competencies, and put in place relapse prevention strategies, in order to increase the client's chances of success.

> 4. Choice theory describes human behavior as determined by:
>   a. total behavior, comparing places, cortex, and needs.
>   b. total behavior, comparing places, quality world, and needs.
>   c. total behavior, comparing places, hypothalamus, and needs.
>   d. total behavior, comparing places, core values, and needs.
>
> 5. Choice theory posits that all human behavior is:
>   a. predictable and conditioned.
>   b. an attempt to meet basic needs at any moment in time.
>   c. both a and b.
>   d. motivated by the external world.

Techniques Overview

The effectiveness of reality therapy is based on your ability to ask effective questions based on the tenets of choice theory. One helpful process that many professionals trained in reality therapy use is "**WDEP Radio**" a mnemonic created by Robert Wubbolding (1988), as noted below:

W (Want)

According to Glasser (2000), self-evaluating questioning occurs throughout the counseling process, because your client's wants and needs change almost daily. Also, the more wants and needs are explored, the clearer the picture of what the client really wants becomes.
Sample questions:

- What do you want?
- What do you *really* want?
- If you had what you want, what would your life be like?
- What is it you do not want to happen?
- What do you know you need in your life to be happy?

D (Direction and Doing)

The goal of this line of questioning is to assist the client in discovering how her present behavior is or is not working.
Sample questions:

- What are you doing these days to get what you want?
- When you do that, what are you thinking?
- Is what you are doing helping or hurting you?
- When you are thinking that, what do you feel?
- How does your body feel when you are feeling this way?

E (Evaluation)

This line of questioning promotes the linkage between actions and self-responsibility.
Sample questions:

- Does your present behavior have a reasonable chance of getting you what you want right now?
- Can these choices take you in the direction you want to go?
- Is what you are doing helping or hurting you?
- How is what you are presently doing helping you for the long term?
- Would you be interested in learning a new way of doing things?

P (Planning and Commitment)

This is where the therapeutic action plan is designed. Reality therapy suggests that all actions need to be simple, measurable, ongoing, immediate, and client-centered (within the client's knowledge and skills). Finally, the plan must have the client's commitment. When a plan does not work, the client and the counselor will work together to modify it. Reality therapy promotes the mantra "never give up."

Sample questions:

- What is it you want to start doing?
- What do you see as a good plan?
- I have a few ideas. Would you be interested in them as a start?
- How will you measure your plan for success?
- What knowledge and skills do you need to achieve this plan?

6. Reality therapy describes setting the environment as:
   a. when the counselor determines if he likes the client.
   b. when the counselor and the client build a relationship.
   c. not important to the counseling process.
   d. both a and b.

7. Reality therapy assists the client in learning how to live from:
   a. a positive frame of reference.
   b. an external locus of control.
   c. an internal locus of control.
   d. all of the above.

RATIONAL EMOTIVE BEHAVIOR THERAPY: ALBERT ELLIS

"Rational Emotive Behavior Therapy (REBT) is a method of psychotherapy that is intrinsically brief and that also aims to help the client achieve intensive, profoundly philosophical and emotional change." (Albert Ellis, 1996, p. 1)

The author of seventy books and more than seven hundred articles that represent a major contribution to cognitive-behavior theory, Albert Ellis is one of the most influential and prolific psychologists alive today. His therapeutic approach can be described as active-directive; that is, actively asking questions to prompt a client to evaluate his own thinking, with the goal of removing destructive thinking and behavior. For nearly fifty years through his Albert Ellis Institute (http://www.rebt.org), Ellis has been active in writing and teaching his theory, as well as seeing clients on a regular basis.

8. The development of Ellis' core theory can be said to originate from:
   a. years of clinical research.
   b. personal perceptions and life experience.
   c. his studies of Beck's work.
   d. both b and c.

9. Ellis' ABC model includes the following:
   a. activating event, beliefs, emotions, disputing, effect, and new feeling.
   b. activating event, beliefs, behaviors, disputing, effect, and new feeling.
   c. activating event, needs, consequences, disputing, effect, and new feeling.
   d. activating event, beliefs, consequences, disputing, effect, and new feeling.

Theory Overview

Ellis (1996) is committed to the belief that all human beings are born with the ability to determine what they want in their life. Rational emotive behavior therapy (REBT) is a direct and efficient problem-solving method, well suited to Ellis' personality. His self-assurance—some would even say arrogance—enables him to confront his clients about their beliefs and tell them what is rational and what is not (http://www.rebt.org/dr/biography.asp). REBT argues that individual preferences are impacted by the interconnection of culture, upbringing, social supports, and environment. In this matrix, Ellis determines that parenting and early child developments are powerful influences of positive mental health. All clients, regardless of history or preferences, can think rationally as well as irrationally, and their thinking will directly impact how they exist or how they may self-destruct. REBT is grounded in the logic that emotional and behavioral consequences originate from an individual's belief system.

Ellis (2001) teaches that many life problems occur because of a client's self-created, negative, and internally self-defeating thinking. REBT provides a vehicle for assisting the client in understanding his thought process in order to eliminate irrational beliefs that have been leading him down a road of despair. The REBT hypothesis is that irrational beliefs come from the client's illogical set of attitudes and values that are not accurate or in synchrony with the real world. Ellis (Ellis & MacLean, 1997) coined the term ***masturbatory thinking*** to categorize inflexible and rigid thinking that originates from irrational beliefs. A client who is trapped in this thinking becomes caught in the illogical belief that he must always be successful and perfect and ought to know better. When a client becomes trapped in this kind of loop, this faulty logic becomes automatic and will negatively impact his life.

Ellis (2001) purports that irrational beliefs can be observed in several different patterns of thinking. The following are examples of several common belief patterns that REBT resolves:

Low frustration tolerance—a client believes that he can no longer cope with a particular situation and gets upset (e.g., child crying)

Self-criticism—a belief system that turns inward and attacks (e.g., blames self for everything that goes wrong)

Over-generalizing—global beliefs (e.g., everybody is angry)

All-or-nothing thinking—defines the world in clear extremes (e.g., peer does not say hello, client assumes peer no longer likes her)

Self-labeling—a self-proclaimed label (e.g., dummy)

REBT explains that invariably these kinds of irrational beliefs have been created without any evidence or facts. A major downside of irrational thinking is that, if left alone, these beliefs become the primary filter that influences how a client interprets the world. If this filter is not corrected, the client is at risk of developing mental health problems such as anxiety or depression.

The foundation for REBT is based on what Ellis calls the ABCs: *A*ctivating events, *B*eliefs, and *C*onsequences (Ellis, 1962). This model identifies the sequence of illogical, self-validating, negative thinking: A peer raises her voice (activating event). A peer raising her voice upsets the client. The client responds based on some irrational belief (belief), and reacts by feeling hurt and yelling back at the peer in anger (consequence). Ellis' point in this model is the client is often only aware of the A (activating event) and C (consequences); in counseling the main outcome is to bring B (irrational beliefs) to the client's level of awareness.

Therapy Overview

In REBT, the counselor is very active in the therapeutic process, and often will encourage the client to do work both in and out of counseling (Ellis, 1997). REBT purports that it is critical for the counselor to accept clients without judging, though that does not mean supporting or excusing negative behaviors. REBT does not stress the need for rapport and warm regard, like Carl Rogers (see chapter 14) and others. In REBT, the ultimate goal of the therapeutic process is permanent cognitive change. REBT facilitates this change by teaching the client the correlation between internal beliefs and behaviors. Acknowledging this linkage will have a positive impact on the client's perception filters, allowing her to live life autonomously and independently. Ellis (Ellis & MacLean, 1997) wants a client to clearly know that the intention of the therapeutic process is to help her change quickly, so that she can see immediate improvement. REBT will often promote this insight at the beginning of the counseling process, to motivate and encourage the client.

As previously mentioned, REBT is clearly grounded in exploring and analyzing illogical thinking, using the ABC model. The following provides an overview. The first three letters (ABC) are the core theory, and all the letters after C represent the therapeutic process REBT follows to assist the client to overcome irrational beliefs:

A—Activating Events: People, places, or things that bring painful associations.

B—Beliefs: Client can create both rational and irrational beliefs. Faulty thinking and irrational beliefs lie at the core of human problems. Most of these beliefs are programmed and over time become automatic. Irrational beliefs directly influence how a person operates and responds to her world.

C—Consequences: These are the self-defeating behaviors and disturbing emotions attached to beliefs in response to an activating event.

D—Disputing: For a client to get out of his negative loops, irrational beliefs must be challenged in a safe manner. REBT teaches that for a client to move forward he first needs to become aware of his irrational thinking. Several examples of how a counselor can challenge and dispute irrational thinking are as follows (Bishop, 2001):

  Functional disputing—a line of questioning to point out the practical realities of irrational thinking in real time (e.g., how is this kind of thinking presently helping you?)

  Empirical disputing—asking the client for evidence to demonstrate how irrational thinking may be misleading her behaviors and emotions (e.g., where does it say he has to treat you this way?)

  Philosophical disputing—exploring the client's internal model of the world to focus on worst case scenarios, to help him move on to evaluate his processing logic (e.g., if you lost your job, are you saying you would never find another?)

  Disputing strategy—"Stands for doing... there may be many other effective behavioral, emotive, and cognitive interventions that may be helpful, such as: role play, analysis of positive and negative effects of various behaviors" (Bishop, 2001, p. 48). This step help the client understand how her present irrational beliefs are not serving her best interests.

E—Effect: A clear awareness of the illogical thinking leads to the development of internal core competencies. The counselor can choose from literally hundreds of cognitive behavioral techniques to teach the client to think more effectively so as to better cope with activating events.

F—Feeling: When the client overcomes irrational thinking and replaces it with new effective thinking, she will be able to create new consequences that will result in healthier behavior choices and more positive feelings.

10. REBT explains the core component of assisting a client in breaking free from his negative thinking loops is that:
    a. his irrational beliefs must be challenged in a safe manner.
    b. his irrational emotions must be challenged in a safe manner.
    c. his irrational behaviors must be challenged in a safe manner.
    d. both a and b.

11. REBT relies on the following:
    a. techniques similar to Rogerian therapy.
    b. no real techniques; uses the ABC model.
    c. REBT techniques.
    d. a wide variety of techniques from various orientations.

12. REBT describes empirical disputing as the:
    a. counselor asking the client for specific evidence.
    b. counselor's exploration of the client's past thinking.
    c. counselor being confrontational because the client has no facts or proof.
    d. none of the above.

Techniques Overview

Ellis and his followers have created many techniques to assist clients in learning how to think more effectively. A few techniques that can be used with REBT to teach new core skills are as follows:

1. *Continuum line*—Provides the client with a baseline as to how his present thinking is impacting his life (e.g., How do you rate your [e.g., present anxiety] on a scale from 1[low] to 10 [high]?).
2. *Humor*—Use of appropriate humor can help a client make an internal shift to assess that perhaps his present thinking is not serving him well. Ellis believes that humor is healthy and helps a client loosen up, as long as it is not offensive (Ellis, 2001).
3. *Use of analogies or images to illustrate problems*—The creative use of analogies or images to illustrate a problem in a different way can help the client take the focus off herself and reframe a current situation from another perspective.
4. *REBT self-help forms*—Forms developed by Ellis to teach the ABC model (Howatt, 2000). Often the client is asked to complete these forms as homework to practice and incorporate the core concepts of the ABC model into his life. (For more information on these forms visit the Albert Ellis Institute Web site: http://www.rebt.org.)

13. REBT purports that irrational beliefs originate from:
    a. childhood experiences.
    b. academic failure.
    c. low self-esteem.
    d. irrational thinking.

14. REBT teaches that the first step for removing destructive thinking is:
    a. successfully disputing irrational beliefs.
    b. moving beyond the past and looking to the future.
    c. committing to being mentally stronger.
    d. none of the above.

15. REBT promotes which of the following concepts in therapy?
    a. internal locus of control
    b. overcoming irrational thought
    c. beliefs impact emotions and actions
    d. all of the above

COGNITIVE-BEHAVIORAL THERAPY: AARON T. BECK

Cognitive therapy consists of all the approaches that alleviate psychological distress through a medium of correcting faulty conceptions and self-signals. (Beck, 1967, p. 214)

Aaron Beck, M.D., was trained in neurology and joined the Department of Psychiatry at the University of Pennsylvania in 1954, where he is currently University Professor Emeritus of Psychiatry. Beck independently developed his cognitive-behavioral theory (CBT) in 1967, but acknowledges Albert Ellis' influence. Beck's approach can be described as goal-directed, structural, time-limited, and emphasizing internal locus of control. He generally defines all techniques that modify faulty thinking as being cognitive-behavioral. Beck continues to contribute to the evolution of cognitive-behavioral therapy and is universally recognized for his commitment to quantitative and qualitative research in treating depression with CBT. CBT as an alternative to medication has been shown to be an effective and powerful treatment strategy for depression and other cognitive issues. Principal at the Beck Institute (http://www.beckinstitute.org), he has published 375 articles and fourteen books.

16. Beck is best known for his research in treatment success using cognitive therapy with which of the following disorders:
    a. anxiety
    b. addictions
    c. depression
    d. ADHD

Theory Overview

CBT considers that negative thinking sours one's experience of the world. Beck (1967) writes that a client's dysfunctional thinking often comes from internal processing errors, or *systemic bias errors*. These occur when the client takes information from the environment and internally processes and defines this information as pain, loss, and hurt. CBT identifies this kind of faulty processing as the driving force in the creation of many current mental health issues. Eight common CBT examples of systemic bias thinking (dysfunctional thinking) are as follows:

1. *Polarized thinking*—dichotomous thinking (black or white)
2. *Overgeneralization*—perceiving a situation in a particular way and applying the same thinking to all future situations
3. *Labeling and mislabeling*—using dysfunctional thinking from the past to define self and present reality
4. *Magnification and minimization*—reporting a particular situation more or less than it actually is

5. *Selective abstraction*—pushing aside the positive parts and focusing only on the negative
6. *Arbitrary interference*—forming conclusions without evidence
7. *Personalization*—connecting information to oneself from an external situation that has nothing directly to do with oneself, without any logical evidence for the connection
8. *Mind reading*—presuming what others are thinking without proof

Beck (1997) compares the client who misinterprets information from her environment to a scientist who bases results on a faulty experiment. The core of CBT is teaching the client to stop misinterpreting the world. This needs to occur before the client can take charge of her life. Beck (1999) expounds that personality is developed and shaped by the client's internal cognitive schemas. *Cognitive schemas* are the drivers that influence personal views, beliefs, internal values, and life assumptions (Clark, Beck, & Alford, 1999). These cognitive schemas determine how a client interacts and processes stimuli in times of stress. Beck teaches that schemas can be either *functional* (supportive) or *dysfunctional* (nonsupportive). CBT explains that clients can develop many different kinds of schemas in either of these two categories. When a client lives by dysfunctional schemas (e.g., "I am dumb and will never be successful"), he negatively impacts his view of the world and potentially his mental health.

To help a client discover how he views the world, Beck (1997) developed the cognitive triad. The triad is made up of three parts: the client's views of himself, the client's view of his world experiences, and the client's view of his future. The triad's purpose is to teach the client how his present cognitive schemas in each of the three areas are impacting him, and the connection to mental health issues such as depression. The triad (Fig. 15.1) provides a visual interpretation of the different origins of dysfunctional thinking that can negatively impact a client's internal logic.

17. Cognitive therapy teaches that Socratic dialogue is:
   a. questions and conversational dialogue to help the client discover why she is depressed.
   b. questions and conversational dialogue to help the client discover her model of the world.
   c. questions and conversational dialogue to help the client discover what she really wants in life.
   d. questions and conversational dialogue to help the client find peace and happiness.

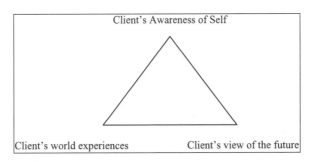

FIG. 15.1. Beck's cognitive triad.

18. Beck calls the dysfunctional thinking that is the root cause for misrepresentation of the environment:
    a. systemic bias.
    b. systemic thinking.
    c. both a and b.
    d. negative cognitive schemas.

Therapy Overview

Beck (1995) believes that it is important for the counselor to build a supportive relationship with the client in the early stages of counseling to dispel fears surrounding the helping process, so the client can derive the maximum benefits from counseling. The therapeutic process of CBT typically follows these stages:

1. *Test the client's present reality.*
2. *Facilitate a reduction of the client's anxiety so that she is ready to grow.*
3. *Teach the client how her beliefs and assumptions are having a negative impact on her present condition.*
4. *Create an action plan to develop the knowledge and skills needed for future success.* (Howatt, 2000)

The success of CBT depends on the client's internal commitment and motivation. For the client to achieve positive outcomes in counseling, she must be an active participant. CBT emphasizes the importance of the counselor and client working together to challenge the sort of wrong-headed thinking that has undermined the client's well-being. Beck terms this process *collaborative empiricism* (Howatt, 2000). Beck asserts that the main outcome of counseling is to assist the client in discovering how her problems originate from faulty thinking that leads her to misinterpret information received from her external environment (Beck, 1997).

To help the client uncover his dysfunctional thinking errors, CBT uses questions and conversational dialogues to gently bring these insights to the surface. A natural two-way conversation, called *Socratic dialogue* (i.e., questioning), accomplishes a natural cognitive reconstruction by providing the client with an opportunity to process and identify his systemic errors in thinking (Clark et al., 1999). Socratic dialogue provides an opportunity for the counselor to question the validity of automatic thoughts. This process is often where **cognitive shifts** occur. Once the client becomes aware of how these thinking errors create automatic thoughts fully accepted as facts, he can begin taking control of his thinking. These shifts allow the client to reframe negative cognitive schemas and recognize cognitive misrepresentations so that he can separate fact from opinion. When the client gets to this point, he is capable of positively interpreting and reframing his present life challenges.

19. Cognitive therapy explains that cognitive shifts occur when:
    a. a person is motivated to consider options.
    b. a person changes his perceptions of the future.
    c. a person refuses to live in the past.
    d. a person changes how he sees his present situation.

20. Beck's work includes which of the following core concepts?
    a. research, schemas, and collaborative empiricism
    b. research, ego strengthening, and collaborative empiricism
    c. research, REBT, and collaborative empiricism
    d. research, schemas, and emotions

Techniques Overview

Beck and his associates developed many different techniques to help clients process the world more effectively. Four samples of some commonly used cognitive-behavioral techniques are as follows:

1. *Beck Inventories—Hopelessness, Suicidal Ideation, Depression*, and *Anxiety*. The counselor uses one of the above diagnostic tools to assess the client's present mental health. The client's situation will determine the appropriate inventory. This inventory, taken at the beginning of counseling, provides real time information for both the counselor and client to track progress. For more information on this tool, visit Beck's Web site.

2. *Redefine the Problem*—The counselor assists the client in redefining her life problems by reducing the perception of doom and failure and empowering the client to see her present situation in a different light.

3. *Cognitive Restructuring*—The client decides on realistic self-enhancing statements to promote problem-solving and effective actions and then practices this statement outside as homework.

4. *Triple Column Technique*—This provides the client with a visual representation and breakdown of his **cognitive distortions**. It teaches him to become more aware of his internal automatic thinking. The format is as follows:

Automatic Thought	*Cognitive Distortion*	*Rational Response*
I am "chicken."	I should be brave all the time.	I am human, and I do not have to be perfect all the time.

21. Which of the following are examples of Beck's systemic errors?
    a. polarized thinking, magical thinking, and mind reading
    b. polarized thinking, regret thinking, and mind reading
    c. polarized thinking, overgeneralizing, and mind reading
    d. none of the above

22. Beck designed which of the following four inventories to assess clients?
    a. hopelessness, anger, sadness, and anxiety
    b. hopelessness, suicidal, depression, and anxiety
    c. hopelessness, anxiety, depression, and fear
    d. hopelessness, addictions, pain, and anxiety

PAVLOV, SKINNER, BANDURA, AND TEN BEHAVIORAL COUNSELING STRATEGIES

It is assumed that all behavior is determined and that the variables determining it can be discovered and changed. (Todd & Bohart, 1994, p. 276)

The development, creation, and learning of new behaviors represent one common link between all behavioral theories (Wilson, 1989). Regardless of the model, the majority of the counseling strategies used today for addictions counseling are designed to assist clients to overcome maladaptive behaviors. Based on an educational model for developing human behavior, these strategies represent a significant commitment to scientific methodologies. This section briefly outlines three well-accepted behavioral strategies, and ten techniques commonly used in behavioral therapy.

Classical Conditioning: Ivan Pavlov

"Essentially only one thing in life is real of interest to us—our physical experience." (Girogian & Pavlov, 1974, p. 431)

Ivan Pavlov's first major publication, *Work of the Digestive Glands*, was published in 1897. As a result of this work, in 1904 he became the first Russian physiologist to win the Nobel Prize. For the next thirty-five years, he devoted his energy to the study of conditioned reflex. His studies of the brain became the underpinning for classical conditioning. For more information, visit www.as.wvu.edu/~sbb/comm221/chapters/pvlov.html.

Theory Overview

Classical conditioning is a process whereby a neutral stimulus (e.g., ringing a bell) is paired with an automatic response (e.g., salivation when food is seen or smelled). In Pavlov's famous experiment, Sam the dog became conditioned to salivate in response to the neutral stimulus (ringing a bell), without the stimulus of food (Pavlov, 1960). Figure 15.2 shows a model of classical conditioning.

Therapy Overview

When using concepts from classical conditioning, the following are important considerations for reinforcing or eliminating conditioning: (a) *Generalization*—something similar to a bell is sounded and triggers the conditioned response; (b) *Discrimination*—opposite of generalization. For example, Sam the dog was able to discriminate between certain bell sounds, and only respond to the original stimulus; (c) *Extinction*—occurs when the bell is sounded and no food follows on a number of occasions. In time, the dog will not salivate automatically. When this occurs, it is said that the bell has gone back to being a neutral stimulus; and (d) *Spontaneous Recovery*—if the bell is sounded and no food is presented, extinction will occur. But if at some time the bell sounds and food is presented, conditioning can spontaneously return.

Operant Conditioning: B. F. Skinner

Operant conditioning focuses on action that operates on the environment to produce consequences (Corey, 2001, p. 257)

STEP 1 – *NEUTRAL STIMULUS*	*UNCONDITIONED STIMULUS*	*UNCONDITIONED RESPONSE*
For example, the ringing of a bell; stimulus, which, when activated alone, does not produce the unconditioned response.	The sight or smell of food; initiates an unlearned, automatic reflex that activates salivation.	The response is salivation.

STEP 2 – Over time (note: can happen with only one exposure), if Step 1 is repeated, the pairing of the neutral stimulus and the unconditioned stimulus can become as one:

NEUTRAL STIMULUS + UNCONDITIONED STIMULUS ⇒ UNCONDITIONED RESPONSE

STEP 3 – To test if the neutral stimulus has become conditioned, activate the neutral stimulus to determine whether it creates the unconditioned response:

CONDITIONED STIMULUS ⇒ CONDITIONED RESPONSE
(previously neutral stimulus)   (previously unconditioned response)

FIG. 15.2. Classical conditioning model.

In the 1930s, B. F. Skinner became interested in how animals learned a concept he called ***operant response*** (Skinner, 1971). In 1948, he joined the faculty of Harvard University, where he was active as a teacher, writer, and researcher until his retirement in 1974. For more information, visit: www.indiana.edu/~edpsych/topics~/behavior.html.

Theory Overview

Operant response is defined as a response that can be modified positively or negatively by a consequence. To understand observable behaviors, Skinner measured and tracked rates of progress. This monitoring provided the information required to predict outcomes by determining how any given consequence impacted behavior. Skinner noticed the impact of both positive and negative reinforcement on animal behavior and developed a formal model for conditioned learning. He used predictable sequences of conditioned learning for *shaping* behavior (the desired behaviors become automatic).

Therapy Overview

The four stages of learning as described by operant conditioning to shape new behavior are: (1) *Goal*—To increase or decrease a chosen behavior, (2) *Voluntary Response*—The desired behavior is voluntary and must be carried out at the learner's own will, (3) *Emitted Response*—The behavior must be acted out in the determined learning environment, and (4) *Consequence*—Once the behavior is emitted, the desired conditioning begins. Conditioning relies on the predetermined consequences (positive or negative). To be effective, the desired consequence must occur directly after the emitted behavior. This begins the conditioning process. An important note: Skinner warned that if there is much delay in the contingent consequence, it might impact the accuracy of the conditioning or lead to conditioning unwanted behaviors.

Social Cognitive Learning: Albert Bandura

Self-belief does not necessarily ensure success, but self-disbelief assuredly spawns failure. (Bandura, 1997, p. 77)

Albert Bandura was the first psychologist to advance the cognitive aspect of learning and, similar to Pavlov and Skinner, was a prolific writer and researcher. In 1973, Bandura became president of the American Psychological Association (APA) and in 1980 he received the APA's award for Distinguished Scientific Contributions. For more information, visit: www. ship.edu/~cgboerre/bandura.html.

Theory Overview

Bandura based his social cognitive learning theory on his research of how children learn aggression. Bandura (1986) taught that clients can learn from observing others, and that there does not always need to be an observable reward (positive or negative) for learning to occur.

Therapy Overview

Bandura's (1977) four stages of social cognitive learning are: (1) *Attention*—The client makes a conscious cognitive choice to observe the desired behavior, (2) *Memory*—The client recalls what he has observed from the modeling, (3) *Imitation*—The client repeats the actions that she has observed, and (4) *Motivation*—The client must have some internal motivation for wanting to carry out the modeled behavior. When he is motivated to repeat the behavior, mastery can occur with practice.

This process will work differently for each client, and it is not easily predictable how long one client will take to learn a task compared to the next. The variable of previously learned skills will impact performance (Bandura, 1969).

23. Bandura's social learning model is made up of which of the following four steps?
    a. attention, memory, repetition, and motivation
    b. attention, IQ, imitation, and motivation
    c. attention, memory, imitation, and motivation
    d. focus, memory, imitation, and motivation

24. Pavlov's theory explains that the first step in classical conditioning includes:
    a. neutral stimulus, unconditioned stimulus, and conditioned response.
    b. neutral stimulus, conditioned stimulus, and conditioned response.
    c. neutral stimulus, unconditioned stimulus, and unconditioned response.
    d. neutral stimulus, unconditioned stimulus, and conditioned stimulus.

25. Skinner's therapy for training a new skill includes:
    a. goal, voluntary response, emitted stimulus, and consequence.
    b. goal, voluntary response, emitted response, and consequence.
    c. goal, involuntary response, emitted response, and consequence.
    d. goal, voluntary response, emitted response, and outcome.

26. Skinner's theory explains new behavior can be conditioned through _____.
    a. shaping
    b. modeling
    c. conditioning
    d. all of the above

Ten Behavioral Counseling Strategies

Techniques Overview

Following are ten commonly practiced behavioral strategies, which provide a sampling of behavioral techniques used in the field of addictions.

1. *Contingency Contract*—A contingency contract defines the desired behaviors, predetermines rewards to be received, and specifies timeframes.
2. *Journaling*—Journaling is a powerful tool for separating facts from opinions. "Using expressive writing reduces intrusive and avoidant thoughts about negative events and improves working memory" (Carpenter, 2001, p. 68).
3. *Behavior Modeling*—The client observes the counselor or someone else performing a specific task, then attempts to imitate.
4. *Behavior Rehearsal*—New behaviors are practiced in a safe place (e.g., counseling).
5. *Bibliotherapy*—The assignment of meaningful educational readings.
6. *Goal Setting*—A process for brainstorming possible goals and implementation strategies, choosing specific goals and strategies, and then putting these strategies into a sequence with timeframes. The outcome of formal goal setting is to mobilize the client's resources and provide support to get the client moving in the right direction.
7. *Activity Scheduling*—Assigning and scheduling specific activities (e.g., work, AA meeting, hug children daily) to support mastery of desired behaviors.
8. *Physical Exercise*—Howatt (1999), reports exercise as being one of the best stress reduction techniques. A client with an addiction often needs to reduce stress levels. Ensure the client consults with her doctor before starting a new physical exercise program.
9. *Self-Monitoring*—The client is assigned to monitor thoughts that can be potentially problematic and can lead to ineffective choices. The client records them for discussion in counseling sessions. The goal is to bring about a conscious awareness of automatic thoughts and the connection to unwanted behaviors.
10. *Counter-conditioning*—A strategy for reducing anxiety. The client practices the opposite emotions of anxiety, such as relaxation. He can be trained in guided imagery (a visual relaxation technique), deep breathing, or listening to music.

27. Pavlov taught that over time, discontinuing the pairing of an unconditioned stimulus and a neutral stimulus would lead to _____.
    a. no effect
    b. extinction
    c. motivation to pair
    d. elevation

28. Bibliotherapy is:
    a. assigned readings for educating the client about a personal challenge.
    b. a form of journaling assigned by the counselor.
    c. a form of prayer.
    d. both a and b.

TABLE 15.1

Summary Table of the 3 Ts

Criteria 3 Ts	Choice Theory and Reality Therapy (William Glasser)	Rational Emotive Behavior Therapy (Albert Ellis)	Cognitive-Behavioral Counseling Theory (Aaron T. Beck)	Pavlov, Skinner, and Bandura and Ten Behavioral Counseling Strategies
Theory— highlights from an addiction counselor's perspective.	All human beings have four basic conscious needs and one unconscious need. All behavior is chosen. Glasser promotes internal locus of control. Client determines his wants.	The vast majority of human mental health issues are a result of the way a person thinks. Ellis promotes the ABC theory to teach a client to think more effectively and stop irrational thinking that is the root cause of many problems.	Beck's core theory promotes working in a partnership with clients to learn how to filter the world more effectively.	Behavioral therapy's main goal is to help clients learn new behaviors.
Therapy— highlights from an addiction counselor's perspective.	The therapy involves asking strategic questions with the goal of self-evaluating.	Ellis' theory is grounded in the ABC model.	Beck's therapy has four steps: reduce anxiety, explore client's beliefs and assumptions, test the client's reality, and develop an action plan.	Pavlov developed classical conditioning. Skinner developed operant conditioning. Bandura developed social learning theory.
Techniques— highlights from an addiction counselor's perspective.	Effectively using the reality therapy process and teaching choice theory.	REBT has many different techniques; the main criterion for selecting a technique is that it must support the client's development in eliminating irrational thinking.	Beck is open to using many different cognitive-behavioral techniques. There are literally hundreds of techniques; this chapter provides a few examples.	Behavioral therapy has many techniques, like journaling, that can be used in many different counseling orientations.

29. Goal setting can best be explained as:
   a. a random strategy to achieve a goal.
   b. a way to motivate a client towards achieving recovery.
   c. a specific course of action to achieve a desired outcome.
   d. a nondirective strategy to assist a client in achieving a desired outcome.

30. Behavioral techniques can be used:
    a. only by a counselor practicing behavioral therapy.
    b. only by a counselor practicing cognitive-behavioral therapy.
    c. in any orientation where the strategy is applicable to a client's needs.
    d. by a counselor willing to study behavioral theory first.

KEY TERMS

cognitive distortions: Automatic, all-encompassing errors in a person's thinking.

cognitive shift: A fundamental and structural shift in how a person perceives the world.

masturbatory thinking: Ellis' term to describe inflexible and rigid thinking that originates from irrational beliefs.

negative reinforcement: Any action or behavior that increases the probability of a response by stopping or withholding an unpleasant stimulus.

operant response: Skinner's term for a response that can be modified positively or negatively by a consequence.

organized behavior: A term developed by William Glasser that represents an individual's learned behaviors and where new behaviors are created.

systemic bias errors: Beck's term for dysfunctional thinking that often comes from the inefficient processing of stimuli.

WDEP radio: A reality therapy training mnemonic created by Robert Wubbolding that stands for Want, Direction/Doing, Evaluation, and Planning.

DISCUSSION QUESTIONS

1. Describe how choice theory could be used to teach a client internal locus of control.
2. How can an addiction counselor use the ABC model on a client with an addiction?
3. How could Beck's work be incorporated into addictions counseling?
4. How could an addiction counselor use Pavlov's model to teach a client about relapse?
5. Using Bandura's model, discuss how it can be used to teach a client a new skill.
6. What do Ellis, Beck, and Glasser all seem to have in common?
7. What are some of the applications of Skinner's model that could be used to support recovery?
8. Select three behavioral techniques and explain how they could be incorporated into addiction counseling.
9. Which of the four theories in this chapter appear to be most congruent with your counseling orientation and why?

SUGGESTED FURTHER READING

All the books recommended here include an overview of the core theories discussed in this chapter.

Corey, G. (2001). *Theory and practice of counseling and psychotherapy* (6th ed.). Pacific Grove, CA: Brooks/Cole.

Corey provides an excellent overview of classical theories, as well as an effective process for developing one's own integrated orientation.

Corsini, R. J., & Wedding, D. (Eds.). (2000). *Current psychotherapist* (6th ed.). Itasca, IL: F. E. Peacock.

This is probably the most technically detailed book on theory on the market today. For those who want to study counseling theory in detail, this is a must.

Howatt, W. A. (2000). *The human services counseling toolbox: Theory, development, techniques, and resources.* Belmont, CA: Brooks/Cole.

Developed with students who were learning to become addiction counselors, it is a reference chock full of information on theory, techniques, and strategies for working with persons with addictive disorders.

REFERENCES

Bandura, A. (1969). *Principles of behavior modification.* New York: Holt, Rinehart and Winston.

Bandura, A. (1977). *Social learning theory.* Englewood Cliffs, NJ: Prentice-Hall.

Bandura, A. (1986). *Social foundations of thought and actions.* Englewood Cliffs, NJ: Prentice-Hall.

Bandura, A. (1997). *Self-efficacy: the exercise of control.* New York: Freeman.

Beck, A. (1967). *Depression: Clinical, experimental and theoretical aspects.* New York: Harper & Row.

Beck, A. (1995). *Biography.* Philadelphia: University of Pennsylvania Press.

Beck, A. (1997). Cognitive therapy: Reflections. In J. Zeig (Ed.), *Evolution of psychotherapy. The third conference* (pp. 149–163). New York: Brunner/Mazel.

Beck, A. (1999). *Prisoners of hate: The cognitive basis of anger, hostility and violence.* New York: HarperCollins.

Bishop, F. M. (2001). *Managing addictions: cognitive, emotive and behavioral techniques.* Northvale, NJ: Jason Aronson.

Carpenter, S. A new reason for keeping a diary. Washington, DC: *APA Monitor On Psychology.* (September, 2001): 68–70.

Clark, D. A., Beck, A. T., & Alford, B. A. (1999). *Scientific foundation of cognitive therapy and therapy of depression.* New York: Wiley.

Corey, G. (2001). *Theory and practice of counseling and psychotherapy* (6th ed.). Belmont, CA: Wadsworth/Thomson Learning.

Ellis, A. (1962). *Reason and emotion in psychotherapy.* Secaucus, NJ: Citadel.

Ellis, A. (1996). *Better, deeper and more enduring brief therapy.* New York: Brunner/Mazel.

Ellis, A. (1997). The evolution of Albert Ellis and rational emotive behavior therapy. In J. Zeig (Ed.), *Evolution of psychotherapy. The third conference* (pp. 107–125). New York: Brunner/Mazel.

Ellis, A. (2001). *Overcoming destructive beliefs, feelings and behaviors: New directions for rational emotive behavior therapy.* New York: Prometheus.

Ellis, A., & MacLean, C. (1997). *Rational emotive behavior therapy: A therapist's guide.* San Luis Obispo, CA: Impact Press.

Girogian, N. A., & Pavlov, I. P. (1974). *Dictionary of scientific biography* (Vol. 10). New York: Charles Schribnera's Sons.

Glasser, W. (1965). *Reality therapy.* New York: HarperCollins.

Glasser, W. (1984). *Control theory: A new explanation of how we control our lives.* New York: HarperCollins.

Glasser, W. (1998). *Choice theory: A new psychology of personal freedom.* New York: HarperCollins.

Glasser, W. (2000). *Reality therapy in action.* New York: HarperCollins.

Glasser, W. (2003). *Warning: Psychiatry can be hazardous to your mental health.* New York: HarperCollins.

Howatt, W. A. (1999). *My Personal Success Coach.* Kentville, NS: A Way With Words.

Howatt, W. A. (2000). *The human services counseling toolbox: Theory, development, techniques, and resources.* Belmont, CA: Brooks/Cole.

Kottler, J. A. (2002). *Theories in counseling and therapy: An experiential approach.* Boston: Allyn & Bacon.

Pavlov, I. P. (1960). *Conditioned reflexes: An investigation of the physiological activity of the cerebral cortex* (G. V. Anrep, Trans.). New York: Dover. (Original translation published 1927)

Rotter, J. B. (1982). *The development and application of the social learning theory: Selected papers.* New York: Prager.

Skinner, B. F. (1971). *Beyond freedom and dignity.* New York: Knopf.

Todd, J., & Bohart, C. B. (1994). *Foundations of clinical and counseling psychology.* New York: HarperCollins.

Wilson, G. T. (1989). *Behavior therapy.* In R. J. Corsini & D. Wedding (Eds.), *Current psychotherapies* (4th ed.) (pp. 205–237). Itasca, IL: F. E. Peacock.

Wubbolding, R. (1988). *Using reality therapy.* New York: Harper & Row.

16

Assessment, Diagnosis, and Treatment Planning

Judith A. Lewis
Governors State University

TRUTH OR FICTION?

___ 1. Screening *is a method for deciding whether clients need treatment so that you can inform them immediately about their placement.*

___ 2. *When you work with people who have addiction problems, you should be warm and respectful.*

___ 3. *Motivational interviewing (MI) helps clients resolve their ambivalence about whether to change their drinking or drug use behaviors.*

___ 4. *In a substance use history, the counselor asks questions about drug and alcohol use and avoids asking about other aspects of the person's life.*

___ 5. *Addiction counselors do not have medical training so they should avoid asking clients about risk for infectious diseases.*

___ 6. *Five percent of people with addiction problems have co-occurring mental health problems.*

___ 7. *Addiction counselors should screen for mental health problems so that they can seek appropriate consultation or make referrals.*

___ 8. *If you try to develop a treatment plan for a client who is not yet contemplating a change you will probably meet with resistance.*

___ 9. *Once a client has been abstinent for a month he or she no longer needs help and support.*

___ 10. *The Diagnostic and Statistical Manual of Mental Disorders includes substance dependence and substance abuse in the category of substance use disorders.*

___ 11. *The only purpose of assessment is to come up with a clear diagnosis of the client's problem.*

truments that clients can fill out themselves provide sufficient information
loping a treatment plan.

iction Severity Index has only two scores: one for alcohol use and one for
?.

ents to assess cognitive-behavioral factors can help clients decide which
  situations are most risky for them.
___ 15. *A treatment plan should always be based on clear outcome statements.*

Thorough and systematic **assessment** and **treatment planning** are at the very heart of successful addiction counseling. Counselors sometimes used to fear that they would be wasting
valuable time if they spent "too much time" on assessment and failed to jump right into action
with their clients. It is not surprising that they felt this way. After all, people grappling with
the pain of addiction do have pressing needs for help. Moreover, in these times of managed
care and dwindling resources, our time with our clients may be severely limited.

Despite these pressures to move ahead, however, you will find in the long run that shortcuts
don't work and that time spent on assessment is time well spent. After all, you will want to
make sure that the action plans you and your clients develop are actually appropriate and that
your clients are committed to them. The treatment plans that work best are the ones that are
developed in true collaboration with the client and that are based on careful analyses of the
client's own needs and goals.

We hope that when you have finished reading this chapter you will feel confident about
your ability to carry out the following steps: (a) comprehensive assessment, (b) **screening**
and diagnosis, and (c) treatment planning. This chapter guides you through this step-by-step
process, provides you with a list of commonly used screening and assessment instruments, and
then discusses treatment plans.

The Addiction Technology Transfer Centers (ATTC) National Curriculum Committee
(1998, p. 29) laid out the competencies underlying successful addiction counseling. Their
list begins with *clinical evaluation*, which involves "the systematic approach to screening and
assessment."

SCREENING

The ATTC National Curriculum Committee (1998, p. 29) defines *screening* as "the process
through which counselor, client and available significant others determine the most appropriate
initial course of action, given the client's needs and characteristics and the available resources
within the community." Exhibit 16.1 lists the competencies you need to carry out a successful
screening process.

1. The primary purpose of screening is:
   a. for the counselor to decide whether the client fits into the specific treatment offered
      in the treatment setting.
   b. for the counselor to tell the client whether he or she needs treatment.
   c. to use data to prove to the client that he or she has a problem.
   d. for the counselor and client to decide together on an initial course of action.

EXHIBIT 16.1

Screening Competencies*

1. Establish rapport, including management of crisis situations and determination of need for additional professional assistance.
2. Gather data systematically from the client and other available collateral sources, using screening instruments and other methods sensitive to age, developmental level, culture, and gender. At a minimum, data should include current and historic substance use; physical health, mental health, and substance-related treatment history; mental status; and current social, environmental, and economic constraints.
3. Screen for psychoactive substance toxicity, intoxication, and withdrawal symptoms; aggression or danger to others; potential for self-inflicted harm or suicide; and co-existing mental health problems.
4. Assist the client in identifying the impact of substance use on his or her current life problems and the effects of continued harmful use or abuse.
5. Determine the client's readiness for treatment and change as well as the needs of others involved in the current situation.
6. Review any treatment options that are appropriate for the client's needs, characteristics, goals, and financial resources.
7. Apply accepted criteria for diagnosis of substance use disorders in making treatment recommendations.
8. Construct with client and appropriate others an initial action plan based on client needs, preferences, and resources available.
9. Based on initial action plan, take specific steps to initiate an admission or referral and ensure follow-through.

*From *Addiction Counselling Competencies: The Knowledge, Skills, and Attitudes of Professional Practice* (pp. 29–34), by Addiction Technology Transfer Centers National Curriculum Committee, 1998, Rockville, MD: Center for Substance Abuse Treatment.

2. The competent screener:
   a. gathers data about the client's substance abuse.
   b. establishes rapport.
   c. uses culturally sensitive instruments.
   d. all of the above.

The list of competencies might seem daunting at first glance. It is true that screening is a complex undertaking, but it all boils down to the idea of establishing a respectful and collaborative relationship with the client and gathering enough information to make sound decisions as treatment is initiated.

Establishing the Relationship

The kind of relationship you establish with the client will be a key factor in the success of the counseling process. In the past, many treatment providers believed that people with addiction-related problems had to be confronted aggressively as a means of "breaking down their denial" about the reality of their addiction. Now, however, the idea that "treatment must be respectful and empowering to the individual" (Center for Substance Abuse Treatment, 2000, p. 20) is widely accepted. Counselors working with addictions should demonstrate the same facilitative

cteristic of other counseling relationships. These facilitative qualities

ity to take the feelings, sensations, or attitudes of another person into
ity for experiencing vicariously the other's feelings and thoughts
: ability to be oneself in a situation, to avoid playing a false role
ability to stay in the here-and-now, to be focused on the current situation
lity to demonstrate openness and responsiveness, to help the client feel
a so... accepted

- *Respect*—the ability to communicate to clients the expectation that the clients are capable of taking responsibility for their own lives, to treat clients as competent adults
- *Cultural sensitivity*—the ability to reach out across difference, to appreciate the role of cultural context, and to recognize the cultural factors that affect the development and resolution of life problems

> 3. The facilitative qualities of effective addiction counselors include:
>   a. directiveness and the ability to confront negative behaviors.
>   b. the ability to break through dishonesty and denial.
>   c. empathy and respect.
>   d. expert knowledge of the cause of addiction.

People grappling with addictions are understandably ambivalent about the prospect of change. When counselors try to coerce their clients into treatment they often engender defensiveness. When you use a respectful and supportive approach, you might be surprised at the willingness of your clients to participate honestly in the screening and assessment process. This approach makes your job easier, too. Now you have collaborators (your clients) to work with—and they are clearly the best experts on their own lives and goals.

Most addiction counselors find the practice of **motivational interviewing** (Miller & Rollnick, 2002) helpful as they begin the process of clinical evaluation. *Motivational interviewing* is a "directive, client-centered counseling style for eliciting behavior change by helping clients to explore and resolve ambivalence" (Rollnick & Miller, 1995, p. 325). At its core, motivational interviewing is an interpersonal style. The counselor tries to elicit motivation, not impose it; to acknowledge that the task of resolving ambivalence lies mainly in the hands of the client, not the counselor; to recognize that denial is a product of the interaction between counselor and client, not part of the client's innate character; and to build a true partnership.

> 4. Motivational interviewing is:
>   a. a method for convincing clients that they should be in treatment.
>   b. an interpersonal style.
>   c. a technique for the counselor to resolve the client's indecisiveness.
>   d. a nondirective approach.

Gathering Data: Substance Use History

When a counselor's interactive style is one of respect and collaboration, he or she can move smoothly through an initial interview with the client. Addiction professionals generally focus on taking what is called a *substance use history* but which also covers a variety of additional

EXHIBIT 16.2

Substance Use History

- Client's motivation for participating in interview
- Client's cultural identities
- Client's perception of his or her strengths and resources
- Client's perception of current problems related to substance use
- Impact of current substance use on the client's life
- History of substance use and abuse
- Current life situation, including living arrangements, family, and work
- Family history
- Legal issues
- Physical health
- Mental status

---

factors that affect the potential for treatment. Exhibit 16.2 shows a list of common topics that might be covered in this history.

5. The substance use history includes:
   a. finding out about the client's substance abuse.
   b. finding out about the client's legal issues.
   c. finding out about the client's cultural identities.
   d. all of the above.

Gathering Data: Screening for Risk of Infectious Diseases

Barthwell and Gilbert (1993) say that addiction counselors have an important role to play in screening for infectious diseases. They suggest that counselors should be alert to the presence of risk factors, including the following (pp. 8–9):

- *Injection drug use*
- *Having sexual partners who are injection drug users*
- *Having unprotected sexual contact*
- *Having multiple sex partners*
- *Poor urban environment* (People who lack access to good medical care and live in substandard housing are vulnerable to many diseases.)
- *Homelessness* (According to Barthwell & Gilbert [p. 8], "poor hygiene, inadequate nutrition and medical care, chronic drug use, crowded shelters, and unsanitary living conditions contribute to the incidence of infectious diseases among the homeless.")
- *History of incarceration or institutionalization*
- *Lower socioeconomic status* (Poor access to health care increases the risk for all health problems, including infectious diseases.)
- *Disease history*

Barthwell and Gilbert encourage counselors to try to solicit this sensitive information as part of an initial intake interview.

6. Urban poverty is a risk factor for infectious disease because:
   a. The urban setting encourages drug use in the population.
   b. Poverty is often the result of risky health behaviors.
   c. The urban poor lack access to good medical care.
   d. People in cities account for most of society's use of illicit drugs.

Gathering Data: Screening for Co-Occurring Mental Health Problems

According to Ries (1994) about one-third of patients with psychiatric disorders experience substance abuse and more than one-half of substance-abusing clients have met the diagnostic criteria for a psychiatric disorder. The fact that so many people have co-occurring problems makes treatment exceedingly complex. Clients' needs can be met most effectively through interdisciplinary collaboration between addiction specialists and mental health specialists. Exhibit 16.3 presents a conceptualization of how this might work.

Note from Exhibit 16.3 that the skills of establishing rapport, carrying out screening and assessment processes, and making treatment recommendations are common to the addictions and mental health specialties. Addictions counselors have the following as central responsibilities: taking substance use histories, making in-depth assessments regarding substance use, diagnosing substance abuse and dependence, and making recommendations for addiction treatment. Addictions counselors also have a secondary responsibility—carrying out a brief screening for mental health problems and seeking consultation and coordination with mental health specialists as needed. Similarly, mental health counselors carry out in-depth assessments of mental health issues but also have an important secondary responsibility to screen for substance use and arrange for appropriate consultation with addiction specialists.

EXHIBIT 16.3

Screening for Co-Occurring Disorders

Addiction Specialists	Mental Health Specialists	Both
Central Responsibility		
Carry out in-depth assessments of client's substance use, abuse, and dependence	Carry out in-depth assessments of client's mental health history	Establish rapport
Apply accepted criteria for diagnosis of substance use disorders in making treatment recommendations	Apply accepted criteria for diagnosis of mental illness in making treatment recommendations	Carry out comprehensive screening and assessment process
		Document findings and make treatment recommendations.
Adjunct Responsibility		
Screen for co-existing mental health problems	Screen for co-existing addiction problems	
Seek consultation and make treatment/referral recommendations	Seek consultation and make treatment/referral recommendations	

7. The percentage of substance abuse clients who also have a psychiatric
   a. less than 5%.
   b. about 25%.
   c. over 50%.
   d. 90%.

Gathering Data: Exploring the Client's Readiness for Change

Prochaska, DiClemente, and Norcross (1992) described stages that people tend to go through as they change problematic behaviors, including addictive behaviors. The **stages of change** they conceptualize include precontemplation, contemplation, preparation, action, and maintenance. Through the process of establishing a relationship with the client and taking the substance use history you will begin to get a sense of where your client stands in this behavior change process. You will find it helpful to focus on this because otherwise it is difficult to determine how and when to move toward developing a treatment plan. For instance, if you tried to begin the development of an action plan while your client was still in the precontemplation stage, you would almost certainly face resistance. You will find that your clients are willing to share their thoughts about the pros and cons of change as long as they don't feel they are being pushed toward change for which they don't feel ready.

8. According to the stages of change model:
   a. Counselors should be direct in moving clients from precontemplation to contemplation as quickly as possible.
   b. A client in precontemplation is not ready to participate in treatment planning.
   c. Once people reach the action stage they can assume that their addiction problem is under control.
   d. Clients are seldom willing to share with you their "pro and con" thoughts about changing their substance use behaviors.

DIAGNOSIS

At this point you will have gathered enough data to develop a diagnostic impression. Arriving at a "diagnosis" assists in communication with third-party payers as well as other professionals, but it is wise to treat a diagnosis as tentative and subject to change. It is also important to remember that although a diagnosis does provide a shorthand for communication, it never tells the whole story.

Keep these caveats in mind as you apply diagnostic criteria. The most commonly used approach to diagnosis comes from the *Diagnostic and Statistical Manual of Mental Disorders*, or *DSM–IV* (American Psychiatric Association, 1994). According to the *DSM–IV*, psychoactive substance use is considered a *disorder* only when (a) the individual demonstrates an inability to control his or her use despite cognitive, behavioral, or physiological symptoms, and (b) the symptoms have been present for at least one month. The criteria are the same across all types of drugs. Within the category of **substance use disorder**, the *DSM–IV* makes a distinction between *substance dependence* and *substance abuse*.

To be diagnosed as *substance dependent*, a client must have exhibited at least three of the following seven symptoms (American Psychiatric Association, 1994, pp. 177–178):

1. Substance often taken in large amounts or over a longer period of time than the person intended.
2. Persistent desire or one or more unsuccessful efforts to cut down or control substance use.
3. A great deal of time spent in activities necessary to obtain the substance (e.g., theft), take the substance (e.g., chain smoking), or recover from its effects.
4. Important social, occupational, or recreational activities given up or reduced because of substance use.
5. Continued substance use despite knowledge of having a persistent or recurrent social, psychological, or physical problem that is caused or exacerbated by the use of the substance (e.g., keeps using heroin despite family arguments about it, cocaine-induced depression, or having an ulcer made worse by drinking).
6. Marked tolerance: need for markedly increased amounts of the substance (i.e., at least a 50% increase) in order to achieve intoxication or desired effect, or markedly diminished effect with continued use of the same amount.
7. Characteristic withdrawal symptoms and substance is often taken to relieve or avoid withdrawal symptoms.

9. The *Diagnostic and Statistical Manual of Mental Disorders* identifies seven symptoms of substance dependence. In order to have a diagnosis of substance dependence, the client must have exhibited:
   a. any one of the symptoms.
   b. three of the symptoms.
   c. all of the symptoms.
   d. five of the symptoms.

If a person exhibits three or more of the seven symptoms, he or she receives the substance dependence diagnosis. Even then, however, you should take into account differences in the severity of the problem. According to the *DSM–IV*, the following distinctions can be made (American Psychiatric Association, 1994, p. 168):

- *Mild*—few, if any, symptoms in excess of those required to make the diagnosis, and the symptoms result in no more than mild impairment in occupational functioning or in usual social activities or relationships with others.
- *Moderate*—symptoms or functional impairment between "mild" and "severe."
- *Severe*—many symptoms in excess of those required to make the diagnosis, and the symptoms markedly interfere with occupational functioning or with usual social activities or relationships with others.
- *Early full remission*—for at least one month but less than twelve months, no diagnostic criteria have been met.
- *Early partial remission*—for at least one month but less than twelve months, some, but not all, diagnostic criteria have been met.
- *Sustained full remission*—no diagnostic criteria met for one year or more.
- *Sustained partial remission*—not all criteria for dependence are met for one year or more, but one or more criteria are met.

- *On agonist therapy*—using a prescribed medication, like Antabuse, to avoid substance use.
- *In a controlled environment*—for instance, a jail or hospital.

10. According to the *Diagnostic and Statistical Manual of Mental Disorders*:
    a. If someone has substance dependence, his or her problem is automatically considered severe.
    b. If someone has only one of the symptoms of substance dependence, he or she is diagnosed as mildly substance dependent.
    c. A substance dependent person is considered to be in *sustained full remission* if the diagnostic criteria have not been met for one year or more.
    d. Remission is not possible for a person with a diagnosis of substance dependence.

The diagnostic category of **substance abuse disorder** is used for a person whose patterns of use are maladaptive but whose use has never met the criteria for *dependence*.

11. According to the *Diagnostic and Statistical Manual of Mental Disorders*:
    a. Substance abuse disorder is a subcategory of substance use disorders.
    b. Substance abuse disorder is identical to substance dependence disorder.
    c. Substance abuse disorder is a diagnosis reserved for someone who was previously substance dependent but has shown no recent symptoms.
    d. Substance abuse disorder may be diagnosed for people whose drug of choice is heroin but not for people whose problem relates to alcohol.

You may have noticed as you reviewed the *DSM–IV* criteria that diagnosis is much more intricate than a simple yes-or-no answer to the question of whether an individual is "an addict" or "an alcoholic." People sometimes oversimplify this question, creating a dichotomy that does not exist in real life. One might think, for instance, that if an individual is identified as an "alcoholic," his or her problems, drinking patterns, and future progress are readily predictable and that we should know how to treat him or her. In fact, however, people with problems related to alcohol vary widely in their consumption, personalities, social environments, gender, culture, and many other factors that affect treatment.

As you move toward the more in-depth assessment that can guide treatment planning, you should keep in mind that your procedures should always involve flexibility on your part. It is the client's progress toward the life he or she desires that is important—not the naming of the problem.

12. If a person has been labeled as an *addict* or *alcoholic*:
    a. it is easy to predict the future progress of his or her behavior.
    b. we know what treatment he or she should have.
    c. we might overlook important variations in factors that could affect treatment.
    d. the counselor's role is to make sure the client accepts this diagnosis.

COMPREHENSIVE ASSESSMENT

The Addiction Technology Transfer Centers National Curriculum Committee (1998) defines *assessment* as "an ongoing process through which the counselor collaborates with the client

EXHIBIT 16.4

Assessment Competencies*

---

1. Select and use a comprehensive assessment process sensitive to age, gender, racial and ethnic cultural issues, and disabilities that includes, but is not limited to the following:
   - History of alcohol and other drug use
   - Physical health, mental health, and addiction treatment history
   - Family issues
   - Work history and career issues
   - History of criminality
   - Psychological, emotional, and worldview concerns
   - Current status of physical health, mental health, and substance use
   - Spirituality
   - Education and basic life skills
   - Socioeconomic characteristics, lifestyle, and current legal status
   - Use of community resources.
2. Analyze and interpret the data to determine treatment recommendations.
3. Seek appropriate supervision and consultation.
4. Document assessment findings and treatment recommendations.

---

*From *Addiction Counseling Competencies: The Knowledge, Skills, and Attitudes of Professional Practice*, by Addiction Technology Transfer Centers National Curriculum Committee, 1998, pp. 35–37, Rockville, MD: Center for Substance Abuse Treatment.

and others to gather and interpret information necessary for planning treatment and evaluating client progress." Exhibit 16.4 lists the competencies that underlie effective assessment.

13. An assessment:
    a. is completed before treatment begins and, once set, should not be revised.
    b. is an ongoing process both for planning and for evaluating client progress.
    c. should focus on the addictive behavior without regard to side issues.
    d. should be kept confidential from the patient and his or her family.

At first glance, it may seem as though much of the information being gleaned at this point duplicates data that were gathered through the screening process. It is true that the history taken at the time of the initial screening will still be very useful as you move through the helping process with your client. Now, however, you will be examining the client's concerns, goals, and characteristics in more depth. You and your client will now be searching for ways to apply the information toward a specific, individualized treatment plan. Moreover, the assessment process will continue through treatment as you appraise the client's progress toward his or her goals.

14. The assessment process:
    a. is identical to the screening process.
    b. should be a clean slate that does not pay attention to data that were gathered through the screening process.
    c. builds on the screening process and goes into more depth about the client's individual goals and needs.
    d. all of the above.

Through the screening process, you have helped and advised your client as he or she grappled with very difficult questions. The client has pondered whether using alcohol or other drugs has been standing in the way of the life he or she would like to have, balanced the pros and cons of change, and considered the connection between substance use and other life issues. Finally, the client has made an initial decision about whether professional help is needed and what kind of help that should be.

15. Looking back at the screening process, the client may now have tentative answers to questions such as:
   a. Is substance use an issue for me?
   b. Are there other physical or mental health problems that I should address?
   c. How much of a commitment am I ready to make?
   d. All of the above.

If you and the client have found answers to these questions, the client might now be ready to embark on a journey toward change. The client has made a tentative decision to work with you. Now you will need to provide advice and support as the client considers a new set of questions. He or she may ask any or all of the following:

- Exactly what outcome should I envision for myself in terms of my substance use?
- Of the treatments and techniques my counselor says are available, which seem to be the best fit for me?
- What about my goals regarding other aspects of my life?
- Are there changes I should seek in my family life?
- Are there things I need to learn to have better relationships with other people?
- What things should I change in the way I manage my life? Are there things I need to learn to make better decisions? Deal with stress more effectively? Solve personal problems?
- What are my goals in terms of education or work? Are there things I should do to improve my life in this area?
- Are there legal or medical problems I should address at this point in my life?

The client and counselor can answer these questions most effectively if the interview process is supplemented with assessment instruments. This comprehensive exploration lays the groundwork for treatment planning.

16. Through the assessment process, it is important that clients:
   a. think about the goals and outcomes they envision for themselves in terms of their substance use.
   b. avoid being influenced by their families.
   c. follow the counselor's advice about what their treatment plans should be.
   d. avoid thinking about issues other than their drug and alcohol use.

INSTRUMENTS

Devices commonly used in addiction counseling settings include (a) brief, self-administered instruments with a narrow focus on substance use behaviors, (b) assessment instruments that help lay the ground work for comprehensive treatment planning, and (c) instruments that focus on cognitive and behavioral factors associated with substance use.

Self-Administered Instruments

When you practice addiction counseling you are likely to observe fairly heavy use of very brief instruments designed to make an initial determination about whether a particular problem exists. These devices are often used in medical, mental health, educational, criminal justice, or social service settings to help professionals make decisions about whether a referral to specialized addiction treatment should take place. Historically, more of the instruments have tended to relate to alcohol use than to other drugs.

The Michigan Alcoholism Screening Test (MAST), for instance, has twenty-four "yes-or-no" items that address alcohol use behaviors. Each item is scored differently, and 53 is the highest possible score. People who score more than twenty points are identified as exhibiting "severe alcoholism." The short form of the MAST (the SMAST) is made up of seventeen questions found to be the best at discriminating between people with and people without alcohol problems.

17. The Michigan Alcoholism Screening Test:
    a. is an in-depth assessment tool that can be the basis of a treatment plan.
    b. is a brief, self-administered instrument that is meant to make an initial estimate of whether an individual's alcohol use is problematic.
    c. screens for alcohol and drug problems.
    d. is always administered in the context of an interview with an addiction professional.

The Alcohol Use Disorders Identification Test (AUDIT) is used most commonly in medical settings. This brief instrument is made up of ten items, so it is easy to administer and score. People who score eight or above out of a possible ten points are considered to have alcohol problems that should be addressed.

The CAGE is another instrument that is often used in medical settings. It has only four items:

1. Have you ever felt you should **C**ut down on your drinking?
2. Have people **A**nnoyed you by criticizing your drinking?
3. Have you ever felt **G**uilty about your drinking?
4. Have you ever had a drink first thing in the morning (**E**ye opener)?

The Alcohol Use Inventory (AUI) is much more extensive than either the AUDIT or the CAGE. The AUI's multiple choice items measure a number of factors related to alcohol use. Scales are derived for several factors, including the quantity and frequency of alcohol use, the client's perceptions of the benefits and negative consequences of drinking, and the client's awareness of the degree to which an alcohol problem exists.

Several brief instruments have been developed for use with drugs other than alcohol. The Drug Abuse Screening Test (DAST) is similar to the MAST. It has twenty yes-or-no items. In the case of the DAST, however, the items are not weighted, so twenty is the highest score. The Substance Abuse Problem Checklist is also self-administered, but is more extensive than most instruments of this type. The checklist lists more than three hundred problems in the following eight categories: (a) motivation for treatment, (b) health, (c) personality, (d) social

relationships, (e) job-related problems, (f) misuse of leisure time, (g) religious or spiri
problems, and (h) legal problems.

18. Brief, self-administered instruments that are meant to provide an initial estimate of the
    degree to which people's substance use might be problematic include the following:
    a. the CAGE
    b. the Alcohol Use Inventory
    c. the Substance Abuse Problem Check List
    d. all of the above

Comprehensive Assessment Instruments

The self-administered instruments discussed can provide a useful start, but you will need to use more comprehensive assessment processes to guide the development of your clients' treatment plans. The assessment normally takes place in an interview setting, with the counselor and client working together in a structured interview format. The Addiction Severity Index and the Comprehensive Drinker Profile are two examples of assessment devices with strong research behind them.

Addiction Severity Index (ASI)

The ASI is used very widely to guide the treatment planning process for people grappling with addiction-related issues. The instrument is administered through a very structured interview. The problems assessed are organized into seven categories: (a) medical status, (b) employment status, (c) alcohol use, (d) drug use, (e) legal status, (f) family/social relationships, and (g) psychological status. The interview is structured so that each section covers a separate category (alcohol and drug use are addressed together). For each issue, a clear distinction is made between problems experienced recently and problems experienced at some time in the person's life. Another interesting aspect of this instrument is that, for each category, clients have an opportunity to express the degree to which they see the issue as problematic for them (e.g., not at all, slightly, moderately, considerably, or extremely problematic). Interviewers take these responses into account when they make their own appraisals in each category. For each section of the instrument, the interviewer devises a severity rating that can guide treatment planning. The severity ratings, which are influenced both by the interviewer's assessments and by the client's ratings, are measured on a 9-point scale, from 0 (no treatment necessary for this issue) to 9 (treatment needed immediately to intervene in a life-threatening situation). The ideal outcome of this process is the development of a treatment plan that immediately addresses issues that are most severely problematic while placing a lower priority on less pressing concerns.

19. The Addiction Severity Index:
    a. assesses problems in seven categories.
    b. assesses only drinking and drug use behaviors.
    c. once scored, provides a single index of the severity of all of the client's problems.
    d. assesses all of the client's life problems except drug use, which is assessed by different
       instruments.

20. The Addiction Severity Index:
    a. is completed by the client on his or her own as a paper-and-pencil inventory.
    b. is administered and scored by a counselor without input from the client.
    c. takes into account the views of both the counselor and the client regarding the severity of problems.
    d. is not administered to clients until they have completed treatment.

Comprehensive Drinker Profile (CDP)

The CDP does include questions about other drugs, but its main focus is on alcohol-related problems. Carried out as a structured interview, the CDP provides an unusually broad and deep array of information that can help in the process of treatment planning. Embedded within the instrument is a series of objective questions from which the counselor can derive two scores: the equivalent of the MAST score on the presence of alcohol problems and a separate score that measures physical dependence on alcohol. Through a series of questions about current alcohol use, the interviewer can derive a very clear and specific picture of the amount and pattern of the client's drinking. A primary strength of this device, however, lies in its qualitative dimensions. With the use of card sets, clients are able to provide information about their most common drinking settings, the people with whom they tend to drink, their beverage preferences, their reasons for drinking, the effects of drinking, the life problems related to drinking, and their own definitions of alcoholism. This kind of information goes beyond the questions of the existence and severity of the problem. The counselor and client can use the data to guide specific behavioral interventions once the change process begins. Exhibit 16.5 provides a summary of the subject matter addressed through the CDP.

EXHIBIT 16.5

Comprehensive Drinker Profile

Demographic Information
- age and residence
- family status
- employment and income information
- education history

Drinking History
- development of the drinking problem
- current drinking pattern
- history of drinking pattern
- alcohol history
- preferred drinking settings
- associated behaviors
- beverage preferences
- relevant medical history

Motivational Information
- reasons for drinking
- effects of drinking (positive and negative)
- other life problems
- motivation for treatment
- rating of type of drinker

---

21. The Comprehensive Drinker Profile:
    a. is self-administered by the client.
    b. includes motivational information as well as a drinking history.
    c. works equally well if the client's drug of choice is alcohol or cocaine.
    d. all of the above.

Instruments to Assess Cognitive-Behavioral Factors

The assessment process is meant to guide treatment planning, so you might want to consider the use of instruments that shed light on your clients' thoughts and behaviors in relationship to substance use. Unfortunately, the devices that are currently available tend to focus solely on drinking, rather than on the use of other drugs. The instruments are useful, however, in that they lead to an understanding of the risky situations that tend to be associated with problematic behaviors.

The Inventory of Drinking Situations (IDS) helps clients identify situations in which they would normally drink. These situations are placed in eight categories: (a) negative emotional states, (b) negative physical states, (c) positive emotional states, (d) testing of personal control, (e) urges and temptations, (f) interpersonal conflict, (g) social pressures to drink, and (h) pleasant times with others. The profile that emerges shows high- and low-risk situations for this particular client. This instrument is especially helpful because it highlights the tremendous variation among clients. One person may tend to drink alone at home when feeling depressed, another might drink to celebrate successes, and still a third might drink primarily in social situations. With this information in hand, you and your client are able to make plans for coping strategies to deal with the situations that are problematic for that individual.

The Situational Confidence Questionnaire also examines drinking situations. In this case, however, clients are asked to imagine themselves in the situation and to rate the degree to which they feel confident to handle the situation without drinking. This instrument, like the IDS, helps in the development of behavioral strategies. Thus, you and your clients are able to create hierarchies of drinking situations such that the client can move gradually toward participating in situations that seem more daunting.

22. The Inventory of Drinking Situations is useful because:
    a. It helps clients identify situations in which they would normally drink.
    b. It shows that most people with drinking problems are troubled by the same risk situations.
    c. It shows that people with drinking problems must avoid all situations in which they would normally drink.
    d. All of the above.

TREATMENT PLANNING

The ATTC National Curriculum Committee (1998) defines treatment planning as follows:

> ...A collaborative process through which the counselor and client develop desired treatment outcomes and identify the strategies for achieving them. At a minimum the treatment plan addresses the identified substance use disorder(s), as well as issues related to treatment progress, including relationships with family and significant others, employment, education, spirituality, health concerns, and legal needs. (p. 39)

EXHIBIT 16.6

Treatment Planning Competencies*

---

1. Obtain and interpret all relevant assessment information.
2. Explain assessment findings to the client and significant others involved in potential treatment.
3. Provide the client and significant others with clarification and further information as needed.
4. Examine treatment implications in collaboration with the client and significant others.
5. Confirm the readiness of the client and significant others to participate in treatment.
6. Prioritize the client needs in the order they will be addressed.
7. Formulate mutually agreed upon and measurable treatment outcome statements for each need.
8. Identify appropriate strategies for each outcome.
9. Coordinate treatment activities and community resources with prioritized client needs in a manner consistent with the client's diagnosis and existing placement criteria.
10. Develop with the client a mutually acceptable plan of action and method for monitoring and evaluating progress.
11. Inform client of confidentiality rights, program procedures that safeguard them, and the exceptions imposed by regulations.
12. Reassess the treatment plan at regular intervals or when indicated by changing circumstances.

---

*From *Addiction Counseling Competencies: The Knowledge, Skills, and Attitudes of Professional Practice* (pp. 39–45), by Addiction Technology Transfer Centers National Curriculum Committee, 1998, Rockville, MD: Center for Substance Abuse Treatment.

The competencies underlying successful treatment planning are outlined in Exhibit 16.6.

23. The treatment planning process:
    a. should be carefully controlled by the counselor to make sure that issues other than drug use are put aside.
    b. should reflect a collaboration in which the counselor and client identify outcomes and strategies.
    c. should not be reassessed once it has been written down.
    d. should focus on how the client can benefit from the program offered to all clients of the facility.

24. Treatment planning competencies include:
    a. explaining assessment findings.
    b. prioritizing client needs.
    c. informing clients of confidentiality rights.
    d. all of the above.

Collaboration

In examining Exhibit 16.6 you probably notice the close association between assessment and treatment planning. The first steps in deciding on the nature of treatment for a particular client are completing a comprehensive assessment *and making sure that the results of that assessment are understood by the client.* I highlight the importance of helping clients understand the results of the assessment because these clients will be close collaborators in the development of their treatment plans. As you saw, treatment planning is, by definition, a collaborative process!

The value of collaboration in the treatment planning process may seem readily apparent. In the past, however, many treatment providers assumed that the treatment plan should be developed by the professional and given to the client. The attitude underlying that approach was that addiction clients could not be trusted to know what should be done to change their own lives. A different set of attitudes is at play in the collaborative approach. Consider, for example, some of the attitudes that the ATTC National Curriculum Committee (1998) identified as necessary for competent practice in treatment planning:

- Recognition of the client's right and need to understand the assessment results
- Willingness to communicate interactively with the client and significant others
- Willingness to negotiate with the client
- Respect for input from client and significant others
- Respect for client values and goals
- Sensitivity to the client's needs and perceptions
- Sensitivity to gender and cultural issues
- Recognition of the value of client input into treatment goals and process
- Willingness to consider multiple approaches to recovery and change
- Open-mindedness toward a variety of approaches

25. The results of the client's assessment should be understood by the client because:
    a. he or she will need to use the information in order to work on the treatment plan.
    b. it is a legal requirement.
    c. it will prevent the client from complaining later that treatment was not actually needed.
    d. it will prove to the client that his or her problem is severe.

Outcomes

When your attitude is one of respect for your clients, you welcome their ideas about how to transform their assessed problems into positive outcome goals. Certainly, one of the outcomes you and your client will seek as a result of treatment is a dramatic change in substance use and abuse. You will also find, however, that clients have other priorities they want to address. Rather than insisting that clients put off addressing other goals until they have a certain amount of "clean and sober" time, you should make sure that some of the client's most pressing concerns are included in the initial treatment plan. Following are some of the kinds of goals that your clients might feel are high priorities:

- Resolving legal problems.
- Attaining financial stability
- Attaining positive and stable family relationships
- Setting and meeting career goals
- Improving social skills
- Improving life management skills
  - Relaxation
  - Stress management
  - Problem-solving and decision-making
  - Recognizing and dealing with emotions
- Enhancing physical health and fitness
- Adapting more effectively to work or school
- Developing social-support systems

- Increasing involvement in recreation and other social pursuits
- Dealing with psychological issues such as depression or anxiety

When you and your client explore the results of the comprehensive assessment, take note of problem areas in the individual's life. You should work together to set some priorities. The result of this process should be a set of goals—about three to five—*each of which is stated as a positive outcome*. Keep in mind that the outcome statement should reflect a change in the client—not a service that you plan to provide! "Participate in eight hours of drug counseling" is *not* an outcome. "Maintain abstinence from mood-altering drugs" *is* an outcome. "Participate in career counseling" is *not* an outcome. "Obtain employment in a retail establishment" *is* an outcome. You and your client should then agree on the methods that will be used for achieving each outcome.

26. Outcomes listed in a treatment plan might include:
    a. abstinence from mood-altering substances.
    b. improving life management skills.
    c. enhancing physical health and fitness.
    d. all of the above.

Methods

Once you and your client have delineated the outcomes you hope to achieve, you can address the question of what methods would be most likely to work.

Among the counseling methods most frequently used in the substance abuse field are behavioral self-control training (teaching clients the techniques they need to monitor and change their own behaviors); contingency management (identifying and manipulating environmental contingencies that reward or punish the substance use behaviors); relaxation, assertion, and social skills training; couple and family therapy; career counseling; cognitive restructuring (helping clients alter their appraisals of self and environment); assistance with problem solving and decision making; aversive conditioning (coupling substance use with a real or imagined unpleasant experience); stress management training; group counseling; lifestyle and recreational planning; provision of information about the effects of psychoactive drugs; and referral to such self-help organizations as Alcoholics Anonymous and Narcotics Anonymous. (Lewis, Dana, & Blevins, 2002, p. 11)

In addition to strategies that take place within counseling or treatment are methods that occur in the context of the client's daily life. Sometimes the best way to achieve one's goals is through going to church or returning to school or starting an exercise program or joining a club. These methods, too, should find their way into the treatment plan.

27. When identifying methods for achieving the outcomes listed in a treatment plan, the counselor should:
    a. help the client make decisions about the methods for achieving each of the outcomes listed.
    b. list the methods normally used in the treatment setting and consider how they might apply to the client's goals.
    c. present the client with a list of approved treatments.
    d. make sure that each method listed is one that can take place within the treatment setting.

Treatment Plan Example

If you are employed in an addiction treatment setting you will probably have an official treatment plan form that is used consistently among the counselors and other treatment providers in that organization. In general, such treatment plan forms include a version of the following components:

- Demographic information about the client.
- Diagnosis (from the *DSM*)
- Brief history
- Case formulation
- Short-term and long-term goals
  - Interventions
  - Time frame
  - Measurement devices

You should be familiar with this type of format. For counseling purposes, however, you might consider using a simplified plan that can guide the counseling process. The simplified treatment plan that I like to use includes outcome statements and methods for achieving each outcome. This approach is practical and manageable for a client and counselor. It is also realistic, in that the current environment does not tend to give the counselor and client much control over the length of short- and long-term treatment. Consider the following example.

> *John Smith has had a long history of heavy drinking. In recent years, this behavior has become more pronounced. His wife is upset about his drinking. She also feels that he is in danger of losing his job because of absences and lateness. After numerous attempts to confront him about it, she has moved out of their home. John is surprised and sad about this situation. With his wife away, he finds himself at loose ends. He hasn't found any way to fill in his time. The only friends he has are people with whom he drinks and he's trying to cut back on drinking in order to win back his wife. He feels depressed and lonely at home alone at night so his drinking has actually increased. Although he feels "down," he worries that he'll be anxious and unable to sleep without alcohol. He doesn't believe that his job in the insurance business is in danger but he does feel that he no longer gets much satisfaction from it.*

John has gone to the employee assistance program at his place of employment. The employee assistance counselor has diagnosed John as alcohol dependent and referred him to you for counseling. John doesn't really accept this diagnosis, but he does know that he will have to have at least a period of being abstinent from alcohol in order to reconcile with his wife. Exhibit 16.7 shows an example of the kind of short-term treatment plan that might evolve if you worked with this client.

Keep in mind that this treatment plan is designed so that a period of abstinence can be achieved. The methods described involve steps to be taken immediately. In the longer term, the steps the client takes will change. If John is successful in achieving a period of abstinence, he will then move toward ways to maintain this life change, including relapse prevention planning. In the treatment plan shown, his desired outcome of reconciliation with his wife remains in the future. The steps he takes now are small steps designed only to reestablish communication and trust. His career planning efforts are clearly focused on the future, with an immediate job change explicitly identified as something to be avoided in the short term.

As you examine Exhibit 16.7 you may notice that sometimes one desired outcome is actually a step toward achievement of another outcome. For example, achieving abstinence, while an important outcome in itself, is also a step toward marital reconciliation. Some of the methods

EXHIBIT 16.7

Sample Treatment Plan

Desired Outcome: Attain abstinence from alcohol
- Monitor alcohol use and cravings for alcohol.
- Identify situations usually associated with drinking (e.g., at home alone at night).
- Identify ways to avoid or cope with these high-risk situations.
- Participate in training sessions to learn the skills for successful coping.
- Practice new ways of thinking about himself and his environment.
- Learn relaxation techniques to cope with anxiety and insomnia.

Desired Outcome: Increase social contacts
- Attend an Alcoholics Anonymous (AA) meeting and identify a potential sponsor.
- Participate in social skills training sessions.
- Identify and follow through on at least one evening activity, in addition to AA, that involves social contact with other people.

Desired Outcome: Reconcile with spouse
- Contract for a period of abstinence.
- Participate in couple communication training.
- Invite spouse to open AA meeting.
- Invite spouse to social evening activity.

Desired Outcome: Initiate career planning
- Improve work habits in current position.
- Participate in career assessment at local community college.
- Analyze the pros and cons of career change.
- Generate ideas for long-term career goals.
- Avoid immediate change.

---

identified for one outcome will also help in achieving another outcome. Participating in AA and social activities will lead not only to improving John's social life but also to improving his chances for success in achieving abstinence.

28. In the counseling setting, a simplified treatment plan might include only:
    a. outcomes and methods.
    b. diagnoses and formulations.
    c. descriptions of methods to be used.
    d. a general case formulation.

29. In the treatment plan, it is important that:
    a. one of the outcomes relates specifically to changes in alcohol or drug use.
    b. none of the methods for one outcome affects the other outcomes.
    c. outcome #1 be achieved completely before Outcome #2 is considered.
    d. all of the above.

30. In the treatment plan for John Smith:
    a. the outcomes listed reflect changes in Mr. Smith's behavior and life situation.
    b. the outcomes reflect his own goals, particularly with regard to his spouse.
    c. the methods for achieving the outcomes are largely behavioral.
    d. all of the above.

We hope that reading this chapter helps you see the possibility for a seamless helping process. Ideally, your work with all your clients begins with the process of learning as much as you can about their current situations, the issues that confront them, and the personal goals that give their lives meaning. Once you and your clients participate in this exploration, you are ready to move toward the hard work of change. At every point along the way from screening to assessment to treatment planning, the process should involve a true, collaborative partnership between you and your clients.

KEY TERMS

assessment: An ongoing process through which the counselor collaborates with the client and others to gather and interpret information necessary for planning treatment and evaluating client progress.

Diagnostic and Statistical Manual: A manual published by the American Psychiatric Association to guide diagnoses of mental health disorders, including substance use disorders.

motivational interviewing: A directive, client-centered counseling style for eliciting behavior change by helping clients explore and resolve ambivalence.

screening: The process through which counselor, client, and available significant others determine the most appropriate initial course of action, given the client's needs and characteristics and the available resources within the community.

stages of change: The stages identified by Prochaska, DiClemente, and Norcross that people tend to go through as they change problematic behaviors. The stages include precontemplation, contemplation, preparation, action, and maintenance.

substance abuse disorder: Diagnostic category for a person whose substance use interferes with functioning but has never met the criteria for substance dependence (see substance dependence disorder).

substance dependence disorder: A diagnosis based on the criterion that the client exhibits three or more of the following symptoms: (a) substance taken in larger amounts or over a longer period of time than intended; (b) persistent desire or unsuccessful efforts to cut down, (c) a great deal of time spent in activities necessary to obtain the substance or recover from its effects; (d) important social, occupational, or recreational activities given up or reduced, (e) continued substance use despite social, psychological, or physical problems; (f) marked tolerance or markedly diminished ability to achieve effect; (g) substance often taken to avoid withdrawal symptoms.

substance use disorder: A diagnosis based on the following criteria: (a) the individual demonstrates an inability to control his or her use despite cognitive, behavioral, or physiological symptoms; and (b) the symptoms have been present for at least one month.

substance use history: A method, usually performed as part of an initial interview, in which the counselor obtains information about the client's substance use, life situation, and related concerns.

treatment planning: A collaborative process through which the counselor and client develop desired treatment outcomes and identify strategies for achieving them.

DISCUSSION QUESTIONS

1. In this chapter, the section on screening states that one of the competencies needed by the counselor is the ability to establish rapport with the client. Some people still doubt that it is possible to develop a warm, positive relationship with a drug-addicted client. What do you see as the barriers that might prevent you from developing rapport with a client? How might you overcome these barriers?

2. Motivational interviewing is based on the assumption that "denial" is not a characteristic of the client but is, instead, a function of the way we choose to interact with the client. What is your reaction to this assertion? Do you feel that you will be able to set aside your own views of what the client should do and recognize that the control is truly in his or her hands?

3. The chapter states that addiction counselors have an important role in screening for infectious diseases, including sexually transmitted diseases. How do you feel about your ability to discuss these sensitive questions with clients? What barriers will you need to overcome?

4. The stages of change model recognizes that clients have different counseling needs, depending on whether they are at precontemplation, contemplation, preparation, action, or maintenance. What basic approaches might you use with clients at each of these stages?

5. In what ways might a *DSM–IV* diagnosis be helpful as you develop a treatment plan for a client? How can you avoid overemphasizing the label of the diagnosis?

6. What do you think are the most important client characteristics to consider in carrying out a truly comprehensive assessment?

7. If your job entailed carrying out assessments of an agency's new clients, what kinds of assessment instruments would you want to have available for use with your clients?

8. The Addiction Severity Index allows you to assess the severity of a client's concerns in seven categories. How might this be useful to you in planning treatment?

9. The chapter suggests that the treatment plan should include the client's desired outcomes for various areas of his or her life in addition to the substance use behavior. Some people believe, however, that the client should achieve abstinence first and then consider other life changes. Where do you stand on this? What is your rationale?

10. The chapter briefly mentions a number of different methods that can be used to help a client change his or her substance use behaviors. At this point, which of these methods do you feel you would like to learn more about? What attracts you about these particular interventions?

SUGGESTED FURTHER READING

How to Obtain Screening and Assessment Instruments

Michigan Alcoholism Screening Test (MAST)

See the National Institute on Alcohol Abuse and Alcoholism Web site for a review and contact information related to this instrument: http://www.niaaa.nih.gov/publications/mast-text.htm.

Addiction Severity Index (ASI)

A wealth of information regarding the Addiction Severity Index can be found at http://www.tresearch.org. On this Web site you can find the instrument itself, the manual, and a short guide.

Comprehensive Drinker Profile (CDP)

Information about the CDP can be found at the following Web site: http://casaa.unm.edu. At this Web site (the on Alcoholism, Substance Abuse, and Addictions at the University of New Mexico) you will be able to obtain the Comprehensive Drinker Profile and its accompanying manual.

Alcohol Use Disorders Identification Test (AUDIT)

See the Web site of National Institute on Alcohol Abuse and Alcoholism for a review and contact information: http://www.niaaa.nih.gov/publications/audit.htm.

Alcohol Use Inventory (AUI)

This instrument is available from Pearson Assessments: http://assessments.ncspearson.com/assessments/tests/aui.htm.

Drug Abuse Screening Test (DAST)

This instrument can be seen in its entirety on the Schick Shadel Hospital Web site: http://www.schick-shadel.com/drug-test.html.

Inventory of Drinking Situations (IDS)

A review and contact information can be found on the Web site of the National Institute on Alcohol Abuse and Alcoholism: http://www.niaaa.nih.gov/publications/ids.htm.

Situational Confidence Questionnaire (SCQ)

See the National Institute on Alcohol Abuse and Alcoholism: http://www.niaaa.nih.gov/publications/scq.htm.

REFERENCES

Addiction Technology Transfer Centers National Curriculum Committee. (1998). *Addiction counseling competencies: The knowledge, skills, and attitudes of professional practice. Treatment Assistance Publication #21* (DHHS Publication No. SMA 98-3171). Rockville, MD: Center for Substance Abuse Treatment.

American Psychiatric Association. (1994). *Diagnostic and statistical manual of mental disorders* (4th ed.). Washington, DC: Author.

Barthwell, A. G., & Gilbert, C. L. (1993). *Screening for infectious diseases among substance abusers. Treatment Improvement Protocol #6* (DHHS Publication No. SMA 93-2048). Rockville, MD: Center for Substance Abuse Treatment.

Center for Substance Abuse Treatment. (2000). *Changing the conversation: Improving substance abuse treatment: The national treatment plan initiative* (Vol. 1). Rockville, MD: U.S. Department of Health and Human Services.

Lewis, J. A., Dana, R. Q., & Blevins, G. A. (2002). *Substance abuse counseling.* Pacific Grove, CA: Brooks/Cole.

Miller, W. R., & Rollnick, S. (Eds.). (2002). *Motivational interviewing: Preparing people to change addictive behavior* (2nd ed.). New York: Guilford Press.

Prochaska, J. O., DiClemente, C. C., & Norcross, J. C. (1992). In search of how people change. *American Psychologist, 47,* 1102–1114.

Ries, R. K. (1994). *Assessment and treatment of patients with coexisting mental illness and alcohol and other drug abuse. Treatment Improvement Protocol #9* (DHHS Publication No. SMA 95-3061). Rockville, MD: Center for Substance Abuse Treatment.

Rollnick, S., & Miller, W. R. (1995). What is motivational interviewing? *Behavioural and Cognitive Psychotherapy, 23,* 325–334.

Case Management

Harvey A. Siegal
Wright State University

TRUTH OR FICTION?

___ 1. Managed care *and* case management *are essentially the same.*
___ 2. *The more resources a client can mobilize for recovery, the more case management is needed.*
___ 3. *A single practice model of case management will serve most clients well.*
___ 4. *Client advocacy is an important function for case managers.*
___ 5. *Case management can assist substance abuse treatment clients with problems other than their drug or alcohol use.*
___ 6. *A detailed case management and clinical assessment are essentially interchangeable.*
___ 7. *Case management establishes a single point of contact for accessing multiple health and human services in a community.*
___ 8. *The presenting pathologies that a client presents with must be substantially diminished before a case management plan can be formulated.*
___ 9. *When dealing with clients with special needs, a case manager needs an appropriate attitudinal set and skills.*
___ 10. *Comprehensive case management is needed because in most communities health and human services are fragmented in scope and can have complex admissions criteria.*
___ 11. *Only persons possessing advanced academic training (Master's level) can effectively provide case management services.*
___ 12. *Case management interventions are best delivered by a professional who has no clinical responsibility for the client.*
___ 13. *Case management is effective in diminishing barriers to treatment engagement.*

___ 14. *Studies have demonstrated that case management itself does not improve treatment*
outcomes but helps retain clients in treatment that does.
___ 15. *Case management is a relatively hard intervention to evaluate.*

As a professional in the substance abuse treatment field, you've probably come to appreciate that in-treatment substance abusers typically need more than counseling and other clinical activities they are participating in to support their recovery. This seems to be especially the case for multiply challenged populations such as substance abusers involved with the criminal justice system, people infected with HIV/AIDS, the substance abuse and mental illness (SAMI) or people with dual diagnoses of psychiatric illnesses and chemical dependency, pregnant drug abusers, very economically deprived people, and those with dependent children. Here, in addition to the usual therapeutic services, assistance with obtaining and maintaining employment, housing, education, medical/psychiatric/psychological care, child care, and transportation, to name but a few, is frequently required. The goal of **case management** as a social service discipline is to help those in need obtain the services and resources that can facilitate and support their recovery.

Human services in most communities are diversely and often complexly distributed between numerous agencies and providers, each with its own access requirements. Significant barriers to accessing and ultimately using needed services are not uncommon. Moreover, substance abusers often carry with them the added barrier that they are a marginalized, stigmatized group of people who may be viewed as being self-indulgent, morally deficit, and not necessarily suffering from an illness. Hence, they may find many doors closed and they are not provided services that are desperately needed. A striking example of this is HIV/AIDS treatment in which many providers will refuse to treat an active drug user. Client-oriented case management is a method to ensure that appropriate, accessible services can be obtained from a complex, fragmented, and often indifferent human services delivery system.

Because substance abuse negatively affects so many parts of a person's life, we believe that recovery is built around a comprehensive continuum of services whose goal is to attenuate drug use, rebuild self-image and relationships, and reintegrate into pro-social activities. These ancillary services must be consonant with the patient's position in the treatment continuum thereby supporting and encouraging continued involvement with therapeutic services. Case managers can help ensure that all therapeutic and supportive activities are structured and sequenced to facilitate seamless transitions to progressive levels of care, avoid gaps in service, and be responsive to events that increase the potential for relapse or dropping out. As a treatment professional, think of case management as your client's "on ramp," or way into the human service delivery system and then perhaps the coordinating or fine tuning mechanism—once your client is receiving therapeutic and perhaps other rehabilitative services.

The origin of case management as a recognizable social service discipline in the United States might be dated from around the 1920s and 1930s. Social work as a profession in the United States partially emerged as a response to the strains engendered by the tremendous immigration to this country beginning in the late nineteenth century and reaching a crescendo during the early part of the twentieth century. Traditional assistance organizations, such as religious institutions and family, were overburdened by demands being made upon them. Urban neighborhoods virtually exploded with arriving people who all had needs. **Settlement houses** and **neighborhood centers** were established and staffed by volunteers sometimes known as *Friendly Helpers* who were replaced by paid workers. This system ultimately developed into a new profession. One important goal for volunteer, paid worker, or professional was helping the neighborhood residents find and access health care, employment, and other such services.

Ultimately this became known as what we today call "case management" (Rose & Moore, 1995, p. 335).

With the arrival of the New Deal as the vehicle that would drive the nation out of the Great Depression, government emerged as the overwhelming provider of welfare and social services. Beginning dramatically with the Social Security Act of 1939 and then the Federal Community Mental Health Center Act of 1963, followed by the flowering of social-oriented programming during the Great Society initiative of the late 1960s, the range of helping services available in the community expanded exponentially. Fueled by the overarching belief that helping people with problems was the "right thing to do" and converging federal, state, and even local funding streams, services sometimes were even duplicative. Persons needing these services found it sometimes very confusing and even difficult to access the assistance that was, at least theoretically, there for the asking. What was needed was a way of operating in a very large, diffuse service arena. A "case manager" who understood both client needs and the system's components and operations, seemed to offer the best promise for bringing client and resource provider together in a rational, comprehensive, and (hopefully) cost effective way.

The early 1960s also marked the large-scale deinstitutionalization of persons with mental illnesses. These were unquestionably among the most vulnerable of our nation's people. If community living was to be sustained, a whole range or safety net of clinical and social services would be required. It was the case manager who assumed the responsibility of helping these vulnerable, not infrequently troubled people successfully navigate through a community's human service delivery system (Center for Substance Abuse Treatment, 1998).

While drug abuse has been seen as a public health and social problem since the Civil War, substance abusers were typically not institutionalized like persons suffering from mental illness. In the 1970s, however, a much decried heroin epidemic was afflicting the nation's cities. Linked very strongly to it was an increase in property (which came to be known as "street") crime as opiate dependent people committed crimes to obtain money to purchase drugs. The criminal justice system found itself the very visible focal point as the connection between drugs and crime was recognized. Political leaders looked to the justice system in tandem with the public health system for the solution to the street crime problem. One very prominent initiative to emerge was the Treatment Alternatives to Street Crime (**TASC**); now known as Treatment Accountability for Safer Communities (also TASC). Here, arrested and convicted drug offenders could receive treatment and other helping services in lieu of incarceration. Naturally, it was expected that these services would address the offender's substance abuse or dependency as a way to reduce the risk of future criminal behavior. At the heart of TASC were case managers who were charged with developing a comprehensive recovery plan for each offender. The TASC case manager would be responsible for fully monitoring his or her client and documenting that the plan was being followed. TASC catapulted the discipline into virtually every part of substance abuse treatment programming. Accrediting bodies soon made case management services a required aspect of service provision.

A precise definition of case management as a service delivery modality still remains elusive. For example, several definitions of case management are mentioned in the Center for Substance Abuse Treatment's (**CSAT**) Treatment Improvement Protocol entitled *Comprehensive Case Management for Substance Abuse Treatment* (1998). In other publications, case management is described as:

- "Planning and coordinating a package of health and social services that is individualized to meet a particular client's needs." (Moore, 1990, p. 444)
- "[A] process or method for ensuring that consumers are provided with whatever services they need in a coordinated, effective, and efficient manner." (Intagliata, 1981)

- "Helping people whose lives are unsatisfying or unproductive due to the presence of many problems which require assistance from several helpers at once." (Ballew & Mink, 1996, p. 3)
- "Monitoring, tracking and providing support to a client, throughout the course of his/her treatment and after." (Ogborne & Rush, 1983, p. 136)
- "Assisting the patient in re-establishing an awareness of internal resources such as intelligence, competence, and problem solving abilities; establishing and negotiating lines of operation and communication between the patient and external resources; and advocating with those external resources in order to enhance the continuity, accessibility, accountability, and efficiency of those resources." (Rapp, Siegal, & Fisher, 1992, p. 83)
- "Assess[ing] the needs of the client and the client's family, when appropriate . . . arranges, coordinates, monitors, evaluates and advocates for a package of multiple services to meet the specific client's complex needs. (National Association of Social Workers, 1992, p. 5)

As you can probably see, these descriptions actually do converge in the appreciation of assisting the client in obtaining resources that could support their efforts at recovery.

There is, however, more general agreement on what constitutes the stages or "Functions" that case managers perform in doing their work. Below, we will describe these and then offer several common operational or practice models of the modality. As a counselor and substance abuse treatment professional, depending upon the agency or organization that employs you, you will either have to be competent in delivering these core case management functions yourself, or work with case managers who do.

This raises another important issue for case managers in substance abuse treatment services. Unlike formal organizational accreditation in mental health programming, there is as of yet, no universally recognized formal academic degree, credential, or licensure for case managers in the specialty substance abuse field. Specific requirements vary by state treatment service credentialing or licensure boards. Private managed care organizations (MCOs) and other reimbursement organizations including governmental ones may have stated criteria for paying for the service of case management. However, at this time, both governmental and private accreditation organizations are in the process of promulgating standards that they hope will be universally adopted by the substance abuse treatment field.

Case management presents its practitioners—whether they are substance abuse counselors or dedicated full-time case management specialists—with unique challenges. Case managers, like other professionals, recognize that patience and perseverance is often necessary to helping clients realistically identify and articulate their needs. Then, once accomplished, some creativity in locating and accessing those resources that can adequately meet these needs might be required as well. However, with these challenges also come significant rewards. For example, the case manager can immediately help clients improve their quality of life by getting safer, stable housing, linking with a provider for needed medical care for themselves or their children, or getting legal assistance. In the longer term, the assistance and support of a case manager can help clients learn how to set goals and develop feasible, practical plans for achieving them. Helping our clients remove themselves from the destructive, chaotic lifestyle that chemical dependency engenders supports their long-term recovery.

Case management is best described as a general or nonspecific intervention and its practitioners therefore need to view themselves as *generalists* rather than *specialists*. The goals of this chapter are to help you understand: (a) what case management is, (b) how case management is delivered to substance abuse treatment clients in its operational practice models, (c) what case managers who work with chemically dependent people do, (d) some of the challenges that case managers face when assisting persons with multiple problems, and (e) the minimal skills and knowledge needed to be effective at the craft. An understanding of these will assist you in preparing for your credentialing examinations.

1. Case management is best described as a:
   a. narrow specialty.
   b. a way to help people.
   c. a "generalist intervention."
   d. a way to limit costs.

2. Case management is particularly useful for:
   a. resource-rich clients.
   b. poly-substance abusers.
   c. multiply challenged clients.
   d. angry or hostile clients.

3. Case management can assist clients in:
   a. making seamless transitions to different levels of care.
   b. avoiding gaps in services.
   c. reducing barriers to accessing and obtaining resources that can support recovery.
   d. all of the above.

4. Case management is best described as employing a:
   a. set of social service functions.
   b. a precise technical language.
   c. a readily recognizable approach.
   d. uniform documentation procedure.

5. Case management is useful in substance abuse treatment because chemically dependent people:
   a. are typically powerless.
   b. have cognitive dysfunctions throughout early recovery.
   c. can have character deficits.
   d. have problems other than their use of drugs or alcohol.

6. Which of the following is necessary for effective case management?
   a. case management certification
   b. a license to case manage
   c. good communication skills
   d. ability to read and understand contracts

7. In conveying referral information to a community agency, the case manager always:
   a. shares "gut level" impressions with the corresponding professional.
   b. offers an informed prognosis of success.
   c. respects confidentiality.
   d. provides necessary assurances.

8. Effective referrals are assured by:
   a. iron-clad agency agreements.
   b. a full understanding of the community agency providing the service.
   c. filling out all the client's paperwork in advance.
   d. all of the above.

9. Which of the following skills are important for case managers?
   a. data collection
   b. communication
   c. documentation
   d. all of the above

10. The case manager should have knowledge about which of the following?
    a. the community human service delivery system
    b. the specific agency to which a referral is being made
    c. federal confidentiality laws
    d. all of the above

WHAT IS CASE MANAGEMENT?

Case management is a set of social services functions whose goals are to help clients access resources they need to support their recovery from substance abuse and other pathologic conditions. Case management is also used to ensure that chemically dependent persons will receive the therapeutic services they need and transition effectively from one level of care to another (e.g., residential treatment to outpatient services) as their recovery proceeds. The resources may be external or even tangible—for example, housing, transportation, child care, vocational training, steady employment, and so forth—or internal—identifying strengths, setting goals, or acquiring and practicing interpersonal or social skills. The seven social service core functions comprising case management—*engagement, assessment, planning, linkage, monitoring, advocacy and disengagement*—remain intact regardless of the specific practice model employed or the goals of the case management intervention. Different practice models do, however, vary the depth, intensity, and extent with which these core functions are delivered. Different practice models also require different practitioner training and experience (Ballew & Mink, 1996).

The specific goals of the case management intervention are usually determined by the client's needs and the agency or setting in which the client and case manager interact. In some settings, the case manager's responsibility is limited to assessment and then referral of substance abusers to primary treatment in a community based agency. Increasingly, communities are establishing centralized outreach, assessment, and referral agencies as a way of centralizing resources (Stephens, Scott, & Muck, 2003). For clients involved with the criminal justice system, the case manager may be responsible for assessing the client, developing a management plan, and referring him or her to a variety of community-based or even criminal justice system–operated treatment programs. Here, the case manager is expected to work closely with the probation officer responsible for the client's community supervision. Remember, the overarching goal for the case manager is assisting clients to define those things that will support and sustain recovery; however, the challenge is doing so effectively given the limitations imposed by the availability of clinical treatment and other human service resources.

While proficiency in all of the core functions is important for delivering effective case management, *linkage* and *advocacy* constitute the hallmarks of the modality. Regardless of the specific practice model employed, the case manager—to one extent or another—attempts to make available services "fit" the needs of the client and not visa versa. Case management is widely regarded as a client-centered intervention, with clients determining and defining their own needs. However, in most settings, a professional works as part of an interdisciplinary team of specialists. As such it is the setting in which the case management is delivered that sets the parameters of the practice. Clients, for example, receiving services in the criminal justice system certainly have less voice in defining their goals than those receiving services in a community-based organization.

A fuller description of these functions can be found throughout the case manager literature. One of the clearest and most concise is in a text by Ballew and Mink, entitled *Case Management In the Human Services*. These core functions can also be seen as the stages of the case management intervention that the case manager and client work and progress through as their professional relationship proceeds.

The beginning stage of the relationship is *engagement*. Here, the case manager initially meets with the client and engenders a positive working relationship. The case manager must offer the client an understandable description of what case management entails and how this service might contribute to the overall goal of recovery. Providing this kind of description helps your client structure realistic expectations about the service, its benefits, and your professional relationship. Often, a brief written statement that the client keeps after the conclusion of the meeting explaining what a case manager does and how the client can benefit from the service can be very helpful for both the client and their significant others. Very early in the relationship, the case manager needs to be able to demonstrate that he or she can actually help the client obtain something of value. The classic example is offering the homeless client a pair of warm socks on a wet, freezing day. However, since the case manager's goal is to support the client's recovery, an example of an immediate benefit of case management might be providing or helping the client obtain transportation tokens or vouchers enabling them to attend counseling and other services. Another example of immediate assistance might be helping the client complete employment applications and insurance forms or find safe, drug-free housing.

Assessment provides the professional with a clear understanding of a client's needs, existing resources, and perceived barriers to meeting these needs. Keep in mind that the goal of the case management assessment is to support the recovery process. Therefore, the assessment necessarily focuses on identifying more proximal goals such as locating stable, safe housing, child care, transportation to the treatment agency, medical care, or employment in a drug free environment. The identification of longer-range goals—such as education or advancement— are appropriately formulated later in the treatment and recovery process.

Communication between case manager and client is very similar to that of substance abuse counselors, social workers, and other human service professionals. The case manager is attentive and respectful of the client's cultural, gender, and sexual orientation issues. It is important to be professional and nonjudgmental and employ empathic listening skills. Confrontation is avoided as in any client-centered approach. The case manager only "confronts" the client with factual information such as helping clients clarify that their drug or alcohol use is responsible for many of the difficulties he or she may be experiencing. As in all professional-client relationships, the case manager may have to be definitive and consistent about setting appropriate boundaries.

Planning involves helping the client develop a feasible, concrete plan to obtain specific services or resources. It states a goal, action steps, who to contact, and usually a time frame to accomplish it. Depending upon the case management practice model employed, it will identify who (i.e., case manager or client) will execute the action steps and if others, such as family members, are to be involved. Case management plans are typically sequential with different goals identified as treatment progresses. Case management planning is, of course, fluid and must be modified as client needs dictate. It is vital that the client not only understands the plan but that he or she actively buys into it and feels some ownership of the plan.

Linkage is "hooking up" the client with an agency/program that can provide the needed service or resource. Again, depending on the practice model of case management employed, linkage may entail the case manager simply identifying the agency, perhaps initiating contact, or perhaps even accompanying the client to the agency and advocating for the client to obtain the needed service or resource.

Monitoring involves the case manager keeping track of the client's progress through the case management plan. It may focus on the treatment continuum, ensuring that a seamless transition is made from service level to service level. Monitoring also entails evaluating the client's success in obtaining the services and resources outlined in the plan that can sustain the recovery process. Based upon the data obtained by the monitoring process, the case management plan can be revised to reflect changes in the client's situation. Naturally, you'll negotiate these carefully with your client and obtain the same kind of "buy-in" and ownership that you had with the original plan.

Advocacy: Because of the complex, fragmented nature of the human service system and the marginalized or devalued status that substance abusers are relegated to, the case manager frequently needs to be an advocate for the client. As an advocate, the case manager morally represents the client and assertively helps him or her obtain the services or resources they are entitled to.

Disengagement, like discharge planning in any clinical service, including chemical dependency treatment, signifies the approaching end of the active professional or formal relationship between case manager and client. Depending on agency regulations, it may occur once linkage with treatment has been effected, or at the end of the primary phase of treatment, or, perhaps even extend through postprimary or aftercare activities. Disengagement is, of course, a process and not a discrete event. Recall that your goal as a case manager is to prepare the client for the change by emphasizing that it will ultimately be the client's responsibility to satisfy their own needs and remember how to find assistance that they need in the community. Your planning may call for linking the client with a community ombudsman agency or similar service or agency.

As a helping intervention, case management is clearly characterized by these social service functions. How these social service functions are actually delivered is determined by the mission and resources of the agency responsible for providing the case management services. In some practice situations there will be a designated case manager, separate from the client's counselor, who performs the functions; in others, it may be the primary counselor or therapist. This may engender stresses and strains as practitioner and client negotiate the boundaries of a productive therapeutic relationship. For example, in criminal justice system operated programs such as Treatment Accountability for Safer Communities (TASC), clients may have difficulty in reconciling the fact that their case manager will be reporting to the sentencing judge (or designee) information about the client's progress or noncompliance. An unfavorable report may result in the imposition of sanctions, such as imprisonment or more intensive urine surveillance. On a more practical level, the integration of clinical and case management activities by the same professional may be incompatible from a time-management perspective. For example, certain case management practice models call for the service to be brought directly to the client in the community and is not facility/office-bound as is typical of most clinical interventions. This kind of intense involvement means a significant reduction in case load and can result in scheduling problems. Though difficult, none of these problems are insurmountable. Careful planning, precisely articulated activities and responsibilities, comprehensive training, and attentive supervision will assist practitioners in providing quality services.

On the philosophical level, substance abuse treatment and case management are complementary and wholly compatible. Perhaps the major difference between the two is that case management focuses on service and resource acquisition, while therapy is directed at helping the client achieve intra- and interpersonal change that facilitates the removal of dysfunctional behaviors including drug use. As we review how case management service is actually delivered as a specific practice model, you'll get a clearer picture of the ways in which it differs from counseling and other clinical activities. What you will appreciate is how each richly contributes to initiating and sustaining your clients' recovery.

One final and very important distinction should be offered. Case management is clearly separate from *managed care* which emphasizes gate-keeping functions to limit access to service as a way to control costs. A persistent criticism of case management, especially in these increasingly resource-strapped times, relates to its strong traditions of being client-driven and advocating for the client. Critics claim that effective case management challenges a community human service system already operating at full capacity to both accommodate new populations of clients that it is ill equipped to serve, along with increasing services demanded by existent clients. This can force the community to obtain new fiscal resources to support these services or reallocate existent ones. However, because case management seems to be an effective substance abuse treatment enhancement, supporting positive outcomes such as decreased drug use, better employment, and less criminal justice involvement, the potential added costs are justified.

11. Which of the following is *not* a social service function employed in case management:
    a. planning
    b. diagnosis
    c. monitoring
    d. advocacy

12. Which of the following is typically *not* done by case managers:
    a. client advocacy
    b. client mentoring
    c. client assessment
    d. service linkage

13. The hallmarks of the case management intervention are client:
    a. assessment/diagnosis
    b. linkage/advocacy
    c. linkage/success
    d. motivation/confrontation

14. Communications between client and case manager are similar to:
    a. doctor and patient.
    b. attorney and client.
    c. counselor and client.
    d. provider and customer.

15. The goals of a case management assessment are to:
    a. ensure that the client is fully aware of the severity of their substance abuse problem.
    b. determine what resources are needed to support recovery.
    c. determine whether the therapeutic modality assigned is the most effective.
    d. determine the cost effectiveness of the range of services to be provided.

16. In case management provided in a criminal justice setting, as an *advocate* for the client, the practitioner should:
    a. help the client avoid sanctions for violating very minor rule regulations.
    b. obtain all the services that he or she is entitled to.
    c. modify probation requirements.
    d. all of the above.

17. In reference to *case management* and *managed care*, which of the following statements best describes the comparison?
    a. They are entirely comparable.
    b. Managed care seeks to restrict services; case management evaluates them.
    c. Managed care assures services are of comparable quality; case management assures that services are appropriately sequenced.
    d. Case management identifies needed services; managed care provides gate- keeping services.

PRACTICE MODELS OF CASE MANAGEMENT SERVICE WITH SUBSTANCE ABUSERS

Although case management uses several social service functions, these are actually organized, or to be more precise, *operationalized* into four more or less recognizable practice models. These practice models are commonly designated as: (a) broker/generalist, (b) strengths-based, (c) clinical/rehabilitation, and (d) assertive community/treatment.

Case management models, like the definitions of case management, vary with the context and setting within which the intervention is offered. Some models focus on delivering social services, others on coordinating the delivery of services. Some will provide both. The models result, as much from the needs of specific client populations and the demands of service settings as they do from distinct theoretical differences about what case management should be. It must be emphasized that a single model is not universally better than another but is, in fact, chosen by the needs of the clients to be served and the resources available to the providing agency.

For substance abuse treatment, the following represent the most commonly applied case management practice models.

Broker/Generalist

In *broker/generalist models* the case manager identifies the clients' needs and then helps them access either clinical services or community resources to address these needs. Rather than an intensive long-term relationship between case manager and client, brokerage models emphasize the acquisition of resources and focus on sequenced, client goal setting and planning and may include social and psychological skills development. Ongoing monitoring, if provided at all, is relatively brief and does not typically include active advocacy.

In discussions of case management, broker/generalist models are sometimes disparaged because of the limited, focused nature of the client–case manager relationship and the absence of active, ongoing advocacy. Nonetheless, this approach employs the basic case management social service functions and is useful and cost effective in selected situations. The relatively limited nature of the case manager–client relationship in this model allows the case manager to provide services to many more clients and consequently caseloads are large. Brokerage approaches work best in settings where treatment and social services are integrated and the need for close monitoring and ongoing advocacy is minimal. The brokerage model works best with clients who are not economically deprived, more psychologically intact, well motivated, and have the internal and social resources that can be readily mobilized to support recovery.

Generalist approaches to working with substance-abusing clients have taken several forms. For example, case managers practicing in a central intake facility are responsible for assessing substance abuse/chemical dependency problems, determining their extent and/or severity, and then referring the person to a community-based substance abuse treatment program and perhaps other human service providers as well. The contact is typically limited to a visit or two and essentially terminates upon the delivery of a referral. Some treatment agencies employ a *case management specialist* who is responsible for referring clients to other human service providers or other resources as well as monitoring the client's progress through treatment at their agency.

In criminal justice programs, case managers often work as generalists making referrals for clinical and other services such as job training and employment. In these settings however, case managers are additionally responsible for closely monitoring their clients' progress in treatment as well as their compliance with other court directives such as drug abstinence (verified by urine surveillance), employment, or approved job training. In the event of noncompliance (e.g., dropping out of treatment), the case manager is required to notify the client's probation officer who may impose sanctions including incarceration.

Strengths-Based Perspective

The **strengths-based perspective** of case management was originally developed at the University of Kansas School of Social Welfare to help a population of persons with persistent mental illness make the transition from institutionalized care to independent living. The model emphasizes: (a) encouraging and then supporting clients to assert direct control over their search for resources, such as housing and employment; and (b) having clients identify their own strengths and assets as the vehicle for resource acquisition. To further help clients take control and find their strengths, this model of case management encourages the use of informal helping networks (such as family, social and church support, and other such noninstitution services), encourages clients to identify their own goals, promotes the primacy of the client–case manager relationship, and provides an active, ongoing form of outreach to clients.

Strengths-based case management appears to be effective for three reasons. First is case management's usefulness in helping clients access the resources they need to support recovery. Second, the strong advocacy component that characterizes the strengths-based approach is especially useful in countering the bias that substance abusers are simply in denial or morally deficient—perhaps even unworthy of needed services. Last, the emphasis on helping clients identify their strengths, assets, and abilities can counterbalance treatment models that focus on pathology and disease and therefore may help retain substance abusers in treatment who would be likely to drop out if they feel overwhelmed by their problems.

Strengths-based case management, however, is more labor intensive than brokerage/ generalist approaches. As such, it requires considerably smaller caseloads. Also, typically case managers who possess greater academic credentials and who are more comfortable in interacting with substance abusers. This practice model is best used as a *treatment enhancement* in which a separate case manager operates side-by-side with the client's primary counselor.

Strengths-based case management has been effectively implemented with crack cocaine users. It has demonstrated effectiveness in retaining substance abusers in treatment, which in turn supports better outcomes such as reduced drug use, less criminal justice involvement, and more employment (Siegal, Li, & Rapp, 2002; Siegal et al., 1996; Siegal, Rapp, Li, Saha, Kirk, 1997).

Clinical/Rehabilitation

Clinical/rehabilitation approaches to case management combine clinical and resource acquisition activities. Typically, a single professional is designated to handle both simultaneously.

This model is built on the premise that the separation of these two activities is really not feasible. Case managers must be capable of responding to client-focused issues as well as what are seen as primarily environmental issues. Client-focused services include psychotherapy, cognitive/ behavioral therapies, and family therapy. In addition to mastering the usual repertoire of case management skills (e.g., assessment, monitoring, etc.), proficiency in this model requires that the case manager be aware of numerous and complex clinical issues such as transference, countertransference, how clients internalize what they observe, and theories of psychotherapy and ego functioning. The clinical rehabilitation approach has been most widely used for the treatment of persons diagnosed with both substance abuse and severe psychiatric problems.

An increasingly popular variation of the combination of clinical and case management activities is *multisystemic therapy*, which is being used with adolescent substance abusers involved with the juvenile justice system. Case managers provide their clients primary therapy, family therapy, and work with others such as school personnel and even the adolescent's peers to help establish a more positive, healthy environment to sustain recovery.

Because this approach demands very small case loads and highly trained and experienced practitioners it can be very expensive to deliver. However, given the extent of problems that many multichallenged clients present with, this offers an effective way to maintain them in the community and minimize their being victimized or involved with the criminal justice system.

Assertive Community Treatment

This is the most intensive case management model and is most appropriate for use with the least intact client such as those suffering from severe substance abuse problems and severe mental illness requiring daily doses of medication. The mentally ill, substance-abusing, homeless, HIV-infected individual who is taking multiple medications might exemplify persons in need of this practice model.

The *program of assertive community treatment* (PACT) model, originally developed in Wisconsin in response to the de-institutionalization of severely mentally ill persons, emphasizes the following components:

- Making contact with clients in their homes and natural settings
- Frequent, typically daily, contact between case manager and client
- Assuring that medication is taken on schedule and correctly
- Focusing on the practical problems of daily living
- Assertive advocacy
- Very small caseload sizes
- Team approach with shared caseloads
- Long-term commitment to clients

Case managers provide direct substance abuse counseling services and work with clients to try to help them develop the skills necessary to function successfully in the community. Case managers also provide family consultations and crisis intervention services and function as group facilitators to provide skills training in areas such as living and work skills and relapse prevention.

In most "real world" (i.e., community-based treatment settings), a blend of the elements of each of the practice models is likely to be delivered by the case manager. Specific activities are always determined by meeting the needs of the client, which is, of course, the primary concern of any professional.

18. Strengths-based case management is so designated because it:
    a. breaks the strengths of addictive diseases.
    b. effectively brings case managers' strengths to bear in the solution of clients' problems.
    c. helps clients identify and use their own strengths.
    d. mobilizes the strengths of the community to deal with chemical dependency problems.

19. The brokerage model of case management might best be characterized as being:
    a. the most intensive of the practice models.
    b. the most widely implemented of the practice models.
    c. the most useful for substance abusers presenting with multiple pathologies.
    d. particularly useful for impoverished substance abusers.

20. Assertive community treatment or program of assertive community treatment would be most appropriate for:
    a. alcohol abusers receiving outpatient treatment who were convicted of offenses like DUI.
    b. homeless, mentally ill substance abusers.
    c. crack cocaine users.
    d. opiate abusers.

21. Client needs and agency resources will typically determine:
    a. which practice model of case management will be adopted.
    b. which of the universal social service functions will be used.
    c. which community resources will be used.
    d. all of the above.

22. Having case managers advocate for their clients is part of which practice model?
    a. brokerage
    b. strengths-based
    c. PACT/ACT
    d. all of the above.

23. Effective case management necessarily rests upon a foundation including which of the following?
    a. respect for clients' cultural, ethnic, gender, and sexual orientations.
    b. good communication skills
    c. the ability to analyze and synthesize data
    d. all of the above

24. To help develop a holistic picture of a client, the case manager might organize data into:
    a. finely differentiated sociodemographic categories.
    b. major traumatic life events.
    c. major life domains.
    d. a detailed enumeration of every drug abused.

25. In developing a case management plan, the case manager should have:
    a. knowledge of the community's human service system.
    b. up-to-date information about the agency program the client is being referred to.
    c. knowledge of the program's admissions criteria.
    d. all of the above.

26. Once a case management plan has been developed and the client signs it, it is:
    a. reviewed regularly and modified as appropriate.
    b. used as the grounds for client termination.
    c. becomes an important measure of case management productivity.
    d. is the basis for agency MCO reimbursement.

27. Documentation of case manager activities and client experiences is important for which of the following?
    a. services reimbursement
    b. agency licensing or accreditation
    c. evaluation and planning
    d. all of the above

CASE MANAGEMENT PRACTICE ACTIVITIES

To provide effective case management, the professional, regardless of the practice model employed, needs an intact core of knowledge, skills, and capabilities. These are conceptually organized as actual *practice activities*. They group themselves into three large service provision areas or dimensions: (1) assessment and planning, (2) referral, and (3) service coordination and documentation. These are really not dissimilar to the skills you already possess as a counselor. Each requires developed communication skills; an understanding of appropriate professional and ethical relations between the case manager, client, and other community professionals, along with a strong commitment to practice within them; and the specific technical knowledge making it possible to successfully fulfill the activity. Case managers, counselors, and other human service providers need to understand applicable federal and state laws and how they affect practice activities. For example, practitioners must know about the regulations governing the confidentiality of information—especially in the substance abuse area—and requirements to report suspected child abuse. Supporting all are professional attitudes such as respect for the client; appreciation of clients' cultural, ethnic, gender, sexual orientation and other differences; being nonjudgmental; and respect for the client's sensibilities.

Assessment and Planning

Obtaining valid and reliable data and knowing how to analyze and synthesize it are at the heart of all helping disciplines. Again, as a counselor, you are well equipped to obtain information from clients about their history, current situation, and needs. Your theories of human behavior and substance abuse classes have taught you how to make sense of it and organize it. Because case management is a *generalist* discipline, the case manager endeavors to develop a holistic picture of the client and this necessarily extends well beyond the negative impact their substance use has had on them. To facilitate planning, however, it is useful to conceptually organize this information into *life domains* such as family, legal status, occupation and education, health, financial situation, spirituality, and so forth. Because clients are receiving treatment services for substance abuse problems, an additional domain—*recovery*—is included. The case manager's goal is to help the client identify and access the resources that will support the recovery process. In terms of this case management planning, however, recovery is not an event but a lifelong process of discovery, support, and change.

Once the case manager obtains the necessary information to develop a plan, judgments are made about what factors might impede your client's recovery. A productive way of visualizing them is seeing them as "barriers to recovery" which can be removed or at least diminished. Removing such barriers may be as immediate and concrete as helping the client leave his or her current living situation because it encourages drug use and finding the client stable, safe, and sober housing; obtaining transportation to the agency that provides the substance abuse treatment services; or finding reliable child care so that a parent can attend treatment and support activities. Or, approaches may be more future-oriented, such as defining and then achieving educational goals that could improve your client's situation and might diminish the prospect of relapse.

The case manager, in consultation with those providing the actual clinical services, develops a plan to help the client achieve identified goals. Naturally, the case management plan is consistent with the client's overall recovery plan. It may include identifying, accessing, and then coordinating clinical services such as medical care, vocational rehabilitation, and psychological services, in addition to the substance abuse–specific ones. The plan needs to ensure that services are appropriately sequenced, meaningfully coordinated, and that gaps in service do not occur.

For effective planning and service coordination, the case manager needs to have an overall understanding of the community's human service delivery system and specific knowledge of the helping services available, agency eligibility criteria, and how admissions procedures (along with waiting lists) operate. Knowledge of other community resources such as 12-step groups, support groups, and what kind of assistance is available from the faith community can help and can become important in formulating a comprehensive case management plan. Resources should be broadly identified and creatively used. Never forget that informal ones can be as useful as those provided through the publicly and privately funded human service network.

Recall that the case management plan should be in writing and identify specific activities, initiation, achievement dates and milestones, and who is responsible for effecting them. Like other clinically oriented plans, it should be reviewed on a regular basis and modified as appropriate. Moreover, the plan needs to have the necessary detail to meet formal/official certifying, licensing review, and services reimbursement and managed care organizations criteria. The client's active involvement in the formulation of the plan and appropriate modification is vital; typically, a client signs his or her plan and is provided an actual copy of the document at the time it is formulated or revised.

Referral

Referral should never be seen as a simple "handoff." Referral involves more than simply selecting an appropriate service and providing the client with contact information. To begin, the case manager has a responsibility to have extensive, firsthand information about the services the agency provides, its admissions and other requirements, and who the client is likely to be working with there. Also, because there is likely to be fluidity in the service actually provided by publicly and privately supported programs, the case manager needs to have up-to-date information on each agency. This kind of information makes the transition easier for the clients and avoids the frustration that clients feel when presenting at an agency only to learn that the service they're seeking is no longer offered, or they no longer meet the agency's eligibility requirements. Helping to set realistic expectations about what the client is likely to encounter when presenting for the service makes it more likely that the client will engage with the agency and therefore benefit from the services.

Personal networking is a vital tool for making effective referrals for case managers. Nothing of course, is as effective as identifying a personal contact that the client can interact with at the agency. This kind of person-to-person service goes a long way toward overcoming the resistance of your clients to engaging in services purportedly offered by a large, impersonal, bureaucratically driven system that not infrequently views substance abusers, their problems, and their needs negatively.

Once a referral has been made, the case manager should follow up, in a timely way, contacting *both* the client and the agency or professional who received the referral. This is part of case management's ongoing monitoring function. If the referral was executed successfully, the case manager need maintain contact as determined by protocol and professional custom in that community, being sensitive to the boundaries imposed by rules of confidentiality and respect for the client's sensibilities and privacy. However, in the case of a "no-show," or *nonlinkage*, the case manager will have to determine why the referral was not successful and work with the client—and sometimes even the agency—to remediate the problem. If necessary, the planning process may have to be reinitiated and a new strategy developed. Problems with linkage and engagement should not be viewed simply as coming from your clients' lack of motivation or deficiencies. A much more productive frame of reference is to see them as barriers that can be removed or reduced using some creativity.

The amount of time and effort that the case manager is able to devote in either referral or monitoring activities is determined by the case management practice model employed, agency directives, and the actual caseload the case manager maintains. Broker/generalist case managers will have the largest case loads and consequently devote the least time to these functions. As in all human service provisions, the client presenting with the greatest problems will take the largest amount of time and effort.

Case managers need to document all services and follow-up activities in which clients participate. Although documentation can be tedious, it is necessary for clinically sound service delivery. Additionally, it is important to obtain and record data that satisfies the requirements of the sponsoring agency, official (governmental or professional) oversight body, and now third-party payers. Finally, the information that the case manager obtains is useful as well, for planning purposes for both the sponsoring agency and community policy makers. Agency protocols determine how such information is obtained.

Service Coordination and Documentation

Because substance abuse treatment programs typically specialize in providing chemical dependency–specific therapeutic services, other assistance (e.g., mental health problems, vocational rehabilitation, and medical care) are appropriately provided elsewhere in the community. The case manager coordinates and monitors the client's progress through these, using regular contacts with the participating agencies or professionals. This requires good communication and documentation skills. The goal is to assure that the overall client management plan is progressing, that client needs will not slip through the cracks, and that rehabilitation and other services are rationally sequenced and coordinated with the client, moving as seamless as possible from one level of care to another.

Ideally, services throughout the community would be of uniform quality and clients could easily access what they needed. Often, however, service acquisition and coordination may call for the case manager to serve as an advocate for his client. Sometimes clients may not fully understand that each agency is autonomous and has its own fee, policies, and procedures. Case managers may find themselves having to intervene on the part of their clients between agency gatekeepers and actual service providers if effective linkage is not occurring. Minimally, the case manager can help reduce the client's frustration and anxiety by educating him or her about the agencies and the services they provide and help formulate realistic expectations about what might happen on the clients first visit and thereafter.

The final aspect of recovery services coordination involves working with those individuals surrounding and supporting the client. Family and significant others can play a vital role in the recovery process. Here, of course, the case manager's challenge in involving these other people is fully respecting the client's privacy and confidentiality as well as the privacy of others who might become involved. These issues require particular sensitivity in assisting HIV-positive drug abusers who may have not yet revealed their serostatus. It requires excellent communication skills through which the case manager helps the client appreciate the benefits of family or significant other involvement.

28. Those factors that might impede your client's recovery are best conceptualized as being:
    a. pathogenomic factors.
    b. facilitators of distractions.
    c. barriers.
    d. antimotivational factors.

29. Planning in case management entails:
    a. the creative use of informal as well as officially provided resources.
    b. the rational sequencing of clinical and supportive services.
    c. identifying and filling potential gaps in services delivery.
    d. all of the above.

30. As in other clinical or client-oriented activities which of the following is necessary?
    a. services documentation
    b. constructive confrontation
    c. didactic education
    d. insight extension

The goal of this chapter is to offer you, a chemical dependency treatment specialist, some insight into the discipline of case management. As you may have perceived, and, like virtually everything else you'll encounter in your career in human services, what initially appears to be simple actually proves to be very complex. Definitions are elusive and the actual delivery of service is nuanced by client need, the availability (or dearth) of community resources, agency specifications, and other mandates or restrictions imposed by funding or regulatory bodies.

In today's service environment, the professional is likely to be called upon to perform (and most likely will be performing) overlapping tasks. The chapter has attempted to demonstrate how the same skills will serve you well as both chemical dependency counselor and case manager. By the same token, you have hopefully gained some appreciation into what case managers do and the processes they employ to accomplish their objectives.

And the final and perhaps most important words: as front-line professionals, we have the privilege of offering our help to people whose lives have been damaged or perhaps even nearly destroyed because of their alcohol or drug use. Often our clients come to us knowing that they are in trouble and believing that a professional can help initiate recovery. Others, however, may not be there yet. They present at our offices upon the order of a court or after an ultimatum delivered by a spouse or employer. Regardless of where they start, we can help; we do have something to offer. As individuals providing case management services, our help may be as modest as the pair of warm socks given to the homeless client, or as far-reaching as helping someone find employment or housing in a drug-free setting. We do know that the treatment and other assistance we offer helps people recover. Case management and those offering the service is a part of this helping process.

KEY TERMS

assertive community treatment model: Very intensive case management practice model typically used for multiply challenged persons.

broker/generalist model: Practice of case management service delivery which strives to help the client obtain services and resources.

case management: A set of social service functions typically including assessment, planning, linkage, monitoring, and disengagement having the goal of helping human services clients obtain the resources they need.

clinical/rehabilitation model: Practice model of case management services in which the case manager provides both clinical and case management services.

CSAT: Center for Substance Abuse Treatment, a division of the Substance Abuse and Mental Health Services Administration. The federal agency whose charge is to assist communities with providing improved and more comprehensive treatment services.

settlement houses and neighborhood centers: Late nineteenth Century/early twentieth century social work institutions established to assist those arriving in the United States.

strengths-based model: More intensive service delivery model which helps clients identify their own strengths and mobilize them to acquire the services of resources they need.

TASC: Criminal justice system–related programming; now known as Treatment Accountability for Safer Communities.

DISCUSSION QUESTIONS

1. While a single, universally accepted definition for case management remains elusive, how might you describe the discipline to a colleague?
2. As practitioners, case managers employ an agreed-upon set of social service functions. Please list and describe them.
3. A crack cocaine abuser presents to your agency for treatment. Intake data indicates that he is homeless, has a history of serious mental illness requiring several episodes of hospitalization over the past two years, and is minimally compliant in taking his prescribed psychiatric medications. Which case management approach would you recommend and why.
4. What does the discipline of case management have to offer the field of substance abuse treatment?
5. When a case manager discusses "reducing barriers to treatment" what is meant? What are some of the barriers and how does the case manager learn about them?
6. Providing case management services to a criminal justice system–involved population will likely entail making some modifications in how the services are to be delivered. What kinds of accommodations will have to be made and how might the case manager structure the services to be delivered?
7. *Advocacy* is seen as one of the hallmarks of the case management intervention. What is advocacy and how do case managers advocate for their clients?
8. Why is it important for the case manager to be personally acquainted with social and human services that are available in their community?

9. When considering assessment and planning, what are *life domains*?
10. What are the points of similarity and difference in case management and treatment planning?

SUGGESTED FURTHER READING

Ballew, J. R., & Mink, G. (1986). *Case management in the human services.* Springfield, IL: Charles C. Thomas.

> This is the standard text for the front-line case management practitioner. It provides a detailed description of every aspect of the intervention and is a "must read" for those who specialize in case management.

Center for Substance Abuse Treatment. (1998). *Comprehensive case management for substance abuse treatment* (Treatment Improvement Protocol (TIP) Series, No. 27, DHHS Pub. No. SMA 98-3222). Rockville, MD: U.S. Department of Health and Human Services.

> This is an excellent reference. The volume provides comprehensive overview of the discipline of case management and how it is integrated into substance abuse programming services. It provides information relevant to the needs of the front-line practitioner as well as program administrator.

Mullahy, C. M. (1995). *The case manager's handbook.* Gaithersburg, MD: Aspen Publications.

> This is an excellent advanced text for case managers. It provides an overview of clinical operations and procedures. It also offers a good perspective on the organizational and fiscal aspects of case management.

REFERENCES

Ballew, J. R., & Mink, G. (1996). *Case management in social work: Developing the professional skills needed for work with multiproblem clients.* Springfield, IL: Charles C. Thomas.

Center for Substance Abuse Treatment. (1998). *Comprehensive case management for substance abuse treatment* (Treatment Improvement Protocol (TIP) Series No. 27, DHHS Pub. No. SMA 98-3222). Rockville, MD: U.S. Department of Health and Human Services.

Intagliata, J. (1981). Operationalizing a case management system: A multilevel approach. *National Conference on Social Welfare: Case Management: State of the Art.* Washington, DC: U.S. Department of Health and Human Services.

Moore, S. T. (1990). A social work practice model of case management: The case management grid. *Social Work, 35*(4), 444–448.

National Association of Social Workers. (1992). Case management's cost, benefits eyed. *National Association of Social Workers News.* Washington, DC: NASW Press.

Ogborne, A. C., & Rush, B. R. (1983). The coordination of treatment services for problem drinkers: Problems and prospects. *British Journal of Addiction, 78,* 131–138.

Rapp, R. C., Siegal, H. A., & Fisher, J. H. (1992). A strengths-based model of case management/advocacy: Adapting a mental health model to practice work with persons who have substance abuse problems. In R. S. Ashery (Ed.), *Progress and issues in case management* (NIDA Research Monograph Series No. 127, DHHS Pub. No. ADM 92-1946; pp. 79–91). Rockville, MD: National Institute on Drug Abuse.

Rose, S. M., & Moore, V. L. (1995). Case management. In *Encyclopedia of social work* (19th ed). Washington, DC. National Association of Social Workers.

Siegal, H. A., Fisher, J. H., Rapp, R. C., Kellehev, C. W., Wagner, J. H., O'Brien, W. F., et al. (1996). Enhancing substance abuse treatment with case management: Its impact on employment. *Journal of Substance Abuse Treatment, 13*(2), 93–98.

Siegal, H. A., Rapp, R. C., Li, L., Saha, P., Kirk, K. D. (1997). The role of case management in retaining clients in substance abuse treatment: An exploratory analysis. *Journal of Drug Issues, 27*(4), 821–831.

Siegal, H. A., Li, L., & Rapp, R. C. (2002). Case management as a therapeutic enhancement: Impact on post-treatment criminality. *Journal of Addictive Diseases, 21*(4), 37–46.

Stephens, R. C., Scott, C. K., & Muck, R. D. (Eds.). (2003). *Clinical assessment and substance abuse treatment: The target cities experience.* Albany, NY: State University of New York Press.

18

Crisis Management

Jeffrey T. Mitchell
International Critical Incident Stress Foundation;
University of Maryland

TRUTH OR FICTION?

___ 1. *Mental health professionals are adequately prepared in graduate schools to manage emotional crises in their clients.*

___ 2. *Critical incidents are events which overwhelm either a person's or a group's ability to function normally.*

___ 3. *A crisis is not the event itself but the acute emotional reaction to the event.*

___ 4. *Crisis intervention is equivalent to any long-term therapy.*

___ 5. *Crisis intervention is a active but temporary supportive entry into the life of an individual or a group during a period of extreme distress.*

___ 6. *Crisis intervention is only about thirty years old as an organized branch of behavioral science.*

___ 7. *Crisis intervention can only be used with individuals.*

___ 8. *Two key characteristics of a crisis is that the person in a crisis is demonstrating some level of impairment and his or her coping mechanisms are failing.*

___ 9. *Intensity and duration of exposure have little to do with a person's response to a crisis.*

___ 10. *The principle of expectancy is one of the most important in crisis intervention.*

___ 11. *Crisis workers should never "unbox" anything that cannot be "reboxed" in the allotted time.*

___ 12. *A main goal of crisis intervention is to eliminate all symptoms in all people under all circumstances.*

___ 13. *Assessment, developing rapport, and exploring the problem are the first three steps in crisis intervention.*

___ 14. *Strategic planning is absolutely vital in managing a client's crisis reaction.*

> ___ 15. At the end of a crisis there should be either evidence of recovery or a level of
>   continuing impairment that indicates a referral.

*A relatively minor force, acting for a relatively short time, can switch the balance to one side or
another, to the side of mental health or the side of mental ill health.*

— Gerald Caplan (1961, p. 293)

The average mental health professional receives little formal training to deal with the chaos produced by an emergency situation or a severe emotional **crisis.** Emotional crises are common in clinical practice, but mental health professionals are rarely equipped to manage these disturbances that interrupt, complicate, and threaten treatment regimens for their clients. And, at times, such situations may even threaten your safety.

This chapter will fill some of the knowledge gaps in the field of crisis intervention. If nothing else, it should serve as a reminder of essential crisis intervention concepts and as a useful tool in preparing you for one or more of the certifying or licensing examinations you are about to face.

The chapter focuses on several important crisis intervention issues. They include: (a) assessment, (b) **strategic planning**, (c) practical individual and group interventions to manage a crisis, (d) follow-up and referral mechanisms, and (e) staff care after the crisis.

You have probably heard the old adage, "Good theory makes for good practice." It applies to crisis intervention. If you know the theory, and if you have practiced the skills, you will be able to apply that theory in difficult or novel situations to the benefit of your clients. We will start with some essential definitions and a brief historical overview and then present some core principles of crisis intervention.

CRITICAL INCIDENTS, CRISES, AND CRISIS INTERVENTION

Critical incidents are emotionally powerful events that overwhelm an individual's or a group's ability to function normally. They are the starting point for a crisis reaction. Critical incidents are perceived to be overwhelming, threatening, frightening, disgusting, dangerous, or grotesque. Accidents, disasters, deaths, violence, threats, unwanted pregnancies, drug overdoses, financial losses, public humiliations, personal rejections, diseases, and property losses are but a few of the critical incidents that may occur in the course of a person's life. Needless to say to you, alcohol and drug abuse presents as both a crisis in itself or as a backdrop for other crises. One or more of the disturbing situations listed above can throw a person into a state of emotional turmoil known as a crisis.

A *crisis*, defined as an acute emotional reaction to some powerful stimulus or demand in your life or in the life of one of your family members or clients, is not the event itself, but it is the person's perception of and response to the situation that is the essence of a crisis (Parad, 1971, p. 197). There are three conditions for a crisis: (1) a stressful or hazardous situation, (2) the person senses that the stressful situation will lead to considerable disruption or emotional upset in their normal lives, and (3) the person is unable to resolve the situation by their usual coping means.

Most clinicians agree that a person in a crisis has the following five characteristics (Roberts, 2000)—look for them in the people you help.

1. They perceive the event as threatening, powerful, or critical.
2. They are unable to manage the impact of the event with their usual repertoire of coping skills.

3. They experience increased fear, tension, and mental confusion.
4. They experience considerable subjective discomfort.
5. In a short time they can proceed to an intense state of crisis or emotional imbalance (*disequilibrium*).

Add alcohol or any abused substance to a crisis reaction and the situation becomes more dangerous as well as far more difficult to manage or resolve. When psychological disequilibrium appears—that is, when one's thinking ability is suppressed and one's feelings explode out of control—outside crisis intervention may be required to rebalance the person and assist in resolving the situation.

1. A crisis is:
   a. a life-changing event.
   b. a period of conflict.
   c. an act of violence.
   d. an acute emotional reaction to powerful event.

Crisis intervention is an active but temporary entry into the life situation of an individual or group during a period of extreme distress. Its primary goals are to: (a) mitigate the impact of a critical incident, (b) facilitate the normal recovery processes of people who are experiencing an emotional crisis, and (c) restore people to an acceptable level of adaptive function. Crisis intervention is most helpful in the most acute phases of a state of emotional turmoil, but it is not psychotherapy nor is it a substitute for psychotherapy. Crisis intervention works to alleviate the impact of a crisis experience and to assist people in mobilizing appropriate **resources** to manage both the situation and the emotional reactions to it (Everly & Mitchell, 1999; Mitchell & Resnik, 1981, 1986).

BRIEF HISTORICAL PERSPECTIVE

Although the emotional turmoil of human crises has been recognized for many centuries, crisis intervention *theory* was not laid out until the early 1900s. Edwin Stierlin used crisis intervention techniques to assist people after a European mining disaster in 1906 (Stierlin, 1909). Also in 1906, the National Save-a-Life League for the prevention of suicides was formed in New York City (Roberts, 2000).

Four major factors influenced the development of crisis intervention theory: warfare, disasters and terrorism, law enforcement, and medicine. Two world wars, an increasing incidence of suicide, and a series of horrific disasters introduced many crisis intervention developments (Caplan, 1961, 1964; Farberow & Frederick, 1978; Frederick, 1977; Kardiner & Spiegel, 1947; Lindemann, 1944; Parad & Parad, 1968; Salmon, 1919).

2. Major historical influences on crisis intervention were:
   a. the printing press, street gangs, and invention of the gun.
   b. warfare, disasters and terrorism, law enforcement, and medicine.
   c. sexual assault, drugs of abuse, street violence, and suicide.
   d. suicide prevention, violence control, HIV, and trauma centers.

Crisis Intervention Developments in the 1960s

- Social pressures caused law enforcement, hospitals, and emergency medical services to develop crisis services.
- In 1963, the **Community Mental Health Centers Act** required community mental health centers to provide crisis services (Foley & Sharfstein, 1983).
- **Paraprofessionals** used in crisis response (Bard, 1970; Bard & Ellison, 1974).
- Crisis intervention stages outlined (Parad & Parad, 1968; Rapoport, 1962).
- Crisis management steps for sexual assault, suicide, and child abuse developed (Ruben, 1976; Salby, Lieb, & Tancredi, 1975).

Crisis Intervention Developments in the 1970s, 1980s, and 1990s

- Group crisis intervention developed beyond battlefield applications (Appel, Beebe, & Hilger, 1946; Holmes, 1985).
- Group crisis work with families initiated (Hill, 1958).
- Development of Critical Incident Stress Management services (Everly, Lating, & Mitchell, 2000).
- Distinct crisis services developed for emergency services, schools, businesses, and communities.
- More than ten thousand victim assistance centers, crisis centers, rape crisis programs, hospital emergency departments, police-based crisis programs, and pastoral counseling centers received nearly 4.5 million annual contacts for crisis services (Roberts, 2000; Roberts & Camasso, 1994).
- Including crisis intervention services such as hotlines and shelters for battered women, programs for troubled teens, drug abuse programs, and programs for employees brings the actual number of crisis contacts to nearly 35 to 40 million a year (Roberts, 2000). In one hundred years' time, crisis intervention has truly been woven into the fabric of everyday life.

3. Crisis intervention may be used with:
   a. any individual or group.
   b. individuals only.
   c. emergency and disaster workers.
   d. businesses and corporations.

GENERAL CRISIS CONCEPTS

- Any person is vulnerable to a crisis at almost any time in his or her life.
- A crisis reaction is always distressing to the person involved even if others do not see the crisis event as upsetting.
- Most crises are sudden and unexpected and people are not adequately prepared to manage them.
- Crises are temporary. Most acute crisis reactions subside in 24 to 72 hours.
- The usual coping methods to cope day to day tend to fail during a crisis.
- Crisis events produce at least a potential for dangerous or unacceptable behaviors for the victims.

- Most distressed people react positively to the support provided by others (Mitchell & Resnik, 1986).

4. Most people in a state of crisis:
   a. become violent.
   b. are completely dysfunctional.
   c. react positively to help.
   d. never recover.

AN OVERVIEW OF CRISIS INTERVENTION SERVICES

Crisis intervention services are provided in the early stages of a state of emotional turmoil (usually the first four to six weeks). But, there are times that are well outside that time range when crisis services are beneficial because the situation has been unresolved and remains "raw" over an extended period of time. Crisis intervention is, therefore, a logical starting point in some circumstances before professional longer-range psychotherapy can be instituted. Many crisis services are 24-hour operations and can thus provide immediate, but temporary, assistance by trained personnel.

Here are some examples of crisis intervention services:

- Information, guidance, education, and instruction
- Emergency psychiatric assessments
- General crisis assessments
- Immediate supportive interventions such as food and other necessities
- Peer support (paraprofessional) programs
- Individual crisis support
- Crisis telephone hotlines
- Walk-in crisis clinics
- Mobile crisis services
- Poison control centers
- Group crisis support for both large and small groups
- Immediate crisis counseling
- Family support services
- Hospital emergency room social services
- Disaster services
- Referrals for depression, suicidal ideation, alcohol and other drug abuse, AIDS, violence, child abuse, sexual assault, psychiatric emergencies, significant other battering, and crime victimization (Roberts, 2000).

5. Crisis services are usually provided within:
   a. a year.
   b. four to six weeks after the event.
   c. within 24 hours.
   d. within 4 hours.

CRISIS REACTIONS

Every person reacts to a critical situation with an individualized response. Relatively common patterns of response, however, can be found in the acute phase of a crisis shortly after the critical incident. People may react with one or more of the following:

- Helplessness
- Mental confusion and disorganization or disorientation
- Decision-making and problem-solving difficulties
- Intense anxiety
- Shock, denial, and disbelief
- Anger, agitation, and rage
- Lowered self-esteem
- Fear
- Withdrawal from others
- Emotionally subdued, depressed
- Grief
- Apathy
- Physical reactions such as nausea, shakes, headache, intestinal disturbance, chest pain, or difficulty breathing. *Any person who is experiencing chest pain, difficulty breathing, or any other severe physical symptoms should be evaluated by medical staff as quickly as possible.*

Keep in mind that a typical crisis reaction is characterized by three main features:

1. Thinking recedes and feelings become dominant. A state of disequilibrium is established as a result of the crisis.
2. Usual coping mechanisms fail to resolve the situation. The person then feels more out of control.
3. There is evidence of impairment of normal functions. The simultaneous presence of alcohol and other drugs can further impair the person and set the stage for severe deterioration in performance and emotional control.

6. In a crisis, a person' performance is usually:
    a. enhanced.
    b. aroused.
    c. effective.
    d. impaired.

FACTORS THAT INTENSIFY OR LESSEN A CRISIS REACTION

Many factors heighten or reduce a crisis reaction. Factors such as a person's age or social status may play a significant role. Very young people or the elderly may suffer a more intense crisis reaction than those in their middle years. People who perceive themselves to be in a higher social or economic status and are used to being in control of their environment may be seriously impacted by any event when they have no control. Other crisis enhancing or limiting factors are:

- A more *intense exposure* to an incident usually generates a more powerful reaction.
- The longer the *duration* of a critical incident, the more severe the reaction.
- The greater the *support* from family and friends, the less the crisis reaction.
- *Previous traumatic experience* can be a two-edged sword, generating more self-confidence or intensifying the reactions to the current situation.
- The more helpful *resources* available, the better.
- People generally do better if they feel that they had *some control* over a situation.
- A pile-up of *concurrent stressful events* cuts down on personal resistance and causes an earlier collapse of resistance and ineffective situation management.

7. Previous experience in a crisis reaction is typically:
   a. a two-edged sword that may either help or hurt depending on the circumstances.
   b. always a good thing.
   c. always a bad thing.
   d. has no influence one way or the other.

THE PRIMARY PRINCIPLES OF CRISIS INTERVENTION

There are seven primary principles of crisis intervention. **Proximity** is the first principle of crisis intervention. The best crisis work is often provided in surroundings familiar to the victims. The second is **immediacy**. People in a crisis cannot wait long for help. The longer they wait, the less likely crisis intervention will be effective. The third principle is that of **expectancy**. Early in the intervention the provider of crisis intervention has to instill hope that the situation can be managed and resolved (Salmon, 1919).

The fourth principle is **brevity**. No one has the luxury of abundant time in a crisis so crisis management actions have to be brief.

8. *Proximity* means:
   a. you do not have to be exact; approximate interventions will be good enough.
   b. it does not matter where the services are provided.
   c. you can do all of the work by mail.
   d. you should provide support services close to the person's operational area.

People do not handle complexity very well in the midst of a crisis. Therefore crisis interventions have to focus on **simplicity**. Simple, well thought out interventions will be the most effective in the majority of cases.

Crisis workers must have **creativity**. The ability to be innovative in the face of unusual and disturbing situations is a key to good crisis intervention. Appropriate helpful interventions have to be developed on the spot.

Finally, whatever actions are chosen in a crisis should be **practical**. Impractical solutions are no solutions at all. People struggling through a painful experience will see them as insensitive and uncaring.

9. Three essential principles of crisis intervention are:
   a. immediacy, expectancy, sensitivity.
   b. brevity, immediacy, creativity.
   c. simplicity, brevity, kindness.
   d. practicality, creativity, intensity.

Several other principles can serve you well when you are helping a person in a crisis. The first is *stay within your training levels*. Do not attempt to do things for which you have not been adequately trained. If you lack the experience necessary, call for help.

We advise the crisis intervener to *avoid "unboxing" anything that cannot be "reboxed" in the time available*. It can be quite disturbing to a person for a helper to try to engage in a discussion of complex and painful personal information only to cut off the distressed person partway through the discussion because there is insufficient time. It is better to say something like, "It sounds like you are having a very difficult time with that issue. I think it is so important that I would like to meet with you for a longer period of time than we have right now. That way, we can thoroughly discuss it and help you work out a solution. Can we meet today at 1:00 PM? I will have much more time available then."

Although it is often therapeutic, crisis intervention is neither therapy nor a substitute for therapy. One cannot achieve substantial, long-lasting life changes in the midst of a crisis. Keep your expectations reasonable. *Do not encourage discussions of excessive details of old psychological material when dealing with a crisis*. Focus on the "here and now." Delving deeply into excessive details about a past situation is time consuming, unhelpful, and often counterproductive.

After crisis intervention, a reasonable degree of improvement or movement toward recovery is usually apparent; if it is not, consider a referral. Crisis intervention is, by nature, brief. We should see some calming of the person and the development of a crisis plan as well as some efforts to resolve the problem in a fairly short period of time. Positive results typically appear with a minimal number of contacts (usually three to five contacts lasting between 5 and 15 minutes each). Make a referral if the distress is extreme, no calming or recovery is evident, or impairment persists.

10. An important guideline for crisis intervention is:
    a. never call a client at home.
    b. never break a confidence even if the person is suicidal.
    c. never work with anyone alone.
    d. never go beyond your training levels.

Keep the primary objectives of crisis intervention in mind. Crisis intervention is a limited therapeutic strategy. Do not establish outcome expectations that are far beyond the program's capacities. The primary objectives are:

1. Mitigation of the impact of a critical incident or traumatic event.
2. Facilitation of recovery processes.
3. Identification of individuals who may need additional support or a referral for psychotherapy.

CRISIS INTERVENTION GOALS

There are five main goals of crisis intervention:

1. To stabilize, confine, and control both the crisis situation and the reactions to it.
2. To mitigate the impact of the distressing event on those involved.
3. To mobilize the resources necessary to manage the traumatic experience.
4. To normalize or "demedicalize" or "depathologize" a person's reaction to the traumatic experience.
5. To restore the person to an acceptable level of adaptive function.

Crisis intervention does not attempt to eliminate all symptoms of distress that a person may be experiencing. Furthermore, it is unreasonable to expect that the limited techniques and processes of crisis intervention will be able to cure any psychopathology. It may contribute to lessening the effects of psychological trauma, but crisis intervention's greatest benefit is that it provides practical methods through which people may resume normal daily functions while they work their way through a crisis.

11. A primary goal of crisis intervention is:
    a. to cure a wide range of psychopathologies.
    b. to eliminate all symptoms in all people and at all times.
    c. to mobilize appropriate resources to manage the crisis reaction.
    d. to make dramatic changes in a person's life.

STAGES OF CRISIS INTERVENTION

Dr. Albert R. Roberts (1991, 2000), a noted crisis intervention specialist, developed a seven stage crisis intervention model. You may find it helpful.

Stage 1: Crisis Assessment

Any crisis assessment covers two important features. The first is a *situational assessment*. What has just happened or is happening now? The second is to determine the *severity of emotional distress* felt by those involved in the situation. The severity of emotional distress provides insight into how assertively and how quickly we need to act to assist the person.

1. Obtain basic information. What is the situation (auto accident, overdose, sexual assault, sudden death of a loved one, suicidal threat, a violent act, other criminal acts, severe illness, fire, flood, property loss, terrorist act, loss of job, physical injury, psychiatric breakdown, etc.)? Are alcohol or other drugs involved? Is there a history of psychiatric disturbance? Are there witnesses who can help inform you if the person is impaired?

2. Are any life threatening conditions present (drug overdose, suicidal or homicidal threat, a weapon)? If so, the person needs immediate transport to a hospital for further evaluation. Many times police need to be called to protect the worker and the person who needs help. Do not hesitate to call police, emergency medical services, or other forms of assistance. Never endanger yourself. If it is a homicidal or suicidal threat, you do not want to be the only person helping.

3. How severe is the impact on those involved (mild, moderate, severe)?

4. Are the symptoms a part of a typical crisis response or are they very unusual? (Expected symptoms are increased heart rate and breathing rate. Unusual symptoms would be hallucinations and chest pain. The more symptoms are out of the ordinary, the more likely a person needs immediate professional medical or psychiatric assistance.)

5. Who needs help (just the individual or are there children or family members involved; group, community or other involvement)?

6. What type of help is best (police, emergency medical assistance, hospitalization, family involvement, or crisis worker support only)?

7. When should that help be given (immediate or delayed for a few hours up to a day or so)?

8. What resources are necessary to provide the right help at this time?

---

12. The first stage in managing a crisis is:
    a. preventing dysfunction.
    b. resolving the problem.
    c. assessment.
    d. refinement of a plan.

Stage 2: Establish Rapport

This step is often accomplished simultaneously with the assessment stage.

1. Make contact and introduce yourself.
2. Convey respect for and acceptance of the person.
3. Assure the person that you want to help and that other help is available.
4. Listen carefully to the person.
5. Do not rush the person.
6. Be friendly, kind, and concerned, but maintain a professional attitude.
7. Use appropriate body positioning and try to get on the same eye level.
8. Speak in a calm, confident, and controlled manner.

Stage 3: Explore the Crisis Problem

1. Ask if some event just occurred that started the crisis response.
2. Ask if this the first time an event like that has happened or is there some previous experience of such an event.
3. Ask how the person has coped with stressful experiences in the past.
4. Discuss any dangerous or possibly lethal aspects of the current crisis experience.
5. Use a series of open-ended questions to get the best information from the person.
6. Ask the person to tell his or her own story of the current crisis experience.
7. Listen carefully and empathetically.
8. Use reflection of emotional content and paraphrase to communicate with the person.

---

13. Exploring the problem means:
    a. listening carefully and asking questions to determine the nature of the problem.
    b. an in-depth discussion of every detail of the problem.
    c. exploring a person's past to determine why they would have the current problem.
    d. writing detailed notes so that they can be reviewed later and a cause of the problem found.

Stage 4: Explore Feelings and Emotions

1. Although much of the emotional distress related to a critical incident is spontaneously discussed when the crisis problem is being reviewed in Stage 3, it is important to discuss the main emotional features of the situation if they have not been brought up.

2. Active and intense listening coupled with concern and support for the person are the best techniques to generate expressions of emotionally laden content.

3. Try to mentally put yourself into the person's situation. Ask yourself, "What would help me?" If you cannot relate to their particular situation, you might ask, "If this person were someone I love what would help my loved one through the situation?" In most cases you will pick something that is supportive and helpful.

Stage 5: Generate and Explore Alternatives

1. Ask questions about the person's previous coping methods during crisis situations.
2. Ask the person if they know what things would be helpful to them right now.
3. Ask the person if they have tried those things.
4. Encourage the person to do some of those things if they have not tried them yet.
5. Be prepared to offer some suggestions about managing the crisis event if the person is unable to generate any practical options on their own.

Stage 6: Develop and Implement a Crisis Action Plan

1. Formulate a list of possible options based on the assessment of the crisis. The list is most likely to be mental list because one rarely has the time to write anything down in a crisis situation. It is important to put on the list any possible solutions to the crisis. Even include options that are more than likely to be rejected. This helps to avoid overlooking potential helpful solutions. It also helps to identify any potential failure points before going too far along in developing a crisis plan.

2. Pick out the very best options and develop an action plan that has the best chance of being successful.

3. Implement the chosen crisis plan immediately. Delays often allow complications to creep in which then inhibit a successful resolution of the crisis.

4. Provide whatever assistance appears necessary to quickly implement the action plan.

14. Crisis action plans should be implemented:
    a. within 24 hours.
    b. immediately.
    c. within a week.
    d. anytime because the plan does not expire.

Stage 7: Check on the Plan's Success and Follow Up

Getting an action plan implemented immediately is not enough. The crisis intervener must monitor the progress of the plan. Alterations to a course of action may need to be made. One should never be so caught up in a specific plan that he or she rigidly adheres to it even when it is failing.

1. Check on the success of the plan.
2. Change or refine the plan, if necessary.
3. Maintain a successful plan until resolution of the crisis reaction is achieved or until a handoff to other qualified mental health providers is achieved.
4. Follow up with the person or group which has experienced the crisis event.
5. If the crisis is resolved, the plan can be abandoned and crisis intervention is closed out.
6. If significant and continued impairment is evident, refer for further assessment and possible professional care.

15. A crisis action plan continues:
    a. indefinitely.
    b. without modification.
    c. up to a week.
    d. until the crisis resolves or until it needs to be altered to resolve the crisis.

STRATEGIC CRISIS PLANNING

In strategic crisis planning we must decide who needs what type of help and when. Strategic planning requires us to consider the resources required to provide the appropriate help. A simple model can help to organize our thinking in developing a strategic plan for crisis intervention. Here is one such model:

TARGET, TYPE, TIMING, THEME + RESOURCES

The **target** represents specific individuals or groups who need some assistance. The **type** represents one or more forms of helpful interventions. The proper **timing** of any intervention is very important, but not easy to determine. If the help comes too early or too late, it will be essentially unhelpful. In addition, people have to be psychologically ready to accept help. Ask the client how ready he or she is for help. **Theme** refers to background issues such as suddenness of event, feelings of betrayal or past personal experiences associated with the current crisis. Finally, once we have determined the target, type, timing, theme we need to make sure the *right resources* are available to intervene.

Effective strategic crisis intervention plans have the following characteristics:

- Practical
- Short-term
- Immediately implemented
- Action oriented
- Well thought out and organized
- Within the capabilities of the person(s) involved in the crisis situation
- Within the capabilities of the crisis worker
- Coordinated with other agencies involved in the crisis event
- Developed with referrals in mind

16. A strategic plan should be:
    a. action oriented, complete, total, and comprehensive.
    b. focused on resources, assessment, contact, and conclusion.
    c. based on target, type, timing, theme and resources.
    d. systematic, integrated, assertive, and comprehensive.

PRACTICAL CRISIS INTERVENTION APPLICATIONS

Individual Applications

Individual crisis intervention is the most common of all crisis interventions. It is basically a conversation with a distressed person to calm the heightened emotions and to develop an action plan to manage both the crisis event and the individual's reaction to that event. There are many ways to approach and assist an individual in a state of crisis. Many of the principles and guidelines in the above paragraphs can be put to good use when dealing with an individual. A specific outline or a model can be helpful. Dr. George Everly, Jr. has developed such a model specifically for use with individual crisis intervention. It is called the SAFER-R model (Everly & Mitchell, 1998).

Here is a summary of the model:

S—*Stabilize the situation*. Cut down on stimuli, protect the person, limit interference.
A—*Acknowledge* that a crisis event has occurred and that a person is distressed over it.
F—*Facilitate* an understanding of the situation and develop a list of options.
E—*Encourage* the person to develop and implement, with the helper, an action plan.
R—*Recovery* is in evidence and, if so, close out the individual crisis intervention process.
R—*Referral* for professional care is indicated if significant impairment is evident.

17. The SAFER-R model of crisis intervention is:
    a. a substitute for psychotherapy.
    b. another form of group intervention.
    c. the safest approach to take with distressed people.
    d. for use with individuals in a state of crisis.

18. There are two *Rs* in the SAFER-R model. One stands for recovery. The other stands for:
    a. retrieval.
    b. reconstruction.
    c. referral.
    d. retribution.

Group Crisis Interventions

Group-based crisis intervention has been utilized since World War II. Group interventions have become especially popular since the development of **Critical Incident Stress Management** (CISM) programs in the 1970s. When applied by knowledgeable and skillful interveners who adhere to the standards of practice within the CISM field they have been very successful (Everly & Mitchell, 1999).

There are several group crisis intervention models. The American Red Cross uses one type and the National Organization for Victim Assistance uses another. The International Critical Incident Stress Foundation (ICISF), which endorses the most widely utilized group crisis intervention processes in the world, uses several different types of group crisis interventions for different purposes. Two of ICISF's group processes, *demobilization* and *Crisis Management Briefings*, are effective in large-group situations such as disasters. Another two, *defusing* and *Critical Incident Stress Debriefing*, are most useful in small-group crisis situations.

Overview of the Four Main Group Interventions

This discussion concentrates on group interventions within the CISM crisis intervention model. We can compare different group crisis intervention services to tools in a tool box. As each specific tool in a tool box has a different function, so too do different group processes have different purposes.

Demobilization. **Demobilization** is a very brief, large-group informational session specifically used for operations personnel (e.g., firefighters, police officers, and other first responders) who are being released from their first work-related exposure to a disaster. The main purpose is to provide about 10 minutes of useful information (i.e., common symptoms, suggestions for coping, and directions for obtaining additional help). The demobilization session is quite passive in that information is provided but the group members have little or no interaction with the presenter. Demobilization helps to normalize reactions and to guide personnel toward recovery from the critical incident. Once the information segment is completed, personnel may also receive food and rest for 20 minutes in another room before being released.

> 19. *Demobilization*, in crisis intervention terms, is:
>   a. a form of intense group psychotherapy.
>   b. a large-group informational session provided to operations personnel after a disaster.
>   c. a process of taking care of crisis workers when they have completed interventions.
>   d. a set of guidelines given to disaster workers before deployment to the field.

Crisis Management Briefing. **Crisis Management Briefing** is a large-group informational session provided to twenty or more people who have been exposed to a distressing traumatic event. Although similar to demobilization described above, there are some differences. For example, demobilization is a very passive process. Information is presented to group members, but no discussion is encouraged by the leaders. In the Crisis Management Briefing, on the other hand, questions are taken from group members and answers are provided. It is usually provided to employees of a corporation or community members where a tragedy has occurred. Accurate, current, and practical information is the primary goal of this particular group crisis intervention service. People need to know what happened in their community and what the fire and law enforcement or relief services are doing about it. Community leaders or representatives of the police, fire service, or other organizations join together with mental health professionals to present information and to guide people. Suggestions are provided regarding safety and health issues and handouts are distributed to the group members. Despite the fact that the Crisis Management briefing usually contains a brief question and answer period, the primary objective is to provide information. The entire Crisis Management Briefing lasts about 45 minutes. It is rarely longer than one hour. It requires a good team of facilitators to field questions and keep the program moving.

20. A crisis management briefing is very similar to demobilization. There is one substantial difference:
    a. There is a question and answer period.
    b. The participants go into great detail about their experiences.
    c. Everything is written down.
    d. Investigators are present who can use the material in a final report.

Defusing. **Defusing** is a small-group process used within hours after a homogeneous group has endured the same traumatic event. It is a shortened version of a Critical Incident Stress Debriefing and is always done on the same day as the critical incident. Because it is so close in time to the crisis event, the participants are usually noticeably distressed. Opportunities are offered for people to participate actively if they so choose, but no one is pressured to speak.

Some providers refer to defusing as a guided, short (30–45 minute) storytelling time. Key to its success is its use only with homogeneous groups who have experienced the same traumatic event. Mixed groups of people who either do not know one another or who have very different levels of exposure to the crisis event should be avoided entirely. The primary objective of the defusing is to foster a brief discussion of the crisis event and to supply the group with practical information that may move them toward recovery. Unlike demobilization or Crisis Management Briefing, defusing is a much more interactive process between the crisis team and the group members. Brief stories are related by the group members and the leaders react to what is brought out. Defusing aims at *processing* a common group experience. Group members are informed that their reactions are normal and that most will recover fairly quickly. The team (often made up of specially trained peer support, paraprofessional personnel) offers suggestions regarding sleeping, eating, activity levels, and contact with loved ones. Defusing is useful in assessing the group to determine who needs further assistance.

21. Defusing is:
    a. a large-group process used after a disaster.
    b. an individual crisis intervention process.
    c. a process reserved only for emergency personnel.
    d. a shortened version of a critical incident stress debriefing used within hours of a traumatic event.

Critical Incident Stress Debriefing. The **Critical Incident Stress Debriefing** (CISD) is a specific, seven-phase group crisis intervention process provided by a specially trained team. Some describe it as a structured storytelling time. After a short introduction, participants are asked to briefly describe the event, their thoughts about it, and the very worst part for them personally. Then the group is asked to list a few of the signals of distress they are encountering. The team will then provide practical information about the signs and symptoms of distress and the best ways to manage those symptoms. A summary segment wraps up the CISD.

The CISD is designed to mitigate the impact of a traumatic event on a homogeneous group. It is typically provided several days after the crisis and lasts between two and three hours. The extended time allows a more detailed discussion of the event than does defusing. The team leadership, which usually comprises a mental health professional and several specially trained peer support personnel, provides information on the typical physical and psychological impact of the event and the many techniques that can be used to reduce stress reactions. Efforts

TABLE 18.1

Group Intervention Summary

Intervention	Type	Target	Timing	Objectives
Demobilization	Large-group informational	Homogeneous operations operations	Immediately after first disaster exposure	Inform/guide
Crisis Management Briefing	Large-group informational	Any large group as homogeneous as possible	Before, during, or after exposure	Inform/guide; answer questions; brief
Defusing	Small-group process	Only homogeneous with same exposure	Within hours of event	Process experience; guide/inform; normalize
CISD	Small-group process	Only homogeneous; same event	24–72 hours after	Process experience; Guide/inform; normalize; direct

are made to normalize those reactions and specific suggestions are offered to enhance an individual's stress management capabilities.

A CISD mitigates the impact of a traumatic event and facilitates the recovery of normal people who are having normal reactions to an abnormal event. It is also useful as a screening tool to determine if group members need additional support or a referral for therapy.

All four of the group crisis interventions are simply components of a comprehensive, systematic, integrated package of crisis services (see Table 18.1). Each has a specific purpose, but none is designed to be used in isolation from other support services (Mitchell & Everly, 2001).

22. A Critical Incident Stress Debriefing is:
    a. a cure for posttraumatic stress disorder.
    b. a specific, seven-step, structured small-group discussion of a traumatic event.
    c. a stand-alone group process that does not need any other intervention.
    d. an intense, detailed reliving of a traumatic experience.

23. A Critical Incident Stress Debriefing's goals include:
    a. mitigation of impact, facilitation of recovery, and identification of those who need more.
    b. direct cause-effect prevention of posttraumatic stress disorder.
    c. cure of posttraumatic stress disorder from past events.
    d. elimination of all stress symptoms.

24. All four group crisis interventions discussed in this chapter are:
    a. powerful enough to be used independently of other forms of crisis intervention.
    b. powerful enough to be substitute for therapy.
    c. part of a systematic and integrated package of crisis interventions.
    d. always harmful and should be avoided.

FOLLOW-UP AND REFERRAL

In some ways, crisis intervention is similar to physical first aid. Not everyone who receives physical first aid needs to go to surgery. For many, the first aid is enough to manage a minor medical problem. Likewise, not everyone who receives "emotional first aid" needs to go to psychotherapy. For most the "emotional first aid" will be enough to stabilize them and allow them to return to an acceptable level of adaptive function.

25. Crisis intervention is known as:
    a. poor man's therapy.
    b. emotional first aid.
    c. snake oil for the masses.
    d. the quick recovery system.

Follow-up needs to be part of the systematic package of crisis interventions. Follow-up begins immediately after the first contact with the distressed person. If a group contact was the first contact, then the crisis intervener needs to connect with those individuals within the group who are showing signs of obvious distress. Individual contacts should occur immediately after the group session. Opportunities for individual contacts should be pursued in the days following the initial contact. Phone numbers of crisis interveners or at least organizations where people can seek further assistance should be made available to the participants in a crisis group. Visits to the work site by crisis interventionists to check on the welfare of distressed people should be encouraged. Phone calls are often made to check on people who have expressed sufficient distress to make the crisis worker concerned.

26. Follow-up for crisis intervention:
    a. starts after 24 hours have passed.
    b. should be continued for at least three months.
    c. is very costly and should be considered carefully before a decision is made.
    d. starts immediately after the first contact.

Many crises can be managed by contacts from the crisis workers and that support may be enough to restore them to adaptive functions. With that being said, we must then turn our attention to those who actually need more than what the support services of crisis intervention can provide. Some people will need psychotherapy or some other resource.

The National Institute of Mental Health (NIMH; 2002) suggests that there are six categories of people who should receive referrals for further evaluation for possible psychotherapy.

1. The bereaved.
2. Those with preexisting psychiatric disorders.
3. Those who required medical or surgical intervention. Many people who experienced a life-threatening medical crisis suffer long term psychological disruption and need psychotherapy.
4. Those with acute stress disorder. *Acute stress disorder* is a set of severe stress-related symptoms that come about as a result of an exposure to a highly traumatic event. It is an early form of posttraumatic stress disorder (PTSD) and needs professional care.
5. Those for whom the exposure was especially chronic or intense.
6. Those who request it.

27. In crisis intervention, people are referred for:
    a. a medical diagnosis.
    b. psychiatric reasons only.
    c. further evaluation.
    d. punishment if they have resisted crisis intervention.

Fortunately, there are several very effective psychotherapies that can help resolve the pain and disruption produced by crisis events. Eye movement desensitization and reprocessing, cognitive-behavioral therapy, and trauma incident reduction are among the most successful trauma therapies. It is beyond the scope of this chapter to present detailed descriptions of these therapies. The interested clinician is therefore urged to review original source material describing those therapies (Foa, Keane, & Friedman, 2000; Shapiro, 2001). More important, clinicians interested in specific therapies should take appropriate training courses so they will be properly prepared to assist their clients.

28. One psychotherapy that is known to be very effective with the aftereffects of traumatic stress is:
    a. psychoanalysis.
    b. EMDR.
    c. flooding.
    d. thought field therapy.

STAFF CARE

Crisis work is difficult. Most providers feel emotionally and physically drained when they complete an intense intervention particularly if there was a threat to human life. At times, hearing painful stories may cause crisis interventionists to experience vicarious trauma. Crisis work should be rounded out with support for the helper.

29. Listening to the stories of people in pain may cause the helper to feel:
    a. lucky.
    b. supported.
    c. elation.
    d. vicarious traumatic stress feelings.

Here are some suggestions to obtain emotional support after you provide crisis intervention:

- Discuss with a supervisor or a colleague the interventions you have provided and the effects you feel.
- Utilize fellow CISM team members to discuss a difficult crisis intervention experience.
- Meet as a group after a CISD to go over three things: (1) how the group process worked and who is responsible for following up with specific participants, (2) what lessons have been learned from the CISD experience, and (3) any aspects of the CISD that generated distressful reactions in the team members themselves.
- Have a trusted colleague or friend to whom you can turn for support.

- Take workshops and attend conferences to enhance your knowledge and skills. Education helps to build self-confidence and trust in your abilities to help others.

30. Staff care for crisis workers should include one important element:
    a. vacations after every ten crisis interventions.
    b. as much sleep as possible.
    c. a trusted colleague with whom to discuss the distressing case.
    d. a quiet room where the crisis worker can cry without interruption.

This chapter reviews the hundred-year history and essential principles of crisis intervention. Specific simple and easily applied steps are offered to assist individuals or groups. Crisis intervention accomplishes three things. It (1) mitigates impact, (2) facilitates recovery, and (3) helps identify individuals who need additional care. When used by trained personnel who adhere to well-published standards of care, crisis intervention positively influences the live of others. In some circumstances, it has even saved some of those lives. As Swanson and Carbon (1989) said, when writing for the American Psychiatric Association Task Force Report on Treatment of Psychiatric Disorders, "Crisis intervention is a proven approach to helping in the pain of an emotional crisis" (p. 2520).

KEY TERMS

brevity: The best interventions during a crisis reaction appear to be the shortest.

Community Mental Health Centers Act: A 1963 act of the U.S. Congress that established community-based mental health centers with emergency crisis intervention services.

creativity: Because it is impossible to have every direction and instruction for every situation at hand, the crisis intervener has to be innovative.

crisis: An acute emotional response to some intense stimulus or demand.

critical incident: The event that triggers the crisis response.

Critical Incident Stress Debriefing (CISD): A specific, seven-stage, *group* crisis intervention process developed to mitigate the impact of a traumatic event, facilitate recovery, and identify individuals who need additional support or a referral for therapy. It is but one small part of the CISM program.

critical incident stress management (CISM): A comprehensive, systematic, integrated, and multi-component crisis intervention package.

crisis intervention: An active, but temporary, entry into the life of an individual or a group during a period of extreme distress. It mitigates the impact of an event, facilitates recovery, and identifies individuals who need additional assistance.

crisis management briefing: A large-group, crisis intervention, informational or educational session similar to the demobilization session except the facilitators encourage questions from the community participants.

defusing: A small-group crisis intervention process provided to homogeneous groups within a few hours of the impact of a traumatic event. It is a shortened form of a critical incident stress debriefing.

demobilization: A large group educational or informational session that helps to take the edge off of a traumatic event. The demobilization is specifically aimed at operations personnel (police, firefighters, and emergency personnel) exposed to a disastrous event.

expectancy: People do best when they are assured that help is available and that recovery is possible.

immediacy: People do better in managing and recovering from a traumatic event if help is provided immediately.

paraprofessional: People who have specialized crisis intervention training but who do not hold professional academic degrees. They actively participate in many crisis intervention services.

practicality: Advice to a person in crisis must be useful and applicable.

proximity: People do better if their crisis intervention services are provided in a safe area close to their normal area of operations.

resources: The support services required to assist a person in a state of crisis.

simplicity: People cannot manage complex mental processes during a crisis. Keep things simple. Concise, precise terminology and instructions are more helpful than long, complex instructions.

strategic planning: Crisis management plans that assist the crisis interventionist in knowing *who* needs *what* kind of help and *at what time* that help is best delivered and by *which resources*.

target: Those individuals or groups that need help.

theme: The issues or concerns that are in the background of any critical incident. Themes may include intense human vulnerability, speed of onset, knowing the victim or feeling responsible for the critical incident.

timing: Refers to the best time to apply the various interventions to the people who need them the most.

type: Refers to the category of interventions that are likely to be applied to help resolve the crisis response.

DISCUSSION QUESTIONS

1. Why do you think many mental health professionals receive inadequate preparations for dealing with crises in their work? What should graduate programs be doing, if anything, to properly prepare mental health professionals to deal with crises?
2. How does the presence of alcohol or other drugs complicate a crisis situation such as a suicidal threat? What should be the course of action?
3. crisis intervention has a long history of using paraprofessionals to provide many of its services. Please discuss the benefits and possible problems of using paraprofessionals.
4. Why did it take roughly forty years for crisis intervention procedures to be adapted to groups such as families, military operations personnel, and work groups?
5. Why is a combination of multiple crisis intervention techniques stronger than any single isolated intervention?
6. Why is positive outcome expectancy so important?
7. Why is it important to know how to apply the right crisis intervention techniques to specific populations in a timely fashion?
8. Why do small-group processes require homogeneous groups?
9. Why is it so important to have linkages between crisis interventionists and psychotherapists?

10. People who do crisis intervention work are more vulnerable to vicarious traumatization than most other "people workers." Why is this the case?

SUGGESTED FURTHER READING

Caplan, G. (1964). *Principles of preventive psychiatry.* New York: Basic Books.

This old book explores the foundations of crisis intervention. The essential principles of modern day crisis intervention are laid out by a true pioneer and in the field.

Everly, G. S., Jr., & Mitchell, J. T. (1999). *Critical incident stress management: A new era and standard of care in crisis intervention.* Ellicott City, MD: Chevron Publishing.

The book presents the strategy of critical incident stress management. It clarifies how the many tactics of individual, family, and group crisis interventions tie together into a comprehensive, systematic, integrated, and multifaceted approach to managing traumatic incidents within organizations and communities.

Mitchell, J. T., & Everly, G. S., Jr. (2001). *Critical incident stress debriefing: An operations manual for CISD, defusing and other group crisis intervention services* (3rd ed.). Ellicott City, MD: Chevron Publishing.

This operations manual details the four primary CISM group crisis intervention tactics. It describes demobilization, crisis management briefing, defusing, and critical incident stress debriefing. Some chapters cover advanced crisis interventions and CISM teams.

National Institute of Mental Health. (2002). *Mental health and mass violence: Evidence-based early psychological intervention for victims/survivors of mass violence. A workshop to reach consensus on best practices.* Washington, DC: NIMH.

The National Institute of Mental Health held a conference to review two main questions: (1) Should early intervention (within 4 weeks) be practiced? and (2) What should early intervention consist of? The conference delivered these conclusions: (1) there is a rationale for providing early psychological intervention, (2) intervention should be systematic, integrated, and multi-component, (3) follow-up services should be provided for those in greater need, and (4) mental health and paraprofessionals can provide the services.

Roberts, A. R. (Ed.). (2000). *Crisis intervention handbook: Assessment, treatment, and research.* New York: Oxford University Press.

This is a comprehensive crisis intervention manual. It contains carefully written, practical crisis intervention material by the top experts in the field. This book is primary source material for anyone with an interest in crisis intervention.

REFERENCES

Appel, J. W., Beebe, G. W., & Hilger, D. W. (1946). Comparative incidence of neuropsychiatric casualties in World War I and World War II. *American Journal of Psychiatry, 102*, 196–199.

Bard, M. (1970). *Training police as specialists in family crisis intervention.* Washington, DC: Law Enforcement Assistance Administration, National Institute for Law Enforcement and Criminal Justice.

Bard, M., & Ellison, K. (1974). Crisis intervention and investigation of forcible rape. *The Police Chief, 41*, 68–73.

Caplan, G. (1961). *An approach to community mental health.* New York: Grune and Stratton.

Caplan, G. (1964). *Principles of preventive psychiatry.* New York: Basic Books.

Everly, G. S., Jr., Lating, J. M., & Mitchell, J. T. (2000). Innovations in group crisis intervention. In A. Roberts (Ed.), *Crisis intervention handbook: Assessment, treatment, and research* (pp. 77–97). New York: Oxford University Press.

Everly, G. S., Jr., & Mitchell, J. T. (1998). *Critical incident stress management: Assisting individuals in crisis, a workbook.* Ellicott City, MD: International Critical Incident Stress Foundation.

Everly, G. S., Jr., & Mitchell, J. T. (1999). *Critical incident stress management: A new era and standard of care in crisis intervention.* Ellicott City, MD: Chevron Publishing.

Farberow, N. L., & Frederick, C. J. (1978). Disaster relief workers burnout syndrome. In *Field manual for human service workers in major disasters.* Washington, DC: U.S. Government Printing Office. DHEW Publication No. (ADM) 78-537.

Foa, E. B., Keane, T. M., & Friedman, M. J. (Eds.). (2000). *Effective treatments for PTSD*. New York: Guilford Press.

Foley, H. A., & Sharfstein, S. S. (1983). *Madness and government: Who cares for the mentally ill?* Washington, DC: American Psychiatric Press.

Frederick, C. J. (1977). Crisis intervention and emergency mental health. In W. R. Johnson (Ed.), *Health in action* (pp. 376–411). New York: Holt, Rinehart and Winston.

Hill, R. (1958). Generic features of families under stress. *Social Casework, 39*(2–3), 139–150.

Holmes, R. (1985). *Acts of war: The behavior of men in battle*. New York: Free Press.

Kardiner, A., & Spiegel, H. (1947). *War, stress, and neurotic illness*. New York: Hoeber.

Lindemann, E. (1944). Symptomatology and management of acute grief. *American Journal of Psychiatry, 101*, 141–148.

Mitchell, J. T., & Everly, G. S., Jr. (2001). *Critical incident stress debriefing: An operations manual for CISD, defusing and other group crisis intervention services* (3rd ed.). Ellicott City, MD: Chevron Publications.

Mitchell, J. T., & Resnik, H. L. P. (1981). *Emergency response to crisis*. Englewood Cliffs, NJ: Robert J. Brady Company, Subsidiary of Prentice Hall.

Mitchell, J. T., & Resnik, H. L. P. (1986). *Emergency response to crisis*. Ellicott City, MD: Chevron Publishing (reprinted from original).

National Institute of Mental Health. (2002). *Mental health and mass violence: Evidence-based early psychological intervention for victims/survivors of mass violence. A workshop to reach consensus on best practices*. Washington, DC: NIMH.

Parad, H. J. (1971). Crisis intervention. In R. Morris (Ed.), *Encyclopedia of social work* (Vol. 1, pp. 196–202). New York: National Association of Social Workers.

Parad, L., & Parad, H. J. (1968). A study of crisis oriented planned short-term treatment: Part II. *Social Casework, 49*, 418–426.

Rapoport, L. (1962). The state of crisis: Some theoretical considerations. *Social Service Review, 36*(2), 211–217.

Roberts, A. R. (1991). Conceptualizing crisis theory and the crisis intervention model. In A. R. Roberts (Ed.), *Contemporary perspectives on crisis intervention and prevention* (pp. 3–17). Englewood Cliffs, NJ: Prentice Hall.

Roberts, A. R. (2000). An overview of crisis theory and crisis intervention. In A. Roberts (Ed.), *Crisis intervention handbook: Assessment, treatment, and research* (pp. 3–30). New York: Oxford University Press.

Roberts, A. R., & Camasso, M. (1994). Staff turnover at crisis intervention units and programs: A national survey. *Crisis Intervention and Time-Limited Treatment, 1*(1), 1–9.

Ruben, H. L. (1976). *CI: Crisis intervention*. New York: Popular Library.

Salby, A. E., Lieb, J., & Tancredi, L. R. (1975). *Handbook of psychiatric emergencies*. New York: Medical Examination Publishing Company.

Salmon, T. S. (1919). War neuroses and their lesson. *New York Medical Journal, 108*, 993–994.

Shapiro, F. (2001). *Eye movement desensitization and reprocessing (EMDR). Basic principles, protocols and procedures* (2nd ed.). New York: Guilford Press.

Stierlin, E. (1909). *Psycho-neuropathology as a result of a mining disaster March 10, 1906*. Zurich: University of Zurich.

Swanson, W. C., & Carbon, J. B. (1989). Crisis intervention: Theory and technique. In *Task force report of the American Psychiatric Association: Treatments of psychiatric disorders*. Washington, DC: APA Press.

TREATMENT RESOURCES

19

Addiction Recovery Tools

Robert H. Coombs
UCLA School of Medicine

William A. Howatt
Nova Scotia Community College

Kathryn Coombs
Los Angeles Unified School District

TRUTH OR FICTION?

___ 1. *The goal of a motivational intervention is to persuade the addict to accept treatment and aftercare.*

___ 2. *An effective strategy during a motivational interview is to push the client when he expresses resistance.*

___ 3. *An opioid addict who relapses following detoxification will actually be at greater risk for an overdose.*

___ 4. *There are two medications currently available to assist with cocaine withdrawal.*

___ 5. *When testing recovering addicts, hair samples provide the most accurate information regarding long-term drug use.*

___ 6. *A recovery contract is useful for drug and behavioral addictions.*

___ 7. *In contingency management programs, counselors offer clients incentive vouchers based on self-reported abstinence from substance use.*

___ 8. *In cue exposure treatment, a counselor might have the client handle paraphernalia or watch someone prepare a syringe.*

___ 9. *As you coach them in developing a recovery lifestyle, your clients should maintain old associations, especially for business purposes.*

___ 10. *One problem in group therapy is that addicts tend to support one another's denial mechanisms.*

___ 11. *As a counselor whose client is involved in a 12-step program, you should read basic 12-step literature and attend some of the public meetings.*

___ 12. *As a family therapist, you will find that the addict's family often denies the addiction as much as the user does.*

___ 13. *Although a client's eating habits may be poor, treatment for drug addiction should be undertaken before moving on to nutritional counseling.*

_____ 14. *Counselors should not suggest specific visualizations to clients.*
_____ 15. *Acupuncture can be used to treat withdrawal from any drug except cocaine.*

This chapter reviews some of the most common, time-tested therapeutic modalities—or tools—to help your clients recover from their addictions. Though not an exhaustive list, these include *motivational tools* (motivational interventions and motivational interviewing), *medical-pharmaceutical tools* (detoxification, medications, disease orientation, and drug testing), *cognitive-behavioral tools* (recovery contracts, contingency management, cue exposure treatment, and affect regulation and coping-skills training), *psychosocial tools* (lifestyle planning and monitoring, group therapy, peer support groups, and family counseling), and *holistic tools* (nutritional counseling, meditation, and acupuncture). Most treatment programs utilize a variety of these therapeutic tools.

MOTIVATIONAL TOOLS

Motivational Intervention

The *motivational intervention* allows a group of people who care about the client to alter the inevitable course of addiction (Johnson, 1978). According to interventionist Edward Storti (2001), the short-term goal of an intervention is to persuade the patient to listen to the concerns of a gathered group of family and friends. The long-term goals are for the patient to accept the gift of full-time treatment and to apply aftercare recommendations (Storti, 1988, 1995).

Storti (2001) describes his method of motivational intervention as consisting of five steps: (1) the *inquiry*—a concerned associate of the addicted person contacts the therapist and provides basic information; (2) the *assessment*—key group members assist the therapist in tailoring the intervention to the specific patient's needs; (3) the *preparation*—all group members learn their assignments and collect their thoughts (*not* a rehearsal); (4) the *intervention* itself—the group expresses their love, concerns, and hopes to the patient with the guidance of the therapist; and (5) the *follow-up* or case management—ideally, the client enters a treatment program.

Even when a client does not agree to the treatment, group participants have usually found the intervention to be positive and even therapeutic. Storti (2001) points out that while an intervention is rightly considered a wake-up call, it is not necessary to wait until a patient hits rock-bottom to implement it. Rock-bottom can be too late. However, he also cautions that an intervention should not be carried out if certain red flags are present: a strong tendency toward violence or vindictiveness (especially involving a spouse or children), a lack of sufficient documentation of the problem, or a psychiatric disorder requiring treatment in its own right. Otherwise, motivational interventions are effective in bringing patients suffering from addictions into treatment and also give them a foundation of support on which to rebuild their lives.

1. Which of the following is *not* a red flag indicating that a motivational intervention is inadvisable?
   a. a strong tendency toward violence or vindictiveness
   b. the individual has not yet hit rock bottom
   c. lack of sufficient documentation of the problem
   d. a psychiatric disorder requiring treatment in its own right

Motivational Interviewing

Addicted clients are often ambivalent about changing a behavior that provides some benefits to them, even though that behavior may be inconsistent with their basic values, beliefs, and goals. Because committing to, making, and maintaining changes in long-standing behavior is difficult, clients may defend themselves against the therapist's unwanted advice and judgment. *Motivational interviewing* (MI) addresses this challenge.

2. Motivational interviewing may best be defined as:
   a. a confrontational approach intended to clarify how a client's behavior affects those around him.
   b. an examination of family history issues contributing to the client's addiction.
   c. a person-centered intervention meant to resolve ambivalence about change.
   d. a cataloguing of client weaknesses to be overcome in order to facilitate change.

One guide for motivational interviewers is *GRACE*, an acronym developed by Chris Dunn (1996). *G* stands for the *gap* between the client's present state and his or her desired state. *R* represents *rolling* with *resistance*—when the client resists, the therapist shifts the focus rather than countering (which tends to strengthen the resistance). *A* is for *argue not*, reminding the therapist that people ambivalent about what they believe often discover their beliefs by hearing themselves speak. The therapist should listen even though he or she may disagree with the client's stated views. *C* stands for *can do*, that is, using a client's small successes to build a sense of personal competence. *E* means *expressing empathy*, or sincerely understanding the client's position (Rosengren & Wagner, 2001).

3. Counselors practicing motivational interviewing must especially focus on:
   a. creating a list of life goals with the client.
   b. addressing childhood traumas that have contributed to the addiction.
   c. avoiding taking a confrontational stance with the client.
   d. resolving ambivalence toward change as quickly as possible.

Chris Dunn (1996) suggests the acronym *OARS* to remind therapists of four key skills: *Open-ended questions, Affirmations, Reflective listening*, and *Summaries*. In addition, four exercises are often effective. Rollnick, Heather, and Bell (1992) call the first exercise *good and less good things*. It addresses the pros and cons of a specific behavior without forcing the client to label it as problematic before she is ready to do so. The activity also gives the counselor information about perceived benefits of the current pattern. Another set of exercises allowing a client to consider the impact of his choices is *looking forward* and *looking back*. First, the client considers how his life has changed since he began this course of action. Next, he envisions two futures—one following his current path and another on a new path *if* he should decide to change. A third exercise involves going over relevant standardized scales and inventories with the client in order to offer *personalized feedback* (Rosengren & Wagner, 2001). The fourth, from Rollnick, Mason, and Butler (1999) is *importance and confidence*. The counselor asks clients to rate how *important* it is to them to change their behavior, as well as how *confident* they feel about their ability to make changes. At this stage, such changes are discussed strictly in hypothetical terms to avoid making the client feeling threatened or pressured while considering options.

Motivational interviewing has proven effective with clients who are mildly or moderately addicted (Burke, Arkowitz, & Dunn, 2002). Other research shows that the results of a four-session form of MI compare with those of longer 12-step facilitation and cognitive-behavior treatments for severely addicted individuals (Project MATCH Research Group, 1997). One particular strength of MI is that it works within the bounds of the client's particular cultural orientation.

MEDICAL-PHARMACEUTICAL TOOLS

Detoxification

Detoxification, the first step in treating addiction, is the removal of drugs from the addicted client's system (Inaba & Cohen, 2000). When physical dependence is present, medical interventions are used to counter the uncomfortable and, in some cases, high-risk symptoms of withdrawal (Graham & Schultz, 1998). These tools include medications to treat symptoms, to rebuild the patient's damaged system, and to combat cravings (Smith & Seymour, 2001). Some addictions can be treated using a *substitution and tapering* process, such as phenobarbitol for sedative-hypnotic detoxification or methadone for opioid detox. Methadone is also sometimes used for maintenance purposes until a patient is better prepared for detoxification.

4. Medications are used during the client's withdrawal to:
   a. treat symptoms, rebuild the individual's damaged system, and combat cravings.
   b. treat symptoms, induce a relaxed state, and combat cravings.
   c. minimize the withdrawal timeframe, rebuild the individual's damaged system, and induce a relaxed state.
   d. combat cravings, substitute and taper, and minimize the withdrawal timeframe.

Different types of drugs require different types of detoxification. For example, discontinuation of opioids and sedative-hypnotic substances causes well-defined withdrawal symptoms. In contrast, withdrawal symptoms from stimulants are less well-defined. Opioid withdrawal is so painful and uncomfortable that without medical intervention, the patient is likely to return quickly to using. Yet, opioid withdrawal is not often fatal, whereas sedative-hypnotic withdrawal can be life-threatening due to the risk of *grand mal* seizures.

5. Without medication, withdrawal symptoms from which of the following drugs can be so severe that addicts tend to quickly revert to using?
   a. marijuana
   b. sedatives
   c. cocaine
   d. methadone

The list of possible withdrawal symptoms is long; however, as Smith and Seymour (2001) explain:

As a rule of thumb, the symptoms of withdrawal from a drug are usually the opposite of the desired effects from use. For example, opioid use may be characterized by cessation of pain, feelings of euphoria, and general constipation. Withdrawal symptoms may include onset of pain, feelings of dysphoria, and loose bowel. The dynamic of withdrawal can be visualized as being like a pendulum that has been pulled as far as it will go in one direction and is then released. (p. 66)

When patients are diagnosed with psychiatric disorders as well as drug addiction, medical management poses additional challenges. Another factor to consider is tolerance levels, especially relative to levels of potential overdose. An opioid addict who relapses following treatment will be at greater risk for an overdose, as his level of fatality will have shifted along with his level of tolerance.

Although addiction is a chronic disease with a powerful tendency toward recurrence, each incident of treatment helps to plant the seeds of eventual recovery.

Medications

The use of medication is standard for detoxification from physically addictive psychoactive drugs. In addition to addressing withdrawal symptoms during detoxification, medications appear to have the potential to support a client in harm reduction (Ziedonis & Krejci, 2001). Medications are also used to treat co-occurring psychiatric disorders—some 25% to 75% of all clients have a current or past non–substance-use psychiatric disorder—and to manage acute and chronic pain syndromes and related medical problems such as HIV, diabetes, and pneumonia.

Medications are effectively used in three ways: (1) *symptomatic treatment*—using a drug whose pharmacological action is unrelated to the abused drug but whose effects ameliorate emotional and/or physical symptoms related to the use of the abused drug (e.g., to ease discomfort when detoxifying), (2) *agonist substitution*—treatment with a medication that has pharmacological actions similar to those of the abused drug (e.g., nicotine chewing gum for tobacco dependence), and (3) *antagonist treatment*—utilizing pharmaceuticals to inhibit or block the chemical effects of the abused drugs (Coombs, 1997).

Antagonist medications commonly prescribed to facilitate addiction recovery include: **antabuse** for alcoholism, creating an unpleasant physical response to drinking; naltrexone (Revia) and nalmefene for heroin/opioid and alcohol dependence, blocking the opiate receptors; and agonists methadone, LAAM, and buprenorphine for addiction to heroin and other opiates, reducing cravings and blocking euphoria. (Unfortunately, there are no effective medications currently available to assist in cocaine withdrawal.) Nicotine addiction is generally treated through tapering alternate delivery systems that avoid the harmful byproducts of smoking. Without medication and psychosocial interventions, only about 3% of smokers succeed in quitting. Ironically, the primary cause of death among successfully recovering addicts is tobacco dependence (Ziedonis & Krejci, 2001).

6. The use of medications in addiction treatment is:
   a. not useful for nicotine addiction.
   b. not necessary for detoxification because cold turkey withdrawal, while unpleasant, is generally more effective.
   c. helpful for cocaine withdrawal.
   d. standard for detoxification.

Disease Orientation

Historically, drug dependency was considered a moral failing, a behavior demonstrating weakness of character (Jellinek, 1960). In 1945, however, the American Medical Association formally accepted the view promoted early in the nineteenth century by Benjamin Rush, founder of the American Psychiatric Association, that addiction is a *disease*. Since then the disease model has been officially endorsed by the World Health Organization, the American Psychiatric Association, the National Association of Social Workers, the American Public Health Association, the National Council on Alcoholism, and the American Society for Addiction

Medicine. The medical model got further support when it was discovered that there are clear genetic markers that can make a person susceptible to alcoholism.

Defining addiction as a disease relieves addicts of the overwhelming shame and responsibility for having caused the addiction and its devastating consequences; at the same time, they are empowered to do something about it. When the moral baggage society attaches to addiction is lifted, the client can focus on getting better (Miller, 2001).

In addition, the client finds it easier to accept a hard truth: abstinence is the solution. Just as victims of lung cancer are expected to stop smoking, or diabetics to avoid sugary foods, addicts must altogether avoid alcohol and other psychoactive drugs as part of their cure.

7. Which of the following is *not* true of the disease model of addiction?
   a. Generally, the disease model makes it easier for clients to embrace abstinence.
   b. The disease model relieves the client of the overwhelming responsibility for having caused the addiction.
   c. The disease model is understood by most addicts except clients with paranoia or personality disturbances.
   d. The disease model is based in part on the concept of addiction as a genetic predisposition.

Drug Testing

Drug testing, used to promote accountability, determine compliance, and measure success, is most often in three settings: among employees whose contracts require them to remain drug-free, in criminal justice applications such as DUI or probationary screenings, and in clinical treatment programs (Coombs & West, 1991; Mieczkowski, 2001).

Performance-based testing such as the familiar field sobriety test for drivers suspected of being under the influence is a type of prescreening, as it cannot accurately show the presence of substances in a person's body. This type of test may be influenced by fatigue, illness, medication, or a combination of factors other than drugs or alcohol. Still, it is a convenient, inexpensive, and noninvasive means of identifying impairment thereby demonstrating whether further testing is required (Mieczkowski, 2001).

More specific drug testing is conducted in order to chemically ascertain the presence of one or more substances in a person's body. The specimens (*matrices*) most often used in drug testing are blood, urine, sweat, saliva, and hair. As Mieczkowski (2001) explains, a matrix is chosen on the basis of factors such as invasiveness and time window. For example, the breath analysis test is convenient and noninvasive. In contrast, obtaining a blood sample is invasive and also carries a risk of infection. Related issues are transportation, storage, and specimen stability. Keep in mind that invasiveness can be psychological as well as biological. Giving a urine sample or a hair specimen can be a disturbing experience for some clients. On the other hand, be aware of the possibility of your clients cheating on their drug tests; determined users have been known to substitute the urine of drug-free relatives or even dogs for their own contaminated urine.

8. Matrices for drug testing are selected on the basis of factors such as:
   a. local ordinances.
   b. psychological invasiveness.
   c. client's history of cheating on such tests.
   d. location of the testing facility.

Each substance has a time window based on how long it takes to reach the matrix and how long it is in evidence there. After crack cocaine is inhaled, for example, it appears in the blood within a few minutes and in the urine after 20 to 30 minutes, but it doesn't show up in the hair and nails for 3 to 5 days (Mieczkowski, 2001). To detect recent drug use, a fluid sample is a better choice than a hair sample. To consider long-term use or obtain a more quantitative picture, however, a hair sample is more useful. Due to differences in biological functioning, quantitative analysis is only possible in rough terms when comparing two individuals, but a clinic can track the course of a particular client's drug ingestion by using her as a control: repeated testing of hair samples over time should show progressively smaller concentrations of the drug.

9. Crack cocaine appears:
   a. in the bloodstream within 30 minutes and in the urine after 60 to 80 minutes.
   b. in the bloodstream within a few minutes and in the urine after 20 to 30 minutes.
   c. in the bloodstream within 60 minutes and in the urine after about two hours.
   d. in the bloodstream within 90 minutes and in the urine after three or four hours.

Select a sophisticated laboratory with a proven track record to ensure that strict protocols are followed to avoid errors such as contamination, clerical error, improper execution, or cross-reactivity.

COGNITIVE-BEHAVIORAL TOOLS

Recovery Contracts

Behavioral contracts monitor and support patient recovery by reinforcing positive behaviors. Citing a 22% relapse rate among a group of one hundred recovering addicts on a contract system, Talbott and Crosby (2001) praise recovery contracts as "the core of primary treatment and continuing care" (p. 127). These contracts can also be used to address a variety of related issues, such as sexual harassment or anger in the workplace.

There are seven key components of effective recovery contracts (Talbott & Crosby, 2001). The first is *presenting the contract* in a serious and compassionate manner, preferably with the significant other and any program representatives in attendance. The second is *releases of information*—the patient must sign privacy releases for family members, co-workers, and so forth to be involved in contract reporting. The third key is *leverage* through clearly understood consequences when expectations are not met. Note that behaviors should be highly specific, for example, "Will attend physicians' support group the second and fourth Thursday of each month and submit attendance form to Jane Doe by the first of each month." Leverage will vary depending on what the patient cares about most—divorce or loss of employment, for example. Talbott and Crosby suggest a general noncompliance clause in the contract, such as:

> *Failure to comply with any of the above recommendation/agreement guidelines may be perceived as a relapse and comprehensive assessment requested. Noncompliance may also result in un-satisfactory discharge from the program, and information may be forwarded to the appropriate licensing board. (Talbott & Crosby, p. 134)*

The fourth key is the *client's support system*. The fifth is a *short timeframe* so that the client feels capable of compliance. Most contracts are designed to cover a five-year span, but they are renewed annually, biannually, or even quarterly. The sixth is *contract review*, which should take place formally at least every six months and informally on an ongoing basis. Changes such as a death in the family, for example, can have a highly adverse effect on the client and her contract. The seventh key is a *"slip"/ relapse clause*. Patients need to be educated regarding warning signs so they can seek help *before* they head into a full-blown relapse.

10. Which of the following is *not* a key for using recovery contracts?
    a. The patient should sign privacy release forms allowing friends, family members, and co-workers to report his behavior.
    b. Clear, specific consequences will provide the counselor with leverage.
    c. A long timeframe will encourage the client to practice big-picture thinking.
    d. Ongoing review allows the counselor to make changes to the contract in response to crises such as a death or divorce in the client's life.

Clients do sometimes attempt to sabotage their contracts. Also, if monitoring programs or consequences are poorly supported, contracts lose their impact. When properly managed, contracts can be an effective means of facilitating patient recovery.

Contingency Management

"Contingency management (CM) interventions can motivate and facilitate change in the most challenging substance abuse treatment populations" (Budney, Sigmon, & Higgins, 2001, p. 147). Put simply, CM strategies reward desired behaviors, providing incentive to recovering addicts.

Positive reinforcement means delivering a reward. *Negative reinforcement*, not to be confused with punishment or a negative outcome, means removing an undesirable restriction or situation. *Positive punishment* means delivering an undesirable consequence, while *negative punishment* means removing a desirable one. In contingency management, reinforcements are generally considered more effective than punishments.

11. Positive punishment means:
    a. removing an undesirable restriction or situation.
    b. delivering an undesirable consequence.
    c. removing a desirable consequence.
    d. delivering a reward.

CM strategies are valuable for three reasons. First, they tell the client that his difficult efforts to remain drug free are recognized and honored. Second, the rewards can be designed to foster participation in healthy activities. Third, the interaction required by a CM contract provides the therapist with valuable feedback regarding a client's progress.

12. When using contingency management programs, it is helpful to:
    a. make the rewards available of a similar quality or magnitude.
    b. require that clients can't recoup their losses after a slip-up, but must work their way back up the ladder again.
    c. let clients accumulate points for a series of positive behaviors before receiving their rewards.
    d. make behavioral as well as tangible rewards available.

Depending on the treatment program and the client's needs, reinforcements can consist of behavioral outcomes as well as tangible rewards. For example, some methadone clinics reward abstinence with the option to self-administer every other day, saving clients the time and trouble of additional trips to the clinic.

Other incentive programs use a voucher system. The client can earn points and then select a reward purchased or provided through the treatment practitioner. The list of incentives should be long enough to please a variety of clients, and its focus should be healthy recreation. For example, in a sample dialogue with a client, Budney et al. (2001) wrote, "The vouchers that you earn can be used in whatever way you and I agree would support the lifestyle changes that we discuss in our counseling sessions" (p. 158).

Although CM can be used with goals such as attendance at therapy sessions, Budney et al. (2001) encourage treatment professionals to use this strategy first and foremost to reward clients for staying drug free. It is also important that CM rewards be of sufficient magnitude, that they quickly follow the clean drug test or other successful behavior, and that they are based on accurate monitoring procedures.

CM gives the recovery more firepower by competing with the rewards of the addict's drug or behavioral habit. This is especially important for the many users who resent authority figures and regulations. As Budney et al. (2001) tell their clients, "We use this program not to catch you being bad but rather to catch you being good (i.e., not using cocaine)" (Budney, 2001, p. 156).

Cue Exposure Treatment

Drug use is rightly known as a *habit*, with addicts responding to accustomed cues and contexts by ingesting their substance of choice. Based on Pavlov's theories of classical conditioning, *cue exposure treatment* focuses on training clients not to respond to their traditional triggers.

Conklin and Tiffany (2001) explain, "Extinction is the process of eliminating a conditioned response through unreinforced exposure to a conditioned stimulus" (p. 174). Under the supervision of a counselor, a client is exposed to cues such as drug paraphernalia, but does not then ingest the drug. After repeated exposures (the theory goes), reaction to the cue is eliminated.

According to Conklin and Tiffany (2001), cue exposure treatment is often ineffectual, though its drawbacks can be overcome. Studies show that the original conditioning stays intact, but that cue exposure treatment layers a new association on top of it. Cue exposure treatment is thus challenged to create a very strong level of conditioning in order to overcome or supplant the original learned response.

13. Researchers no longer believe:
    a. extinction training can dispel the bond between a conditioned stimulus and an unconditioned stimulus.
    b. original conditioning stays intact following cue exposure treatment.
    c. cue exposure treatment layers a new association on top of the previous training.
    d. context is a factor in cue exposure treatment.

The counselor should be aware of specific threats to extinction. It helps to vary the contexts in which treatment occurs. Giving clients a memory trigger also strengthens the effect of the treatment. To further avoid spontaneous recovery of original conditioning, it is vital to repeat the extinction, with sufficient time elapsed between sessions. Another threat is *reinstatement*, when exposure to the original conditioning triggers it all over again. For this reason, slip-ups must be addressed immediately. A further concern is the drug administration ritual itself, often overlooked as a cue by treatment specialists, but very powerful in its own right.

14. In cue exposure treatment, threats to extinction include:
    a. the slip-up, a difference in setting, and the drug administration ritual.
    b. a difference in setting, a memory trigger, and a time lapse between sessions.
    c. the drug administration ritual, a memory trigger, and spontaneous proximity.
    d. varied contexts, spontaneous proximity, and a time lapse between sessions.

Of course, a counselor can't possibly treat every cue for a given client; therefore, the most prominent cues must be the focus of the program. A counselor should discuss the context of use thoroughly in order to identify powerful cues and discard peripheral information. Note that cues can include emotional states or stressful situations along with more tangible triggers.

When administering cues, the counselor will need to track the client's responses, usually by asking her to self-report cravings, negative mood, and physiological responses on a scale of 1 to 10 (Conklin & Tiffany, 2001). Treatment for a particular cue is ended when a client no longer responds to the cue, though an occasional review to ensure continued extinction is helpful. Properly administered, cue exposure treatment can strengthen the client's resistance to relapse.

Affect Regulation and Coping-Skills Training

Coping-skills training acknowledges that addicts generally use addictive substances or behaviors to regulate their own moods; they self-medicate to avoid uncomfortable feelings (Scott, Kern, & Coombs, 2001). This technique focuses on helping the client learn positive coping skills for addressing challenges and the unpleasant emotions they invoke.

15. Affect regulation is based on the premise that addicts use drugs:
    a. to escape from adult responsibilities.
    b. to block out painful childhood memories.
    c. to manage their emotions.
    d. to enhance their social interactions.

The F-A-N model helps the client understand that Feeling + Action = New Feeling (Kern & Lennon, 1994) He *can* alter his unwanted mood, not only through a self-defeating choice of psychoactive drugs, but by taking other, more constructive actions. His self-confidence will grow as a result.

16. Which is *not* one of the principles of affect regulation and coping-skills training?
    a. The client must stop avoiding unpleasant emotions.
    b. The client learns he can alter an unwanted mood in a constructive way.
    c. The client adopts new coping strategies such as exercise.
    d. The client is encouraged to stop altering her own biochemistry, instead altering thinking, behavior, and environment.

Another useful concept is the pyramid model of emotional well-being (Scott, Kern, & Coombs, 2001). The apex of the pyramid—*feelings*—is supported and influenced by four fundamental corners: *thinking, behavior, environment*, and *biochemistry*. In the past, the client has relied on altering only biochemistry through artificial means. Now he will practice altering the other three factors. In addition, he will learn that he can alter biochemistry in healthy ways, such as changes in diet. Your role as his counselor is partly that of a lifestyle coach as you assist him in thinking of alternative coping techniques. How, for example, can he build a new social support structure (environment)? Setting up an exercise program and using a calendar to schedule positive activities are other strategies you will help him adopt.

The client must also learn to identify and deal with his feelings specifically. As he becomes more comfortable with his own emotions, he will be able to accept "that painful feelings will not kill [him] and will, with time, diminish in intensity" (Scott, Kern, & Coombs, 2001, p. 198). After spending several sessions exploring basic emotions such as anger, happiness, fear, depression, anxiety, and shame, you can assign the client to monitor his own feelings on an hourly basis (e.g., "How am I feeling now?"). Then you can teach the client strategies such as Ellis's (1999) ABCs of rational emotive behavior therapy, in which the client learns that feelings are not simplistically caused by events. Rather, beliefs (B) about activating events (A) actually trigger the consequent feelings or actions (C). The client then learns that he can (D) dispute unproductive beliefs and (E) produce a new effect, or healthy consequence. The client is given specific homework for practicing these strategies, and his progress is tracked over the course of the treatment.

PSYCHOSOCIAL TOOLS

Lifestyle Planning and Monitoring

The two key features in the big-picture approach to addiction recovery are getting off drugs and creating a healthy new life (Zackon, McAuliffe, & Chien, 1993). As a counselor, one of your most vital roles is to assist clients in constructing a drug-free life. Zackon (2001) identifies three common barriers to success: the *people* problem (building a satisfying new social network), the *work* problem (finding rewarding employment), and the *pleasure* problem (acquiring new means of entertainment and excitement). He points out that the drug lifestyle, with its immediate gratification and highs, is not easily replaced by a straight life, which may seem inherently dull and unsatisfying to users.

17. Which of the following is *not* one of the three primary issues lifestyle planning must address?
    a. the people problem
    b. the work problem
    c. the pleasure problem
    d. the motivational problem

18. One important issue in lifestyle coaching is that:
    a. the key to readiness is a change of attitude.
    b. a toxic environment will hold the client back.
    c. the drug-free life can seem boring.
    d. extensive involvement in a recovery community is vital.

According to Zackon (2001), a recovery lifestyle needs eight vital elements: (1) participation in a community that supports abstinence and nourishes moral or spiritual values, (2) productive work (or appropriate training or education) that yields sustenance and social approval, (3) social activities with friends who offer drug-free recreation and support, (4) a home setting that is comforting and relatively free of strong "triggers" (incitements to use), (5) personal growth activities in any or all of the above, (6) standard practices for avoiding high-risk (trigger-laden) situations, (7) standard practices for coping with unavoidable high-risk situations, and (8) regularity in one's personal routines and schedules.

Zackon (2001) further identifies four steps that indicate readiness for recovery: (1) acknowledging one's addiction and the need for major personal change, (2) becoming drug free or largely drug free, (3) accepting a guide for the journey ahead, and (4) joining a pro-recovery community. Without taking these steps, the client probably isn't ready for a full-scale commitment to being drug free.

In resisting positive lifestyle change, clients often resort to one of four excuses. The first is *dangerous liaisons*—retaining a piece of the old lifestyle supposedly for purely social or business purposes. A second dodge is the *toxic environment*—the client feels helplessly surrounded by drugs on every side. The third is *"That's not me"*—the client tries to avoid healthy new alternatives by arguing that they don't fit her personality. The fourth, oddly enough, is a *career in recovery*—the client who hides from real life at the halfway point of the recovery subculture and never quite moves on (Zackon, 2001). As a counselor, you need to address these avoidance techniques firmly yet compassionately.

19. Which of the following is *not* an excuse given by addicts to avoid changing their lifestyle?
    a. They need to retain associates from their drug-using lifestyle.
    b. Drugs are ever-present in their environment.
    c. They cannot perform their work without being in an altered state.
    d. Health alternatives to drug use are not appropriate for them.

Group Therapy

Group therapy can be an effective tool for two basic reasons: first, the substance habit is typically maintained by what Arnold Washton (2001, p. 240) calls "the addict's massive wall of denial," and second, recovering addicts need a strong social support system. When you group several addicts together in a therapeutic atmosphere, they can call one another's bluffs even as they provide an encouraging recovery community.

Washton (2001) finds it most productive to have different groups for differing stages of recovery. Some counselors run *self-evaluation groups* (SEGs) for clients who are not yet ready to commit to abstinence and need motivation enhancement. A second type of group is the *early recovery group*. In this setting, members work on acknowledging their addiction, achieving abstinence, and stabilizing their lives. Participation typically lasts from several months to a year. A third type is the *relapse prevention*, or *advanced recovery*, group. These individuals have maintained abstinence for some time and are ready to focus specifically on issues which make them vulnerable to relapse.

20. Self-evaluation groups (SEGs) are for:
    a. clients who have been abstinent for a period of months and need to assess the direction of their new, drug-free lives.
    b. clients who are not yet ready to commit to abstinence and need motivation enhancement.
    c. clients who need mentoring in terms of strategies for avoiding relapse.
    d. clients who are involved in meditation practice and need a setting in which to discuss their insights.

Make sure each group is small (eight–ten members is ideal) and consists of a diverse mix in terms of gender, ethnicity, social status, drug of choice, and so forth. On occasion, certain clients should not be assigned to group work because they are particularly volatile or may be too different from the group's population to feel truly comfortable (Washton, 2001).

21. Group therapy:
    a. breaks through addicts' denial.
    b. provides strong social support for recovery.
    c. is done with a diverse group of addicts.
    d. All of the above.

Prior to entering the group, a new member should meet with you for a briefing about what to expect and how to contribute appropriately to the group. You can ask her to sign a form agreeing to abide by the rules of the group. One rule is to come to meetings clean and sober— for this reason, it is helpful to require group members to take an on-the-spot drug test at the beginning of each meeting. When a new member first attends, each group member should briefly introduce himself, commenting on his own life and addiction history as well as his experience in the group (Washton, 2001).

22. Among the keys to conducting therapy group with recovering addicts is:
    a. involving at least fifteen to eighteen group members.
    b. briefing new members on expectations prior to their first meeting.
    c. including participants at various stages of recovery to act as models and mentors for each other.
    d. spending sufficient time on issues such as the role of 12-step programs.

As group leader, your role is to facilitate a productive interaction among group members. Washton (2001) explains:

> Topics for group discussion should be largely patient driven so that members' problems, crises, and recovery issues can be dealt with as they arise in the course of daily life. Your main responsibilities are to help keep the group focused on relevant issues, encourage participation of all members, and ensure that members provide helpful therapeutic feedback to one another and refrain from lecturing, advice giving, hostile confrontation, and other negative behaviors that do more harm than good. (p. 245)

You may also wish to suggest topics of discussion on occasion for the early recovery group.

Another important role is to subtly overcome pockets of resistance. You will sometimes need to ask overly aggressive group members to tone it down. Other issues to address are slips, lateness and absenteeism, hostility and chronic complaining, lack of participation, reporting that avoids either details or emotional content, and proselytizing for Alcoholics Anonymous (AA). Many concerns can successfully be turned back over to the group. For example, "I wonder if anyone else is experiencing Jim's remarks as hostile and devaluing? Can someone give Jim feedback?" (Washton, 2001, p. 253). With wise guidance and the good will of participants, a recovery group can become a source of strength for the addict who is attempting to turn her life around.

Peer Support Groups

Client participation in peer support groups can be a key to successful recovery (Kurtz, 2001). Studies have shown that AA and other 12-step programs are at least as effective as other treatment modes; in fact, they tend to have a higher rate of abstinence as well as lower health care costs (Humphreys & Moos, 2001; Project MATCH Research Group, 1997).

Borkman (1999) asserts that support groups are a store of "experiential knowledge," the firsthand knowledge that comes from personally facing a life challenge:

> When I got there [to his first AA meeting] I saw individuals that I thought were either dead or in prison, but they weren't. They were doing good—had jobs, back with their families. They were looking real good to me. With their support and their encouragement it helped me to see that recovery was a possibility. (Kurtz, 2001, p. 265)

In addition to hope, the peer group provides the recovering addict with a social support system to take the place of his network of drug-using friends. Support groups also offer the client a new model for understanding the role of substances in his life, along with strategies for attaining and maintaining sobriety. AA's famous twelve steps address the fundamental issues of addiction, beginning by breaking down denial and resistance to change and moving on to requiring members to take personal responsibility for their actions. The groups hold frequent meetings—it is suggested that newcomers strive to attend ninety meetings in ninety days. Considering the difficulty of addiction recovery, the frequency of these meetings makes them a practical source of support (Kurtz, 2001).

23. Peer support groups:
    a. are not as effective as other therapeutic recovery tools.
    b. provide the addict with a social support system.
    c. are expensive to join.
    d. meet only occasionally.

At the meetings, members may share their recovery stories, discuss insights and concerns, or study literature such as AA's "Big Book." Service is an important component, particularly in terms of senior members serving as sponsors to newer, struggling participants (Alcoholics Anonymous World Services, 1981). When a client knows he can call a sponsor any time—day or night—for help in resisting relapse, his recovery process is automatically strengthened.

Because some clients are uncomfortable with the spiritual aspect of the 12-step programs, a few non-spiritual alternatives have sprung up. However, AA, Narcotics Anonymous (NA), and similar groups emphasize that the client selects his own concept of a higher power when working the steps. And its nondenominational approach makes it consistent with a variety of belief systems. The spiritual component should not be taken lightly, as it seems to help participants break through discouragement and move forward with their lives (Kurtz, 2001).

24. Which of the following is *not* true of 12-step programs such as Alcoholics Anonymous (AA)?
    a. The programs' spiritual component advocates reliance on a traditional Judeo-Christian version of God.
    b. Twelve-step programs are generally as effective as other treatment options, and sometimes more so.
    c. Twelve-step programs offer the strength of "experiential knowledge."
    d. Newcomers to AA are encouraged to attend meetings daily for the first few months.

You will be better able to encourage your client's progress if you become well-acquainted with the basic 12-step literature and attend those meetings open to the public.

Family Counseling

With a new client, consider the possibility that she may have a substance abuse problem, and also determine whether she is involved with an addict or alcoholic. Co-alcoholism or **co-dependence** is an adaptation paralleling addiction, and it can be treated through stage-appropriate psychotherapy, based on Brown's developmental model of addiction (Brown, Lewis, & Liotta, 2000). As Schmid and Brown (2001) explain, "In this model, addiction is viewed as a 'central organizing principle' governing individual, couple, and family dynamics and development in addicted families" (p. 274).

If you suspect addiction is part of the family system, Schmid and Brown (2001) suggest you try to ascertain the following:

- To what extent have alcohol and drugs taken on a central organizing role in the family?
- To what extent does the client use cognitive distortion, rationalization, and denial about the family member's substance use?
- What behaviors contribute to maintaining alcohol and drug use?
- What functions are served by the substance use?
- What are the family members' thoughts, perceptions, feelings, and behaviors about the addict's drinking and using drugs?

25. When counseling an addict's family, it's useful to consider the other family members as:
    a. allies in supporting the addict's recovery.
    b. a dysfunctional construct that created the addiction.
    c. a group who is most likely fed up and ready for change.
    d. a parallel system of psychological addiction.

The following stages refer to co-dependent family members rather than to the addict (Schmid & Brown, 2001). Stage I is *active addiction,* when family members are firmly entrenched in a system marked by adaptation, compensation, and denial. At this stage, treatment is primarily educational and cognitive.

Stage II, *transition,* is movement toward recovery. Its substages are the *addicted mode* and the *recovery mode.* In the addicted mode, as family members begin to acknowledge the user's addiction, they are likely to upset existing protocols with frantic attempts to control the addict. They may also be overwhelmed by feelings of helplessness and despair. Schmid and Brown (2001) warn: "When family members reach this point, be ready: Things can get worse. Some of them will eventually give up on recovery and sink back into active addiction" (p. 280).

26. In Stage II of a family's recovery process, you can expect:
    a. continued denial of the addiction.
    b. root issues such as trust to be addressed.
    c. family members to react less impulsively.
    d. overwhelming feelings of helplessness and despair.

In the recovery mode, family members will finally admit that they cannot change the addict and will begin to focus on their own potential for change. While continuing cognitive work, you should now shift to a largely behavioral focus. Schmid and Brown (2001) point out that family members need your guidance in replacing old behaviors, which are almost entirely based on impulse, with new, considered, patterns of behavior. Attending a support group like Al-Anon is also very helpful at this point.

Like addicts, family members may revert to the old family system more than once. In time, they should move on to Stage III, *early recovery.* At this stage, the family is no longer reacting on impulse. They have begun to create a calmer, more structured life for themselves, whether or not they continue their contact with the addict. Behavioral work continues to be key at this stage. However, at Stage IV, *ongoing recovery,* you can use more psychodynamic work to address root issues as the client begins to develop a self separate from the addictive system (Schmid & Brown, 2001).

HOLISTIC TOOLS

Nutritional Counseling

Many addicts are malnourished, and their addiction represents a severe imbalance in the bio-chemistry of their bodies. Adding nutritional counseling to your repertoire will close what tends to be a glaring gap in the addict's treatment needs.

Early studies with animal subjects showed that well-nourished subjects demonstrated "wisdom of the body" by rejecting alcohol in favor of water, while malnourished subjects were more likely to consume alcohol (Rogers et al., 1955, cited in Beasley, 2001). In another study, even bacterial cultures were better able to resist the toxic effects of alcohol when they were better nourished (Ravel et al., 1955, cited in Beasley, 2001). Guenther (1983) treated two groups of addicts, differentiating in her approach only by incorporating a nutritional component into one program. Six months later, 81% of the individuals in the nutrition group were not drinking, as opposed to 38% of the control group. Patients in the nutrition group also claimed to experience fewer cravings.

Beasley (2001) built on Guenther's (1983) work in a program for 111 patients in New York:

> *[All] had severe and chronic alcoholism. All had long and difficult histories of alcohol and drug abuse, with many failed treatment attempts . . . All their diets were deficient; 80% were overtly clinically malnourished, almost two thirds had liver disease, and almost half were also addicted to other drugs. (p. 294)*

After twelve months of a treatment program including a strong nutritional component, 91 patients were still participating, and 74% of these patients were sober (Beasley, 2001).

27. In a study of addicts in a treatment program in New York City:
    a. 25% were clinically malnourished.
    b. 40% were clinically malnourished.
    c. 80% were clinically malnourished.
    d. 65% were clinically malnourished.

As a counselor, educate yourself about nutrition. At a minimum, encourage clients to avoid refined sugar and carbohydrates, highly processed foods (with many additives), fatty foods, and caffeine. Beasley (2001) notes that caffeine "contributes to fatigue, depression, and cravings for addictive substances" (p. 300). Instead, clients should eat regular meals with a protein component to help stabilize their erratic body chemistry and moods. They should eat more fresh fruits and vegetables, whole grains, and meats free from hormones and other additives whenever possible. They should take nutritional supplements to revitalize their depleted systems. Of course, a regular exercise program will not only strengthen their bodies, but will also lift their spirits during the ups and downs of recovery.

You may consider asking your clients to be tested for respiratory and food allergies, as these can further distort biochemistry. In fact, because patients with food allergies often crave the very foods they are allergic to, some allergy specialists suspect that alcoholism is partly an allergic reaction. Take the time to support your client's nutritional well-being. Beasley and Knightly's book, *Food for Recovery* (1994) is an excellent guide.

Meditation

Meditation, defined as "a specific state of attending to a particular focus while withdrawing one's attention from the outside world . . . [as] a way of tapping into the inner wisdom inherent in us all" (Snarr, Norris, & Fahrion, 2001, p. 307), is used effectively to support recovery. Because meditation requires a kind of discipline and thoughtfulness that has been missing from the addicted client's life, it helps stabilize him. It also gives him opportunities for self-analysis.

Breathing and hand temperature training are two basic meditation techniques. Regulating breath is the first skill learned by beginning students of meditation. The goal is to replace shallow thoracic breathing with deeper diaphragmatic breathing, a calming practice. Hand temperature training, in which the client learns to adjust the warmth and blood flow in her hands, is an example of *biofeedback*. "Learning to regulate the autonomic nervous system is powerful. It gives your client a direct experiential knowing of self-regulation, of the capacity for choice, for self-control" (Snarr et al., 2001, p. 310).

28. Meditation:
    a. can stabilize a client.
    b. includes biofeedback techniques.
    c. provides an opportunity for self-analysis.
    d. all of the above.

These techniques are intended to lead to the further practice of *deep reverie*, the state of mind that precedes sleep. In this case, its orientation is toward befriending and accessing the inner self—the subconscious mind—enhancing self-awareness as well as problem-solving capabilities. Because reverie also tends to produce images meaningful to the subconscious self, the therapist deliberately utilizes **visualization** and **imagery** in treating the addicted client. Visualizations must be sincere and positive, representing what the client wants to bring into her life. Once the client is accustomed to visualization practice, three key visualizations suggested by Snarr et al. (2001) are the substance rejection scene, the enjoyable abstinence scene, and a visualization representing unconditional positive self-regard.

29. Deep reverie is:
    a. the dream state during REM sleep.
    b. usually only attained by meditation masters.
    c. the state of mind experienced shortly after awakening.
    d. a desired state for tapping into the subconscious.

The therapist can guide some visualization especially in early sessions, but the client should ultimately conduct her own visualizations. According to Lohman (1999), meditation strengthens recovery motivation and supports detoxification. It also helps clients manage stress, increasing self-confidence and a sense of well-being (Snarr et al., 2001).

Acupuncture

Some one thousand treatment programs use *acupuncture* in treating addictions, both to ease withdrawal symptoms and to prepare clients for psychosocial recovery (Smith & White, 2001). Acupuncture has been found to have a calming effect on patients and to improve treatment retention; in addition, it is safe and cost efficient. In two studies, Bullock, Culliton, and Olander (1989) found significantly better outcomes for alcoholism recovery among clients receiving acupuncture, specifically in terms of treatment participation, self-reported need for alcohol, and drinking episodes. Lipton, Brewington, and Smith (1994) achieved similar results in supporting withdrawal among cocaine abusers. Their findings are particularly significant because pharmaceutical treatment options have yet to be discovered for cocaine addiction. Wen and Cheung (1973) found early success in treating opium addicts for withdrawal symptoms in Hong Kong, while Washburn et al. (1993) reported better program attendance for clients receiving acupuncture as compared to a control group (all studies in this paragraph also cited in Smith & White, 2001).

Smith and White (2001) define acupuncture as "the stimulation of specified locations on the surface of the body that alters and improves bodily function" (p. 340). Each *zue*, or point, is physiologically distinct from the flesh around it, having greater electrical conductivity and warmth detectable both by the touch and by instruments. Acupuncture at the correct points produces measurable changes in EEG, GSR, blood flow, and breathing, unlike needling at placebo sites. Other studies relate acupuncture to changes in neurotransmitters—the release of endogenous opiate peptides, for example, might help explain how the treatment alleviates withdrawal symptoms (Smith & White, 2001).

30. Which of the following is *not* true of acupuncture?
    a. Acupuncture points are identified through patient response, as they are not physiologically distinct from the flesh around them.
    b. Acupuncture supports cocaine withdrawal.
    c. Acupuncture is safe and cost efficient.
    d. Acupuncture has been found to improve addiction treatment retention and reduce withdrawal symptoms.

During treatment, needles are inserted smoothly and shallowly. Other than a brief pinching sensation, pain is rarely experienced. Bleeding is also rare. The technique generally produces a sense of relaxation almost immediately. Clients may also feel warmth, tingling, electrical movement, or heaviness either in the application area (usually the ears) or some other part of the body. Touch, movement, heat, and electricity can also stimulate the points. Related procedures therefore include acupressure, shiatsu, reiki, and tai ji chaun.

In addition to treating the addict's obvious need for relaxation and for relief of withdrawal symptoms, acupuncture addresses her general state of physiological imbalance and ill health. It also supports treatment of coexisting psychiatric disorders ranging from depression to paranoia. The Lincoln Recovery Center has found a group setting to be most successful, and has trained a range of clinicians to administer the treatment. The National Acupuncture Detoxification Association (NADA) assists programs with an interest in applying the Lincoln model.

Though not an exhaustive review of addiction recovery tools, this chapter provides a brief overview of some of the best-known therapeutic methods used to help addicts. Your therapeutic results will improve as you learn to use these tools effectively. The main questions are: (a) Which therapeutic tool will work best with each client? and (b) How can I effectively incorporate these tools into my practice to better serve them?

KEY TERMS

affirmations: Statements of recognition about client strengths.

antabuse: Popular name for *disulfiram*, a chemical antagonist used to discourage alcohol ingestion; produces nausea, extreme flushing, and decreased blood pressure when alcohol is consumed.

agonist substitution: Replacing an abused drug with a prescribed medication that has the same pharmacological effects.

antagonist treatment: Utilizing pharmaceuticals to block the desired chemical effects of the abused drug.

co-dependence: A pathological adaptation, involving a sacrifice of self, by the addict's family members and other intimate associates, which reinforces and enables the addictive behavior.

imagery: Spontaneous messages from the unconscious to the conscious, much like dreams, that are typically quite meaningful.

negative reinforcement: Removing a desirable reward.

positive reinforcement: Delivering a reward.

symptomatic treatment: Utilizing a drug whose effects ameliorate the symptoms related to the use of the abused drug.

visualization: The consciously chosen, intentional instruction to the unconscious mind about the will to wellness, to change.

DISCUSSION QUESTIONS

1. Some psychotherapists suggest that addiction and psychosocial health seem to have a "chicken or egg" relationship because it is often unclear which truly precedes or causes the other. Ziedonis and Krejci state that at least 25% of addicts have coexisting psychiatric conditions. What, then, are the implications for therapeutic practice?

2. In the section on motivational interviewing, Rosengren and Wagner emphasize that your goal as a counselor is to gently assist clients in exploring their ambivalence toward changing their addicted lifestyles. A basic paradox of counseling is that clients both desire and fight against change. How will you go about encouraging someone to make major life changes without pushing so hard that they push back?

3. Explore the controversy surrounding the use of medication in recovery treatment. Which is more important—alleviating withdrawal symptoms and supporting recovery with medications or avoiding the paradox associated with using drugs to treat drug addiction?

4. The disease model teaches clients to lay at least some of the blame for their habit on genetic predisposition, thus lifting the burden of shame so that clients are more free to fight their addiction. Yet one negative characteristic typical of addicts is their avoidance of adult responsibility. To what extent should clients take responsibility for their own addiction?

5. One challenge in treating addiction is the high incidence of relapse. As a counselor faced with relapsing clients, how will you keep from become discouraged and even cynical about your work?

6. Some might argue that contingency management trivializes recovery or turns it into a childish game. In what ways is offering clients rewards for their progress a justifiable therapeutic strategy?

7. Cue exposure treatment is sometimes considered problematic because it layers new conditioning on top of old conditioning rather than replacing it and can also easily be extinguished. What are the benefits of using this treatment?

8. The section on affect regulation and coping-skills training explains that clients use drugs to avoid uncomfortable feelings. It also offers new ways for clients to think about their feelings. Design two therapeutic exercises which might assist your clients in handling unpleasant feelings when they arise.

9. In talking about group therapy, Arnold Washton warns against getting bogged down in debates about 12-step programs. In the section on AA and similar programs, Linda Kurtz suggests ways that counselors can support their clients' participation. How do you feel about 12-step programs? What do you think of their spiritual component? In what ways might such programs seem to "compete" with your work as a counselor? In what ways might they complement it?

10. In this chapter, you have read about eighteen different approaches to addiction treatment. Which methods most appeal to you and why? How would you go about selecting the best options for meeting a given client's needs? What strategies might work well in concert with one another?

SUGGESTED FURTHER READING

Coombs, R. H. (Ed.). (2001). *Addiction recovery tools: A practical handbook*. Thousand Oaks, CA: Sage.

This edited book offers more extensive elaboration on each of the recovery tools briefly reviewed in this chapter. It also discussions ways to match clients with recovery tools.

National Institute on Drug Abuse. (2000). *The NIDA clinical toolbox: Science-based materials for drug abuse treatment providers*. 2000. CLN Box.

A compilation of publications based on NIDA-supported research regarding effective drug treatment approaches and strategies.

REFERENCES

Alcoholics Anonymous. (1976). *Alcoholics Anonymous: The story of how many thousands of men and women have recovered from alcoholism* (3rd ed.). New York: Alcoholics Anonymous World Services.

Alcoholics Anonymous. (1981). *Twelve Steps and twelve traditions.* New York: Alcoholics Anonymous World Services.

Beasley, J. D. (2001). Nutritional counseling: How to get the big high. In R. H. Coombs (Ed.), *Addiction recovery tools: A practical handbook* (pp. 291–306). Thousand Oaks, CA: Sage.

Beasley, J. D., & Knightly, S. (1994). *Food for recovery: The complete nutrition comparison for recovering from alcoholism, drug addiction, and eating disorders.* New York: Crown.

Borkman, T. J. (1999). *Understanding self-help/mutual Aid: Experiential learning in the commons.* New Brunswick, NJ: Rutgers University Press.

Brown, S., Lewis, V., & Liotta, A. (2000). *The family recovery guide: A map for healthy growth.* Oakland, CA: New Harbinger.

Budney, A. J., Sigmon, S. C., & Higgins, S. T. (2001). Contingency management using science to motivate change. In R. H. Coombs (Ed.), *Addiction recovery tools: A practical handbook* (pp. 147–172). Thousand Oaks, CA: Sage.

Bullock, M., Culliton, P., & Olander, R. (1989). Controlled trial of acupuncture for severe recidivist alcoholism. *Lancet,* 1435–1439.

Burke, B. L., Arkowitz, H., & Dunn, C. (2002). The effectiveness of motivational interviewing and its adaptations: What we know so far. In W. R. Miller & S. Rollnick (Eds.), *Motivational interviewing: Preparing people to change* (2nd ed., pp. 217–250). New York: Guilford Press.

Conklin, C. A., & Tiffany, S. T. (2001). Cue exposure treatment: New thoughts about an old therapy. In R. H. Coombs (Ed.), *Addiction recovery tools: A practical handbook.* (pp. 173–190). Thousand Oaks, CA: Sage.

Coombs, R. H. (1997). *Drug-impaired professionals.* Cambridge: Harvard University Press.

Coombs, R. H., & West, L. J. (Eds.). (1991). *Drug testing: Issues and options.* New York: Oxford University Press.

Dunn, C. (1996). Packaging. *Motivational Interviewing Newsletter for Trainers, 3,* 5.

Ellis, A. (1999). *How to make yourself happy and remarkably less disturbable.* Atascadero, CA: Impact.

Graham, A. W., & Schultz, T. K. (Eds.). (1998). *Principles of addiction medicine* (2nd ed.). Chevy Chase, MD: American Society of Addiction Medicine.

Guenther, R. M. (1983). The role of nutritional therapy in alcoholism treatment. *International Journal of Biosocial Research, 4*(1), 5–18.

Humphreys, K., & Moos, R. (2001). Can encouraging substance abuse patients to participate in self-help groups reduce demand for health care? A quasi-experimental study. *Alcoholism: Clinical and Experimental Research, 24*(5), 711–16.

Inaba, D. S., & Cohen, W. E. (2000). *Uppers, downers, all arounders: Physical and mental effects of psychoactive drugs.* (4th ed.). Ashland, OR: CNS Publications.

Jellinek, E. M. (1960). *The disease concept of alcoholism.* New Haven, CT: College and University Press.

Johnson, V. E. (1978). *I'll quit tomorrow.* New York: Harper & Row.

Kern, M., & Lennon, L. (1994). *Take control now!* Los Angeles: Life Management Skills.

Kurtz, L. F. (2001). Peer support: Key to maintaining recovery. In R. H. Coombs (Ed.), *Addiction recovery tools: A practical handbook* (pp. 257–272). Thousand Oaks, CA: Sage.

Lipton, D., Brewington, S., & Smith, M. (1994). Acupuncture for crack-cocaine detoxification: Experimental evaluation of efficacy. *Journal of Substance Abuse Treatment, 11,* 205–215.

Lohman, R. (1999). Yoga techniques applicable within drug and alcohol rehabilitation programmes. *Therapeutic Communities: International Journal for Therapeutic and Supportive Organizations, 20*(1), 61–72.

Mieczkowski, T. (2001). Drug testing: A review of drug tests in clinical settings. In R. H. Coombs (Ed.), *Addiction recovery tools: A practical handbook* (pp. 111–126). Thousand Oaks, CA: Sage.

Miller, N. S. (2001). Disease orientation: Taking away the shame and blame. In R. H. Coombs (Ed.), *Addiction recovery tools: A practical handbook* (pp. 99–110). Thousand Oaks, CA: Sage.

Project MATCH Research Group. (1997). Matching alcoholism treatments to client heterogeneity: Project MATCH post-treatment drinking outcomes. *Journal of Studies on Alcohol, 59,* 113–522.

Ravel, J. M., Felsing, B., Lansford, E. M., Jr., Trubey, R. H., & Shive, W. (1995). Reversal of alcohol toxicity by glutamine. *Journal of Biological Chemistry, 214,* 497.

Rogers, L. L., Pelton, R. B., & Williams, R. J. (1955). Dietary deficiencies in animals in relation to voluntary alcohol and sugar consumption. *Quarterly Journal of Studies on Alcohol, 16,* 234–244.

Rollnick, S., Heather, N., & Bell, A. (1992). Negotiating behaviour change in medical settings: The development of brief motivational interviewing. *Journal of Mental Health, 1,* 25–37.

Rollnick, S., Mason, P., & Butler, C. (1999). *Health behavior change: A guide for practitioners.* Edinburgh: Churchill Livingstone.

Rosengren, D. B., & Wagner, C. C. (2001). Motivational interviewing: Dancing, not wrestling. In R. H. Coombs (Ed.), *Addiction recovery tools: A practical handbook* (pp. 17–34). Thousand Oaks, CA: Sage.

Schmid, J., & Brown, S. (2001). Family treatment: Stage-appropriate psychotherapy for the addicted family. In R. H. Coombs (Ed.), *Addiction recovery tools: A practical handbook* (pp. 273–290). Thousand Oaks, CA: Sage.

Scott, R. L., Kern, M. F., & Coombs, R. H. (2001). Affect-regulation coping-skills training: Managing mood without drugs. In R. H. Coombs (Ed.), *Addiction recovery tools: A practical handbook* (pp. 191–206). Thousand Oaks, CA: Sage.

Smith, D. E., & Seymour, R. B. (2001). Detoxification: Opening the window of opportunity to recovery. In R. H. Coombs (Ed.), *Addiction recovery tools: A practical handbook* (pp. 63–80). Thousand Oaks, CA: Sage.

Smith, M. O., & White, K. P. (2001). Acupuncture: A venerable nonverbal therapy. In R. H. Coombs (Ed.), *Addiction recovery tools: A practical handbook* (pp. 339–366). Thousand Oaks, CA: Sage.

Snarr, C. A., Norris, P. A., & Fahrion, S. L. (2001). Meditation: The path to recovery through inner wisdom. In R. H. Coombs (Ed.), *Addiction recovery tools: A practical handbook* (pp. 307–322). Thousand Oaks, CA: Sage.

Storti, E. A. (1988). *Crisis intervention: Acting against addiction*. New York: Crown.

Storti, E. A. (1995). *Heart to heart: The honorable approach to motivational intervention*. New York: Carlton.

Storti, E. A. (2001). Motivational intervention: The only failure is the failure to act. In R. H. Coombs (Ed.), *Addiction recovery tools: A practical handbook*. Thousand Oaks, CA: Sage.

Talbott, G. D., & Crosby, L. R. (2001). Recovery contracts: Seven key elements. In R. H. Coombs (Ed.), *Addiction recovery tools: A practical handbook*. Thousand Oaks, CA: Sage.

Washburn, A. M. et al. (1993). Acupuncture heroin detoxification: A single-blind clinical trial. *Journal of Substance Abuse Treatment, 10*, 345–351.

Washton, A. M. (2001). Group therapy: A clinician's guide to doing what works. In R. H. Coombs (Ed.), *Addiction recovery tools: A practical handbook* (pp. 239–256). Thousand Oaks, CA: Sage.

Wen, H. L., & Cheung, S. Y. C. (1973). Treatment of drug addictions by acupuncture and electrical stimulation. *Asian Journal of Medicine, 9*, 139–141.

Zackon, F. (2001). Lifestyle planning and monitoring: Readiness, guidance, and growth. In R. H. Coombs (Ed.), *Addiction recovery tools: A practical handbook* (pp. 207–222). Thousand Oaks, CA: Sage.

Zackon, F., McAuliffe, W., & Chien, J. (1993). *Recovery training and self-help*. Rockville, MD: National Institute on Drug Abuse.

Ziedonis, D., & Krejci, J. (2001). Medications: One tool in the toolbox. In R. H. Coombs (Ed.), *Addiction recovery tools: A practical handbook* (pp. 81–98). Thousand Oaks, CA: Sage.

20

Drug Treatment and Aftercare Programs

Yih-Ing Hser
M. Douglas Anglin
University of California, Los Angeles

TRUTH OR FICTION?

___ 1. Drug addiction is a chronic relapsing disorder.

___ 2. Patients come to drug treatment because they are eager to achieve drug abstinence.

___ 3. Drug treatment only treats drug-use problems. Hence, there is no need to assess patients' functioning in other areas of life.

___ 4. The Addiction Severity Index is the instrument most used for patient assessment.

___ 5. The American Society of Addiction Medicine Patient Placement Criteria is used for diagnosing psychiatric disorders.

___ 6. After patients have been successfully detoxified, they are unlikely to relapse because they are no longer physically dependent on the drug.

___ 7. Methadone maintenance is an effective treatment for heroin abuse.

___ 8. Day treatment is designed for treating adolescents with cocaine disorder.

___ 9. It is important to develop and implement a treatment plan for the patient at intake and to make reassessments and revised plans regularly throughout the treatment.

___ 10. Urine monitoring should apply only to criminal justice referrals as they have the least motivation for drug treatment.

___ 11. Most therapeutic community programs rely on pharmacotherapy for treating drug abuse disorders.

___ 12. Many patients don't stay to complete their treatment; this is usually because they are able to quit on their own.

___ 13. Treatment retention is positively related to treatment outcome.

___ 14. Drug addicts are criminals, and it is impossible for drug treatment counselors to establish a positive, therapeutic relationship with them.

___ 15. Aftercare programs are for those losers who cannot remain drug-free.

Drug addiction is a complex illness. Individuals with drug addiction problems often persist in their use despite adverse health, legal, and social consequences. The past three decades of efforts to curtail drug use and related problems in the United States have given rise to a wide range of treatment options. Individuals with drug problems may choose from a host of treatment programs including single approaches and combinations of hospital-based inpatient stays, residential care, outpatient care, and self-help group meetings. Services available at such programs include drug education; individual, group, and family counseling and cognitive-behavioral therapy; specialized medical care; educational and vocational training; relapse prevention training; social and community support; and pharmacotherapy. Formal treatment programs usually provide a combination of such service components, although the quality and quantity of these services vary greatly from program to program. The increasing recognition that drug addiction is a chronic relapsing disorder has also resulted in increased availability of aftercare programs. In the previous chapter, you were introduced to some of the effective treatment approaches. In this chapter, our goals are to (a) familiarize you with the elements or components of a comprehensive treatment system, including formal programs and aftercare programs, (b) summarize what is known about treatment effectiveness, (c) prepare you to deliver effective treatment by letting you know the critical issues involved in doing that, and (d) provide you with guidelines on steps to ensure that patients receive the most appropriate and effective treatment(s).

1. Many patients have multiple treatment episodes, which means:
   a. treatment is ineffective most of the time for most people.
   b. drug addiction can be a chronic relapsing condition.
   c. drug addiction is hopeless.
   d. treatment is a waste of social resources.

WHAT CONSTITUTES A COMPREHENSIVE DRUG TREATMENT DELIVERY SYSTEM?

A drug treatment delivery system can be described as a four-part model (Simpson, 1997) including *referral, induction, intervention,* and *transition* to aftercare. Treatment referral strategies and sources often involve the criminal justice system, community health and social service agencies, HIV/AIDS community outreach programs, centralized treatment intake units, self or family, and employee assistance programs. Induction into treatment often involves assessment of patient problems and needs and development of a treatment plan for appropriate intervention strategies. The major objective of this phase is to help patients develop a commitment to treatment and recovery and to comply with therapeutic plans. During the intervention phase, drug treatment strategies usually involve detoxification/stabilization, commitment, and rehabilitation. Generally, the first few weeks focus on detoxification from street drugs and engagement in treatment, followed by compliance and increased commitment as the patient becomes regularly involved in counseling and related therapeutic activities. Assessments of individual functioning are continued periodically throughout treatment to monitor personal progress, and adjustments are made to the treatment plan, if needed. In the later phase of treatment, the patient is prepared for independent drug-free living after discharge, which often involves a transition to aftercare.

A comprehensive treatment delivery system should have a variety of treatment programs and services available (see Fig. 20.1) to meet patients' diverse needs and stages or phases of

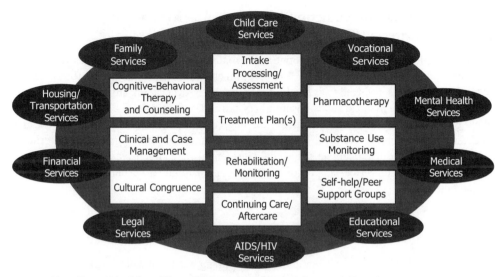

Note. From *Principles of Drug Addiction Treatment: A Research-Based Guide* (p.14), by National Institute on Drug Abuse, 1999, NIH Publication No. 99-4180.

FIG. 20.1. Components of comprehensive drug abuse treatment.

recovery. Effective drug treatment programs typically incorporate many services, each directed to a particular aspect of the illness and its consequences. The best treatment programs provide a combination of (a) pharmacotherapy to eliminate or reduce the side effects of withdrawal, (b) cognitive or behavioral therapy to address the psychosocial problems of addiction, and (c) supportive services to address other needs, such as employment, transportation, child care, and medical care. Additionally, programs can help the patient withstand urges to use drugs by objective monitoring of a patient's drug and alcohol use during treatment, such as through urinalysis or other tests. Such monitoring also can provide early evidence of drug use so that the individual's treatment plan can be adjusted. Feedback to patients who test positive for illicit drug use is an important element of monitoring.

2. When a patient tests positive for drug use, the addiction counselor should:
   a. report the result to criminal justice officials and have the person locked up immediately.
   b. discuss the urine results with the patient and adjust the treatment plan if necessary.
   c. kick the patient out of treatment for violating program rules.
   d. tell other patients to criticize the patient in group sessions.

WHAT ARE THE TOOLS FOR ASSESSMENT, REFERRAL, AND THE DEVELOPMENT OF A TREATMENT PLAN?

An ideal process of assessment, referral, and the development of a treatment plan involves the use of standardized tools to assist the determination of appropriate levels of care and needs for treatment services for a particular patient. The most commonly used tools or instruments are described below.

American Society of Addiction Medicine (ASAM) Patient Placement Criteria (PPC)

The **ASAM PPC** has been devised to define appropriate levels of treatment services, to measure individual patient needs, and to standardize program characteristics (Gastfriend, 1999). Levels of treatment services, referred to as *levels of care* in the ASAM criteria, are specified treatment settings and levels of medical and counseling services and staffing patterns. The ASAM criteria allow clinicians to systematically evaluate the degree of a patient's need for treatment and to determine the appropriate level of care for the patient. The four original ASAM criteria levels of care were placement in a hospital, residential care, intensive outpatient care, or outpatient care. The empirical support of this placement matching procedure is currently under investigation.

Addiction Severity Index

Addiction often involves not only compulsive drug-taking but also a wide range of problematic behaviors in other key life areas such as health, mental health, or employment. A patient may require a combination of services and treatment components, including medical services, family therapy, parenting instruction, vocational training, and social and legal services, to address these areas during the course of treatment and recovery. The **Addiction Severity Index** (ASI; McLellan, Luborsky, Woody, & O'Brien, 1980; McLellan et al., 1992) is a structured interview that assesses problem severity, both in the previous thirty days and lifetime, in seven domains: alcohol use, drug use, employment, family and social relationships, legal, psychological, and medical status. A high severity score indicates a greater need for services in that domain. These severity scores can be used to identify service needs and as a basis for developing an individualized treatment plan that meets a patient's needs. ASI is also commonly used to assess during-treatment progress and after-treatment status.

Most other assessment instruments of drug use are variations of the ASI. The ASI does not provide a diagnosis, however. The diagnostic manual of the *International Classification of Diseases (ICD–10)* and the American Psychiatric Association's *Diagnostic and Statistical Manual of Mental Disorders (DSM)* set criteria for diagnoses based on signs and symptoms. In the United States, the *DSM* is more widely used than the *ICD*. The *DSM–IV* (the fourth edition of the *DSM*) lists seven signs and symptoms of psychoactive substance use disorders. Any combination of three signs or symptoms qualifies for a diagnosis. The *DSM* also distinguishes between *abuse* and *dependence*. Methods of making diagnoses within the contexts of these systems, such as the Diagnostic Interview Schedule (DIS; Robins, Helzer, Croughan, & Ratcliff, 1981) or Structural Clinical Interview for the DSM (SCID) may be useful. These assessment tools provide detailed diagnoses that help with clinical decisions. However, users who do not meet abuse or dependent criteria should not be excluded for treatment because they may need treatment to avoid the development of a more severe drug problem.

3. Clinicians use ASAM criteria:
   a. to determine the appropriate diagnostic category for the patient.
   b. to determine the appropriate international classification of diseases for the patient.
   c. to determine the appropriate level of care for the patient.
   d. none of the above.

4. Addiction Severity Index is used to obtain:
   a. a drug dependence diagnosis.
   b. a psychiatric diagnosis.
   c. problem severity in seven key life areas.
   d. all of the above.

5. The most commonly used tool to assess patient problems in multiple key life domains is the:
   a. American Society of Addiction Medicine Patient Placement Criteria.
   b. Addiction Severity Index.
   c. Structural Clinical Interview for the *DSM*.
   d. Diagnostic Interview Schedule.

6. To develop an adequate treatment plan, patient assessment should include:
   a. drug use history and patterns.
   b. psychosocial functioning.
   c. medical condition.
   d. all of the above.

Motivation and Readiness

Compliance to treatment referral or a treatment plan (e.g., attendance, taking medication) among substance abuse patients has been extremely problematic. A high percentage (as high as 70%) of referrals do not show up at treatment, and among those who do, many do not complete treatment. Dropout rates range from 40% to 60%. During the assessment and referral, care needs to be taken to identify and remove potential barriers (e.g., geographic accessibility, transportation problems, child care needs) so as to facilitate participation. Low or unstable motivation is common among drug addiction patients and is a common predictor of dropping out. Especially during the beginning phase of the treatment, when dropout is most likely to occur, an important task for counselors is to develop a trusting therapeutic relationship with patients and help them to become committed to treatment and recovery. Successful engagement in treatment depends on finding ways to help individuals enhance and sustain their motivation for treatment.

Several instruments are available for measuring motivation and readiness. The Circumstances, Motivation, Readiness, and Suitability (CMRS) questionnaire developed by De Leon, Melnick, Kressel, and Jainchill (1994) is composed of four primary scales as noted in its title: *circumstances* (external motivation), *motivation* (internal motivation), *readiness* (for treatment), and *suitability* (perceived appropriateness of the treatment modality). An instrument developed by Simpson and Joe (1993) identifies three dimensions: self-perceived *severity* of drug-use problems, *desire* for help, and treatment *readiness*.

7. Clinicians should focus on patients' motivation and readiness:
   a. particularly during the beginning phase of the treatment.
   b. because most patients do not comply with treatment referral or treatment rules.
   c. by identifying and removing potential barriers.
   d. all of the above.

WHAT TYPES OF DRUG TREATMENT PROGRAMS ARE CURRENTLY AVAILABLE?

Drug treatment programs vary in many ways, but they generally can be characterized in terms of modality or setting, structured phases, services and staffing, and orientation or philosophy.

Modality or Setting

Treatment for drug abuse and addiction can be delivered in specialized drug treatment facilities, in mental health clinics, in the general medical sector, by human services professionals, and in jails or prisons. Most drug treatment is community-based and can occur in a variety of settings (residential, outpatient, inpatient) and for different lengths of time. Treatment programs have typically been classified into several types or modalities. These modalities are *detoxification programs, residential treatment* (including therapeutic community or other long-term residential programs and short-term residential programs), *outpatient drug-free* (non-methadone) *treatment, day treatment*, and *methadone maintenance* (see Gerstein & Harwood, 1990).

Detoxification programs, whether inpatient or outpatient, are concerned with the medical management of symptoms associated with drug withdrawal in preparation for referral of the patient to a longer-term treatment program. **Inpatient** detox is delivered within a hospital setting and emphasizes medical care during a typically short period of stay (three to twenty-eight days, but usually seven).

Residential programs typically provide a highly structured environment with intensive personality restructuring and socialization efforts. The *therapeutic community* (TC) is a type of residential program that uses a hierarchical model of treatment in which patients are given increased levels of personal and social responsibility as they move through the recovery process. Self-help and peer influence, mediated through a variety of group processes, are used to help individuals learn and assimilate social norms and develop more effective social skills. Traditionally, stays in TCs have varied from eighteen to twenty-four months. Recently, funding restrictions have forced many TCs to significantly reduce stays to twelve months or less or to develop alternatives to the traditional residential model.

Outpatient care can be provided by drug-free, day treatment, or methadone programs. **Outpatient drug-free programs** typically provide six to twelve months of drug education and counseling. Nationally and in most local communities, outpatient drug-free programs account for the largest capacity and broadest use. **Day treatment** is more intensive than the typical outpatient drug treatment program in that patients spend most of each day in intensive program activities and then go home at night; this circumvents expensive hospital or residential costs. Most day treatment programs have a short planned treatment duration, usually less than six months. Outpatient methadone (detoxification and maintenance) programs displace heroin dependence by substituting methadone within (ideally) the context of medical, social, and psychological services. **Methadone maintenance** is long-term; patients may be expected to stay with the treatment indefinitely.

The number of jail- and prison-based treatment programs has increased in recent years. Offenders with drug disorders may encounter a number of treatment options while incarcerated, including drug education classes, self-help programs, and therapeutic community models. Those in treatment should be segregated from the general prison population and should continue treatment after returning to the community.

The drug court is a criminal justice alternative to incarceration for drug offenders. Drug courts mandate and arrange for drug treatment, actively monitor progress in treatment, and arrange for other services to drug-abusing offenders.

Structured Phases

A structured program usually provides treatment in accordance to several phases that patients may go through during the recovery process. These phases typically include *engagement and stabilization, early recovery, maintenance of recovery*, and *transition to aftercare*. The main goal of the engagement and stabilization phase is to help stabilize the acute symptoms and motivate patients to continue in treatment. The phase of early recovery involves participating in treatment activities, learning to cope with desires to use drugs, and other related issues. During the maintenance phase, patients who are abstinent continue to work on issues addressed earlier and on any new clinical issues that emerge. Finally, before the end of the formal treatment, patients are prepared to transition to drug-free life in the community.

Services and Staffing

Most treatment programs provide a combination of services in addition to their modality-specific ones. These services may include vocational training, mental health services, medical services, educational services, child care services, housing services, legal services, or AIDS/HIV services. Many programs monitor patients' drug use during treatment through urinalysis or other tests. Most treatment programs encourage patients to participate in self-help groups during and after formal treatment.

The majority of treatment programs provide some form of counseling services, and in many programs counseling is the only service component. Therapeutic approaches vary widely, but most programs focus on drug counseling. Counseling can be applied in individual, group, or family modes by a variety of types of therapists. The staff may include people in recovery who have become counselors, certificate-level counselors specializing in substance abuse counseling, and licensed clinical social workers, psychologists, and psychiatrists. Most programs have a mix of degreed and nondegreed staff who provide the counseling services. Many programs offer group therapies solely or in addition to individual therapies; some because of their therapeutic belief in group methods, others for the low-cost advantage of group methods.

Orientation or Philosophy

Programs also vary in their orientation toward addiction and its treatment. Some program philosophies argue that past experience with drug use is necessary for understanding and engaging patients; therefore, there is an emphasis on recruiting ex-addicts as counselors. Programs also vary in their emphasis on the importance of medication and counseling. Some programs focus on the importance of building skills. Others emphasize internal changes in patients. Still others attribute addiction to the influence of environmental factors and emphasize the necessity of making changes in the client's environment.

8. A comprehensive drug treatment system should include which type(s) of programs?
   a. methadone maintenance
   b. residential treatment
   c. outpatient treatment
   d. all of the above

9. Which of the following is not included in a therapeutic community program?
   a. personality restructuring and socialization
   b. peer influence
   c. residential treatment
   d. medical management

10. Detoxification programs:
    a. are mostly for cocaine disorder.
    b. usually last more than three months.
    c. are concerned with the medical management of symptoms associated with drug with-
       drawal.
    d. are concerned with the substance use monitoring and continuing care.

11. Methadone maintenance programs are usually:
    a. outpatient programs.
    b. residential programs.
    c. day treatment programs.
    d. drug court programs.

12. Which of the following type of programs are only for individuals with heroin prob-
    lems?
    a. outpatient drug-free programs
    b. methadone maintenance programs
    c. therapeutic community programs
    d. 12-step programs

WHAT ARE AFTERCARE PROGRAMS AND
WHY ARE THEY NEEDED?

Although some individuals with drug disorders are able to achieve sustained recoveries after receiving treatment, for many others, drug addiction is a chronic disorder, characterized by periods of abstinence followed by relapse and reentry into the treatment system. Thus, individuals are generally encouraged to participate in some form of aftercare extending beyond the formal treatment episode. The primary goal of this phase is to maintain the gains that have been achieved in treatment and to prevent relapse. Most **aftercare programs**, regardless of the treatment setting of the primary care, usually consist of outpatient aftercare group therapy sessions and participation in self-help programs such as Alcoholics Anonymous (AA), Cocaine Anonymous (CA), or Narcotics Anonymous (NA). These 12-step programs support the individual's efforts to become and remain drug free. Correlational studies that have examined the relationship between participation in aftercare programs and substance use outcomes have consistently generated positive results (McKay, 2001). Likewise, attendance in self-help programs has been found to be associated with better outcomes.

Self-help programs explicitly discourage use and offer a supportive social network of individuals who do not use drugs. Self-help programs are widely available and can be attended for extended periods. Many 12-step programs view themselves as neither a treatment alternative nor as an appendage to drug abuse treatment (Brown, Kinlock, & Nurco, 2001). Nevertheless, these programs can join forces with drug abuse treatment to provide additional support for abstinence during treatment and/or to provide aftercare for the patient. Self-help programs can be a long-term "way of living and being" (Miller & Kurtz, 1994, p. 161) well-matched to a long-term disorder such as addiction.

There is increasing evidence that aftercare is an essential aspect of eff. treatment and that relapse prevention is a critical aspect of the treatment process. In o sustain the benefits achieved from formal treatment, it is important to encourage participation in aftercare following completion of formal treatment.

13. Twelve-step programs:
    a. are led by psychologists.
    b. are led by priests.
    c. are for Catholics only.
    d. explicitly discourage use.

14. Aftercare programs:
    a. are for religious patients.
    b. are most effective for female patients.
    c. help the patient remain drug-free.
    d. are not necessary for those patients who have successfully completed treatment.

15. Patients are most likely to relapse even after completing treatment if they:
    a. do not continue in some self-help or aftercare program.
    b. have a job.
    c. are married.
    d. are a parent.

WHAT DO WE KNOW ABOUT TREATMENT EFFECTIVENESS?

Numerous studies conducted over the past three decades have concluded that drug treatment is effective and that treatment produces measurable and significant changes in drug use and other behaviors, compared with no treatment (or minimal treatment) or compared with pretreatment status (e.g., Anglin & Hser, 1990; Finney & Moos, 1998; Gerstein & Harwood, 1990; Hubbard, Craddock, Flynn, Anderson, & Etheridge, 1997; McLellan et al., 1996; Simpson, Joe, Fletcher, Hubbard, & Anglin, 1999; Simpson, Joe, & Broome, 2002).

Taking into account that any given study will have some methodological and generalizability problems, reviews of the literature typically draw similar conclusions regarding the effectiveness of drug treatment, including:

1. There are reductions in drug use during and after treatment compared with no treatment or compared with pretreatment status.
2. Treatment effects tend to decline after patients leave treatment, but patients do not return to pretreatment levels of use.
3. Improvements are found in use-related behaviors (e.g., use by injection, drug dealing, property crime, domestic violence) and in positive social functioning such as employment.
4. None of the major treatment approaches is more effective than any of the others for all users, but some are better suited to different types of users.
5. Within treatment modalities, the effectiveness of programs varies considerably, which appears to be related to differences among patients in diverse programs; differences in

program management, staffing, and policies; and differences in the local social service "ecology" in which programs are situated.

6. Effectiveness of treatment is positively related to the length of time that patients spend in treatment and to the provision of sufficient services at adequate levels of intensity to meet patient needs.

7. Treatment has a favorable ratio of costs to benefits as compared to the health, criminal justice, and other costs associated with untreated drug dependence.

Many local and national studies have confirmed these findings. The National Treatment Improvement Evaluation Study (NTIES) reported twelve-month posttreatment outcome results for 4,411 patients selected from seventy-eight programs across the country. This study found statistically significant reductions in patients' use of their primary drug and related behaviors. In addition to decreases in drug and alcohol use and criminal activity, the rate of employment significantly improved among individuals who completed their treatment plans, those who received more intensive treatment, and those who were treated for longer periods (SAMHSA, 1997).

The Drug Abuse Treatment Outcome Studies (DATOS) collected one-year follow-up data on 2,966 patients in ninety-six programs in eleven cities from 1991 to 1993. DATOS found declines in drug use (Hubbard et al., 1997). Other analyses of DATOS data found that within the same treatment modality, programs differed considerably in the number of services they offered and in the amount of time their patients remained in treatment. This national evaluation of treatment for cocaine dependence also showed that 25% of the patients reported weekly cocaine use in the previous year during the five-year follow-up interviews (Simpson et al., 2002), which is slightly higher than the rate for the first year after treatment (21%), but still much lower than the rate that reported weekly use in the year before admission (73%; Simpson et al., 1999). Similarly, Drug Abuse Treatment Outcome Studies for Adolescents (DATOS-A) followed 1,167 adolescents who were consecutively admitted during 1993 to 1995 to twenty-three community-based treatment programs in four U.S. cities (Hser et al., 2001). The study found that adolescents in treatment were typically troubled with multiple problems (e.g., 58% of them were involved in the legal system and 63% met diagnostic criteria for a mental disorder). Nevertheless, less than half (44%) of all patients reported weekly marijuana use in the year following treatment (dropping from 80% in the year before admission). There were decreases in heavy drinking (from 34% to 20%), use of other illicit drugs (48% to 42%), and criminal involvement (76% to 53%). Additionally, patients reported better psychological adjustment and school performance after treatment.

The California Drug and Alcohol Treatment Assessment (CALDATA) collected data at intake and at an average of fifteen months after treatment discharge from a representative sample of 1,850 patients. CALDATA found that drug use declined by about 40% after treatment, criminal activity decreased by about 66%, and hospitalization rates fell by about 33%. According to this study, the benefits of treatment exceeded the costs of treatment by ratios ranging from 4:1 to 12:1, depending on the type of treatment, with an average return of $7 on every dollar invested (Gerstein et al., 1994).

16. Treatment evaluation research has shown that:
    a. patients reduce drug use during and after treatment, compared to no treatment or pretreatment status.
    b. drug treatment is ineffective.
    c. residential treatment is the most effective modality of treatment.
    d. only outpatient treatment is effective.

17. The relationship between effectiveness of treatment and the length of time that patients spend in treatment is:
    a. positive.
    b. negative.
    c. dependent on the age of the patient.
    d. none of the above.

18. Which of the following is the best predictor of treatment outcome?
    a. gender
    b. age
    c. type of drug used
    d. length of stay in treatment

19. Most evaluation studies on drug treatment have shown that:
    a. the benefits of treatment exceed the costs of treatment.
    b. treatment works for adults but not adolescents.
    c. treatment reduces drug use at the expense of public safety.
    d. all of the above.

WHAT ARE SOME OF THE CRITICAL ISSUES YOU NEED TO KNOW TO DELIVER EFFECTIVE TREATMENT?

Treatment outcomes depend on the extent and nature of the patient's presenting problems, the appropriateness of the treatment components and related services provided to address those problems, and the degree of active engagement of the patient in the treatment process. Factors possibly influencing treatment outcome can be broadly discussed in terms of treatment characteristics and patient characteristics. Past literature on treatment effectiveness has consistently shown positive outcomes associated with drug treatment, but most studies have focused on patient characteristics to account for the variation in treatment outcomes (Anglin & Hser, 1990). Patients who have less extensive drug use and higher levels of social adjustment (e.g., are employed, have more family and social support and fewer psychiatric problems, are less criminally involved) generally are more likely to have favorable outcomes.

Although the effects of program characteristics have seldom been quantitatively evaluated, most researchers and clinical observers believe that substantial differences in outcome can be attributed to program policies and protocols, the quality of therapeutic staff and program management, the breadth of services provided, and general staff and facility-wide morale (Anglin & Hser, 1990; Ball & Ross, 1991). It is also commonly believed that effective treatment counselors are knowledgeable, empathetic, and culturally competent in meeting their patient needs.

Next we provide more in-depth information on three of the most critical issues you need to know in delivering effective treatment.

Issue 1: Patients With Special Needs

Certain patient characteristics, including patients with co-occurring mental disorders, patients who are women, adolescent patients, and patients who are involved in the criminal justice system can present additional complications to treatment processes and outcomes.

Psychiatric Disorders

Psychiatric disorders commonly co-exist with addictive disorders. These include anxiety disorders, psychotic disorders and affective disorders such as depression. Typically, greater psychiatric severity is associated with poorer treatment response. A co-existing psychiatric disorder generally complicates treatment; this is especially true for patients diagnosed as having antisocial personality disorder. These substance abuse and mental disorders may be interactive and mutually reinforcing over time. Medications such as antidepressants, mood stabilizers, or neuroleptics may be critical for treatment success when patients have co-occurring mental disorders. Medication may eliminate or reduce symptoms as well as help patients address their problems during counseling sessions. For example, a severely depressed patient may be unable to focus on learning cognitive or behavioral skills until the depressive symptoms are under control.

20. Individuals with co-occurring drug and mental disorders:
    a. are best treated with medication only.
    b. are best treated with medication and behavioral interventions.
    c. are best locked up because no treatment can help.
    d. are best kept at home because no treatment can help.

21. When you encounter a drug-abusing patient who also appears to be mentally disturbed, you should:
    a. ignore it because the patient is likely to be faking.
    b. notify his or her probation officer to prevent the patient from committing a crime.
    c. ensure that the patient is examined by a mental health professional.
    d. make sure that the patient takes methadone to stabilize his or her emotions.

Women

The special problems and vulnerabilities of women in substance-abuse treatment have been increasingly recognized. For example, drug policy for pregnant women has frequently taken on a coercive and punitive character, raising a variety of ethical issues in formulating drug and alcohol abuse treatment policies for pregnant women. Women face several practical and logistical barriers to accessing treatment, such as lack of transportation and child care, which stem from their generally lower levels of income or employment and the fact that they are usually the primary caregiver for children. Specialized drug treatment programs and services for women substance abusers typically stress their psychosocial problems and need for comprehensive services, particularly regarding parenting issues and history of victimization. Sexual abuse represents an additional key issue for women that may both play a role in the etiology of substance abuse and have implications for effective treatment. The high rates of sexual abuse among drug-dependent women argue for the importance of integrating therapy for sexual abuse into treatment for such women.

22. Pregnant addicts should be:
    a. put in jail to prevent harmful drug use.
    b. kept in treatment regardless of whether they stop drug use immediately.
    c. handled by law enforcement officials.
    d. allowed to continue drug use to prevent harmful withdrawal.

23. Gender differences found among addicts suggest that:
    a. women and men need to be treated separately.
    b. women and men need to be treated together.
    c. treatment should be tailored to address the issues salient to each gender.
    d. treatment needs to emphasize gender differences in tolerance to drugs.

Adolescents

Treatment for adolescents is complicated by factors such as age, level of maturity, and family and peer environment, in addition to those factors normally considered, such as severity of drug use and presence of co-existing disorders. The use of drugs may also compromise the adolescent's mental and emotional development because drug use interferes with how people approach and experience social interactions. The treatment process must address each adolescent's experience, including his or her cognitive, emotional, physical, social, and moral development and must make connections to academic performance, self-esteem, and social interactions. The involvement of family members or a foster parent or legal guardian is considered essential to successful treatment outcome. Most adolescent programs also provide an educational program that could include tutorial or graduation equivalency diploma (GED) preparation. Vocational training is also an important intervention and should be part of an adolescent's treatment. Without appropriate skills, many youths may support themselves through illegal activities and thus be more prone to relapse.

Until recently, most assessment and intervention approaches for adolescents have been modeled after those for adults. Knowledge about their effectiveness for adolescents is limited. Although certain approaches are effective, many currently used instruments and programs are not. Wagner and Waldron (2001) documented the best-known and effective assessment, prevention, and treatment programs that are developmentally appropriate for substance use problems among adolescents.

24. Drug treatment for adolescents should:
    a. avoid family involvement.
    b. consider developmental issues.
    c. be modeled after that for adults.
    d. be confrontational to be effective.

25. Developmental appropriate treatment for adolescents should consider:
    a. types of drug used.
    b. educational services.
    c. parental involvement.
    d. all of the above.

Criminal Justice–Involved Drug Treatment Patients

The practice of mandating treatment for substance abusers as an alternative or adjunct to incarceration within the criminal justice system is now commonplace. By some estimates, legal sanctions account for as much as 70% of all referrals to community substance abuse treatment programs (Marlowe, 2002). The criminal justice system and drug treatment system, however, have evolved as separate service entities in this country, with highly divergent philosophies and practice standards. The criminal justice system views drug users as criminals and the correctional action is to punish, whereas most treatment communities view drug use as a disease that needs to be treated. Neither approach alone has proven to be sufficient for rehabilitating drug-abusing offenders; correctional strategies have generally had a small impact on criminal recidivism and virtually no impact on drug use, and community-based treatments have generally failed to retain offenders in treatment or reduce recidivism or drug use among offenders (see a recent review by Marlowe, 2002). Research has shown that *combining* criminal justice sanctions with drug treatment can be effective in decreasing drug use and related crime. Offenders treated in their community of origin but supervised by the criminal justice system tend to stay in treatment for a longer period of time, adhere to treatment rules, and avoid drug use and criminal activity, while maintaining family and social contacts and seeking gainful education or employment.

26. The most effective treatment approach to drug offenders is:
    a. criminal justice supervision only.
    b. drug treatment only.
    c. to combine criminal justice supervision and drug treatment.
    d. no treatment because nothing works.

27. From the perspective of a disease model, relapse after treatment indicates that:
    a. treatment is a failure.
    b. the individual should be locked up.
    c. the individual needs additional treatment.
    d. the individual is hopeless.

Issue 2: Treatment Compliance, Engagement, and Retention

Patient compliance is an important component in pharmacotherapy. Like the treatment of many chronic diseases or psychological disorders (e.g., diabetes, hypertension, mental illness), treatment for drug dependence is beset with problems of patient noncompliance with intervention protocols (McLellan et al., 1996). Poor patient compliance often accounts for the lack of success of medication use in treatment settings.

Whereas patient engagement in treatment (attendance, adherence to program rules, etc.) is understudied, it is well known that many drug abusers prematurely quit treatment, and subsequent relapse to drug use and related negative behaviors are common among dropouts from all types of drug treatment programs. For example, the national Drug Abuse Treatment Outcome Studies (DATOS) reported that more than 50% of patients in residential and outpatient drug-free programs remained in treatment fewer than three months (Simpson et al., 1999). Studies have consistently demonstrated that treatment retention is positively correlated with such posttreatment outcomes as reduced drug use and improved psychosocial functioning (Hubbard et al., 1997; Simpson et al., 1999). Thus, dropout represents a major obstacle to effective treatment and is a major concern in the drug treatment field.

Whether a patient stays in treatment depends on factors associated with both the individual and the program. Personal factors related to engagement and retention include motivation to change drug-using behavior, degree of support from family and friends, and whether there is pressure to stay in treatment from the criminal justice system, child protection services, employers, or the family. Program factors related to retention are program policies and protocols, quality of clinical staff and program management, breadth of services provided, and morale among staff and patients (Ball & Ross, 1991).

Because successful outcomes often depend upon retaining the person long enough to gain the full benefits of treatment, the following strategies are important for programs to keep an individual in a treatment program.

Services

Some studies have revealed that enhancements to standard treatment services, such as increasing the frequency, intensity, and types of treatment services and increasing the opportunity for patients to participate in group and individual counseling, had a significant impact on treatment retention (Hoffman et al., 1994; McLellan et al., 1996). For example, McLellan and colleagues (1996) demonstrated that patients who received a broader array and frequency of services stayed in treatment longer and showed 15% better outcomes than patients who did not. Simpson and colleagues (Simpson et al., 1997) also found that greater counseling session attendance is associated with better treatment retention and outcomes.

Client Satisfaction

Another potential indicator of treatment engagement is client satisfaction with treatment. Health and human service agencies routinely use this information as a measure of accountability. With some exceptions (McLellan & Hunkeler, 1998), studies have found that patients who are engaged in and satisfied with their treatment experience tend to stay in treatment longer, which may contribute to positive outcomes. Hser, et al. (2004) also found that patients who received a greater number of services or had their needs met were more satisfied and stayed in treatment longer.

Other Program Factors

Several other program factors may also influence patient retention. For example, use of contingency management strategies has been shown to increase retention and compliance (Higgins, Wong, Badger, Ogden, & Dantona, 2000). High counselor turnover rates and high levels of caseloads per counselor are expected to negatively impact service quality and retention. Some studies (Maddux, Prihoda, & Desmond, 1994) have shown that elimination of fees significantly increased retention among patients in methadone maintenance programs.

28. Patients who are most likely to drop out of treatment prematurely:
    a. are not sure they want to change.
    b. are not satisfied with the treatment or staff.
    c. have poor counseling session attendance.
    d. all of the above.

29. Treatment programs can increase patient treatment retention by:
    a. increasing services needed by patients.
    b. offering better training for staff.
    c. applying behavioral principles.
    d. all of the above.

30. Patients who are likely to have better treatment outcomes are those who:
    a. are highly motivated to change.
    b. stay in treatment longer.
    c. participate in scheduled activities.
    d. all of the above.

Issue 3: Patient–Treatment Matching

Evaluation research has established that no single treatment approach is effective for all patients with drug use problems and that a range of alternatives need to be available to suit individual needs (Gerstein & Harwood, 1990). Therefore, optimum treatment depends on the effective matching of the treatment or treatments to a particular individual's needs. Although empirical support is not abundant, several studies have shown that congruence between patient problems and actual services received will improve patient outcomes. For example, studies showed that those patients who received their desired or needed services do better than those who do not, and consequently, are more likely to remain in and benefit from the treatment provided (Hser, Polinsky, Maglione, & Anglin, 1997; McLellan et al., 1997).

WHAT STEPS DO YOU NEED TO FOLLOW AS AN ADDICTION COUNSELOR TO ENSURE PATIENTS RECEIVE APPROPRIATE AND EFFECTIVE TREATMENT?

As noted previously, because of the complex and chronic nature of addiction and the diversity of patient needs, no one form of treatment is likely to be effective for all persons with drug problems. However, effective treatment requires these elements:

- Comprehensive assessment and diagnosis of patients seeking treatment
- Development and maintenance of an individualized treatment plan
- Provision of needed services
- Reassessment and revision of the treatment plan on a regular basis
- Establishment of a support system (including aftercare programs) after formal treatment is completed.

The typical patient evolves from a drug user, to an abuser, to a dependent or addicted person over a period of years. During this lengthy period of time, it is common for them to develop social, health, mental health, and legal problems. Those psychosocial complications affect how responsive the patient will be to treatment and the likelihood of relapse after treatment. An individual's treatment and services plan must be assessed continually and modified as necessary to ensure that the plan meets the person's changing needs. A comprehensive treatment service delivery system must effectively address the individual's problems and needs. Additionally, because drug addiction is typically a chronic disorder characterized by occasional relapses, a short-term, one-time treatment often is not sufficient. Many addicted individuals require prolonged treatment and multiple treatment episodes to achieve long-term abstinence and fully restored functioning. An effective treatment delivery system needs to incorporate strategies to sustain longer-term treatment effectiveness.

KEY TERMS

Addiction Severity Index: A standardized assessment instrument designed to gather data on the status of the following seven domains: medical, employment/support, alcohol, drug, family/social, legal, and psychological.

aftercare programs: Aftercare programs offer some form of care after the formal treatment has ended. The primary goals of this phase of the treatment are to maintain the gains that have been achieved in the initial phase of care and to prevent relapse. Most aftercare programs, regardless of the treatment setting of the primary care, consist of outpatient aftercare group therapy sessions and participation in self-help programs.

ASAM PPC (American Society of Addiction Medicine Patient Placement Criteria): A standardized assessment designed to guide treatment providers in determining the level of care needed for clients.

day treatment programs: Day treatment is more intensive than the typical outpatient drug treatment program. Day treatment patients usually spend most of each day in intensive program activities and then go home at night; this avoids expensive hospital or residential costs. The planned treatment duration of most day treatment programs is usually less than six months.

detoxification programs: A detoxification program can be delivered either in an inpatient or outpatient setting and is concerned with the medical management of symptoms associated with drug withdrawal in preparation for referral of the client to a longer-term therapeutic treatment program.

inpatient programs: Inpatient programs are delivered within a hospital setting and include a greater emphasis on medical care than other treatment modalities during a typically short period of stay (three to twenty-eight days, but generally seven days).

methadone maintenance: Methadone (detoxification and maintenance) programs are usually outpatient, and displace heroin dependence by substituting methadone within (ideally) the context of medical, social, and psychological services. Methadone maintenance is designed as a long-term program and patients may be expected to stay with the treatment indefinitely.

outpatient drug-free programs: Outpatient drug-free (nonmethadone) programs typically provide six to twelve months of drug education and counseling.

residential programs: Residential programs typically provide a highly structured environment with intense personality restructuring and socialization efforts. Therapeutic community (TC) is one type of residential program that uses a hierarchical model in which patients are given increased levels of personal and social responsibility as they move through the recovery process. Many TCs have planned stays of about twelve months or less.

DISCUSSION QUESTIONS

1. Why is it said that drug addiction is a chronic relapsing condition? Do you agree or disagree with this statement, and why?
2. Do you consider drug addiction a disease or a matter of a lack of willpower? Why? And how would addiction be approached differently by the two perspectives?
3. How would you design and describe a comprehensive drug treatment delivery system?
4. How would you help patients select the most appropriate treatment program? How would you develop an effective treatment plan?
5. What is the Addiction Severity Index? How can it help you clinically?
6. What are the pros and cons of using urinalysis to monitor patients' drug use?
7. How, as an addiction counselor, should you respond to a positive urine test?
8. How, as an addiction counselor, should you engage and treat an unmotivated patient?
9. How would you prepare patients to stay clean after they have successfully completed treatment?
10. What is your understanding and view of drug treatment effectiveness?

SUGGESTED FURTHER READING

Gerstein, D. R., & Harwood, H. J. (1990). Treating drug problems. Institute of Medicine Report. Washington, DC: National Academy Press.

Comprehensive description of drug treatment and findings.

National Institute on Drug Abuse. (1999). *Principles of drug addiction treatment: A research-based guide* (NIH Publication No. 99-4180). Washington, DC: U.S. Government Printing Office.

A concise document on what works in drug treatment.

Wagner, E. F., & Waldron, H. B. (Eds.). (2001). *Innovations in adolescent substance abuse interventions.* Amsterdam, Netherlands: Elsevier Science Ltd.

A most current document on interventions for adolescent substance abuse.

REFERENCES

Anglin, M. D., & Hser, Y. (1990). Treatment of drug abuse. In M. Tonry & Q. Wilson (Eds.), *Drugs & crime* (pp. 393–458). Chicago: The University of Chicago.

Ball, J. C., & Ross, A. (1991). *The effectiveness of methadone maintenance treatment.* New York: Springer-Verlag.

Brown, B. S., Kinlock, T. W., & Nurco, D. N. (2001). Self-help initiatives to reduce the risk of relapse. In F. M. Tims & C. G. Leukefeld (Eds.), *Relapse and recovery in addictions* (pp. 275–302). New Haven, CT: Yale University Press.

De Leon, G., Melnick, G., Kressel, D., & Jainchill, N. (1994). Circumstances, motivation, readiness and suitability (the CRMS scales): Predicting retention in therapeutic community treatment. *American Journal of Drug & Alcohol Abuse, 20,* 495–515.

Finney, J. W., & Moos, R. H. (1998). Psychosocial treatments for alcohol use disorders. In P. E. Nathan & J. M. Gorman (Eds.), *A guide to treatments that work* (pp. 156–166). New York: Oxford University Press.

Gastfriend, D. (1999). Patient placement criteria. In M. Galanter & H. D. Kleber (Eds.), *Textbook of substance abuse treatment* (pp. 121–127). Washington, DC: The American Psychiatric Press.

Gerstein, D. R., & Harwood, H. J. (1990). *Treating drug problems.* Institute of Medicine Report. Washington, DC: National Academy Press.

Gerstein, D. R., Johnson, R. A., Harwood, H. J., Fountain, K., Suter, N., & Malloy, K. (1994). *Evaluating recovery services. The California Drug and Alcohol Treatment Assessment (CALDATA) general report.* Sacramento, CA: California Department of Alcohol and Drug Problems.

Higgins, S., Wong, C., Badger, G., Ogden, D., & Dantona, D. (2000). Contingent reinforcement increases cocaine abstinence during outpatient treatment and 1 year of follow-up. *Journal of Consulting and Clinical Psychology, 68*(1), 64–72.

Hoffman, J. A., Caudill, B. D., Koman, J. J., III, Luckey, J. W., Flynn, P. M., & Hubbard, R. L. (1994). Comparative cocaine abuse treatment strategies: Enhancing client retention and treatment exposure. *Journal of Addictive Diseases, 13*(4), 115–128.

Hser, Y., Evans, E., Huang, D., & Anglin, D. (2004). Relationship between drug treatment services, retention, and outcomes. *Psychiatric Services, 55*(7), 767–774.

Hser, Y., Grella, C. E., Hubbard, R. L., Hsieh, S. C., Fletcher, B. W., Brown, B. S., et al. (2001). An evaluation of drug treatments for adolescents in four U.S. cities. *Archives of General Psychiatry, 58,* 689–695.

Hser, Y., Polinsky, M. L., Maglione, M., & Anglin, M. D. (1997). Matching patients' needs with drug treatment services. *Journal of Substance Abuse Treatment, 16*(4), 299–305.

Hubbard, R. L., Craddock, S. G., Flynn, P. M., Anderson, J., & Etheridge, R. M. (1997). Overview of 1-year follow-up outcomes in the Drug Abuse Treatment Outcome Study (DATOS). *Psychology of Addict Behaviors, 11,* 261–278.

Maddux, J. F, Prihoda T. J., & Desmond, D. P. (1994). Treatment fees and retention of methadone maintenance. *Journal of Drug Issues, 24*(3), 429–443.

Marlowe, D. B. (2002). Effective strategies for intervening with drug abusing offenders. *Villanova Law Review, 47*(4), 989–1024.

McKay, J. R. (2001). Effectiveness of continuing care interventions for substance abusers: Implications for the study of long-term treatment effects. *Evaluation Review, 25*(2), 211–232.

McLellan, A. T., Cacciola, J., Kushner, H., Peters, F., Smith, I., & Pettinati, H. (1992). The fifth edition of the Addiction Severity Index: Cautions, additions and normative data. *Journal of Substance Abuse Treatment, 5,* 312–316.

McLellan, A. T., Grissom, G. R., Zanis, D., Randall, M., Brill, P., & O'Brien, C. P. (1997). Problem-service "matching" in addiction treatment: A prospective study in 4 programs. *Archives of General Psychiatry, 54*(8), 730–735.

McLellan, T. A., & Hunkeler, E. (1998). Patient satisfaction and outcomes in alcohol and drug abuse treatment. *Psychiatric Services, 49*(5), 573–575.

McLellan, A. T., Luborsky, L., Woody, G. E., & O'Brien, C. P. (1980). An improved diagnostic evaluation instrument for substance abuse patients. The Addiction Severity Index. *Journal of Nervous and Mental Disease, 168*(1), 26–33.

McLellan, A. T., Woody, G. E., Metzger, D., McKay, J. R., Durrell, J., Alterman, A. I., et al. (1996). Evaluating the effectiveness of addiction treatments: Reasonable expectations, appropriate comparisons. *Milbank Quarterly, 74*(1), 51–85.

Miller, W. R., & Kurtz, E. (1994). Models of alcoholism used in treatment: Contrasting AA and other perspectives with which it is often confused. *Journal of Studies on Alcohol, 55*(2), 159–166.

Robins, L. N., Helzer, J. E., Croughan, J. L., & Ratcliff, K. S. (1981). National institute of mental health diagnostic interview schedule: Its history, characteristics, and validity. *Archives of General Psychiatry, 38*(4), 381–389.

Simpson, D. D. (1997). Effectiveness of drug-abuse treatment: A review of research from field settings. In J. A. Egerson, D. M. Fox, & A. I. Leshner (Eds.), *Treating drug abusers effectively* (pp. 41–73). Malden, MA: Blackwell.

Simpson, D. D., & Joe, G. W (1993). Motivation as a predictor of early dropout from drug abuse treatment. *Journal of Psychotherapy, 30*, 357–368.

Simpson, D. D., Joe, G., & Broome, K. (2002). A national 5-year follow-up of treatment outcomes for cocaine dependence. *Archives of General Psychiatry, 59*(6), 538–544.

Simpson, D. D., Joe, G., Fletcher, B., Hubbard, R., & Anglin, M. (1999). A national evaluation of treatment outcomes for cocaine dependence. *Archives of General Psychiatry, 56*(6), 507–514.

Simpson, D. D., Joe, G. W., & Rowan-Szal, G. A. (1997). Drug abuse treatment retention and process effects on follow-up outcomes. *Drug and Alcohol Dependence, 47*, 227–235.

Substance Abuse and Mental Health Services Administration (SAMHSA). (1997). *NTIES: National Treatment Improvement Evaluation Study final report.* Chicago, IL: The National Opinion Research Center.

Wagner, E. F., & Waldron, H. B. (Eds.). (2001). *Innovations in adolescent substance abuse interventions.* Amsterdam, Netherlands: Elsevier Science Ltd.

e Prevention: Tools
d Programs

Karol L. Kumpfer
Rose Alvarado
Paula Smith
University of Utah

(rotated text, left margin:)

- It is common – rather than the exception
- Prevalence rates vary from 2 to 83%
- Such clients often experience poorer treatment outcomes (higher rates of re...
- They are often excluded by treatment services
- Specialist services focus on one or other problem – "ping-pong" effect

---

TRUTH OR FICTION?

_____ f U.S. funding for the "War on Drugs" goes for supply reduction

_____ easing vulnerability to addiction has been identified.

_____ o" and "scare tactics" programs in school are highly effective for
       drug use.

_____ risk factor of adolescent substance abuse is peer influence.

_____ l supervision and monitoring are even more important for preventing drug
       nong older adolescents than preteens.

_____ nary prevention can be divided into three types: universal, selective, and indi-
       ted.

_____ Knowledge and affective education programs are the most effective "child-only"
       prevention approaches.

_____ 8. Community prevention approaches can include individual, school, workplace, and
        family programs.

_____ 9. Effective policy strategies are increasing taxes, the cost of tobacco and alcohol, and
        the minimum legal age of use.

_____ 10. An effective strategy for reducing alcohol use in college age students is to teach
        them how to deal with the stressors of college life.

_____ 11. Seniors are resistant to counseling on the appropriate use of alcohol and prescrip-
        tion drugs.

_____ 12. Most physicians feel comfortable diagnosing alcoholism and drug abuse.

_____ 13. Recruitment and retention of ethnic clients improves if prevention programs are
        culturally sensitive.

___ 14. *Prevention approaches work equally well for girls as they do for boys.*
___ 15. *The most effective prevention approaches are usually those that are commercially marketed.*

WHY IS SUBSTANCE ABUSE PREVENTION NEEDED?

Drug and alcohol use in adolescents in the United States is unacceptably high. Despite small decreases in the past few years, a higher number (but not percent) of young people are using drugs than during the psychedelic 70s. You may be aware that drug use substantially decreased during the 1980s, partially due to increased prevention efforts by worried parents. However, the mid-1990s produced a major increase in drug use in teenagers. Between 1992 and 1997, regular marijuana use (thirty-day use) increased 99% (from 11.9% to 23.7%) among twelfth graders and 154% (from 8.1% to 20.5%) among tenth graders (Johnston, O'Malley, & Bachman, 2002). Tobacco, alcohol, and illegal drug use (particularly of uppers) has also risen at even faster rates in young girls, partially because of a "Virginia Slims" effect and a dramatic reduction in parental monitoring. Many girls are smoking cigarettes or using methamphetamines, amphetamines, or cocaine to reduce their weight and self-medicate depression. American Indian youth have the highest alcohol and drug use rates with 58% having used alcohol or illegal drugs in the past month. These rates are almost three times higher than the 20% use rate for White youth, 18% for Hispanic youth, 16% for African American youth, and 12% for Asian youth (DHHS/OAS, 2002).

1. The highest alcohol and drug use rates are reported in _____.
   a. adolescent girls
   b. American Indian youth
   c. Caucasian youth
   d. African American youth

The economic costs of alcohol and drug abuse are estimated by the White House Office of National Drug Control Policy (ONDCP, 2001) at more than $450 billion for 2000. Lost earnings because of incarceration, premature death, unemployment, and impaired productivity comprise the largest portion of these costs; however, health care costs, law enforcement, and treatment also contribute to this economic loss. You may have noticed ONDCP's recent media campaign highlighting the relationship between illegal drug use and increased drug production, crime, guns, and international terrorism.

TRENDS IN FUNDING DRUG PREVENTION
OR DEMAND REDUCTION

The "War on Drugs" has been criticized for its failure to reduce drug use despite increased funding (Klein, 2000). Whereas the National Drug Control Budget increased by 57% between 1994 and 2001—from $12.2 billion to $19.2 billion—drug prevention funding rose only 33% and funding to reduce international supply increased 175% (ONDCP, 2001). The majority (about 90%) of U.S. funding for the "War on Drugs" goes for interdiction, crop eradication, border patrols, and so forth. Despite this massive funding, adolescents report drugs are as available as they were in 1989 (Johnston, O'Malley, & Bachman, 2002). Demand reduction approaches are more effective in reducing drug use than supply reduction, yet only about 10% (1.5 billion) is devoted to drug prevention programs or research. The fiscal year (FY) 2002 budget includes $1.725 billion for State Substance Abuse Block Grants (with only a 20% set aside for prevention), $180 million for the ONDCP National Anti-Drug Media Campaign and $50 million for the Drug-Free Communities Act. Safe and Drug-Free Schools and Communities received $746 million in FY 2002, but much less has been requested by Congress this year. Funding for substance abuse research increased at the National Institute on Drug Abuse (NIDA) to $888 million and $384 million at the National Institute on Alcohol Abuse and Alcoholism (NIAAA), but very little funding is available for alcohol and drug prevention grants compared to biomedical, genetic, and drug treatment grants.

2. What percentage of the U.S. budget is devoted to drug prevention programs or research?
   a. 1%
   b. 10%
   c. 50%
   d. 90%

The Center for Substance Abuse Treatment's (CSAT) budget has doubled in the last few years to $298 million, whereas the Center for Substance Abuse Prevention's (CSAP) budget has increased only $30 million to $198 million for state and community drug and HIV/AIDS prevention.

FAMILY AND SOCIETAL CORRELATES AND CAUSES OF SUBSTANCE ABUSE

It is said that addiction is a "family disease" passed on from one generation to another. We do know that addictions run in families. But why? Drug addiction or dependency is clearly not a disease of infection, but a disease of lifestyle—similar to heart disease, diabetes, skin cancer, and other chronic diseases we have not yet conquered. These diseases involve a genetic predisposition combined with environmental toxins or stressors. Although the specific genes that make a person highly vulnerable to alcohol and drug dependency have not yet been discovered, there are enough twin, adoption, and family history studies to demonstrate a highly inheritable form of alcoholism and possibly drug dependency, called *Type II Alcoholism* or *early onset alcoholism* (Kumpfer, 1987). This type of alcoholism affects about 25% of all alcoholics in treatment. About 75% of all addicts are suffering from a type of addiction caused primarily by environmental causes that are easier to prevent and treat. For instance, bingeing on alcohol or drugs can lead to *brain disease*, a condition characterized by deficits in the neurotransmitters associated with the drugs abused. Medications are an important element in treating drug dependence because they help increase these neurotransmitters and thereby help prevent relapse and self-medication of the withdrawal symptoms of anxiety and depression.

3. It is said that addiction is a _____ disease.
   a. childhood
   b. adult
   c. short-term
   d. family

eeds assessment helps prevention to programs _____.
>re money
ngitudinal data
_____ the best approaches
d. follow NIDA guidelines

The highest risk group are children of substance abusers—particularly those with a family history of early onset substance dependency (prior to 15 years of age). The highest risk youth in this group are those who are: (a) over-stressed due to autonomic hyperreactivity and higher frequency brain waves resulting in self-medication using alcohol and drugs, (b) struggling in school because of verbal learning disorders from inherited pre-frontal cognitive dysfunction, and (c) thrill seeking and have poor problem-solving skills resulting in risky choices of activities and friends (Tarter & Mezzich, 1992). Northern European boys who begin delinquent behaviors and regular use of alcohol or drugs prior to 15 years of age are the most likely to become drug dependent. American Indian youth are also at risk because some have inherited liver enzymes that break alcohol down rapidly and contribute to a high build-up of acetaldehyde in the blood stream that leads to loss of control. Although some Asian youth also have this genetic risk factor, the hopelessness, poverty, and breakdown of the American Indian family make them more vulnerable to substance abuse.

5. The highest risk group for substance abuse is _____.
   a. children of substance abusers
   b. young girls
   c. college students
   d. the elderly

Prevention is now a science that has moved well beyond the days of ineffective "scare tactics," or one shot drug prevention assemblies to an abundance of effective programs. Prevention practitioners are encouraged to select the best evidence-based programs addressing local risk and protective factors as determined by standardized needs assessment systems (see examples on www.preventiondss.org). Communities also use the Communities That Care (Hawkins & Catalano, 1999) needs assessment survey and matching system to select evidence-based prevention programs.

6. Prevention science recommends _____.
   a. "scare tactics" programs
   b. "Just Say No" campaigns
   c. evidence-based programs
   d. drug prevention assemblies

PRIMARY RISK AND PROTECTIVE FACTORS FOR ADOLESCENT ALCOHOL OR DRUG USE

In the mid-1980s, risk researchers determined that the final pathway or proximal cause of substance abuse was association with drug-using peers or peer influence. Hence, the first truly effective prevention programs, the peer resistance social skills training programs, were designed. In 1990, Kumpfer and Turner tested the causes of adolescent drug abuse and found that family environment was the root distal cause of substance abuse even if the final proximal risk factor was drug-using peers (1990–1991). By 1998, a more refined model was tested with about ten thousand students and discovered three strong family protective factors: (1) positive parent–child relationships characterized by love, care, respect, and support; (2) parent or caretaker monitoring, supervision, and discipline; and (3) communication of prosocial family values and expectations for not using tobacco, alcohol, or drugs (CSAP, 2000). Supervision and monitoring were even more important in preventing drug abuse in older adolescents than in preteens. Also, girls and ethnic minorities were slightly more influenced by their families than were Caucasian boys, who were more influenced by their community and neighborhood environment. Self-control, school bonding, and achievement are also important protective factors.

7. Family protective factors include all *except* _____.
   a. positive parent–child relationships
   b. authoritarian parenting
   c. parent monitoring
   d. prosocial family values

THREE TYPES OF PRIMARY PREVENTION

The Public Health Service (PHS) and the prevention field have for some time differentiated *primary* prevention, which targets nonusers, from *secondary* prevention, which targets initiates or drug users, and *tertiary* drug treatment, which targets addicts. Recently, primary prevention was separated into three types (IOM, 1995):

1. *Universal prevention*—targeting general populations (i.e., students, families, or everyone in a community)
2. *Selective prevention*—targeting subgroups of at-risk individuals (i.e., children of substance abusers or prisoners, American Indian children, etc.)
3. *Indicated prevention*—targeting those with identified precursors of alcohol or drug abuse such as aggression, conduct disorders, thrill seeking, or delinquency.

8. Primary prevention includes all *except* _____.
   a. universal prevention
   b. drug treatment
   c. selective prevention
   d. indicated prevention

In 2003, ONDCP began stressing secondary prevention approaches in its demand reduction themes because nondependent users do not perceive the negative consequences of drug use and introduce friends to drugs. This type of secondary prevention will require the adoption of effective early identification and intervention programs by school, workplace, social service, justice, and primary healthcare settings (Fleming, 2002). The training of health care and social services professionals in substance abuse is critical to broadening this approach of early identification and referrals for services. Most university professional training programs do not have adequate coverage of substance abuse issues and many have no courses preparing doctors, nurses, public health or health educators, social workers, psychologists, or psychiatrists in diagnosing, referring, or treating substance abuse disorders (Haack & Adger, 2002). In an attempt to rectify this problem, the U.S. Health Resources and Services Administration's Bureau of Health Professions collaborated with the Association for Medical Education and Research in Substance Abuse (AMERSA) to conduct a needs assessment and develop a Strategic Plan for Interdisciplinary Faculty Development (AMERSA, 2002).

WHAT WORKS IN SUBSTANCE ABUSE PREVENTION?

Most of the research on the prevention of substance abuse has focused on junior high school–aged students, because most students initiate substance use during this time. Less is known about the other developmental periods; however, we discuss what is known about the most effective approaches for children, adolescents, and college-aged youth (or young adults) in separate sections.

9. Most prevention programs are designed for _____.
   a. junior high students.
   b. college students
   c. adults
   d. the elderly

Funding agencies are increasingly requiring that funds be used only or primarily for evidence-based strategies. These best practices are those with research evidence in decreasing substance use, delaying age of onset of use, improving protective factors, and decreasing risk factors related to later use. Fortunately, the research literature contains many research-based prevention strategies with sufficient program effectiveness in Phase III controlled intervention trials to warrant dissemination and adoption by schools and communities. Effective prevention approaches have been identified by federal reviews and are listed on these Web sites: www.samhsa.gov/csap/modelprograms and www.strengtheningfamilies.org. Syntheses of best practices in research-based prevention practices have been published by the Institute of Medicine (IOM, 1995), CSAP (1998), NIDA (1997), and researchers (Hawkins & Catalano, 1999; Kumpfer & Alder, 2003).

10. Best practices improve all of the following *except* _____.
    a. substance use
    b. age of onset
    c. protective factors
    d. attitudes

Effective Approaches for Children and Adolescents

The different types of approaches generally included in a comprehensive prevention plan include: child-only approaches, family-focused approaches, and community or school environmental change approaches.

11. Comprehensive community prevention plans can include all *except* _____.
    a. drug treatment
    b. family-focused approaches
    c. community coalitions
    d. school prevention programs

Child-Only Approaches

According to meta-analyses (Tobler & Stratton, 1997), the most effective approaches for working with only youth include social skills and life skills training (Botvin, 1995) implemented in many settings (e.g., schools, community centers, churches, youth clubs, etc.). Other types of social competency programs include: mentoring, tutoring, alternative activities, recreation and leisure programs, wilderness challenge programs, and community service programs. School-based programs are most successful in reducing tobacco use, followed by drug use and then alcohol use.

Characteristics of effective programs include involvement with positive role models or mentors, sufficient dosage or number of contact hours, interactive and cooperative learning, and booster sessions. Interventions run by mental health clinicians are two to three times more effective than programs implemented by peers, teachers, police officers, or "others." The average **effect size** for all these child-only programs (N = 206) was .10, which is quite small. The least effective program type is a combination of knowledge-only and affective education programs with a slight negative effect size of −.05. DARE-type programs have only a very small positive effect size of .08. The recent highly publicized failure to prevent drug use of one of the most widely used school-based substance abuse prevention programs, DARE (Ennett, Tobler, Ringwalt, & Flewelling, 1994; Harrington, Hoyle, Giles, & Hansen, 2000), highlights the importance of enhanced dissemination of programs that work. See Table 21.1 for a summary of various programs' effectiveness (Tobler & Kumpfer, 2000; Tobler & Stratton, 1997).

12. School-based programs are least successful in reducing _____.
    a. alcohol use
    b. drug use
    c. tobacco use
    d. marijuana use

TABLE 21.1

Rank Ordering of the Most Effective Types of Programs

1. In-home family support (1.62 ES)
2. Family skills training (.82 ES)
3. Behavioral parent training (.31 ES)
4. Comprehensive life skills training (.30 ES)
5. "Other" programs—peer-counseling, parent involvement, behavioral token economy, community partnerships, etc. (.21 ES)
6. Social influences (.20 ES)
7. Health education (.18 ES)

13. The most effective child-only approach is _____.
    a. DARE
    b. life skills training
    c. health education
    d. affective education

14. The least effective child-only approach is _____.
    a. DARE
    b. life skills training
    c. health education
    d. affective education

Comprehensive life skills training programs include refusal skills components, life skills such as communication, problem solving, coping, social/dating, goal-setting, stress management, media literacy, and public commitments not to use. Prevention programs, such as life skills training using *interactive, skills training methods* to change behaviors as opposed to didactic lecture methods to change knowledge were more effective, particularly for minority youth.

15. The essential ingredient in child-only prevention is _____.
    a. refusal skills
    b. school bonding
    c. social skills
    d. knowledge

Family-Focused Approaches

The CSAP Prevention Enhancement Protocols System (PEPS; 1998) review of family-focused approaches found that four approaches had sufficient research evidence to claim effectiveness for substance abuse prevention: (1) behavioral parent training, (2) family skills training, (3) family therapy, and (4) in-home family case management or support programs. Parent involvement in substance abuse prevention homework assignments with their children are recently showing promise as a cost effective approach (Bauman, Foshee, Ennett, Hicks, & Pemberton, 2001). For additional reviews of effective family strengthening approaches see Kumpfer and Alvarado (2003), Taylor and Biglan (1998), or the Office of Juvenile Justice and Delinquency Prevention (OJJDP) Strengthening America's Families Web site at the University of Utah (www.strengtheningfamilies.org).

16. Evidence-based family-focused approaches include all *except* _____.
    a. parent education
    b. in-home family support
    c. behavioral parent training
    d. family skills training

The last national review of family strengthening approaches conducted in 2000 for OJJDP found about thirty-five evidence-based practices (Kumpfer & Alvarado, 2003). Fourteen family programs had been tested in randomized control trials, but only seven independently replicated, thus meeting the criteria for the highest level of evidence of effectiveness, and thereby qualifying as an Exemplary I program. The Exemplary I family programs for children 0 to 5 years old include: Helping the Noncompliant Child and the Parent and Children's Training Series: The Incredible Years. The only Exemplary I–rated program for families with children 6 to 12 years old is the Strengthening Families Program (SFP). The only preteen and adolescent programs included in this category are: Functional Family Therapy, Multisystemic Family Therapy, Preparing for the Drug Free Years, Treatment Foster Care, & SFP (10–14 years), which was found by Foxcroft & Associates (2003) for the Cochrane Collaboration reviews to be the most effective school-based substance abuse prevention program in the world based on longitudinal studies. Overall, family-focused approaches average effect sizes that are nine times larger than child-only prevention approaches (.96 ES versus .10 ES) as shown in Table 21.1.

17. The only Exemplary I family program for children 6 to 12 years old is _____.
    a. Nurturing Program
    b. Strengthening Families Program
    c. Functional Family Therapy
    d. Preparing for the Drug Free Years

18. Family-focused approaches average effect sizes that are _____ times larger than child-only prevention approaches.
    a. 3
    b. 6
    c. 9
    d. 12

In selecting the best family-focused program, the prevention practitioner must consider whether the target population needs a universal, selective, or indicated prevention program; the age of the child; and ethnicity or special need. A matrix of these programs by prevention level and age is available on the abovementioned Web site (Strengthening America's Families) along with program descriptions and links to program developers' Web sites.

Community or School Environmental Change Approaches

Research suggests that comprehensive, coordinated community approaches are the most effective in reducing drug use. They can include individual, school, workplace, and family approaches. Community coalitions that are effective in reducing substance use and abuse are those that implement proven prevention strategies and have strong, empowering leadership that promotes a comprehensive shared vision among a broad membership (Yin, Kaftarian, Yu, & Jansen, 1997).

19. A shared vision, broad membership, and empowering leaders improve _____.
    a. family-based approaches
    b. affective education
    c. community coalitions
    d. life skills training

Examples of evidence-based community partnership or coalition approaches include the Midwestern Prevention Program (Pentz, 1995) and the Communities That Care (CTC) model (Hawkins & Catalano, 1999). Research on the CTC model is being conducted on forty-one matched communities in the seven states participating in their federally-funded Diffusion

Consortium Project (Hawkins, Catalano, & Arthur, 2000). This project seeks to track the natural history of diffusion of risk- and protection-focused prevention planning and to assess the effectiveness of the CTC coalition model in reducing risk factors, increasing protective factors, and reducing youth substance abuse. The CTC community coalition model is based on six phases: (1) needs assessment using standardized CTC school and community leader surveys, (2) prioritization of risk and protective factors for intervention, (3) selection of tested interventions to address priority risk and protective factors, (4) implementation of research-based prevention interventions, (5) monitoring changes in targeted risk and protective factors, and (6) adjustment of interventions as indicated by performance monitoring data.

20. The first phase of the CTC community coalition model is _____.
    a. prioritizing needs
    b. monitoring changes
    c. selection of effective interventions matching needs
    d. needs assessment

Policy Strategies. Community coalitions often focus on improving the environmental climate by advocating for changes in community policies and laws related to age of legal purchase, cost of tobacco or alcohol, availability, density of outlets, keg registration, server training, counteradvertising, warning labels, and other environmental changes (Grube & Ny-gaard, 2000). Only a few policy approaches, such as increasing the age of purchase and the taxes and cost of tobacco or alcohol have been subjected to research; both were found to be effective (Toomey & Wagenaar, 2002). Many of the alcohol misuse interventions are implemented through an overall community coalition mobilization approach (NIAAA, 2000). Some examples of effective alcohol prevention-focused coalitions include the Community Trials Project (Holder et al., 1997), Saving Lives (Hingson et al., 1996), and Project Northland (Perry et al., 1996).

School Climate Change Strategies. Comprehensive school change approaches operate much like community coalitions, but in schools. A comprehensive needs assessment of risk and protective factors is conducted with planning task forces developing a strategic plan after exposure to evidence-based models. This approach also includes alcohol policy changes, awareness campaigns, improvements in teaching methods to include cooperative learning, tutoring, in-school suspension, recovery groups, personal growth classes for high-risk youth (NIDA, 1997), and recreation and competency-building after-school activities. Examples of effective school climate change approaches include Project Positive Action Through Holistic Education (PATHE) (Gottfredson, 1986), Project HI PATHE (Kumpfer, Turner, & Alvarado, 1991), and the Child Development Project (Schaps, Battistich, & Solomon, 1997). The goal of the 21st Century Schools funded by the Department of Education is to modify the school climate and co-ordinate services between schools and mental health and treatment services in the community.

Effective Prevention Approaches for College Students

About 40% of college students **binge drink** and 25% drive while drunk resulting in 1,400 fatalities, 500,000 injuries, and 70,000 cases of sexual assault per year (Hingson, Heeren, Zakocs, Kopstein, & Wechsler, 2002). Colleges experience higher rates of alcohol problems if they foster a drinking culture where Greek systems (fraternity and sorority) or sports teams predominate and they don't enforce minimum use age laws (Toomey & Wagenaar, 2002).

21. How many injuries result annually from college students' drinking?
    a. 500,000
    b. 70,000
    c. 1,400
    d. 100

Few prevention strategies aimed at college-age drinking have been tested in research and found successful (NIAAA, 2002). In the last decade the Department of Education's Fund for the Improvement of Post-secondary Education (FIPSE) was very successful in funding drug prevention centers on college campuses nationwide. Many colleges continued these prevention centers when the seed funding ended. The primary prevention approaches adopted in colleges are media campaigns, alcohol and drug policy revisions, and early identification and referrals to counseling. Changing the perception that most college students are substance users through normative education by publishing needs assessment surveys is another approach (Perkins & Berkowitz, 1989) thought to be effective.

22. A primary prevention approach adopted by colleges is _____.
    a. mentoring
    b. alcohol and drug policy revisions
    c. skills training
    d. parent education

The NIAAA Task Force (2002) suggests that generalized strategies effective with adults should work (e.g., increasing taxes and cost of alcohol, increasing enforcement and consequences of minimum legal drinking age laws and driving under the influence). Strategies recommended specific for college/university students include normative education and stress-coping strategies as well as correcting their false beliefs about the positive effects of alcohol and increasing their motivation to reduce drinking. Combining approaches into a comprehensive campus-wide approach should be more effective. More information on the NIAAA Task Force's report can be found at http://www.collegedrinkingprevention.gov/Reports/.

Prevention in Workplaces: Effective Approaches

Workplaces focus more on secondary rather than primary prevention. Employee assistance programs (EAPs) with early identification, screening, and referrals for treatment are the most popular approaches. Drug testing upon hire is being required by many employers today. Some employers have treatment aftercare groups, self-help groups, and also provide parent support or training groups on-site. General health and wellness employee programs can also be considered as prevention programs for substance abuse although they have generally not been evaluated this way (Poole, Kumpfer, & Pett, 2001).

23. Workplaces are more focused on _____ prevention.
    a. primary
    b. secondary
    c. tertiary
    d. treatment

FAS/FDS Prevention for Pregnant Women

Because of the increasing incidence and prevalence of **fetal alcohol** and drug syndrome (FAS/FDS), particularly for American Indian women (Streissguth, 2001), Congress has earmarked funding in the past few years for effective detection and prevention programs. Little is known about how to prevent alcohol and drug use in pregnant women, other than to increase education and public awareness concerning the negative effects of substance use on the developing fetus. Preventing substance use altogether in girls is the most effective prevention approach. Many women think they have to be heavy drinkers or drug users to have a negative effect on their fetus. In fact, you can just be unlucky and drink on a critical day when the effect of alcohol will have a devastating impact on the baby. Hence, the best prevention of FAS/FDS is to avoid all alcohol and drug use during pregnancy.

> 24. The best prevention of FAS is _____.
>   a. to avoid drinking alcohol during pregnancy
>   b. early detection
>   c. education
>   d. none of the above

Substance Abuse Prevention in the Elderly

Substance misuse by the elderly is a growing health concern in the United States. Heavy alcohol consumption is as high as 16%, which is concerning because of seniors' increased vulnerability to harmful drug interactions and negative side effects (e.g., depression, sleep problems, cognitive impairment, liver disease, and accidents and injury). The elderly account for one-third of all prescription drug purchases and 40% of over-the-counter drug purchases, but comprise only 13% of the U.S. population Lisansky-Gomberg (2000, p. 280). There is a low prevalence of illicit drug use among the elderly; however, as baby boomers age, this trend may increase particularly for cannabis use.

> 25. The elderly account for _____ of all prescription drug purchases, but comprise only 13% of the population.
>   a. one-fifth
>   b. one-fourth
>   c. one-third
>   d. one-half

Because seniors seek health care more often, the most effective prevention approaches for the elderly focus on training health care professionals to monitor medication misuse and to educate seniors about alcohol and drug interactions (Fink, Beck, & Wittrock, 2001). Interpersonal communication skills training for the elderly, listing or bringing in a "brown bag" all drugs (prescription, over-the-counter, and herbal drugs) being taken, and asking health care professionals about possible drug interactions is also effective (Beisecker, 1991). Seniors are willing to read extensively about the relationship between drinking, medication use, and their health and act upon this information. Education and counseling have proven to be the most effective preventive measures for this population. Prevention approaches should be tailored to the unique needs, stressors, social, cognitive and physical losses, and delivery systems typical of seniors (Lisansky-Gomberg, 2000).

26. Effective prevention for the elderly includes _____.
    a. counseling
    b. tutoring
    c. values-based strategies
    d. setting goals

The Michigan Alcohol Screening Test-Geriatric Version (MAST-G) or Short MAST-G (Blow et al., 1992) or CAGE can be administered if alcohol misuse is a concern. It should be combined with a brief intervention, education, and referral for further assessments and treatment services, such as the Clear Horizons smoking cessation program adapted for the elderly and the Community Older Persons Alcohol (COPA) Program (Oslin & Holden, 2002).

HEALTH CARE PROVIDERS: TRAINING, SCREENING, REFERRALS FOR TREATMENT

It has been estimated that nearly 50% of health care costs are related to substance abuse. Although addressing substance abuse is considered a vital strategy for improving the nation's health (Healthy People 2010, 2000), very few health care providers identify, diagnose, refer, or treat substance abuse disorders as readily or accurately as they do other chronic diseases or illnesses. For example, only 19% of physicians feel comfortable about diagnosing alcoholism and 17% about diagnosing drug abuse (Haack & Adger, 2002). Few health care provider training programs offer workshops or training in substance abuse diagnosis, early intervention, referral, or treatment (Fleming, 2002). However, 91% of health care workers who have attended such training report using the techniques learned even five years later.

The Strategic Plan developed by AMERSA (Haack & Adger, 2002) recommends four core competencies in substance use disorders (SUDs). All health professionals should: (1) receive education to enable them to understand SUDs and accept the importance of treating SUDs to improving health and wellbeing, (2) have basic knowledge of SUDs and of evidence-based prevention approaches, (3) be aware of the benefits of SUD screening and appropriate intervention methods, and (4) have core knowledge of treatment methods and be able to initiate treatment or refer patients for further evaluation and treatment.

27. AMERSA's Strategic Plan to improve professional training in SUDs includes _____.
    a. basic knowledge of SUDs
    b. education on effective prevention and treatment programs
    c. knowledge of benefits of SUD screening
    d. all of the above

The core knowledge, skill, and attitude competencies for substance abuse specialists are also listed in the Strategic Plan. Among twelve recommendations for federal policy makers are creating a Secretary's Advisory Committee on Health Professions Education in SUDs, developing and disseminating a Surgeon General's Report on the State of Substance Use Disorders Prevention and Treatment in the United States, convening a National Forum on Health Professions Education on Substance Use Disorders, expanding federal support for faculty development programs in SUDs including regional centers of excellence, and reviewing substance abuse specialist certification requirements to include core competencies.

MENTAL HEALTH CARE PROVIDERS AND DUAL DIAGNOSES

Mental health care specialists including psychiatrists, psychologists, psychiatric nurses, and social workers are rarely trained in the treatment of addictions. Although 91% of psychologists see addicted clients daily, 75% have received no formal coursework in SUDs, and 50% have no addiction training (Anavai, Tauge, Ja, & Duran, 1999). Many are trained to refer clients with SUDs to substance abuse specialists, despite the high overlap of substance abuse and mental health problems they do treat regularly. Very few specialty clinics treat clients with dual diagnoses. Substance abuse prevention programs provided by mental health care providers is even rarer, but some community mental health clinics are beginning to offer parenting and family skills training interventions for the prevention of substance abuse in children with conduct disorder problems.

WHAT ARE THE PRINCIPLES OF EFFECTIVE PREVENTION PROGRAMS?

When judging the potential effectiveness of different prevention programs, certain principles should be used. Nation and associates (2003) employed a "review of reviews" approach when extracting effectiveness principles from research articles on prevention programs in four content areas (e.g., substance abuse, risky sexual behavior, school failure, and juvenile delinquency and violence). Nine program characteristics were consistently associated with effective prevention programs: theory-driven, comprehensive, appropriately-timed, socioculturally relevant, sufficient dosage, varied teaching methods, positive relationships, well-trained staff, and outcome evaluation. Fifteen similar Principles of Prevention were also developed from research by a subcommittee of White House Office of National Drug Control Policy.

CULTURE AND GENDER SPECIFICITY IN PREVENTION

Very few prevention interventions are adapted to be gender or culturally specific. Research suggests improved recruitment and retention if programs are culturally adapted (Kumpfer, Alvarado, Smith, & Bellamy, 2002). Whether outcomes are improved is unknown because little research exists comparing a generic prevention program with a culturally-sensitive version of the same program. Harachi, Catalano, and Hawkins (1997) found that culturally-adapted, but equivalent dosage versions of their family program were more locally acceptable, and slightly more effective. Botvin, Schinke, Epstein, Diaz, and Botvin (1995) reported slight improvements at the two-year follow-up (but not the one-year follow-up) for a culturally-modified version of their life skills program compared to the generic, standard version.

28. Cultural adaptations primarily improve _____.
    a. outcomes
    b. retention
    c. generalizability
    d. implementation

Culturally-specific programs should address deep-structure cultural values and practices (Resnicow, Soler, Braithwaite, Ahulwalia, & Butler, 2000). According to Santisteban,

Muir-Malcom, Mitrani, and Szapocznik (2001), these deep-structure adaptations would include sensitivity to diverse cultural values of relational orientation, human nature, a person's relationship to nature, activity orientation, and time orientation.

Likewise, few gender-specific drug prevention programs have been tested. Many of the effective prevention programs were developed primarily for conduct disordered boys. Problem-prone girls are more likely to manifest depression, shyness, and be less identifiable as outwardly aggressive in the early grades, making identification and referral to selective or indicated prevention programs for high-risk youth more difficult. Little attention has been paid when developing prevention programs to addressing the unique risks or strengths of girls (Amaro, Blake, Schwartz, & Flinchbaugh, 2001). For instance, when early-maturing girls are provided social skills training their drug use *increases*, because their social networks change to include older drug-using friends.

29. Substance use by girls has _____ compared to boys in the past decade.
    a. increased
    b. decreased
    c. stayed equal
    d. decreased then increased

Guthrie and Flinchbaugh (2001) have developed principles to guide the development of effective programs for girls, such as: (a) select a physically and emotionally safe place, (b) create opportunities for girls to develop trusting relationships with other women, (c) focus on cultural strengths or resiliency rather than risks, (d) develop a comprehensive program covering mental, spiritual, emotional, social, and physical health and wellness, (e) involve family and friends, and (f) actively involve girls in the design, implementation, and evaluation.

WHY IS IT IMPORTANT TO DISSEMINATE AND ADOPT EVIDENCE-BASED PREVENTION PROGRAMS?

Despite the existence of a number of effective prevention programs, a gap exists between what practitioners are doing and what works resulting in a need for improved dissemination of effective prevention programs (Biglan, Mrazek, Carnine, & Flay, 2003). Only about 10% of all substance abuse prevention programs are research-based and possibly only about 25% of these are implemented with fidelity. Academically based researchers are not trained in marketing. They need federal and state government support in marketing and training. National and regional conferences have been conducted by federal agencies to showcase their pick of the most effective prevention programs. CSAP hosted a symposium with written papers on how to improve dissemination of evidence-based practices (Backer & Rogers, 1999).

30. Only about _____ of all substance abuse prevention programs implemented in the United States are research based and possibly only about _____ of these are implemented with fidelity.
    a. 5%; 5%
    b. 10%; 25%
    c. 10%; 75%
    d. 50%; 75%

In an ideal world, the proposed flow of research models would be smooth from basic biomedical research through the five phases of research to implementation in nationwide prevention systems (Jansen, Glynn, & Howard, 1996). Unfortunately, the most commonly used programs are synonymous with the most highly commercially marketed programs, not the evidence-based models. Although based on similar prevention principles, ineffective programs are generally shorter, with poor fidelity and poorly trained implementors.

Research-based programs are generally tested in clinical trials by university researchers who rarely have the time or knowledge to become commercial marketers to disseminate their programs. The funding sources should also support the dissemination of research-based approaches. Practitioners also have a responsibility to ask about program effectiveness and find the best match to the participants' needs when selecting programs.

WHY IS PREVENTION ADVOCACY IMPORTANT?

Prevention funding is not increasing as much as drug treatment funding because of the lack of advocacy by the prevention field compared to the drug treatment field. Also, most of the State Block Grant substance abuse funds are controlled by more powerful drug treatment providers, who also provide drug prevention programs so as to historically maintain their funding levels. Prevention providers who have federal funding were warned inappropriately in the early 1990s that they could not educate or advocate for substance abuse prevention if they received federal funding. This is not true. What is true is that a prevention agency cannot use their federal funding to lobby congressional staff or members to vote for a specific bill. However, they can use other funds to educate and advocate more generally for the importance of drug prevention in a comprehensive National Drug Control Strategy.

A good first step in advocacy is joining a national advocacy organization such as CADCA, the Community Anti–Drug Abuse Coalitions of America, which educates members with e-mail alerts, training institutes and national or regional conferences.

Because of the lack of strong advocacy groups for substance abuse prevention, prevention specialists and health care professionals are encouraged to advocate individually and en mass at the county, state, and national level. Because of the highly publicized lack of effectiveness of the DARE program, many school boards and mayors are looking for more effective approaches. Educating mayors, county commissioners, and state legislatures that substance abuse prevention programs not only work in reducing alcohol and drug misuse, but can substantially reduce crime, violence, delinquency, teen pregnancy, school failure, and health care costs is a role that prevention specialists can play. In addition, these professionals, who often serve on boards of directors of private, nonprofit agencies serving children and families, can advocate for the implementation of evidence-based practices.

KEY TERMS

binge drinking: Consuming five or more drinks in one sitting.
effect size: A statistic designed to quantify the effectiveness of a specific intervention relative to comparison interventions.
fetal alcohol syndrome (FAS): Fetal exposure to alcohol which can cause physical, mental, and neurobehavioral birth defects.

DISCUSSION QUESTIONS

1. Identify and discuss potential community and environmental factors that impact the different rates of substance use among various ethnic groups. Link these directly to the various ethnic groups.
2. If prevention approaches are effective, why would funding be more heavily directed at other methods such as supply reduction or treatment? Is funding directly linked to political attitudes and agendas?
3. Discuss, from your perspective, why supervision and monitoring are more important to preventing drug abuse as preteens mature into older adolescents. What changes during this developmental period?
4. Discuss the specific positive effects social/life skills training could have on building resistance to drug abuse.
5. Because there is scientific evidence indicating that families are a vital link in preventing substance abuse in adolescents, how could you as a practitioner encourage and promote family involvement in meaningful and effective ways?
6. Identify the steps you would take as a service provider to select programs for your community or for the target population with which you work? What would be the logic of practitioners for not utilizing science-based approaches to provide prevention services?
7. Explore how and why the inaccurate perception that most college students are substance users is perpetuated on college campuses.
8. What are some of the social considerations (longevity, death of spouse) in relation to the extensive senior prescription and over-the-counter drug use and how could social services or community support for seniors improve this situation?
9. Specifically, how might you change prevention programs (e.g., more group discussion) to make them more meaningful to adolescent females and why do you think these changes would be beneficial?
10. Discuss methods that could be used to influence policy makers to increase funding for the application and research of substance abuse prevention technology.

SUGGESTED FURTHER READING

Haack, M., & Adger, H. (Eds.). (2002). Strategic plan for interdisciplinary faculty development: arming the nations health professional workforce for a new approach to substance use disorder. *Substance Abuse*, Suppl, *23*(3); pp. 1–345.

Articles written by experts on how to improve substance abuse education for those who do not specialize in the addictions yet routinely see patients and clients who use alcohol, tobacco, and other drugs in a risky, problematic manner.

Hansen, W. B., Giles, S. M., & Fearnow-Kenney, M. D. (Eds.). (2000). *Improving Prevention Effectiveness*. Tanglewood Research, Inc., Greensboro, North Carolina.

Written by leading experts, these chapters present evidence-based practices which strictly focus on school prevention.

Sloboda, Z., & Bukoski, W. (Eds.). (2003). *Handbook for Drug Abuse Prevention*. New York: Kluwer Academic/ Plenum.

Chapters written by leading experts in the field of substance abuse prevention, which demonstrate their knowledge of prevention theory, intervention design, and development and prevention research methodology.

Wagner, E., & Waldron, H. (Eds.). (2001). *Innovations in Adolescent Substance Abuse Interventions.* Pergamon. Elsevier Science Ltd, Kidlington, Oxford, UK.

> Chapters written by researchers and clinicians to present developmentally appropriate approaches to the assessment, prevention, or treatment of substance use among adolescents.

Weisserg, R., & Kumpfer, K. (Eds.). (2003). Special issue on primary prevention for children and youth. *American Psychologists, 58*(1).

> This journal presents reviews on current primary prevention research and practice for children and youth. Specialists summarize key prevention findings across family, school, community, health-care, and policy efforts and highlight their implications for practice.

REFERENCES

Amaro, H., Blake, S. M., Schwarz, P. M., & Flinchbaugh, L. J. (2001). Developing theory-based substance abuse prevention programs for young adolescent girls. *Journal of Early Adolescence, 21*(3), 256–293.

Anavai, M. P., Tauge, D. O., Ja, D. Y., & Duran, E. F. (1999). The status of psychologists' training about and treatment of substance-abusing clients. *Journal of Psychoactive Drugs, 31*, 441–444.

Backer, T., & Rogers, E. (1999). Dissemination best practices workshop briefing paper: State-of-the-art review on dissemination research and dissemination partnership. Encino, CA: National Center for the Advancement of Prevention (NCAP).

Bauman, K. E., Foshee, V. A., Ennett, S. T., Hicks, K., & Pemberton, M. (2001). Family matters: A family-directed program designed to prevent adolescent tobacco and alcohol use. *Health Promotion and Practice, 2*, 81–96.

Beisecker, A. (1991). Interpersonal communication strategies to prevent drug abuse by health professionals and the elderly: Contributions of the health belief model. *Health Communication, 3*(4), 241–250.

Biglan, A., Mrazek, P., Carnine, D., & Flay, R. (2003). The integration of research and practice in the prevention of youth problem behaviors. In R. Weissberg & K. Kumpfer (Eds.), Special Issue *American Psychologist, 58*, 433–440.

Blow, F. C., Brower, K. J., Schulenberg, J. E., Demo-Danenberg, L. M., Young, J. P., & Beresford, T. P. (1992). The Michigan Screening Test-Geriatric Version (MAST-G): A new elderly specific screening instrument. *Alcoholism: Clinical and Experimental Research, 16*(2), 372.

Botvin, G. J. (1995). Drug abuse prevention in school settings. In G. T. Botvin, S. Schinke, & M. A. Orlandi (Eds.), *Drug Abuse Prevention with Multiethnic Youth* (pp. 169–192). Thousand Oaks, CA: Sage.

Botvin, G. J., Schinke, S. P., Epstein, J. A., Diaz, T., & Botvin, E. M. (1995). Effectiveness of culturally-focused and generic skills training approaches to alcohol and drug abuse prevention among minority adolescents: Two-year follow-up results. *Psychology of Addictive Behaviors, 9*, 183–194.

Center for Substance Abuse Prevention (CSAP). (1998). *Preventing substance abuse among children and adolescents: Family-centered approaches. Prevention Enhancement Protocols System (PEPS)*, (DHHS Publication No. SMA 3223). Washington, DC: U.S. Government Printing Office.

Center for Substance Abuse Prevention (CSAP). (2000). The national cross-site evaluation of high-risk youth programs: Final report (pp. 4.18–4.22). Prepared for CSAP by EMT Associates, Inc. and ORC Maco.

Ennett, S. T., Tobler, N. S., Ringwalt, C., & Flewelling, R. (1994). How effective is Drug Abuse Resistance Education? A meta-analysis of Project DARE evaluations. *American Journal of Health, 84*(9), 1394–1401.

Fink, A., Beck, J., & Wittrock, M. (2001). Informing older adults about non-hazardous, hazardous, and harmful alcohol use. *Patient Education and Counseling, 45*(2), 133–141.

Fleming, M. F. (2002). Screening, assessment, and intervention for substance use disorders. *Substance Abuse, 23*(Suppl.)(3), 47–66.

Foxcroft, D. R., Ireland, D., Lister-Sharp, D. J., Lowe, G., & Breen, R. (2003). Longer-term primary prevention for alcohol misuse in young people: A systematic review. *Addiction, 98*(4), 397–411.

Gottfredson, D. (1986). An empirical test of school-based environmental and individual interventions to reduce the risk of delinquent behavior. *Criminology, 1986*(24), 705–730.

Grube, J., & Nygaard, P. (2000, February). *Adolescent drinking and alcohol policy.* Paper presented at The Alcohol Policy and the Public Good: An International Conference, Copenhagen, Denmark.

Guthrie, B. J., & Flinchbaugh, L. J. (2001). Gender-specific substance prevention programming: Going beyond just focusing on girls. *Journal of Early Adolescence, 21*(3), 354–372.

Haack, M. R., & Adger, H. (2002). Executive summary. *Substance Abuse, 23*(Suppl.)(3), 1–24.

Harachi, T. W., Catalano, R. F., & Hawkins, J. D. (1997). Effective recruitment for parenting programs within ethnic minority communities. *Child and Adolescent Social Work Journal, 14*(1), 23–39.

Harrington, N., Hoyle, R., Giles, S., & Hansen, W. (2000). The All-Stars Prevention Program. In W. B. Hansen, S. M. Giles, & M. D. Fearnow-Kenney (Eds.), *Increasing prevention effectiveness* (pp. 121–129). Greensboro, NC: Tanglewood Research.

Hawkins, D., & Catalano, R. (1999). *Communities that care* (2nd ed.). San Francisco: Jossey-Bass.

Hawkins, D., Catalano, R., & Arthur, M. (2000). *Diffusion consortium project briefing for federal funding agencies.* Washington, DC: Social Development Research.

Healthy People 2010. (2000). Healthy People 2010: National disease prevention and health promotion objectives. U.S. Surgeon General's Office.www.healthypeople.gov.

Hingson, R., Heeren, T., Zakocs, R. C., Kopstein, A., & Wechsler, H. (2002). Magnitude of alcohol-related mortality and morbidity among U.S. college students ages 18–24. *Journal of Studies on Alcohol, 63*(2), 136–144.

Hingson, R., McGovern, T., Howland, J., Heeren, T., Winter, M., & Zakocs, R. (1996). Reducing alcohol-impaired driving in Massachusetts: The Saving Lives Program. *American Journal of Public Health, 86*, 791–797.

Holder, H., Saltz, R., Grube, J., Treno, A., Reynolds, R., Voas, R., et al. (1997). Summing up: Lessons from a comprehensive community prevention trial. *Addiction, 92*(Suppl. 2), S293–S301.

Institute of Medicine (IOM). (1995). *Reducing Risks for Mental Disorders: Frontiers for Preventive Intervention Research.* In P. J. Mrazek, & R. J. Haggerty, (Eds.). Washington, DC: National Academy Press.

Jansen, M. A., Glynn, T., & Howard, J. (1996). Prevention of alcohol, tobacco, and other drugs abuse: Federal efforts to stimulate prevention research. *American Behavioral Scientist, 39*(7), 790–801.

Johnston, L. D., O'Malley, P. M., & Bachman, J. G. (2002). *Monitoring the Future national survey results on drug use, 1975–2001. Volume I: Secondary school students* (NIH Publication No. 02-5106). Bethesda, MD: National Institute on Drug Abuse.

Johnston, L. D., O'Malley, P. M., & Bachman, J. G. (1996). National survey results on drug use from the Monitoring the Future study, 1975–1994. Volume I: Secondary school students (NIH Publication No. 95-4026). Bethesda, MD: National Institute on Drug Abuse.

Klein, D. (2000). Ending the war on drugs: Serious challenge for the field of prevention. *Journal of Primary Prevention, 21*, 147–151.

Kumpfer, K. L. (1987). Special populations: Etiology and prevention of vulnerability to chemical dependency in children of substance abusers. In B. S. Brown & A. R. Mills (Eds.), *Youth at high risk for substance abuse* (pp. 1–71). (National Institute on Drug Abuse Monograph, DHHS Publication No. ADM 90-1537). Washington, DC: U.S. Government Printing Office.

Kumpfer, K. L. (2002). Prevention of alcohol and drug abuse: What works? *Substance Abuse, 23*(Suppl.)(3), 25–47.

Kumpfer, K. L., & Alder, S. (2003). Dissemination of research-based family strengthening interventions for the prevention of substance abuse. In Z. Sloboda & W. Bukoski (Eds.), *Handbook for drug abuse prevention, theory, science, and practice* (pp. 75–100). New York: Kluwer Academic/Plenum.

Kumpfer, K. L., & Alvarado, R. (1998, November). *Effective family strengthening interventions.* Juvenile Justice Bulletin, Family Strengthening Series. Office of Juvenile Justice and Delinquency Prevention.

Kumpfer, K. L., & Alvarado, R. (2003). Family interventions for the prevention of drug abuse. In R. Weissberg & K. Kumpfer (Eds.), Special Issue *American Psychologist, 58*, 457–465.

Kumpfer, K. L., Alvarado, R., Smith, P., & Bellamy, N. (2002). Cultural sensitivity in universal family-based prevention interventions. In K. Kavanaugh, R. Spoth, & T. Dishion (Special Edition Eds.), *Prevention Science, 3*(3), 241–244.

Kumpfer, K. L., & Turner, C. W. (1990–1991). The social ecology model of adolescent substance abuse: Implications for prevention. *The International Journal of the Addictions, 25*(4A), 435–463.

Kumpfer, K. L., Turner, C. W., & Alvarado, R. (1991). A community change model for school health promotion. *Journal of Health Education, 22*(2), 94–110.

Lisansky-Gomberg, E. (2000). Substance abuse disorders. In S. K. Whitbourne (Ed.), *Psychopathology in later adulthood. Wiley series on adulthood and aging* (pp. 277–298). New York: Wiley.

Nation, M., Cursto, C., Wandersman, A., Kumpfer, K. L., Seybolt, D., Morrissey-Kane, E., et al. (2003). What works in prevention: Principles of effective prevention programs. In R. Weissburg & K. Kumpfer (Eds.), *American Psychologist, 58*, (special issue), 449–456.

National Institute on Alcohol Abuse and Alcoholism (NIAAA). (2000). Community-based prevention approaches. In *Prevention Research* (pp. 397–411). Rockville, MD: NIAAA.

National Institute on Alcohol Abuse and Alcoholism (NIAAA). (2002). *A call to action: Changing the culture of drinking at U.S. colleges* (NIH Publication No. 02-5010). Bethesda, MD: National Institute on Alcohol Abuse and Alcoholism Publication Distribution Center.

National Institute on Drug Abuse (NIDA). (1997). *Preventing drug use among children and adolescents: A research-based guide.* (NIH Publication No. 97-4212). Rockville, MD: National Clearinghouse for Alcohol and Drug Information.

Office of National Drug Control Policy (ONDCP). (2001). *Agency accomplishments and significant actions, January 1993–December 2000.* Washington, DC: White House, Executive Office of the President of the United States.

Oslin, D. W., & Holden, R. (2001). Recognition and assessment of alcohol and drug dependence in the elderly. In A. M. Gurnack, R. Atkinson, & N. J. Osgood (Eds.), *Treating alcohol and drug abuse in the elderly* (pp. 11–31). New York: Springer.

Pentz, M. (1995). Prevention research in multiethnic communities: Developing community support and collaboration and adapting research methods. In G. J. Botvin, S. Schinke, & M. O. Orlandi (Eds.), *Drug abuse prevention with multi-ethnic youth* (pp. 193–214). Thousand Oaks, CA: Sage.

Perkins, H., & Berkowitz, A. (1989). Stability and contradiction in college students' drinking following a drinking age law change. *Journal of Alcohol Drug Education, 35*(1), 60–77.

Perry, C. L., Williams, C. L., Veblen-Mortenson, S., Toomey, T., Komro, K. A., Anstine, P. S., et al. (1996). Project Northland: Outcomes of a community-wide alcohol use prevention program during early adolescence. *American Journal of Public Health, 86,* 956–965.

Poole, K., Kumpfer, K., & Pett, M. (2001). The impact of an incentive-based worksite health promotion program on modifiable health risk factors. *American Journal of Health Promotion, 16*(1), 21–26.

Resnicow, K., Soler, R., Braithwaite, R., Ahulwalia, J., & Butler, J. (2000). Cultural sensitivity in substance use prevention. *Journal of Community Psychology, 28,* 271–290.

Santisteban, D. A., Muir-Malcom, J. A., Mitrani, J. B., & Szapocznik, J. (2001). Integrating the study of ethnic culture and family psychology intervention science. In H. A. Liddle, D. A. Santisteban, R. F. Levant, & J. H. Bray (Eds.), *Family psychology: Science-based interventions* (pp. 331–351). Washington, DC: American Psychological Association.

Schaps, E., Battistich, V., & Solomon, D. (1997). School as a caring community: A key to character. In A. Molnar (Ed.), *The construction of children's character: 96th yearbook of the National Society for the Study of Education, Part 2* (pp. 127–139). Chicago, IL: The National Society for the Study of Education.

Streissguth, A. (2001). Recent advances in fetal alcohol syndrome and alcohol use in pregnancy. In Agarwal, D. P. & Seitz, H. K. (Eds.), *Alcohol in health and disease* (pp. 303–324). New York: Marcel Dekker.

Tarter, R., & Mezzich, A. (1992). Ontogeny of substance abuse: Perspectives and findings. In M. Glantz & R. Pickens (Eds.), *Vulnerability to drug abuse* (pp. 149–177). Washington, DC: American Psychiatric Association.

Taylor, T. K., & Biglan, A. (1998). Behavioral family interventions for improving child rearing: A review of the literature for clinicians and policy makers. *Clinical Child and Family Psychology Review, 1,* 41–60.

Tobler, N. S., & Kumpfer, K. L. (2000). *Meta-analysis of family based strengthening programs.* Report to CSAP/SAMHSA, Rockville, MD.

Tobler, N., & Stratton, H. (1997). Effectiveness of school-based drug prevention programs: A meta-analysis of the research. *Journal of Primary Prevention, 18*(1), 71–128.

Toomey, T. L., & Wagenaar, A. C. (2002). Environmental policies to reduce college drinking: Options and research findings. *Journal of Studies on Alcohol.* Vol. 63, Suppl., 193–205.

Yin, R. K., Kaftarian, S., Yu, P., & Jansen, M. (1997). Outcomes from CSAP's community partnership program: Findings from the national cross-site evaluation. *Evaluation Program Planning, 20,* 345–355.

22

Harm Reduction Tools and Programs

Patt Denning
Harm Reduction Therapy Center

TRUTH OR FICTION?

___ *1. Needle exchange is legal in most states in the United States.*
___ *2. Harm reduction strategies were first developed and used in the Netherlands.*
___ *3. Drug addicts did not benefit from the early syringe exchange efforts.*
___ *4. The Harm Reduction movement has policy, advocacy, and treatment segments.*
___ *5. Starting at the client's level is a major principle of harm reduction.*
___ *6. Drug, set, and setting is a way of understanding the complex interactions of drug use.*
___ *7. Motivational interviewing is a new assessment tool.*
___ *8. There are three major areas of substance use management.*
___ *9. LAAM is an ultra-short acting drug used for detoxification from heroin.*
___ *10. Methadone is often used in outpatient drug treatment programs.*
___ *11. Drug users can learn to moderate or change the amount of a drug they use.*
___ *12. The stages of change model can be applied to behavior changes other than addiction.*
___ *13. Childhood trauma increases the likelihood of substance abuse.*
___ *14. The decisional balance helps a person quit using drugs.*
___ *15. Our culture's attitudes about pleasure influence our attitudes towards drugs.*

WHERE AND WHY DID HARM REDUCTION ORIGINATE?

The history of **harm reduction** is a lesson in the important principles of public health. During the late 1970s and early 1980s, Hepatitis B was killing thousands of injection drug users throughout Europe. The Netherlands began the first coalition of health care providers and consumers to develop life-saving strategies. In Rotterdam and Amsterdam, intravenous (IV) drug users formed "junkie unions" to meet with public health officials to ensure that whatever public health departments decided to do to curb the epidemic would actually benefit them, not just society at large. It became obvious very quickly to public health workers that sharing dirty syringes was the most likely cause of the epidemic.

When HIV hit in 1982 to 1983, these same drug users began to die from a mysterious disease that also appeared to be blood borne. Once again, the Dutch public health system turned to the people who were dying and asked a simple question: "What do you need to stay alive?" The response was very specific:

> We need clean syringes and an ample supply of them. We need easy access to medical care for other deadly non–IV-related problems (e.g., abscesses, vein care, tuberculosis, etc.). And we need more drug treatment. But some of us want to get totally clean and some of us don't. Some of us want to quit shooting dope, but we aren't about to stop smoking pot.

The Dutch government and its people made a crucial decision that everyone deserved to live, no matter what their behaviors, even if those behaviors created some societal harm. In 1986, the Dutch enacted Harm Reduction as its public health policy. Since that time, the HIV infection rate has plummeted, drug use has not increased, and costs of medical services have remained steady.

1. Harm reduction began in response to:
   a. the HIV epidemic in Europe.
   b. the high death rate from overdoses.
   c. action by drug treatment staff in the United States.
   d. the rise of burglaries in the Netherlands.

During this time, the United Kingdom and Australia were also responding to the new AIDS crises in their IV drug–using communities. Government-sponsored programs experimented with a number of radical strategies, including providing free syringes and offering drug substitution therapies in addition to methadone. This allowed the addict to decide to go on "maintenance" with his or her drug of choice, if this is what it would take to keep them healthy and keep the community at large safer from co-infection, burglary, and so forth. By 1989, in Liverpool, England, syringe exchange alone was responsible for a new HIV infection rate of less than 1% of active IV drug users, while, during the same years in London and New York, the infection rates were closer to 60%.

2. As a result of syringe exchange in Liverpool, England:
   a. drug use decreased by 10%.
   b. the rate of new HIV infection plunged to less than 1%.
   c. more people quit using needles.
   d. the government came out in favor of harm reduction.

Needle exchange programs have sprung up all over the world and in many major American cities since the late 1980s. New York was the first state to issue waivers so that five community groups could legally operate a syringe exchange. Since then, only a few states and some local communities have either legalized syringe exchange or given public health emergency waivers to groups. The North American Syringe Exchange Network (NASEN) was established and continues to advocate for research about the benefits of syringe exchange.

3. The first syringe exchange program in the United States:
    a. was a great success in lowering rates of drug use.
    b. was organized in such a way that very few addicts used it.
    c. operated out of a drug treatment program in New York.
    d. was open seven days a week.

Despite such success in reducing HIV and other harms, syringe exchange networks in the United States continue to operate illegally in most states and with constant police threats and raids. This, despite the fact that few people achieve abstinence with or without treatment.

4. Outcomes in substance abuse treatment:
    a. indicate that treatment is usually successful.
    b. are typically poor in terms of abstinence rates.
    c. show that motivated clients get better than do involuntary clients.
    d. indicate that women do better than men.

Until about 1988, the major focus of drug policy activists was syringe exchange. But that changed when a disheartened social worker, Edith Springer, went to Amsterdam and England to learn more about their drug treatment models. She transformed the large agency in her charge in New York into a Harm Reduction agency (which to her meant welcoming people into treatment even if they were still using). Although many staff revolted at this notion, many became persuaded by her arguments. "Dead addicts don't recover," Edith said to her staff, and to anyone else who would listen. This is the first principle that drove the development of harm reduction from a political and needle-exchange-only movement, to the creation of alternative treatment strategies.

At its heart, harm reduction is a public health philosophy that uses a multitude of strategies to reduce drug-related harm, ranging from syringe exchange to drug substitution therapies, to abstinence, to controlled use. These methods have proven effective in helping people make lasting changes in a variety of health related behaviors: nutrition, exercise, smoking cessation, weight control, and preventive medical care.

5. What is the most common outcome of substance abuse treatment?
    a. abstinence from drug of choice
    b. abstinence from all drugs and alcohol
    c. relapse to substance abuse
    d. reduction in substance use and improvement in other health indices

PEER-BASED HARM REDUCTION

Syringe exchange is probably the most well-known harm reduction strategy (other than condoms) to prevent the spread of HIV and other sexually transmitted diseases. These programs have taught us that even people with serious drug addictions are interested in protecting themselves and others and that addicts can make rational choices and significant behavior changes, despite continuing to still use or drink. Most of these programs began as, and continue to be, grass roots and peer based.

Many needle exchange programs now offer, in addition to clean syringes, instruction in proper injection techniques and vein care, warnings about bad drugs that are in circulation, wound care, and social services that connect IV drug users with treatment, housing, and employment. Workers in these programs, often current and past IV drug users, are especially suited to be knowledgeable and empathic.

The Harm Reduction Coalition (HRC), with offices in New York and Oakland, California, is the largest peer-based, consumer-led harm reduction group in the world. It has nurtured the development of three major areas in the harm reduction movement: (1) policy and advocacy, (2) street outreach, and (3) treatment revision. HRC publishes newsletters and drug information brochures and holds conferences to disseminate the latest ideas. (For more information, visit www.harmreduction.org.)

Several other local and national harm reduction groups provide services ranging from education to research. DanceSafe (dancesafe.org), one such group, provides excellent information through their Web site about the recent flow of "rave drugs." They offer technical assistance to dance clubs by testing samples of the drug Ecstasy to determine if it's actually pure Ecstasy rather than adulterated. They also offer instructions in safe use while dancing and have been successful in forcing club owners to offer free water and a "cool down" room to prevent deaths from overheating.

Another peer-based harm reduction strategy is the formation of new self-help groups such as Moderation Management and Drink Link (www.moderation.org)—both hold meetings in which people develop plans to control and monitor their alcohol use to reduce problems they might have had in the past. Many of these groups use the Internet to facilitate people meeting and sharing their ideas.

PROFESSIONALLY DEVELOPED HARM REDUCTION

Many psychologists have been researching and developing harm reduction clinical techniques long before the phrase *harm reduction* became used. Because most of these clinicians come from a cognitive-behavioral model, they are comfortable examining the components of complex behaviors and planning specific strategies to help people make changes. One of the leaders in the field, G. Alan Marlatt (of The Addictive Behaviors Research Center at the University of Washington in Seattle), is best known for his groundbreaking research (with Judith Gordon) on relapse prevention (Marlatt & Gordon, 1985).

Many other professional chemical dependency specialists in this country are developing effective treatment strategies: William Miller and Stephen Rollnick (1987), who developed Motivational Interviewing (MI), continue to research and train clinicians in this method. Fred Rotgers (Rotgers, Keller, & Morgenstern, 1996) is known for his research on evidence-based practices in substance abuse treatment and for his clinical practice with moderation techniques. Reid Hester is developing Web-based software applications that can be used as self-help modules. The Drinkers Check-Up is one such program (download from rhester@ behviortherapy.com). Marc Kern has been instrumental in developing SMART Recovery as an abstinence-based alternative to 12-step programs (see http://www. addictionalternatives.com and http://smartrecovery.org).

6. Many of the harm reduction therapy techniques have come from:
   a. learning theory
   b. freudian analysis of defenses
   c. counterconditioning
   d. cognitive-behavioral approaches

In addition to these behavioral oriented professionals, many psychodynamically trained clinicians have contributed to what is now called *harm reduction psychotherapy* (HRP). Andrew Tatarsky in New York, for example, edited a book that contains moving cases from experts treating people with significant substance abuse problems (Tatarsky, 2002). I have also written a book on HRP outlining a formal assessment and treatment program that is especially useful for dually diagnosed clients (Denning, 2000) A new book, written with Jeannie Little and Adina Glickman, addresses the drug-using person directly and can be used as a self-help guide for change (Denning, Little, & Glickman, 2004). The Harm Reduction Therapy Center in San Francisco has recently opened to provide both direct clinical services as well as training for substance abuse counselors and psychotherapists in this new model.

PRINCIPLES AND TECHNIQUES OF HARM REDUCTION PSYCHOTHERAPY

Why Should We Use Harm Reduction in Treatment?

HRP refers to several clinical models for treating addictions based in the international harm reduction public health movement. The very mention of harm reduction often causes more heat than light, with people taking sides for or against. But when you think about it, it is almost impossible to be *against* harm reduction. It's what we do every day. We all find ways to reduce the risks of life. When I drive to work each day, for example, I reduce my risk by wearing a seat belt. Abstaining behavior may sometimes be the best harm reduction strategy, and yet most of us choose, for a multitude of reasons, to practice other harm reduction methods.

7. What is an everyday harm reduction strategy?
   a. going to school
   b. keeping your room clean
   c. using seatbelts in your car
   d. having a spiritual practice

On the other hand, it is sometimes difficult to be *for* harm reduction, to allow your client the freedom to make choices that may lead to his personal disaster, or watch her struggle with impulses that we suspect will cause pain to others. In many of these circumstances, we sometimes feel right to weigh in with strict rules for our clients' behaviors, hoping to forestall disaster to them and reduce our own sense of personal discomfort or failure. (i.e., "If only they would listen to us . . . ").

Drug treatment in the United States is currently based on the American disease model, which asserts that addiction is a primary disease, not caused by any other condition, is characterized by loss of control and denial, and is only treatable by immediate abstinence, usually before treatment is even begun. In addition, despite calling addiction a medical disease, most people also think that successful treatment requires that the client "work the program" within a 12-step fellowship that emphasizes spiritual development.

Requiring abstinence as a condition of entering treatment and terminating clients who relapse are two examples of setting too high a threshold for treatment. By doing so, we dramatically limit the range of people who can and will come to treatment. Substance abuse is the only mental health problem where the client is required to give up his symptom (drug use) before entering treatment.

HRP, by contrast, founded on the basic principle of the harm reduction movement, respects peoples' choices. A basic HRP principle is to meet clients "where they're at"; and offer **low threshold treatment**. This means removing barriers (such as lack of child care) or eliminating the traditional "hoops" (requiring abstinence prior to entry) that people have to "jump through" in order to access services.

What Are the Basic Principles of Harm Reduction Psychotherapy?

Harm reduction efforts respect the client's autonomy and develop a relationship of mutual collaboration with the goal of reducing drug- and alcohol-related harm. In addition, HRP suggests that the concept of denial be replaced by the more accurate idea of ambivalence regarding drug use. This allows the person to fully explore the adaptive reasons for his drug use as well as the harms that are accruing as a result of it. Additional principles stress the need to develop a hierarchy of client needs—a list including all other services, with the importance for each set by the client.

Principles

1. *Harm reduction is any action that attempts to reduce the harm of drug abuse and drug prohibition.* Reducing harm can take on many different strategies. Some of the more common strategies include syringe exchange, which reduces the spread of blood-borne diseases such as HIV and hepatitis. Other strategies include managing one's use by reducing the frequency of use, switching to a different drug, or abstaining from one or several or all drugs that one uses. These techniques are referred to as substance use management (SUM) and is described in detail later in this chapter.

2. *There can be no **punitive sanctions** for what a person puts in their body or refuses to put in their body.* Punishing people for doing drugs is not just a matter of the criminal justice system, but is a problem within our treatment system. When we punish people for drug use while in treatment, we set up a dynamic of dishonesty that undermines any effort to get better. We can only hope to foster honesty and self-examination if we encourage a client to talk openly about all of their experiences with alcohol and drugs in order to develop appropriate treatment plans.

8. What is a harm reduction method of getting people to be honest in treatment?
   a. point out the dangers of lying
   b. confront all obvious inconsistencies
   c. never punish acknowledged substance use
   d. don't ask direct questions

3. *People use drugs for many reasons and not all drug use is abuse.* People are drawn to different drugs for different reasons. There is no disease process that results in a person's "drug of choice." People tend to experiment with different substances until they find one that gives them the results they are looking for—relief from emotional suffering, improved social or

sexual performance, etc. This is known as Khantzian's *self-medication hypothesis* (Khantzian, 1999). While economics and one's peer culture certainly influence the drug of choice, most people develop relationships with specific drugs (Leonard & Blane, 1999).

9. What is the self-medication hypothesis?
   a. the belief that people use drugs to medicate underlying mental illness
   b. people usually pick a drug that they feel is good for them
   c. addiction is always dual diagnosis
   d. people are drawn to a particular drug because it solves some emotional problem

4. *People can, and do, make rational decisions about important life issues while still using.* We tend to think of people with substance abuse problems as being out of control and unable to think about their use. The fact is, most people who decide to quit using have done so when either intoxicated or in a state of withdrawal. These altered states of consciousness do not prevent a person from rationally assessing her situation and deciding to change it. We, as counselors, should not send the message that a person cannot take steps toward changing their use while still using.

5. *Denial is not actually denial. It is a product of shame and punitive sanctions and is usually quite conscious.* Most people know if they have a drug problem; they are not in denial. Admitting this is difficult mostly because of the punishments that can be levied against the person who admits to having a problem. When we demand immediate and total abstinence, and if the person cannot maintain it, we accuse them of not trying or of being in denial. In fact, the person is hiding or minimizing, or outright lying to us because they are trying to avoid suffering more harm at the hands of drug treatment rules.

10. How does harm reduction psychotherapy (HRP) view denial?
    a. Denial is usually an attempt to hide from others, not from oneself.
    b. People who use drugs tend to lie a lot.
    c. Denial is a central part of addiction.
    d. Denial must be talked about early in treatment.

6. *Ambivalence and resistance to change are "human" qualities. It is our job to work with someone's ambivalence and explore it, not confront it.* Hitting bottom is not necessary for change. In fact, most people do not get motivated by hitting bottom, they adjust to the bottom, leading to increased harm in their lives. People are always ambivalent about making changes because it is about leaving the relative comfort of how they're used to doing things for the unknown fears of what will happen if they change. Ambivalence and resistance are not barriers to our work with clients. These psychological factors are an integral part of our work and are to be welcomed and respectfully discussed.

7. *Addiction is a relationship, an attachment that offers significant support to the person. Treatment must offer that same support, with the understanding that therapists cannot actually offer a relationship that is as consistently useful as the addiction relationship.* Addiction is not a disease. People who are addicted to drugs have developed a relationship to the drug, a relationship that, like those with people, may have more or less healthy and harmful aspects (Walant, 1995). We as counselors need to acknowledge the benefits that a client might get from this relationship to alcohol or drugs as well as notice the harms that are occurring. We need to examine the biological roots, but not forget the psychological and social roots of drug abuse.

11. Rather than seeing addiction as a disease, HRP views it as:
    a. a relationship that may have healthy as well as unhealthy aspects.
    b. a psychological disorder.
    c. a compulsive behavior pattern.
    d. a result of early childhood trauma.

8. *Change is typically slow, incremental, with many setbacks.* **Relapse** *is the rule, not the exception. Plan for it. Help people stay alive and healthy and connected to treatment during their relapses.* People generally do not make lasting changes in large leaps, but by small steps. Each person goes through a predictable process that takes place in stages until stable change is achieved. The **stages of change** model is explained later in this chapter (Prochaska, DiClemente, & Norcross, 1992). Expecting abstinence immediately means that the important work that needs to be accomplished in the earlier stages has been missed. Relapse, though a typical part of the change process, can be made worse by not paying attention to the work of stages prior to the action stage. Recovery does not begin with abstinence. It begins the moment that a person becomes worried about their use, or begins to think about making a change.

9. *Success is any positive change—any step in the right direction.* Harm reduction redefines success. Instead of success only being recognized when a person quits using and doesn't relapse, success is seen as any step in the right direction. Any reduction in harm, any improvement in health and well-being is seen as a step toward permanent change. This new definition of success allows you and your clients to celebrate improvements rather than feel discouraged by a lack of perfection.

12. How does HRP define success?
    a. consistent reduction in amount of drug used
    b. any reduction in drug-related harm
    c. being able to refuse alcohol or drugs
    d. not using every day

What Are the Primary Techniques of Harm Reduction Psychotherapy?

- The use of *Motivational Interviewing* (MI) to establish an honest therapeutic relationship, with the goal of influencing the client toward change
- An assessment of the client's place in the *stages of change model*
- Active encouragement of the expression of ambivalence and resistance to change
- Developing a *decisional balance* that shows the pros and cons of changing and not changing
- Developing a *hierarchy of needs* in which the client and therapist together decide on the relative importance of different problems and agree on the order in which they are addressed
- Psychiatric evaluation and medications to reduce psychiatric symptoms and to promote and maintain abstinence from drugs of abuse, or reduction in use.
- Psychological treatment of emotional disorders such as depression, anxiety, trauma, or psychosis that interact with substance abuse problems

HRP defines addictions as biopsychosocial phenomena. It recognizes that most people who use drugs problematically when young will stop abusing them as they get older. Only tobacco users tend to use more over time. The general framework comes from Norman Zinberg's *drug, set, and setting model* (1984), described later.

Knowledge about how people make behavioral changes is essential to any treatment process. Prochaska and DiClemente's (1992) stages of change model provides this. They describe the stages through which a person passes on their road to behavior change, the lessons that must be learned, and suggest the techniques that can be used in working with people relative to which stage they are in.

These concepts and strategies are central to HRP and are especially useful when engaging a person whose drug abuse is intertwined with significant emotional problems. All of the methods follow from a particular style of talking—a style that decreases resistance in the client.

13. Which drug use continues to be a problem with people as they age?
   a. alcohol
   b. marijuana
   c. tobacco
   d. crack cocaine

Motivational Interviewing

Motivational interviewing (MI) is both a treatment strategy and a technique for interviewing clients (Miller & Rollnick, 1987). Information gathering per se is only a small part of the interview. The development of a therapeutic relationship is of primary importance.

Much chemical dependency literature relies on the concepts of denial and lack of **motivation** for treatment to explain the difficulties of working with people with substance use disorders. In contrast, MI is based on several assumptions that contrast with those traditionally used in chemical dependency work. Motivation is not a stable trait residing within the individual, but rather, a flexible state existing within an interpersonal matrix. If motivation is viewed this way, the counselor has a unique ability and responsibility to enhance a client's motivation for change. This is an inherently hopeful stance.

14. Miller and Rollnick see motivation as:
   a. an ever changing state that both counselor and client are responsible for.
   b. essential before real treatment can proceed.
   c. inherent in the person coming for help.
   d. something that family pressure can increase or decrease.

The two phases of MI are: first, building motivation to change, and second, strengthening the client's commitment to change. The techniques reflect genuine respect for the client and a belief that the client can, with help, arrive at a responsible decision about addictive behaviors. No time line is suggested for developing motivation that leads to change. For some people the process will be relatively quick, taking only a few sessions. Others may need a year or more before significant motivation is built.

15. Motivational interviewing techniques include all *except*:
   a. goal setting.
   b. avoiding confrontation.
   c. support self-efficacy.
   d. asking open-ended questions.

The Stages of Change

Any time a person wishes to make a change in her life, whether it involves a complex series of decisions (like switching jobs), or a relatively straightforward choice (like quitting smoking), she goes through several stages of change. Changing drug use is essentially an internal and external process despite the fact that we tend to see it as only as an overt behavior. Researchers have focused specifically on how behavior change takes place. Not surprisingly, they have found that a person tends to go through the same process and stages when trying to change drug or alcohol use as he does when deciding to change jobs or start an exercise program (Prochaska, DiClemente, & Norcross, 1992). The stages are **precontemplation**, **contemplation**, **preparation**, **action**, **maintenance**, and **termination**.

Important concepts in this theory include the fluidity of change and the importance of self-efficacy in both the initiation and maintenance of change. Clinical assessment of the client's place along the continuum of change provides a broader view of the person and creates possibilities for the development of interventions specific to the individual at a particular point in her treatment process. For example, a person is in the contemplation stage when ambivalence and resistance are highest. Thus, clinical interventions can be designed to match the client's current stage of change and assist in the natural process of changing.

16. What stage of change is most characterized by ambivalence and resistance?
    a. contemplation
    b. relapse
    c. reworking
    d. maintenance

Drug, Set, and Setting

This model helps explain how some people get into trouble with drugs and others don't. Problems with drugs result from interactions—interactions among three phenomena—the drug one uses, the set (meaning the person using), and the setting, or the environment influencing that person. It's not that any one of these things is the truth. It's that if you try to simplify a drug or alcohol problem, you are likely to miss the interactions and the relative importance of several different factors. For example, a person who has suffered trauma as a child may have a brain that is damaged in the areas that control pleasure and emotional tolerance. Drug use will make such a person feel "normal."

17. Which parts of the brain are damaged by early childhood trauma?
    a. the "thinking areas"
    b. the areas that control balance
    c. the areas that affect pleasure and tolerance of feelings
    d. the memory centers

The *drug* itself influences the relationship. Each drug has its own unique chemistry and produces widely varied effects. A drug's action is the first important element, the second is dosage. How a drug is taken—the route of administration—also affects the experience. The rate of onset is different when a drug is smoked, injected, absorbed through mucous membranes, or eaten (in order of rapidity.) The faster the drug comes on, the more compelling it is, which is why smoking cocaine has become a larger problem than snorting it was. Finally, a drug's legality influences our relationship as illegal drugs have poor to nonexistent quality control.

Set refers to the influence of the characteristics of each individual user on their drug experience—one's unique personality, motivation for using, and hopes for a good effect. Is the client a risk taker? Does she love a challenge? This personality trait may make it easier for people to experiment with different drugs than it would be for someone who is more cautious in their life. Does the person want a new experience of life? A search for meaning may motivate people to try LSD or some other hallucinogen. Has the client been abused as a child? Abuse tends to cause a child to develop different coping styles that may or may not be healthy.

18. How many people with substance abuse problems have a history of childhood trauma?
    a. fewer than half
    b. almost all
    c. about 30%
    d. up to 80%

Settting refers to the environment in which one drinks or uses drugs. Who is she usually with and where does she use? Alone? With friends or family? Outside under a freeway overpass or inside an apartment? The setting will determine not only what drug a person might use, but the effect it will have on him or her (shooting heroin in a back alley is not as safe as shooting it at home).

The setting also refers to the larger context of a person's life—the attitudes and beliefs of their community and the dominant culture around them, especially when it comes to pursuit of pleasure. Community is a term that has come to describe everything from one's religious affiliation to one's local political and social climate. Many people define their community primarily by their personal relationships with their families and friends. For example, in the United States, the youth culture is very tolerant of drug experimentation. This could account for the fact that drug use is not on the rise among any other group of people except youth.

19. Drug use is increasing among which group of people?
    a. young, urban minorities
    b. rural adults
    c. urban adults
    d. young people from all areas of the country

20. In the drug, set, and setting model, *set* refers to:
    a. the place where a person uses a drug.
    b. the personality traits of the person.
    c. coming down from using.
    d. getting ready to use after a period of abstinence.

Decisional Balance

Another HRP technique, *decisional balance*, is a conceptual, behavioral, and affective "display" of the ambivalence a person feels about her substance use. Many clinicians view this ambivalence as either a source of potent resistance or a denial of problems, either of which foretells treatment failure. A more productive way of understanding this is to acknowledge that drugs are used for adaptive reasons, for example, a client began to use psychoactive agents to prevent feelings of sadness or anger, or to enhance social interactions. Despite the fact that considerable negative consequences may have accrued over time, these original (positive) adaptive reasons for substance use persist in the unconscious life of even the most motivated client. What this means in terms of treatment is that most people retain significant conscious or unconscious ambivalence about their drug or alcohol use, no matter what stage of change she's in when she first presents.

While the client's ambivalence is most obvious during the contemplation stage, it is operative in all stages. The systematic use of decisional balance communicates the counselor's acceptance of the client's ambivalence while reminding the counselor of the need to work on many different levels at once.

There are several ways to construct a decisional balance worksheet but it is preferable to begin with a worksheet that is not too conceptually complex. People who are using drugs, or who have recently stopped, may have hidden cognitive problems even when they are not obviously impaired. Abstract reasoning is often diminished in a client whose drug use includes heavy alcohol intake or excessive use of tranquilizers. Paranoid thinking may be evident in the long-term stimulant user. For these reasons it is best to avoid complex cognitive tasks until you know the client better and have assessed cognitive functions.

To begin, take a sheet of blank paper and divide it into two halves that represent pros and cons. Typical questions include:

- "You've said you want to quit drinking. What do you think will be good for you if you do quit?"
- "What positive things do you expect to gain?"
- "On the other hand, can you imagine what might be the down side of quitting? What might not be so good for you?"

On an entirely different note, one might ask these questions:

- "What have you noticed about your drug use that you like?"
- "How do you think the amount of speed you're using may affect your sleep problems?"

Record your client's responses or use what information you already have from his or her chart to fill in the worksheet. Then ask if your statements fit her beliefs and feelings. It is interesting to note that if you "misquote" the client while attempting to help articulate pros and cons of drug use, she will probably revert to a previous stage of change.

This method of conceptualizing the decisional balance process places responsibility on you to conduct the interview in a way that builds rapport and elicits cooperation. Although the client has a concurrent responsibility, he may be incapable of full participation in the process because of the very problems that brought him into treatment or because of the stigma attached to using drugs.

21. The decisional balance:
    a. helps the person see the complexity of their ambivalence to change.
    b. takes the counselor out of the role of confrontation.
    c. is difficult to use when a person's cognitive functions are diminished.
    d. all of the above.

The Hierarchy of Needs

Each person comes to treatment with their own agenda regarding what problems they view as most important. Even when a person comes specifically to a drug treatment program, we cannot assume that drug issues are at the top of their list. Each person has created, or needs to create, their own rank ordering of concerns—their *hierarchy of needs*. For one person it might look like this: get housing, find child care, quit smoking crack, and go back to school. If we jump in with quit smoking crack, we may lose the client, or cause a false compliance with our version of their treatment plan. It is important to help the client articulate what is most important to them and then negotiate which of those needs can actually be addressed in your particular setting. Attending to the problems that the person lists on the top end of their hierarchy, even if it only means giving them a referral to another program for that specific purpose, will improve trust and solidify the therapeutic relationship.

22. Attending to a person's hierarchy of needs means:
    a. helping them see that their drug use is the primary cause of other life problems.
    b. making sure that the most severe problems are addressed first.
    c. assisting the person in developing a rank order of problems in their lives and plan how to address each one in order of importance to the client.
    d. starting with the appropriate level of care (detox, inpatient, outpatient, etc.).

Attention to Therapist Pitfalls

Therapist pitfalls fall into the category of *countertransference* (those reactions to the client that come from our own biases, lack of knowledge, or unresolved emotional problems). The most common reactions to watch for:

- Bringing a moralizing tone to therapy
- Being overeager to capitalize on a client's wishes to change without giving due attention to his attachment to drugs and his resistance to change
- Not eliciting enough detailed information about drug use for fear of producing craving or of appearing to support pathological drug use (i.e., enabling)
- Colluding with the client's resistance to change. In an effort to develop or protect the therapeutic alliance, being afraid to be challenging enough
- Underestimating the negative aspects of a client and his life. In an effort to support the client's strengths and self-efficacy, not acknowledging and giving space for the depth and extent of his hopelessness and despair

23. One of the common counselor pitfalls is:
    a. paying too much attention to the person's motivation.
    b. asking specific questions about private behaviors.
    c. using a moralizing or punishing tone or attitude.
    d. not confronting denial strongly enough.

SPECIFIC SUBSTANCE USE MANAGEMENT TECHNIQUES

You have many different clinical interventions available to form an ongoing treatment plan for your client (psychoeducation, coping skills training, stress reduction, nutrition, relapse prevention training, family therapy). At least three other major interventions are standard in harm reduction–oriented treatment and may not be utilized in more traditional treatments.

Psychiatric Medications

Routinely used in mental health settings, medications are often controversial in drug treatment settings. Some outpatient and most residential programs will not allow a person to be on psychotropic medications, claiming that it undermines the drug-free lifestyle that is at the heart of most recovery programs. Increasingly, programs that focus on the dually diagnosed do allow medications, but even then there may be restrictions placed on the type of medication (programs usually allow antipsychotic and antidepressant medications, but often ban the antianxiety drugs because of a fear of cross-addiction).

The field of addiction medicine is not unanimous on the timing of the use of medications, nor on the appropriate medications to use. It is often difficult to arrive at an accurate diagnosis if a person is still using or recently abstinent and the physician often fears contributing to an overdose. For example, despite research showing that anti-anxiety medications can be safely used with alcohol or drug abuse clients if they are accurately diagnosed and monitored, most addiction physicians will not prescribe benzodiazepines (e.g., Valium, Klonopin, etc.), partly out of fear of interfering with the person's recovery, and partly out of fear of making the symptoms worse.

24. Difficulties working with dually diagnosed clients include:
    a. a firm diagnosis may be difficult to establish.
    b. they may not be able to tolerate intense interpersonal interactions.
    c. street drugs may make symptoms better or worse.
    d. all of the above.

Many physicians require that a client be at least thirty days clean and sober before they will prescribe antidepressants. There is a belief that most depressive symptoms will clear up once the person stops using (especially alcohol). Some also believe that it is dangerous to combine these medications with alcohol or street drugs. In fact, many of the newer antidepressant medications (SSRIs such as Prozac, Celexa, Paxil, etc.) can be safely prescribed if the person is drinking, or using sedatives or marijuana, or some club drugs. Stimulants, however, usually cause drug interaction problems with SSRIs. Antipsychotic medications can be safely given even when the person is still using.

A third rationale for limiting the use of medications with people who are not abstinent is the belief that the meds will not work. Again, many patients receive significant relief, if not complete remission, when they take appropriate psychiatric medications prior to a period of abstinence. In fact, such psychological relief may help the person get off drugs if one of their primary reasons for using is relief from emotional pain.

25. What is the reason that psychiatric medications are not often used with clients who are not abstinent?
    a. fear of overdose or other drug interactions
    b. medications don't work if the person is still using
    c. interferes with "clean and sober" recovery
    d. all of the above

Drug Substitution Therapies

Methadone, LAAM, buprenorphine, marijuana, and so forth are increasingly being used as drug substitutes as the field of addiction medicine gains acceptance. However, these therapies are still a controversial part of many traditional drug treatment programs. The fear of relapse and the belief that real recovery means being absolutely drug free makes staff reluctant to recommend these interventions, even to people who relapse frequently. The message that clients often receive is that these treatments are second best, with abstinence still being the gold standard of success. Most drug substitution strategies are for opiate dependence. These are legal and stringently controlled by federal law. The stigma that is associated with methadone often keeps people from using it. Most Americans see heroin users as chaotic criminals, despite the fact most are working, and that only about 23% of those who use heroin become dependent on it, and thus may need drug substitution therapies. Marijuana, however, is still illegal for any medical purpose, including drug substitution therapy.

26. Of people who have ever used heroin, how many will develop dependence?
   a. up to 75%
   b. at least 50%
   c. fewer than 1%
   d. about 23%

The history of methadone in this country shows shifting opinions; from hailing it as a lifesaver to seeing it as a racist ploy to keep African Americans enslaved by drugs. The fact is that the majority of clients who use methadone dramatically reduce their use of opiates and of other drugs as well. Methadone is used either as a short-term intervention with the aim of eventual detoxification or as a long-term treatment in order to prevent relapse to heroin use. For short-term treatment, termed *brief maintenance*, federal regulations allow up to 180 days of methadone, with gradual reductions to a drug-free state. In the past five years, even briefer protocols of methadone maintenance have been developed, some as short as one week. The long-term efficacy of these strategies have not been adequately studied, but many clinicians feel that such rapid detoxification does not contribute to stable abstinence.

In addition, it is thought that those who continue to use methadone have a better long-term outcome in other areas of life than do those who are heavily addicted and use it for detoxification only. People on methadone are able to work, take care of their families, and contribute to society in more consistent ways than are those who continually relapse after short-term methadone detoxification. LAAM has similar actions, but is longer acting (up to 72 hours) and has similar success rates. San Francisco has just begun an office-based methadone pilot project (OBOT), where clients will receive their methadone from local pharmacies after a physician in a health center or private practice orders it. This practice, if ultimately approved for widespread use, will greatly increase the numbers of clients willing to participate in this treatment. The inconvenience, stigma, and expense of going to federally licensed methadone facilities keep many heroin addicts from making use of this life-saving treatment.

Buprenorphine has just been approved by the Food and Drug Administration for office-based use by private physicians who undergo specialized training. It is a *partial opiate agonist*, which means that it mimics the action of opiates such as heroin without causing euphoria. Because it is only a partial agonist, though, it can only be used for people who would need 30 mg. or less of methadone. It can also be mixed with an antagonist such as Narcan to prevent diversion to the street or the use of increasing doses in an attempt to get high. This new treatment should dramatically increase the numbers of people willing to use this opiate replacement therapy, because it allows for private practice visits rather than clinic attendance.

27. Which of the following is not a drug substitution therapy?
    a. Prozac
    b. LAAM
    c. methadone
    d. buprenorphine

A Psychoeducational Process[1]

Substance use management (SUM) is a term widely used in the harm reduction movement to describe any steps taken to control the use of, and the harms associated with, alcohol or other drugs. SUM relies on your ability to be honest with yourself and on your willingness to observe yourself. It also assumes that you and only you are responsible for what you put into your body. The suggestions offered here are culled from interviews with physicians and pharmacologists, Web sites, public health pamphlets, harm reduction videos, professional books and lectures, my clients and their families and friends, and my general experience as a therapist. If you have decided to quit, but want to take it slow, you can also use these suggestions as steps toward abstinence.

28. What is substance use management?
    a. a new program of slow detoxification
    b. random urinalysis
    c. relapse prevention training
    d. a method to help a person change dangerous ways of using drugs

SUM is based on three principles: being honest with yourself about your drug use and the impact of drugs in your life, being willing to make some changes, and, finally, learning skills to help you make concrete, beneficial changes in your alcohol or other drug use.

Specific SUM techniques include helping clients change the amounts of alcohol or drug use, the numbers and types of drugs used together, the frequency that they drink or use, the route of administration (how they put it in their bodies), and the situation (alone versus with others). It also entails helping clients plan their use.

Changing the Amount

Less is more. You are more likely to actually enjoy your drug experience if you don't do it all the time or in large quantities. This is because of *tolerance*. If you've been drinking or using for a while, chances are that you're using a lot more now than when you started. Your body has gotten used to some of the effects and made changes to keep the drug from having too dramatic an effect on you. So you continue to need more to get high as your body tries to balance you out. In order for you to decrease the amount, you'll have to deal with the fact of tolerance. Your goal is to decrease your tolerance so that you can actually control your use without suffering. If you're not totally physically dependent, the best and easiest way to decrease tolerance is to quit using for a while. Even a few days can make a difference, but a few weeks are much better. If you are physically dependent (you get sick or shaky when you try to quit), lowering

---

[1] Note: This section is written directly to a drug-using client to give information to the reader, and to directly teach the psychoeducational model that has been developed by those of us who work in the field. I owe a special thanks to Dan Bigg of the Chicago Recovery Alliance.

your tolerance will be harder, and may actually be dangerous. If you try to "tough it out," your chances of success go down and your risk of medical problems goes up. If you are dependent on alcohol, benzodiazepines (like Valium, Xanax, Ativan, Klonopin, or barbiturates), you run the risk of serious medical problems—convulsions or death—if you quit abruptly or drastically cut down. Going "cold turkey" or "kicking" is a very stressful thing to do. You might be better off going the traditional medical detoxification route until your tolerance is safely lowered, especially if you have HIV, diabetes, a heart condition, or other problems that are made worse by stress.

Once you know how much you are drinking or using, you can begin a reduction plan. You might want to start by writing the details of your current use in a journal or notebook—how much, how often, and so on. Keep track for a week or two. That way you will know how much you typically use and then can really keep track of your progress. The general rule of thumb is: "Start low and slow until you know." This means cutting down a little at a time in order to reduce the stress on your body. Stay at each new level until it feels comfortable or normal to you. (You might notice that as you cut down more and more, you won't be able to do it as quickly as you could in the beginning.)

Changing the Number/Types of Drugs Mixed Together

Many of the short-term adverse effects of alcohol and drug use are related to interactions when you take more than one drug at a time. Some drugs cancel out the action of another. Other drugs may actually slow down the metabolism of another drug, so you are in more danger of overdose even if you haven't taken much. Still other drugs speed up the metabolism and get rid of the drug effect much faster. The biology can get really complicated. The *Physician's Desk Reference* (PDR) has a companion volume that describes all of the possible drug interactions of prescribed medications, and usually of alcohol as well.

If you use one drug (like cocaine) for recreation, but then add alcohol on top of it to take the edge off or to help you sleep, you're more likely to run into problems. Some drugs that are relatively safe even in large quantities (benzodiazepines like Valium) can turn deadly when mixed with another drug (like alcohol). Some HIV antiviral medications and protease inhibitors (Norvil is one example) are notorious for not mixing well with street drugs, alcohol, and some other legal drugs. Medications that help control blood pressure can be made less effective with excessive use of stimulants (like coffee, too, not just things like speed). Or, you could experience a dangerous lowering of blood pressure with some of the sedatives.

You can reduce the harm of mixing drugs if you do one at a time. If you pay attention to your first drug and control it, you might not feel the need to counteract one with another.

Changing the Frequency

If you've tried to cut down on the amount that you use and haven't had consistently good results, changing how often you use might be more satisfying. The fact is, the less often you use, the less chance that you will experience harm over the long run. Daily use causes a number of problems, but perhaps the most insidious is that you get used to the behavior of using, so that it becomes an automatic habit, and you stop paying attention to whether it's doing what you want (bringing pleasure, numbing pain, etc.). Think about drinking coffee in the morning. If you do it every day, you probably could prepare it in your sleep, right? *Paying attention is the fundamental rule of harm reduction. If your drug use is automatic (a habit), you're not thinking.*

Some drugs lend themselves better to changing frequency than others. If you are a maintenance heroin or other opiate user, this is a ridiculous suggestion. You can't change your frequency—you dose whenever the last dose is running out. You should go back to reducing the amount gradually. If you are a daily heavy drinker, depending on the level of your physical dependence, it may be impossible to stop for a day. You also might have to either reduce the amount or be medically detoxed.

Ideally, drugs should be used in moderation. But some cause brain changes that lead us to be concerned about frequency of use. Ecstasy's effect on serotonin cells is becoming a concern for those who use high doses frequently. Ketamine and other dissociatives (dextromethorphan, nitrous, and PCP) have been discovered to cause brain lesions (holes in the brain like Swiss cheese). The less you do these drugs, the better. However, they provide many users with wonderful experiences, either of closeness to others, hallucinatory visions, lessening of self-consciousness, or insights into self or the world. If you don't want to give up those experiences, try treasuring them more and doing them less.

Changing the Route of Administration

There are as many ways to get a drug into your body as there are creative people to think about it! Some are considerably more risky than others. You can swallow a drug, smoke it, snort it, put it in other mucous membranes, inhale the fumes, rub it on your skin, or use a needle to put it in a vein, a muscle or under your skin. Some drugs are "naturally" taken only in certain forms. Most drugs, however, can be prepared in several different ways and used by various routes of administration. In general, eating a drug is the safest route and shooting up into a vein is the most dangerous. But any way you use can be made more or less safe.

If you use needles, you probably realize that smoking is not a very efficient use of your drug, because, well, a lot of it goes "up in smoke." But it is the fastest. Some ways of shooting are always dangerous. For example, does your drug of choice come in a pill form? Opiates often do. Eat pills if you can, but don't crush pills to inject. The particles are often too big and cause trauma to your veins or to the smaller vessels in your lungs. Oxycontin (an oral opiate) is time released. Shooting that one will give you a much stronger dose than swallowing it but can easily cause you to overdose. Cocaine can only be injected into a vein—you can't "skin pop" it or put it into a muscle without risking a toxic skin infection. Can you do your drug by some other route and save the IV for special occasions?

If it comes down to your liking to shoot because it gets you off better, then safe injection is the harm reduction practice for you. There are numerous pamphlets and a good video that teaches how to make your injections safer (for example, The Straight Dope Education Series, put out by the Harm Reduction Coalition in New York has a booklet called *Getting off Right*). The first thing to put into practice is using a clean needle for each shot. Not only the needle, but the cooker and cotton and tie must be absolutely clean to prevent the spread of diseases like HIV and hepatitis and also to prevent nasty skin and heart infections. It is always risky to share any of your equipment with others. If you don't have a choice, remember that sharing needles requires scrupulous hygiene to prevent problems. If you're using an unknown potency of drug, test a little of it before you give yourself the whole shot. It'll act like an early warning signal if it's too strong or mixed with junk. The bottom line: Shoot safe. The Chicago Recovery Alliance, one of the oldest syringe exchange networks, has produced a 30-minute video that teaches safe injection techniques (www.anypositivechange.org).

If you smoke, be aware that for short-acting drugs like cocaine (and, of course, nicotine), smoking is the fastest way for it to get to your brain, but the drug doesn't last long. That will make you want to do more and more, faster and faster. This is where overdose becomes a problem. Try slowing down your use. Set a schedule. Distract yourself. The point is to stay high, not to have muscle spasms and heart attacks.

If you snort, take care of your poor nose. Heroin is not abrasive, but cocaine is, and so is speed. Mix the powder with a little water and spray it in. Or rub the inside of your nose with vitamin E oil before using. Crushed pills won't pass into the blood vessels in your nose very well, so you might as well just swallow them, or mix in water and drink.

If you drink or eat, what you have in your stomach can make a lot of difference. If you drink alcohol on a full stomach, it will take longer to be absorbed. This is a good thing because your judgment isn't as impaired so you can make better decisions about the next drink.

If you are eating marijuana, figuring out how much is enough will take a bit of experimenting. When in doubt, eat just a little (1/4 of a small brownie, for example) and wait an hour to see how you feel.

If you are taking pills, the important thing is to know whether or not they are standard legal drugs or if they have been manufactured in someone's home chemistry lab. You can look up standard drugs in textbooks and online to see what you've got and how strong they are. You can also research how a particular drug interacts with others. For homemade pills, like Ecstasy or LSD, you'll have to ask around. Does anyone know what it is and how strong? Has anyone taken this particular pill before? Take only one if you're not sure. You can always do more later.

If you feel weird or sick after taking something, don't go off by yourself. Find someone fast. Sometimes just talking to someone will calm you down and help you assess if you're really in danger. Don't worry about your pride or the cops or anyone's opinion. Take care of yourself. If you don't want anyone to know, call 911. Call poison control. And next time, try to use unknown drugs only when you are with people who can take care of each other if things go bad. Never leave a person who is clearly overly intoxicated or sick. They might not sleep it off. They might just die.

Changing the Situation

If you're in a bar, the drug that's available is alcohol! If you are at a certain street corner, whatever the person is selling is what you can have. Sometimes changing the situation will automatically change your drug use. Decide what you want and don't want to use. Decide what effect you want to have. Make sure that you have what you want and so are less tempted by whatever else is offered. Most people have a drug of choice. Don't settle for second choice!

This is all about the environmental factors surrounding your drug use. Where you use and with whom can either increase or decrease the risk of using the very same drug. For example, shooting drugs under the freeway or in a bathroom makes it harder to take your time and use good hygiene. Try to arrange places and times when you can have some privacy, light, access to water, etc. Make sure that you can see what you're taking. Get to know yourself in different situations. You'll find it easier to manage your drug or alcohol use if you are in charge of where you use.

29. All of the following are substance use management techniques *except*:
    a. detoxification.
    b. changing the route of administration.
    c. using less frequently.
    d. changing the type of drug used.

Planning Your Use

There are some simple rules you could make for yourself that will certainly reduce harm and might even save your life. Planning when and where and with whom to use is actually something that you can learn to do pretty easily. Most people think that people who use alcohol and drugs, especially people who have problems, or abuse these substances, can't possibly think rationally or control themselves in any way. You might even think this about yourself. But we have learned that people can, and do, plan how to use in order to maximize the benefits and minimize the harms. Some simple guidelines that you might make for yourself include:

- Designated driver—either literally have someone to drive you and others who are using, or someone to guide the experience and make sure no one gets hurt (and to call 911 if they do).
- Clean equipment—pack up your stuff ahead of time if you're going out, or get extra syringes at the exchange when you go. Make sure you have enough cotton, cookers, pipes, etc. before people come over so no one has to share.
- Who you're with and where (especially for psychedelic use)—being with friends or being alone in a place that feels good to you can make an enormous difference, and save you from a traumatic trip.
- Have enough water and food—start your fun out with some food and water, and keep more handy.
- NOT eating too much if you're using psychedelics that can make you vomit—it's pretty uncomfortable.
- Alternate alcohol with something else—if you start by drinking a glass of water or juice, then an alcoholic beverage, you can space things out a bit. Then have a glass of water in between each drink. You'll feel better the next day for sure.

You can probably come up with a lot more ideas that are particular to you situation. Be creative about your health and your fun!

30. What is accurate about SUM?
    a. It rarely works with true addicts.
    b. It's goal is to move from gradual reduction to abstinence.
    c. It relies on the client being mindful (paying attention to) and planning their use of alcohol or drugs.
    d. It doesn't work well in treatment groups.

The field of harm reduction psychotherapy, while new, has already developed specific guiding principles and techniques that are evidence-based practices. Client retention and satisfaction are high in these types of programs, and improvement in functioning is impressive even for those who do not achieve or maintain abstinence. The practice of harm reduction psychotherapy challenges us to radically redesign not only our treatment programs, but our attitudes as well.

Hopefully I have been able to challenge some old beliefs and offer ways of working with clients that are engaging and keep them in treatment. As mentioned previously, *dead addicts don't recover!*

KEY TERMS

harm reduction: Any strategy that aims to reduce alcohol and drug-related harm to the individual, their family, or society at large without necessarily stopping drug use.

harm reduction therapy: A clinical model that uses harm reduction techniques to help the person achieve lasting change along the continuum of drug use from abstinence to controlled use.

low threshold treatment: Removing barriers to treatment, such as limited hours of operation, no child care, requiring person to be clean and sober prior to entering treatment.

motivation: A fluid state characterized by changing feelings and decisions about changing behavior.

precontemplation: The person does not associate their drug use with problems in their life.

preparation: The person has decided to make some change and is actively making plans to do so.

punitive sanctions: Rules or punishments that remove a person from treatment if they continue to use alcohol or drugs.

relapse: A return to previous behavior. A broken promise. Most people relapse several times before stable change is achieved. Should be seen as a learning opportunity, not as "backsliding."

stages of change: The series of steps that a person goes through in order to make lasting changes in behavior.

contemplation: The "yes, but" stage. Person is ambivalent about problems and about a wish to change.

action: The person has decided upon a goal and has made the initial change.

maintenance: All of the other changes that must be made to keep the change going (new friends, therapy, learning to deal with cravings, etc.).

termination: The time at which the change is solid and the person doesn't need to think too much about it. Some people don't get to this point.

DISCUSSION QUESTIONS

1. What is harm reduction?
2. What are the basic principles of harm reduction?
3. What are some objections and criticisms of harm reduction?
4. How would you answer those if you were convinced that harm reduction is a viable alternative?
5. In what ways does harm reduction–based treatment differ from traditional substance abuse treatment?
6. What is important about the therapeutic relationship in harm reduction?
7. What specific techniques can be used to help a person make changes in maladaptive substance use?

8. What are the principles behind substance use management (SUM)?
9. In general, what are your personal beliefs about whether or not people should be allowed to use mind-altering substances?
10. How much do you think your beliefs should be reflected in social and legal policy?

SUGGESTED FURTHER READING

Denning, P. (2000). *Practicing harm reduction psychotherapy: An alternative approach to addictions.* New York: Guilford Press.

This is the first book to describe a comprehensive treatment model using the principles of harm reduction. Beginning with a critique of existing treatments, it takes the reader step-by-step through assessment and treatment protocols. Many extensive case histories are used to describe the approach.

Denning, P., Little, J., & Glickman, A. (2004). *Over the influence: The harm reduction guide for managing drugs and alcohol.* New York: Guilford Press.

This book is written for the general public and describes how people can assess their own alcohol and drug use, the harms and problems, and begin to make decisions about changing.

Horvath, A. T. (1998). *Sex, drugs, gambling, and chocolate.* San Luis Obispo, CA: Impact.

The definitive guide to understanding one's relationship with many significant substances and behaviors. A self-help manual that people can use to discover the reasons for their behavior and explore their motivation for change. Action plans are also included.

Peele, S. (1991). *The truth about addiction and recovery.* New York: Simon & Schuster.

This is a classic critique of traditional substance abuse treatment ideas and models. While often extremely vitriolic and anti-AA, it contains important references to little-known research findings about traditional treatment. The second half of the book is devoted to a self-help program that is extremely useful—the life skills approach.

Rotgers, F., Kern, M., & Hoeltzel, R. (2002). *Responsible drinking: A moderation management approach for problem drinkers.* Berkeley, CA: New Harbinger.

The most recent and comprehensive self-help manual based on moderation management. It includes sections on how to decide if moderation or abstinence is a better choice, and gives a specific, lifelong set of rules to live by.

Shavelson, L. (2001). *Hooked: Five addicts challenge our misguided drug rehab system.* New York: The New Press.

This is the book that blew the cover of treatment programs in San Francisco. Dr. Shavelson follows five seriously mentally ill substance abusers for two years as they try to access and make use of various treatment programs, both mental health and substance abuse. Particular emphasis is on the policies of Walden House, one of the largest residential programs in the area.

REFERENCES

Denning, P. (2000). *Practicing harm reduction psychotherapy: An alternative approach to addictions.* New York: Guilford Press.

Denning, P., Little, J., & Glickman, A. (2004). *Over the influence: The harm reduction guide for managing drugs and alcohol.* New York: Guilford Press.

Khantzian, E. (1999). *Treating addiction as a human process.* Northvale, NJ: Aronson.

Leonard, K., & Blane, H. (1999). *Psychological theories of drinking and alcoholism* (2nd ed.). New York: Guilford Press.

Marlatt, G. A., & Gordon, J. (Eds.). (1985). *Relapse prevention.* New York: Guilford Press.

Miller, W. M., & Rollnick, S. (Eds.). (1987). *Motivational interviewing: Preparing people to change addictive behaviors.* New York: Guilford Press.

Prochaska, J., DiClemente, C., & Norcross. J. (1992). In search of how people change: Applications to addictive behaviors. *California Psychologist, 47*(9), 1102–1114.

Rotgers, F., Keller, D., Morgenstern, J. (Eds.). (1996). *Treating substance abuse: Theory and technique.* New York: Guilford Press.

Tatarsky, A. (2002). *Harm reduction psychotherapy.* Northvale, NJ: Aronson Press.

Walant, K. (1995). *Creating the capacity for attachment: Treating addictions and the alienated self.* Northvale, NJ: Aronson.

Zinberg, N. (1984). *Drug, set, setting: The basis for controlled intoxicant use.* New Haven, CT: Yale University Press.

CAREER ISSUES

23

Disclosure Dilemmas: Legal Compliance for Counselors

Renée M. Popovits
Popovits & Robinson

TRUTH OR FICTION?

___ 1. *I can acknowledge whether someone was a patient as long as I do not discuss the details of the counseling or diagnosis.*

___ 2. *The federal confidentiality regulations protect only written records.*

___ 3. *The Privacy Standards under HIPAA protect only electronic records.*

___ 4. *An address is patient identifying information.*

___ 5. *A client number is protected health information under the Privacy Standards.*

___ 6. *Height, weight, race, hair, and eye color are patient identifying.*

___ 7. *A photograph is patient identifying information.*

___ 8. *If the police arrive with a search warrant, this type of court order allows me to reveal information without breaching confidentiality.*

___ 9. *A general release of medical information is not valid for substance abuse treatment records.*

___ 10. *A fax of a consent is valid.*

___ 11. *Persons receiving information pursuant to written consent cannot redisclose.*

___ 12. *Consent and informed consent mean the same thing.*

___ 13. *Psychotherapy notes must be kept in a separate file to have protection under the HIPAA Privacy Standards.*

___ 14. *A client is entitled to access his or her record.*

___ 15. *Federal regulations require consents to terminate in one year.*

An entire book could be dedicated to counseling counselors of the legal landmines that lie ahead for you in your career. There is a paucity of counselors in the substance abuse field and persons suffering from addiction so desperately need your intervention. Attorneys—not necessarily the good ones—are a dime a dozen. When I pondered the advice that I would share with you as a **health care** attorney who has been almost exclusively dedicated to counseling behavioral **health care providers** for the last fourteen years, I did not want your enthusiasm and your interest in the field to be tempered by fear of liability or clouded with risk management issues. Of course, you should be mindful of those issues, but they should not be the sole driving force in your daily business and clinical decisions. Balance is key. Legal, as well as clinical, medical, ethical, social, financial, and quality of care issues should be considered when making decisions in the treatment setting. The law is just one piece of the puzzle.

What is most difficult to accurately convey is a brief legal analysis of key issues. A legal analysis depends upon the specific facts and circumstances of each situation; laws, regulations and caselaw in existence at a particular point in time; and the applicable legal mandates of specific jurisdictions. Because those laws change from time to time and vary from state to state, and because additional facts may alter a legal outcome, I thought it would be most helpful if this chapter focused on the fundamental legal principle underlying substance abuse treatment: *confidentiality*. This chapter will highlight key provisions of the two sets of federal regulations establishing the national standards for confidentiality and privacy: federal confidentiality regulations (42 C.F.R. Part 2) and the Privacy Standards promulgated under the Health Insurance Portability and Accountability Act (**HIPAA**). These regulations are predicated on the view that persons with substance abuse problems are more likely to seek treatment if they have assurances that their need for treatment will be kept confidential. These federal regulations should serve as your guidepost for legal compliance. You will also need to be mindful of state laws and regulations that are more stringent.

ISSUES OF "CONSENT"

Before I address the specific requirements of the confidentiality regulations, a few legal concepts are important for background. These terms are often misused, misapplied, and misunderstood. These concepts are not interchangeable and each has its own legal significance.

Consent means the voluntary agreement by a person in the possession and exercise of sufficient mental capacity to make an intelligent choice to do something proposed by another. Consent is implied in every agreement and is an act unclouded by fraud, duress, or mistake. Consent, for example, requires a physician to obtain a patient's permission prior to treating; without it, physical touching constitutes battery. This is often why virtually all treatment facilities have consents to treatment. This document typically describes the informed consent process and the voluntary nature of the treatment **program,** references client rights and confidentiality, addresses cooperation in treatment, expressly authorizes specific treatment services, including a number of psychiatric and medical services, discusses withdrawal of consent, and may include specific consent provisions relating to minors, photographs, transportation, personal property, participation in program evaluation studies, and financial responsibility.

Informed consent is a fundamental principle grounded in both the law and ethics. The principle was developed by court decisions in the 1950s and significantly expanded in the 1970s with the explosion of malpractice litigation. More recently, some states have adopted statutes relating to informed consent. Courts have traditionally imposed on physicians the obligation to provide patients sufficient information to enable them to make an informed choice regarding a proposed course of treatment by balancing the probable risks against the probable benefits. This principle of informed consent requires that you tell your clients: (a) the nature and purpose of the procedure/treatment, (b) the risks and consequences, (c) the alternatives, and (d) the risks of no treatment.

Consent for disclosure is yet another separate and distinct legal term. Federal confidentiality statutes and regulations, as well as the HIPAA Privacy Standards govern written consents for disclosure. These legal documents are governed by the federal confidentiality regulations and authorize you to **disclose** information that you would otherwise not be able to legally disclose. To satisfy the requirements under the Privacy Standards, many treatment facilities are now referring to consents for disclosure as *authorizations*. Your facility may call these legal documents *releases*. As disclosed below, what is important is not the title or name on the document but the elements included.

CONFIDENTIALITY AND PRIVACY

Confidentiality protections exist to encourage people to seek treatment for addiction to alcohol or other drugs or a mental illness. Mental health confidentiality is generally governed by state law as well as the federal HIPAA Privacy Standards. On the other hand, substance abuse programs meeting certain criteria are governed by very stringent federal regulations (42 C.F.R. Part 2) which, in most cases, are far more protective of patient confidentiality than the HIPAA Privacy Standards.

The drug and alcohol confidentiality regulations restrict both the disclosure and the use of information about individuals in federally assisted drug or alcohol abuse treatment programs (42 C.F.R. Part 2.3(a)). **Records** of the identity, diagnosis, prognosis, or treatment of any patient maintained in connection with the performance of any program or activity relating to alcoholism or alcohol abuse or in connection with the performance of any drug abuse prevention function, which is conducted, regulated or directly or indirectly assisted by any department or agency of the United States, must be kept confidential (42 C.F.R. Part 2.12(a) and (b)).

1. The federal confidentiality regulations govern what kind of records?
   a. drug treatment records
   b. mental health records
   c. drug and alcohol treatment records
   d. drug, alcohol, and mental health records

2. Where are the federal confidentiality regulations found?
   a. 26 U.S.C. 2
   b. 42 C.F.R. Part 2
   c. U.S. Constitution
   d. 45 C.F.R. Part 164

Patient Identifying Information

Patient identifying information is defined broadly to include any information whereby the identity of a patient can be determined with reasonable accuracy and speed either directly or by reference to other publicly available information.

The Privacy Standards also protect information that identifies or could reasonably be used to identify an individual. The Privacy Standards contain many of the same identifiers as 42 C.F.R. Part 2, as well as numerous additional "identifiers" which are afforded protection (i.e., client ID numbers). See "Key Terms" for definitions of **Protected Health Information** (PHI) under HIPAA and patient identifying information under Part 2.

It is worthy to note 42 C.F.R. Part 2 covers any information (written or oral) relating to a patient that is received or acquired by a federally assisted alcohol or drug abuse program. The Privacy Standards cover PHI about an individual (oral, written, etc.) and only when maintained, collected, used, or disseminated by or for a **covered entity.**

Federally assisted programs, as used in 42 C.F.R. Part 2, includes programs funded by the federal government, as well as programs conducted under a license, certification, registration, or other authorization granted by any federal department or agency, including Medicare certification or authorization to conduct methadone maintenance treatment. Federal assistance also includes tax exemption granted by the IRS. Even if the program does not meet the definition of a federally assisted program, state law or state licensure regulations may require adherence to 42 C.F.R. Part 2.

3. Is a client ID number considered PHI under the Privacy Standards?
   a. yes
   b. no, as long as the number is random and includes information such as a social security number
   c. no
   d. no, as long as the client ID number is kept separate from the list linking it to a patient name

4. Which of the following is *not* covered by 42 C.F.R. Part 2?
   a. a federally funded residential substance abuse treatment facility
   b. a Medicaid certified private facility that provides treatment for alcohol and substance abuse
   c. a community-based methadone maintenance treatment facility
   d. an Alcoholics Anonymous meeting

Disclosing Patient Records

Records are broadly defined to include verbal communications as well as what is typically thought of as written medical records. Therefore, patient records include any information relating to the patient, written or oral. In addition to disclosing any of the patient identifying information above, there are other ways of disclosing patient information (e.g., giving written records with a patient's name on it, or answering a telephone and informing the caller that the person to whom the caller wishes to speak is present).

Federal confidentiality regulations permit a facility to acknowledge the presence of an identified patient only if the facility is not publicly identified as only an alcohol or drug abuse diagnosis, treatment, or referral facility and the facility does not identify the patient as an alcohol or drug abuser. This restriction applies even if a caller appears to already know the person is receiving treatment. In addition, any answer to a request for disclosure of patient identifying information that is not permitted under the federal confidentiality regulations must be made in a manner that does not reveal that the patient is a current or former substance abuse patient. The regulations do not prohibit a disclosure that an identified individual is not and never has been a patient.

42 C.F.R. Part 2 strictly governs the disclosure of any information, whether recorded or not, that would identify a client as an alcohol or drug abuser either directly or indirectly. Protection is afforded to "patients" in a program, meaning any individual who has applied for or been given diagnosis or treatment for alcohol or drug abuse at a federally assisted program and includes any individual who, after arrest on a criminal charge, is identified as an alcohol or

drug abuser in order to determine that individual's eligibility to participate in a program. The restrictions on disclosure apply even if you believe that the person seeking the information: already has the information, has other means of obtaining it, is a law enforcement or other official, has obtained a subpoena, or asserts any other justification which is not permitted by the regulations (42 C.F.R. Part 2.13(b)).

The Health Insurance Portability and Accountability Act of 1996 (HIPAA)

HIPAA was enacted to provide better access to health insurance and to toughen the law concerning health care fraud. Additionally, it created national standards to facilitate the electronic exchange of health information and protect the privacy of any patient-identifying health information. A substance abuse "program" required to comply with 42 C.F.R. Part 2 is not automatically a covered entity under the Privacy Standards of HIPAA. A covered entity is a health plan, health care clearinghouse, or a health care provider who transmits any health information in electronic forms in connection with a covered transaction.

> 5. Which one of these is *not* a covered entity?
>   a. health plan
>   b. health care clearinghouse
>   c. patient
>   d. health care provider

Privacy Standards

The Privacy Standards establish a federal floor of safeguards to protect the confidentiality of medical information by limiting the disclosure of PHI. PHI is any **individually identifiable health information** in *any* form: electronic, written, oral, and any other. Protected health information may not be used or disclosed except as authorized by the patient or as permitted by the regulations. In other words, if the provider does not transmit any health information electronically, the provider is not a covered entity under the Privacy Standards. If the provider transmits health information in connection with **covered transactions** (see "Key Terms") electronically via the Internet, extranet, private networks, e-mail, or by transmissions that are physically removed from one location to another using magnetic tape, disk, compact disk, etc., then the privacy standards apply, even if all other information is kept in paper form.

> 6. Which one of these is *not* considered a method of transmitting health information electronically?
>   a. via the Internet
>   b. via e-mail
>   c. via computer disk
>   d. via fax

Like 42 C.F.R. Part 2.13(a), the Privacy Standards require that only the "minimum necessary" information be disclosed. However, the Privacy Standards also direct covered entities to take specific actions to document the minimum necessary for certain job classifications, for routine disclosures, and for nonroutine disclosures.

A concept in the Privacy Standards that is not in 42 C.F.R. Part 2 is that of incidental uses and disclosures. *Incidental uses and disclosures* include being overheard while engaged in a confidential conversation, using sign-in sheets in waiting rooms or maintaining client charts at bedside. Incidental uses and disclosures are not considered a violation of the Privacy Standards as long as the covered entity addresses the minimum necessary rule and implements reasonable safeguards to limit unintended uses or disclosures.

Another unique aspect of the Privacy Standards is that they go beyond the acknowledgment of patient's rights in 42 C.F.R. Part 2 by establishing specific patient's rights including:

- The right of access to inspect or copy the client's own PHI in most cases
- The right to request amendment of the client's own record
- The right to an accounting of disclosures of PHI made by the covered entity
- The right to request certain restrictions on the disclosure of PHI
- The right to request that communications be made in a certain manner
- The right to receive a copy of a Notice of Privacy Practices (see below)
- The right to file a complaint with the covered entity or with the Secretary of the Department of Health and Human Services

The Notice of Privacy Practices describes the potential uses and disclosures of a client's PHI. The Privacy Standards dictate a number of elements that must be included in a Notice of Privacy Standards.

7. Which of the following is *not* required to be included in the Notice of Privacy Practices?
   a. fees for copying
   b. the effective date of the notice
   c. a statement of the patient's right to amend PHI
   d. privacy officer or privacy office contact information

8. Which of the following is *not* a patient right established by the Privacy Standards?
   a. the right to access or copy patient's own PHI
   b. the right to treatment free of charge if the patient cannot afford treatment
   c. the right to an accounting of disclosures
   d. the right to file a complaint with the covered entity or the Secretary of the Department of Health and Human Services

The Privacy Standards also contain numerous administrative requirements and require the creation of policies for implementation and monitoring of the implemented requirements.

Furthermore, the Privacy Standards condition a covered entity's disclosure to its **business associates** (see "Key Terms") on the provider or plan obtaining, typically by contract, satisfactory assurances that the business associate will: use the information only for the purposes for which they were engaged by the covered entity, safeguard it from misuse, and help the covered entity comply with the covered entity's duties under the Privacy Standards.

Confidentiality and Privacy Standards Protections

Under 42 C.F.R. Part 2, the confidentiality protections extend to "patients" in a program. Once an individual becomes a patient, all individually identifiable information about that patient is protected. Applicants for substance abuse treatment services are patients even if not admitted to the program. However, a person who does not show up for an appointment for an assessment to determine whether a substance abuse problem exists is not a patient. Former patients and deceased patients remain protected as well.

Assuming the treatment agency is both a *program* under 42 C.F.R. Part 2 and a *covered entity* under the HIPAA Privacy Standards, PHI becomes protected upon its creation or receipt by the substance abuse provider.[1] The person does not have to be admitted as a patient. If a person calls and makes an inquiry and the substance abuse agency documents identifying information about the individual, the information would be considered PHI. This protection applies to any PHI in any form and remains protected for as long as the covered entity transmits or maintains it.

9. When does PHI become protected for someone seeking substance abuse treatment?
   a. upon application for treatment
   b. upon admission to the program
   c. upon completion of the program
   d. once the information is stored electronically

Disclosing Information

There are a number of ways to share protected health information without breaching a client's confidentiality. The most obvious is to use de-identified information or to disclose the information without identifying the person as a recipient of substance abuse treatment services. If you need to include patient identifying information, you may legally disclose: (a) with written patient authorization, (b) with a valid court order, (c) to a **qualified service organization**, (d) to staff within the program, (e) under a child abuse reporting exception, (f) to law enforcement for a crime on program premises or against program personnel, (g) to health care personnel for medical emergencies, (h) for research, and (i) for audit and evaluation activities. Each of these disclosures is further discussed below.

10. Which of the following could be used by a program to share communicable disease information with a public health agency?
    a. written consent
    b. court order and subpoena
    c. QSO
    d. all of the above

11. Which of the following is *not* an exception to the general rule that substance abuse patient identifying information may not be disclosed?
    a. written consent
    b. audit and evaluation activities
    c. internal communications
    d. external communications to an individual who knows that the patient is in treatment

Patient Authorization

The basic premise of both 42 C.F.R. Part 2 and the Privacy Standards is that disclosure of confidential information is impermissible unless authorized in writing by the client. The

---

[1] In cases where 42 C.F.R Part 2 and the Privacy Standards apply and conflict, the more stringent of the two laws will apply.

Privacy Standards call this written client document an *authorization* whereas 42 C.F.R. Part 2 refers to it as *consent*. I will use *authorization* in this chapter to indicate a form that meets *all* the requirements of both the Privacy Standards and 42 C.F.R. Part 2.31(a).

Although both laws contain several exceptions that permit disclosure without written authorization, if an exception does not apply, then written client authorization is required. 42 C.F.R Part 2.31 specifies the following required elements for a valid written consent:

- The specific name or general designation of the program or person permitted to make the disclosure
- The name or title of the individual or the name of the organization to which disclosure is to be made
- The name of the client
- The purpose of the disclosure
- How much and what kind of information is to be disclosed
- The signature of the client or personal representative
- The date on which the consent is signed
- A statement that the consent is subject to revocation at any time except to the extent that the program has already acted in reliance on it
- The date, event, or condition upon which the consent will expire if not revoked before

The required elements under the Privacy Standards are essentially the same as those listed above, except that the Privacy Standards require a few additional elements as follows (45 C.F.R. Part 164.508(c)):

- If a personal representative, rather than the client, signs the authorization, then the authorization, must specify why the representative is authorized to act for the client.
- The authorization must describe when and how a person may revoke the authorization and include instructions for revocation. Under the Privacy Standards, an individual is allowed to revoke an authorization at any time except to the extent that an entity has taken action in reliance on the authorization.
- The authorization must include a statement concerning redisclosure. For substance abuse treatment providers, disclosure is prohibited unless expressly permitted by 42 C.F.R. Part 2 (see 42 C.F.R. §2.32).
- The authorization must also address the ability or inability to condition treatment, payment, enrollment, or eligibility for benefits on the authorization. With the exception of treatment for research purposes or for fitness for duty examinations, the Privacy Standards do not permit a provider to condition the provision of treatment on the receipt of an authorization. Therefore, the authorization should state that the provider will not so condition treatment, payment, or eligibility for benefits.

12. Which of the following does *not* have to be included in an authorization form?
    a. person or agency to whom disclosure is made
    b. purpose for disclosure
    c. date on which consent expires
    d. recipient's date of birth

13. An authorization valid under both 42 C.F.R. Part 2 and the Privacy Standards may never:
    a. be combined with another authorization.
    b. contain elements in addition to the required elements.
    c. be a multi-party authorization.
    d. provide that the authorization may not be revoked.

An authorization must include all the thirteen elements described above to be valid under both 42 C.F.R. Part 2 and the Privacy Standards. The authorization must be written in plain language and may contain additional elements as long as they do not contradict the required elements. An authorization may be combined with another authorization to create a compound authorization, except authorizations for use or disclosure of psychotherapy notes may be combined only with another authorization for psychotherapy notes. An authorization cannot be combined with any other type of document, except that a research authorization may be combined with any other type of written permission for the same research study. A multi-party authorization is permissible if the information to be disclosed and the purpose for the disclosure are the same for all parties. However, if the client revokes the authorization for one party, the entire authorization is revoked.

14. Under the federal confidentiality regulations, can patient consent be verbal?
    a. yes, if the patient is competent
    b. yes, if the patient signs a written consent letter
    c. no, unless the patient is a minor
    d. no, never

If you have an authorization that was executed prior to April 14, 2003, the effective date of the Privacy Standards, PHI may be used or disclosed based on that authorization as long as the authorization is otherwise valid (e.g., not expired, addresses the disclosure). If the authorization expires, or it is revoked, you cannot release information. Similarly, if the person or agency on the authorization wants information that the client has not included on the form, you cannot release it. It is critical to discuss with the client how much and the types of information they want to share.

15. Protected health information may be shared without breaching a client's confidentiality only:
    a. with consent of the client's primary physician.
    b. for research purposes, even if it contains client identifying information.
    c. to staff within the program.
    d. under an elder abuse reporting exception.

16. Can you say anything if a release has expired?
    a. yes, if you have already released information to the person/organization
    b. no, never
    c. no, unless the person/organization is listed on the release
    d. yes, within thirty days of the expiration date

42 C.F.R. Part 2.32 requires each disclosure made with the patient's written consent to be accompanied by a notice informing the recipient of the following:

- The information has been disclosed to the person from records protected by federal confidentiality regulations.
- The federal confidentiality regulations prohibit the person receiving the information from making any further disclosure of the information unless further disclosure is expressly permitted by the written consent of the person to whom it pertains or as otherwise permitted by the federal confidentiality regulations.
- A general authorization for the release of medical or other information is not sufficient for disclosure of the information.
- The federal confidentiality regulations restrict any use of the information to criminally investigate or prosecute any alcohol or drug abuse patient.

Information may be redisclosed with patient authorization, pursuant to appropriate court order, or pursuant to another exception contained within the federal confidentiality regulations.

17. 42 C.F.R. Part 2 prohibits redisclosure of information. HIPAA does not. What should you do?
    a. follow HIPAA and allow redisclosure
    b. allow redisclosure of information if a warning is included in a consent
    c. follow 42 C.F.R. Part 2 and prohibit redisclosure
    d. allow BAs and QSOs to only redisclose information a provider has disclosed to them because they are not covered entities

Court Orders for Criminal Investigations or Prosecutions

42 C.F.R. Part 2.65 governs the procedures for using or disclosing patient records pursuant to a court order.

Where a court orders disclosure for civil proceedings and investigation, 42 C.F.R. Part 2.64 requires that the patient and the person holding the records be given:

- Adequate notice in a manner which will not disclose patient identifying information to other parties
- An opportunity to file a written response to the application or to appear and be heard for the limited purpose of providing evidence on the statutory and regulatory criteria for the issuance of the court order

A court may enter an order authorizing disclosure for civil proceedings if it determines that good cause exists, by finding:

- Other ways of obtaining the information are not available or would not be effective
- The public interest and need for the disclosure outweigh the potential injury to the patient, the physician–patient relationship, and the treatment services

The procedures governing disclosure pursuant to a court order for criminal investigations and prosecutions differ somewhat from the procedures for disclosure of civil proceedings (see 42 C.F.R Parts 2.65 and 2.66).

Qualified Service Organizations

Qualified service organizations (QSOs) that enter into a QSO agreement are permitted to receive protected information without client authorization. A business associate (BA) is similar to a QSO but is an organization defined under the Privacy Standards (see "Key Terms"). The Privacy Standards require that BAs enter into a BA agreement, which is subject to more extensive requirements than a QSO agreement.

18. What is a QSO?
    a. quality service order
    b. qualified substance abuse organization
    c. qualified subpoena option
    d. qualified service organization

19. Entity A is a qualified service organization. Is entity A also a business associate?
    a. yes
    b. no
    c. not necessarily
    d. yes, unless they do not transmit PHI in electronic form

Communications Within a Program

Communications within a program or between a program and an entity having direct administrative control over the program are permitted. The information must be in conjunction with duties that arise out of the provision of diagnosis, treatment, or referral. Under this provision, an alcohol or drug abuse program, within a larger structure such as a general hospital, may disclose drug or alcohol abuse information to other components of that larger organization if that information is needed to provide services to that patient. Similarly, where a community mental health center has separate alcohol or drug abuse units, those organizations could share communications as long as the entity has direct administrative control over the substance abuse program. Disclosures to third parties outside the overall organization would still be prohibited. This exception allows the information to be shared with employees as well as volunteers of the treatment programs.

Under the Privacy Standards, treatment programs need to be cognizant of the *minimum necessary standard*. Briefly, providers may disclose the minimum necessary amount of PHI to staff of the agency for the purposes of carrying out their duties. However, programs must identify the staff persons or classes of persons who need access to PHI, the categories of PHI they need access to, and any conditions appropriate to such access. The provider must also make reasonable efforts to limit access based on these determinations. This includes limiting any use or disclosure of PHI to the minimum amount necessary to accomplish the intended purpose. The minimum necessary standard does not apply to uses and disclosures: to a healthcare provider for treatment, to the patient, made pursuant to an authorization, required by law, required for compliance with applicable requirements of the Rule, or required by the Secretary of the Department of Health and Human Services (DHHS).

20. In order to share PHI with program staff, a provider must do all of the following *except:*
    a. de-identify all PHI.
    b. identify staff or classes of staff that need access.
    c. make reasonable efforts to limit access.
    d. identify the categories of PHI that will need to be accessed.

Child Abuse Reporting

Reports of incidents of suspected child abuse or neglect made to the appropriate state or local authorities as required by state law are permissible. No patient consent, court order, or other authorization is needed. However, the restrictions on disclosure continue to apply to the original alcohol or drug abuse patient records maintained by the program, including their disclosure and use for civil or criminal proceedings that may arise out of the report of suspected child abuse and neglect. Note that this exception does not apply to the reporting of other types of suspected abuse or neglect, such as elder abuse or domestic violence.

21. For an appropriate court order to be issued in a civil proceeding, the court must:
    a. determine that good cause exists to disclose the information.
    b. limit disclosure to the parts of the record that are essential.
    c. limit persons who may receive the information.
    d. all of the above.

22. In the case of suspected child abuse or neglect, which of the following information remains protected?
    a. the client's name
    b. the client's records
    c. your name
    d. the child's name

Law Enforcement Disclosures

Limited information (for example, circumstances of the incident, name, and address of a client who committed a crime, or the reason for committing the crime) may be released to law enforcement for a crime committed by a client on program premises or against program personnel.

Note that threats by a client to commit a crime may be the basis for releasing information to law enforcement only if the threat itself is a crime or the program director, in good faith, believes the disclosure to law enforcement is necessary to prevent or lessen a serious and imminent threat to the health or safety of a person or the public, and that law enforcement may reasonably be able to prevent or lessen the threat. If the crime involves another client as the victim, you should ask the client victim whether he or she wishes to press charges. If so, you should obtain a written authorization allowing disclosure of the relevant information.

Inquiries from law enforcement can create an awkward situation, because the only permitted disclosures without client authorization are those discussed above. Any other disclosures to law enforcement require an authorization or a valid court order, unless the information does not identify any individual as a recipient of drug or alcohol abuse services.

23. When can protected health information concerning a patient be given to the police?
    a. if the patient commits a crime on program premises
    b. if the patient admits to a crime that occurred before seeking treatment
    c. if the police go to the facility with a search warrant and request information regarding the patient
    d. if the police call and ask if the patient is in the program

24. A program may only release records when it has received which of the following?
    a. search warrant
    b. arrest warrant
    c. a proper court order
    d. subpoena

Medical Emergencies

42 C.F.R Part 2 also allows disclosures to be made without patient authorization if the disclosure is to medical personnel who require the information for the purpose of treating a condition which poses an immediate threat to the health of any individual and which requires prompt medical intervention.

Immediately following a medical emergency disclosure, you must document the following information in the patient's chart:

- The name of the medical personnel to whom disclosure was made and their affiliation with any health care facility
- Your name
- The date and time of the disclosure
- The nature of the emergency

The Privacy Standards also allow PHI to be disclosed in the event of a medical emergency. However, the covered entity must provide the patient with a notice of the entity's privacy practices as soon as reasonably practicable after the emergency treatment situation is resolved.

25. In a medical emergency, disclosures of substance abuse information may be made to all of the following without patient consent *except*:
    a. mental health experts.
    b. law enforcement personnel.
    c. EMTs.
    d. emergency room physicians.

Research Activities

The federal confidentiality regulations permit patient identifying information to be disclosed for the purpose of conducting scientific research if certain criteria are met. There are also a number of HIPAA provisions that apply to research. For an in-depth discussion of those requirements, see DHHS Office of Civil Rights Guidance on the Privacy Rule published December 3, 2002.

Audit and Evaluation

Patient identifying information may be disclosed for audit or evaluation by any federal, state, or local government agency, third-party payers, or peer review organization performing a utilization or quality control review. Before an entity is permitted to review records for audit and evaluation activities, the entity must sign an audit and evaluation agreement. Examples of entities that conduct audit and evaluation activities are the state licensing and funding authorities,

Joint Commission on Accreditation of Healthcare Organizations, other accreditation agencies, and third-party payers.

Duty to Warn

Although a growing number of state statutes and common law are finding therapists liable when they failed to warn someone threatened by a patient, the federal confidentiality laws supercede those state obligations (see 42 C.F.R. Part 2.20). The federal regulations prohibit this disclosure about a patient in a covered drug or alcohol program unless you obtain a court order or you can make the report without identifying the individual who threatens to commit the crime as a patient.

When faced with this type of situation, ask yourself the following questions:

- First, is there a way to report without identifying the client? If so, do so.
- If not, then determine if there is a way to report without identifying the client as a participant in a drug or alcohol treatment program. For instance, by naming the client and providing any other information necessary for the report without identifying yourself or the agency's name.
- If there is no possible way to keep the client anonymous, is there an exception under the confidentiality laws?
- If there is an exception, you must also determine if there is a limit to the information that can be shared under the exception.
- If there is not an exception, is it possible to get the client's written authorization to the disclosure or even convince the client to self-disclose?
- If there is not an exception and the client will not grant consent, decide if, ethically, you or the agency should pursue a court order to disclose.
- In a situation where there is no time to obtain a court order, then ask yourself whether you strongly feel you should warn someone despite the potential liability for breach of confidentiality because you believe a specific person is in imminent danger and the client has a history of committing such violence, is capable of the violence, and has a specific plan.

If a clear and imminent danger to a particular person exists because a client has identified that person and communicated a specific plan to harm him or her, it is wise to err on the side of warning about the danger. Just recognize that such a warning most likely violates federal and possibly some state laws or regulations.

26. It is *not* okay to disclose confidential patient identifying information without consent even if:
    a. the person already knows the recipient is receiving treatment.
    b. it is a medical emergency.
    c. the recipient threatens suicide or harm to others.
    d. it is for quality control review.

27. Which of the following is *not* a factor in a *duty to warn* analysis?
    a. Has the client admitted to past crimes?
    b. Has the client threatened a specific person?
    c. Is there a way to report without identifying the client?
    d. Does the client have a specific plan?

28. When making a child abuse report, which of the following is *not* considered protected under the regulations?
    a. interviews with the client
    b. any verbal and mandated written report required under applicable state law
    c. interviews with treatment staff about the client
    d. copies of the patient's records

Minor Patients

The rules pertaining to minors are driven by state law. If a minor patient has the legal capacity under applicable state law to apply for and obtain alcohol and drug abuse treatment, written consent for disclosure or authorization may be given only by the minor patient.

The federal regulations do provide an exception if a minor has applied for services and refuses to consent to parental notification. The program may contact the parent without the minor's consent only if the program director: believes that the minor, because of extreme youth or medical condition, does not have the capacity to decide rationally whether to consent to parental notification, and the disclosure is necessary to cope with a substantial threat to the life or well-being of the minor or someone else.

Security

Written records that are subject to the regulations must be kept in a secure room, locked file cabinet, safe, or other container when not in use. Each program must adopt procedures in writing that regulate and control access to and use of written records that are subject to the federal regulations. The HIPAA Security regulations 45 C.F.R. Part 162 were published on February 21, 2003. Providers will have twenty-six months from that date to comply.

Penalties for Violations

If you violate 42 C.F.R. Part 2, you are subject to a criminal penalty of up to $500 for the first offense and up to $5,000 for each subsequent offense. Moreover, under state laws, drug or alcohol treatment programs that violate the law could also lose a facility license, certification, or accreditation. A medical professional or licensed psychologist, social worker, or counselor who violates the law jeopardizes his or her professional license. Additionally, a patient may sue for civil damages for violating confidentiality requirements under various theories such as breach of privilege, violation of privacy, etc.

Penalties for noncompliance with the Privacy Standards can be even more severe. Civil penalties include a fine up to $100 per violation and up to $25,000 per year. Criminal penalties can include fines up to $250,000 and ten years in prison.

Complaint Process

42 C.F.R. Part 2 provides that suspected violations of the regulations may be reported to the United States Attorney for the judicial district in which the violation occurs. The Privacy Standards provide for a complaint process whereby individuals may file a complaint with the Secretary of DHHS if they believe a covered entity is not complying with the applicable requirements of the regulations. The complaint must be filed in writing, must name the entity that is the subject of the complaint, describe the violation of the Privacy Standards, and be filed

within 180 days of when the action leading to the complaint occurred. Complaints may also be filed with a covered entity's privacy officer. The covered entity must state in its privacy notice the procedure for filing complaints. A covered entity can require that complaints be made in writing. A covered entity must also document all complaints received and their disposition, if any, in written or electronic form and retain such documents for six years.

Psychotherapy Notes

42 C.F.R. Part 2 is silent on psychotherapy notes. However, the HIPAA Privacy Standards address the protection of psychotherapy notes. Psychotherapy notes are notes recorded (in any medium) by a health care provider who is a mental health professional documenting or analyzing the contents of conversation during a private counseling session or a group, joint, or family counseling session and that are separated from the rest of the individual's medical record. Psychotherapy notes exclude medication prescription and monitoring, counseling session start and stop times, the modalities and frequencies of treatment furnished, results of clinical tests, and any summary of the following items: diagnosis, functional status, the treatment plan, symptoms, prognosis, and progress to date. Notes may include the following types of information:

- Intimate personal content or facts
- Details of fantasies and dreams
- Process interactions
- Sensitive information about other individuals in the client's life
- The formulations, hypotheses, or speculations of the therapist
- Topics or themes discussed in therapy sessions

To receive special protection under the Privacy Standards, the psychotherapy notes must be kept separate from the rest of the medical record. Note also that applicable state mental health laws may impose even stricter limitations on the disclosure of information included within the definition of psychotherapy notes. Generally, covered entities must obtain an individual's authorization to use or disclose psychotherapy notes.

29. Psychotherapy notes exclude which of the following?
    a. process interactions
    b. sensitive information about other individuals in the client's life
    c. summary of diagnosis, functional status, treatment plan, symptoms, prognosis, and progress to date
    d. details of fantasies and dreams

As stated in the beginning, there are a number of legal issues you will encounter in your counseling practice. However, I believe the fundamental legal principles focus on confidentiality and privacy issues. Without your commitment to protect the confidentiality of your clients, the client will not trust you enough to share information. Your promise of confidentiality has many exceptions under the law. It is important for you to understand those exceptions to facilitate communication with necessary funding sources, referral agencies,

TABLE 23.1

Common Disclosures for Substance Abuse Clinical Staff

Type of Disclosure	Permissible Under 42 C.F.R. Part 2 and HIPAA Privacy Standards?
Audit and Evaluation 42 C.F.R. §2.53	Disclosure to government licensing and funding agencies, to third-party payers for quality/peer review or financial audit or to accreditation agencies (JCAHO, CARF) with signed audit and evaluation agreement permitted.
Business Associate (BA) 45 C.F.R. §160.103 45 C.F.R. §164.502(e) 45 C.F.R. §164.504(e)	Disclosure not permitted unless the BA is also a QSO or fits within the audit and evaluation exception and a BA agreement is signed.
Child Abuse or Neglect Report 42 C.F.R. §2.12(c)(6) 45 C.F.R. §164.512(b)(1)(ii) and (c)	Disclosure for mandated child abuse reporting under state law permitted. Follow-up information may only be disclosed with patient authorization or appropriate court order.
Court Orders and Subpoenas 42 C.F.R. §2.61–2.66 45 C.F.R. §164.512	Disclosure only permitted with subpoena *and* court order meeting the requirements of 42 C.F.R. Part 2. Subpoenas alone, search warrants, or arrest warrants are not enough.
Crime on Program Premises or Against Program Personnel 42 C.F.R. §2.12(c)(5) 42 C.F.R. §2.02 45 C.F.R. §164.512(f) and (j)	Disclosure to law enforcement permissible if limited to: • Circumstances of the incident • Patient's status • Name and address of the patient who committed the crime • Last known whereabouts of the patient
Deceased Persons 42 C.F.R. §2.15(b) 45 C.F.R. §164.512(g)	Disclosure of information relating to the cause of death to a coroner or medical examiner for the purposes of identifying a deceased person, determining the cause of death, or collecting vital statistics relating to death permitted.
Domestic Violence 42 C.F.R. §2.12 (c)(6) 45 C.F.R. §164.512(c)	Disclosure to report domestic violence only permitted: • With patient authorization • With appropriate court order • If does not identify the individual as a recipient of drug or alcohol treatment services
Elder Abuse 42 C.F.R. §2.12(c)(6) 45 C.F.R. §164.512(c)	Disclosure to report elder abuse only permitted: • With patient authorization • With appropriate court order • If does not identify the individual as a recipient of drug or alcohal treatment services
Employers 42 C.F.R. §2.12 and §2.13	Disclosure to employer about patient requires patient authorization.
Family Members 42 C.F.R. §2.12, §2.13 and §2.14 45 C.F.R. §164.502(a) 45 C.F.R. §164.510(b)	Disclosure to family members about patient requires patient authorization. Check state law for rules on minors' rights and disclosure to parents.
Funding/Licensure/Government Oversight Agencies 42 C.F.R. §2.53 45 C.F.R. §164.512(d)	Disclosure only with: • Patient authorization • Signed audit and evaluation agreement
Insurance/Managed Care 42 C.F.R. §2.12	Disclosure for payment requires patient authorization.

(Continued)

529

TABLE 23.1

(Continued)

Type of Disclosure	*Permissible Under 42 C.F.R. Part 2 and HIPAA Privacy Standards?*
Law Enforcement (Not Crime on Program Premises) 42 C.F.R. §2.12(c)(5) 45 C.F.R. §164.512(f) and (j)	Disclosure only: • With appropriate court order • With patient authorization (if referral from criminal justice system, use criminal justice system authorization) • If does not identify the individual as a recipient of drug or alcohol treatment services
Marketing 42 C.F.R. §2.12 and §2.13 45 C.F.R. §164.508(a)(3)	Disclosure for marketing purposes only with patient authorization.
Medical Emergencies 42 C.F.R. §2.51 45 C.F.R. §164.510(a)(3)	Disclosure to medical personnel who have a need to know the information for the purpose of obtaining treatment for a condition that poses an immediate threat to the patient or any other individual is permitted. Need to document: • Name of medical personnel and facility • Name of treatment staff making disclosure • Date and time of disclosure • Nature of emergency Staff should provide a notice of privacy practices when it is practical to do so after the emergency if such notice has not already been given to the patient.
Psychotherapy Notes 45 C.F.R. §164.501 45 C.F.R. §164.508(a)	Notes only protected if kept in a separate file. Disclosure permitted only with patient authorization, except in very limited circumstances.
Public Health/Safety Reports 42 C.F.R. §2.51(b) 45 C.F.R. §164.512(b) and (j)	Disclosure for any public health or public safety purpose only permitted: • With patient authorization • With appropriate court order • If does not identify the individual as a recipient of drug or alcohol treatment service
Qualified Service Organization 42 C.F.R. §2.11 42 C.F.R. §2.12(c)(4) 45 C.F.R. §160.103 45 C.F.R. §164.502(e)	Disclosure permitted to QSO with signed QSO agreement.
Research 42 C.F.R. §2.12(b) 42 C.F.R. §2.52 45 C.F.R. §164.512(i)	Disclosure permitted with patient authorization or without patient authorization if Institutional Review Board has approved a waiver of the authorization requirement.
Treatment Purposes: *Communication Within a Program* 42 C.F.R. §2.12(c)(3) 45 C.F.R §164.506	Disclosure permitted between staff within the same program who have a need for the information in connection with their duties that arise out of the provision of diagnosis, treatment, or referral for treatment permitted.
Treatment Purposes: *Communication Outside a Program* 42 C.F.R. §2.12(c)(3) 42 C.F.R. §2.51 45 C.F.R §164.506 45 C.F.R. §164.510(a)(3)	Disclosure only with patient authorization unless: • Medical emergency • Outside entity has direct administrative control over the program • Outside provider qualifies as a QSO to the program

Note. From Popovits & Robinson, PC. Copyright 2002. Reprinted with permission.

licensing entities, criminal justice system representatives, and other collaborating partners that may be integral to a multi-disciplinary treatment team that will improve outcomes for your clients. To assist you in this effort, a detailed chart (Table 23.1) is included in this chapter that summarizes common disclosures and the general rules if you are both a program under 42 C.F.R. Part 2 and a covered entity under the HIPAA Privacy Standards. This chart also contains regulatory references so you can consult the direct source if you need additional information.

It is also important to be honest with your clients about the limitations on confidentiality. This should be integrated into your consent to treatment and/or informed consent process. This chapter and the following chapter contain a number of discussion questions that should be analyzed from both a legal and an ethical perspective. You will find that in many cases the legal and ethical answers are consistent. However, there are a number of situations that will arise in your practice that will be legally correct but will feel ethically wrong. When you enter these zones of vulnerability, I encourage you to seek supervision and consultation. You are a substance abuse counselor, not an attorney. Those counselors who have gone solo in those situations or did not take the time to research or attempt to follow the law have cost themselves turmoil, sleepless nights, uninvited lawsuits, added expenses for their agency, and have even lost their jobs. Use your resources and trust your instincts!

KEY TERMS

business associate (BA): A person who on behalf of such covered entity, but other than in the capacity of a member of the workforce, performs a function or activity involving the use or disclosure of individually identifiable health information, including claims processing or administration, data analysis, processing or administration, utilization review, quality assurance, billing, benefit management, practice management, and repricing; or provides, other than in the capacity of a member of the workforce of such covered entity, legal, actuarial, accounting, consulting, data aggregation (as defined in 45 C.F.R §164.501), management, administrative accreditation, or financial services to or for such covered entity, where the provision of the service involves the disclosure of individually identifiable health information from such covered entity.

covered entity: A covered entity is a health plan, health care clearinghouse, or health care provider who transmits any health information in electronic form in connection with a covered transaction.

covered transactions: Covered transactions include health care claims or equivalent encounter information, health care payment and remittance advice, coordination of benefits, health care claims status, enrollment and disenrollment in a health plan, eligibility for a health plan, health plan premium payments, referral certification and authorization, first report of injury, health claims attachments, and other transactions that the Secretary may prescribe by regulation.

disclose or disclosure: A communication of patient identifying information, the affirmative verification of another person's communication of patient identifying information, or the communication of any information from the record of a patient who has been identified.

health care: Includes, but is not limited to: preventive, diagnosis, therapeutic, rehabilitative, maintenance, or palliative care, and counseling, service, assessment, or procedures with respect to the physical or mental condition, or functional status, of an individual or that affects the structure or function of the body and the sale or dispensing of a drug, device, equipment, or other item in accordance with a prescription.

health care provider: A provider of services, a provider of medical or health services, and any other person or organization who furnishes, bills, or is paid for health care in the normal course of business.

HIPAA: Health Insurance Portability and Accountability Act.

individually identifiable health information: Includes information that identifies or could reasonably identify an individual. The following information is considered individually identifiable information, or that which can identify a patient and which is protected under the Privacy Standards: names, all geographic subdivisions smaller than a state, all elements of dates (except year) directly related to the individual (i.e., birth date, admission date, discharge date, and date of death), all dates that would indicate an individual is 89 years of age or older, telephone numbers, fax numbers, e-mail addresses, social security numbers, medical records number, health plan beneficiary number, account numbers, certificate/license numbers, vehicle identifiers and serial numbers, including license plate numbers, device identifiers and serial numbers, Web Universal Resource Locators (URLs), Internet Protocol (IP) address numbers, biometric identifiers, including finger and voice prints, full face photographic images and any comparable images, and, any other unique identifying number, characteristic, or code.

patient identifying information: The name, address, social security number, fingerprints, photograph, or similar information by which the identity of a patient can be determined with reasonable accuracy and speed either directly or by reference to other publicly available information. The term does not include a number assigned to a patient by a program, if that number does not consist of or contain numbers that could be used to identify a patient (such as social security or driver's license number) with reasonable accuracy and speed from sources external to the program.

program: (a) An individual or entity (other than a general medical care facility) that holds itself out as providing, and does provide, alcohol or drug abuse diagnosis, treatment, or referral for treatment; (b) an identified unit within a general medical facility that holds itself out as providing, and does provide, alcohol or drug abuse diagnosis, treatment, or referral for treatment; or (c) medical personnel or other staff in a general medical care facility whose primary function is the provision of alcohol or drug abuse diagnosis, treatment, or referral for treatment and who are identified as such providers.

protected health information (PHI): Individually identifiable health information (including patient identifying information) that is transmitted by or maintained in any form or media. Health information is any information that is created or received by an organization and that relates to: past, present, or future physical or mental health of an individual; the provision of health care to an individual; and the payment of health care. Identifying information is any information that identifies the individual or can be used to identify the individual. PHI does not include education records or employment records (including employee health records) maintained by the employer in its role as the employer.

qualified service organization (QSO): A person or entity that provides services to a program, such as data processing, bill collecting, dosage preparation, laboratory analyses; legal, medical, accounting, or other professional services; or services to prevent or treat child abuse or neglect, including training on nutrition, child care, and individual and group therapy, and has entered into a written QSO agreement with a program.

records: Any information, whether recorded or not, relating to a patient received or acquired by a federally assisted alcohol or drug program.

DISCUSSION QUESTIONS

1. Mary, a counselor, suspects that her patient, Ruth, is abusing her children. Mary is required by state law to report any suspected child abuse to the state child welfare agency.
   a. Can Mary report this suspicion of child abuse under 42 C.F.R. Part 2 and HIPAA?
   b. If Mary does make a report, is she allowed to provide any follow-up information to the agency under 42 C.F.R. Part 2 or HIPAA?
2. Jan, a fourteen-year-old adolescent, has contacted your agency requesting counseling services for problems that include alcohol and drug use. She is adamant, however, in her refusal to allow you to contact her parents. Jan states that she will seek counseling only under the condition her parents know nothing about it. From the brief information you have collected so far, she is clearly in need of services.
   a. Can minors provide consent for their own treatment or must such consent come from parents or legal guardians?
   b. Can minors access services without the knowledge of their parents?
   c. Do you have any ethical or legal responsibilities to the parent in this situation?
3. A client you saw briefly in counseling discontinued therapy and some months later committed suicide. The parents of this adult client approach you with a request for any information that would help them understand why their son killed himself. They are in great pain and are each experiencing guilt over real and imagined sins of commission and omission in their respective relationships with their son. You possess information gained from the therapy relationship with their son which could absolve them of this guilt.
   a. How would you respond to this request?
   b. Is sharing information about the deceased client with his parents a breach of confidentiality?
   c. Could similar information be shared with legal authorities investigating the client's death?
   d. Does the moral imperative to not share confidentially disclosed information continue even after the death of a client?
4. Bernie, a client you are seeing in outpatient counseling, reports today during his counseling session that he needs you to write a summary of your intake assessment and a progress in treatment summary for his upcoming court date. To comply with this request, you prepare a letter to the probation officer briefly summarizing the material upon which you based Bernie's need for addiction treatment services and a brief synopsis of the course of treatment. Prior to sending the letter, you review its contents with Bernie and ask him to sign a written consent for release of the information to his probation officer. After reviewing the content of the letter, Bernie says he will sign a release for all information except the reference to one episode of relapse which he experienced during the early stage of his treatment. He is concerned that the mention of the relapse episode may result in a revocation of his probation rather than his release from probation.
   a. How do you respond? Can a client selectively delete portions of clinical information to be disclosed to an outside source?
   b. How would you respond if the deletion of the material the client refused to have released substantively altered the overall content and meaning of the communication?

   c. Would it be an ethical breach for the counselor to forward the report to the probation department with the relapse episode deleted?

5. FBI agents knock on the door and indicate that they saw Charlie Chan walk into your treatment facility. Charlie has two outstanding federal warrants, one for bribery and one for armed robbery. The FBI wants to come in and take Charlie into custody.

   a. Should you allow the FBI access?

   b. Should you confirm that Charlie is in the building so the FBI does not kick down the door?

   c. Does it make a difference if the FBI has a search warrant in addition to an arrest warrant?

   d. D. What if the FBI were chasing the person and were in hot pursuit and Charlie entered the facility—would that alter your decision?

SUGGESTED FURTHER READING

Legal Action Center. (2000). *Confidentiality and communication: A guide to the federal & alcohol confidentiality law.* New York: Legal Action Center of the City of New York.

   An in-depth analysis of the federal confidentiality regulations.

Thompson, A. (1990). *Guide to ethical practice in psychotherapy.* New York: Wiley.

U.S. Department of Health and Human Services, Substance Abuse and Mental Health Services Administration. *Confidentiality of patient records for alcohol and other drug treatment.* (Technical Assistance Publication Series #13)

U.S. Department of Health and Human Services, Substance Abuse and Mental Health Services Administration. *Checklist for monitoring alcohol and other drug confidentiality compliance.* (Technical Assistance Publication Series #18)

U.S. Department of Health and Human Services, Substance Abuse and Mental Health Services Administration. *Addiction counseling competencies: The knowledge, skills, and attitudes of professional practice.* (Technical Assistance Publication Series #21)

U.S. Department of Health and Human Services, Substance Abuse and Mental Health Services Administration. *Welfare reform and substance abuse treatment confidentiality: General guidance for reconciling need to know and privacy.* (Technical Assistance Publication Series #24)

U.S. Department of Health and Human Services, Substance Abuse and Mental Health Services Administration. *Confidentiality of alcohol and drug abuse patient records regulation and the privacy rule: Implication for alcohol and substance abuse programs.*

White, W., & Popovits, R. (2001). *Critical incidents: Ethical issues in the prevention and treatment of addiction.* Bloomington, IL: Lighthouse Institute. (A book of vignettes designed for substance abuse staff addressing common ethical and legal dilemmas.)

REFERENCES

Code of Federal Regulations, Title 42, Part 2 (2002). (federal confidentiality regulations governing substance abuse treatment records)

Code of Federal Regulations, Title 45, Parts160 and 164 (2002). (HIPAA Privacy Standards)

24

Professional Ethics

William L. White
Chestnut Health Systems

TRUTH OR FICTION?

___ 1. An act that is unethical and alegal is one that is ethically prohibited but about which the law is silent.

___ 2. Fiduciary relationships are equal and reciprocal.

___ 3. Boundary management is the delineation of the role of the addiction counselor from that of other professionals.

___ 4. Legal reductionism is the process of reducing the question, "Is it ethical?" to the question, "Is it legal?"

___ 5. When an addiction counselor is governed by two or more ethical codes, the least restrictive standard applies.

___ 6. Informed consent is an issue only for clients who can clearly understand the potential benefits and risks of treatment.

___ 7. NAADAC's twelve ethical principles are based on the twelve steps of Alcoholics Anonymous.

___ 8. Refusal to disclose information about a deceased client reflects the ethical principles of fidelity and discretion.

___ 9. The two most common ethics complaints filed with state counselor certification boards involve breaches of confidentiality and having an inappropriate social or business relationship with a client.

___ 10. NAADAC's Ethical Standards for Addiction Counselors require that counselors not have sexual contact with a client for at least two years following the point of last service contact.

___ 11. The ethical value of obedience demands that the addictions counselor comply with a supervisory directive to commit an unethical or illegal act.

_____ 12. *When a client poses an imminent threat of violence to one or more identified individuals, that client's right to confidentiality regarding that verbalized threat is ethically trumped by the need to prevent immediate harm to another individual—even when such disclosure is judged to be a legal violation of confidentiality.*

_____ 13. *Dual relationships with clients must be avoided at all costs.*

_____ 14. *A counselor has an ethical obligation to declare to his or her supervisor the existence of any preexisting relationship with a client that could affect the counselor's objectivity or the client's comfort.*

_____ 15. *A counselor is free to share any information about a client with others inside the treatment agency as long as such information is not disclosed outside the agency without client consent.*

The goals of this chapter are to: (a) introduce you to some of the basic terms and concepts related to professional **ethics** in addiction counseling, (b) increase your ethical sensitivities by orienting you to the ethical terrain of addiction counseling, (c) enhance your ethical decision making abilities through exposure to one model of ethical decision making, and (d) provide you with guidelines about how to reduce your ethical vulnerability as an addictions counselor. I encourage you to apply the ethical standards of your own agency and your state certification/ licensure board in your reflections on the dilemmas discussed in this chapter. Standards from two national bodies will be referenced in our discussions: NAADAC, The Association for Addiction Professionals' ethical standards for counselors (www.naadac.org), and the International Certification and Reciprocity Consortium (ICRC), Alcohol & Other Drug Abuse, Inc.'s codes of ethics for clinical supervisors and prevention specialists (www.icrcaoda.org).

WHAT DO WE MEAN WHEN WE USE TERMS LIKE *ETHICS*, *ETHICAL*, AND *UNETHICAL*?

There are many judgments that others can make about what you as an addictions counselor do or fail to do. A single act could be judged by others to be immoral, illegal, professionally inappropriate, or unethical, with each of these terms springing from very different frameworks of reference. Striving for a high level of ethical conduct is at its most aspirational level about *beneficence*—promoting the health of all parties touched by the counseling process. At its most basic level, it is about preventing harm to: (a) your clients and their families, (b) yourself, (c) your agency, (d) your profession, and (e) and your community. The best interests of these multiple parties can conflict with one another, which is what makes ethical decision making difficult. Three terms help distinguish the ethical from other frameworks of judging professional conduct.

1. The value of *beneficence* calls upon the addiction counselor to:
   a. promote the health of all parties touched by the counseling process.
   b. maintain loyalty to the client.
   c. keep their promises to the client.
   d. not do any harm.

The first term, ***iatrogenic***, is a medical term that means physician-caused, or treatment-caused, harm or injury. The term suggests that actions you initiate as an addictions counselor could have unintended and harmful effects. In the past two hundred years, there have been many such iatrogenic practices within addiction treatment: multi-year legal commitments, mandatory sterilizations, invasive psychosurgeries, drug insults of numerous varieties (e.g., treating morphine addiction with cocaine), emotional and sexual exploitation of clients, and financial exploitation of clients and their families.

2. Which of the following is an example of an iatrogenic effect within the history of addiction treatment?
   a. multi-year legal commitments
   b. mandatory legal sterilization
   c. psychosurgery
   d. all of the above

In professions where there is a potential for such harm, services to clients are delivered within the context of a *fiduciary relationship*. This means that as an addictions counselor, you take on a special duty and obligation for the care of the client or family, and that this relationship must be governed by the highest standards of competence and objectivity. Most importantly, it means that the needs and interests that drive decision making in this relationship are those of the client or family. Unlike most other relationships in your life, the fiduciary relationship is not a relationship of equal power nor is it reciprocal like most family and social relationships. Everything you do as a counselor should flow out of this special duty and obligation.

3. An addiction counselor has a fiduciary relationship with his or her clients because:
   a. the counselor is being paid contractually to do the counseling.
   b. the counselor is a professional.
   c. the counselor has assumed a duty and obligation for the care of the client.
   d. the counselor has achieved a high degree of education and training to perform this job.

Another term governing the relationship between you and your clients is that of *boundary*. Boundary management reflects the relative pace and degree of intimacy in your service relationship with a client. If we were to construct a continuum of intimacy within the relationship between yourself and your clients, three zones could be plotted. First, a **zone of safety** for both you and your clients (actions that are always okay). Second, a **zone of vulnerability** in terms of increased attachment or disengagement (actions that are sometimes okay and sometimes not okay). Third, a **zone of abuse** in terms of harmful intimacy or detachment (actions that are never okay; Milgrom, 1992). The boundaries between these zones are not well marked and may vary with different clients and even with the same client at different stages of the service relationship.

4. A zone of vulnerability designates an area of intimacy and activity that:
   a. is never okay.
   b. is always okay.
   c. is okay if its okay with the client.
   d. is sometimes okay and sometimes not okay.

5. A zone of abuse designates an area of intimacy and activity that:
   a. is never okay.
   b. is always okay.
   c. is okay if its okay with the client.
   d. is sometimes okay and sometimes not okay.

WHAT DISTINGUISHES WHAT IS *ETHICAL* FROM WHAT IS *LEGAL*?

Ideally, standards of legal and ethical conduct are congruent (what is ethical is also legal and what is unethical is also illegal). But the relationship between ethics and law is actually quite complex. There are situations in which: (a) what is ethical is illegal (breaking an unjust law), (b) what is unethical is legal (complying with an unjust law), and situations in which (c) what is ethical or unethical is *alegal* (not addressed in law) (Thompson, 1990). The question of what is ethical or unethical is thus a more complicated issue than the question of what is legal or illegal. To rely only on the latter would constitute a process of *legal reductionism* that shrinks ethical complexities to the arena of legal interpretation. The best models of ethical decision making integrate questions of ethics and law within the decision making process.

WHAT ARE THE MAJOR ZONES OF ETHICAL VULNERABILITY IN THE PRACTICE OF ADDICTION COUNSELING?

A review of the two primary texts on ethical issues in addiction treatment (Bissell & Royce, 1987; White & Popovits, 2001) reveals seven zones of vulnerability in the practice of addiction counseling: (1) personal conduct, (2) conduct related to business practices, (3) professional conduct unrelated to clinical services, (4) conduct in relationships with clients and families, (5) conduct in professional peer relationships, (6) conduct involving threats to safety, and (7) ethical issues in special roles and functions (e.g., prevention, early intervention, training, and research).

When examined in terms of their prevalence within the field of addiction counseling (as measured by complaints regarding ethical breaches filed with state licensing boards), the three most common complaints are sexual exploitation of a current client, personal impairment due to substance use or another condition, and practicing addiction counseling without a certificate (St. Germaine, 1996).

> 6. Which of the following is *not* among the three most common complaints lodged against addiction counselors?
>   a. sexual exploitation of a current client
>   b. personal impairment due to substance use or another condition
>   c. breach of confidentiality
>   d. practicing addiction counseling without a certificate

WHAT FACTORS MUST BE CONSIDERED IN ETHICAL DECISION MAKING?

There are many models of ethical decision making that you might find helpful in your role as an addictions counselor (Wagner, 2001). The model proposed by myself and Renée Popovits (2001) involves three steps. The first step is to analyze the situation in terms of who will potentially benefit and who could potentially be harmed. This requires detailing both the probability and degree of benefit and harm to multiple parties. This first step also examines whose interests in the situation might be in conflict, for example, what is best for the client in a particular situation may not be what is best for you or your agency.

The second step is to examine whether there are any universal or culturally relevant values that apply to the situation and what actions those values might dictate that you take in the situation (see table later in this chapter). The question of culturally relevant values suggests that ethical standards might differ across different cultural contexts, for example, an action that could be beneficial in one cultural context might do harm or injury in another context.

The third step is to explore how existing ethical codes, laws, regulations, organizational policies, or historical practices apply to the situation in question. This model provides a framework for individual decision making, but also underscores the need for seeking consultation on **ethical dilemmas**.

WHAT ARE THE MAJOR CODES OF ETHICAL CONDUCT GOVERNING THE PRACTICE OF ADDICTION COUNSELING?

As an addictions counselor, you may be accountable to multiple codes of ethics. You may be bound by codes of ethics linked to: (a) state and/or national addictions counselor certification or licensure systems, (b) state and national professional associations (e.g., NAADAC: The Association for Addiction Professionals), (c) professional licenses or certificates held in addition to addiction counseling (e.g., ethical codes for psychologists, social workers, professional counselors, employee or student assistance professionals), and (d) agency codes of ethics that are a condition of your employment. The existence of multiple and qualitatively different standards to which you may be held accountable raises the question of which standards apply in particular situations. To afford the greatest protection for your clients, yourself, your employing agency, the addiction counseling profession and the public, it is generally best to be guided by the more stringent standard, except where the application of the more stringent standard would do harm to the client/family to whom we have pledged fiduciary responsibility.

7. When an addiction counselor is bound by two or more codes of ethics whose standards differ, the counselor should:
   a. ignore all standards.
   b. adhere to the strictest standard.
   c. adhere to the less stringent standard.
   d. use their own judgment.

WHAT ETHICAL PRINCIPLES UNDERLIE THE PRACTICE OF ADDICTION COUNSELING?

The codes of ethics that have evolved to guide the practice of addiction counseling draw heavily upon earlier traditions of ethical standards development in the fields of medicine, psychology, and social work. Typical of the principles that undergird addiction counseling are the following twelve principles within the NAADAC Code of Ethics: (1) nondiscrimination, (2) responsibility (for objectivity and integrity), (3) competence, (4) legal and moral standards, (5) public statements, (6) publication credit, (7) client welfare, (8) confidentiality, (9) client relationships, (10) interprofessional relationships, (11) remuneration, and (12) societal obligations (NAADAC, 1994).

TABLE 24.1

Universal Professional Values

Autonomy (freedom over one's destiny)	Honesty and Candor (tell the truth)
Obedience (obey legal and ethically permissible directives)	Fidelity (keep your promises)
	Loyalty (don't abandon)
Conscientious Refusal (disobey illegal or unethical directives)	Diligence (work hard)
	Discretion (respect confidence and privacy)
Beneficence (do good; help others)	Self-improvement (be the best that you can be)
Gratitude (pass good along to others)	Nonmaleficence (don't hurt anyone)
Competence (be knowledgeable and skilled)	Restitution (make amends to persons injured)
Justice (be fair; distribute by merit)	Self-interest (protect yourself)
Stewardship (use resources wisely)	

Note. From *Critical Incidents: Ethical Issues in the Prevention and Treatment of Addiction* (p. 28), by W. White and R. Popovits, 2001, Bloomington, IL: Chestnut Health Systems. Used with permission.

8. Which of the following is *not* one of the twelve principles within NAADAC's Code of Ethics?
   a. nondiscrimination
   b. reciprocity
   c. competence
   d. confidentiality

The universal values considered within the White and Popovits (2001) model of ethical decision making are displayed in Table 24.1.

9. The ethical value of *nonmaleficence* is a mandate for the addiction counselor to:
   a. not hurt anyone.
   b. keep his/her promises.
   c. respect privacy.
   d. obey legal directives.

10. Which of the following is *not* a universal value found within codes of professional ethics?
    a. courage
    b. competence
    c. loyalty
    d. autonomy

11. Which universal value should be applied to a situation in which you are ordered by a supervisor to do something that is unethical or illegal?
    a. loyalty
    b. obedience
    c. discretion
    d. conscientious refusal

WHAT PROFESSIONAL DUTIES AND OBLIGATIONS DO YOU HAVE AS AN ADDICTIONS COUNSELOR DURING NONWORKING HOURS?

As an addictions counselor, you have rights to privacy—areas of your life that are not open to professional scrutiny or accountability, but you also have duties and obligations that transcend an 8-hour work shift. The question then is where and how one draws this line between your rights to privacy and your professional duties and obligations. The concept of *nexus* has been used to define this boundary. The principle upon which it is based is that what you as an addictions counselor do in your own private life is exactly that—*private*—until such time as there is an inextricable nexus—linkage or connection—between that private behavior and your professional performance. What you implicitly pledge when you enter this field is to not do anything in your personal life that destroys your ability to function as an addictions counselor. You must, for example, avoid private conduct (e.g., illegal or immoral behavior) that threatens your reputation and the reputation of your employing agency (e.g., making clients less comfortable seeking services with you or the agency). This principle also calls upon you to notify your supervisors when any issue in your private life threatens to compromise your professional performance (e.g., the existence of preexisting relationships or other conflicts of interests with persons seeking service).

12. The term *nexus* as discussed in this chapter refers to:
    a. a hair product.
    b. the linkage between private behavior and professional performance.
    c. the link between ethical and legal conduct.
    d. an incident in which one ethical value trumps another ethical value.

13. For an agency to hold a counselor accountable for private behavior unrelated to their work performance is an example of:
    a. a high standard of ethical conduct.
    b. the application of a code of ethics beyond the workplace.
    c. the growing concern about ethics in all areas of American life.
    d. an invasion of the privacy of the counselor.

WHAT ETHICAL ISSUES MAY ARISE RELATED TO THE PROFESSIONAL CONDUCT OF THE ADDICTIONS COUNSELOR (OUTSIDE THE ARENA OF RELATIONSHIPS WITH CLIENTS)?

There is a wide variety of ethical and professional practice issues for addictions counselors that occur outside the context of relationships with clients and families. Some of the more troublesome issues you could encounter include:

- Misrepresenting your education, training, or experience via self-report, resumé, or failing to correct others who mistakenly inflate your credentials
- Practicing beyond the boundaries of your education, training, and experience

- Misusing agency resources
- Conflicts over ownership of work products
- Conflicts of interest involving secondary employment

14. The professional mandate to accurately represent one's education, training, and experience would preclude:
    a. misrepresenting one's recovery status.
    b. claimed education that was not completed.
    c. exaggerating the length of one's work experience.
    d. all of the above.

NAADAC Principle 5 ("public statements") explicitly calls upon you to respect the limits of present knowledge and to "state as facts only those matters which have been empirically validated as fact. " (NAADAC, 1995, p. 2) This is not to say that you can never express your opinion, but that you must be very clear in your separation of fact and opinion in communications to clients, families, professional colleagues and the public and express the basis of those opinions.

WHAT ARE SOME OF THE MOST CRITICAL ETHICAL ISSUES THAT WILL ARISE IN YOUR RELATIONSHIPS WITH CLIENTS AND FAMILIES?

There are virtually hundreds of ethical and boundary issues that can arise within your relationships with clients and their families. While there is a tendency to define appropriate responses to many of these issues in very prescriptive terms, subtler and sometimes dramatic changes occur in what is ethically appropriate as we move across the boundaries of cultures, different client populations, and even across different developmental stages of the same counselor–client relationship.

What follows is a discussion of some of the most troublesome areas within the ethical territory of the counselor–client relationship.

Definition of Client

Helping professionals are bound by all kinds of regulations and standards defining what they should and should not do in their relationships with clients, but many of these regulations and standards fail to define *client*. When does a person's status as a client begin and end? Does a client always remain a client? Does the term *client* include family members of those being counseled? Do addiction counselors working in nonclinical positions (e.g., prevention, training, research, supervision) have clients?

There are several trends relating to the definition of client. One is the position of "once a client, always a client." This stance, which takes the position that you as a counselor never lose the power to potentially exploit the counseling relationship, is reflected in NAADAC's Principle 9d: "The NAADAC member shall not under any circumstances engage in sexual behavior with current or *former* clients" (emphasis added; NAADAC, 1995, p. 4). This position may be particularly apt for the addiction counselor given the chronic, relapsing nature of addiction. The ethical codes of some other helping professions and some criminal statutes prohibit sexual contact before a prescribed period (usually two years) following service termination. A growing number of these codes are also explicitly including family members in the definition of client. As for the application of ethical codes to nonclinical staff, a growing number of agencies are developing codes of professional practice that apply to all board members, staff, consultants, and volunteers, and some professional organizations are developing standards that apply specifically to those in specialty roles such as prevention (e.g., the ICRC Code of Prevention Ethics).

15. The prohibition against engaging in sexual behavior with clients in the NAADAC Code of Ethics extends:
    a. until the client is discharged.
    b. until two years after the client is discharged.
    c. until five years after the client is discharged.
    d. forever.

16. In most codes of professional practice, the prohibition against sexually exploiting clients encompasses:
    a. only those working as counselors.
    b. only those working in clinical roles.
    c. only physicians, nurses, and doctors.
    d. all staff, board members and volunteers.

Informed Consent

The goal of the informed consent process is to ensure that all persons considering entry into treatment are fully informed of the exact nature of the treatment and, having been apprised of all potential benefits and risks of treatment, are free to participate or refuse to participate. The ethical prerequisites of informed consent are that the client is competent to provide informed consent (e.g., developmental maturity, absence of cognitive impairment), is free from coercion in providing informed consent, has been given objective information related to the potential risks and benefits of treatment and treatment alternatives, and is informed that he or she is free to revoke informed consent and withdraw from treatment at any time (McCrady & Bux, 1999).

17. The focus of informed consent is on:
    a. negotiating reimbursement for treatment services.
    b. getting consent to talk to other parties about the client's progress.
    c. informing the client about potential risks and benefits of treatment.
    d. informing the client about the history of the treatment program.

Confidentiality

Special procedures (federal and state statutes) have been developed to ensure the confidential nature of addiction counseling. The ethics textbooks and major journals in the addictions field have paid special attention to the issue of confidentiality, and this issue is also addressed in chapter 23 of this book. It is the responsibility of every addictions counselor to clearly inform every client of the scope *and exceptions* to confidentiality and to rigorously adhere to these boundaries. There are quite subtle areas in which confidentiality can be commonly violated.

Internal Confidentiality

Disclose information inside the agency only to those in a "need to know" situation and disclose only role-appropriate information. Communication beyond these boundaries constitutes professional gossip and violates the ethical principles of privacy and discretion. NAADAC principle 8d calls upon the addictions counselor to "discuss the information obtained in clinical, consulting or observational relationships only in the appropriate settings for professional purposes that are in the client's best interest." (NAADAC, 1995, pp. 3–4)

18. Casual discussion about particular clients with staff not in a "need to know" role breaches which professional values?
    a. privacy and discretion
    b. loyalty and stewardship
    c. self-interest and justice
    d. fidelity and self-interest

Casual Interagency Encounters

There are a growing number of multiple-problem clients and families who bring extensive service histories with many community agencies. Shared experience with these clients and families breeds an informality of communication across agency boundaries that can lead to nonmalicious breeches in confidentiality. Avoiding such breeches requires discipline and rigorous self-monitoring.

19. During a casual interchange at a training event, a probation officer asks you the following, "Has your agency had much contact with the Brown family that lives on Clayton Street?" Your best response is to:
    a. answer the question honestly.
    b. change the subject.
    c. inform the worker that you would not be able to disclose such information.
    d. disclose the information if he or she promises not to disclose the information to anyone else.

Casual Encounters With Clients in Public

Another potential area in which confidentiality can be violated is during encounters with clients outside of the professional setting. For counselors residing in smaller communities, such encounters are common. Problems resulting from these encounters can be minimized by talking about the possibility of such encounters with each client and working out a mutually agreeable etiquette for such situations.

Dual Relationships

Dual relationships occur when you agree to counsel someone with whom you have another relationship or connection that could compromise your objectivity or the client's comfort. Most professional associations and certification/licensure bodies prohibit or strongly discourage entering into counseling relationships with persons with whom one has a preexisting, nonclinical relationship or connection. NAADAC, for example, prohibits its members from entering into counseling relationships with family members, current or former intimate partners, friends, close associates, and "others whose welfare might be jeopardized by such a dual relationship" (NAADAC, 1995, p. 4).

The fact is that dual relationships will be inevitable for many addiction counselors, particularly those working in isolated rural communities or whose practice focuses on members of a "small town" within a larger community (e.g., a gay therapist working primarily with gay, lesbian, bisexual, and transgender clients). Prohibiting all dual relationships would be impractical under those circumstances and would deny many people access to services. Such relationships must be individually evaluated based on their degree of intimacy and the extent to which the nature of the relationship would compromise your effectiveness and the client's psychological safety and comfort.

20. A dual relationship occurs when:
    a. a counselor sees two clients at the same time.
    b. two counselors interview a single client.
    c. a counselor jointly interviews a client and his or her partner.
    d. a counselor has one or more roles with the client outside of the counseling setting.

21. Dual relationships are secondary relationships that occur:
    a. prior to the counseling relationship.
    b. during the counseling relationship.
    c. after the counseling relationship.
    d. any or all of the above.

Preexisting Relationships

A good working principle is that you should declare any preexisting relationship with a client to your supervisor and use the supervision process to determine whether this client should be transferred to another counselor or another agency. Where such transfer is not possible (e.g., where no other service alternatives exist), it is possible that counseling will need to be done in spite of such dual relationships. In this case, other protections must be used to minimize the potential harm, for example, informed consent (including a discussion of the preexisting relationship and its potential effect on counseling), increased supervision, and more meticulous documentation of the counseling process.

Social and Business Relationships

Addiction counselors are discouraged from working with people with whom they have social or business relationships and to not initiate such relationships with clients. Such relationships compromise the counseling relationship by shifting the fiduciary relationship (decisions made in the best interest of the client) to a reciprocal relationship (decisions made to meet the mutual interests of both parties). Such dual relationships inevitably spill clinical material into the social relationship and social interactions into the clinical relationship, leaving both counselor and client confused as to which roles they are occupying at any point in time. Such confusion usually produces poor friendship and poor counseling.

Recovery Peer Relationships

One of the most frequent dual relationship questions that arises in the field of addiction counseling is the question of contacts between a recovering counselor and his or her clients in outside-of-work recovery activities. The most common questions include: How should I handle social contact with clients at recovery meetings? How should I respond when current or former clients ask for a ride to a meeting or ask me to sponsor them? How should I handle my own disclosures at meetings in which current or former clients are present?

The folk wisdom that has grown up over the years is designed to protect the integrity of the counseling relationship and the sobriety of the counselor. Such folk wisdom has been canonized within the *AA Guidelines for AA Members Employed in the Alcoholism Field* (n.d.). These guidelines emphasize the importance of separating one's role as an Alcoholics Anonymous (AA) member from one's role as an addictions counselor. To do this, AA members are encouraged to avoid using professional jargon in their AA role, speaking for AA in their professional role, and sponsoring people with whom they have a professional relationship. (The ICRC code of ethics specifically prohibits sponsorship of current or former clients or their family members.) They are encouraged to clarify with clients and their fellow professionals when they are speaking as a counselor and when they are speaking as an AA member.

22. The folk wisdom regarding the advisability of serving as both a counselor and a sponsor for the same client is that:
    a. such relationships strengthen both the counseling and sponsorship relationship.
    b. sponsorship should not be taken on until at least six weeks after the counseling relationship has terminated.
    c. such dual roles are advisable only of the client and the counselor are of the same sex.
    d. it is best to keep the role of counselor and the role of sponsor separate.

Individuals whose personal recoveries have been aided by their affiliation with AA, Narcotics Anonymous (NA), or other recovery mutual aid groups bring assets that can contribute to their effectiveness as counselors, but such affiliations can also create areas of blindness and bias. It is essential that the recovering counselor not push all clients into his or her own pathway or style of recovery. This requires developing knowledge, tolerance, and respect for alternative frameworks of recovery.

Sexual Relationships

A sexual relationship between a counselor and a client can emerge from a confluence of conditions: unmet needs in the counselor's personal life, the counselor's manipulation of the work environment to meet these needs, weak or nonexistent clinical supervision, and "closed, incestuous organizations" that poorly define boundaries between staff and clients (White, 1995, 1997, p. 46). Sexual intimacies between a counselor and client are best viewed as processes rather than events—acts that are the last stages of a progressive violation of intimacy barriers within the service relationship. This understanding provides an opportunity for self-monitoring of early drift within the counseling relationship (see Table 24.2).

23. Which of the following is a potential warning sign of increased enmeshment with a client:
    a. increased frequency/duration of sessions.
    b. sexualization of session content.
    c. resistance to supervision.
    d. all of the above.

TABLE 24.2

Warning Signs of Boundary Drift (Overinvolvement)

Preoccupation with/possessiveness of client
Resistance to referral when clinically indicated
Increased frequency/duration of sessions
Sexualization of session content
Excessive self-disclosure
Escalation of touch
Evidence of client dependency
Resistance to supervision
Contact outside the professional setting
Courtship behaviors (e.g., increased phone contact, dressing
    up for appointments, personal gifts)

Self-Disclosure

There is an extensive body of professional literature on the question of whether and when counselor self-disclosure is an effective clinical technique. The question we will address here is under what conditions your self-disclosures could actually do harm to the client, yourself, or your organization. Such harm can occur when your self-disclosure breaks the fiduciary promise by shifting the focus of the counseling session to yourself, or when the nature of your disclosure (by its nature or timing) injures the service relationship. In general, self-disclosure should be used sparingly, selectively, and strategically. When used, self-disclosures should be brief, appropriate to the developmental stage of the client and the client–counselor relationship, end with an opening for the client to link the disclosure to their own experience, and involve only material over which the counselor has achieved distance and emotional control. In terms of potential threat to you and your agency, you should also understand that confidentiality is not reciprocal. Clients are under no obligation to hold secret what you share with them, and the rediclosure (and frequent misinterpretation) of this information could result in unanticipated harm to your reputation and the reputation of your agency.

24. Which of the following is a warning sign related to counselor self-disclosure?
    a. a prolonged self-disclosure
    b. self-disclosure that is not clinically strategic
    c. self-disclosure of current material from the counselor's life
    d. all of the above

Disengagement

Whereas problems of overinvolvement between the addictions counselor and his or her clients have garnered much attention in the ethics literature, little attention has been paid to the ethical issues inherent in a counselor's *underinvolvement* in such relationships. Significant harm can occur from failure to engage a client or from the premature disengagement of the counselor from the helping relationship (clinical abandonment). Such acts can result from many conditions—personal depletion or impairment of the counselor, excessive caseloads, or negative countertransference in the counselor–client relationship. Warning signs of disengagement are illustrated in the Table 24.3.

TABLE 24.3

Warnings Signs of Disengagement

Lack of preparation for interviews
Drift of counselor attention during interviews
Aversion to seeing particular clients
Failure or delays in returning client phone calls
Decreased frequency/length of sessions
Unfocused, superficial content of sessions
Disrespect of clients
Adversarial relationships with clients
Depersonalization of clients (e.g., use of labels)
Precipitous, unprocessed terminations

Experimental Techniques

New techniques lauded for their clinical effectiveness but which lack empirical support raise two issues for the addictions counselor: (1) practicing within the boundaries of competence in the mastery of such techniques, and (2) the potential iatrogenic (harmful) effects of these techniques even when competently executed. Counselors should maintain a critical skepticism regarding fads in treatment and counseling; popularly reported breakthroughs in the treatment of addiction have been notoriously unreliable for more than two hundred years.

NAADAC Principle 3a demands that the addictions counselor "recognize boundaries and limitations of the member's competencies and not offer services or use techniques outside of these professional competencies" (NAADAC, 1995, p. 2). Even where experimental procedures are delivered with a level of assured fidelity, steps need to be taken to prevent potential harm to clients. These steps include the use of informed consent prior to implementation of the procedure, rigorous supervisory review, and reasonable efforts to assess the degree of effectiveness of the procedures and the presence of any harmful side effects of the intervention.

Documentation

There are several ethical issues related to documentation you may encounter over the course of your career as an addictions counselor. Some of the most common and more difficult of these include:

- Failure to adequately document service activity
- Breaches of confidentiality related to inadequate security of documents (e.g., loss of an appointment book, briefcase or laptop containing client information)
- Documentation of clinically irrelevant information that could do potential harm to the client (e.g., details of criminal activity)
- Unethical and fraudulent service documentation/billing

This list underscores the potential ethical problems inherent in underdocumentation, overdocumentation, and undue attention to the disposition of any information about clients whether that information is in the form of paper, electronic documents, audio/video-tapes, or photographs. Special care must be taken to assure the security of clinical information stored and transmitted via computer.

25. A client has disclosed embezzlement of funds from his employer to support his cocaine addiction. You should:
    a. notify the employer immediately of the embezzlement.
    b. document the details of the embezzlement in the clinical record.
    c. document that the client was involved in illicit activity related to his addiction but note no details related to that activity.
    d. pretend the client didn't disclose this information.

WHAT ARE THE MOST COMMON ETHICAL ISSUES THAT ARISE WITHIN THE PROFESSIONAL PEER RELATIONSHIPS OF THE ADDICTION COUNSELOR?

Some of the most frequent ethical issues that arise within professional peer relationships include the following: responding to allegations of unethical conduct of a peer, impairment of a professional peer, intra-agency confidentiality, intra- and interagency conflict management, fee-splitting (accepting financial or other incentives for referrals), abuses of power in supervisory relationships, dual relationship conflicts involving supervisors and supervisees, and "**whistle blowing**."

NAADAC's Principle 2d calls upon the addictions counselor to report allegations or observations of unethical conduct by other service professionals to appropriate authorities (NAADAC, 1995, p. 2). It is *not* the counselor's responsibility to determine whether such an allegation is true or not true before reporting it.

26. If you hear an allegation that a therapist in your local community has sexually exploited a client, you should:
    a. report the allegation along with the client and therapist's names and contact information.
    b. determine if the allegation is true before reporting it to anyone.
    c. communicate the allegation to the therapist about whom the allegation was made.
    d. report the allegation and the therapist's name to an appropriate authority but provide the client's name only with the client's permission.

The NAADAC code of ethics (Principle 10c) explicitly prohibits addiction counselors from emotionally, sexually, or financially exploiting relationships of unequal power (e.g., with supervisees, student interns, research participants, or volunteers). Addiction counselors have a responsibility to ethically manage sexual feelings toward those they supervise in the same way they would be expected to manage such feelings toward clients. The principles governing dual relationships with clients have direct applicability to the supervisor–supervisee relationship. The ICRC Code of Ethics for Clinical Supervisors, for example, explicitly prohibits entering into dual relationships in supervision, exploiting the supervision relationship, or transforming clinical supervision into psychotherapy. Regarding the latter, the Code states: "Personal issues should be addressed in supervision only in terms of the impact of these issues on clients and professional functioning." (ICRC, 1999, p. 2)

HOW SHOULD YOU RESPOND WHEN YOU ENCOUNTER SITUATIONS IN WHICH A CLIENT POSES A THREAT TO THEMSELVES OR OTHERS?

Situations involving potential harm to self or others require a *clinical* response (assessment or degree of risk and interventions to lower risks) and an *ethical* response (interventions to protect the interests of multiple parties). The latter often involves weighing the client's right to confidentiality versus the potential threat of imminent harm to other parties. Two terms are invoked in the literature of law and ethics regarding such situations. ***Duty to report*** is a phrase used to denote the counselor's responsibility to disclose to a responsible authority either self-reported or observed injury by a client to another party (e.g., the abuse of a child or an elder). Addiction counselors are defined as *mandatory reporters* in most states, which means that promises of confidentiality do not include client disclosure of or observation of abuse of the client's children or aging relative. (See chapter 23 for more details on this complex issue.) In this case the child or elder's right to be protected outweigh the client's right to confidentiality. To manage these co-existing loyalties to the client and other parties, it is important for each client to know when the rights of others take precedence over their own. This is managed by discussing with each client of the exclusions to confidentiality.

> 27. Which of the following would generally fall under a *duty to report* provision for an addiction counselor?
>   a. disclosure by a client that he or she robbed a bank a year ago
>   b. disclosure by a client that they shot and killed someone four years ago
>   c. disclosure by a client that he or she is sexually abusing his or her child
>   d. disclosure of generalized fear that they might "lose it" in the future and hurt someone

A second term, ***duty to warn***, describes the addiction counselor's responsibility to intervene to thwart a client's threat of harm to other individuals. Such interventions, like duty to report, pit the client's rights of confidentiality against the threatened parties' rights to be warned of the threats to their safety. This is an area in which legal and ethical interpretations of counselor responsibilities can differ dramatically. A literal interpretation of most confidentiality statutes would preclude the counselors breaking confidentiality to disclose such a threat. Ethicists, however, often argue that the counselor has a responsibility to prevent harm to others and that this responsibility supercedes the right to confidentiality when two conditions are met: (1) there is a *clear target* of the threat (one or more persons have been named) and (2) the threat of harm to the individual is judged to be *imminent*.

> 28. Ethical mandates related to duty to warn are usually invoked in the presence of what two conditions?
>   a. The potential victim is named and the threat of harm is judged to be imminent.
>   b. The potential perpetrator has a prior risk of violence and is threatening violence again.
>   c. The potential victim is particularly vulnerable and judged to be unable to defend him- or herself.
>   d. The potential perpetrator has a prior history of illness-induced violence and has stopped taking his or her medication.

WHAT ETHICAL ISSUES ARISE IN THE PERFORMANCE OF SPECIAL ROLES WITHIN THE ADDICTIONS FIELD?

Over your career, you may work in many different roles and different modalities of addiction treatment and in such specialty roles as prevention, early intervention (student assistance, employee assistance), training, or research. These specialty areas differ from arenas in which ethical responsibilities are more clearly defined. They may involve areas where elaborate structures of ethical compliance exist (such as in human research) or areas in which very little of the ethical territory has been charted (such as prevention). When you move into such specialty areas, you have a responsibility to prepare yourself for the ethical issues that can arise in this new professional territory. (Those addiction counselors who are also working in the prevention arena are strongly encouraged to review ICRC's Prevention Ethics Standards (ICRC, 1994)). Mastering the ethical nuances within these specialty roles requires reading, seeking out training, interviewing peers experienced in the area, and actively pursuing supervision and consultation.

29. If the "client" of a preventionist is the community and the works within an agency that prohibites sexual intimacies with clients, this means that:
    a. the counselor/preventionist must be celibate or have relationships only with individuals outside the community.
    b. these standards should be ignored.
    c. preventionists do not have clients, therefore the prohibition against sexual contact does not apply.
    d. preventionists may not use their prevention position to sexually exploit consumers of prevention services.

WHAT STEPS CAN HELP THE ADDICTION COUNSELOR ELEVATE HIS OR HER LEVEL OF ETHICAL PRACTICE AND WHAT STRATEGIES CAN BE USED TO PROACTIVELY MANAGE AREAS OF POTENTIAL ETHICAL VULNERABILITY?

If I were to offer some closing advice to the aspiring addiction counselor, it would include these key points:

- Take care of yourself! Effective self-care is an essential precursor to ethical conduct; it is the physically, emotionally, and spiritually depleted counselor who is most vulnerable to using clients to meet these unmet needs.
- Get ethically educated! Ethical decision making is as much about skill as it is about character. Seek out self-instructional reading and training that provides a safe environment for rehearsing and sharpening your basic ethical decision making skills.
- Utilize mentors! Develop a small cadre of consultants that can provide a sounding board and objective advice on difficult ethical dilemmas.
- Know thyself! Practice rigorous self-monitoring in order to identify when you are moving into periods of heightened personal vulnerability and when you are entering a zone of ethical vulnerability in your relationship with one or more clients,
- Ask for help! Seek formal consultation when you are in a zone of vulnerability and when there appears to be an exception to the normal ethical prescriptions.

- Protect yourself! There are times when it is clinically warranted to be in the zone of vulnerability we have described. Just don't be there alone, and create a paper trail (e.g., a journal) within zones of vulnerability that document your ethical decision making processes and decisions.
- Finally, respect your clients, your co-workers, your craft, and yourself by adhering to the ultimate ethical mandate, "First, do no harm!"

30. When a counselor moves into the *zone of vulnerability* in their relationship with a client or family, they should:
    a. increase supervisory consultation.
    b. avoid self-monitoring.
    c. decrease documentation.
    d. talk it over with your family.

KEY TERMS

boundary: Demarcation of the level of intimacy in the counselor–client relationship.
code of professional practice: An organizational code of standards that defines aspirational values, ethical mandates ("Thou shalt or shalt not . . ."), folk wisdom ("It has been our experience that . . ."), procedural directives, and organizational etiquette.
conscientious refusal: Refusal to comply with a directive to commit an unethical or illegal act.
dual relationship: Simultaneous or sequential involvement in two or more roles between a counselor and a client, e.g., counselor–client relationship, counselor and client are also next door neighbors, and client-neighbor is also the teacher of the counselor's child.
duty to report: The ethical obligation to report harm to others that has already occurred, e.g., reporting the abuse of a child.
duty to warn: The ethical responsibility to report the threat of harm to another person.
ethics/ethical: A body of values, principles, and standards developed by a profession to guide its member's fiduciary service relationships.
ethical dilemma: A situation in which the ethical course is unclear and which different course of action could be ethically justified.
fiduciary: The assumption of professional responsibility for the care of another.
iatrogenic effect: Interventions that produce inadvertent harm or injury to a client, family, or community.
informed consent: The process through which potential clients are educated about the risks and benefits of addiction counseling prior to their decision to participate or not participate in such counseling.
nexus: The linkage between private behavior and professional role performance.
whistle blowing: A counselor's disclosure of unethical or illegal activity within their organization to an outside investigative body.
zone of abuse: A zone in which the service relationship (either from too little or too much intimacy) has the potential of doing great harm to the client, the counselor and the agency.
zone of safety: A zone of routine service delivery in which a high degree of physical and psychological safety exists for the client and the counselor.
zone of vulnerability: A zone of heightened or diminished intimacy in the client–counselor relationship in which the vulnerability of both parties has increased.

DISCUSSION QUESTIONS

1. Iatrogenic effects of treatment interventions are glaring within the hindsight of history, but are often difficult to see within one's era. What areas of practice within addiction treatment over the past twenty years might have resulted in inadvertent harm to individual clients, their families, or local communities? If you have not yet worked or have just begun working in the field, ask some of your more tenured co-workers to reflect on this question with you.

2. In which of the following situations (all occurring during non–work hours) do you feel there is a nexus between the personal conduct and the professional obligations or performance of an addiction counselor? An addictions counselor is:
   - arrested or convicted of driving while intoxicated.
   - addicted to nicotine.
   - a member of a club that prohibits membership of women and ethnic minorities.
   - observed to be drinking away from work (in spite of his or her alleged recovery status) with no observable changes in performance at work.
   - found to have used information obtained from a client to further his personal financial interests.

3. Brad works as an addiction counselor at a public agency and also conducts a private addiction counseling practice. Discuss potential ethical issues related to the following practices. Brad: (a) refers clients he sees at the agency into his private practice, (b) conducts emergency appointments with his private clients at the agency office, (c) sees some clients both at the agency and in his private practice, and (d) uses the agency reception services to receive calls to reschedule private practice appointments.

4. While being interviewed for a live television program, you are asked to comment on a subject about which you have very strong opinions, but about which you have neither direct experience nor any research-based knowledge. How do you respond to the question?

5. Many states legally allow minors to provide informed consent for entry into addiction treatment. Such legal permission does not mean that the universal application of this permission is ethical. What procedures could you use to help ensure that a minor is competent to provide informed consent?

6. Two weeks ago, a co-worker left your agency to assume another professional position, but, before leaving, transferred a client to you. Today, the co-worker stopped by to say hello to everyone and asks you, "How's Joe?" (the client). How do you respond?

7. A large and exotic-looking client approaches you in a local shopping mall, gives you a bear hug, and expresses his delight at seeing you. After this brief encounter, one of your family members, witnessing this interesting interaction, inevitably asks, "Who was that?" How do you respond?

8. For purposes of agency billing, you have been asked by a supervisor to sign off on time worked that far exceeds the actual hours. When you object to this, the supervisor explains that this billing is necessary to keep the agency funded and is crucial to continued services to clients. Describe how the following universal ethical values would or would not apply to this situation: obedience, conscientious refusal, honesty, loyalty, self-interest?

9. A client you have just interviewed reports having been sexually exploited by a very prominent local therapist over the course of the past year of treatment. What is your response to this client's disclosure? To whom, if anyone, do you report this allegation? Do you have any responsibility to the person about whom the allegation has been made? What do you say three weeks later when another professional coincidentally asks for your opinion of this particular therapist?

10. You are extremely attracted to a clinical intern that you supervise. Given the inequality of power, would pursuing this relationship at this time be a breach of ethics even if the intern reciprocated your feelings and wished to pursue a relationship? What is the difference between the definition of sexual harassment (which emphasizes unwanted sexual advances) and abuse of power (which includes the manipulation of personal vulnerability for sexual gain)?

ACKNOWLEDGMENT

I would like to acknowledge Michael Wagner, one of the leading ethics trainers in the addictions field, for his helpful review of an early draft of this chapter.

SUGGESTED FURTHER READING

Barker, M. (1996). The ethical dilemma of the two-hatter. *The Counselor, 14*(3), 15–16.

  Highly recommended for counselors in recovery.

Brooks, M. K. (1997). Ethical and legal aspects of confidentiality. In J. H. Lowinson, P. Ruiz, R. B. Millman, & J. G. Langrod (Eds.), *Substance abuse: A comprehensive textbook* (3rd ed., pp. 884–899). Baltimore, MD: Williams and Wilkins.

  A good primer on confidentiality issues.

Chapman, C. (1997). Dual relationships in substance abuse treatment: Ethical implications. *Alcoholism Treatment Quarterly, 15*(2), 73–79.

  Well-written, insightful article.

Chapman, C. (2000). Ethical issues in the use of self-disclosure for substance abuse professionals. *Counselor, 18*(1): 18–22.

  Should be a handout in every addiction studies program.

Imhof, J. (1991). Countertransference issues in alcoholism and drug addiction. *Psychiatric Annals, 21*(5), 292–306.

  An exploration of how our own feelings toward clients can interfere with effective counseling.

Keith-Spiegel, P., & Koocher, G. (1985). *Ethics in psychology*. NY: Random House.

  An excellent discussion of whistle blowing.

VandeCreek, L., & Knapp, S. (1989). *Tarasoff and beyond: Legal and clinical considerations in the treatment of life-endangering patients*. Sarasota, FL: Professional Resource Exchange, Inc.

  One of the best books on legal and ethical issues involving duty to warn.

White, W., & Popovits, R. (2001). *Critical incidents: Ethical issues in the prevention and treatment of addiction*. Bloomington, IL: Chestnut Health Systems.

  More than two hundred ethical case studies, including discussions of most of those presented in this chapter.

REFERENCES

AA guidelines for AA members employed in the alcoholism field. (n.d.). New York: General Service Office.
Bissell, L., & Royce, J. (1987). *Ethics for addiction professionals*. Center City, MN: Hazelden.
ICRC. (1994). Prevention Ethics Standards. Falls Church, VA: International Certification & Reciprocity Consortium Alcohol and Other Drug Abuse, Inc.

ICRC. (1999). Code of ethics for clinical supervisors. Falls Church, VA: International Certification & Reciprocity Consortium Alcohol and Other Drug Abuse, Inc.

McCrady, B. S., & Bux, D. A., Jr. (1999). Ethical issues in informed consent with substance abusers. *Journal of Consulting and Clinical Psychology, 67*(2), 186–193.

Milgrom, J. H. (1992). *Boundaries in professional relationships: A training manual.* Minneapolis, MN: Walk-In Counseling Center.

(NAADAC): The Association for Addiction Professionals. (1994). Ethical standards of alcoholism and drug abuse counselors: Specific principles. *Counselor, 12*(3), 22–24.

(NAADAC): The Association for Addiction Professionals. (1995). Ethical standards for counselors by the NAADAC, The Association for Addiction Professionals. Retrieved May 6, 2004 from http://naadac.org/documents/display.php?DocumentID=11

St. Germaine, J. (1996). Dual relationships and certified alcohol and drug counselors: A national study of ethical beliefs and behaviors. *Alcoholism Treatment Quarterly, 14*(2), 29–44.

Thompson, A. (1990). *Guide to ethical practice in psychotherapy.* NY: Wiley.

Wagner, M. (2001). Practical application of ethical principles. *Counselor, 2*(6), 62–63.

White, W. (1995). A systems perspective on sexual exploitation of clients by professional helpers. In J. Gonsiorek (Ed.), *Breach of trust: Sexual exploitation by health care professionals and clergy* (pp. 176–192). Thousand Oaks, CA: Sage.

White, W. (1997). *The incestuous workplace: Stress and distress in the organizational family.* Center City, MN: Hazelden.

White, W., & Popovits, R. (2001). *Critical incidents: Ethical issues in the prevention and treatment of addiction.* Bloomington, IL: Chestnut Health Systems.

25

Professional Development

Michael J. Taleff
University of Hawai'i at Mānoa

TRUTH OR FICTION?

___ 1. A practice model of professional development is a recent phenomena and centers on obtaining internal knowledge.

___ 2. Research has established that the development of a professional relationship is the single most significant element affecting counseling outcomes.

___ 3. One building block needed for ongoing professional development involves continuing education.

___ 4. In traditional addiction professional development, passing some certification or licensing process comes before the educational requirements.

___ 5. These days the basic educational requirements to be an addiction counselor vary from an associate's degree to a graduate education.

___ 6. To become certified, an addiction counselor generally needs about three years of field experience.

___ 7. Among other things, professional organizations allow its members to come together to support a common philosophical belief.

___ 8. According to the addiction professional development hierarchy, a true expert is able to prove his or her competence via the case study or single system design.

___ 9. The single-system design requires a sophisticated knowledge of statistics.

___ 10. Years of counseling always amount to better counseling expertise.

___ 11. Because we all work in the same profession, a genuine antidote for burnout is a set of processes that work best for all addiction counselors.

___ 12. Reasonable freedom from impairments that would interfere with clinical performance or abilities that compromise counseling status are professional ethical requirements.

___ *13. An addiction counselor who has made it to the highest level of the addiction professional development hierarchy not only has empirical support for his or her competency, but gives back to the field in terms of publications and training.*

___ *14. The single-system research design is a reliable method to determine whether one is truly competent.*

___ *15. The addiction professional development hierarchy has six main levels.*

An estimated 80,000 addiction counselors practice in the United States (J. Ayers, personal communication, 2002). Most aspire for ***professional development***, a process whereby counselors craft themselves from one level of competency to progressive, advanced levels.

Why do this? Why would you spend a considerable amount of time and effort in professional development? The answer may seem obvious, but let's go ahead and spell it out anyway. For one, there certainly are the tangible rewards of advancement, pay raises, and even prestige. Perhaps more central to the professional development quest lies an answer within addiction science itself. For all its forms, addiction has an extraordinarily complex set of operating dynamics. Discoveries occur almost daily, producing new information begging to be understood. Shortly after a discovery comes some new treatment idea to engage the new finding. This discovery/application cycle requires the counselor to stay at the forefront of information and skills. The core reason, then, why you would spend time and energy in professional development is to provide your clients with the best possible treatment. The alternative is to stay comfortably tied to old ideas, treatments, or feel smugly above the need for improvement. Those opinions, in today's addiction field, are unacceptable and unethical.

1. The key reason for becoming as professionally developed as possible is to:
   a. provide substantial reasons for promotion.
   b. provide the best possible treatment for clients.
   c. provide a base of prestige for colleagues to model.
   d. provide a base of personal growth.

This chapter examines this frequently overlooked subject from:

1. A general professional development perspective
2. An addiction development slant
3. A more novel, scientific approach

GENERAL SCHEMAS OF PROFESSIONAL DEVELOPMENT

The concept of growing expertise dates from the time of Aristotle (O'Byrne, Clark, & Malakuti, 1997). Throughout history, professionals have journeyed from novice status to high levels of expertise. Some authors indicate that there is a dearth of literature on professional development (Vacc & Loesch, 2000). Other reviews indicate some twenty-two different professional development models now exist (Sakai & Nasserbakht, 1997). Many of these models adopt a linear approach, that is, a person grows from one stage (**novice**) to more advanced stage (**expert**) (Neufeldt, 1999; Sakai & Nasserbakht). The usual time thought to achieve these higher levels of development vary anywhere from ten to fifteen years (Neufeldt; Shovholt, Rønnestad, & Jennings, 1997).

2. How many years does it generally take an addiction counselor to become an expert?
   a. around five years
   b. between seven to ten years
   c. between ten and fifteen years
   d. between fifteen and twenty years

A detailed examination of these professional development theories and their criticisms are beyond the scope of this chapter. But suffice it to say, the theories abound, and all outline varying paths from no knowledge or skills to more (Sakai & Nasserbakht, 1997). The professionally developed counselor is said to be self-regulated, quick, able to attend to important problem elements, has access to large stores of knowledge, and processes client information differently than novices (Ericsson & Smith, 1991; O'Byrne & Goodyear, 1997). Moreover, he or she is able to comprehensively process the nuances of one's work. This form of scientific inquiry or searching is called *continuous professional reflection* (Shovholt et al., 1997).

Blocher (1987) notes that effective counselors are more aware of themselves in terms of personal characteristics. They develop a keen sensitivity to others and acquire patience and a cognitive complexity about the way they think.

Tied to professional reflection and personal understanding is a certain level of awareness that comes with experience. This idea is, in part, adapted from Troxell and Snyder (1976). They indicate that awareness is not the same as the simple accumulation of facts, but revolves around several ideas. For example:

- Assimilating ideas that contrast to a counselor's preferred way of making sense of the world. This assimilation allows for a much wider perspective on the dynamics of a client than would be allowed with a more closed set of ideas.
- Using this new awareness to focus on aspects of the world that are different. This awareness helps counselors differentiate one client from another and at the same time gain perspective—that is, see the evolution of addiction studies from the predominate ideas of yesterday's to today's ideas and then use that perspective in counseling.

3. Professional reflection and awareness is best characterized by:
   a. an accumulation of important facts.
   b. making sense of the world with an open perspective.
   c. knowing the dynamics of one's employment.
   d. considering the feelings of others.

General Training Schemas to Achieve Professional Development

Attaining an advanced status has historically been driven by two educational perspectives. First is the practice approach, which has been around for centuries. The practice approach is simply working as an apprentice. This model emphasizes learning by working with experts in the field. Here the trainee engages real life problems and is given support and direction (O'Byrne, Clark, & Malakuti, 1997). This translates into today's version of supervised practicums and internships.

4. Becoming an expert through the old apprenticeship method is based on today's counseling experience with:
   a. practicums and internships.
   b. postgraduate work.
   c. role playing.
   d. addiction technology transfer methods.

The second, more recent, training approach rests on obtaining internal knowledge. Today, that knowledge base comes mostly from colleges and universities. There is a large amount of information, facts, concepts, and principles to learn in the counseling business. To review all this material takes years. Further, the business of obtaining a foundation of internal knowledge is not limited to a specialty. There are always the college requirements of language, reasoning, multicultural perspectives, as well as the arts, humanities, and natural sciences.

Most colleges and universities incorporate both schemas (practice and internal knowledge) into their curriculum. Yet, this signifies only the beginning of professional development.

What happens in the years following graduation?

Ongoing Professional Development

Certainly professional development does not stop at graduation. The next tangible development process entails obtaining some kind of certification or license. This process evaluates, via a standardized examination, whether the counselor knows most of the information obtained from college and workshops (O'Byrne, Clark, & Malakuti, 1997). On top of that, most certification and licensing require a period of actual work in your specialty. Once all this is achieved, you are able to place some letters behind your name signifying that you have demonstrated some level of minimum **competence**. All forms of human science have their own version of this process.

5. Attaining a certification or license is intended to tell the public and clients that:
   a. the counselor has achieved some minimum level of competency.
   b. the counselor has achieved an expert level.
   c. the counselor is still working toward competency.
   d. the counselor has finished his or her basic educational requirements.

Following this are the usual continued development requirements of ongoing supervision, continuing educational requirements needed between recertification or relicensing periods, and personal development.

The individual development element has traditionally been based on models proposed by Erickson, Perry, and others (Neukrug, 1999). Professional development presupposes that counselors should also personally grow. For example, Erickson claims we develop through eight lifespan stages. We start with building trust versus mistrust and toward the end of our lives craft a sense of integrity versus despair (Erickson, 1968).

Certainly this is not the only development model given the context of culture, but the idea of growth remains the same. The counselor ought to develop in some personal manner that keeps pace with his or her professional side. Wisdom, perspective, and awareness are only some of the qualities to come from personal growth. Any counselor would value such qualities in his or her professional life.

Behind Professional Development Is the Driving Influence of Counseling Competence

A fundamental point intertwined with professional development and expertise is the concept of competence. But, let's define all these terms a bit more before moving on. Professional development needs to be seen as a process, course of action, or method. The aim of that process is to become an expert who possesses a certain set of measurable capabilities. Demonstrating these capabilities is *competence*. Thus, the more competence demonstrated, the higher the expertise and overall professional development. A measured level of competence then is a key factor in professional development. So:

The greater the $\longrightarrow$ The greater the $\longrightarrow$ The higher the professional
competence expertise development

6. Fill in the appropriate professional element, competency $\longrightarrow$ _____ $\longrightarrow$ professional development.
   a. published research record
   b. ongoing education
   c. supervision
   d. expert

What, then, are the parameters of competence? Well, the answer is not simple. There is a horde of standards outlined in many books and journal articles. For example, Boylan, Malley, and Scott (1995) outline ninety-eight different abilities in which counselors should clearly show some proficiency. These abilities range from personal characteristics such as having a people orientation, to communication proficiencies such as showing the ability to show positive regard and clarify the client's sentiments, to counseling skills such as keeping eye contact and presence, to personal characteristics such as maintaining structure within the counseling session, to adjunctive functions such as keeping good case notes and being organized, to ethical standards such as maintaining professionalism.

These proficiencies, in turn, are to be found in any number of licensing and certification examinations and within counseling and psychotherapy standards.

Having established a basic summary of professional development from the traditional counseling perspective let's move on to examine what constitutes professional development in the addictions field.

PROFESSIONAL DEVELOPMENT SPECIFIC TO THE ADDICTION FIELD

It is interesting that in the background research for this chapter few books spoke directly to the issue of professional development in the addiction counseling profession. Some would ask, does not Treatment Improvement Protocol (TAP) #21 (CSAT, 1998) address development? It certainly lists a set of demonstrated competencies, including a whole collection of knowledge, skills, and attitudes. It does not, however, address a true professional development model that utilizes described stages or levels. It was not designed to do so. This chapter makes that attempt.

Professional Identity

To establish a professional development model for addiction counselors, we have to start with some very basic issues. For example, when asked what it means to be a professionally developed addiction counselor, many addiction counselors can surely rattle off some basic educational requirements, some state or national certification process, longevity, and the never ending continuing credit hours needed to maintain their certification or license status.

Not a bad answer, but we need to get a little broader vision of addiction counseling. That means we need to ask, where in the greater scheme of things, is the addiction field, or the addiction counselor to be found?

Recall we are attempting to establish what is it means to be *competent*. This translates into the question of who are we? And, this little question raises some troublesome problems. The issue is that we as a field have never come to some nice, agreed-upon theoretical definition of who we are. We have loads of state and national certifying bodies and professional organizations, which often discuss what we do, but not often who we are. Who then are we?

For example, are we a specialty to be found within the general field of psychology (the study of human behavior)? Are we a freestanding profession? Maybe we are covered within social work. Maybe we are covered within general counseling. Perhaps, we are variants of rehabilitation. Anyway, you get the picture. We have no firm, agreed-upon identity at this time.

7. Which of the following best explains who we are as a profession?
   a. a subdivision of psychology
   b. indefinite at this time
   c. a subspecialty of social work
   d. a subspecialty of rehabilitation

Each of the abovementioned disciplines has its own version of what it means to be competent. They have developed a detailed set of mechanics of how to get there. Examine any professional social science organization and scrutinize what it means to develop professionally and you will generally find conditions that require:

- Certification and licensing requirements that entail test taking
- Fundamental education requirements
- Continuing education beyond the basic education level
- Experience in the field
- Adherence to existing ethical standards

8. Most forms of professional development require all but which of the following?
   a. foundational education
   b. years of experience
   c. a sponsored mentor
   d. adherence to a set of ethical standards

As stated, all forms of behavior/social sciences have their own version of professional development. By virtue of their own professional process, they are able to define themselves more clearly. Yet, they do so from a central idea. The addictions field, however, has yet to decide on a central defining concept.

This argument, interesting though it may be, is not the direct focus of our discussion. Despite not having a clear answer, we can proceed. Perhaps this short discussion will give some guidance for a future author to resolve this issue.

Addiction Professional Development

The standard addiction field professional schemas have organized around several themes not that much different from general counseling models. Let's examine each of these main schemas and move into new realms.

Beginning Counselors

First, all addiction counselors begin their professional life as novices. It goes without saying, that at this point these individuals display little in the way of standard competency practices, hence have little expertise, and are not long on professional development. At best, they have hopes and dreams, and some natural but unrefined abilities. For an addiction counselor novice, what does the road to competence look like?

9. Which best describes a novice?
    a. someone with little expertise and little professional development
    b. someone who has the beginning elements of an addiction counselor
    c. someone with a minimum of appropriate education
    d. someone who is able to sit for a certification examination

Educational Requirements

From a traditional addiction point of view, the second level, and arguably most important element to be an addiction counselor is **academic preparation**. This requirement has grown in terms of academic preparation in the past decade. Not too many years ago, little education save a high school degree, or personal recovery was needed to become a frontline addictions counselor (Stevens & Smith, 2001). With the advent of state and national certifying and licensing bodies, managed care, and the cries for accountability from consumers, the basic education requirements now range between an associate's degree to a graduate degree (Taleff, 2003). Whatever the degree, it is usually centered in a social or behavioral science department (psychology, counseling, social work, etc.). Because addiction counseling has become a major industry around the world, more and more colleges are now offering degrees with a set of courses or specific programs in addiction counseling (Taleff, 2003). This has led to some attempts to establish how future addiction counselors should be taught.

10. Most state certification/licensing boards require the basic educational requirements of:
     a. graduate degrees only.
     b. high school or equivalent degree.
     c. some college.
     d. between an associate's to graduate degree.

Educational Standards

What are the standards for a quality addictions education? As of today, no official curricula exist. However, Deitch and Carlton (1997), and Taleff and Swisher (1997) did set out models of addiction education. The Deitch and Carlton model revolves around a broad set of competencies that include: foundation knowledge; clinical evaluation; treatment planning; referral; case management; client, family, and community education; documentation; and professional and ethical responsibilities. The Taleff and Swisher model is specifically directed at graduate addiction education. It encompasses seven core functions that include: an understanding and application of research principles, high level assessment, matching treatments to clients, evaluating program effectiveness, supervision, leadership, and ethics.

11. Which of the following best describes the parameters of a basic addiction education?
    a. foundations, case management, counseling
    b. foundations, mathematics, written composition
    c. case management, humanities, biology
    d. counseling, ethics, medical aspects

Certification or Licensing

The third level of addiction professional development centers on **certification** or **licensing**—licensing being a state-sanctioned law that recognizes a particular professional, certification being a private version.

The idea behind a license, or more likely in the addictions field, a state or national certification, is that it provides some assurance to clients and others that counselors can competently deliver the services they offer (Moyers & Hester, 1999). The licensing or certification process usually revolves around knowledge, skills, and attitudes of certain core counseling areas. The latest of these proposals is called TAP # 21 (Center for Substance Abuse Treatment, 1998).

12. The main idea behind certification/licensing is:
    a. to ensure payment to managed care.
    b. to assure clients and others that counselors are competent to deliver the services they offer.
    c. to bring counselors together who have the same concerns and philosophy of their field.
    d. to help improve the standards of addiction counselors.

Each state has its own version of either a certified addictions credential or a state-sanctioned license. Moreover, there are a number of national certifying bodies, which offer addiction certificates for some specialization. Those specialized positions include counselors, physicians, social workers, and psychologists (Moyers & Hester, 1999).

The issues that make certification and licensing third on the professional development hierarchy are those of experience and the ability to pass a comprehensive test. These requirements generally follow the basic education (second) level.

Many addiction certifying bodies presently have a standard of around three years of full-time working experience before you are permitted to take the state or national certifying exam (see next chapter). Some states require more or less years of experience, but once these years are accumulated, you are then eligible to sit for a test.

13. The general number of years required by most state certification boards is around:
    a. one year
    b. two years
    c. three years
    d. four years

To pass the test, and finally achieve the certification or license status, you must demonstrate a minimum knowledge of:

- General principles
- Assessment/evaluation
- Treatment planning
- Referral
- Counseling
- Record keeping
- Ethics

14. To pass most state addiction certification examinations you must demonstrate a minimum base knowledge of:
    a. general principles, assessment, treatment planning.
    b. general principles, pharmacology, psychology.
    c. assessment, mental status examination, test construction.
    d. treatment planning, problem statements, toll/care statements.

Ethics

The ethics of addiction counseling is covered extensively in the preceding chapter, so we will say just a few words about this important issue and its relation to professional development. Essentially, the professional developmental ethical focus is directed toward ensuring that the addiction counselor is reasonably ready and able to do the job (Myers & Salt, 2000). Competency in this realm includes:

- Reasonable freedom from *impairments* that would interfere with clinical performance that would compromise counseling status (e.g., counselor psychiatric infirmities, relapse from a previous addiction, neurological problems).
- Being reasonably *prepared* to handle the multiple issues that people with an addiction face. (Preparedness is most often directed at educational competence.)
- Acting in a *responsible* manner that would otherwise compromise the health and well-being of people with dependency problems. Such issues are generally covered quite well in state or national certification requirements.

15. In terms of professional development, the ethical focus is on ensuring that the addiction counselor is reasonably ready and able to do the job. This translates into:
    a. reasonable freedom from debt.
    b. reasonable freedom from a criminal record.
    c. reasonable freedom from religious/political bias.
    d. reasonable freedom from impairments.

Other Elements Found in Addiction Counseling Professional Development

This three-tiered (novice, basic education, certification/licensing) process constitutes what many consider the manner by which addiction professionals arrive at some minimum standard of competency. Yet, other professional development elements continue in tandem with these stages. They generally revolve around a few other conditions. They include:

1. Ongoing education
2. Joining relevant professional organizations
3. Collaboration with other professionals and programs
4. Research utilization

16. Continuing professional development is best described as:
    a. the refinement of a career goal.
    b. ongoing education and belonging to the appropriate organizations.
    c. maintaining the basic knowledge found in foundational training.
    d. maintaining minimum competencies.

Ongoing Education

It goes without saying that the education one receives in college will soon become obsolete. Addiction research is progressively uncovering more data about the dynamics of addiction. With these discoveries comes more clarity about addiction and not far behind are better treatments to offer our clients.

In order to stay abreast of such vital information, the addiction counselor's obligation is to continual education. This generally consists of attending quality (empirically based) conferences, participating in workshops, and completing additional academic coursework. All this training can be delivered in person, online, or via teleconferencing. Other methods of staying current with new addiction material include reading journals, quality based magazines, and newsletters (Myers & Salt, 2000).

17. A good method to stay current with the discoveries made in the addiction field is to:
    a. read the latest pop psychology books.
    b. read the empirically based journals.
    c. read any online site.
    d. read and review those books you like.

Affiliations With Professional Organizations and Agencies

Addiction counselors join germane professional organizations as part of the traditional professional development process. They do it for a number of reasons (see Neukrug, 1999). They including:

- To fellowship and support a common philosophical belief
- To take advantage of special membership benefits such as having access to professional journals and newsletters that discuss relevant issues
- To provide avenues for contacts, networking, and mentoring
- To provide access to malpractice insurance

- To provide a code of ethics and practice standards
- To provide employment information
- To protect the interests of the organization and members through hired lobbyists

18. One main reason to join appropriate professional organizations is:
    a. to talk to people who understand you.
    b. to maintain one's prestige.
    c. to network in case you need a job someday.
    d. to come together, and support a common philosophical belief.

A partial list of organizations with direct addiction connections and some with addiction subdivisions include:

- The National Association of Drug and Alcohol Abuse Counselors (NAADAC)—http://www.naadac.org/
- The American Counseling Association (ACA)—http://www.counseling/org/
- The American Psychological Association (APA)—http://www.apa.org/
- The American Psychiatric Association (APA)—http://www.psych.org/
- The National Association of Social Workers (NASW)—http://naswdc.org/
- The American Association of Marriage and Family Therapists (AAMFT)—http://www.aampt.org/
- The American Psychiatric Nurses Association (APNA)—http://www.apna.org/
- The International Coalition of Addiction Studies Education (INCASE)—http://incase/org/

Collaboration With Other Health Service Professionals

An addiction professional not only knows his or her field, but also has a basic knowledge of what other allied professions do. Clients with addiction problems generally have other problems that require an array of services. These services may be provided by case managers, social service organizations, judicial affairs, employment services, mental health and medical services, and so forth. Knowing what these services and professionals really do tends to decrease misunderstandings about parallel professions. More important is that such knowledge can greatly assist addictions counselors in a referral process, as well as promote active, cordial relationships with those agencies.

19. The main reason to collaborate with other heath professionals is for:
    a. maintaining cordial relations.
    b. referral purposes.
    c. the many training functions that are offered.
    d. future contacts.

Understanding and Using Clinical Research

There certainly is a need to transfer addiction research to practice. Such practices should be at the forefront of any modern addiction counselor's collection of interventions. Often, however, they are not (CSAT, 2000).

Things change in the field. How treatment is practiced now will not be the same as it was practiced ten or even five years ago. Addiction counselors can certainly attend workshops and seminars to obtain the newest information about addiction dynamics and strategies. However, a regime of continuous personal reading, especially in empirical journals, is the mark of a developing counselor.

Reading these journals means that the developing addiction counselor has a fundamental comprehension of research, which includes research methods, designs, and statistics. Moreover, there is an appreciation of what research can and cannot do. With this appreciation comes the professional trait of actively searching and finding the latest research to put into practice. This constant reading is an integral part of any developing addiction professional, but is not often overtly stated.

20. Applying research to practice in the addiction field:
    a. rarely happens.
    b. is an established fact.
    c. is being held up by the lack of appropriate articles.
    d. is underfunded.

Counselor Burnout and Impairment

No discussion of professional development and addiction counseling would be complete without a word about **burnout**. Vacc and Loesch (2000) note that counseling is an emotionally taxing activity. It can extract heavy tolls from the counselor. This comes as no surprise to anyone working in the field. We commonly called it *burnout*.

General symptoms of burnout include such feelings as emotional lethargy, boredom, decreased motivation to do the job, less productivity, high turnover, and underutilization of talent and skills (Kottler & Hazler, 1997; Stevens & Smith, 2001). Specific stressors to the addiction field are the poignant cases of high mortality rates from drug cases, court-mandated cases, excessive paperwork, and little time to really spend with clients (Stevens & Smith, 2001).

All of this comes with the job. Yet, to gain some level of success despite these constant sources of stress requires a certain level of personal development. That means experts find things that, more often than not, work well for themselves. The skills generally accrue from trial and error until the expert comes upon a set of options that are just right for that individual.

Certainly, there is the usual set of suggestions a colleague or supervisor hands out. These include the ever-popular "take a vacation" "leave your work at the office" "set your boundaries" or "attend to your personal needs" All, however, are generic. If for example, you take a vacation the question needs to be asked, does it really relax and revitalize? And more importantly, does that feeling carry over to work for a sustained period of time? Counselors with expertise ask these types of questions. As a result, they find things that work for them.

The better-developed professionals find individual ways to revitalize the spirit. This ability renews energy and excitement about work and self. If something really works, it inflames the passions. These moments come from heart-to-heart discussions with trusted colleagues and friends, readings that offer something fresh and stimulating, or deep reflection. Whatever the process, it does one thing—it works.

21. Symptoms of burnout can include:
    a. boredom, lack of money, search for self.
    b. lethargy, boredom, decreased motivation.
    c. decreased motivation with periods of elation.
    d. lethargy, foolish laugher, disturbing dreams.

MOVING BEYOND THE TRADITIONAL

Everything stated thus far makes sense conceptually. But, there is scant data to support the notion that our present criteria of professional development actually improve the ways counselors do their job (Vacc & Loesch, 2000). In addition, the traditional and addiction approach to professional development has not been researched to demonstrate empirical links to better clinical outcomes. For example, psychology research has consistently noted no strong correlation between years of experience and better clinical results (Beutler, Machando, & Neufeldt, 1994; Dawes, 1994). Moreover, there are no strong correlations between higher levels of education and improved clinical results (Dawes). There is a lack of similar outcome data for the addiction field.

22. The correlation between years of counseling experience and better treatment outcome is:
    a. strong.
    b. strong in some cases, weak in others.
    c. weak in some cases, strong in others.
    d. weak.

REALLY DETERMINE IF YOU ARE PROFESSIONALLY COMPETENT: AN ALTERNATIVE PROCEDURE

The lack of evidence of how most of us strive to grow professionally leaves us with a predicament. If the traditional models are not fulfilling their goals, what do professional development models need to do in order to demonstrate stronger correlations or better, demonstrate a set of causal factors that affect clinical outcomes?

First, consider that professional development is a hypothetical concept. In other words, a theory based on concepts. As such, the traditional method of explaining and requiring professional development can turn into a problem. The problem is that traditional developmental models are in danger of becoming reified. That is, the concept turns to stone. Soon all sorts of tests and "evidence" are presented to support the validity of the concept. Then all sorts of supervision, workshops, and academic programs follow with methods that further reify the concept even more.

Blocher (1987) has been one of a small number of authors suggesting that professional development be more than merely passing tests and meeting minimal educational requirements. His option, however, is still a traditional one. It involves ongoing supervision, professional seminars, and lab experiences. Parallel with this line of thinking are the suggestions of McLeod (1994) who suggests professional development be augmented by having others rate sessions, utilizing client satisfaction surveys, and utilizing interviews by expert clinicians.

Second, and to keep matters in perspective, any concept, especially professional development, needs to be modified every now and then. The modifications will hopefully better fit what the concept is attempting to describe. As such, this chapter introduces a new wrinkle on professional development.

The initial step in this process is to operationalize key development concepts. And a good way to do that is to keep the emphasis of development on demonstration or simply doing a better job. That means asking questions like, "How do you best measure doing a better job?" "With more continuing credit hours?" (Not necessarily.) "More certified hours of training?" (Not necessarily.) "More experience?" (Perhaps.) How you measure your development is through individual outcome research. That is, you should be able to document through case studies that you gain some significant effect in the outcome of a client. And this process gets better with time. Demonstrate this ability consistently over time and you truly gain the title of expert and achieve a fifth level of professional development.

23. Professional development is:
    a. an established fact.
    b. in today's terms, something that is easily measured.
    c. a hypothetical concept.
    d. costs money.

24. Demonstrate _____ and do it consistently over time, and you truly gain the title of expert and achieve a fifth level of professional development.
    a. a personal reading base
    b. competency
    c. willingness to improve yourself
    d. accrued training hours

Qualities of an Effective Counselor

Certainly some evidence exists for what counselors should do to improve their outcomes. An array of research has revealed that the single most important factor in the counseling domain is the ability to create a very *positive working relationship* with clients (Hubble, Duncan, & Miller, 1999; Lambert, 1992; Sexton, Whiston, Bleuer, & Waltz, 1997). This type of relationship is built on empathy, caring, and kindness (Miller & Rollnick, 2002; Volpicelli & Szalavitz, 2000). Interestingly enough, very little emphasis is placed on this from professional development venues such as national examinations or continuing education. For our purposes, the ability to create a working relationship with a client needs to be at the forefront of supervision and education. This would take place in the second and third levels of traditional addiction professional development.

25. An array of research has revealed that the single most important factor in the counseling domain is the ability to:
    a. create a very positive working relationship with clients.
    b. match treatment to the client.
    c. appear confident.
    d. maintain a toolbox of counseling techniques.

Proving Competency

How is one to assess this level of competency? It is established through evaluation practices, specifically case studies and/or single-system designs (Bloom, Fischer, & Orme, 1999; Lundervold & Belwood, 2000). Such designs are not attached to any particular model. They are theory free and can be used with just about any intervention or clinician.

As an in-depth investigation of an individual, group, or system, *case studies* provide clinicians with intimate knowledge of a subject's feeling, cognitive, and behavioral states that can be subjected to some level of research rigor (Polit & Hungler, 1995).

At the most basic level, **single-system designs** involve an observation procedure of the client or system (e.g., family, group) before, during, and after the application of some therapeutic intervention. Certainly, this procedure requires a little more technical information than can be contained in a single chapter. Yet, for determining a base by which a clear level of competency can be assessed for the addiction counselor, this outline will do. The idea is to observe changes in an identified target (e.g., problem behavior, treatment objective).

The design has few statistical elements. First, specify the *target*. In addiction counseling, a fundamental component of an assessment is to determine the problem (target). The main question at this point is, "What are you out to change?" Second, measure the target via some *operational definition*. This definition will contain elements of an operational base (e.g., the *Diagnostic and Statistical Manual of Mental Disorder*, 4th ed.) intensity, duration, and so forth. Third, establish a *baseline phase* where no target intervention is applied, then establish a *intervention phase* in which a helping practice is introduced. This is a pivotal point in the single-system design. This evaluation procedure looks for change between the baseline measurement phase and the intervention phase as a key indicator of change. Fourth, to assess whether target change is directly related to an intervention, a time series or reversal design is applied (Ray, 2000). Simply, that as an intervention is applied the target behavior should change over a unit of time (e.g., days, weeks, months). Without the intervention, the target behavior whould return to its baseline measure. Fifth, whatever practice was used that had an affect on the target behavior, that practice should be plainly evident (Lundervold & Belwood, 2000). So, if the treatment results are positive, you should be able to clearly know what services were applied and under what conditions. In other words, there should be a clear link between the intervention and the target behavior. Sixth, and last, little analysis of the data is required. In the single-system design, this process relies on simple visual analysis of change on a plot chart. The plot will note change, deterioration, or no change. If a positive change occurs, the chart will note marked differences between baseline and intervention phases. Data from the single-system method also does not necessarily require the use of statistical techniques. And to date, no consensus exists as to an appropriate statistical formula to use with the single-case method (Lundervold & Belwood, 2000).

26. An easy nonrigorous statistical method that can adequately assess competency is called:
    a. regression analysis.
    b. multiple analysis of variance.
    c. analysis of variance in pretest, posttest design.
    d. single-system designs.

Advantages to this approach include the ability to generate scientifically based evidence that is directly relevant to counseling practice (Lundervold & Belwood, 2000). Advantages include developing the capacity to promote a broad band of research and scholarship within addiction counseling practice that in turn would shape emerging counselor skills. Another advantage would be the enhanced research understanding side-effect generated by single system practice.

27. A major advantage of using the single-system design in professional development:
    a. includes the ability to direct funding where it is most needed.
    b. includes the ability to generate scientifically based evidence showing that counseling practice is related to outcome.
    c. includes a baseline from which promotions can more readily made.
    d. includes a factor analysis of variables in the schema of addiction counseling to a broad understanding of general counseling.

Furthermore, once a case is determined to be correlated to a counselor's intervention, then a portfolio of similar cases can be collected. The portfolio could conceivably provide a longitudinal analysis of counselor's work, as well as a means of collecting, organizing, and displaying professional materials (James & Greenwalt, 2001). It would clearly demonstrate the evolution of competency from the novice stage to the more advanced. It would also clearly show which clients with which problems are treated successfully by which counselor. This portfolio can be more indicative of competency than the traditional resume or vita. This information can be applied to better promotion practices and managed care utilization.

Disadvantages certainly include the extra work (time consumption) this level of competency will require from an already busy schedule. This extra work could divert time away from needed attention to a troubled client (Bloom, Fischer, & Orme, 1999). There is no question that this method of determining level of competency requires time, but the effort will eventually give the counselor (and future clients) a big return.

Another possibility for clinical research lies in the accumulated results of many case study scores. A meta-analysis could add significantly to outcome studies for our field. Utilizing an ethnographic-inductive design, or the grounded approach an emerging picture of best practices, would develop around certain themes found in the many case studies (Hayes, 2000; Kellehear, 1993).

Years of accumulated national case histories and similar cases from around the globe should be able to clarify the dynamics of treatment outcomes. These findings would set empirical standards for future professional development models.

The Highly Developed Addiction Counselor

This is the last stage of the hierarchy. At this level, it is suggested that the truly developed addiction counselor is one who is not only able to supply levels of proof that he or she is competent, but who gives back to the field through the production of material. This production is best seen through publications and scientific output. Essentially, all those confirmed abilities found in level five need to be put into print or a dialectic format and shared with others. This sixth and final professional development level marks the pinnacle of expertise.

28. A counselor who arrives at the sixth level of the addiction professional hierarchy:
    a. gives back important information to the field via publications and educational venues.
    b. has established years of experience and hours of training.
    c. has established themselves in directorships of professional organizations.
    d. has authored books and articles based on personal knowledge and awareness of the field.

The overall hierarchy of addiction professional development appears in Table 25.1.

TABLE 25.1

The Addiction Professional Development Hierarchy

First Level	Novice (little or no relevant experience, education, or training)
Second Level	Academically prepared (has completed a basic addiction specialization or educational degree, ranging from an associate's level to a graduate degree)
Third Level	Achieves state/national certification/licensing
Fourth Level	Joins relevant professional organizations, continues training and education
Fifth Level	Establishes proof of competence
Sixth Level	Proof of competence is maintained, gives back to the field

29. The chief difference between a professional counselor at level three and level five is:
    a. the counselor at level five probably has years of experience.
    b. the counselor at level five has demonstrated competence.
    c. counselors at level five give back to the field.
    d. counselors at level three are just starting off in the field.

This hierarchy represents a tall order for addiction counselors who wish to be truly professionally developed. When a large number of addiction counselors attain the fifth level of this hierarchy, the field will be closer to answering the questions of who we are at our best, and what does a competent addiction counselor look like?

30. Moving the counselors or the addiction field through all six levels of the professional hierarchy will:
    a. be a relatively easy task.
    b. never occur.
    c. be a very tall order.
    d. become unimportant in lieu of managed care.

KEY TERMS

academic preparation: Completing a basic addiction specialization and higher education degree. This degree may range from an associate's level to a graduate degree.

addiction professional development hierarchy: A six-leveled hierarchy outlining the professional development of an addiction counselor from novice to one who can prove competence and give knowledge back to the field.

burnout: The emotionally taxing by-product of counseling. General symptoms include lethargy, boredom, decreased motivation to do the job, less productivity.

certification/licensing: Licensing is a state-sanctioned law that recognizes a particular professional, while certification is a private version. The idea behind a license or a state/national certification is that it provides some assurance to clients and others that counselors are competent to deliver the services they offer.

competence: Demonstrating a certain set of measurable capabilities.

expert: an individual who possesses a certain set of measurable capabilities—the aim of professional development.

novice: Individuals display little in the way of standard competency practices and hence have little expertise.

professional development: A process or method by which counselors craft themselves from what they are now into improved addiction professionals.

single-system design: A procedure involving observation of the client or system (e.g., family, group) before, during, and after the application of some therapeutic intervention.

DISCUSSION QUESTIONS

1. Are there core problems associated with a professional identity in the addiction field? Note them and what suggestions you would pose to help resolve these issues.
2. List the traditional elements for achieving counseling competency in the addiction field. How would you improve this process?
3. Speculate as to why it takes years to become an expert addiction counselor.
4. Based on the professional development information provided in this chapter, what courses you include in a higher education curriculum?
5. Expand on the possibilities that a meta-analysis of an accumulation of single case studies would provide the addiction field.
6. How would you describe professional addiction counseling development from a multi-cultural perspective?
7. Using any of the models mentioned in the chapter, how would you describe your own professional development to date. What concrete steps do you think you need to take to move on to different levels of your own professional development?
8. Explain the advantages of demonstrated competence via the single-system design to managed care workers, prospective clients, or referral sources.
9. How reasonable is it to expect most addiction counselors to gain the fourth and fifth level of the addiction professional development hierarchy?
10. If you were the chairperson of a national addictions organization, how would you modify the professional development requirements of your organization, if at all?

SUGGESTED FURTHER READING

Center for Substance Abuse Treatment (CSAT). (1998). *TAP #21, Addiction counseling competencies: The knowledge, skills, and attitudes of professional practice.* (DHHS Publication No. SMA 98-3171). Rockville, MD: Author.

A set of the latest and greatest addiction counselor competency standards. It is a must read.

Deitch, D. A., & Carlton, S. A. (1997). Education and training of clinical personnel. In J. H. Lowinson, P. Ruiz, R. B. Millman, & J. G. Langrod (Eds.), *Substance abuse: A comprehensive textbook* (3rd ed., pp. 801–811). Baltimore: Williams & Wilkins.

A worthwhile book chapter that outlines a core curriculum for addiction studies. The suggestions are basic to addiction education knowledge and professional development.

Shovholt, T. M., Rønnestad, M. H., & Jennings, L. (1997). Searching for expertise in counseling, psychotherapy, and professional psychology. *Educational Psychology Review, 9,* 361–369.

This is an interesting short piece on what constitutes an expert. The references alone are worth the read.

Taleff, M. J., & Swisher, J. D. (1997). The seven core functions of a master's degree level alcohol and other drug counselor. *Journal of Alcohol and Drug Education, 42,* 1–17.

A speculative description on what would constitute the core material of a graduate addiction education. The core functions are felt to be key components of a graduate addiction education and hence core knowledge of one's professional development.

REFERENCES

Ayers, J. (2002). Personal communication.

Beutler, L. E., Machando, P. P. P., & Neufeldt, S. A. (1994). Therapist variables. In A. E. Bergin & S. L. Garfield (Eds.), *Handbook of psychotherapy and behavior change* (4th ed., pp. 229–269). New York: Wiley.

Blocher, D. H. (1987). *The professional counselor*. New York: MacMillian.

Bloom, M., Fischer, J., & Orme, J. G. (1999). *Evaluation practice: Guidelines for the accountable professional*. Boston: Allyn & Bacon.

Boylan, J. C., Malley, P. B., & Scott, J. (1995). *Practicum and internship: Textbook for counseling and psychotherapy* (2nd ed.). Washington, DC: Accelerated Development.

Center for Substance Abuse Treatment (CSAT). (1998). *TAP #21, Addiction counseling competencies: The knowledge, skills, and attitudes of professional practice* (DHHS Publication No. SMA 98-3171). Rockville, MD: Author.

Center for Substance Abuse Treatment (CSAT). (2000). *Changing the conversation. Improving substance abuse treatment: The national treatment plan initiative.* (DHHS Publication No. SMA 00-34-79). Rockville, MD: Author.

Dawes, R. M. (1994). *House of cards: Psychology and psychotherapy built on myth*. New York: The Free Press.

Deitch, D. A., & Carlton, S. A. (1997). Education and training of clinical personnel. In J. H. Lowinson, P. Ruiz, R. B. Millman, & J. G. Langrod (Eds.), *Substance abuse: A comprehensive textbook* (3rd ed., pp. 801–811). Baltimore: Williams & Wilkins.

Erickson, E. H. (1968). *Identity: Youth and crises*. New York: Norton.

Ericsson, K. A., & Smith, J. (1991). *Toward a general theory of expertise*. Cambridge: Cambridge University Press.

Hayes, N. (2000). *Doing psychological research*. Buckingham, England: Open University Press.

Hubble, M. A., Duncan, B. L., & Miller, S. D. (1999). *The heart and soul of change: What works in therapy*. Washington, DC: American Psychological Association.

James, S. H., & Greenwalt, B. C. (2001). Documenting success and achievement: Presentation and working portfolios for counselors. *Journal of Counseling and Development, 79*, 161–165.

Kellehear, A. (1993). *The unobtrusive researcher: A guide to methods*. St. Leonards, Australia: Allen & Unwin.

Kottler, J. A., & Hazler, R. J. (1997*). What you never learned in graduate school: A survival guide for therapists*. New York: W.W. Norton & Co.

Lambert, M. J. (1992). Implications of outcome research for psychotherapy integration. In J. C. Norcross & M. R. Goldfried (Eds.), *Handbook of psychotherapy integration* (pp. 94–129). New York: Basic Books.

Lundervold, D. A., & Belwood, M. F. (2000). The best kept secret in counseling: Single-case ($N = 1$) experimental designs. *Journal of Counseling & Development, 78*, 92–102.

McLeod, J. (1994). Doing counseling research. London: Sage Publications.

Miller, W. R., & Rollnick, S. (2002). *Motivational interviewing: Preparing people for change*. New York: Guilford Press.

Moyers, T. B., & Hester, R. K. (1999). Credentialing, documentation, and evaluation. In B. S. McCrady & E. E. Epstein (Eds.), *Addiction: A comprehensive guidebook* (pp. 414–420). New York: Oxford University Press.

Myers, P., & Salt, N. R. (2000). *Becoming an addictions counselor: A comprehensive text*. Boston: Jones and Bartlett Publishers.

Neufeldt, S. A. (1999). *Supervision strategies for the first practicum*. Alexandra, VA: American Counseling Association.

Neukrug, E. (1999). *The world of the counselor: An introduction to the counseling profession*. Pacific Grove, CA: Brooks/Cole.

O'Byrne, K., Clark, R. E., & Malakuti, R. (1997). Expert and novice performance: Implications for clinical training. *Educational Psychology Review, 9*, 321–333.

O'Byrne, K. R., & Goodyear, R. K. (1997). Client assessment by novice and expert psychologists: A comparison of strategies. *Educational Psychology Review, 9*, 267–278.

Polit, D. F., & Hungler, B. P. (1995). *Nursing research: Principles and methods* (5th ed.). Philadelphia: J.B. Lippincott Company.

Ray, W. J. (2000). *Methods: Toward a science of behavior and experience* (6th ed.). Belmont, CA: Wadsworth/Thomson Learning.

Sakai, P. S., & Nasserbakht, A. (1997). Counselor development and cognitive science models of expertise: Possible convergences and divergences. *Educational Psychology Review, 9*, 353–359.

Sexton, T. L., Whiston, S. C., Bleuer, J. C., & Waltz, G. R. (1997). *Integrating outcome research into counseling practice and training*. Alexandria, VA: American Counseling Association.

Shovholt, T. M., Rønnestad, M. H., & Jennings, L. (1997). Searching for expertise in counseling, psychotherapy, and professional psychology. *Educational Psychology Review, 9*, 361–369.

Stevens, P., & Smith, R. L. (2001). *Substance abuse counseling: Theory and practice* (2nd ed.). Upper Saddle River, NJ: Merrill Prentice Hall.

Taleff, M. J., & Swisher, J. D. (1997). The seven core functions of a master's degree level alcohol and other drug counselor. *Journal of Alcohol and Drug Education, 42*, 1–17.

Taleff, M. J. (2003). The state of addictions education programs: Results of a cross-sectional survey. *Journal of Teaching in the Addictions*, (2), 1, 59–66.

Troxell, E. A., & Snyder, W. S. (1976). *Making sense of things: An invitation to philosophy*. New York: St. Martin's Press.

Vacc, N. A., & Loesch, L. C. (2000). *Professional orientation to counseling* (3rd ed.). Philadelphia, PA: Brunner-Routledge.

Volpicelli, J., & Szalavitz, M. (2000). *Recovery options: The complete guide*. New York: Wiley.

26

Professional Examinations in Alcohol and Other Drug Abuse Counseling

James P. Henderson
CASTLE Worldwide, Inc.

TRUTH OR FICTION?

___ 1. *The real value of certification or licensure for alcohol and other drug abuse professionals is to enhance the profession's respectability and provide a basis for third-party reimbursement.*

___ 2. *The public's interest in alcohol and other drug abuse counseling is broad ranging and affects the training and credentialing in the profession.*

___ 3. *Certification for alcohol and other drug abuse counselors is a more rigorous process than licensure or registration because it implies a higher standard.*

___ 4. *Using job analysis or a role delineation study to validate the content of certification and licensure tests is optional for the provider of the test, according to pertinent psychometric standards.*

___ 5. *Candidates for an examination should obtain information about test specifications because they are useful in studying for the test.*

___ 6. *It is valid for candidates who achieve extremely high scores on certification or licensure tests in alcohol and other drug abuse counseling to promote themselves as more highly qualified than others whose scores are lower.*

___ 7. *Multiple choice questions are written so that you can eliminate one option as obviously wrong.*

___ 8. *Questions that require application or analysis in order to derive the correct answer are about the same difficulty as questions that require only recall of factual information, maybe even easier.*

___ 9. *It is possible for the provider of an oral examination to address the issues of validity, reliability, and fairness satisfactorily, even though this testing format is scored using subjective models.*

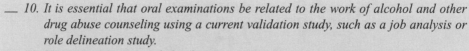

___ 10. It is essential that oral examinations be related to the work of alcohol and other drug abuse counseling using a current validation study, such as a job analysis or role delineation study.

___ 11. Using scoring criteria helps focus evaluators' attention during an oral examination to help ensure standardized scoring.

___ 12. Rules for most oral examinations prohibit you from adding clarification to a topic addressed in a previous question while answering a subsequent question.

___ 13. If you know one of the evaluators for your oral examination, you can request reassignment to a different team without having to give an explanation.

___ 14. It is the test provider's ethical responsibility to give detailed feedback about performance to candidates who fail a certification or licensure examination.

___ 15. A standardized examination measures all candidates for a license or certificate against a common benchmark.

Alcohol and other drug abuse (AODA) counselors, like you, play a critical role in the lives of their clients. Clients seek AODA counseling because they have experienced a complex problem with addiction—an often debilitating situation from which they may be unable to recover without competent assistance. Because addiction frequently affects clients' ability to live productively, interrupting careers and interfering with obligations to family and friends, the competent AODA counselor provides essential direction in their clients' efforts to recover. The counselor who lacks the necessary **competence,** despite the completion of training courses and supervised experience, might do more harm than good.

Competency assurance is the mission of **certification** and **licensure** programs in the United States and many other countries. In AODA counseling and other critical professions, practitioners such as yourself are asked to complete a required course of study to master professional knowledge and to demonstrate their ability to perform competently by passing a practice-related examination. Successful performance on such an examination qualifies you for professional licensure or certification, designations that clients and other stakeholders can rely on as evidence that the AODA counselor has met standards that are appropriate for the discipline and linked to a standard of competence. Certification and licensure examinations provide a common and standardized benchmark for evaluating counselor competence.

1. Which is the purpose of licensure and certification for alcohol and other drug abuse counselors?
   a. They satisfy the demands of third-party payers concerning reimbursement.
   b. They assist employers in hiring the best applicants from those who apply.
   c. They identify individuals who meet standards for professional competence.
   d. They ensure that AODA counseling is equal to other professions.

Many factors work together in determining how much individuals learn in training and supervised experience. Some training programs are better than others. Some people learn easily whereas others may have difficulty with professional subject matter. Supervised experience might or might not expose the novice counselor to a wide variety of situations and equip the counselor well to confront them. As a standardized benchmark, a certification or licensure examination is valuable because of the clear variation along these other dimensions. The **standardized examination** compares everyone against a consistent and well-defined standard so that key stakeholder groups, including clients and the people who support and depend on them, can be assured of the counselor's ability to provide competent and professional service.

2. Why is it valuable that alcohol and other drug abuse counselor licensure and certification agencies require examinations?
   a. They assist in identifying highly qualified AODA counselors.
   b. They hold all applicants to a uniform standard.
   c. They give useful feedback about the quality of training programs.
   d. They ask job-related information based on job analysis studies.

Credentialing structures in the United States address the matter of competency assurance through three traditional, distinct systems: licensure, certification, and **registration**. *Licensure* is the most restrictive of the three because individuals cannot practice their chosen professions (under practice acts) or identify themselves with the legally protected professional designation (under title acts) unless they meet specified criteria and pass the required examinations. Official governmental action, most frequently at the state level, establishes the licensure program as well as protection for the scope of practice and/or title in the jurisdiction. *Certification* typically is voluntary regulation, established by professions as the system of private law through which they police themselves. While there may not be a statutory mandate, often third-party payers and employers require professional certification. (This is currently the most common situation in AODA counseling, although there appears to be slow progress toward licensure.) *Registration* is a system under which individuals who practice in a particular profession simply list their names and contact information in a registry of practitioners, without having to meet eligibility criteria or pass an examination. Registration can be governmental or voluntary, but it offers little in the way of competency assurance because registration does not normally involve a professional examination. At the present time, no jurisdiction is known to require only registration for AODA counselors.

3. Which type of professional regulation determines which services alcohol and other drug abuse counselors can offer to the public?
   a. Practice Act
   b. Title Act
   c. Certification
   d. Regulation

In reality, however, credentialing structures do not always follow these definitions. The terms *licensure*, *certification*, and *registration* are indistinct in that a certified teacher and a registered nurse are actually licensed, a registered environmental professional is actually certified, and a certified financial planner is licensed to use the protected designation. In AODA counseling, the systems are varied and rather complex: some states license AODA counselors; some states require certification; and other states have no statutory credentialing requirement but state-funded counseling programs require private certification. In still other states, credentialing is voluntary but preferred by employers and third-party payers.

Although as the credentialing system for AODA counselors varies from state to state, there is substantial consistency in examination requirements. Whether statutory or voluntary, state credentialing systems for AODA counselors use one of two national examination programs, both of which feature multiple choice and oral components. The International Certification and Reciprocity Consortium/Alcohol and Other Drug Abuse (IC&RC), headquartered in Falls Church, VA, provides the written and oral examinations used in forty-one states, the District of Columbia, the three branches of the U.S. military, the Indian Health Service, Puerto Rico,

TABLE 26.1

Summary of Certifications in the Alcohol and Other Drug Abuse Professions

Organization	Program(s)	Education Requirements	Experience Requirements	Other Requirements	Types of Examination
American Academy of Health Care Providers in the Addictive Disorders	Certified Addiction Specialist (CAS)	Advanced or doctoral degree from an accredited health care training program	Three years of postgraduate, supervised experience providing direct health care services to those identified with an addictive disorder	Portfolio of clinical training with 120 hours of training in basic counseling skills and a minimum of 60 hours of training in each area of specialization; three professional recommendations	200-item multiple choice examination
	Gambling Specialist Certification (GSC)	Minimum 60 hours of pathological gambling–specific clinical training	Documented, clinically supervised experience in treating clients with a gambling addiction	Successful completion of all CAS minimum eligibility requirements, including passing the CAS examination	200-item multiple choice examination
American Society of Addiction Medicine	Certification in Addiction Medicine	Graduation from a medical school in the United States	One year of full-time involvement in the field of alcoholism and other drug dependencies; 50 hours of Category I credit toward the American Medical Association (AMA) Physician Recognition Award	License to practice medicine; three letters of recommendation; certification through a member board of the American Board of Medical Specialties	350–400-item multiple choice examination
CASTLE Worldwide, Inc.	Examination for Counselors of Problem Gamblers	Established by credentialing authority	Established by credentialing authority	Established by credentialing authority	150-item multiple choice examination
International Certification and Reciprocity Consortium	AODA Counselors	270 hours of AODA-specific training	6000 hours of supervised experience	300-hour practicum	150-item multiple choice examination; oral examination

Organization	Certification	Education/Training	Experience	Other requirement	Examination
	Advanced AODA Counselors	Master's or equivalent; 180 hours AODA-specific training	2000 hours of supervised experience	300-hour practicum	150-item multiple choice examination
	Alcohol, Tobacco, and Other Drug (ATOD) Prevention Specialists	100 contact hours in ATOD prevention	One year of experience in ATOD prevention		150-item multiple choice examination
	Clinical Supervisors	30 contact hours in clinical supervision	Five years as an AODA counselor and two years experience as a clinical supervisor	AODA counselor certification	150-item multiple choice examination
NAADAC: National Association for Addiction Professionals	Nationally Certified Addiction Counselor I	270 hours of AODA-specific training	6000 hours of supervised experience	Current state licensure or certification; references	250-item multiple choice examination
	Nationally Certified Addiction Counselor II	Bachelor's degree; 450 hours of AODA-specific training	10000 hours of supervised experience	Current state licensure or certification; references	250-item multiple choice examination
NAADAC & National Board for Certified Counselors (jointly sponsored)	Master Addiction Counselor	Master's degree in the healing arts or related field; 500 contact hours of AODA-specific training	6000 hours of experience (4000 of which must be post-master's)	References	200-item multiple choice examination
Substance Abuse Program Administrators Certification Commission	Substance Abuse Program Administrator	40 hours of substance abuse–related training	6000 hours of experience (4000 with bachelor's degree)		150-item multiple choice examination
	Substance Abuse Providers (as defined in 49 CFR 40.281)	Training as required under 49 CFR 40.281		Current state licensure or certification under NAADAC or IC&RC	150-item multiple choice examination

and other nations (Canada, Germany, Greece, Malaysia, Sweden, Israel). All IC&RC-member credentialing bodies require written and oral assessments of competence for reciprocal certification or licensure, which enables the credentialed individual to relocate within IC&RC jurisdictions without having to retest. The National Association of Alcoholism and Drug Abuse Counselors (NAADAC) Certification Commission, which is located in Alexandria, VA, provides the written and optional oral examination for fourteen states and the U.S. Bureau of Prisons. Credentialing programs supported by IC&RC (2001) and NAADAC (1986) examinations are recognized by the U.S. Department of Transportation as acceptable qualification for counselors wishing to work under its approved **Substance Abuse Provider** designation. The Substance Abuse Program Administrators Certification Commission (SAPACC) offers specific certification for service as a Substance Abuse Provider under 49 CFR 40.281.

Along with IC&RC and NAADAC, a variety of organizations sponsor examinations that are used for various professional certifications in addiction-related professions. These include advanced qualifications and specialty practice areas (e.g., counselors for individuals addicted to gambling, program administrators, clinical supervisors, forensic counselors, prevention specialists). Please refer to Table 26.1 for a summary of these programs. Professional certification and licensure programs in AODA counseling are designed to offer assurance to clients and other stakeholders that certified or licensed individuals have demonstrated competence in comparison to a reasonable standard. Whether the responsible jurisdiction requires licensure or certification, the examination requirement imposes a standard that is linked to the level of ability that corresponds with competent practice in this critical profession. For much of the following discussion, IC&RC is used as a case study because its examinations are the most widely used in the field—more than 6000 individuals take an IC&RC examination each year. IC&RC's strategies conform to accepted practice in the development of standardized examinations and represent a useful model. Other programs, however, follow similar practices in their test development activities.

WHAT IS INVOLVED IN THE DEVELOPMENT OF PROFESSIONAL AODA EXAMINATIONS?

Certification and licensure examinations required by states or other entities for practice in a professional discipline such as AODA counseling are considered *high-stakes examinations* because decisions based on an individual's score have serious consequences for both clients and practitioners. If an incompetent AODA counselor were to pass the examination and be credentialed, clients would receive inadequate service and run an unacceptable risk in their recovery. If a competent AODA counselor were denied a valuable credential, then that individual would unfairly be denied the right to serve clients.

4. What distinguishes a high-stakes examination from a low-stakes examination?
    a. the types of decisions that are based on scores
    b. the amount candidates spend on training for the profession
    c. how readily the public can be damaged from incompetence
    d. how tight security is before, during, and after test administrations

High-stakes examinations must meet certain standards to ensure high quality and fairness. These standards are defined in such documents as the *Joint Technical Standards for Educational and Psychological Tests* (AERA, APA, & NCME, 1999), the *Standards for Accreditation of Certification Programs* (National Commission for Certifying Agencies, 2002), and the

Guidelines for Employee Selection Criteria (United States Equal Employment Opportunity Commission, 1977, 1999). Key among the requirements of these standards are that professional examinations be related to practice and that procedures that ensure the measurement quality and fairness of the examinations be implemented in a manner that is faithful to accepted psychometric principles and practice.

Content Validation Study

The examinations used for the certification and licensure of AODA counselors must demonstrate *content validity,* or a demonstrable linkage to the practice of AODA counseling. This requirement is reasonable given that the individuals passing these tests will provide such services to the public. The requirement is all the more reasonable given that U.S. Supreme Court decisions mandate that professional examinations document job relatedness. Practice or **job analysis studies** supply the essential documentation for content validity.

5. What part does job analysis (role delineation study) play in the development of licensure and certification examinations?
   a. It identifies the characteristics of individuals who currently practice in the profession.
   b. It provides a well-researched basis for required entry-level training programs.
   c. It identifies the number of questions that a person must answer correctly to pass.
   d. It defines what content is appropriate to include in the examination.

Test Development and Scoring

IC&RC introduces new versions of its examinations each year. Its methodology is described in this section to illustrate the intense process that is employed in any high-quality credentialing examination program.

Questions for the multiple choice examinations and **prompts** for the oral examinations are written by qualified AODA counselors, and then reviewed, revised, and approved by other qualified AODA counselors. Questions and prompts are coded to knowledge and skill, or competencies, as defined in the validation study and required in **test specifications**. All questions are referenced to published documents (textbooks, monographs, etc.) in AODA counseling and reviewed for importance to practice, criticality (potential that harm might result if the counselor does not know the information), and relevance (frequency with which the information is used).

6. What is the reason that questions and prompts are written, revised, and validated by experts in alcohol and other drug abuse counseling?
   a. Experts use test development as an opportunity to build their professional reputations.
   b. Experts can articulate philosophies about addiction and counseling very clearly.
   c. Experts help to raise the status of the profession by adhering to new and high standards.
   d. Experts are knowledgeable about current trends in research, practice, and regulations.

7. Which of the following groups should be included in the test development and review teams in order for the test sponsor to demonstrate the strongest possible relationship to practice?
   a. researchers in alcohol and other drug abuse counseling
   b. professional alcohol and other drug abuse counselors
   c. alcohol and other drug abuse clinical supervisors
   d. administrators of alcohol and other drug abuse counseling programs

8. What type of reference is appropriate to verify the correctness of an examination question or problem?
   a. article in a research journal
   b. common knowledge among professionals
   c. widely distributed books
   d. outline for a training course

Experts in AODA counseling play the central role in preparing questions and prompts (items) for the examination. They write, review, edit, and validate them and make the key decisions concerning their use. Without the involvement of experts in AODA counseling, it would be difficult to defend the appropriateness and integrity of the questions. The process followed in making the selections should ensure that participants in test development are well qualified for this responsibility and representative of the profession of AODA counseling in a number of critical ways. At a minimum, considerations for the selection of panelists include region, culture, and practice setting, in addition to clearly defined professional qualifications.

MULTIPLE CHOICE EXAMINATIONS

The training of panelists for multiple choice examination development is based on the logic that the role of the questions is to distinguish between candidates who know the material being tested and those who do not. This expectation is consistent with the purpose of the test in identifying candidates who possess the required level of knowledge. Panelists are reminded that the examination provides an opportunity for the candidates to demonstrate their knowledge, and that accurate assessment of candidates' abilities dictates that the questions be clearly written, fair, and targeted at the appropriate level of difficulty. Training also addresses the process for test development and the strategies employed to organize the effort as well as the manner in which panelists are expected to work together.

9. Which statement characterizes the purpose of questions on multiple choice examinations used in licensure and certification for alcohol and other drug abuse counselors?
   a. They distinguish between candidates who know the material and those who do not.
   b. They separate the most competent candidates from those who are minimally competent.
   c. They challenge the test-wise candidates who know how to use item content to identify the answer.
   d. They promote Western thought and research on alcohol and other drug abuse counseling.

The vocabulary of multiple choice items is straightforward. The first part of an item is referred to as the *stem*, which presents the premise or the question. The stem should present enough information so that the candidate can clarify specifically what information, judgment, or ability is required to make a successful response. Stems might be direct questions or they might end as sentence fragments to be completed by the correct answer. The stem is followed by response options. The IC&RC multiple choice test provides five response options for each question while the NAADAC examination provides four. Only one of the response options is correct, and it is referred to as the *answer* or ***keyed response***. The remaining response options, which are incorrect, are called ***distracters*** or *foils*.

The language of multiple choice items must be clear and fair. That is, each question must state unambiguously what is being asked without any attempt to be tricky or unnecessarily difficult in any way. The terminology of the question, which may include abbreviations and terms of art that are key to accurate and efficient communication within the profession, must be widely understood by the intended candidate population and consistent in meaning throughout the profession. Sentence structure must be kept as simple as possible. These steps are important to the readability of the test, as it is important that the test measure knowledge of AODA counseling and not reading ability. (Of course, what is clear to one person may be unclear to another, and for this reason questions should be reviewed thoroughly and revised as necessary by groups of panelists who did not write them.)

Item writer training also focuses on ways to avoid unintended barriers to candidates who know the concept being tested. If a question is written well, knowledgeable candidates should be able to read and understand clearly what it is asking and then identify the correct answer among the response options presented. Unintended barriers confuse the knowledgeable candidate and may cause him or her to mark an incorrect option. They are, thus, a source of measurement error and should be edited out.

10. Why should the language of a multiple choice question be clear and fair?
   a. so that knowledgeable candidates can recognize the answer from the options presented
   b. so that unknowledgeable candidates can understand the question and try to identify the answer
   c. so that test-wise candidates cannot use the way the question is written to identify the answer
   d. so that the least-qualified candidates can answer questions about advanced topics

Just as unintended barriers create measurement error, unintended clues are unfair to clients and other stakeholders. Unintended clues assist candidates who do *not* know the concept evaluated in a question. Such a candidate should read a question and, depending on how unknowledgeable he or she may be, understand or not understand what is being asked. Ideally, the unknowledgeable candidate should be faced with equally attractive response options. Unintended clues are likely to change the probability of answering the question correctly. If unintended clues are not removed from an examination, skilled test takers who are not sufficiently knowledgeable in AODA counseling might answer enough questions to pass the test, a result that is clearly counter to the purpose of the assessment.

11. What role do unintended clues play in licensure and certification examinations?
   a. They increase the probability that unknowledgeable candidates will eliminate the answer.
   b. They increase the probability that unknowledgeable candidates will identify the answer.
   c. They increase the probability that candidates who know the answer will miss it.
   d. They increase the probability that candidates who know the answer will select it.

Another topic of considerable importance in panelist training concerns the **cognitive task** that candidates must perform in responding to test questions. To answer some questions on the examination the candidate is expected simply to *recall* information he or she has learned in courses and training programs or to demonstrate basic *understanding* of concepts. For other questions, the candidate must not only recall or understand information but use it to solve a problem posed by the question. The cognitive task required of candidates in these questions is *application* because candidates must apply their knowledge and use information presented to draw correct conclusions or implement sets of procedures in order to derive the correct answers. A third cognitive task that questions can require of candidates is *analysis*. In analysis questions, candidates have to break a problem into its components in order to formulate a diagnostic impression or identify the correct explanation for some malfunction. Including application and analysis questions on the test is appropriate in that AODA counselors must possess *and apply* a large body of information in their work with clients. Because competent counseling involves problem solving and trouble shooting, it is important to include these cognitive tasks in the professional examination.

12. What cognitive task does the following question require of candidates taking a multiple choice test?

Which individual named below is considered a developmental psychologist?
- Jean Kinney
- Erik Eriksen
- Carl Rogers
- B.F. Skinner

a. recall
b. understanding
c. application
d. analysis

13. What cognitive task does the following question require of candidates taking a multiple choice test?

Your work with the family of a client you have been counseling identifies that the thirteen-year-old daughter often helps around the house, keeps quiet during arguments, and relieves stress by engaging in sports activities when she is with friends. What role is she playing in family systems theory?
- scapegoat
- mascot
- lost child
- family hero

a. recall
b. understanding
c. application
d. analysis

14. What cognitive task does the following question require of candidates taking a multiple choice test?

The case record you have developed about your alcoholic client offers the following observations: avoids exposure to alcohol by staying away from certain friends and from bars, binges, occasionally blacks out, was passed over for a promotion at work, and his wife has moved out. How would you characterize the stage he is in?
- prodromal
- crucial
- chronic
- severe

a. recall
b. understanding
c. application
d. analysis

After the training is concluded, panelists work individually and in groups, depending on the test development **task**. They apply the rules and strategies to prepare and validate the questions and to select questions for the test in accordance with test specifications. The questions also undergo an intense grammatical and technical review. In this process, qualified editors analyze the questions for writing style and mechanics. The *technical study*, conducted by a *psychometrician* (a test development professional), is an analysis of the questions in light of the measurement qualities of effective multiple choice items. This analysis involves statistics describing the characteristics and performance of each question designed to discern the degree to which the question conforms to desirable patterns.

Taking the Multiple Choice Examination

After documenting eligibility to take the certification or licensure examination, candidates register for the test administration. Given the nature of certification and licensure decision making based on scores, test administration must be secure. Currently, all AODA counselor multiple choice examinations are administered in a paper-and-pencil format. There are rules for taking the test designed to ensure that responses are the result of the individual's own knowledge. It is critical to the validity of the score for the certification or licensure board to know that the individual taking the test is the person who will be granted the credential. It also is essential that the testing environment promote the individual's ability to exert his or her best effort on the test, and there are conditions concerning the time allowed for the test.

15. Why must you show identification for yourself when being admitted to take a licensure or certification examination?
    a. to ensure the address on file for you is correct
    b. to verify that the person taking the test is the one who applied for the credential
    c. to prevent unauthorized people from entering the testing room
    d. to match names on the roster to names on the test booklets

Rules serve two purposes: (a) to ensure that candidates work independently and without aid as they take the test, and (b) to create equal opportunity for all candidates to work to their best ability. No candidate is allowed to bring books or other reference materials into the room. This rule prohibits resources on AODA counseling, dictionaries, and even blank paper. Calculators (which are not required), computers, and electronic devices such as PDAs are also not permitted. Cellular telephones must be turned off. Purses and other handbags must be placed in a location to which candidates are not permitted access during the examination. Candidates are not permitted to talk during the examination, except to the proctors who are responsible for careful monitoring and supervision throughout the examination. It is important to understand that proctors answer only procedural questions and do not discuss test questions. During the examination, proctors circulate to monitor candidate behavior and to ensure the security of test materials.

16. Which policy during test administration ensures that candidates work independently, without aid, and with equal opportunity to perform to their best ability?
    a. supervision during the test
    b. accurate timing of the test
    c. prohibition on books and notes
    d. proctors answer only procedural questions

Security of the test materials is of paramount concern. Materials are counted multiple times, stored in a secure section of the testing room, and monitored carefully by test administration personnel. All test booklets are marked with an identification number. When test materials are distributed, candidates are directed to sign the cover. Candidates are not permitted to remove test materials from the room under any circumstance.

Candidates are provided with directions regarding test location and reporting time several weeks prior to the announced test date. Upon arrival, candidates go through a process of admission to the testing room(s). This involves checking personal identification with photographs and signatures to verify that the correct person will be answering the questions. Additionally, each candidate is required to show his or her admission letter (which contains an identifying number) as well as the address to which scores on the test will be mailed. As part of the identification check, candidates are asked to sign a roster of registered candidates. The final stage of the admissions process is a visual check by the testing staff to ensure that the candidate is not bringing prohibited materials into the testing room. At this point, directions are given to the candidate for entering the room and the supervision process begins.

When candidates enter the door of the testing room they are advised about the location in the room where they are to sit. Candidates are not permitted to sit next to other candidates and they especially are not allowed to sit near friends or acquaintances. Candidates who are observed engaging in inappropriate behavior at any time are addressed by the proctors and may be asked to leave the testing center. The test administration personnel then read directions, distribute test materials, answer general questions, and announce the beginning of the examination.

There is a specified time period during which candidates are permitted to work on the test—three-and-one-half hours for the IC&RC examination and four hours for the NAADAC examination. Once the time has begun, candidates may work at their own pace. Candidates who desire a break outside the testing room for any reason during the time period are required to surrender their test materials to the proctor. These candidates are permitted only in certain areas of the building where they are supervised; they are not permitted access to any materials. Upon readmission to the testing room, candidates can retrieve their test materials and resume work. It is critical to understand that the permitted time is unaffected by breaks taken by candidates, and they are not allowed to make up the time lost. When the specified time has transpired, testing personnel require all candidates to stop working. They then collect the test materials in an orderly and secure fashion and conduct a careful inventory to ensure an accurate accounting before dismissing candidates.

Candidates are invited to offer comments about test questions directly in the test booklets. Comments must be written during the time that candidates are permitted to work on the test, however, and candidates should not expect to receive an answer to their comments. All comments are reviewed as part of the scoring process.

17. What should you do if you have a comment about a test question?
   a. discuss the question with the proctor
   b. make a note on your answer sheet
   c. record a note on your test booklet
   d. write a note on your admission ticket

Scoring the Multiple-Choice Examination

During the test administration, candidates record their responses by marking the response option of their choice on an answer sheet. The answer sheets are then scanned for computerized scoring. Following checks on the accuracy of scanning, an initial *item analysis* occurs. Classical item analysis statistics describe the performance of the question and how it works to distinguish between knowledgeable and unknowledgeable AODA counselors. In general, it is anticipated that the greatest number of candidates will answer the question correctly—the **difficulty** of the question is determined as the percentage of candidates marking the right answer. It is also anticipated that a smaller number of candidates will mark each of the distracters (incorrect response options), and this also is described with percentages and distracter effectiveness statistics. Although there can be reasonable variation in the percentage of candidates answering a question correctly relative to distracters, a useful question must also follow the pattern that the group answering the question correctly is more knowledgeable than candidates answering incorrectly, as expressed in the total number of questions answered correctly on the test. This characteristic of performance for a question is called its *discrimination power*, in that it distinguishes well between knowledgeable and unknowledgeable individuals.

18. What information is given by the difficulty estimate for a test question?
    a. the percentage of candidates who answer the question correctly
    b. the degree to which incorrect responses attract unknowledgeable candidates
    c. the degree to which incorrect responses attract knowledgeable candidates
    d. the percentage of questions that candidates answered correctly

19. What is meant by the discriminating power of a test question?
    a. Candidates from ethnic populations answer the question incorrectly more often than general population.
    b. Candidates from the general population answer the questions incorrectly more often than those from ethnic populations.
    c. Unknowledgeable candidates tend to answer correctly whereas knowledgeable candidates tend to answer incorrectly.
    d. Knowledgeable candidates tend to answer correctly whereas unknowledgeable candidates tend to answer incorrectly.

20. Why are item analysis statistics useful during the scoring of a licensure or certification examination?
    a. They identify improvements to make in the wording of questions.
    b. They maximize the reliability of scores on the test.
    c. They select which questions to use again on future forms of the test.
    d. They validate that questions on the test are keyed correctly.

Item analysis information is useful in evaluating the correctness of the keyed response (*key verification*). Based on how candidates respond to a question, item analysis can reveal instances where it appears that a response option other than the correct might merit credit. In these rare instances, those involved in scoring the test work with experts in AODA counseling to review the statistics and evaluate what changes, if any, should be made in the scoring key.

Following key verification and final item analysis, other statistics are generated to describe the measurement quality of the test. Some statistics describe how candidates as a group perform as raw scores: the high score, low score, range of scores, average score, variance and standard deviation (which describe how scores are dispersed around the average—whether the score distribution is flat and wide or tall and thin). Other statistics describe measurement qualities: internal consistency **reliability** (the manner in which all questions contribute to the raw score), standard error of measurement (a description of the true score distribution), and decision consistency reliability (which estimates the degree to which candidates who are truly knowledgeable pass while unknowledgeable candidates fail).

21. What step is it essential to take when licensure and certification examinations are updated regularly with new versions?
    a. equate the forms
    b. revise the role delineation study
    c. publish a new study guide
    d. make a public announcement

Armed with this information, those responsible for scoring then take steps to equate the version administered to all other versions of the test. *Equating* as a statistical process is quite involved and a detailed explanation is well beyond the scope of this chapter; however, two sources of variability have to be accounted for in the equating process, regardless of the methods used. One is the difference in the overall ability of the different candidate populations. That is, the group of candidates taking the *anchor test* (the base test to which new versions are equated) might be more or less knowledgeable than the group taking the new version. The differences attributable to the groups will have an impact on the number of questions candidates answer correctly and must be accounted for in the equating study. The second source of variability is due to the fact that different questions are used on the anchor and new versions—and because they are different, they will vary the overall difficulty of the test. Equating and the scaling that results account for the differences in the two groups and determines the unique differences in the difficulty of the questions. Equating is an essential element of fairness, because candidates would otherwise be penalized for taking a harder version of the test whereas others would be rewarded for taking the easier version.

22. What are the principal sources of variance between versions of an examination that is used for licensure/certification?
    a. test dates and stakeholders
    b. candidates and questions
    c. policies and procedures
    d. stakeholders and eligibility criteria

It is only after all of these steps are completed that final statistical reports are prepared and score reports are issued. IC&RC scores are reported on a scale of 200 to 800 points, with the **criterion-referenced** passing standard anchored at 500. Score reports include the scaled score, pass/fail standing, and the percentage of questions answered correctly in each **domain** of the test.

THE ORAL EXAMINATIONS

AODA counselors use oral communication in their work. They also employ a wide range of professional skills that are critical to the therapeutic relationship and the development of, implementation of, and follow through on treatment plans. The purpose of the oral examination as a component of licensure and certification for AODA counselors is to assess whether the candidate's explanation of critical skills used in a real case demonstrates competence. As a performance examination, the development and scoring of the oral interview addresses both the issues of validity and reliability, but in ways that are quite different from the multiple choice examinations.

23. What is the primary justification for an oral examination for alcohol and other drug abuse counselors?
    a. The content tested seems to resemble steps in the counseling process.
    b. It has been an essential component of counselor credentialing for twenty-five years.
    c. Counselors interact with clients using spoken language.
    d. It is the best way to assess the quality of a counselor's educational background.

In 1979, IC&RC defined twelve **core functions** as the basis for the first generation of the Case Presentation Method (CPM) oral interview. The core functions identified the major phases of AODA counseling, beginning with the process of screening candidates for eligibility for treatment and ending with discharge. (When IC&RC completes updates to its **role delineation study** for AODA counselors, it also undertakes a review in which the core functions are linked to performance domains and tasks.) With prompts for each core function and a scoring guideline based on forty-six **global criteria**, the current oral interview is required in every member jurisdiction of IC&RC and a similar examination based on fourteen dimensions is required in a portion of the jurisdictions in which NAADAC's oral interview is employed. The IC&RC and NAADAC tests are similar as they interface with candidates but very different in the processes followed in validating the tests and scoring candidates' responses.

For IC&RC, some member boards require that candidates prepare and submit a written summary of an actual case in their own experience. When this is required, candidates must follow an outline of topics to address, and representatives of the IC&RC member board evaluate the written case along the required mechanical dimension. If the written case does not comply with the stated requirements, it is returned to the candidate for revision. If the written case is found to comply, then the candidate is informed of the time and place of the oral interview based on the case.

Whether or not the IC&RC member board requires the written case, all candidates for certification or licensure through an IC&RC member board are asked to report to the testing location, where they will be admitted to the test after showing a picture identification with signature and a second signature identification, as well as signing a roster. After other procedures required by the member board are satisfied, the candidate is greeted by a member of the testing team and rules are explained using a script, which ensures standardization in the type and quantity of information given to the candidate. The candidate then is ushered into the testing room where he or she is introduced to the team of three **evaluators**. The lead evaluator follows a script explaining the 45-minute examination and the responsibility of the candidate to manage time during his or her response to the prompts.

Taking the Oral Examination

The format of the IC&RC oral interview centers on twelve prompts, one for each core function. The prompts permit the candidate to address the manner in which pertinent skills were implemented in a case drawn from the candidate's experience. In addressing the prompts and core functions, candidates must explain how they employed key skills that work together to define the core function. Although some core functions are obviously more complex than others and might require relatively more time to explain, candidates should understand that, on average, they must complete their response for each in less than four minutes. Consequently, candidates should focus clearly on the points to address and provide sufficient detail to convince evaluators that they are capable of implementing the scoring criteria in a competent manner. The forty-six global criteria, weighted in accordance with the current role delineation study, provide the framework for scoring.

24. What should you emphasize in your responses to the prompts in the oral examinations for alcohol and other drug abuse counselors?
    a. your opinion about the client's prognosis
    b. how you implemented relevant counseling skill
    c. background information about the client
    d. community resources you drew upon on behalf of the client

Key in taking the examination is keeping the global criteria (or other scoring criteria) for each core function in mind, making sure to illustrate with examples how the core function and global criteria were implemented in the case being presented. If the core function was not relevant in the specific case, it is important for the candidate to say so and then describe how the core function *would have been implemented* in compliance with the global criteria. While that expectation may seem artificial, candidates must understand that they will not receive credit unless they satisfactorily address the global criteria. No credit can be awarded for a global criterion if a candidate fails to explain its competent implementation.

25. When taking the oral examination, what should you do if one or more of the scoring criteria do not apply to the case you are presenting?
    a. State that the criteria did not apply and move on to the next question.
    b. Address the criteria in a manner that makes it appear the criteria did apply.
    c. Explain that the criteria did not apply and ask for a different question.
    d. Say that the criteria did not apply and give a general explanation of them.

The oral nature of the examination may provoke anxiety for candidates and the anxiety may cause candidates to lose their focus or forget to explain everything they wish. It is only natural to be anxious during an oral examination and candidates should not worry that the observation of nervous behavior will in and of itself affect their score. Although the evaluator's task is easier when candidate responses are well organized and presented sequentially, there is nothing in the rules to prevent candidates from revisiting topics that they have previously addressed to elaborate further or offer corrections. Doing so may improve one's score. In this instance, it is beneficial to alert the evaluators that earlier topics are about to be revisited, and then, when finished with the additional elaboration, to inform the evaluators when returning to the current topics.

26. What should you do if during your response to one of the last problems on the oral examination you remember something you intended to say in an earlier problem that you have already finished?
    a. Tell the evaluators which problem you have in mind and give your complete answer to that prompt over again, making sure to include the explanation you need to add.
    b. Recognize that the impact of a portion of one response will play a minimal influence in your pass/fail standing and proceed without giving the additional explanation.
    c. Ask for additional time from the evaluators and tell them you want to go back to the problem to give a more complete explanation.
    d. Give the information after alerting the evaluators that it applies to the earlier problem and then proceed where you left off.

Scoring the Oral Examination

Evaluators record their ratings (yes or no) independently for each global criterion during the live oral interview. In doing so, they use the oral response as a source of data, concentrating on what is actually said (not implied) to determine if the response demonstrates competence with respect to the criteria. Evaluators do not compare ratings or consult with each other in any way. This process, a very complex task, requires a great deal of concentration. Consequently, many candidates will observe that evaluators do not make frequent eye contact with them and they do not attend to the usual courtesies of social interaction. It is not their role during the examination to interact in a friendly manner with candidates, but to ensure that the ratings constitute an accurate accounting of the candidate's response. Interaction with evaluators should be professional, but candidates should not expect it to be affable.

27. What demeanor should you expect from evaluators for the oral examination?
    a. stern
    b. friendly
    c. relaxed
    d. neutral

Even in highly populated jurisdictions, it is possible that candidates will recognize evaluators who are assigned to their oral interviews. In such an event, evaluators are expected to inform the test site administrator and request reassignment without explanation. It is possible, however, that evaluators may not recognize such situations. Perhaps the evaluators do not recognize the candidate or recall the earlier acquaintance. Then, it is the privilege of the candidate to request assignment to different evaluators. Candidates' requests for reassignment are honored without question.

Each global criterion for the IC&RC oral examination is linked to the current role delineation study and weighted in accordance with importance, criticality, and frequency ratings collected in that study. The **weighting** allocated to each criterion is added to the total number of points awarded by each evaluator for a candidate, and totals for each of the three evaluators are averaged to derive candidate scores. The score that candidates must achieve in order to pass the test is determined using criterion-referenced methods that link the required score to minimally acceptable competence.

28. What reason is there for giving different weight to the scoring criteria for the oral examination?
    a. The response time needed for some criteria exceeds the time required for others.
    b. Role delineation study data indicate that some criteria are more important than others.
    c. Some elements of counseling take a longer time to implement than others.
    d. Item analysis studies indicate that candidates find some criteria to be more difficult than others.

IC&RC has conducted studies to determine the reliability of scores on the oral examination. Of primary interest is the degree to which the three evaluators agree with each other (all three recording *yes* or all three recording *no* for the global criteria). A high level of evaluator agreement—*inter-rater reliability*—supports the argument that scores are accurate depictions of candidate competence. All studies conducted to date indicate inter-rater reliability statistics that exceed psychometric requirements. Candidates wishing to appeal their scores can do so if they believe there have been violations of required procedure, such as noise or incorrect timing of the examination. Simply failing the examination is not seen as acceptable grounds for appeal. Candidates may retake the examination after a waiting period designated by that member board jurisdiction.

Scoring procedures for the IC&RC oral examination include statistical feedback that member boards give to evaluators after scoring for the purpose of improving their scoring abilities. This feedback describes patterns that might be observed in scoring, such as whether the evaluator tends to score relatively harshly or generously (in comparison with the other evaluators). When this type of information is made available to evaluators, they can assess the manner in which they implement prescribed expectations for evaluating responses and make informed adjustments. This information also can be used by the licensure or certification board to identify evaluators who require additional training and others who should no longer be permitted to evaluate candidate responses.

Evaluator Training

When candidates take the multiple choice examination, they read the various questions, decide on the correct responses, and mark them for objective scoring. *Objective scoring* means that there is no human judgment involved in determining candidate scores—responses selected by the candidate are read by a computer, compared with a scoring key, and counted as either correct or incorrect. However, the oral examination follows a different scoring model, one that involves the subjective judgment of experts in AODA counseling in a process whereby assessments of each candidate's responses are made and recorded. Because of the professional judgment exercised in scoring the oral examinations, evaluator training is critical.

29. What is the compelling reason that evaluators for an oral examination should be thoroughly trained?
    a. to ensure that the rules for the examination are followed precisely
    b. to enhance the probability that scoring adheres to established standards
    c. to improve their knowledge of alcohol and other drug abuse counseling
    d. to reduce the likelihood that candidates will experience test anxiety

A final important element of IC&RC evaluator training is the requirement for periodic retraining. Evaluators undertake *recalibration training* about every six months, during which they view, rate, and discuss video segments and demonstrate a satisfactory level of agreement with criterion ratings set for the segments. This process helps to ensure accuracy in the scoring process.

> 30. What steps help to ensure that evaluators maintain current knowledge of the oral examination process?
>   a. newsletters
>   b. telephone conversations
>   c. periodic retraining
>   d. postexamination evaluations

Professional examinations serve a serious purpose, identifying for the public which individuals possess sufficient knowledge and skill to provide effective addiction counseling services. For this purpose, the certification decisions based on pass/fail performance on the tests are considered high stakes. If you are preparing for professional licensure or certification, then you will find it helpful to be aware of the procedures for developing, administering, and scoring the examination(s) to be taken because these procedures are essential to the tests' quality and fairness.

KEY TERMS

certification: A professional credential awarded by a private organization, often a freestanding nonprofit organization whose mission is specifically certification or a professional association, but also may be a for-profit corporation.

cognitive task: The type of thought that an individual engages in to respond to information given or asked about in an examination. A variety of classification systems, or taxonomies, exist to describe different cognitive tasks, the most popular of which is Bloom's.

competence: The ability to perform in a field or discipline at a level consistent with accepted practice and research.

core function: One of twelve major activities that constitute the basic services provided to alcohol and other drug abuse clients.

criterion-reference: The type of standard set for certification, licensure examinations, and for a number of other types of tests. Criterion-referenced standards impose the same standard of difficulty for all candidates and demonstrate a linkage to protection of consumers.

difficulty: The percentage of candidates who answer a test question correctly, or the probability of answering a question correctly.

discrimination power: The ability of a test question to distinguish effectively between knowledgeable and unknowledgeable candidates. It is frequently estimated as a point-biserial correlation.

distracter: In a multiple choice question, an incorrect response option.

domain: A large category of content in an examination. For professional examinations, domains are defined as part of the role delineation study or job analysis.

equating: A process through which one version, or form, of an examination is made comparable in content and difficulty to other forms of the same examination.

evaluator: A person who has been trained to score an oral examination and who has been found to agree with criterion ratings.

global criteria: The elements that standardize the analytical scoring model for an oral examination. Global criteria form the focus of evaluators' attention and scoring during the oral examination.

item analysis: The process of evaluating the function of a test question statistically. Item analysis statistics normally include estimation of difficulty, discrimination, and different ways of looking at distracter effectiveness.

job analysis study: A research project in which the content for a licensure or certification examination is defined and validated. *Validation* involves collecting data from a scientifically determined sample of the certified population. Validation data normally lead to specifications for the test.

keyed response: The correct answer to a test question.

licensure: The regulatory means through which states protect the public by establishing standards and examination procedures for individuals wishing to offer professional services in the state.

prompts: Questions that direct candidates in constructing and delivering their response in an oral examination.

psychometrics: The science of measuring human capabilities. Psychometrics helps to ensure that the inferences based on scores made by candidates on an examination are valid and reliable.

registration: The process through which individuals offering services to the public in a particular occupation, profession, or trade list their names with a registry, such as may be required by a state or offered by a private entity.

reliability: The consistency in scores obtained using a measure, like a test. There are different ways of thinking about reliability, depending on the purpose of the assessment. For certification and licensure examinations, reliability analysis typically involves internal consistency, standard error of measurement, and pass/fail consistency.

role delineation study: A type of job analysis normally used when the work is defined in terms of responsibilities and there is not a definite product or outcome of the work.

standardized examination: A test, often used for licensure or certification, that is developed according to pertinent standards to provide a consistent examination and test administration experience for all candidates: standardization involves comparability in content, comparability in difficulty (equating), criterion-referenced passing point determination, and consistent test administration (e.g., time permitted, environmental conditions).

stem: The part of a multiple choice question that presents information to the candidate along with the question to be answered.

substance abuse provider: A certified or licensed professional as defined under U.S. Department of Transportation regulations recorded in 49 CFR 40.281.

task: A statement of professional responsibility that is more finite and specific than a domain statement, but more general than a knowledge or skill statement.

test specifications: A plan for an examination, normally based on data collected during the validation study phase of a job analysis or role delineation study. Test specifications may be thought of as a blueprint for the construction of the examination, detailing the purpose of the examination, the number and type of items to be presented, and the appropriate weighting structure for scoring the examination.

validity: The degree to which an examination serves the purpose for which it is intended. The purpose of certification and licensure examinations is to make decisions about which individuals possess the required level of competence; this purpose determines the types of validation that are appropriate. For instance, content validity requires job relatedness.

weighting: The system of points to be awarded for successful performance, or in some instances partially acceptable performance, for items on a test. For most multiple choice tests, the weighting structure gives equal value to each question. For oral examinations, each scoring criterion may be weighted differently, based on test specifications.

DISCUSSION QUESTIONS

1. Who are the stakeholder groups in the delivery of alcohol and other drug abuse counseling services? What interests does each stakeholder group have? Which stakeholder group has the most important interests?
2. If licensure for alcohol and other drug abuse counselors restricts who can practice and what services fall within the scope of the profession, why do counselor associations promote it?
3. Are the training and experience standards for alcohol and other drug abuse counselors commensurate with the level of competence required for safe and effective service?
4. Many professions have only one national examination that is used for licensure and certification. Why does alcohol and drug abuse counseling have more than one? Is having more than one examination program good or bad? What reasons do you have for your position?
5. Role delineation studies and job analysis studies provide the basis for licensure and certification examinations in alcohol and other drug abuse counseling. Are they the best way to define content for the tests? What other source can you suggest that would be defensible for the examinations for this profession, and what reason(s) support your response?
6. In taking multiple-choice tests, candidates work independently to understand the questions and to select the best answer. Does this format of examination affect the performance of ethnic groups on the test? If not, why not? If so, what suggestions do you think would address the issue and still satisfy the objectives for licensure and certification?
7. What variables influence how people perform on standardized examinations? Should there be different passing standards for people from different backgrounds? Why or why not?
8. Oral examinations in alcohol and other drug abuse counseling are scored using subjective procedures. What threats does such a model introduce to the validity of scores and licensure and certification decision making?
9. Why have certification programs for advanced- or masters-level alcohol and other drug abuse counselors developed? Are these programs helpful or harmful? To whom? How?
10. The public protection mission of certification and licensure programs drives examination policy and procedure. What other considerations should licensure and certification boards take into account when setting policy and procedure? Why?

SUGGESTED FURTHER READING

National Organization for Competency Assurance. (1995). *Certification: A NOCA handbook*. Washington, DC: Author.

For the reader interested in the various steps in developing certification examinations.

National Commission for Certifying Agencies. (2002). *Standards for accreditation of certification programs*. Washington, DC: National Organization for Competency Assurance.

Standards pertaining to certification examinations.

International Certification and Reciprocity Consortium (IC & RC). (2003). *AODA counselor study guide*. Falls Church, VA: Author.

Information about the examinations of the International Certification and Reciprocity Consortium.

National Association of Alcoholism and Drug Abuse Counselors (NAADAC). (2003). *Basics of addiction counseling desk reference and study guide*. Alexandria, VA: Author.

Information about the examinations of the National Association of Alcoholism and Drug Abuse Counselors examinations.

REFERENCES

American Educational Research Association (AERA), American Psychological Association (APA), and National Council on Measurement in Education (NCME). (1999). *Joint technical standards for educational and psychological tests*. Washington, DC: American Educational Research Association.

International Certification and Reciprocity Consortium/Alcohol and Other Drug Abuse (IC&RC). (2001). *Role delineation study for alcohol and other drug abuse counselors*. Falls Church, VA: Author.

National Association of Alcoholism and Drug Abuse Counselors (NAADAC). (1986). *Competencies of alcoholism and drug abuse counselors*. Reston, VA: Author.

National Commission for Certifying Agencies. (2002). *Standards for accreditation of certification programs*. Washington, DC: National Organization for Competency Assurance.

United States Equal Employment Opportunity Commission. (1977, 1999). *Guidelines for employee selection criteria*. Washington, DC: Author.

About the Authors

EDITOR

Robert H. Coombs, PhD, CAS, Professor of Biobehavioral Sciences at the UCLA School of Medicine, is trained as a sociologist (PhD), medical behavioral scientist (postdoctoral), counseling psychologist (postdoctoral MS), family therapist (California licensed), certified addiction specialist and certified group psychotherapist. A Fellow of the American Association for the Advancement of Science, he serves on the International Certification Advisory Committee of the American Academy of Healthcare Providers in the Addictive Disorders. Author or editor of more than two hundred publications, including eighteen books, he is currently co-editing (with William A. Howatt) a book series on *Treating Addictions* for John Wiley & Sons. He received the Award for Excellence in Education from the UCLA School of Medicine and the Distinguished Faculty Educator Award from the UCLA Neuropsychiatric Hospital.

CONTRIBUTING AUTHORS

Mark J. Albanese, MD, a graduate of Harvard College and Cornell University Medical College, completed an internship in medicine at Brighman and Women's Hospital and a psychiatry residency at Massachusetts Mental Health Center. Certified by the American Board of Psychiatry and Neurology in psychiatry and addiction psychiatry, he is Medical Director of Addictions at Cambridge Health Alliance. He is also on the faculty of Harvard Medical School's Division on Addictions, and is Assistant Clinical Professor of Psychiatry at Harvard Medical School. His special area of interest is research on those who drive while intoxicated (DWI).

Rose Alvarado, PhD, Research Assistant Professor in the Department of Health Promotion and Education, University of Utah, directs a project funded by the Office of Juvenile Justice and Delinquency Prevention focusing on the nationwide dissemination of model family-based juvenile delinquency prevention programs. She is also the Co-Principal Investigator for a National Institute on Drug Abuse grant to strengthen inner-city families in Washington, DC.

M. Douglas Anglin, PhD, Professor in Residence, Department of Psychiatry and Biobehavioral Sciences, and Associate Director of Integrated Substance Abuse Programs at UCLA, has been conducting research on substance abuse and treatment evaluation since 1972. Author or co-author of more than two hundred published articles, he has advised many prominent treatment evaluation studies and consulted to the following agencies: NIDA, the Office of National Drug Control Policy, CSAT (SAMHSA), the National Academy of Sciences Institute of Medicine, the National Institute of Justice, the California Office of Criminal Justice Planning, and the Los Angeles County Alcohol and Drug Program Administration.

Christopher Barrick, PhD, Project Director of an NIAAA-funded research project at the University of Buffalo's Research Institute on Addictions, is author of more than a dozen peer-reviewed articles and book chapters, and has served as an ad hoc reviewer for many journals in the fields of psychology and addictions research. He currently serves on the board of directors of the University at Buffalo's Graduate School of Education's Alumni Association. A recipient of the 1997 Mental Health Association in New York State's Edna Aimes Memorial Scholarship, he was awarded the Mark Diamond Research Grant in 1999. His research interests include substance abuse treatment, clinical interventions, geropsychology, and computer-based knowledge dissemination.

Kathryn Coombs, MA, a teacher for the Los Angeles Unified School District in California, works with inner-city children who cannot attend school for medical reasons. A writer and editorial consultant on numerous articles and chapters, she is also a poet and author of children's books.

Dharma E. Cortés, PhD, Clinical Instructor and Research Associate at Cambridge Health Alliance/Harvard Medical School, Department of Psychiatry and a senior research associate at the Mauricio Gaston Institute for Latino Community Development and Public Policy at the University of Massachusetts, Boston, received her doctorate in sociology from Fordham University. A member of the National Hispanic Science Network on Drug Abuse, funded by NIDA, she has published on health, acculturation, mental health, and substance abuse among culturally diverse populations, especially Latinos in the United States. The focus of her current work is on the impact of acculturation on substance abuse and HIV risk and incorporating cultural factors into substance abuse treatment.

Patt Denning, PhD, Director of Clinical Services and Training for the Harm Reduction Therapy Center in San Francisco, California, received her doctorate in clinical psychology from the San Francisco Professional School of Psychology and is a board certified diplomate-fellow of Prescribing Psychologists Register. She specializes in treating dually diagnosed patients as well as training others about this population.

Lynn F. Field, PhD, LPC, a Licensed Professional Counselor in Northern Virginia specializing in treating eating disorders and in working with adolescents, received her doctoral training at George Mason University in Fairfax, Virginia. Her clinical work has also included supervision, administering grant programs, and providing training for clinicians who work with eating disorders. She is a member of the Academy for Eating Disorders.

Robert F. Forman, PhD, Assistant Professor of Psychology and Director of Technology Transfer at the University of Pennsylvania School of Medicine's Treatment Research Institute, received his doctoral training in counseling psychology at Bryn Mawr College. He is the Co-Principal Investigator for the National Institute on Drug Abuse Clinical Trial Network, has authored several peer-reviewed research publications, and chairs the Consensus Panel, CSAT Treatment Improvement Protocol (TIP) #8: Intensive Outpatient Treatment.

Kyle J. Frantz, PhD, Assistant Professor and Science Educator in the Department of Biology at Georgia State University, received her doctorate in psychobiology from the University of Florida. A Fulbright Scholar at the Karolinska Institute in Stockholm, Sweden and a postdoctoral fellow at the Scripps Research Institute in La Jolla, CA, she received a National Research Service Award from NIDA. Her current research involves social, behavioral, and biochemical factors modulating drug self-administration and the long-term effects of drugs of abuse in developing rats. An active member of the Center for Behavioral Neuroscience, she also guides initiatives in Neuroscience Outreach and Education.

James P. Henderson, PhD, Executive Vice President of Castle Worldwide, has been involved in the development of the International Certification and Reciprocity Consortium (IC&RC) examination since 1991, the year it was first used, ensuring that all IC&RC tests and test development procedures adhere to or exceed the requirements set forth by the American Educational Research Association (1999) and the U.S. Equal Employment Opportunity Agencies (2002). Under his leadership, Castle has conducted numerous content validation and role delineation studies for clients of both national and international scope. Chair and psychometrician to the National Commission for Certifying Agencies (NCCA), the accreditation body of the National Organization for Competency Assurance (NOCA), he is a member of NOCA's Leadership Council and of NOCA's Board of Directors. A recipient of the NOCA's Leadership Award, he also serves on the North Carolina Commission on Workforce Development.

William A. Howatt, PhD EdD, recently completed a postdoctoral fellowship at the UCLA School of Medicine and has more than sixteen years experience as an internationally certified alcohol and drug addictions specialist, gambling addictions specialist, registered professional counselor, and registered social worker. A faculty member of the William Glasser Institute, he developed and designed the Human Services Counseling and Addictions Counseling Program at the Nova Scotia Community College, Annapolis Campus, where he teaches. Author of *The Human Services Counseling Toolbox: Theory, Development, Techniques, and Resources,* he is co-authoring *The Addiction Counselor's Desk Reference* and co-editing a Book Series on Treating Addictions, both with R. H. Coombs.

Yih-Ing Hser, PhD, Adjunct Professor in Psychiatry and Biobehavioral Sciences at UCLA, has authored publications in treatment evaluation, epidemiology, natural history of drug addiction, and innovative statistical modeling development and application. She is Principal Investigator for numerous studies, such as *Evaluation of California Treatment Outcomes Project; Cost Analysis and Operations Assessment of Community-based Alcohol and Drug Treatment Programs; A 12-year Follow-Up of A Cocaine-Dependent Sample; and Treatment System Impact and Outcomes of Proposition 36 in Five California Counties.* Other projects include the *California Statewide Evaluation of the Substance Abuse and Crime Prevention Act of 2000 (Proposition 36), Drug Abuse Treatment Outcome Studies (DATOS): A Treatment Careers Perspective,* and *the Persistent Effects of Treatment Studies (PETS).*

Valerie L. Johnson, PhD, Associate Research Professor at the Rutgers University Center of Alcohol Studies, has been involved in a longitudinal research project studying psychosocial correlates and predictors of substance use and other problem behavior patterns among adolescents and young adults as they develop across the lifespan. A sociologist, her research interests also include the study of children from alcoholic and dysfunctional families, the documentation of long term outcomes of diverse drug-using patterns, and the evaluation of prevention and intervention programs. She directs a substance use research program within the Transdisciplinary Prevention Research Center and has provided assistance to both employers in the design of drug-free workplace initiatives and to the university's sports medicine department in curriculum development.

George F. Koob, PhD, Professor and Director, Division of Psychopharmacology, Department of Neuropharmacology at The Scripps Research Institute and Adjunct Professor of Psychology and Psychiatry at the University of California, San Diego, has published more than 560 scientific papers and is an authority on addiction and stress. His current research focuses on the neurobiological bases for the neuroadaptations associated with drug dependence and stress. He is U.S. Editor-in-Chief of the journal *Pharmacology Biochemistry and Behavior*, Director of the National Institute on Alcohol Abuse and Alcoholism Alcohol Research Center at the Scripps Research Institute, and Consortium Coordinator for NIAAA's multi-center Integrative Neuroscience Initiative on Alcoholism.

Cynthia M. Kuhn, PhD, Professor of Pharmacology at Duke University Medical Center, received her bachelor's in biology from Stanford University and doctorate in pharmacology at Duke. The head of the Pharmacological Sciences Training Program at Duke, she is a retired member of an NIH study section which reviews graduate training grants and a study section for the National Institute of Drug Abuse. She teaches about drug abuse, opiates, antidepressants and antipsychotics for medical pharmacology; and an undergraduate course entitled, Drugs and the Brain. She coauthored three books for the lay public about drugs: *Buzzed: The Straight Facts About the Most Used and Abused Drugs From Alcohol to Ecstasy, Pumped: Straight Facts for Athletes About Drugs, Supplements and Training, and Just Say Know: Talking with Kids about Drugs and Alcohol.*

Karol L. Kumpfer, Ph.D., Associate Professor in the Department of Health Promotion and Education at the University of Utah is a former Director (1998–2000) of the Center for Substance Abuse Prevention, Substance Abuse and Mental Health Services Administration, Department of Health and Human Services, Washington, DC. She is also a past president of the Society for Prevention Research. Her doctorate is in psychology from the University of Utah. She is nationally and internationally known for her research and publications on effective family strengthening interventions, including her Strengthening Families Program for children of addicted parents. Her areas of expertise include substance abuse and delinquency prevention, measurement instruments, program evaluation, and grant writing.

Ann W. Lawson, PhD, CAS, Professor and Coordinator of Clinical Training for the Marriage and Family Therapy programs at California School of Professional Psychology, Alliant International University, is a licensed Marriage and Family Therapist, Certified Addiction Specialist, and a Diplomate in Professional Chemical Dependency Counseling. President of the California Division of the American Association of Marriage and Family Therapists, she is the former director and founder of the Children From Alcoholic Families Program, Lincoln, Nebraska, and also of the Addictions Counselor Training Program at U.S. International University. Her books include *Essentials of Chemical Dependency Counseling, Alcoholism and the Family: A Guide to Treatment and Prevention, Alcoholism and Substance Abuse in Special Populations,* and *Adolescent Substance Abuse: Etiology, Treatment and Prevention.*

Gary W. Lawson, PhD, CAS., Professor of Clinical Psychology and Coordinator of Clinical Training for the clinical PsyD program at California School of Professional Psychology, Alliant International University, is a psychologist, Certified Addiction Specialist, and Diplomate in Professional Chemical Dependency Counseling. Former director of the doctoral and master's programs in chemical dependency at U.S. International University, his books include *Essentials of Chemical Dependency Counseling, Alcoholism and the Family: A Guide to Treatment and*

Prevention, Alcoholism and Substance Abuse in Special Populations, Adolescent Substance Abuse: Etiology, Treatment and Prevention, Family Dynamics of Addiction Quarterly, and *Clinical Psychopharmacology: A Practical Reference for Non-Medical Psychotherapists.*

Judith A. Lewis, PhD, Chair of the Department of Addictions Studies and Behavioral Health at Governors State University, University Park, Illinois, is past president of the American Counseling Association and the International Association of Marriage and Family Counselors. She has been active in the addictions field at the national level, where she participated in the development of *Treatment Improvement Protocol 21: Addiction Counselor Competencies* and served on the workforce panel for *Improving Substance Abuse Treatment: The National Treatment Plan Initiative.* Her many books, including *Addictions: Concepts and Strategies for Treatment, Substance Abuse Counseling,* and *Management of Human Service Programs* focus on substance abuse, community, family, adolescence, and health counseling.

Delinda E. Mercer, PhD, Clinical Psychologist at the Regional West Medical Center in Nebraska treats patients, trains counselors in addiction treatments, and studies rural mental health and addiction issues. A former researcher in the Department of Psychiatry at the University of Pennsylvania, she received her PhD in counseling psychology from the University of Pennsylvania. Author of numerous scientific articles, manuals, and chapters on HIV and addiction treatment, she has also authored manuals on drug counseling. A researcher in the NIDA-sponsored Cocaine Collaborative Study and the Clinical Trials Network, she developed and researched the efficacy of treatments for substance abuse. Her clinical HIV prevention research resulted in an innovative treatment to reduce sexual HIV risk among drug-using women.

Jeffrey T. Mitchell, PhD, CTS, Clinical Associate Professor of Emergency Health Services at the University of Maryland in Baltimore County, Maryland, and President Emeritus of the International Critical Incident Stress Foundation, earned his PhD in human development from the University of Maryland. After serving as a firefighter/paramedic he developed a comprehensive, systematic, integrated, and multi-component crisis intervention program called "Critical Incident Stress Management." He has authored more than 250 articles and ten books in the stress and crisis intervention fields. He serves as an adjunct faculty member of the Emergency Management Institute of the Federal Emergency Management Agency. He is a reviewer for the Journal of the American Medical Association and the International Journal of Emergency Mental Health.

Bernice Order-Connors, MSW, Special Projects Coordinator for the Tobacco Dependence Program at The University of Medicine and Dentistry of New Jersey (UMDNJ) School of Public Health, provides policy and clinical consultation to the staff who provide addictions treatment, and mental health services to young people to develop and implement nicotine addiction treatment. A national trainer on this topic, she has served as a consultant to several states' departments of addiction services as they move to integrate tobacco dependence treatment into clinical treatment. Ms. Connors was the lead author of the manual, *Drug-Free is Nicotine-Free.* She is a faculty member of the UMSNJ School of Public Health and an adjunct professor at Monmouth University's Graduate School of Social Work. A licensed clinical social worker and certified alcohol and drug counselor, she received her MSW from Rutgers University in 1991.

Robert J. Pandina, PhD, Professor of Psychology and Director of the Rutgers University Center of Alcohol Studies, is President of Alcohol Research Documentation, Inc., the corporation that publishes the *Journal of Studies on Alcohol.* Director of the Transdisciplinary Prevention

Research Center, a newly created center for the development and testing of promising alcohol and drug use prevention initiatives, he has received grants from several sources including the National Institute on Alcohol Abuse and Alcoholism and the National Institute on Drug Abuse. Scholar in Residence at the National Institute on Drug Abuse, he serves on several advisory and editorial boards.

Christi A. Patten, PhD, Associate Professor of Psychology and Associate Director of the Nicotine Research Program at the Mayo Clinic, received her doctorate in clinical psychology from the University of California, San Diego. She completed a clinical psychology internship at Western Psychiatric Institute and Clinic in Pittsburgh followed by a two-year postdoctoral fellowship at the Mayo Clinic Nicotine Research Program. Her research interests focus on nicotine dependence treatment outcome studies with smokers with co-morbid alcoholism and depression, adolescent smokers, and Alaska Native tobacco users.

Melvin I. Pohl, MD, Medical Director of Chemical Dependency Services, Behavioral Health-care Options, Inc., and also the Clinical Director of Chemical Dependency Programs, Montevista Hospital, in Las Vegas, Nevada, is board certified in family practice. Certified by the American Society of Addiction Medicine (ASAM), he co-chaired ASAM's Third, Fourth, and Fifth National Forums on AIDS and chemical dependency. A Fellow of the American Academy of Family Practice, he is Chairman of ASAM's Infectious Disease Committee and has published several books and articles about AIDS and addiction, including *The Caregivers Journey: When You Love Someone with AIDS* (Hazelden, 1990) and *Staying Sane: When You Care for Someone with Chronic Illness* (Health Communications, 1992).

Renée M. Popovits, JD, a health care attorney, founded the Chicago-based law firm Popovits & Robinson, a firm that provides regular legal consultation to a number of behavioral health care providers as well as to state and federal government agencies impacting substance abuse treatment and prevention policy. A member of the Illinois Governor's Forum on Substance Abuse and the Women's Committee of the Illinois Advisory Council on Alcoholism and Other Drug Dependence, she is Co-Chair of the Legal Advisory Committee and a board member of the National Association of Addiction Treatment Providers. Formerly General Counsel of BHS Management Corp., a company serving multi-state human service and behavioral health care providers, she published, with William L. White, *Critical Incidents*, an award-winning book that addressed ethical and legal issues in substance abuse prevention and treatment.

Jennifer P. Schneider, MD, PhD, lives in Tucson, Arizona, where she practices addiction medicine and chronic pain management. Certified by the American Board of Internal Medicine, the American Society of Addiction Medicine, and the American Academy of Pain Management, she received the 1998 Patrick Carnes Award for lifetime contribution to the advancement of the sex addiction field. Associate Editor of *Sexual Addiction and Compulsivity*, she has published several books including *Back From Betrayal: Sex, Lies, and Forgiveness* (with Burt Schneider); *The Wounded Healer* (with Richard Irons); *Cybersex Exposed* (with Robert Weiss); and *Disclosing Secrets* (with M. Deborah Corley), a step-by-step guide for all types of addicts on how to disclose addiction secrets to their families. Her latest book, *Embracing Recovery from Chemical Dependency* is also co-authored with M. Deborah Corley.

Linda Seligman, PhD, Director of the Center for Counseling and Consultation, has a private practice in Fairfax, Virginia. She is a faculty member at Walden University, a faculty associate at Johns Hopkins University, and professor emeritus at George Mason University where she co-directed the doctoral program in Education and was Coordinator of the Counseling and Development Program. After receiving her PhD in counseling psychology from

Columbia University, she edited *The Journal of Mental Health Counseling* and was selected as a Distinguished Professor by George Mason University and Researcher of the Year by the American Mental Health Counselors Association. She is the author of more than seventy-five professional articles and chapters and ten books such as *Technical and Conceptual Skills for Mental Health Professionals; Systems, Strategies, and Skills of Counseling and Psychotherapy; Selecting Effective Treatments; Diagnosis and Treatment Planning in Counseling;* and *Promoting a Fighting Spirit.*

Howard J. Shaffer, PhD, CAS, Associate Professor and Director of the Division on Addictions at Harvard Medical School and The Cambridge Hospital, is the founder of the American Academy of Health Care Providers in the Addictive Disorders. Principal or co-principal investigator on five government or foundation sponsored research projects, he established the Institute for Research on Pathological Gambling and Related Disorders within the division on addictions at Harvard Medical School. Editor of *The Psychology of Addictive Behaviors,* he has more than 150 professional articles and book titles include *Quitting Cocaine* (with Dr. Stephanie Jones); *Compulsive Gambling,* edited with Dr. Blasé Gambino, Sharon Stein, and Thomas Cummings; and *Youth, Gambling, and Society,* edited with Matthew Hall, Joni Vander Bilt, and Elizabeth George.

Harvey A. Siegal, PhD, Professor in the Department of Community Health and the Department of Sociology and Anthropology, is Director of the Center for Interventions, Treatment, and Addictions Research at Wright State University School of Medicine. He earned his doctorate from Yale University and areas of specialization include alcohol and other substance abuse, alcohol, drugs and highway safety and medical sociology. A NAADAC National Certified Addiction Counselor II and IC&RC/AODA Internationally Certified Alcohol and Drug Counselor, he serves on the Ohio Corrections Substance Abuse Advisory Board and is a member of the board of trustees, University Medical Services Association, Inc. He is Principal Investigator on a five-year study funded by NIH/NIDA, "Crack Cocaine and Health Services Use in Rural Ohio."

Paula Smith, PhD, Assistant Professor of Human Development in the Department of Family & Consumer Studies at the University of Utah, was a NIDA postdoctoral research associate at the Health Research and Policy Centers at the University of Illinois at Chicago where she obtained her doctorate in psychology. Her current research focuses on female juvenile offenders.

Steve Y. Sussman, PhD, FAAHB, Professor of Preventive Medicine and Psychology at the University of Southern California, received his doctorate in social-clinical psychology from the University of Illinois at Chicago. Co-Principal Investigator and Co-Director for the Transdisciplinary Drug Abuse Prevention Research Center (TPRC) at University of Southern California, he conducts research in the prediction, prevention, and cessation of tobacco and other drug abuse. With more than two hundred publications, his projects include Towards No Tobacco Use (young teen tobacco use prevention), Towards No Drug Abuse (older teen–targeted drug abuse prevention), and EX (teen tobacco use cessation), all three of which are considered model programs at numerous agencies (including the CDC, NIDA, CSAP, NCI, Health Canada, and the U.S. Department of Education).

Michael J. Taleff, PhD, a Certified Substance Abuse Counselor in Hawaii, and a Certified Master's Addictions Counselor, is an instructor at the University of Hawaii at Manoa and West Oahu. Editor of the *Journal of Teaching in the Addictions,* he recently completed his third book, *A Critical Thinking Primer for Addiction Counselors,* serves on the editorial board of *The Journal of Counseling and Development,* and is on the editorial board of *The Counselor* and the *Journal of Offenders and Addiction Counseling*. Instructor of addiction studies courses, he also teaches national workshops and is President of the *International Coalition of Addiction Studies Education* from 2003 to 2005.

Rodolfo R. Vega, PhD, Senior Research Scientist at John Snow, Inc., Boston, Massachusetts, received his doctorate in community psychology from the University of Texas at Austin and completed a National Institute on Drug Abuse postdoctoral fellowship program at the University of Miami. He is Co-Investigator in a project sponsored by the Center for Substance Abuse Prevention that provides capacity building assistance to forty-seven grantees around the nation in integrating substance abuse and HIV/AIDS prevention strategies. A member of the National Hispanic Science Network on Drug Abuse funded by the National Institute on Drug Abuse, he is also Principal Evaluator of another project, funded by the Center of Substance Abuse Treatment, which facilitates access to HIV/AIDS treatment services to Latinos in Massachusetts.

Kimberly S. Walitzer, PhD, Deputy Director of the Research Institute on Addictions and Research Associate Professor in the Department of Psychology at the University at Buffalo, The State University of New York, received her doctorate in clinical psychology from the University of Missouri–Columbia. Her postdoctoral clinical internship was completed at Brockton Veterans Affairs Medical Center. Her research interests are in prevention and treatment of alcohol problems, couples therapy in alcohol treatment, and Alcoholics Anonymous. She is Principal Investigator and Co-Investigator on several National Institute on Alcohol Abuse and Alcoholism grants on these topics.

William L. White, MA, Senior Research Consultant at Chestnut Health Systems/Lighthouse Institute, has a master's degree in addiction studies and more than thirty-five years of experience in the addictions field. Author of more than 140 articles and monographs, his books include *Slaying the Dragon—The History of Addiction Treatment and Recovery in America*, which received the 1999 McGovern Family Foundation Award for the best book on addiction recovery, and *Critical Incidents* (with Renée Popovits). He was featured in the Bill Moyers PBS special, "Close to Home: Addiction in America" and the Showtime documentary, "Smoking, Drinking and Drugging in the 20th Century."

Wilkie A. Wilson, PhD, Medical Research Professor in the Department of Pharmacology & Cancer Biology at Duke University Medical Center, Veteran's Administration Medical Center, Durham, North Carolina, completed his postgraduate training at the Epilepsy Center at Durham Veterans Administration Medical Center. A physiologist, biomedical engineer and associate in the departments of physiology and pharmacology at Duke University Medical Center, he is also a research scientist at the Durham Veterans Administration Center, an associate medical research professor of medicine and supervisor of medical students in the Neuroscience Training Program where he has trained many postdoctoral fellows. He received a Research Career Scientist Award in 1985 and has served as a consultant for Icagen Pharmaceuticals for analysis of drug actions in small neural networks.

Appendix: Answer Key

CHAPTER 1

Truth or Fiction Answers

1. T		9. F	
2. T		10. F	
3. F		11. T	
4. T		12. F	
5. F		13. T	
6. T		14. T	
7. F		15. F	
8. T			

Multiple Choice Answers

1. d		16. c	
2. a		17. b	
3. b		18. d	
4. d		19. a	
5. c		20. d	
6. c		21. c	
7. a		22. d	
8. d		23. a	
9. c		24. b	
10. a		25. c	
11. c		26. c	
12. c		27. b	
13. b		28. a	
14. c		29. c	
15. a		30. d	

CHAPTER 2

Truth or Fiction Answers

1. T		9. T	
2. T		10. F	
3. F		11. T	
4. F		12. T	
5. T		13. F	
6. F		14. T	
7. F		15. T	
8. F			

Multiple Choice Answers

1. b		16. a	
2. a		17. d	
3. c		18. c	
4. d		19. a	
5. a		20. a	
6. c		21. c	
7. a		22. d	
8. d		23. a	
9. c		24. c	
10. c		25. b	
11. b		26. d	
12. c		27. c	
13. b		28. c	
14. b		29. d	
15. d		30. d	

CHAPTER 3

Truth or Fiction Answers

1. T		9. T	
2. T		10. F	
3. F		11. T	
4. T		12. F	
5. T		13. T	
6. F		14. T	
7. T		15. F	
8. F			

Multiple Choice Answers

1. b	16. a
2. b	17. b
3. d	18. a
4. c	19. c
5. c	20. d
6. d	21. c
7. c.	22. b
8. d	23. a
9. b	24. b
10. c	25. a
11. d	26. b
12. a	27. d
13. c	28. c
14. b	29. b
15. b	30. c

CHAPTER 4

Truth or Fiction Answers

1. F	9. T
2. F	10. T
3. T	11. T
4. T	12. T
5. F	13. F
6. F	14. T
7. F	15. T
8. T	

Multiple Choice Answers

1. a	16. b
2. a	17. b
3. c	18. a
4. c	19. b
5. c	20. c
6. a	21. c
7. b	22. d
8. c	23. b
9. a	24. d
10. b	25. a
11. c	26. a
12. b	27. b
13. d	28. b
14. d	29. d
15. a	30. b

CHAPTER 5

Truth or Fiction Answers

1. T	9. T
2. F	10. F
3. T	11. T
4. F	12. F
5. T	13. T
6. F	14. T
7. F	15. F
8. F	

Multiple Choice Answers

1. d	16. c
2. d	17. c
3. d	18. a
4. a	19. d
5. b	20. c
6. c	21. b
7. d	22. c
8. d	23. a
9. d	24. b
10. c	25. d
11. b	26. d
12. a	27. c
13. b	28. a
14. c	29. d
15. a	30. d

CHAPTER 6

Truth or Fiction Answers

1. T	9. F
2. T	10. T
3. F	11. T
4. F	12. T
5. F	13. T
6. F	14. F
7. T	15. T
8. T	

Multiple Choice Answers

1. c		16. c
2. b		17. c
3. b		18. d
4. a		19. a
5. d		20. d
6. d		21. a
7. d		22. a
8. d		23. a
9. a		24. d
10. d		25. b
11. c		26. a
12. a		27. d
13. b		28. d
14. a		29. d
15. d		30. a

CHAPTER 7

Truth or Fiction Answers

1. F		9. F
2. F		10. T
3. F		11. T
4. F		12. F
5. F		13. T
6. T		14. F
7. F		15. F
8. F		

Multiple Choice Answers

1. b		16. d
2. d		17. a
3. b		18. c
4. c		19. c
5. b		20. b
6. d		21. d
7. a		22. b
8. d		23. c
9. b		24. a
10. d		25. d
11. a		26. a
12. c		27. d
13. d		28. b
14. d		29. a
15. c		30. d

CHAPTER 8

Truth or Fiction Answers

1. T	9. T
2. T	10. F
3. T	11. T
4. F	12. F
5. T	13. T
6. F	14. T
7. T	15. F
8. T	

Multiple Choice Answers

1. a	16. b
2. b	17. d
3. a	18. a
4. c	19. a
5. a	20. a
6. b	21. d
7. d	22. b
8. d	23. c
9. a	24. d
10. a	25. a
11. c	26. a
12. c	27. a
13. c	28. c
14. b	29. c
15. a	30. d

CHAPTER 9

Truth or Fiction Answers

1. T	9. F
2. F	10. T
3. F	11. T
4. F	12. F
5. T	13. T
6. F	14. F
7. F	15. F
8. T	

Multiple Choice Answers

1. b		16. b	
2. d		17. c	
3. c		18. a	
4. d		19. d	
5. c		20. b	
6. d		21. c	
7. a		22. d	
8. a		23. d	
9. d		24. d	
10. b		25. d	
11. d		26. a	
12. a		27. c	
13. d		28. a	
14. d		29. d	
15. d		30. b	

CHAPTER 10

Truth or Fiction Answers

1. T		9. F	
2. F		10. T	
3. F		11. F	
4. T		12. T	
5. F		13. T	
6. T		14. F	
7. F		15. T	
8. F			

Multiple Choice Answers

1. b		16. b	
2. c		17. d	
3. d		18. c	
4. b		19. a	
5. b		20. c	
6. c		21. b	
7. d		22. a	
8. a		23. c	
9. c		24. d	
10. c		25. a	
11. a		26. c	
12. c		27. b	
13. d		28. d	
14. d		29. c	
15. a		30. a	

CHAPTER 11

Truth or Fiction Answers

1. F		9. T	
2. F		10. T	
3. T		11. F	
4. T		12. F	
5. T		13. T	
6. F		14. T	
7. T		15. F	
8. T			

Multiple Choice Answers

1. c		16. d	
2. a		17. a	
3. b		18. b	
4. d		19. c	
5. b		20. b	
6. c		21. c	
7. b		22. a	
8. d		23. a	
9. a		24. b	
10. c		25. c	
11. c		26. a	
12. b		27. c	
13. d		28. d	
14. d		29. b	
15. a		30. c	

CHAPTER 12

Truth or Fiction Answers

1. T		9. F	
2. T		10. F	
3. T		11. T	
4. F		12. T	
5. T		13. T	
6. T		14. F	
7. F		15. F	
8. T			

Multiple Choice Answers

1. c	16. d
2. a	17. b
3. e	18. b
4. d	19. e
5. b	20. c
6. b	21. b
7. b	22. e
8. a	23. a
9. e	24. c
10. c	25. a
11. c	26. e
12. c	27. c
13. d	28. d
14. d	29. b
15. d	30. b

CHAPTER 13

Truth or Fiction Answers

1. T	9. F
2. T	10. T
3. F	11. F
4. T	12. T
5. T	13. T
6. F	14. F
7. F	15. F
8. T	

Multiple Choice Answers

1. c	15. c
2. a	16. a
3. d	17. b
4. c	18. b
5. b	19. b
6. a	20. a
7. b	21. b
8. c	22. d
9. d	23. b
10. d	24. d
11. a	25. a
12. d	26. b
13. b	27. c
14. c	28. b

CHAPTER 14

Truth or Fiction Answers

1. F	9. T
2. F	10. F
3. T	11. T
4. F	12. F
5. T	13. T
6. T	14. T
7. T	15. T
8. T	

Multiple Choice Answers

1. a	16. a
2. a	17. b
3. b	18. d
4. a	19. d
5. c	20. d
6. d	21. b
7. c	22. a
8. a	23. c
9. c	24. d
10. b	25. a
11. d	26. a
12. d	27. a
13. d	28. a
14. c	29. a
15. a	30. b

CHAPTER 15

Truth or Fiction Answers

1. F	9. T
2. F	10. F
3. T	11. T
4. T	12. F
5. T	13. T
6. T	14. T
7. F	15. F
8. F	

Multiple Choice Answers

1. c		16. c	
2. d		17. b	
3. a		18. a	
4. b		19. d	
5. b		20. a	
6. b		21. c	
7. c		22. b	
8. b		23. c	
9. d		24. b	
10. a		25. b	
11. d		26. a	
12. a		27. b	
13. d		28. a	
14. a		29. c	
15. d		30. c	

CHAPTER 16

Truth or Fiction Answers

1. F		9. F	
2. T		10. T	
3. T		11. F	
4. F		12. F	
5. F		13. F	
6. F		14. T	
7. T		15. T	
8. T			

Multiple Choice Answers

1. d		16. a	
2. d		17. b	
3. c		18. d	
4. b		19. a	
5. d		20. c	
6. c		21. b	
7. c		22. a	
8. b		23. b	
9. b		24. d	
10. c		25. a	
11. a		26. d	
12. c		27. a	
13. b		28. a	
14. c		29. a	
15. d		30. d	

CHAPTER 17

Truth or Fiction Answers

1. F		9. T	
2. F		10. T	
3. F		11. F	
4. T		12. F	
5. T		13. T	
6. F		14. T	
7. T		15. T	
8. F			

Multiple Choice Answers

1. c		16. b	
2. c		17. c	
3. d		18. c	
4. a		19. b	
5. d		20. b	
6. c		21. a	
7. c		22. d	
8. b		23. d	
9. d		24. c	
10. d		25. d	
11. b		26. a	
12. b		27. d	
13. b		28. c	
14. c		29. d	
15. b		30. a	

CHAPTER 18

Truth or Fiction Answers

1. F		9. F	
2. T		10. T	
3. T		11. T	
4. F		12. F	
5. T		13. T	
6. F		14. T	
7. F		15. T	
8. T			

Multiple Choice Answers

1. d	16. c
2. b	17. d
3. a	18. c
4. c	19. b
5. b	20. a
6. d	21. d
7. a	22. b
8. d	23. a
9. b	24. c
10. d	25. b
11. c	26. d
12. c	27. c
13. a	28. b
14. b	29. d
15. d	30. c

CHAPTER 19

Truth or Fiction Answers

1. T	9. F
2. F	10. F
3. T	11. T
4. F	12. T
5. T	13. F
6. T	14. F
7. F	15. F
8. T	

Multiple Choice Answers

1. b	16. c
2. c	17. d
3. a	18. d
4. d	19. a
5. c	20. c
6. b	21. b
7. c	22. b
8. b	23. d
9. a	24. a
10. d	25. c
11. c	26. d
12. c	27. d
13. b	28. b
14. a	29. b
15. d	30. d

CHAPTER 20

Truth or Fiction Answers

1. T
2. F
3. F
4. T
5. F
6. F
7. T
8. F

9. T
10. F
11. F
12. F
13. T
14. F
15. F

Multiple Choice Answers

1. b
2. b
3. c
4. c
5. b
6. d
7. d
8. d
9. d
10. c
11. a
12. b
13. d
14. c
15. a

16. a
17. a
18. d
19. a
20. b
21. c
22. b
23. c
24. b
25. d
26. c
27. c
28. d
29. d
30. d

CHAPTER 21

Truth or Fiction Answers

1. T
2. F
3. F
4. T
5. T
6. T
7. F
8. T

9. T
10. T
11. F
12. F
13. T
14. T
15. F

Multiple Choice Answers

1. b	16. a
2. b	17. b
3. d	18. c
4. c	19. c
5. a	20. d
6. c	21. a
7. b	22. b
8. b	23. b
9. a	24. a
10. d	25. c
11. a	26. a
12. a	27. d
13. b	28. b
14. d	29. a
15. c	30. b

CHAPTER 22

Truth or Fiction Answers

1. F	9. F
2. T	10. F
3. F	11. T
4. T	12. T
5. T	13. T
6. T	14. F
7. F	15. T
8. T	

Multiple Choice Answers

1. a	16. a
2. b	17. c
3. b	18. d
4. b	19. d
5. d	20. b
6. d	21. d
7. c	22. c
8. c	23. c
9. d	24. d
10. a	25. d
11. a	26. d
12. b	27. a
13. c	28. d
14. a	29. a
15. a	30. c

CHAPTER 23

Truth or Fiction Answers

1. F	9. T
2. F	10. T
3. F	11. T
4. T	12. F
5. T	13. T
6. F	14. T
7. T	15. F
8. F	

Multiple Choice Answers

1. c	16. d
2. b	17. c
3. a	18. b
4. d	19. c
5. a	20. d
6. c	21. c
7. d	22. a
8. a	23. d
9. b	24. b
10. c	25. a
11. a	26. c
12. d	27. b
13. d	28. a
14. d	29. b
15. d	30. c

CHAPTER 24

Truth or Fiction Answers

1. T	9. F
2. F	10. F
3. F	11. F
4. T	12. T
5. F	13. F
6. F	14. T
7. F	15. F
8. T	

Multiple Choice Answers

1. a		16. d	
2. d		17. c	
3. c		18. a	
4. d		19. c	
5. a		20. d	
6. d		21. d	
7. b		22. d	
8. b		23. d	
9. a		24. d	
10. a		25. c	
11. d		26. d	
12. b		27. c	
13. d		28. a	
14. d		29. d	
15. d		30. a	

CHAPTER 25

Truth or Fiction Answers

1. F		9. F	
2. T		10. F	
3. T		11. F	
4. F		12. T	
5. T		13. T	
6. T		14. T	
7. T		15. T	
8. T			

Multiple Choice Answers

1. b		16. b	
2. c		17. b	
3. b		18. d	
4. a		19. d	
5. a		20. a	
6. d		21. b	
7. b		22. d	
8. c		23. c	
9. a		24. b	
10. d		25. a	
11. a		26. d	
12. b		27. b	
13. c		28. a	
14. a		29. b	
15. d		30. c	

CHAPTER 26

Truth or Fiction Answers

1. F	9. T
2. T	10. T
3. F	11. T
4. F	12. F
5. T	13. T
6. F	14. F
7. F	15. T
8. T	

Multiple Choice Answers

1. c	16. a
2. b	17. c
3. a	18. a
4. a	19. d
5. d	20. d
6. d	21. a
7. b	22. b
8. c	23. c
9. a	24. b
10. a	25. d
11. b	26. d
12. b	27. b
13. c	28. c
14. d	29. b
15. b	30. d

Author Index

Subject Index